THE ANATOMY OF COMMUNIST TAKEOVERS

The Anatomy
of Communist Takeovers

Edited by

THOMAS T. HAMMOND

Associate Editor: ROBERT FARRELL

Foreword by CYRIL E. BLACK

New Haven and London

YALE UNIVERSITY PRESS, 1975

Printed in the United States of America

by

Murray Printing Co., Inc., Forge Village, Massachusetts

Published in Great Britain, Europe, and Africa by
Yale University Press, Ltd., London
Distributed in Latin America by Kaiman & Polon, Inc., New York City;
in Australasia and Southeast Asia by John Wiley & Sons Australasia Pty.
Ltd., Sidney; in India by UBS Publishers' Distributors Pvt., Ltd., Delhi;
in Japan by John Weatherhill, Inc., Tokyo

To

KENT HAMMOND

and

KATHY, JENNY and CAROL SHESTAK

Contents

Contents

Foreword

We live in an age of revolutions: the great revolutions like the English, American, French, Russian, and Chinese and the equally profound but less publicized revolutions that have occurred in almost all other countries.

All have been political revolutions that have brought to power new leaders seeking to adapt their countries' policies to the requirements and opportunities of the modern era. The revolutions of decolonization have often been more radical than those carried out in states already independent. The leaders have included military and civilians; Jacobins and other nationalists; and socialists and Communists. More often than not, revolutions have followed closely on major wars that have shaken the power and legitimacy of long-established political systems.

Americans have had difficulty understanding these revolutions, perhaps because their own revolution of decolonization, accompanied by radical political and social change, took place almost two hundred years ago. They have been repelled by the violence of contemporary revolutions and confused by their ideologies. While a small minority of Americans has been attracted to foreign revolutions, seeing their goals as applicable to reform in the United States, a great majority has viewed them as a threat to American values and institutions. This threat is usually perceived as a dual one: as examples of illegal political change that if widely adopted might turn a world of constitutional order into one of anarchy and as episodes in a movement that might eventually unite many countries in a common opposition to American interests.

At times the American fear of revolution has come close to hysteria. Revolutions have been seen as fires to be extinguished before they engulf the American community rather than as stages in the political development of countries under the impact of the scientific and technological revolution. As with all great fears in this one there has been a germ of truth; and, in separating this germ from the confusion of generality, it is the task of scholarship to sort out the commonalities and variances of the many different revolutionary episodes.

It was possible in the 1950's to imagine, for example, that the Soviet Union and China might join forces to manipulate Communist revolutions in Europe, Asia, Latin America, and Africa and mobilize the resources of two-thirds of the world's population against the developed countries. This possibility evoked images of the teeming millions of the world's proletariat storming the gates of the privileged few and destroying the fruits of their civilization as well as their property and lives. The germ of truth underlying this fear was the goal of "world revolution" that had been announced by the prophets of reform in the nineteenth and twentieth centuries and that has in fact inspired many revolutionary leaders down to the present time.

For example, in 1958 I had the occasion to ask Mr. Khrushchev about the proposed form of government, economy, languages, and organizational arrangements once the Marxist principles of society as developed in the USSR were in due course adopted throughout the world. He did not for a moment deny the assumption underlying this admittedly loaded question—that world revolution would be successful—and replied that it was too early to state what form a Communist world state would take. When that point was reached, he said, the appropriate means and forms would be found. He regarded the world state as still a field of fantasy and said that it was impossible as yet to describe the organizational arrangements in any detail. The general principles, he asserted, were set forth in the doctrines of Marx, Engels, and Lenin. As to governmental forms, the first step would be to raise the living standards of people so as to equalize conditions of life all over the world. He saw war as a result of capitalism, and with the victory of socialism economic resources would no longer be needed for armed forces and defense, which now consume so much material wealth. If these resources were freed, it would facilitate the development and well-being of all peoples—clothing and housing, as well as political and spiritual needs. The languages of all countries would be preserved, and Russian, English, and Chinese would probably be the world languages. Perhaps eventually a common language would be arrived at. Khrushchev acknowledged that he could not say how long it would take before communism would be established all over the world, but the important thing was to raise living standards before the transition to communism.

There are many interpretations that one can give to these off-the-cuff remarks. Khrushchev's underlying thought was not of Soviet aggression to impose world communism but rather of the gradual evolution of all societies in that direction. It is well known that he believed in "peaceful coexistence," which to Soviet leaders means the gradual development of all societies from capitalism to socialism and communism, without recourse to a general war. The ultimate institutions of a Communist world state seemed to him a matter of fantasy, because the achievement of a Communist world state was in the distant and theoretical future. Soviet resources for the foreseeable future would be devoted to raising domestic social and economic levels, not to promoting world revolution. It is worth noting that Woodrow Wilson also had a vision of a world government—a world parliament formed by the democratic governments that he saw being established after the First World War—and he hoped to see a democratic world government established in his own lifetime.

One of the problems faced by American students of Communist revolutions is to disentangle Marxist and Marxist-Leninist theories based on nineteenth-century conceptions from views of change based on contemporary social science scholarship. More often than not, although they are opponents of Marxism-Leninism, American commentators wrestle with the terminology without having any independent base of interpretation. One frequently ends up with accounts that are anti-Communist but not "pro" anything in particular.

Yet the matter is not all that complex. Through the mechanism of class conflict consequent upon exploitation, in the Marxist-Leninist view, feudal landlords and bourgeois property owners are successively overthrown by the exploited classes until the proletariat comes to power. In this view, the English and French revolutions were classic cases of the bourgeoisie supplanting feudalism, and the Russian revolution represents a turning point in world history as the first occasion when a proletariat supplanted a bourgeoisie. Since there is no exploitation and hence no class struggle under the Marxist-Leninist view of socialism, no further revolutions are necessary or indeed possible. History in this sense comes to an end once all peoples have had their revolutions, and they all live happily ever after.

Contemporary social science in Europe and the United States has developed a much more complex view of the processes of change in the modern era. The central adjustment that they study is that between the long-established and widely varying pre-modern values and institutions of individual societies and the common levels of achievement made possible by the scientific and technological revolution. Each society has to wrestle with this transformation in its own way. It is also an unending process, to the extent that the growth of knowledge that underlies all change is likely to continue as long as human beings retain the capacity for thought. Each society comes to this process with a different capacity to meet the requirements of successful transformation. Russia, along with many of the countries of Central and Eastern Europe, and also Japan, has met these requirements rather well and is now approaching the level of development of the Western countries that had a head start in terms of both time and resources. Most other countries have seemed to lack this capacity and may never catch up.

Another problem faced by students of Communist revolutions is to distinguish between spontaneous and imposed revolutions and between these two categories of successful revolutions and those that have failed. The successful and spontaneous revolutions are distinguished both by their small number and by their diversity: the Soviet Union, Yugoslavia, Albania, China, North Vietnam, and possibly Czechoslovakia and Cuba. Since these revolutions were spontaneous, that is to say won primarily by domestic political forces without decisive outside intervention, they developed through an interaction between indigenous values and institutions and the common guiding principles of communism. The guiding principles of communism, or more specifically Marxism-Leninism, are distinctive chiefly as regards the forms rather than the substance of policy. Communist governments assert a monopoly over all political power and all property, and to this extent they are truly distinctive. When it comes to the substance of policy—the mobilization of resources and their allocation to economic and social ends—Communists have faced the same frustrations as others. Since the indigenous values and institutions have widely differed, the outcomes have also been different; so different, in fact, that they do not have a great deal in common: sufficient disagreement on fundamental issues prevents the formation of lasting alliances even under the pressure of common danger.

These different categories of Communist revolutions are comprehensively treated in this volume, and the tactical similarities that mark the various Communist seizures of power are noted along with the widely differing circumstances under which they were applied.

It is significant that, of the 90–100 countries that have undergone revolutionary transformation since 1917—some 10 in Europe, 8 or 10 in Latin America, 25—30 in Asia, and as many as 45 in Africa—no more than 7 have been successful spontaneous Communist revolutions. The imposed Communist governments were successful as takeovers and had revolutionary consequences, but they belong in the category of power politics or imperialism rather than of domestic revolutions.

Seen in this context, Communist takeovers deserve study as examples of the fulfillment not of a theory of historical transformation but rather of a technique of the seizure of power that has been successful when certain factors have been present and others absent in the various revolutionary situations. This is the subject with which the essays in this volume are concerned.

Cyril E. Black
Princeton, New Jersey

Preface

The systematic study of communism has progressed rapidly during the past three decades, but scholars still tend to concentrate on only a single country or at most a specific part of the world, with the result that comparative Communist studies largely remains in a stage of infancy. Thus, while there are many specialists on the Soviet Union, Communist China, Eastern Europe, or on communism in Latin America, few persons have competence outside of any one of these geographic areas. This situation is illustrated by the fact that the present volume is the first book to be published anywhere that deals in depth with *all* the successful Communist takeovers from 1917 to the present. Beginning with the Bolshevik revolution in Russia and ending with the establishment of communism in Cuba, it tells the story of Communist seizures of power in Europe, Asia, Latin America, and the Middle East. It is also the first work to concern itself extensively with Communist takeovers that failed. More than one-third of the chapters are devoted in part or in full to abortive revolutions: Germany in 1918–1923, Finland in 1918 and 1944–1948, Hungary in 1919, Poland in 1920, China in 1924–1927, Greece in 1944–1949, Austria in 1945, northern Iran in 1945–1946 Guatemala in 1951–1954, Indonesia in 1965, and South Vietnam s'nce World War II. Such emphasis on failures seems appropriate, since the history of communism has by no means been a steady succession of unmitigated triumphs. In fact, more Communist revolutions have been defeated than have not.

It is hoped that by bringing together in one volume essays on both Communist successes and failures and by treating Communist movements in several different parts of the world, the present collection will facilitate the comparative study of Communist revolutions and increase our understanding of why Communists sometimes win and why they sometimes fail. In other words, this volume might be something of a guide to those who wish to prevent Communist takeovers and, incidentally, to those who wish to carry them out (though this is hardly the purpose of the book).

Trying to cover such a broad subject was obviously a rather ambitious project, and it could not have been completed without the co-operation of many scholars from many parts of the globe. Indeed this book is truly a product of international effort: the authors represent, either by birth or long residence, the following countries—the U.S.A., Great Britain, Germany, France, Austria, Albania, Greece, Rumania, Bulgaria, Hungary, Czechoslovakia, Iran, Korea, Vietnam, and Cuba.

While pointing out what this book *does* cover, it might also be helpful to mention what it *does not* cover. For reasons of space (it is already a big book), we decided not to deal at length with the historical background or with the underlying social and economic conditions that prepared the way for revolution. Similarly, we have not discussed what the Communists did after they gained power—the nationalization of industry, the collectivization of agriculture, and so on. Instead we have concentrated on the actual takeovers, with special emphasis on the strategy and tactics of seizing power.

Some readers may wonder why we have generally used the term "takeover" instead of the more common term "revolution." The reason is simply that the process whereby the Communists gained power often cannot accurately be described as a "revolution." For example, in many countries the Communists did not carry out true revolutions but were installed in power by the Red Army. Furthermore, in Kerala and San Marino the Communists got control through free elections rather than through revolutionary coups. In fact, very few countries have become Communist through genuine revolutions.

This book grew out of a seminar in international affairs that was organized by the editors and taught by Mr. Hammond for the Munich branch of the University of Oklahoma. Twelve of the chapters were originally prepared for that seminar. Later it was decided to add more essays and to publish them in a special issue of *Studies on the Soviet Union*, a journal edited by Mr. Farrell under the sponsorship of the Institute for the Study of the USSR. The present volume is a reprinting of that issue with one new chapter added, one chapter completely rewritten, and the addition of a bibliography and an index. Mr. Hammond was responsible for selecting the authors and subjects, as well as for providing overall guidance regarding the scope and emphasis of the book. The editing was performed jointly, while Mr. Farrell bore the burden of ensuring uniformity of style, preparing the copy, and correcting the proofs.

The editors wish to acknowledge the debts they owe to the many people who helped in one way or another with the preparation of this book. First of all, we wish to pay tribute to the contributors, without whose expertise this volume could never have been written. At the Radio Liberty Committee we are especially indebted to the President, Howland H. Sargeant, who came to the rescue when the whole project was threatened with cancellation. Benjamin Peacock, assistant to Mr. Sargeant, helped with many details. At the Institute for the Study of the USSR our greatest debts are to Edward L. Crowley and William C. Thoma, who gave support at crucial moments. David B. Jenkins and Max Klieber provided valuable editorial and technical assistance. In particular, Mr. Klieber is responsible for the typographical presentation of the book.

Mr. Hammond wishes to express his appreciation for financial assistance from the Relm Foundation, the U.S. Office of Education, and the University of Virginia Research Committee. He is also grateful to the Russian Research Center at Harvard University and to the Hoover Institution at Stanford University, both of which provided him with research materials and a place to work. The Alderman Library of the University of Virginia provided services of many kinds. Others who helped in various ways include Hugh Seton-Watson, Warren Nutter, Joseph Rothschild, Paul Shoup, L. A. D. Dellin, and Hermann Gross, as well as Jaromir Netik, Slobodan Stankovich, and James Brown. Research assistants at the University of Virginia who helped with such matters as the index include James Currie, John Kneebone, Sue Taishoff, and John F. Copeley. Finally, thanks should be given to Lottie M. McCauley, Ella M. Wood, Elizabeth C. Stovall, Sharane S. Morgan, and Elizabeth Schuman for secretarial labors.

Thomas T. Hammond   *Robert Farrell*
Charlottesville, Virginia   Munich, Germany

The History of Communist Takeovers
Thomas T. Hammond

Before 1917 there was not a single Communist regime in the world, but since 1917 Communists have gained power in twenty-two countries or parts of countries, so that today about one-third of the people of the globe are ruled by Communist governments. Aside from the successful revolutions, there have also been numerous Communist attempts to seize power, beginning as early as 1918 in Finland and continuing as recently as 1971 in the Sudan. Thus it would appear that there is no aspect in the history of the twentieth century more important than the question of how Communists gain power and why in some cases they fail.[1]

This chapter will attempt to trace briefly the historical evolution of the strategy and tactics used by Communists in gaining power. It is hoped that by first getting a bird's-eye view of the whole panorama of events since 1917 the reader will be better able to understand the chapters that follow on individual countries and to see how each takeover fits into the overall picture. This essay, it should be made clear, will not deal with the social and economic conditions in the various countries on the eve of the Communist takeovers, partly because this subject is too vast, and partly because in many countries the weaknesses and injustices of the old regime were largely irrelevant to the fact that the country became Communist.[2]

---

[1] The footnotes in this chapter refer to only a few of the most basic works. For additional sources see the following chapters or refer to Thomas T. Hammond (ed.), *Soviet Foreign Relations and World Communism. A Selected, Annotated Bibliography of 7,000 Books in 30 Languages*, 2nd printing, with revisions, Princeton, N. J., 1966.

The author wishes to thank his colleague at the University of Virginia, Professor David Powell, for reading this chapter and offering many helpful suggestions.

[2] Two excellent essays dealing with much the same subject as this chapter, although with different emphases and approaches, are: Robert C. Tucker, "Paths of Communist Revolution, 1917–67," in Kurt London (ed.), *The Soviet Union : A Half-Century of Communism*, Baltimore, 1968, and Cyril E. Black, "The Anticipation of Communist Revolutions," in Cyril E. Black and Thomas P. Thornton (eds.), *Communism and Revolution*, Princeton, N. J., 1964. Among the many other fine contributions to the Black and Thornton volume, see: "The Emergence of Communist Revolutionary Doctrine" by Thomas P. Thornton and "Eastern Europe" by R. V. Burks. One side of the picture is provided in Peter A. Toma,

The Bolshevik Prototype

The revolution that started it all and made the others possible was of course the Bolshevik seizure of power in Russia. Most subsequent Communist revolutions were said to have been modeled after the Russian example, but as we shall see, this is only partly true. In what ways *did* the Bolshevik takeover serve as a prototype for revolutions to come?

(1) *The Use of Armed Force.* The Bolshevik coup was like most revolutions in that it was primarily a military operation, carried out by organized armed detachments. This is not the popular view of the Bolshevik revolution, nor is it the picture conveyed by most Soviet books, movies, and paintings. The "official" view is that it was a spontaneous uprising of the toiling masses, but anyone familiar with the facts knows that while the revolution of March, 1917, *was* spontaneous, the Bolshevik revolution of November, 1917, *was not.* The chief reason for the Bolshevik victory was that at the crucial moment more army and navy units stationed in and around Petrograd supported Lenin than supported Kerensky. Except for some workers organized in units of the Red Guard, the masses in Petrograd hardly knew what was happening, while the masses in other parts of the country knew even less. Lenin suffered from no illusions that the Bolshevik coup could be, or had been, a spontaneous revolution. He had studied Clausewitz carefully, and his chief concern in planning the Petrograd uprising was to know which military units would fight on which side. In this respect Stalin was a faithful disciple of Lenin. If anything, Stalin placed even greater emphasis than Lenin on the use of military power in establishing Communist regimes, as shown by his actions in Eastern Europe and North Korea at the end of World War II. Thus in the employment of armed force the Bolshevik revolution served as a model for most of the Communist coups that were to follow.

(2) *The Use of Propaganda.* A second way in which the tactics of 1917 served as a prototype was in the skillful use of propaganda. Lenin was particularly adept at composing slogans that would appeal to the masses, his promise of "Bread, Peace, Land" proving irresistible to many of the Russian people. Years later the Communists of Eastern Europe showed themselves to be equally able propagandists, promising the people almost

"Failures in Communist Revolutionary Strategy," in Andrew Gyorgy (ed.), *Issues of World Communism*, Princeton, N. J., 1966. A standard history of Communist revolutions is Hugh Seton-Watson, *From Lenin to Khrushchev: The History of World Communism*, New York, 1960. The best survey of Soviet foreign relations is by Adam Ulam, *Expansion and Coexistence: The History of Soviet Foreign Policy, 1917–1967*, New York, 1968. See also Feliks Gross, *The Seizure of Political Power in a Century of Revolutions*, New York, 1958.

anything, regardless of whether or not they intended to abide by these promises.

(3) *Ruthlessness*. A third characteristic of Lenin and his cohorts was a willingness to use almost any means to gain power. Lenin was ready to violate democratic principles and to take money from the Kaiser's government; indeed, as events proved, he was willing to kill hundreds of thousands of people in order to maintain Bolshevik rule. By contrast, the members of the Provisional Government were comparatively decent, honorable men, who hoped that democracy would prevail. Lenin's principle that the end justifies any means was applied by his pupils in the Communist takeovers of the 1940's, while their non-Communist opponents innocently abided by the rules of the democratic process. The result might be described in the classic statement of baseball manager Leo Durocher, "Nice guys finish last."

(4) *The Party*. Another important way in which the Bolshevik revolution set the pattern for later Communist takeovers was in the type of political party that was used. As is well known, Lenin created a party that was highly centralized, rigidly disciplined, and led by a carefully selected élite of professional revolutionaries. During the struggle for power in Russia (and later in many other countries), Communist Parties organized according to these principles demonstrated time and again that a well-disciplined minority can easily defeat an unorganized, divided majority. The "organizational weapon" of the Communist Party proved to be of crucial importance in one takeover after another.

(5) *Planning*. One of the reasons why the Bolsheviks triumphed was the simple fact that they made plans to seize power, while the other revolutionary parties did not. Lenin had a profound distrust of spontaneity; the masses, he argued as far back as 1902, could not be depended upon to carry out a revolution on their own. Any seizure of power, therefore, had to be carefully planned and controlled by an élite of Party leaders.

(6) *Use of Camouflage*. The Bolsheviks also served as models for later Communists by camouflaging their true intentions. No Communist Party, it is worth noting, has ever come to power on the basis of a full and frank statement of its program, for the very simple reason that in no country has the majority of the population ever wanted communism. For example, Lenin in 1917 was careful not to proclaim his intention to collectivize agriculture; instead he stole the Socialist Revolutionaries' program of "Land to the Peasants." Similarly, before his rise to power Lenin championed "workers' control" of the factories, even though he had no intention of following such a syndicalist practice in the long run. In like fashion he agreed to the formation of a coalition government with the Left Socialist

Revolutionaries, but only as a temporary tactical maneuver designed to gain peasant support.

However, Lenin did not use camouflage nearly as much as later Communists. In 1917 the Bolsheviks admitted that they were carrying out an illegal seizure of power, whereas the Communists of the 1940's went to great pains to present an appearance of legality. In Eastern Europe, coalition governments supposedly representing several political parties were formed, elections were held, parliaments met, and constitutions were drafted—all in a synthetic aura of democratic procedure. While Lenin boasted that his revolution marked a complete break with the past, later Communists in other countries attempted to give an impression of continuity with all that was good in the past, even to the point of occasionally permitting a king or a president to remain as the figurehead ruler of a Communist-dominated regime.

The Bolsheviks paid a heavy price for not using more camouflage, deception, and gradualism. By boldly proclaiming that they intended to introduce communism, they aroused widespread opposition to their coup, with the result that they had to fight a long and bloody civil war. The Communists of the 1940's were careful to avoid this error.

The commonly used expression, "the Bolshevik revolution of 1917," is of course a gross misnomer, for it implies that with the seizure of the Winter Palace on the night of November 7, 1917, the Bolsheviks became the rulers of Russia. In truth it took them several years to establish their dominion over the vast Russian empire, with armed opposition continuing in some areas until the mid-1920's. Having the support of only a minority, the Bolsheviks soon found themselves at war with socialists, anarchists, liberals, conservatives, and reactionaries, plus non-Russian nationalities of every political coloration, not to mention foreign interventionist armies. Stalin evidently drew the correct conclusions from this bitter and bloody conflict. At the end of World War II, as he directed the new wave of Communist takeovers, he tried to prevent civil wars, not only by effective use of the Red Army, but also by camouflage and gradualism. (For a closer view of the Bolshevik revolution, see the chapter below by John Keep.)

The Export of Revolutions to the Non-Russian Borderlands, 1917–1924

The Russian empire in 1917 was a patchwork of nationalities, most of whom had been conquered by the Russians over the centuries, and many of whom yearned for independence. When Lenin seized power, he was well aware that some of the nationalities were dissatisfied, but he mistakenly assumed that the minorities were opposed to *Tsarist* rule, not *Russian* rule. Thus he promised them the right to self-determination, even to the point of secession, but naïvely believed that none of them would want to secede from the wonderful new regime that the Bolsheviks had instituted. To his surprise, the major nationalities one after another proclaimed their independence and proceeded to form their own governments. The Bolsheviks thus found themselves faced with the task not only of establishing their rule over the Russian population, but also of exporting Communist revolutions to the newly created "foreign" states that sprouted from the ruins of the old Tsarist empire. As a result, the first successful Communist revolutions to follow the Bolshevik coup in Petrograd came not in Germany or the other advanced states of Europe, but in the borderlands of Russia.

These revolutions displayed several similarities to the original Bolshevik coup. First of all, in none of these areas was the majority of the people pro-Communist, and the governments which they created were uniformly anti-Communist. Second, armed force without exception played the decisive role in determining which of these states gained their freedom from Bolshevik rule and which did not. The Red Army was sent into every area that attempted to assert its independence; those areas that became Communist did so because of the overwhelming power of the Red Army, while those that escaped communization obtained military aid from abroad. Despite the efforts of the Red Army, two of the states—Poland and Finland— achieved independence permanently (at least up until the present), while the three Baltic states managed to remain independent until 1940. Other areas, however, were able to break away only for short periods—for example, the Ukraine, Belorussia, the Crimea, Caucasia, and parts of Central Asia.[3]

The Bolsheviks' First Efforts to Foment Revolutions Abroad, 1919–1924

One of the articles of Bolshevik faith in 1917 was the conviction that Communist revolutions would soon break out elsewhere, especially in the advanced countries of Europe. Such revolutions were looked upon as

---

[3] For descriptions of some of the successful and unsuccessful attempts by the Bolsheviks to establish Communist regimes in the borderlands, see the following contributions to this volume: "The Bolshevik Conquest of the Moslem Borderlands," by Alexandre Bennigsen; "Soviet Russia and the Red Revolution of 1918 in Finland," by C. Jay Smith; and "Attempting a Revolution from Without: Poland in 1920," by Warren Lerner. For a comprehensive account dealing with most of the nationalities, see Richard Pipes, *The Formation of the Soviet Union : Communism and Nationalism, 1917–1923*, revised edition, Cambridge, Mass., 1965.

vitally important to the Bolsheviks since they assumed that their regime could not survive in backward, peasant Russia without the support of like-minded regimes in industrially developed countries. It was only natural, therefore, that from the day they seized power the Bolsheviks tried to incite revolts in other lands. Money was appropriated for propaganda, arms, and agents, while prisoners of war in Russia were indoctrinated and sent back to Germany, Austria, Hungary, and other countries. In March, 1919, the Communist International (Comintern) was created for the specific purpose of bringing about world revolution. Yet with one exception, which will be discussed later, all of these efforts by the Bolsheviks to spread communism to other lands failed in the years from World War I to World War II.

Germany. The country which the Bolsheviks considered most ripe for a Communist revolution was Germany, and on several occasions their hopes seemed about to be fulfilled, only to be followed by disappointment. In November, 1918, workers' and soldiers' soviets assumed power throughout Germany, the Kaiser fled, and a republic was proclaimed. There was jubilation in Moscow, but the joy was premature. Germany did not become Communist, or even socialist, because the great majority of the workers and peasants did not want a radical social revolution, while the conservative forces—including the army, the bureaucracy, the businessmen, and the landlords—remained very powerful. Furthermore, most of the socialist leaders were reformists rather than revolutionists, and even the most radical wing—the Spartacists, who later formed the German Communist Party—was opposed to a minority dictatorship *à la* Lenin. In addition, the Red Army was unable to intervene in Germany, and the presence of the Allied occupation forces made the establishment of a radical regime out of the question.

For all these reasons, the German revolution of November, 1918, brought to power a moderate republican government, not a Communist one. Failure also befell the later attempts at Communist revolution in Germany—the left-wing uprising in Berlin in January, 1919; the formation of the Bavarian Soviet Republic in April, 1919; the *"März Aktion"* of the Mansfeld miners in 1921; and the abortive Hamburg revolt in October, 1923. Only a minority of the German people wanted a Communist revolution, and the military power lined up against them was overwhelming. Bolshevik visions of a Communist Germany remained only a fantasy.[4]

---

[4] See the chapter below by Werner T. Angress on the German revolutions of 1918–1923. See also Werner T. Angress, *Stillborn Revolution: The Communist Bid for Power in Germany, 1921–1923*, Princeton, N.J., 1964. One of the most recent accounts is by Francis L. Carsten, *Revolution in Central Europe, 1918–1919*, Berkeley, Calif., 1972.

Hungary. For a few months in 1919 Hungary actually had a Communist regime, led by Béla Kun, a former prisoner of war in Russia, who had been converted by the Bolsheviks and sent back to his native land to carry out a revolution. Placed in power without bloodshed in March, 1919, Kun and his followers proved so inept that they soon antagonized all classes of the population, including even the workers and peasants. Kun was also foolhardy enough to get Hungary involved in wars with Rumania and Czechoslovakia, both of whom had the backing of the Allies. Red Army units operating in the Ukraine were ordered to march into Hungary to support the Kun regime, but the demands of the Russian Civil War forced a cancellation of the order, though on two occasions the Red Army was able to relieve the pressure on Hungary by attacking Rumania. Faced with invasion from abroad and rebellion at home, Kun resigned at the beginning of August and fled the country, while the Hungarian Soviet Republic came crashing down.[5] (On Hungary in 1919, see the chapter by Paul Ignotus in this volume.)

Austria. Before falling from power, Kun exerted great efforts to incite a Communist revolution in nearby Austria. On his orders the Hungarian embassy in Vienna spent large sums of money on propaganda and bribes, but two attempts to stage Communist insurrections—on April 18 and June 15, 1919—failed disastrously. The Austrian Communist Party, which had been created by the Russians, was able to win the support of only a few discontented elements, while the great bulk of the workers remained loyal to the Social Democrats. Partly as a result of their *Putsch* tactics, the Communists remained an insignificant force in Austrian politics.[6]

Slovakia. The Béla Kun regime also attempted to spread Communist revolution to nearby Slovakia. At one time during the course of the fighting between Kun's armies and those of Czechoslovakia, the Hungarians managed to occupy almost all of Slovakia. Under Kun's auspices a "Slovak Soviet Republic" was proclaimed on June 16, 1919, with a government

---

[5] On Hungary in 1919, see Rudolf Toekes, *Béla Kun and the Hungarian Soviet Republic*, New York, 1967; Istvan Deak, "Budapest and the Hungarian Revolutions of 1918–1919," *Slavonic and East European Review*, London, January, 1968, pp. 129–140; Ivan Voelgyes, *The Hungarian Soviet Republic: 1919. An Evaluation and a Bibliography*, Stanford, Calif., 1971, and Andrew C. Janos and William B. Slottman (eds.), *Revolution in Perspective: Essays on the Hungarian Soviet Republic*, Berkeley, Calif., 1972.

[6] See Julius Braunthal, *History of the International, 1914–1943*, London, 1967, pp. 144–147; Franz Borkenau, *The Communist International*, London, 1938, pp. 127–129.

composed of Slovaks, Czechs, and Hungarians. Soon thereafter, however, the Hungarian forces withdrew, and the Communist regime collapsed.[7]

Poland. Aside from Germany, the most important country in Europe that seemed at one time to face the possibility of becoming Communist was Poland. During the Polish-Soviet War of 1920 the Bolsheviks attempted to "export" a revolution on the bayonets of the Red Army, but the "Provisional Revolutionary Committee" which they established as the temporary government of Poland got little support, and it disappeared when Soviet troops were driven out of the country. (For further details on Poland in 1920, see the essay by Warren Lerner in this volume.)

Bulgaria and Estonia. The only other European countries in which Communist revolutions were attempted in the 1920's were Bulgaria (in 1923) and Estonia (in 1924). Both attempts were fiascos, merely adding further evidence to the general conclusion that Europe in the aftermath of World War I was not ripe for communism, regardless of Bolshevik hopes to the contrary.[8]

Iran. If Europe was not ripe for a proletarian revolution, it should have appeared obvious to any Marxist that the Middle East was even less so. However, Lenin was not fussy about ideological niceties if a likely prospect for revolution presented itself, as it seemed to do in northern Iran in 1920. When a revolt broke out against the Shah, Russia sent arms, troops, and warships to the support of the insurgents, and the Soviet Republic of Gilan was proclaimed. However, it soon became evident that the rebellion had little chance of success without massive Soviet intervention, and Moscow came to the conclusion that it would benefit more from collaborating with the Shah than from supporting a rebel chieftan. The Soviet forces were withdrawn, and the Gilan Republic evaporated. In this case, as in many others, Russian national interests were given priority over the cause of world revolution.[9]

---

[7] Peter A. Toma, "The Slovak Soviet Republic of 1919," *American Slavic and East European Review*, New York, April, 1958, pp. 203–215. Zdeněk Eliáš and Jaromír Netík, "Czechoslovakia," in *Communism in Europe*, edited by William E. Griffith, Vol. II, Cambridge, Mass., 1966, pp. 166–167.

[8] On the Bulgarian revolution, see Borkenau, *op. cit.*, pp. 238–242; E. H. Carr, *The Interregnum, 1923–1924*, London, 1954, pp. 190–200; and Joseph Rothschild, *The Communist Party of Bulgaria : Origins and Development, 1883–1936*, New York, 1959. On the Estonian rising, see A. J. Toynbee, *Survey of International Affairs, 1924*, London, 1926, pp. 198–202; W. G. Kritvisky, *I Was Stalin's Agent*, London, 1940, pp. 65–66; Braunthal, *op. cit.*, p. 337; and E. H. Carr, *Socialism in One Country, 1924–1926*, Vol. III, Part I, London, 1964, pp. 284–285.

[9] For further details on the Gilan episode, see Rouhollah K. Ramazani, *The Foreign Policy of Iran, 1500–1941*, Charlottesville, Va., 1966, chap. vii.

The Takeovers
in Outer Mongolia and Tannu Tuva, 1921

All the efforts of the Soviet government and the Comintern to promote revolutions in Europe and the Middle East during the 1920's and the 1930's ended in failure. Indeed throughout its entire existence from 1919 to 1943, the Comintern succeeded in spreading communism to only one country, and this occurred in the most unlikely of places—Outer Mongolia. The case of Outer Mongolia is of interest not only for this reason but also because it embodied a variation on the usual pattern of Communist takeover tactics. As we have seen, when the Bolsheviks seized power in Russia, they did not try very hard to hide the fact that they were carrying out a radical revolution. Similarly, the attempted revolutions in Europe in the years after 1917 followed the Bolshevik pattern insofar as the revolutionaries frankly stated that they intended to establish Communist regimes. The Outer Mongolian revolution in 1921, however, was characterized by quite different tactics: extensive use was made of camouflage and gradualism, thereby minimizing opposition from the population and avoiding the necessity of civil war. In this respect the takeover of Outer Mongolia served as a dress rehearsal for the takeovers in Eastern Europe and North Korea in the 1940's.

The events in Outer Mongolia may be briefly summarized as follows. In 1921 the country was occupied by an army under the command of a White Russian, the Baron von Ungern-Sternberg, who thereby provided the Bolsheviks with an excuse to invade Outer Mongolia and "liberate" it. Before doing so, however, the Bolsheviks helped a small group of Mongols to organize a revolutionary party, a provisional government in exile, and an army. This tiny Mongolian army fought its way across the frontier from Siberia, and the provisional government followed soon after. Once on Mongolian soil, the government issued an appeal to the Soviets for military aid in freeing their country from Ungern's oppressive rule, and the Red Army was glad to comply. Soviet forces quickly defeated Ungern, and under their auspices a new government was established in July, 1921. Since there were very few Communists or proletarians in Outer Mongolia, and since the people in general were extremely backward and conservative, the Bolsheviks realized that the country was far from ripe for a proletarian revolution. Thus the Bolsheviks did not venture to set up a Soviet-style regime at the start, but instead permitted the re-establishment of the theocratic monarchy, headed (in theory) by the chief of the Buddhist church. The real rulers of the country from 1921, however, were the many Soviet advisers on hand. Backed by the Red Army, they gradually transformed Outer Mongolia into a capsular imitation of the Soviet Union. The takeover of Outer Mongolia offers the most extreme example of the use of the tactic of gradualism; the process of sovietization took fifteen or twenty years, as the country was so backward, whereas in Eastern Europe in the 1940's it took only four or five years.

The significance of the Mongolian revolution derives not from the fact that this remote, unimportant country became the first Soviet satellite state, but rather from the new pattern of tactics—gradualism and camouflage—that was employed and that became standard practice in the wave of Communist revolutions at the end of World War II. The Outer Mongolian revolution also served as a model for some of the later takeovers in that it was exported from Russia on the bayonets of the Red Army. (For a comparison of the Outer Mongolian takeover with the takeovers of Poland, Rumania, North Korea, and other countries, see the essay below by Thomas T. Hammond.)

The only other instance in which the Soviets succeeded in exporting a Communist revolution before 1940 was in the tiny district of Tannu Tuva, an area which many consider to be a part of Outer Mongolia. The revolution in Tuva closely followed the pattern in Outer Mongolia proper. In 1921 the Red Army invaded Tuva, drove out the Chinese overlords, and proclaimed the country an independent state. In fact, however, the Soviets merely restored the protectorate over Tuva which Tsarist Russia had established in 1914. Problems soon arose over the desire of many Mongols and Tuvans to unite; in 1924 the foreign minister of Outer Mongolia declared that Tuva should be joined with Mongolia, and Tuvan leaders supported the move. The Soviets promptly sent troops into Tuva to suppress the rebellion and make it clear to both Tuvans and Mongols that a merger of the two countries would not be tolerated. A regime modeled after that of Soviet Russia was imposed, and Moscow's control was strengthened. Tuva remained a nominally "independent" Soviet satellite until 1944, when—in contrast to Outer Mongolia—it was formally annexed to the USSR.[10] (On the annexation of Tuva, see the chapter by Robert A. Rupen in this volume.)

---

[10] The information on Tuva was obtained from Robert A. Rupen, *Mongols of the Twentieth Century*, Bloomington, Ind., 1964, Vol. I, p. 189; Peter S. H. Tang, *Russian and Soviet Policy in Manchuria and Outer Mongolia, 1911–1931*, Durham, N.C., 1959, pp. 416–423; *Novaya Mongoliya; Protokoly pervogo Velikogo khuraldana Mongolskoy narodnoy respubliki*, Ulan-Bator-Khoto, 1925, pp. 81, 87–88; and Xenia Eudin and Robert C. North, *Soviet Russia and the East, 1920–1927*, Stanford, Calif., 1957, pp. 257–259.

The Temporary Abandonment of Efforts to Promote Revolution

In 1917 the attitude of the Bolsheviks towards Communist revolutions in other countries was shaped by three convictions. First of all, the Bolsheviks believed that such revolutions were inevitable. Second, they thought that other revolutions were essential if the Soviet regime was to survive in a hostile capitalist world and succeed in building socialism in backward Russia. Third, the Bolsheviks felt that it was their sacred duty as Marxists to promote revolutions, even if it meant sacrificing Russian national interests. In other words, the Bolsheviks in the early days were partly, if not wholly, internationalist in their outlook.

As time passed, however, the attitude of the Bolsheviks towards revolutions in other countries changed. When their efforts to foment revolutions elsewhere failed except in Mongolia, it became obvious to them that the coming of world revolution was *not* inevitable, at least not in the foreseeable future. Moreover, since the Soviet regime had survived without help from revolutions abroad, many Bolsheviks came to the conclusion that other revolutions were *not* essential for them to retain power and build socialism. Finally, the Bolsheviks decided, even if they did not admit it, that their chief duty was *not* to concentrate their efforts on revolutions abroad, but rather to preserve, protect, and strengthen their own revolution. What this meant is that the Bolsheviks, even if they did not realize it, became more nationalistic, placing the interests of Russia first.

This change in attitude towards world revolution began to take form as early as January, 1918, during the debates over the Treaty of Brest-Litovsk. Bukharin argued that signing a peace treaty with the Kaiser's government would be a betrayal of the German workers, who were hoping to overthrow that government. Lenin, on the other hand, insisted that it would be a blind gamble to risk the downfall of the Bolshevik regime on the chance that a revolution would break out in Germany within the near future. "From the time of the victory of a socialist government in any one country," wrote Lenin, "questions must be decided...exclusively from the point of view of the best conditions for the development and strengthening of the socialist revolution which has already begun."[11] In other words, the preservation of the Russian revolution must come first, and the promotion of other revolutions second.

---

[11] V. I. Lenin, "Theses on the Question of the Immediate Conclusion of a Separate and Annexationist Peace," *Sochineniya*, 3rd ed., Vol. XXII, Moscow, 1936, p. 195.

Lenin won the argument, the Brest treaty was signed, and in the years that followed the Soviet government concluded agreements with numerous capitalist states—often the same states in which the Bolsheviks were trying to provoke revolutions. Thus, from the very beginning there developed a duality in Soviet foreign policy consisting, on the one hand, of attempts to overthrow capitalist governments, and, on the other hand, of conducting normal diplomatic and economic relations with these very governments. Obviously, there was a conflict between the two elements of this dual policy, with one hindering the other. As time passed and one revolution after another aborted, it became evident that diplomatic means were proving to be more successful than revolutionary means. Consequently, the Bolsheviks gradually tended to place less emphasis on fomenting revolutions and more on promoting the interests of Soviet Russia through peaceful coexistence with capitalist states. However, the duality remained a permanent feature of Soviet foreign policy, and the Soviet government still tried to stage revolutions when a favorable opportunity seemed to arise. At certain times and in certain countries the Bolsheviks were willing to abandon the revolutionary path temporarily, but they never gave it up completely.

During Lenin's last years there was a noticeable decline in his optimism regarding the imminence of world revolution and a corresponding rise in his hopes regarding the possibility of building socialism in Russia without help from abroad. It remained for Stalin, however, to formulate this new attitude as official dogma, which he did in 1924 in his famous doctrine of "socialism in a single country." According to Stalin, the world revolution had been temporarily postponed because capitalism had stabilized itself, and attempts to promote revolutions abroad should, therefore, be abandoned for the time being, until conditions became more favorable. In the meanwhile, the Bolsheviks should concentrate their efforts on building up Russia both economically and militarily, on creating an impregnable bastion of communism which would be ready to come to the aid of other revolutions when the moment was ripe. As for the problem of building socialism in backward Russia, Stalin insisted that it could be done and would be done without the help of other countries. In other words, Stalin appealed to the nationalism of the Russian people by insisting that Russian interests should be put first and that Russia did not need the help of foreigners. His theory became in practice a substitution of nationalism for internationalism, although he could not admit it.

This change in Soviet attitude towards other revolutions had a profound impact on the Communist International. The Comintern had been founded mainly for the purpose of promoting revolutions, but as the attempted revolts failed, and as the Bolsheviks became increasingly concerned with Russian national interests, Comintern policy was subordinated completely to Soviet policy. Of course Stalin could not, as a Marxist, openly repudiate the cause of world revolution, and he undoubtedly hoped that other countries would become Communist later on. But for the moment his attention was focused primarily on consolidating his own personal power and in building up the Russian economy. For fifteen years, from 1924 to 1939, the Soviet Union and its tool, the Comintern, made no serious effort to spread communism abroad. There was only one exception—China—and that adventure ended in disaster.[12]

The Attempted Revolution in China, 1924–1927

As mentioned above, Soviet foreign policy has generally been dual in nature, characterized by an attempt to pursue two different, often contradictory lines—trying to overthrow capitalist governments and simultaneously trying to deal peacefully with these same governments. This two-pronged policy was well illustrated in the Middle East and Asia during the early years of the Bolshevik regime. In Iran, as we have seen, the Bolsheviks originally aided the Soviet Republic of Gilan, but abandoned it when they decided that more could be gained by co-operating with the Shah. In Turkey the Bolsheviks at first tried to build up a strong Communist movement, but soon came to the conclusion that Russian national interests would be better served by supporting Ataturk. In other words, Soviet policy towards Iran and Turkey during this period was similar to that followed many years later towards Nasser in Egypt—aiding strong nationalists rather than weak Communists.[13]

Soviet policy in China was not two-pronged but five-pronged, reflecting the political and ideological divisions in that strife-torn country. First, in 1921 the Soviets carried out a revolution in Outer Mongolia (which the Chinese looked upon as an integral part of China), and Outer Mongolia became a colony of Russia, despite Chinese protests. Second, in 1924 the Soviets signed a treaty granting diplomatic recognition to the "Chinese Republic" in Peking. Third, the Soviets also signed a treaty with Chang Tso-lin, the warlord who controlled Manchuria. Fourth, the Soviets

---

[12] On the adoption of the policy of "socialism in a single country" see: Isaac Deutscher, *The Prophet Unarmed. Trotsky: 1921–1929*, London, 1959; Isaac Deutscher, *Stalin: A Political Biography*, London, 1949, and Edward H. Carr, *Socialism in One Country, 1924–1926*, Vol. 2, London, 1959, chap. xii.

[13] For quotations from the debate at the Second Congress of the Comintern over whether or not Communists in colonial countries should co-operate with bourgeois elements, see Eudin and North, *op. cit.*, pp. 36–44 and 63–70.

supported the Chinese Communist Party, which they helped bring into being in 1921. And fifth, the Soviets gave aid to the Kuomintang (Chinese Nationalist Party), which dominated a Chinese government in Canton.[14]

Since both the Communists and the Kuomintang were revolutionary, pro-Soviet, and anti-imperialist, the Soviet Union favored them rather than the other factions in China, and since the Kuomintang was much stronger than the Communists, the Russians concentrated their main efforts on trying to gain control of the Kuomintang. Moscow gave aid to the Kuomintang, first under Sun Yat-sen and later under Chiang Kai-shek, ostensibly for the sole purpose of helping to unite China and drive out the imperialist powers. In fact, however, Stalin hoped that by sending arms, military experts, and political advisers (led by Mikhail Borodin), he would enable the Chinese Communists to gain control of the revolutionary movement. As a result of Soviet pressure, the Communists were admitted to membership in the Kuomintang, which they attempted to subvert from within by allying with the Left Kuomintang against Chiang and his supporters in the Right Kuomintang. Stalin expressed his policy with frank cynicism:

> At present we need the Right...Chiang Kai-shek has perhaps no sympathy for the revolution, but he is leading the army and cannot do other-wise than lead it against the imperialists...the people of the Right...have to be utilized to the end, squeezed out like a lemon, and then thrown away.[15]

Chiang, however, was no lemon. During the Great Northern Expedition of 1926–1927, the Communists tried to curtail most of his powers and take over the leadership of the movement. In April, 1927, however, Chiang attacked the Communists in their greatest stronghold, Shanghai, slaugh-tered them by the thousands, and set himself up as the head of a new government. Stalin thereupon ordered the Communists to seize power, but this only resulted in the killing of more Communists. Subsequently, Chiang ordered all Soviet advisers to leave the country, and broke off diplomatic relations with Russia. Stalin had hoped to use Chiang and then cast him aside; instead Chiang used the Soviets and then threw them out.

The China fiasco was hardly likely to entice Stalin to attempt further revolutionary ventures abroad. Instead it probably strengthened his policy

---

[14] Russia's multifaceted policy in China and the duplicity which Stalin practiced in dealing with the various factions are described in Allen S. Whiting, *Soviet Policies in China, 1917–1924*, New York, 1954.

[15] Stalin, as reported in a speech by Vujo Vujovich at the Eighth Plenum of the Executive Committee of the Comintern. Leon Trotsky, *Problems of the Chinese Revolution*, New York, 1932, pp. 389–390. Quoted in Robert C. North, *Moscow and Chinese Communists*, 2nd ed., Stanford, Calif., 1963, p. 96.

of "socialism in a single country," i.e., of concentrating on building up Russia instead of risking its security by attempting further revolutions. (For details on the Chinese events of 1924–1927, see the chapter by Gottfried-Karl Kindermann in this volume.)

The failure in China apparently also deflated Stalin's optimism regarding co-operation with Asian nationalists. At the Sixth Congress of the Comintern in 1928 the "bourgeois nationalist" forces in the colonies were denounced as reactionary and untrustworthy, while the Communist Parties were described as the only elements in the backward countries that were reliably and consistently anti-imperialist.[16] By and large this was to be Stalin's attitude until his death, it remaining for his successors to institute the policy of courting non-Communist leaders in the Third World like Nasser and Nehru.

The Rise of Hitler
and the Adoption of the "Popular Front" Policy

Stalin's decision to abandon temporarily the cause of world revolution was further strengthened by the rise of Hitler to power in 1933. Fearful of Hitler's plan to seek *Lebensraum* at the expense of Russia, Stalin could ill afford to antagonize any potential allies, whether they be anti-fascist states or anti-fascist parties. Consequently in the years following the Nazi coup there occurred a further change in both Soviet and Comintern policy.

From 1928 to 1933, prior to Hitler's coup, the Comintern had conducted an all-out struggle against the Socialists. The stupidity of this policy was most dramatically demonstrated in Germany, where the Communists refused to co-operate with the Social Democrats against the Nazis, thereby facilitating Hitler's triumph. The following year, in February, 1934, French fascist leagues attempted to storm the Chamber of Deputies, and there was fear that France might be heading in the same direction as Germany. Alarmed by the events in Germany and France, Moscow ordered a complete about-face in the tactics of the French Communist Party. In July, 1934, the Communists persuaded the Socialists in France to join them in a "United Front," and in the following year it was broadened into a "Popular Front" by the addition of the Radical Socialists, a bourgeois party. In May, 1936, the Popular Front won an overwhelming victory in the national elections, and from 1936 to 1938 France was ruled by a succession of Popular Front governments, led by the Socialists and Radical Socialists.

---

[16] Jane Degras (ed.), *The Communist International, 1919–1943: Documents*, Vol. III, London, 1960, pp. 530–541.

Despite the fears of French conservatives, the immediate aim of the Comintern's new Popular Front policy was *not* to stage a revolution in France or anywhere else. Instead the objective was, first, to prevent any more countries from becoming fascist, and, second, to encourage the election of governments that would co-operate with Russia against her foreign foes. But while the Popular Front policy may have helped to prevent a fascist takeover in France, it did not bring about a firm Franco-Russian alliance; mistrust between the two governments persisted, and the Popular Front cabinets were paralyzed by pacifism and appeasement. The French Communist Party definitely benefited from the Popular Front tactic, however, since it won many new members through its moderate, patriotic, and anti-fascist line, and this paved the way for its emergence after World War II as the largest party in France.[17]

The only other country in which the Popular Front policy was of much importance was Spain, where a Popular Front coalition triumphed in the parliamentary elections of February, 1936. The fascist and other right-wing forces were quite strong, however, and they rose up in rebellion in July, 1936, under the leadership of General Franco. Germany and Italy dispatched munitions and troops to the Rightists, and Russia responded by assisting the Loyalists with arms, officers, Soviet troops, and International Brigades recruited by the Comintern.

As in France, the immediate aim of the Soviets in Spain was not to establish a Communist regime, but rather to prevent the country from going fascist and thereby weakening the international position of the USSR. However, a secondary, long-range aim was to increase the influence of the small Communist Party, with the hope that, if the Loyalists won the civil war, the Communists might be able to gain power. This long-range aim was carefully camouflaged, however, in a manner similar to the tactics used later by Communists in other countries during World War II. The Spanish Communist Party advocated moderate policies, designed to attract the broadest possible support for the Popular Front government. "This is not a revolution at all," said a Communist slogan, "it is only the defense of the legal government."[18] Stalin sent a letter to the Socialist Prime Minister in 1936

---

[17] On the Popular Front, see Kermit McKenzie, *Comintern and World Revolution, 1928–1943. The Shaping of Doctrine*, New York, 1964; Kermit McKenzie, "The Soviet Union, the Comintern and World Revolution: 1935," *Political Science Quarterly*, New York, June, 1950, pp. 214–237; Thomas P. Thornton, "The Emergence of Communist Revolutionary Doctrine," in Black and Thornton, *op. cit.*, pp. 58–61; Borkenau, *op. cit.*, pp. 386–400; and Max Beloff, *The Foreign Policy of Soviet Russia, 1929–1941*, Vol. I, London, 1947, pp. 186–196.

[18] Beloff, *Foreign Policy*, Vol. II, p. 34.

advising him to protect the economic interests of the peasants and the bourgeoisie, to respect foreign-owned property, and to retain the support of the Republican leaders so as to prevent the Loyalist regime from appearing to be Communist-dominated.[19]

The two Soviet aims of winning the war and increasing Communist influence in Spain were doomed to failure, however. The Axis powers sent much more assistance to Spain than the Soviet Union could muster, while the democratic powers sent none at all. By mid-1938 the Loyalist cause seemed hopeless, and the Soviets gradually cut off their support. This made Franco's victory inevitable, and the war was finally brought to a close with the fall of Madrid in March, 1939.

The Spanish Civil War was not a total loss for the Soviets, however. Thousands of Communists from France, Italy, Yugoslavia, Greece, and other countries gained combat training that was to help them win control of resistance movements during World War II. In addition, these Communists obtained experience in following Popular Front tactics under wartime conditions, thus preparing them for the "National Fronts" of the 1940's.[20]

During the Popular Front period Stalin tried to create the impression abroad that the Soviet Union had lost all interest in promoting revolutions and, indeed, that it had never had any such intentions. In one of his rare interviews, he spoke as follows to the American journalist, Roy Howard:

> *Howard:* Do you not think there may be a genuine fear in capitalist countries of an intention on the part of the Soviet Union to force its political theories on other nations?
>
> *Stalin:* There is no justification for such fears....
>
> *Howard:* Does this statement of yours mean that the Soviet Union has to any degree abandoned its plans and intentions to bring about a world revolution?
>
> *Stalin:* We never had any such plans or intentions.
>
> *Howard:* You appreciate, no doubt, Mr. Stalin, that much of the world has for long entertained a different impression.
>
> *Stalin:* That is the product of misunderstanding.
>
> *Howard:* A tragic misunderstanding.
>
> *Stalin:* No, comic. Or perhaps tragi-comic. You see, we Marxists believe that revolution will occur in other countries as well. But it will come only when it is considered possible or necessary by the revolutionaries in those countries. Export of revolution is nonsense. Each country, if it so desires, will

---

[19] *Ibid.*

[20] On Spain, see especially the two books by David Cattell, *Communism and the Spanish Civil War*, Berkeley, Calif., 1956, and *Soviet Diplomacy and the Spanish Civil War*, Berkeley, Calif., 1957.

make its own revolution, and if no such desire exists, no revolution will occur.... But to assert that we desire to bring about revolution in other countries by interfering with their way of life is to speak of something that does not exist, and which we have never preached.[21]

But while Stalin attempted to persuade non-Communists that he had abandoned the cause of world revolution *permanently*, Communists looked upon the Popular Front as only a temporary tactic. And not only Communists; many non-Communists viewed statements such as those made by Stalin in his interview with Howard as propaganda designed to hide the reality of continued support for revolution. As on many other occasions, the dual nature of Soviet foreign policy—dealing with capitalist governments while plotting to overthrow them—made it difficult for the Kremlin to achieve either of its two contradictory objectives. The fear of Russia as the center of Communist subversion hindered the Soviets in their search for allies against Germany and Japan; Western leaders like Chamberlain did not trust Stalin and refused to ally with him, choosing instead to appease Hitler. So Stalin played the same game, joining with Hitler in the Nazi-Soviet pact of August, 1939, thereby outappeasing the appeasers.

World War II and the Second Wave of Communist Victories

The Nazi-Soviet pact led to World War II, which in turn led to the greatest expansion of communism in history. Indeed, all of the Communist takeovers that occurred during the years between 1939 and 1949 were made possible by World War II or conditions created by the war. To begin with, the pact of 1939 enabled Stalin to annex several countries and parts of countries in Eastern Europe. Furthermore, the war weakened, discredited, or destroyed many of the old regimes, giving the Communists a chance to organize resistance movements and thereby increase their influence. And, in the later stages of the war, the Red Army swept across Eastern Europe, liberating most of the countries from the Nazis and helping to install Communist governments.

It may be appropriate at this point to ask a fundamental question: In promoting Communist revolutions during the period from 1939 to 1949, was Stalin inspired by revolutionary zeal for world communism or by Russian national interests? Did he install Communist regimes because he considered this his duty as a Marxist? No, not Stalin. If he had ever felt that it was his sacred obligation to extend the blessings of communism to other lands (which is doubtful), he surely was not motivated by such

---

[21] *Pravda*, March 5, 1936, as translated in Jane Degras (ed.), *Soviet Documents on Foreign Policy*, Vol. III, London, 1953, pp. 165–166.

considerations as late as 1939. He annexed the Baltic States to Russia not because of Marxist zeal, but purely for *raisons d'état*. After World War II he insisted upon the establishment of a Communist regime in Poland not because he felt sorry for the poor, oppressed masses of Poland, but because he thought a Communist regime in Poland would be friendly towards the Soviet Union. The dissolution of the Comintern in May, 1943, symbolized the fact that the old Comintern spirit was dead, at least in the Kremlin. The Communist takeovers from 1939 to 1949 were carried out not by the Comintern but by organs of the Soviet state and Party apparatus, especially the Red Army and the secret police. Old Comintern hands like Tito and Georgi Dimitrov did play an important role in the takeovers, however.

Areas Formally Annexed to the USSR, 1939–1945

That Stalin was not inspired by Marxian messianism is particularly clear in regard to the territories which he seized in 1939–1940 as his part of the spoils from the pact with Hitler. The areas involved were western Belorussia and the western Ukraine (annexed from Poland in 1939), Bessarabia and northern Bukovina (annexed from Rumania in 1940), and Estonia, Latvia, Lithuania and parts of Finland (annexed in 1940). In each of these areas the takeover tactics consisted of little more than simple military occupation by the Red Army. While it is true that so-called elections were held in the Baltic States in order to give the takeovers some slight aura of legality, the whole operation was carried out so hurriedly that the camouflage was pretty thin and probably fooled no one.

The takeovers from 1939 to 1940 differed from later Communist coups in another important respect: instead of establishing "independent" puppet regimes, Stalin formally annexed these territories to the USSR. In doing this he may have been motivated by a conviction that he had a *right* to do so, either because these lands had once belonged to Russia, or, in the case of some of these areas, because they were populated by Ukrainians and Belorussians. Thus Stalin was behaving like a Russian nationalist claiming Russia's historical inheritance, not as a Marxist revolutionary fighting for world revolution. And it seems likely that the same claims would have been exercised against Finland if the Finns had not put up such heroic resistance. (The annexation of the Baltic States is described below in the chapter by Edgar Tomson.)

In 1944–1945 several other bits of territory were annexed to the Soviet Union. The annexation attracting the least notice was that of the remote, little-known country of Tannu Tuva, in the heart of Asia, where Russia is bordered by Outer Mongolia. In August, 1944, the government of the Tuvan People's Republic submitted a "spontaneous" request for admission to the USSR, and two months later the Supreme Soviet gave its approval. As Tuva had been a protectorate of Soviet Russia since 1921, the change was a mere formality. (For an account of the annexation of Tuva, see the chapter by Robert A. Rupen in this volume.)

The seizure of Carpatho-Ukraine from Czechoslovakia in 1944–1945 was quite a different story. This area, sometimes called Ruthenia or Sub-carpathian Russia, was populated predominantly by Ukrainians and had been a part of Czechoslovakia since World War I. In 1943 Stalin emphatically promised President Beneš that it would be returned to Czecho-slovakia after the war. However, when the Red Army occupied the area in the fall of 1944, Soviet military and police officials, supported by local Communists, arrested leaders of the democratic opposition and sponsored resolutions requesting that the province be incorporated into the USSR. Beneš protested, but in vain. Stalin explained that he was following a policy of "non-interference" in the internal affairs of Czechoslovakia, and was unable to forbid the population of Carpatho-Ukraine from expressing its "national will." With the Red Army in occupation of the territory, there was nothing that Beneš or the local population could do, and so Ruthenia became a part of the Ukrainian Soviet Socialist Republic.[22]

The only other areas annexed to the Soviet Union as a result of World War II were acquired not by the staging of artificially contrived "revolutions," but by diplomatic agreements with the United States and Great Britain. The Kurile Islands and the southern half of the island of Sakhalin were taken from Japan in accordance with the promises made at the Yalta Conference, while a section of East Prussia including the port of Königs-berg was granted to Russia at the Potsdam Conference.

Was There a Blueprint for the Takeovers of the 1940's ?

The period of the greatest expansion of communism took place, of course, at the end of World War II, when Communist regimes were estab-lished in a total of twelve countries. The marked similarities in the tactics used in these takeovers has caused some writers to suggest that this great

---

[22] A good summary of the events is provided in Josef Korbel, *The Communist Subversion of Czechoslovakia, 1938–1948*, Princeton, N. J., 1959, pp. 78–79, 84–85, 99–108. For a more detailed treatment, see F. Nemec and V. Moudry, *The Soviet Seizure of Subcarpathian Ruthenia*, Toronto, 1955.

spread of communism was carried out in accordance with a "blueprint" prepared in Russia, while others have rejected this notion.[23]

Was there a blueprint? The answer depends, naturally, on how the term is defined. If by a blueprint one means a rigid plan which all Communist leaders were ordered to follow without change, then of course there was no blueprint. If, however, one means a general tactical plan which Stalin expected each Communist leader to adapt and modify to suit local conditions, then it seems clear that there was such a blueprint. Otherwise it would be difficult to explain the striking similarities in the tactics used in the various countries—in countries as distant and as different as, say, Poland and North Korea. (For a comparison of the North Korean takeover with those in Eastern Europe, see the chapter by Dae-Sook Suh in this volume.)

Most of the takeovers of the 1940's were directed by Communists who had spent the war years in Russia, who returned to their native lands with takeover plans carefully worked out in advance, and who received instructions regularly both from Moscow and from Soviet officials on the scene. In some cases (such as in Poland) the nuclei of the future Communist regimes had already been founded on Soviet soil. During the war Communist cadres from Europe and Asia were trained in special schools in the Soviet Union to participate in the communization of their homelands.[24]

The similarities in tactics in the different countries cannot be explained by the argument that these Communists were familiar with the principles of Marxism-Leninism-Stalinism and were simply "doing what comes naturally" for experienced revolutionaries. On the contrary, the Communists in Eastern Europe were ordered *not* to use the tactics which many of them felt were the "natural" ones. For example, Wolfgang Leonhard, who was a member of the first group of Communists sent from Moscow to Germany at the end of the war, says that Walter Ulbricht brought with him from Stalin a tactical plan which many of the local Communists found difficult to swallow. Indeed, Ulbricht and his "Muscovite" compatriots had to force the "native" Communists to follow the tactics of gradualism and

---

[23] Adam Ulam, for example, says: "It is fairly clear that no such blueprint existed, that in fact Soviet policies responded to the specific circumstances and to the wider repercussions of Soviet thrusts in this or that area" (Ulam, *op. cit.*, p. 345.)

[24] Wolfgang Leonhard describes attending such a Comintern school near Ufa in 1942–1943. See his autobiographical account, *Child of the Revolution*, Chicago, 1958, chap. v. The training of Koreans is mentioned by Leonhard on pages 214–215, and is also discussed in the essay by Dae-Sook Suh in the present volume.

camouflage instead of immediately establishing a one-party Communist regime.[25]

Further evidence that a tactical blueprint was drawn up in Russia is provided by the case of Yugoslavia. During the war, Moscow (i.e., Stalin) sent several messages to Tito in which the Yugoslav partisans were criticized for organizing "proletarian brigades" with red stars on their uniforms, as well as for other practices which revealed the Communist orientation of the partisan leaders. Moscow advised Tito that he should avoid acts which justified the suspicions of the British and others that the partisan movement was acquiring a Communist character and aiming at the sovietization of Yugoslavia.[26] Similarly, in September, 1944, Stalin advised Tito to let King Peter return to Yugoslavia until the Communists had consolidated their hold on the country. "You need not restore him forever," said Stalin. "Take him back temporarily, and then you can slip a knife into his back at a suitable moment."[27]

In other words, gradualism and camouflage were the basic principles of the blueprint which Stalin had devised for the postwar Communist takeovers. (For more detailed comments on Stalin's policies towards Eastern Europe, see the chapter by Malcolm Mackintosh.)

The General Pattern of Takeover Tactics, 1944-1949

The general tactical line which the Communists followed in most countries during World War II might be called the "National Front" line. It went into effect in June, 1941, and was at first little more than a revival of the "Popular Front." Whereas the Popular Front had been designed to unite as many countries and as many political parties as possible to *prevent* an attack on the USSR by the fascist powers, the National Front policy was originally instituted to unite all opponents of fascism *after* the German attack on Russia had begun. As the war progressed, however, and it became clear that the Soviet Union would triumph over Germany, the purpose of the National Front changed. Instead of a defensive tactic—i.e., defense of the Soviet Union from collapse—it became an offensive one, designed to facilitate the carrying out of Communist revolutions in as many countries

---

[25] Leonhard, *op. cit.*, chaps. vii–viii.

[26] Vladimir Dedijer, *Tito*, New York, 1952, p. 180. See also p. 174.

[27] *Ibid.*, p. 233. The pamphlet by Mosha Piyade (Moša Pijade) entitled *About the Legend That the Yugoslav Uprising Owed Its Existence to Soviet Assistance*, London, 1950, contains many messages exchanged between Tito and Moscow during the war, including numerous Soviet criticisms of the partisans for not hiding the fact that their movement was Communist-dominated. See especially pages 9–11, 20, and 23.

as possible. Thus the various National Front coalitions which functioned as resistance movements in Axis-occupied countries were transformed at the end of the war into vehicles for Communist seizures of power.

The similarities between the Popular Front and National Front policies made it easy for Communists to shift from one to the other. Indeed, the National Front line at first was simply the Popular Front line with modifications, i.e., a shift in emphasis from political struggle to military struggle. Thus the various political parties, trade unions, and other groups which had worked with the Communists during the Popular Front era often found it natural to co-operate with the Communists again during the war.

The National Front policy as a tactic for seizing power embodied the following characteristics:

(1) *Use of Armed Force.* In the 1940's, as in 1917, the most important reason for the success of Communist revolutions was the use of armed force, usually meaning the Red Army. It is significant that every country that has ever become Communist was invaded by the Red Army except for three—Albania, Vietnam, and Cuba. To look at the other side of the coin, the only countries in Eastern Europe which failed to become Communist (Greece and Finland) were *not* invaded by the Red Army. Furthermore, only two areas occupied by the Red Army during World War II did not have Communist regimes imposed upon them—eastern Austria and northern Iran.

The importance of the Red Army varied from country to country. It was *the* key element in eleven countries—Outer Mongolia, Tannu Tuva, Estonia, Latvia, Lithuania, Poland, East Germany, Hungary, Rumania, Bulgaria, and North Korea.[28] In some countries which it invaded, however, its role was considerably less important. In Yugoslavia and China the Communists probably would have won without Soviet aid since native armies provided the necessary military power. In Czechoslovakia, to cite a somewhat different case, the liberating Soviet armies helped to place the Communists in a dominant position in 1945, and the threat of renewed Soviet intervention played a role in the Communist coup of 1948. But the Commu-

---

[28] The fact that the Communist regime in Poland attained power because of the Red Army is admitted in the preamble to the Polish constitution of 1952. "The historic victory of the U.S.S.R. over fascism liberated Polish soil, *enabled the Polish working people to gain power*, and made possible the rebirth of Poland within new just frontiers" (Hugh Seton-Watson, *The East European Revolution*, 3rd ed., New York, 1956, p. 373; quoted in Tucker, *op. cit.*, p. 34; italics added.). This book by Seton-Watson is an excellent survey of the communization of Eastern Europe. Another highly perceptive account is the one by R. V. Burks in Black and Thornton, *op. cit.* See also Gross, *op. cit.*, chap. xii. For detailed accounts of the events in Poland, Bulgaria, and Rumania, see the essays in this volume by Susanne S. Lotarski, Nissan Oren, and Stephen Fischer-Galati.

nists in Czechoslovakia had so much popular support and used such skillful tactics that they might have been able to take power without Soviet aid.

Stalin seems to have preferred takeovers carried out under the auspices of the Red Army, since this made it easier for him to control the countries involved. Likewise, he appears to have been suspicious of indigenous military movements, for fear that they would act independently, which explains in part his failure to give all-out support to Tito and Mao Tse-tung. Subsequent events demonstrated, of course, that his fears were well-founded.

While recognizing that many Communist takeovers were the direct result of Soviet armed intervention, it would be a gross mistake to overlook the many other elements in Stalin's takeover plans. Except when he was in a great hurry (as in the Baltic States in 1940), Stalin was not so inept as to use naked, undisguised military force. In each country he sought to get as much popular support for the Communists as possible, and he tried to make the takeovers look both legal and democratic. There seem to have been three reasons for this: *First*, Stalin wished to minimize internal opposition and thereby avoid duplicating the civil war that the Bolsheviks had been forced to fight in Russia. In other words, he wished to imitate Hitler's takeover tactics rather than Lenin's. *Second*, Stalin may have wished to reduce the possibility of intervention by the Western powers. *Third*, Stalin preferred to disguise the role of the Red Army for the sake of the Soviet Union's world image. For all these reasons, it was important to Stalin (and to the local Communists) that means other than the Red Army play as prominent a role as possible in the seizures of power. This brings us to the other characteristics of the National Front tactics for seizing power.

(2) *Use of Camouflage.* Stalin wanted the Communists to take over in such a way that the local citizens and the Western powers would not be sure what was happening. In other words, he wanted revolutions that did not look like revolutions. For this purpose it was necessary to form broad coalition governments, with cabinets containing highly respectable elements—nobles, priests, army officers, professors, and the like. In Rumania, King Michael happened to be popular, so he was retained temporarily to lend an air of legitimacy to the new regime. Similarly, in Czechoslovakia the former President, Eduard Beneš, was returned to his post, while Jan Masaryk was given the position of Foreign Minister. However, in all countries the Ministry of the Interior, which controlled the police, was kept in Communist hands.[29]

---

[29] For a description of how these policies were put into practice in East Berlin, see Leonhard, *op. cit.*, pp. 378–385.

Propaganda was also used to camouflage the true objectives of the Communists. The peasants were promised land, but nothing was said about the eventual goal of collectivization. The workers were promised that the big factories and mines would become "theirs," while the small manufacturers and shopkeepers were assured that they could keep their enterprises (a promise that was not fulfilled).[30]

The avoidance of Communist terminology was another important aspect of camouflage. The Communist-dominated regimes were not described as "dictatorships of the proletariat" but rather as "People's Democracies." Local soviets were called "people's committees," while Communist Parties usually hid behind some other name. Even the word "revolution" was avoided; in Czechoslovakia, for example, the Communist coup of February, 1948, was referred to simply as "the February events."

Wherever possible, legal, democratic procedures were simulated so as to camouflage the fact of Communist manipulation. Elections were held in all countries, democratic-sounding constitutions were adopted, and broad, popular support was claimed. Walter Ulbricht, the man who directed the Communist takeover of East Germany, expressed the principle succinctly: "It's got to look democratic, but we must have everything in our control."[31]

---

[30] A perfect example of a Communist leader camouflaging his intention to establish communism is provided by Mao's pamphlet, *China's New Democracy*, written in 1940 and published in New York in 1944 by Workers Library Publishers. On page 29 of this New York edition we read:

> Big banks, big industries and big business shall be owned by this republic...The New Democratic Government will not confiscate other capitalist private property...

> It will adopt certain measures to confiscate the land of big landlords and distribute it to the peasants who are without land or have too little of it...This is different from establishing a socialist agricultural system. It only turns the land into the private property of the peasants. The economy of the rich peasants is allowed to run as usual.

Hungary provides another example. On December 15, 1948, Ernö Gerö, a member of the Hungarian Politburo, declared in parliament that small shops would remain in private hands. When a decree on December 28, 1949, placed a number of enterprises under state ownership, Gerö assured the people that this did not mean that private trade would be nationalized. "The decree on nationalization," he said, "concerns industrial and transportation enterprises exclusively. It does not concern crafts and retail trade, and the government does not intend to nationalize the shops of craftsmen and retail trade in the future either" (*Hungarian Bulletin*, No. 67, January 15, 1950). Three years later, however, on January 19, 1953, the Hungarian Press Service, MTI, reported that ninety-nine percent of all retail trade in Hungary had been nationalized.

[31] Leonhard, *op. cit.*, p. 381.

The various National Fronts were themselves important devices for camouflage. Regardless of the name—"National Liberation Front," "Fatherland Front," or whatever—these coalitions of political parties, trade unions, and other mass organizations helped to disguise the fact of Communist control behind a façade of popular unity. In elections, for example, the Communist candidates usually managed to run as part of a "unity" slate backed by the National Front.

(3) *Use of Gradualism.* Avoiding the mistake made by the Bolsheviks in 1917, and following instead the tactics used in Outer Mongolia in the 1920's, the Communists in Eastern Europe eschewed a sudden, blatant seizure of power, and instead followed a program of "creeping communism," that is, of gradual, bit-by-bit elimination of the opposition, the aim being to get control without the people realizing what was happening. Mátyás Rákosi, the top Communist in Hungary until 1956, described this process as "salami tactics"—cutting off one slice at a time; removing first one opposition leader, then another; eliminating one political party today, and another later. By moving gradually and attacking one foe at a time, the Communists prevented the opposition from uniting and thwarting their plans.

Indeed, one of the important aspects of gradualism was the policy of trying to convince as many people as possible that the Communists did not look upon them as enemies, but rather as allies in a broad, national "United Front." As Mao expressed it in 1949:

> The Chinese revolution is a revolution of the broad masses of the whole nation. Everybody is our friend except the imperialists, the feudalists and the bureaucrat-capitalists, the Kuomintang reactionaries and their accomplices. We have a broad and solid revolutionary front. This united front is so broad that it includes the working class, the peasantry, the urban petty bourgeoisie and the national bourgeoisie.[32]

---

[32] Mao Tse-tung, "Address to the Preparatory Committee of the New Political Consultative Conference, June 15, 1949," *Selected Works*, Vol. IV, Peking, 1961, p. 407. For a similar statement, indicating the desire of the Communists in 1949 to gain the support of all strata of the population, see: Mao Tse-tung, "Proclamation of the Chinese People's Liberation Army, April 25, 1949," *ibid.*, pp. 397–400.

The Chinese Communists made extensive use of the tactic of the "United Front" or "National Front" in their rise to power, and it has since become a part of Chinese Communist dogma, which is said to be applicable to the present day, especially in underdeveloped countries. Typical of Chinese pronouncements is the following by Lin Piao in his famous pamphlet, *Long Live the Victory of People's War!*, Peking, 1966, p. 19:

> History shows that when confronted by ruthless imperialist aggression, a Communist Party must hold aloft the national banner and, using the weapon of the united front, rally around itself the masses and the patriotic and anti-imperialist people who form more than

Gradualism also characterized Communist economic policy. For example, the Communists denied at first that they had any intention of collectivizing agriculture. Instead, they began by confiscating the lands of the landlords, collaborators, and expellees and distributed this land to the peasants. Only later, after Communist rule was firmly established, were the peasants forced into collective farms. Similarly, nationalization of industry and trade proceeded gradually. In the beginning only the largest enterprises were seized, and the small manufacturers and shopkeepers were assured that they would be permitted to operate freely. Within a few years, however, these promises were broken and the small entrepreneurs also lost their properties.

(4) *Use of Planning.* Aside from the general "blueprint" which Stalin apparently had prepared for Eastern Europe, the various Communist leaders seem to have drawn up specific "blueprints" for each individual country. As soon as part of a country was liberated by the Red Army, Communist chieftains arrived from Moscow and put their plans into operation, and this gave them a tremendous advantage over the other political parties. For example, the Communists knew which ministries they wanted most—Interior (the police), Defense (the armed forces), Information (the press and the radio), and Agriculture (which would carry out any land distribution). In addition, they made special efforts to gain preponderant influence in mass organizations such as the trade unions and the peasant unions. Secret Communists and fellow travelers were placed in various branches of the government, as well as in other political parties. The non-Communists, by contrast, tended to place their faith in the democratic process and showed few signs of advance planning.

Exceptions to the General Pattern of Takeovers in the 1940's

Guerrilla Takeovers. In four countries—Yugoslavia, Albania, China, and North Vietnam—Communist takeovers were the outgrowth primarily of World War II resistance movements carried on simultaneously with civil wars. The Soviet army played a relatively unimportant role in Yugoslavia

---

90 per cent of a country's population...If we abandon the national banner, adopt a line of "closed-doorism" and thus isolate ourselves, it is out of the question to exercise leadership and develop the people's revolutionary cause...

History shows that within the united front the Communist Party must maintain its ideological, political, and organizational independence, adhere to the principle of independence and initiative, and insist on its leading role.

On the United Front policy, see also Peter Van Ness, *Revolution and Chinese Foreign Policy : Peking's Support for Wars of National Liberation*, Berkeley, Calif., 1970, pp. 61–66.

and China, while it played no role at all in Albania and Vietnam. The victory of the Communists in these four countries was attained by guerrilla armies, and the regimes established by the Communists were dominated by former military officers. Thus armed force was the key factor in these takeovers also, even though it was not Soviet armed force. (For further details on the takeovers in Yugoslavia, Albania, China, and Vietnam, see the chapters in this volume by Paul Shoup, Stephen Peters, Jürgen Domes, and Dennis J. Duncanson.)

Czechoslovakia. Czechoslovakia was another exception to the general pattern; indeed, in certain respects it was unique. It was the only case in Eastern Europe or the Far East in which the Communists won a plurality of the votes in a free election (thirty-eight percent of the ballots in 1946), and the only case in which the Communists had some chance of eventually winning a majority of the votes. As things turned out, they never achieved this goal, but seized power instead. However, because of their extensive popular support, combined with careful planning and skillful tactics, they were able to take over in a manner that was almost legal. In addition, the coup was virtually bloodless. It was, in fact, the closest thing to a peaceful Communist takeover that has ever occurred except in small states like San Marino and Kerala.

This is not to say that armed force played no role at all in Czechoslovakia. As the Red Army swept across the country in 1944–1945, it placed Communists in dominant positions in organs of government, and Communist influence was greatly enhanced by the fact that most of the country, including Prague, was liberated by the USSR. Furthermore, although there were no Soviet troops in Czechoslovakia when the Communists seized power in February, 1948, everyone knew that Russia could intervene if necessary. In addition, the Communists had their own private army—the "Workers' Militia"—which paraded with rifles slung over their shoulders and helped the Communist-dominated police intimidate the population. Still, the fact remains that the Communist regime in Czechoslovakia gained power primarily by winning a large following, by out-maneuvering its opponents, and by planning its takeover with consummate skill. (For further details on the Prague coup in 1948, see the chapter by Pavel Tigrid in this volume.)[33]

San Marino. While the Communist takeover in Czechoslovakia was almost legal, the takeover in tiny San Marino was completely legal. The

---

[33] An interesting discussion of the similarities between Hitler's "legal revolution" and the Communist takeover in Czechoslovakia is contained in Hugh Seton-Watson, *Neither War Nor Peace*, New York, 1960, pp. 200–205.

smallest republic in the world, with a population of only around 20,000, San Marino, located in northern Italy, is the only independent state that has seen the Communists win a majority in free elections. On August 14, 1945, the people voted the Communists into power, but defections from the Communists in September, 1957, deprived them of their majority in the Grand Council, and since that time the non-Communists have dominated the country.

Communist Takeovers Since 1949

Cuba. The Cuban case is unique because the man who led it was not a Communist when he seized power, but stumbled into communism, apparently without knowing at first where he was going. Before his victory Castro was a professed believer in pluralistic democracy, but he was also anti-capitalist, anti-imperialist, and a radical social reformer, though his notions of how Cuba should be transformed were extremely vague. Having overthrown the Batista regime through a guerrilla struggle, he gradually became a "Communist" himself and made Cuba "Communist" because of a combination of circumstances: (1) His radical economic measures destroyed private enterprise and led to a state-controlled economic system. (2) The Communist Party was the only well-organized, disciplined political force which could provide the cadres needed to administer the government and the economy. (3) Lacking an ideology of his own or the ability to formulate one, he eventually seized upon Marxism-Leninism to fill the ideological vacuum. (4) As his expropriations of United States property brought him into increasing conflict with Washington, he moved ever closer to Moscow. The Soviets bailed out his sinking economy and promised to defend him militarily, thus providing another incentive for him to identify himself as a Communist and Cuba as a Communist country. (For a fuller description of the events in Cuba, see the chapter by Boris Goldenberg.)

India. Local conditions of caste, class, and shifting party alignments in parts of India have produced that great historical rarity: Communist-dominated governments voted into power in free elections. In the Indian state of Kerala the Communists won electoral victories not once but twice— first in 1957 and again in 1967. In both instances, however, the cabinets lasted only two years, being removed on one occasion by the central government of India, while the second time the regime collapsed from internal discord. The Communists remain strong in Kerala, however, and they may well gain power again. That Kerala is a portent of things to come for all of India remains doubtful, however, despite the electoral triumph of the Communists in West Bengal in 1967. (See the chapter on Kerala by Gerald A. Heeger.)

Communist Failures Since World War II

Though the years since 1945 have seen many Communist takeovers, the story is not one of victories alone. There have been failures too, and the reasons for Communist successes are better understood in the context of these abortive revolutions.

Greece. Greece is the only country in Southeast Europe which did not become Communist as an outgrowth of World War II, though the Communists tried hard. As in Yugoslavia, the largest resistance movement during the war was dominated by Communists, and it probably would have seized control of Greece in 1944 or 1945 if British troops had not intervened. (It is notable that Soviet troops did *not* invade Greece, perhaps as a result of the agreement made between Churchill and Stalin in October, 1944.)[34] Undeterred by this defeat, the Communists hid many of their arms and waited until the fall of 1946, when they rose against the conservative, monarchist government. The rebels received munitions from Greece's Communist neighbors, Bulgaria, Yugoslavia, and Albania, who also permitted fleeing guerrillas to escape across their frontiers for rest, medical care, and training. Under such circumstances the Greek government had great difficulty in suppressing the rebellion, even with economic and military aid from the United States under the Truman Doctrine, which was announced in 1947. In the summer of 1949, however, Yugoslavia stopped all assistance to the rebels, and soon thereafter the Communists were forced to give up the fight.[35] (On the Greek civil war, see the chapter by D. George Kousoulas.)

Finland. Besides Greece, Finland was the only other country in Eastern Europe to avoid communization. That Finland escaped again, as it had in 1918 and 1940, would almost lead one to conclude that there is a special department in heaven charged with the task of protecting these plucky people, but other, less fanciful reasons might be suggested. *First* of all, Stalin knew that the Western powers were quite sympathetic towards the

---

[34] For an account of the famous "percentages agreement" whereby Churchill and Stalin divided Southeast Europe into spheres of "predominance," see Winston Churchill, *The Second World War*, Vol. VI, *Triumph and Tragedy*, Boston, 1953, pp. 227–229.

[35] Hugh Seton-Watson states that the revival of the civil war by the Greek Communists in 1946 "no doubt had the approval of Moscow" (*The East European Revolution*, p. 325). However, Milovan Djilas, who was one of Tito's closest associates at the time, told the present author in a private interview that Stalin was not responsible for the resumption of the civil war, and that the Greek Communists probably made the decision without his endorsement. Further evidence to substantiate this view is provided in the chapter by D. George Kousoulas in the present volume.

Finns, so much so that they had planned to aid Finland against Russia in the Winter War of 1939–1940. At the Teheran Conference and on other occasions both Roosevelt and Churchill expressed their continued interest in Finland's independence.[36] *Second,* Stalin's nightmarish memories of the Winter War may have convinced him that the Finns were so tough that he could not impose a Communist regime on them without massive armed intervention, possibly followed by long guerrilla resistance. *Third,* the armistice terms accepted by Finland in 1945 gave Stalin those bits of territory which he considered vital for Russian security, committed the Finns to paying huge reparations, and required that the Finnish army undertake the job of driving the German forces out of the country. Though costly in Finnish blood, the fight against the Germans made it unnecessary for Finland to undergo "liberation" by the Red Army, with all that this might have meant for subsequent political developments. *Fourth,* from the point of view of the Soviet Union, Finland's geographic location was not as strategic as that of Poland, Czechoslovakia, Rumania, or other states. It is no accident that the two countries of Eastern Europe which escaped communization—Greece and Finland—happened to be on the fringes of Russia's western frontier. *Fifth,* Stalin may have hesitated to communize Finland for fear that this would force Sweden to abandon its traditional neutrality and join the Western bloc. *Finally,* since 1945 Finland has behaved towards Russia with utmost circumspection, giving Moscow a veto over Finnish foreign policy, and suppressing any flagrant manifestations of anti-Soviet behavior by its citizens. (It should be noted, however, that a similar pro-Soviet policy on the part of Czechoslovakia from 1945 to 1948 did not save it from communism.)

These explanations leave unresolved the controversy over whether or not there was in fact an attempted Communist takeover in Finland in 1948 and, if so, why it failed. In any event it seems clear that, regardless of whether a coup was tried or not, the Communists got little support from the Soviet Union.[37] And this remains the fundamental fact of life for Finland: if at any time since 1917 the Soviet government had made up its mind to impose a Communist regime on its tiny neighbor, it could have done so, but for one reason or another it has chosen to let Finnish freedom survive. (On Finland since World War II, see the chapter by Kevin Devlin.)

---

[36] Herbert Feis, *Churchill, Roosevelt, Stalin: The War They Waged and The Peace They Sought,* Princeton, N.J., 1957, pp. 268–269, 411–413.

[37] One of the advocates of the view that the Finnish Communists *did* try to seize power in 1948 is James Billington. See his chapter on Finland in Black and Thornton, *op. cit.*

Once again it is worth calling attention to the importance of Soviet military power in Communist takeovers: Finland and Greece were not invaded by the Red Army; Finland and Greece did not become Communist. The importance of Soviet military power is also demonstrated by the fact that only two areas have ever been occupied by the Red Army without becoming Communist—eastern Austria and northern Iran.

Austria. In contrast with Germany, the Soviets never made any determined effort to establish a Communist regime in their occupation zone in Austria, the main reason probably being that the area was too small to survive as a viable political or economic unit. Instead of promoting communism, the Soviets concentrated on extracting as much as possible from their zone economically. After years of disagreement, in 1955 the Russians and the Western powers finally signed an Austrian peace treaty which provided for the evacuation of all foreign troops. The Soviet and Western armies went home, and Austria regained its independence.[38]

Iran. The case of Iran is in one respect unique: it was the only country in which the Red Army established Communist regimes, only later to withdraw and permit them to be overthrown. In the fall of 1945 the Russians sent Azeri and Kurdish agents into northern Iran, arms were distributed to local Communists, and in December, 1945, the "Autonomous Republic of Azerbaijan" and the "Kurdish People's Republic" were established under the protection of the Soviet army. For some months it appeared that Stalin was planning to follow his previously used scenario: the two "republics" would request that they be annexed to the USSR, the Supreme Soviet would accede to the "will of the people," and Iran would lose its two northern districts.

Before the final scenes of the familiar script could be acted out, however, the Soviet Union was subjected to multiple pressures: Iran appealed to the United Nations, while at the same time promising Russia an oil concession if the troops were withdrawn. In the meantime, President Truman, if his memory can be trusted, sent an ultimatum to Stalin stating that he had given orders to American military chiefs to prepare for the movement of ground, sea, and air forces into the area.[39] In any event, all Soviet forces

---

[38] On Austria, see William B. Bader, *Austria Between East and West, 1945 to 1955*, Stanford, Calif., 1966; Sven Allard, *Russia and the Austrian State Treaty: A Case Study of Soviet Policy in Europe*, University Park, Pa., 1970; and Kurt L. Shell, *The Transformation of Austrian Socialism*, New York, 1962. See also the chapter by Hans W. Schoenberg in the present volume.

[39] *The New York Times*, August 25, 1957. See the chapter by Rouhollah Ramazani in this volume. Truman's claim that he sent an ultimatum had been overlooked by scholars until Prof. Ramazani uncovered it.

were evacuated from Iran in May, 1946, and the two puppet regimes collapsed.

Frustrated in its designs on northern Iran and apparently halted in Europe and Turkey by the Truman Doctrine and the Marshall Plan, after 1947 the Soviet Union increasingly turned its attention to Asia as the most promising area for further Communist takeovers. Inspired perhaps by Andrei Zhdanov's militant speech at the founding of the Cominform in September, 1947, and by the revolutionary rhetoric at the Southeast Asian Youth Conference in Calcutta in February, 1948, a wave of Communist insurrections broke out in Southeast Asia in 1948–1949.[40]

Burma. In Burma the Communists started an armed rebellion in March, 1947, almost immediately after their leader had returned from the Southeast Asian Youth Conference. The Communists were able to establish "liberated areas" in several parts of the country, but in the 1950's the insurrection petered out, although the Communists still retained some strongholds.[41]

Malaya. In Malaya the Communists launched a "people's revolutionary war" in 1948. Large numbers of British troops were brought into use, and by the middle of 1950 the prospects of the Communists deteriorated, although the official "state of emergency" was not terminated until the Communists had carried on guerrilla warfare for twelve years.[42]

Philippines. The Communists in the Philippines controlled a strong guerrilla force, the Hukbalahap, which had engaged in intermittent struggle against the government ever since World War II. In January, 1950, the Politburo ordered an all-out civil war, but the rebellion was unsuccessful, and thousands of Huks were killed or captured.[43]

Indochina. The attempt by the Communists to seize power in Indochina erupted into an armed conflict with the French in November, 1946. After years of warfare, culminating in the defeat at Dienbienphu, the French finally decided to get out of Indochina, which they agreed to do at the Geneva Conference in July, 1954. By this agreement the Communists gained complete control of North Vietnam, and in the years that followed they waged a long and bloody struggle to try to take over South Vietnam, as well as Laos and Cambodia. As of the date of this writing, however, they

---

[40] The insurrections and the events which preceded them are described in Charles B. McLane, *Soviet Strategies in Southeast Asia*, Princeton, N. J., 1966, chap. vi. Among other things, McLane discusses the question of whether or not the revolts were carried out on the initiative of Moscow.

[41] *Ibid.*, pp. 371–385.

[42] *Ibid.*, pp. 385–401.

[43] *Ibid.*, pp. 417–432.

have so far failed to attain their goal, largely because of United States aid to the south. (On Vietnam, see the chapter by Dennis J. Duncanson in this volume.)

South Korea. Except for Vietnam the most famous failure of an attempted Communist takeover in Asia was the invasion of South Korea in June, 1950, by the armies of the Communist regime in the north. In several respects the Korean and Vietnamese cases are similar. Both countries were divided along the middle, with a Communist regime in the north and a non-Communist regime in the south. In each case the Communists launched military campaigns aimed at establishing control over the whole country, and the non-Communists were saved from defeat only by the intervention of the United States. In both countries the Communists received aid from the Soviet Union and China.

There were important differences between the two fratricidal wars, however. One was geography: Vietnam consisted largely of jungle, which provided ideal cover for guerrillas, whereas the terrain in Korea was much more open. Furthermore, Vietnam was bordered by Laos and Cambodia, through which supplies and troops could be transported by the Communists to almost any point in the south. Korea, by contrast, was surrounded on all but one side by the sea, which was controlled by United States naval forces, with the result that the Communists could gain access to the south only by crossing the border between North Korea and South Korea. Furthermore, once the Communists had been driven out of South Korea, it was possible to establish a fixed, defensible military position, and South Korea was able to maintain its independence.

There were also differences in the nature of the leadership in each country. Whereas Ho-chi-Minh was a national hero to many people in both parts of Vietnam, Kim Il-song was virtually unknown until the Soviets installed him in power in North Korea. Partly for this reason, the Communists in South Vietnam had more support than in South Korea. Moreover, in South Vietnam there was no one leader who stood out from the rest and was able to retain power for very long, while in South Korea the dominant figure was clearly Syngman Rhee, who also had strong connections with the United States.

Finally, the Communist invasion of South Korea was a case of naked aggression, with the result that the south was immediately able to get military support from both the United States and the United Nations. In Vietnam the issues were not so clear; for many years the war was conducted in guerrilla fashion, without the open participation of North Vietnam, thereby enabling the Communists to claim that the struggle was a civil war, conducted by the people of South Vietnam against their own government.

Whether such claims were true or not (and the point will not be debated here), many people outside of Vietnam accepted them, and this made it more difficult for the South Vietnamese government to secure sustained help from other countries. Although the United States sent hundreds of thousands of soldiers and spent billions of dollars in Vietnam, public opinion finally forced President Nixon to commit himself to the withdrawal of American troops. Unlike Korea, there seemed to be no way to bring the Vietnamese conflict to an end.

Indonesia. In Indonesia the Communists staged an uprising in September, 1948, but it was suppressed by President Sukarno within a few weeks, and most of the top leaders were killed.[44] Surprisingly, however, this proved to be only a temporary setback. Within a few years the Party had regained much of its popular following, and President Sukarno allied himself more and more closely with the Communists. Indeed, during the early 1960's it looked as though Indonesia might follow the same road as Cuba. Sukarno, like Castro, was a charismatic nationalist leader, whose popularity was due in part to his claim that he had freed his country from the bonds of imperialism. Also like Castro, Sukarno was not a Communist, although he defended the Communists from their critics and gave the Party an aura of respectability. Both men found common interests with the Communists, and both came to depend increasingly on the Communists for support. Both established friendly relations with Communist states.

Castro, as we have seen, eventually decided to become a "Communist" and to make his country "Communist." Whether Sukarno would have done the same cannot be said for sure, but there is evidence that he knew about and was sympathetic towards the Communist plot of September 30, 1965, which was designed to push Indonesia far towards becoming a Communist state. Had the coup been successful, it is conceivable that Sukarno also would have decided sooner or later to embrace communism openly.

However, the Communist coup in Indonesia failed, and here the similarities with Cuba end. Unlike the nimble and masterful Castro, Sukarno behaved like an uneasy political juggler, unable to maintain a firm grip on either of the two chief contenders for power, the Communists and the army. He permitted himself to become identified as a partisan of the Communists,

---

[44] *Ibid.*, pp. 401–417. The Indonesian Communist Party seems to have a penchant for building up a considerable popular following and then throwing it away by premature, poorly planned revolts. Already in 1926 and 1927 they had staged several uprisings, which were followed by severe repressions. See Harry J. Benda and Ruth T. McVey (eds.), *The Communist Uprisings of 1926–1927 in Indonesia : Key Documents*, Ithaca, N.Y., 1960.

and when their coup miscarried, he found himself discredited, soon to be cast to the political sidelines.

The Indonesian case provides another example of the crucial importance of military power in Communist revolutions. The attempted coup was predicated on the assumption that the army could be neutralized by assassinating its anti-Communist leaders, but the Minister of Defense escaped and rounded up enough loyal troops to suppress the uprising. There followed a bloody anti-Communist pogrom which effectively destroyed the Party, at least for the foreseeable future.[45] (For a description of the coup in Indonesia, see the chapter below by Justus M. van der Kroef.)

Guatemala. Moving from Asia to Latin America, we find that the only thwarted takeover by Communists in this area occurred in Guatemala in the period from 1951 to 1954. There the Communist Party had considerable support among intellectuals and the working class, and—most important of all—it had great influence over Jacobo Arbenz, who became President in March, 1951. Though not a Communist himself, Arbenz came to depend more and more upon the Communists for advice, cadres, and organizational support, while the Communists used him to strengthen their following throughout the country, hoping eventually to establish a Communist regime.

The United States government, as represented by the Central Intelligence Agency, became alarmed over the possibility that one of its Latin-American neighbors might become Communist, and it plotted with Guatemalan exiles to overthrow Arbenz. An "army" of about 150 Guatemalans invaded the country from Honduras on June 18, 1954, and a few days later an "air force" consisting of a handful of World War II fighter planes with American pilots bombed the Guatemalan capital. Demoralized by the refusal of the army to defend him, Arbenz resigned on June 27. The CIA-financed revolution was over. A regime which was not yet Communist, but which seemed well on the way towards becoming Communist, had been overthrown, and military power was again decisive. Arbenz had made a mistake which Castro was not to repeat: he had failed to gain control of his country's armed forces, thereby making it possible for a piddling group of exiles to overthrow him.[46]

Chile. In October, 1970, Dr. Salvador Allende Gossens, an avowed Marxist but not a Communist, became President of Chile after his coalition

---

[45] Communist China's role in Indonesia is described in the section of this essay entitled "China and Communist Takeovers."

[46] See the chapter by Ronald M. Schneider in the present volume, as well as his book, *Communism in Guatemala, 1944–1954,* New York, 1959. The role of the United States in the overthrow is discussed in David Wise and Thomas B. Ross, *The Invisible Government,* New York, 1964, chap. xi.

of Socialists, Communists, and other leftists won a plurality of thirty-six percent. His program of gradually taking over private enterprise might have led eventually to a Communist-type regime, but this program, combined with inflation, shortages, and strikes, aroused the middle classes, who got financial aid from the CIA. Finally, on September 11, 1973, a military junta ousted Allende and seized power.

Soviet Counter-Revolutions

The postwar era has so far witnessed three instances in which Soviet armed forces have carried out counter-revolutions in countries rebelling against Soviet-style communism—namely, in East Germany in 1953, Hungary in 1956, and Czechoslovakia in 1968. In East Germany the rebellion erupted outside of the Party and was essentially leaderless. For this reason, as well as because the country was already occupied by Soviet troops, the revolt was quickly and totally suppressed.

In Hungary and Czechoslovakia, by contrast, the anti-Stalinist liberalization movements were led by Communists, their aim being to keep the "good" features of communism while removing the "bad," to create "socialism with a human face," as it was called in Czechoslovakia. These movements quickly attracted non-Communist and anti-Communist elements, however, who put forward demands for considerably more than merely a reformed communism. They called for such fundamental changes as the institution of free elections and the establishment of a multiparty system, which were clearly incompatible with communism.

In each country the Party itself removed the old Stalinist bosses (Rákosi in Hungary and Novotný in Czechoslovakia) and replaced them with Party liberals (Nagy in Hungary and Dubček in Czechoslovakia). These well-meaning men tried to initiate reforms in keeping with the confines of communism, but they soon discovered that the majority of the population was not only anti-Soviet and anti-Stalinist but also anti-Communist. Having opened the floodgates of liberalization a bit, they were unable to master the onrushing wave of demands for freedom of speech, freedom of the press, free elections—indeed, all of those troublesome liberties which would make the maintenance of a Communist regime impossible.

In Hungary the situation got out of control and erupted into violence against the hated representatives of the Stalinist regime, especially the police. Imre Nagy, who found himself unexpectedly the leader of the revolt, was swept off his feet by the emotions of the moment and was injudicious enough to take steps certain to frighten the Soviets, such as dissolving the

Communist Party, proclaiming Hungarian neutrality, withdrawing from the Warsaw Pact, and asking for intervention by the United Nations. These measures were looked upon in Moscow as a direct challenge to its dominance of the rest of Eastern Europe as well as of Hungary, and the rebellion was dramatically crushed by Soviet tanks. A Soviet counter-revolution was imposed from above, thereby bringing an end to the popular, democratic revolt from below.

The reforming Communist leaders in Czechoslovakia thought that they could escape Soviet intervention by avoiding some of the mistakes of the Hungarians. They assumed that by professing their loyalty to the Soviet Union in foreign policy they would be permitted some liberalization in domestic policy, and so they repeatedly emphasized Czechoslovakia's devotion to the Soviet bloc and the Warsaw Pact. Furthermore, there was no violence, no lynching of Communists, and no talk of overthrowing Dubček. There were, however, other developments which appeared intoler-able in Soviet eyes—freedom of speech, freedom of the press, proposals for free elections under a multiparty system, tentative steps towards improving relations with West Germany, and even public criticism of the Soviet Union. The Kremlin feared that such subversive notions might spread not only to other Communist states in Eastern Europe, but even to the Soviet Union itself. Since Dubček appeared to be a weak, indecisive man, who was either unable or unwilling to suppress these heresies, the Soviet leaders decided that they would have to restore "order" them-selves. And so, once again, Soviet tanks invaded a "brotherly socialist state" to "suppress fascism." The Soviet army, which had been the principal instrument for establishing Communist regimes, also proved to be the principal instrument for maintaining them. (On the counter-revolutions in Hungary and Czechoslovakia, see the chapters by Andrew Gyorgy and William E. Griffith in this volume.)

China and Communist Takeovers

Prior to 1949 almost all Communist takeovers were inspired and aided by Soviet Russia, but the triumph of communism in China created another base from which the spread of Communist influence might be promoted. The creation of the Chinese People's Republic (CPR) was bound to affect the prospects for further Communist revolutions for at least three reasons. First, China was the largest and most powerful country to become Commu-nist since 1917. Second, China was geographically close to many Asian countries which were more or less ripe for revolution. Third, the Chinese Communists felt that their revolution was more relevant than Russia's to the underdeveloped countries of the world, and they were eager to spread the Maoist gospel to other lands.

In actual practice, however, the Chinese People's Republic has had little success in inspiring revolutions, and it has concentrated primarily on the promotion of China's national interests rather than on the cause of world communism. Its major efforts, and its major successes, have involved either: (1) giving military aid to friendly neighbors on its borders, or (2) establishing Communist rule in areas which it considers to be part of China.

In the first category belongs the Korean War. When victorious United States and South Korean armies approached the frontier between Korea and Manchuria in late 1950, the Chinese felt themselves directly threatened, and they sent hundreds of thousands of troops to help the North Korean regime drive its enemies back across the thirty-eighth parallel and beyond. China thereby saved its Communist neighbor from defeat and prevented the establishment of an American-dominated government along the Chinese frontier.

Tibet falls in the second category. In 1950 the Chinese dispatched their armies to Tibet and imposed a Communist regime on that remote country. Many have argued that this was not a case of Chinese aggression since both Chinese Nationalists and Chinese Communists claim Tibet as an integral part of China. Such an argument is no more convincing (at least to the present writer) than to say that Stalin was justified in annexing Lithuania in 1940 on the grounds that Tsarist Russia had seized that country in the eighteenth century (the same century, incidentally, in which China gained control of Tibet). Regardless of what the Chinese may have felt, the Tibetans assuredly were not Chinese, did not want to be a part of China, and had been independent of China during most of their history, most recently between 1911 and 1950.

Korea and Tibet are the only cases in which the Chinese Communists are known to have employed ground troops in combat outside of China proper. In North Vietnam, however, the Chinese are reported to have sent many thousands of soldiers to maintain roads and rail lines, construct airfields, and even operate anti-aircraft guns.[47] China has also supported North Vietnam by large shipments of food and arms, and has from time to time threatened to intervene with combat troops if North Vietnam should be invaded. As in the case of Korea, Chinese aid to North Vietnam has

---

[47] *The New York Times*, December 1, 1965, p. 1; *Christian Science Monitor* March 8, 1967, p. 4, and April 18, 1968, p. 1, as cited in Van Ness, *op. cit.*, p. 112. Harold C. Hinton in *China's Turbulent Quest*, New York, 1970, p. 145, states that China has stationed "fifty thousand military engineer troops in North Vietnam."

probably been motivated less by ideology than by a desire to eliminate United States influence from a country located on China's frontier.

Elsewhere in Southeast Asia the Chinese have given both moral and material support to Communist movements in Laos, Cambodia, Thailand, Burma, Malaya, Singapore, northern Bornea, and Indonesia.[48] Of these countries the greatest potential prize was Indonesia, whose huge Communist Party was pro-Peking, and whose President, Sukarno, was co-operating with both Peking and the Indonesian Communists. On the night of September 30, 1965, a group of Communists attempted to overthrow the existing cabinet and replace it with a revolutionary council, the aim being to push Indonesia far in the direction of becoming Communist. The coup backfired, however, when army leaders overthrew the rebels, launched an extermination campaign against the Communists, and removed President Sukarno. The extent of China's involvement in the affair is a debated issue. It is known that China endorsed the Indonesian Communist Party's plans to arm the peasants, and China reportedly agreed to send 100,000 small weapons to the Communists, but how many of these arms reached Indonesia or whether China specifically endorsed the planned coup is unclear. In any event, the Communist Party and President Sukarno, both of whom had identified themselves closely with Communist China, lost all political power, and efforts to promote communism in Indonesia were wrecked for the forseeable future.[49]

Aside from Asia, the continent where China has been most active in trying to promote revolutions is Africa. The Chinese have at times won friends in Africa by collaborating with established left-wing (but non-Communist) governments, as in Tanzania and Ghana, while in other countries they have apparently made unsuccessful attempts to support revolutionary movements, as in Burundi, Dahomey, the Central African

---

[48] Hinton, op. cit., pp. 149, 227, 240–242; Van Ness, *op. cit.*, pp. 132–138 and *passim*.

[49] For details on China's role in Indonesia, see the chapter by Justus M. van der Kroef in this volume, as well as Sheldon W. Simon, *The Broken Triangle : Peking, Djakarta, and the PKI*, Baltimore, 1969, pp. 102–109, and Van Ness, *op. cit.*, pp. 101–110. Van Ness seems to get off the track when he argues that "the September 30 Movement clearly did *not* represent a revolutionary attempt to overthrow the Indonesian state or to oust the chief-of-state, President Sukarno" (p. 103) and that "the movement . . . was not involved in making revolution against the Indonesian government . . ." (p. 110). To contend that the plotters were not attempting a revolution simply because they planned to retain Sukarno is no more persuasive than it would be to say that Czechoslovakia did not experience a revolution in February, 1948, because Gottwald remained as Prime Minister and Beneš was kept on as President.

Republic, and the Congo.[50] In Latin America the Chinese have had little success in winning friends or fostering revolutionary movements, partly because they have had to compete with United States and Soviet influence.[51]

Communist China's activities in support of revolutions have taken varied forms, including disbursing arms and money, training guerrillas, bribing officials, disseminating propaganda, forming front organizations, and encouraging political terror, tribal revolts, demonstrations, strikes, and riots, but the results so far have generally been unimpressive.[52]

Any discussion of China's role in promoting Communist takeovers would be incomplete without some mention of the controversies between the Soviet Union and China on the issue of how, when, where, and under what circumstances Communist countries should support revolutionary movements. The chief point to make for the purposes of this essay is that the Chinese accuse the Soviets of having abandoned the cause of revolution and of preaching the following false doctrines: (1) Imperialism can be overthrown peacefully, without violence. (2) War is so terrible, and in the nuclear age so dangerous, that it must be avoided at all costs. By contrast, the Chinese say that their views are the following: (1) Revolutions cannot be carried out by peaceful means, but only through violence, through "people's wars," "national liberation wars," or "revolutionary wars." (2) Such wars do not inevitably escalate into nuclear wars. Revolutionary wars, therefore, must not be feared, for otherwise the peoples of the underdeveloped countries would be doomed to perpetual slavery. If the imperialists or "social-imperialists" (i.e., the Soviets) unleash wars, this will bring revolutions, but if the people overthrow imperialism, there will be no more wars. As Mao expressed it, "With regard to the question of world war, there are but two possibilities: One is that war will give rise to revolution and the other is that revolution will prevent the war."[53]

One of the clearest statements of how the Chinese view the differences between the Soviet and Chinese positions on revolution was contained in the famous article by Lin Piao, *Long Live the Victory of People's War!*:

---

[50] Hinton, *op. cit.*, pp. 151–152; Harold C. Hinton, *Communist China in World Politics*, Boston, 1966, pp. 188–197; Van Ness, *op. cit.*, pp. 114, 139–146.

[51] Hinton, *Communist China in World Politics*, pp. 197–201; Van Ness, *op. cit.*, pp. 146–156, 175, 180.

[52] Hinton, *China's Turbulent Quest*, pp. 151–152, 196; Van Ness, *op. cit.*, pp. 112–121.

[53] Quoted in the pamphlet, *Leninism or Social Imperialism?—In Commemoration of the Centenary of the Birth of the Great Lenin*, Peking, 1970, p. 50. The idea expressed here that a world war is *not* inevitable represents a shift from Mao's earlier position.

The Khrushchov [sic] revisionists claim that if their general line of "peaceful coexistence, peaceful transition and peaceful competition" is followed, the oppressed will be liberated and "a world without weapons, without armed forces and without wars" will come into being. . . . The essence of the general line of the Khrushchov revisionists is nothing other than the demand that all the oppressed peoples and nations and all the countries that have won their independence should lay down their arms and place themselves at the mercy of the U. S. imperialists and their lackeys. . . .

In diametrical opposition to the Khrushchov revisionists, the Marxist-Leninists and revolutionary people never take a gloomy view of war. Our attitude towards imperialist wars of aggression has always been clear-cut. First, we are against them, and secondly, we are not afraid of them. . . . As for revolutionary wars waged by the oppressed nations and peoples, so far from opposing them, we invariably give them firm support and active aid.[54]

Lin's claim that the Chinese "invariably give. . . active aid" to revolutionary wars, while the Soviets do not, is hardly true. In practice there is little if any difference between the Soviet Union's and China's policies towards promoting revolutions, since both give top priority to their own national interests. On occasion the Chinese have found it to their advantage to endorse regimes that are not only non-Communist but even anti-Communist. For example, the Chinese approved the Algerian government of Boumedienne, just as the Soviets have supported the Egyptian governments of Nasser and Sadat.[55] The Chinese have also warmly supported Pakistan.

Similarly, if the Chinese were determined and dogmatic foes of "imperialism" wherever it occurs, they would hardly have tolerated the continuation of the regimes in Hong Kong and Macao. China's attitude towards a particular regime or a particular revolutionary movement has been determined not primarily by ideology, but rather by such simple matters as whether the government of that country has granted diplomatic recognition to Communist China, has supported Communist China's claim to a seat in the United Nations, or in other respects has furthered China's interests. In other words, as Peter Van Ness has remarked, like most Communist states, China has "tended to be predominantly socialistic at home and nationalistic in foreign affairs."[56]

China's attitude towards Communist takeovers has been well summarized by Harold C. Hinton:

---

[54] Lin Piao, *Long Live the Victory of People's War!*, Peking, 1966, pp. 61–63. The article was originally published in *People's Daily* on September 3, 1965. Although Lin has since fallen from favor, these views, which originated with Mao, are still part of the official line.

[55] Van Ness, *op. cit.*, p. 188.

[56] *Ibid.*, p. 196. See the detailed discussion of this point in chapters vi and vii, especially pages 168–169, 176, 188, 190, 196–197.

Peking's desired outcome seems to be a series of Communist-controlled states, in which the local Communist parties have come to power by a Chinese-style "people's war," with just enough Chinese aid, support, and advice to ensure success and a significant degree of Chinese influence (but probably not amounting to control). On the other hand, the extent of Chinese involvement must not be great enough to render the Maoist shibboleth of "self-reliance" obviously inapplicable or to expose Peking to undue risks or costs.[57]

It might be added that in recent years China has placed less stress than before on promoting revolutions because it has been increasingly engrossed by the problem of its relations with the two superpowers, the Soviet Union and the United States.[58]

The Soviet Union and Communist Takeovers Today

Like Communist China, the Soviet Union today tends to look upon the promotion of Communist takeovers in a very realistic way, with primary consideration (perhaps exclusive consideration) being given to the question of whether or not a particular takeover will further the interests of the USSR. In the old days Moscow assumed that the establishment of a Communist regime in any part of the world would automatically be good for Russia, but events in Yugoslavia, Albania, Cuba, and especially in China have dramatically demonstrated the falsity of this assumption. Because of these bitter experiences the Politburo will probably be much more cautious and discriminating in granting support to Communist movements which are trying to seize power or which have already seized power.

---

[57] Hinton, *China's Turbulent Quest*, pp. 175–176.

[58] For further discussion of the complex and changing nature of China's attitude and actions towards revolutions, one might consult (in addition to the sources already cited) the following: Samuel B. Griffith, *Peking and People's Wars*, New York, 1966; Donald Zagoria, *Vietnam Triangle: Moscow, Peking, Hanoi*, New York, 1967; Robert A. Rupen and Robert Farrell (eds.), *Vietnam and the Sino-Soviet Dispute*, New York, 1967; Tang Tsou and Morton Halperin, "Mao Tse-tung's Revolutionary Strategy and Peking's International Behavior," *American Political Science Review*, Washington, D.C., March, 1965; Tang Tsou and Morton Halperin, "Maoism at Home and Abroad," *Problems of Communism*, Washington, D.C., July-August, 1965; Stuart Schramm, *The Political Thought of Mao Tse-tung*, 2nd ed., New York, 1969; Philippe Devillers, *Mao*, New York, 1969.

In getting a better understanding of China's policies, the author has benefited greatly from discussions with his colleagues at the University of Virginia, Professors John Israel, Shao Chuan Leng, and David Powell, although they do not necessarily agree with the views expressed here.

As a general rule of thumb the Soviet leaders will probably assume that a Communist country is more likely than a non-Communist one to be friendly towards the USSR, just as we assume that a Communist country will probably be hostile towards the United States. However, before committing itself to the support of a Communist takeover, the Soviet Union will in all likelihood consider such factors as the following: (1) If this country becomes Communist, will it side with Russia or with China? (This is the unanswered question which haunts the Soviets about Vietnam.) (2) If the Soviet Union supports this Communist movement, or this Communist regime, how much is it going to cost in economic and military aid? (Cuba has cost plenty, and the Soviets must wonder if they could have found some better way to use that money.) (3) If this country becomes Communist, or remains Communist, how much will it weaken the non-Communist powers politically, economically, and militarily? (The Allende regime in Chile, for example, was welcomed by the USSR because it expropriated American business, weakened U.S. influence in Latin America, and popularized the notion that Marxists support the democratic process.) (4) If the Communists take over in this country, will the United States react so strongly that Soviet interests and perhaps even Soviet security, would be threatened? (For example, Moscow probably would discourage any plans for Communist takeovers in West Germany, France, or Italy for fear of what Washington might do.)

Soviet attitudes towards Communist takeovers today are also affected by the realization that the influence of the USSR on a given country is by no means excluded just because that country happens to be non-Communist—witness Egypt, Syria, India, and a number of other states in the Third World. The Soviets are pragmatic enough to see that in such countries they can gain more by supporting non-Communist governments than by engaging in quixotic attempts to incite Communist revolutions. One may safely speculate, to use an unlikely example, that the Kremlin would gladly sacrifice every Communist in Iran for an agreement by the Shah to transfer all Western oil concessions to the USSR.

Nor is the expansion of Soviet influence without revolution limited to the less developed countries. Deals for improved economic and political relations with Germany, France, Italy, Japan, and other advanced countries may well lead to an increase in the Soviet Union's prestige and power, while at the same time weakening the position of the United States. And of course the threat of Soviet military power has much to do with its influence. Finland, for example, is non-Communist, but conducts its foreign policy within the limitations of a Soviet veto. If Soviet military and economic power continues to grow, other European countries may find themselves gradually undergoing a process of "Finlandization."

All these considerations (and others which cannot be mentioned for lack of space) point to the basic fact that while Russia has on the whole benefited from the expansion of communism in the past, Soviet policy today is by no means motivated primarily by a commitment to the cause of world revolution. Kremlin policy towards Communist takeovers has been, is today, and will in the future be determined above all by considerations of Russian national interest.

The Bolshevik Revolution: Prototype or Myth?

John Keep

In what sense, if any, did the Bolshevik revolution[1] in Russia in October, 1917, serve as a model for, or inspire, Communists in other parts of the world when they came to seize power? In answering this question, it seems to me that we are faced at the outset with a substantial difficulty. Is it really possible for persons whose information about the past is drawn mainly, if not exclusively, from sources approved by the Communist Party ever to know what actually took place? Can they ever know the real reasons why such a great event as the Russian revolution took the particular course it did?

Since all writing on the Russian revolution by Communists—from straightforward history to collections of documents and memoirs—is subject to very rigid ideological control, perhaps we may say that Communists cannot come very close to a knowledge of the truth, because this truth is at once more complex and more simple than partisan historians would have us believe. If this is so, what we are dealing with is not a body of concrete experience, which later revolutionaries might apply to their own situations, but an historical myth, which might be as much of an obstacle as a guide to realistic political action.

It may be that we still do not know enough about the ways in which myths affect human behavior to assess the importance of what people have believed happened in 1917. But we can approach the subject by noting that up to the present time all revolutionaries have eagerly sought historical precedents for their actions and have viewed these precedents through a

---

[1] Two popular Western histories of the 1917 Russian revolution are: Alan Moorehead, *The Russian Revolution*, London, 1958, and John S. Curtiss, *The Russian Revolutions of 1917*, Princeton, N.J., 1957; the latter includes basic documents. A more comprehensive standard account is William Henry Chamberlin, *The Russian Revolution, 1917–1921*, 2 vols., New York, 1965 (first published in 1935). A good recent study of the Bolshevik seizure of power is R.V. Daniels, *Red October : The Bolshevik Revolution of 1917*, London, 1968. On Lenin, the biography by Alam B. Ulam, *The Bolsheviks : The Intellectual and Political History of the Triumph of Communism in Russia*, New York, 1965, is the most judicious. For reviews of Western and Soviet historiography on the Russian revolution, see R. D. Warth, "On the Historiography of the Russian Revolution," *Slavic Review*, New York, Vol. 26, 1967, pp. 247–264, and R. H. McNeal, "Soviet Historiography on the October Revolution: A Review of 40 Years," *American Slavic and East European Review*, New York, Vol. 17, 1958, pp. 269–281. Two collections of articles which may be found useful are: Leonard Schapiro and Peter Reddaway (eds.), *Lenin : The Man, the Theorist, the Leader : A Reappraisal*, London, 1967, and Richard Pipes (ed.), *Revolutionary Russia : A Symposium*, Cambridge, Mass., 1968.

distorting prism. The overthrow of an established social and political order is an immense undertaking calling for considerable courage. Traditionally, revolutionaries have felt that the zeal necessary to make a revolution can be gained by studying the past, by looking at it with a heightened political awareness. (This may no longer be true, for Marx seems to have given way to Mao Tse-tung and Herbert Marcuse, and now it is often argued that historical experience may mislead us and that wisdom can best be gained from action itself—a throwback to pre-Marxian anarchistic attitudes.)

Leaving aside such attitudes, the mainstream of revolutionary thinking up to 1917 had been very consistent. Just as in 1830 French revolutionaries worried whether they were emulating the events of 1789 or 1688, the Russian Bolsheviks were much concerned with the alternative precedents of 1848 and 1870. In *The State and Revolution*, Lenin envisaged the reproduction of the Paris Commune, with all that it implied in the way of "direct democracy," on alien Russian soil. The Bolsheviks were also greatly influenced by the events of 1905, which were still very fresh in everyone's mind, for it seemed to them that by studying the lessons of the "first Russian revolution," they might avoid its mistakes—i.e., prevent a triumph of reaction.

It is unfortunate for the theorist that history never repeats itself, even approximately. Each event, each situation is bound to be unique. Any attempt to lay down a particular course of action on the assumption that one can predict at least the basic framework of considerations within which political leaders of the day must operate is bound to invite failure. As proof of this assertion, one need look no further than the history of Communist revolution-making since 1917. Just as the Bolshevik revolution did not bring about the results anticipated by "scientific socialists" of any persuasion (or for that matter by non-Marxists!), so Lenin's guidelines for his disciples in the Comintern (Communist International)—guidelines which governed behavior towards the "social reformers" of the Second International and which were laid down in great detail in the famous Twenty-one Points—were in practice soon discarded.[2] The first "Messianic" efforts to export the Soviet revolutionary model—to Germany and Hungary in

---

[2] On the early years of the Communist International, see: Franz Borkenau, *World Communism : A History of the Communist International*, Ann Arbor, Mich., 1962; Jane Degras (ed.), *The Communist International, 1919–1943 : Documents*, Vol. I, London, 1956; Helmut Gruber, *International Communism in the Era of Lenin : A Documentary History*, Greenwich, Conn., 1967; D. Footman (ed.), *International Communism, St. Antony's Papers*, Vol. 9, Oxford, 1960. On early Soviet relations with Germany, Hungary and Poland, see respectively: A. J. Ryder, *The German Revolution of 1918 : A Study of German Socialism in War and Revolt*, Cambridge, 1967; Rudolf L. Tökés, *Béla Kun and the Hungarian Soviet Republic*, New York, 1967; P. S. Wandycz, *Soviet-Polish Relations, 1917–1921*, Cambridge, Mass., 1969.

1918-1919—were dismal failures. Lenin at least seems to have drawn the appropriate conclusions, for in 1920, when Soviet Russia found itself at war with Poland, he thought that the way to bring a Communist government to power there (and ultimately in Germany as well) lay not so much in encouraging locally based Communist movements, as in relying on the bayonets of the Red Army, with the Polish Communist Party acting as a kind of puppet, dependent in every vital respect on Soviet support. That the Bolsheviks failed to achieve their objective on this occasion was not due to any doctrinal scruples on their part, but to the resistance offered to the Red Army by the soldiers of Marshal Josef Pilsudski.

Stalin adopted the same pragmatic standards as the later Lenin had done, and if he had any lingering doubts about the foolishness of resting hopes for successful revolutions in foreign countries on local Communist forces, these were wholly dispelled by his experience with Germany in 1923 and with China three to four years after, when Chiang Kai-shek outsmarted his Communist rivals. From this time on, the Comintern and its constituent parties were downgraded to the rank of mere instruments of Soviet foreign policy. This foreign policy was preoccupied with the task of safeguarding the security of the Soviet state, and it was thought that Communist influence could be extended only to those areas contiguous to the USSR where there would be no risk of a major war with the capitalist powers (e.g., to Mongolia).

But this did not mean, as some rather naïve Western observers believed at the time, that the ultimate aim of world-wide revolution had been abandoned. On the contrary, Stalin succeeded in harmonizing the national interests of the Soviet Union with what might be called its revolutionary goals. If the two came into conflict with one another, as they sometimes did, the former had priority. However, Stalin's success in reconciling the apparently irreconcilable brought about a change in the nature of the Communist movement itself, and with it a change in the nature of the society the Communists had sought to build. The local parties gradually withered as autonomous units with roots in the masses, and bureaucracy took hold of them. Communism ceased to mean the happy, spontaneous free-for-all of 1917-1918 and came to be identified with Stalin's totalitarian state. The early Bolsheviks had emphasized the boundless joys that would accrue from expropriating the capitalists, but their successors could offer only grim toil, hardship, and scarcity, all of which were inseparable from efforts to build an industrial society at rapid tempo. The emphasis now was on mobilizing the masses for certain ends, on discipline, organization, and planning under the watchful eye of the *apparat*.

Because such prospects hardly seemed attractive to other people, it may be said that the successes of the Soviet Union in foreign policy over the past quarter of a century have not really been caused by popular enthusiasm for "the construction of socialism," but by careful manipulation of the nationalism that has been such a powerful force in modern affairs and by occasional reversions to sheer old-fashioned imperialism. By nationalism is meant here the sentiments that impel some French and Italian workers, or for that matter Egyptian *fellaheen*, to endorse a pro-Soviet, anti-American line because they feel this will serve the interests of their "people," who are conceived of as something abstract, with the class differences among them, which were formerly deemed all-important in building a new social order, now somehow overlooked. This nationalist emotion has very little to do with the world of Marx and Lenin, notwithstanding all the superficial similarities evident in the anti-imperialistic language it generates.

From this follows a point of special importance: in the modern world there can be no spontaneous Communist revolutions in the orthodox Leninist sense. The fact that Communists have come to power largely by their own efforts in Yugoslavia, Cuba, and China does not contradict this point, but actually helps to prove it, because the takeover of power in these countries was the work of men whose primary political instincts were essentially nationalistic. These men only became Communists and declared their solidarity with Moscow for specific historical reasons. None of them was a Communist pure and simple in the way in which the Bolsheviks of 1917 were.

Even in the Bolshevik movement, if one looks back on it closely, there was a certain nationalist undertone. This was what lay behind the sentiment, widespread among the war-weary soldiers, that Russia was fighting for the cause of the Western Allies and not for anything that mattered to Russia. But in 1917 this "patriotic" motif was secondary. What is striking is the force of genuine, perhaps naïve, internationalist feelings alive at the time. The belief that the Russian workers and peasants were not acting in the interests of Russia, but were showing their comrades in the rest of Europe how to carry out the "world-wide socialist revolution" in which all proletarians would take part as equals, makes the Russian revolution seem to belong to a bygone era. Such faith would scarcely be possible today, for history has moved on, and most people have a more cynical, more realistic, and more parochial outlook on life. They can no longer believe to the same extent as their forefathers in generous, self-sacrificing, altruistic actions, in the universal brotherhood of man—that admirable eighteenth-century concept which first the Marxists and then the Bolsheviks took over, modifying it in the process.

Thus, it might be said that 1917 was *par excellence* a time of illusion on both sides of the barricades—among the Bolsheviks as among their opponents. While the former dreamed of an imminent utopia, an international socialist paradise, the anti-Bolsheviks fondly hoped that the Russian revolution was just a temporary aberration in the empire's long history, an artificial consequence of the war; after it was over, they thought, life would sooner or later settle down again into familiar, accepted patterns. Such complacency may seem barely credible to us fifty years afterwards, as we have become so used to rapid change in every walk of life and to political and social convulsions all over the globe. The placid, balanced, orderly world of Europe before 1914, with its belief in human reason and progress by reform, today seems as ancient and remote as the Middle Ages. The First World War and the Russian revolution which it brought forth were the epochal birthpangs of the era of violence in which we live.

One consequence of this general deterioration in harmony throughout the world has been to make governments much more concerned for their safety, much more aware of the threat of subversion than in the easy-going days before 1914. A logical parallel of this development has been the realization by revolutionaries that revolutions will not materialize "in the fullness of time," but have to be forcefully organized by conscious élites. Today governments and the more "responsible" elements of society understand this threat and try to guard against it by timely action. Usually, this involves both repression and reform. Police measures of various sorts are taken against subversive factions, and political maneuvering goes on to exclude these factions from parliaments or to split their alliances with more moderate groups. Positive political action is taken on a variety of "fronts" to allay social discontent, and efforts are made to avoid wars that might bring such unrest to a head.

All this is so familiar to us that we tend to take it for granted. It is difficult for us to imagine that governments did not always act in this way. We find it incredible, for example, that up to 1914 the Tsarist government had virtually no policy at all on some of the serious problems it faced, such as strikes among the workers or separatist tendencies among national minorities, but that it lived improvidently from one crisis to the next, leaving the initiative to its opponents, about whom it knew and cared very little. Today no government in the world, no matter how reactionary it might be, could afford to be so lax. Governments have come to recognize that they have a responsibility to govern, to adopt positive policies to avert their own overthrow, even if they often find it hard to translate these intentions into actions. At the same time, "public relations" has become an inseparable part of political life, and this too—for good or ill—has very largely been a consequence of events in 1914 and 1917, when the power of propaganda to influence a nation's destiny was first shown.

*

Turning to the problems of 1917, it makes sense to look first at the groups that opposed the Bolsheviks, because in this revolution, as in most, it was the mistakes made by those in power, rather than by their enemies, that had the greatest impact upon events. In 1917 Russia was in an extraordinarily chaotic and confused situation. The sudden collapse of the imperial regime, the abdication of the Tsar, and the extinction of the monarchy removed from the body politic the linchpin that had held it together until then. Such a situation was unlikely to recur in other countries where the political traditions had been less absolutist and less monocratic. Left for the first time to their own devices, various groups in Russian society began to ventilate their grievances and demand immediate satisfaction of them. As the country was in the middle of a major war, when all its resources had to be mobilized for defense, these exaggerated aspirations could not possibly be contained within the existing political framework, and whatever the new rulers of the country did was bound to seem wrong from the point of view of one faction or another. The result was a classic "revolutionary situation," in which the governors had lost the ability to govern.

We need not be too hard in judging the democratic liberal and socialist politicians in the Provisional Government, because the revolutionary upheaval was very largely a matter of age-old problems coming home to roost. These men had to bear the consequences of the cumulative shortcomings of the old regime. Even so, it must be noted that they often made a bad situation worse than it need have been by their deplorable lack of realism. In retrospect, the degree of doctrinaire complacency shown by the Provisional Government seems startling. For one thing, the leaders of this government failed to comprehend how important it was to maintain a reasonable degree of stability in the composition of the government and a reasonable degree of consistency in its policies. Within only eight months there were four coalitions, and for long periods the country had no government at all, while the party leaders carried on their mutual intrigues. With each change of government, the central figures tended to become more inept, and to have less support in the country at large. Few of them had any political experience, and many of them automatically carried on the traditions of the underground, with its endless arguments about first principles, its abstract way of thinking, and its impracticality.

In any revolution the struggle for control revolves around the question of legitimacy of power. Revolutionaries seek to deprive the established regime of its natural aura of authority and to appropriate it for themselves. In 1917 Russia was ruled by people who considered themselves no more than caretakers and who had no clear entitlement to exercise power. They deliberately repudiated any connection with the discredited Tsarist regime. (Before Nicholas II abdicated, he did approve Prince Lvov's appointment as the new premier, so that some continuity might plausibly have been claimed.) Instead they sought legitimacy in the popular will, in a vote by a democratically elected, fully representative constituent assembly. In conformity with democratic theory, they held that this assembly alone had the right of sovereignty; until it met, every action by the government was to be considered just as provisional as the government itself. This point of view did credit to their desire to avoid the coercive measures so characteristic of earlier (and later) Russian regimes. But in practical terms it was absurd, for it prevented the Provisional Government from grappling energetically with any of the vital problems that confronted it from day to day: supplying food to the hungry in the cities, solving the land problem, and above all ending the unpopular war. On any of these issues timely action by the Provisional Government might well have moderated the ambitions of the extremists and given the upper hand to democracy, at least for a time. But such action was not forthcoming, and it bears repeating here that one cannot easily imagine any subsequent government committing such folly.

After the abortive Kornilov mutiny in August, 1917, the Kerensky government adopted a left-wing orientation that to an untutored eye seemed little different from the course adopted by the Bolsheviks. It tried to "build a bridge to the masses," to recruit popular support; however, its efforts were characterized not by resolute action but by clouds of revolutionary rhetoric, and by political maneuvering. Kerensky sought to align the government's attitude, but not its policies, with that advocated in the councils (soviets) elected by workers and soldiers, even though the soviets had no legal status and were merely a political façade, behind which the Bolsheviks and other extremists carried on subversive activities. In September and October, 1917, many ordinary Russians thought that the soviets already were the government of the country; indeed, they were not far from right, for in many regions public order had broken down, the regular administration was powerless, and authority was in fact in the hands of these *ad hoc* bodies acting in the name of "revolutionary democracy." When the people in these areas learned that the Bolsheviks had taken over in Petrograd, they understood this event as the completion of a process that had been under way for several months: the transfer of power to genuine representatives of the population. They were, of course, in for a rude shock, because such democratic or anarchic concepts had no place in Lenin's image of socialism.

It is important to realize that in Russia in 1917 the general public and even educated people with some experience of political affairs were almost totally ignorant of the nature or aims of the Bolshevik Party. In general, the Bolsheviks were seen simply as one among several democratic groups, rather more extreme in their "maximalism" than most, but not intrinsically or disturbingly different from others. This widespread underestimation of their potential was to have momentous consequences. A liberal lawyer, Julius Hessen, writes in his memoirs of the weeks just after the revolution: "No one doubted for a moment that the Bolsheviks would be overthrown; the only question was how and when."[3] It was a commonplace among educated people that a "dictatorship of the proletariat" could not last for long in a country such as Russia, which did not have a large proletarian class. A regime predicated on domination by the proletariat would have no popular basis, and was bound to collapse as soon as it was confronted with harsh realities; then the pendulum would swing back to political moderation or perhaps to right-wing authoritarianism. This, it was thought, was the lesson of history: of 1789, of 1848, and of 1905. The accepted wisdom of the day taught that revolutions follow certain ineluctable laws that may be violated only at one's peril.

An extraordinary paradox of the Russian revolution is that the anti-Bolsheviks were, if anything, more Marxist than the Bolsheviks. The thinking of men in all political parties in Russia at the time was strongly colored by rather shallow, deterministic interpretations of Marxism; it was also imbued with vivid memories of the traditions held by the nineteenth-century Russian intelligentsia, with its inherent romanticism. These men believed that class struggle was an inevitable feature of modern society, and could on occasion lead to fruitful results. They believed that the bourgeoisie was naturally self-interested and inclined to be reactionary (or at least they believed that Russia *had* a bourgeoisie, which is an idea that many modern historians might dispute). They thought that the Russian people were a reliable bulwark of democracy and progress. The romantic intelligentsia by and large looked upon the state as a harmful, repressive organism, and not as something politically neutral or necessary to any modern society. They had little regard for normal processes of law; adhering

---

[3] I. V. Gessen, "V dvukh revolyutsiyakh: zhiznennyy opyt," *Arkhiv russkoy revolyutsii*, Berlin, XXII, 1937, p. 382.

to a view which had deep roots in the Russian Orthodox past, they identified justice with truth as an abstract ideal, scarcely attainable by ordinary mortals through such mundane institutions as law courts, with their supposed formalism and indifference to morality.

This shallow, romantic way of thinking was current not only among democratic socialists but also among many liberals and conservatives. Left-wingers deduced from these assumptions that whatever might happen, democracy was bound to triumph in the end, simply because this was what the Russian people wanted. Right-wingers deduced that the worse things became owing to socialist mismanagement, the greater would be the resultant swing of popular sentiment in their favor. It was beyond men's comprehension in 1917 that a single authoritarian party could defy what were taken to be the laws of history by an act of will, that it could seize power, consolidate its control over the population by a combination of propaganda and terror, and attract or manufacture enough mass support to see it through the next half-century. From this lack of imagination sprang that strange "paralysis of will" that afflicted all anti-Bolsheviks in the autumn of 1917 and prevented them from doing anything effective to stop Lenin in his single-minded march to power.

The importance of the hold which this unenlightened, romantic myth had on people in 1917 may become clearer if we compare the situation in Russia then with that in Eastern Europe after the Second World War, when Communist regimes were established there. It is doubtful whether in 1944 or 1945 the Poles, for example, had many illusions about the nature of Soviet power or about what the Lublin government portended for their country. That they failed to resist the patent extension of Soviet influence was due not to ignorance, but to physical weakness, to the pervasiveness of anti-fascist sentiment, which was embarrassing for the conservatives, and above all to the inability of the Western Allies to help them against Stalin. Or again, we find that the overwhelming majority of Yugoslavs who backed the Communists in 1945 did so because they saw in them the only force that could unite the various nationalities, heal the wounds of war and internecine factional strife, and promote the progress and security of the country—a belief in which they were proved right by Tito's eventual split with the Cominform. That one may question whether many people in Poland or Yugoslavia really believed in the utopian elements of the Communist program suggests that the Russian revolution of 1917 belongs to a different order altogether from the revolutions that have succeeded it.

Let us now take a look at the role of the Bolsheviks. In doing so, we need not take too seriously the legend, spread assiduously by their supporters and assisted today by their more ardent adversaries, that depicts them as sinister, subtle geniuses in the art of making revolution. What is closer to the truth is that the Bolsheviks made almost as many mistakes as their opponents and were almost equally prey to illusions. In Lenin, the Bolsheviks had a leader of totally different mettle from his subsequent emulators: a man of immense concentration of will and—what was rarer—of considerable imagination and realism, who knew how to adjust his ideas to a rapidly changing situation, and who kept steadily and firmly in mind, as he put it himself in April, 1917, that "the basic question in any revolution is the question of state power."[4] Lenin was far more closely attuned to the realities of politics than his rivals. His idealism, while no doubt sincere, had a down-to-earth side (some might say a cynical side) which proved to be his salvation. That being said, it must also be noted that at the same time he was helped by a colossal amount of sheer luck. This arbitrary factor should not be left out of account. Supposing Lenin had been arrested after the "July Days," would there have been an October Revolution?

Apart from forceful leadership, the Bolsheviks, unlike their rivals, had a clearly articulated philosophy of organization. They looked upon organization as a matter of principle and not as an incidental or subsidiary concern, as the democratic socialists and the liberals tended to do. This feel for discipline gave the Bolsheviks a decisive margin of advantage over their opponents on the left. Lenin had been urging the merits of "democratic centralism" since 1902. His paramountcy within the Party was generally recognized, but it was compatible with a fair amount of discussion and dissent. Other leaders like Kamenev might object to certain tactical decisions but sooner or later fell into line under the impact of Lenin's charismatic personality. Nobody in other Russian parties had such power of discipline. Kerensky, for example, had a good deal of influence, but it derived chiefly from his abilities as an orator. Among the Socialist Revolutionaries, Chernov was greatly respected as a theorist, but he did not have the ability to exert authority over other people in his party, which was plagued by one schism after another.

The nature of Lenin's authority among the Bolsheviks was such that if something went wrong, as it did in July, he would not be blamed by his followers in public. There might well be some grumbling, but the Party had a knack of adroitly transferring the responsibility for failure to other people, of finding scapegoats. Middle-ranking activists whose reputation was tarnished in this way might well leave the Party in high dudgeon, but their resentment was a small price to pay for the feeling of general

---

[4] V. I. Lenin, *Polnoye sobraniye sochineniy*, Moscow, 1962, Vol. 31, p. 145.

solidarity among those who remained. A schism in the ranks of the Bolsheviks was less disruptive and dangerous than one among their democratic
rivals.

As a tactician, Lenin showed remarkable ability to combine single-
minded determination to achieve his principal objective—power for his
party—with utmost flexibility in day-to-day maneuvering. He was quick
to perceive changes in the balance of political forces and to adjust the
tactical line of his party accordingly, extracting the maximum advantage
from altered or altering circumstances. In the "April Theses" Lenin
recognized the potentialities of the soviets as vehicles for power. Between
April and June, when the revolutionary tide was in full flood, he strongly
backed the cry for "All Power to the Soviets," and rapidly extended Party
influence in the mass organizations (e.g., factory committees and soldiers'
committees at the front). The "July Days" were a kind of reconnaissance
in force, followed by a retreat—for Lenin seems to have underestimated
the government's ability to recover the initiative. After this temporary
defeat, Lenin gave up hope in the soviets, and in exile in Finland he quickly
changed the Party's slogan, proclaiming in its place the need for a transfer
of power to "the revolutionary proletariat, led by its vanguard," i.e, to
the Party. He first saw this insurrection as occurring in the fairly distant
future, but he quickly changed his view a few weeks later, when General
Kornilov challenged the government and public opinion swung sharply to
the left. Not missing his cue, Lenin advanced the time of the insurrection
to the near future, and bombarded the Party's Central Committee with one
request after another for immediate action. When the Petrograd and Moscow
soviets passed into the hands of the Bolsheviks, Lenin reconsidered the
role which the soviets could play in his scheme, but after July he probably
never trusted these bodies again to the extent that he had done in April, or
to the extent that Trotsky did. In all this, one can but admire Lenin's
tactical flexibility, his manipulative skill, his sense for the changing mood
of the masses. These are the ingredients for success in any political system,
particularly in an era of revolution. Lacking Lenin's indefatigable self-
confidence and unchallengeable position in the Party, no later Communist
leader could hope to emulate him in this.

The subtlety of Lenin's leadership can perhaps better be appreciated
by taking a look at the way in which the Bolsheviks treated their allies in
1917. What were later to be called "salami tactics," in reference to events
in Eastern Europe after the Second World War, were applied rather more
spontaneously and with less cynical deliberation in Russia in 1917. That is
to say, like-minded groups were constrained to throw in their lot with the
Bolsheviks, as the most consistently revolutionary party, and to merge

with them organizationally. If they did not do so, then these groups would be split, with the pro-Bolshevik element mobilized against the "reactionary" faction. Those who vacillated would eventually be neutralized and won over by persuasion and pressure, and the hard-core anti-Bolsheviks would gradually be isolated until it was convenient to eliminate them. This very simple basic pattern was often quite complex in its application. It was followed in trade unions, mass organizations, national minority groups (like the Ukrainians), and in other political parties. For example, it did not require much inducement from the Bolsheviks to beget a left-wing faction among the Socialist Revolutionaries, who in 1917 constituted the largest party in the country. This leftist group was pledged to much the same line as the Bolsheviks on the agrarian question, but it remained opposed to them on the question of dictatorship. The "land decree," promulgated immediately after the Bolshevik takeover, stole the clothes of the left-wing Socialist Revolutionaries. A few weeks later, to make it appear as if the new regime was more broadly based than it actually was, Lenin admitted them to a secondary role in the Soviet government. The Left Socialist Revolutionaries were history's first fellow travelers. They were of invaluable service to the Bolsheviks during the first few months of the new regime, when Lenin's government was anxious to consolidate its power, and then, after the signing of the Treaty of Brest-Litovsk, they were discarded as redundant. The split within the Menshevik Party—between the internationalist left wing of Martov, which gave qualified support to the Soviet regime, and the patriotic right wing of Tsereteli—was exploited in much the same way. The railway union VIKZHEL (*Vserossiiskiy ispolnitelnyy komitet zheleznodorozhnikov*) was deprived of popular support until, under coercion, a new executive that would co-operate with the Soviet government was elected. The Bolsheviks found it much harder to implement these "salami tactics" in organizations that had powerful roots in national sentiment. In such cases, as in the Ukraine, they had to use outright violence on a much more extensive scale.

Another advantage the Bolsheviks had over their rivals—one that was never really copied by those who later emulated them—was their insight into the psychology of the people, especially as this affected choice of slogans. For its sheer shock effect in stirring up popular envy and class hatred it would be hard to beat such a slogan as "Peace to the Huts, War to the Palaces." Compare this with the post-World War II slogan "For a Lasting Peace, for a People's Democracy." Another succinct popular slogan of 1917, "Bread, Peace, Land," very conveniently left unsaid what kind of peace was to be signed. Was it to be a separate peace with the Germans, and if so, on what terms? What kind of legal right would the

peasants have to their land, given the fact that the Bolsheviks were committed to nationalization of all means of production? These ambiguities were
deliberate. Lenin understood very well the value of being "all things to all
men." Such crude propaganda could only be effective in a relatively simple
society in which there was a low level of political education and a pervasive
mood of hysteria brought on by war. Each disaffected group artlessly
looked on the Bolsheviks as a band of strong-willed men with the courage
to give them at once what their own leaders might promise them but
could not provide. In the emotional climate of the time, people were prepared
to believe that an ordinary fellow citizen who dared criticize the policy of
the Bolsheviks was "objectively" a class enemy and therefore an outcast
without any rights whatsoever. It was unlikely that these conditions would
arise in countries where there was a higher degree of political sophistication
and more skepticism towards authority.

Lenin's insistence on insurrection becomes more understandable if we
bear in mind his acute insight into the psychology of the people. In purely
political terms, the Bolsheviks stood to lose a great deal by staging an uprising in October, 1917, when the government was already leaning far to
the left, and when public opinion was generally favorable to their designs, to
the extent that these were understood. That a revolution was superfluous was
evident to such men in the top Party leadership as Kamenev and Zinoviev,
who opposed it. It was also apparent to the bulk of middle-ranking activists in the Party, in such measure as they cared about the matter. They
did not see any advantage in needless violence. They had no idea that the
slogan "All Power to the Soviets" did not mean what it said, but that in
Lenin's mind it implied an all-Bolshevik minority government making
use of Soviet power for its own ends. They thought that "Soviet power"
implied a socialist coalition government which would be obliged by
Bolshevik predominance to bring the revolution to completion, carrying
out various radical measures. If the Bolsheviks took power alone, so the
reasoning went, they would have to take the blame for everything that went
wrong, and they would be overthrown. But Lenin was much more sophisticated than the majority of his followers. He insisted on insurrection not for
political but for psychological reasons. An insurrection would, he saw,
serve as an emotional catalyst. It would enforce a clear split between the
Bolshevik insurgents and the rest of the Russian left. After an insurrection
there could be no real return to more moderate forms of socialism, no
compromise with "petty-bourgeois ideology," with its softness and
commitment to democratic principles. The Party's dictatorship would then
be assured by the circumstance that it could claim credit for having made
the revolution. The Bolsheviks would be firmly identified in the popular

mind with the new era of "socialism," and they would be able to act as they saw fit against all alleged "counter-revolutionaries."

Lenin was not troubled by the thought that application of terror might be incompatible with the principles of Marxist socialism, as understood up to this time, since for him, terror—like insurrection—had a kind of positive psychological function. Terror would serve to separate the sheep from the goats, would commit to the revolution by a kind of "blood bond" those who practiced or condoned it. They would leave behind them forever the world of liberal-socialist "bourgeois democracy," with its principles of tolerance, humanism, legality, and respect for the popular will, and would devote themselves whole-heartedly to the tasks allotted them by the party in power. Lenin well understood the mental and physical dynamics of totalitarian rule. In this he had something in common not only with the Stalinists but also with many non-Communist dictators who have established police states based on the principle that an élite is justified in using violence on a massive scale against ordinary individuals.

The political preparation for the October Revolution is to be viewed as much more important than the technical details of the event itself. No other Communist Party was likely to meet the same conditions, the same negligible opposition, as faced the Bolsheviks in 1917. Trotsky tells us that he was surprised how easy it was to seize power in Petrograd.[5] Although he tended to exaggerate, and to dramatize his own role, his account is admirably free of the pompous myth-making that has marred so much Soviet writing on the subject, and it is worth noting the skill displayed by him in particular in the insurrection. He represented the whole operation as a defensive one, to safeguard the gains of the revolution against treachery by the "bourgeois" government and the "petty bourgeois" moderate socialists. The coup was timed to coincide with the long-awaited Second Congress of Soviets. The Congress would be presented with a "Soviet"—in fact a Bolshevik—government as a *fait accompli*, and called upon to sanction it. Such sanction would confer a useful if spurious aura of legitimacy on the new dictatorial regime, as it would make it more acceptable to the broad mass of left-wing opinion. This was a point that Lenin did not appreciate as fully as Trotsky did.

By later standards of insurgency ("coup-ology" as some writers have light-heartedly called it), the Bolshevik uprising of October, 1917, was an amateurish effort. The insurgents omitted to cut off the government's telephone links with military headquarters; they unnecessarily postponed

---

[5] L. Trotsky, *The Russian Revolution* (abridged paperback edn.), New York, 1959, p. 354.

the attack on the Winter Palace, thinking that the opposition was stronger than it actually was; and they were never in full control of their forces, which were allowed to act very much on their own initiative, as their essentially anarchic sentiments moved them. Such laxity would have been unthinkable later, in situations where Communists encountered more serious opposition from experienced, well-entrenched regimes.

Naturally, this truth could never be admitted by the Bolsheviks themselves. Instead they began immediately to build up an heroic legend justifying their claim to possess greater revolutionary experience than their followers abroad. They tenaciously spread the myth that the so-called Great October Socialist Revolution was successful because the valorous Russian proletariat had responded magnificently to the brilliant leadership of Lenin and Trotsky. (Trotsky was of course quietly dropped from the legend as the years went by.) This was, as we have seen, only one element of the situation. Equally, if not more, important was the contribution of the opposition: the assistance given to the Bolsheviks by the apathetic middle segment of the Russian public, and the poor showing of the right wing, all prey to the general atmosphere of illusion, false optimism, and self-deception. Such a state of affairs was most unlikely to come about elsewhere. In subsequent efforts to subvert governments in other countries, Communists were to find that the experience of their Russian comrades was of limited practical value. Indeed it was more likely to prove a hindrance to them than a help, for it took little account even of Russian reality, let alone the realities of their own countries. In the rest of Europe, Communists hardly needed instruction by the Russians on such obvious points as the importance of the peasantry, trade unions, or soviets in carrying out a revolution. What mattered to them was neither Leninist revolutionary strategy nor the details of insurrectionary technique but the historical myth of 1917. That myth enhanced their self-confidence and quickened their feeling that to succeed they should be audacious. It bolstered the voluntarism that is the hallmark of the true revolutionary in any age, however convinced he may be that his conduct is shaped by some deterministic theory.

The Bolshevik Conquest of the Moslem Borderlands

Alexandre Bennigsen

In 1917, at the time of the October Revolution, the Moslem territories of Soviet Russia formed three major areas: Central Asia, the Caucasus, and the Middle Volga-Urals region. Central Asia, where roughly three-fourths of the Moslem population of Russia was to be found, comprised the General Governorate of Turkestan—including Kazakhstan, Kirghizia, Turkmenistan, Tajikistan, and Uzbekistan—that had come under Tsarist domination in the second half of the nineteenth century, and the protectorates of Bukhara and Khiva. In Central Asia, Moslems made up 80 to 90 percent of the total population. (In the Emirate of Bukhara and the Khanate of Khiva they made up almost the entire population, i.e., 99 percent.) The Moslem areas of the Caucasus, comprising two principal territories—eastern Transcaucasia (now Azerbaijan) and the north Caucasian mountains—had strong Russian and Armenian minorities. Of their total population, 60 to 70 percent were Moslems. The third area, the Middle Volga-Urals region, was Tatar and Bashkir country. Politically and culturally, it was more important than Central Asia or the Caucasus. Kazan, a chief cultural center of eastern European Russia, with a famous university attended by Tolstoy and Lenin, was the heart and the brain of Russian Islam. It was also the stronghold of the Tatar nationalist movement. But Russians made up the majority of the population in the area, and Moslems only 40 to 45 percent.

These three areas differed widely in their levels of social, cultural, and political development. Moslems inhabiting them had only two things in common: their religion, which supported a vaguely shared general cultural background, and the existence of a more or less strong national movement, which was directed primarily against the Russians, but also at times against their own backwardness, in an awakening anti-feudal consciousness. Beyond this, the similarity of the three areas ended. In some regions—in Central Asia, for example—the nationalist movement was still in its earliest, purely reformist stages; in others—in Kazan and Baku, in particular—it had already become a strong political force, with heavy socialist coloring. It is not difficult to see that the pattern of Communist conquest in the Moslem borderlands had to vary from one area to another. Clearly, the Bolsheviks could not use the same methods to take over the very modern, bourgeois Tatar country as they could in the medieval Emirate of Bukhara.

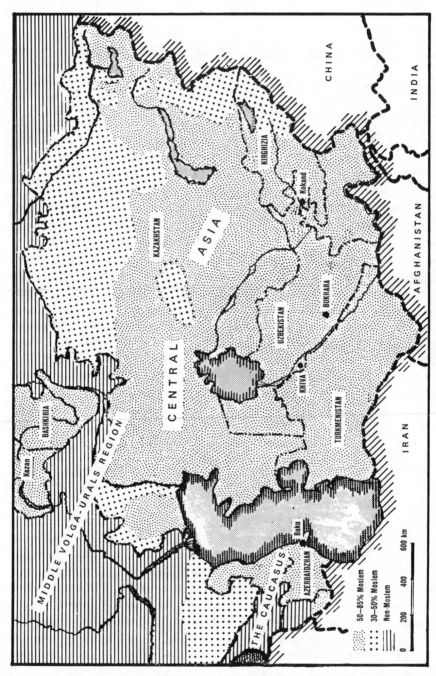

The Moslem Borderlands

But we can gain a better idea of the peculiarity of the Communist takeover in the Moslem lands if we bear in mind the Leninist theory of insurrection, which was successfully applied in Petrograd and Moscow. Except for Marx's advice on what the proletariat should do with the state, made in reference to the Paris Commune of 1871, Lenin found little in the way of a guide to political action in any of the writings of his Marxist predecessors. In a sense the October Revolution was his own invention, improvised to climax the transformation of Marxism, which was essentially an historical analysis, into palpable political power. Lenin's thinking, in highly simplified form, might be put as follows: When the disintegration of the bourgeois regime has reached its lowest point, a small group of professional revolutionaries, politically tried and true, leading small units of workers (to whom Lenin added the peasants after 1904) pushes away the crumbling government and takes power by means of an armed military *Putsch*. There follows the establishment of a strong, monolithic Bolshevik regime.

It hardly needs to be said that nowhere in the Moslem territories of Russia did this pattern apply. What is remarkable is that, contrary to the course of events at the center, the takeover of the Moslem lands happened very gradually. Indeed it is a spectacular if little known fact that it took the Bolsheviks some ten years to establish their power in all the Moslem territories. For purposes of exposition, this protracted period of struggle for power may be divided into six stages, beginning in 1917 and ending sometime between 1927 and 1928.

The First Stage
February to October, 1917

The first stage, which might be called the phase of preparation for the Bolshevik revolution, took place from February to October, 1917. The quick disintegration of the Provisional Government in the peripheral Moslem lands saw the emergence of a variety of competitors for power. There were at least three, sometimes four, contending factions. This circumstance merits special attention, for it is important to realize that the struggle for power in the Moslem lands did not pit just Bolsheviks against counter-revolutionaries, as was the case in purely Russian areas. In addition to the two opposing Russian groups, those asserting claims to power included one or two rival Moslem factions. It is this permutation of adversaries that gives the Bolshevik takeover of the Moslem borderlands its particularity.

Of these adversaries, the first group, the Russian partisans of the Provisional Government, was the weakest. Nowhere was there support for the Provisional Government among the Moslems, largely because one of its war aims was the conquest of Constantinople.

The second Russian group represented a coalition of leftist elements, including Bolsheviks but consisting mostly of Left Socialist Revolutionaries. Only in Tatar country and in Baku were the Bolsheviks in the majority in this coalition. Elsewhere, and specifically in Central Asia, the Socialist Revolutionaries were the leading force. This fact ought not to be overlooked, because the Socialist Revolutionaries were much more inclined to Russian chauvinism than the Bolsheviks and much more hostile to the non-Russian peoples. But what is more important is that with the exception of Baku, where there was a small but active Marxist faction (the Hümmet Party), Moslems everywhere—even the most radical among them—failed to support the Bolsheviks and their allies, not because of ideological antipathy, but because of disinterest in the Bolshevik program of class struggle. The primary aim of the Moslems was, after all, independence or autonomy, not class conflict.

The third group, the Moslem nationalist movement, was politically left of center, embracing Right Socialist Revolutionaries and Mensheviks, but its socialist coloring was more tactical than genuine. Above all it was in varying degrees an anti-Russian phenomenon. Unhappily for its followers, it had no political or military machine to cope with a major crisis. It might be said that for the Moslem nationalists the October Revolution came too early.

A fourth group, the strong right-wing clerical organizations, such as the Naqshbandi Brotherhood of Uzun Hadji in Daghestan, was to be found in parts of Central Asia and the North Caucasus. Together with the established, purely Moslem powers—the Emirate of Bukhara and the Khanate of Khiva—these right-wing conservative and even reactionary (but very popular) organizations turned out to be the strongest, most dangerous adversaries of the Bolsheviks. Their opposition largely determined the pattern of tactics for the Bolshevik takeover.

The Second Stage

The October Revolution

The second stage of the Bolshevik accession to power in the Moslem lands was the October Revolution itself. While the history of the Bolshevik *coup d'etat* in Petrograd and Moscow has been closely and repeatedly studied, the story of the Bolshevik revolution in the Moslem territories is still a largely neglected subject. There are three key aspects of this subject:

(1) Almost everywhere in the Moslem areas, the October Revolution was a purely Russian contest, with the Bolsheviks and their allies easily

outmatching the partisans of the Provisional Government. There was only one curious exception: in Kazan, the reactionary clerical Sufi community—the Vaisi Brotherhood—fought side by side with the Bolsheviks against the Provisional Government in the belief, fostered by Bolshevik propaganda, that it was conducting a holy war against Kerensky. Otherwise, all over Central Asia, the Kazakh Steppe, the Crimea, and the Caucasus, the Moslems largely remained neutral onlookers, passively sympathizing with the Bolsheviks out of distrust for the Provisional Government. It is evident that the Moslems did not realize the historical importance of the Bolshevik revolution.

(2) In Moslem areas where Russians made up only a small minority of the population—in Central Asia, the Kazakh Steppe, the North Caucasus, and even Azerbaijan—the Bolshevik regime won unexpected but unequivocal backing from the local Russians. These Russians, a non-proletarian community of civil service officials, military officers, rich peasants, and even clergymen, looked upon the indigenous Moslems as their principal enemy. Their behavior towards the native population was patently a manifestation of colonialist policy, reflecting as it did the old Tsarist attitude of disdain for backward peoples. Many of these non-proletarian Russians were admitted to the Communist Party and to other local Soviet organizations.

(3) The October Revolution in the Moslem territories did not bring complete victory for the new regime. For three or four months the nationalist organizations of the Moslems, their provincial and central councils and armed detachments, continued to function parallel with the Russian Soviet and Party administration in a strange climate of mounting tension. The turning-point in this situation led directly to the third and most important stage in the Bolshevik subjugation of the Moslem lands: direct confrontation between local Bolsheviks and the Moslem nationalist organizations.

The Third Stage
The Struggle between Bolsheviks and Moslems in the Spring of 1918

The third stage of the Bolshevik rise to power in the Moslem lands consisted of the struggle that took place between local Bolsheviks and Moslem nationalists in the spring of 1918. The break with the Moslem nationalists had been decided on in Petrograd in January, 1918, and in the next few months was carried out in the Moslem territories with the utmost vigor and brutality by local Soviet and Bolshevik organizations. The history of the struggle has been documented elsewhere by this writer, but it would be useful to recall here that the conflict started when the Moslems in Central Asia moved to separate themselves from the Russian state in December, 1917.[1] A Moslem National People's Council met in the city of Kokand and proclaimed the autonomy of Turkestan. Two months later, troops of the Tashkent Soviet, which was composed of Russians only, assaulted the ancient Moslem capital and in a bloody encounter crushed all resistance. Similar forays were made about the same time—from January to March—in the Kazakh Steppe, the Crimea, Kazan, and Baku. In the Crimea and Baku the elimination of the local Moslem nationalist organizations was outright slaughter, with countless numbers killed. A conspicuous feature of the Bolshevik campaign is that it was conducted almost exclusively by Russian troops. Only in Kazan did the Bolsheviks find some of the native population willing to assist in the destruction. Elsewhere the dishonorable work of annihilation had to be done by the Russians themselves.

Thus by April, 1918, the Moslem nationalist movement in Soviet Russia had practically been liquidated. The only exceptions were in Daghestan and in the kingdoms of Bukhara and Khiva, where feudal regimes and the Sufi brotherhood of Naqshbandi had proved to be a stronger force against the Bolsheviks than had the liberal left bourgeoisie in the rest of the Moslem territories. The Bolshevik triumph seemed almost complete, but this was more apparent than real. The representation of Russians in local Communist and Soviet organizations increased even more than it had after the October Revolution, and the posture of these organizations became more overtly hostile towards the native population. In Central Asia, all Moslems were simply excluded from Communist and Soviet organizations, and in Kazan, of the people's commissars in the government, ten were Russian and only one was Tatar. But, though shocked and dispersed, the Moslem nationalist organizations were not definitely defeated. In Central Asia, bands of partisans calling themselves the Basmachis had formed an anti-Russian

---

[1] Alexandre Bennigsen and Chantal Lemercier-Quelquejay, *Islam in the Soviet Union*, with a foreword by Geoffrey E. Wheeler, London, 1967; Alexandre Bennigsen and Chantal Lemercier-Quelquejay, *The Evolution of the Muslim Nationalities of the USSR and their Linguistic Problems*, London, 1961. For works in English by others writing on the establishment of Soviet rule in the Moslem areas of Russia, see: Seymour Becker, *Russia's Protectorates in Central Asia: Bukhara and Khiva, 1865–1924*, Cambridge, Mass., 1968; Charles W. Hostler, *Turkism and the Soviets; The Turks of the World and Their Political Objectives*, New York and London, 1957; Walter Kolarz, *Russia and Her Colonies*, New York and London, 1952; Geoffrey Wheeler, *Racial Problems in Soviet Muslim Asia*, London, 1960; and Serge Zenkovsky, *Panturkism and Islam in Russia*, Cambridge, Mass., 1960. For a general account of how the Bolsheviks established their dominion over both Moslem and non-Moslem nationalities of the former Tsarist empire, see: Richard Pipes, *The Formation of the Soviet Union: Communism and Nationalism, 1917–1923*, revised edition, Cambridge, Mass., 1964.

resistance movement that was spreading into a powerful popular uprising. Similarly, in the Crimea, Bashkiria, and Azerbaijan, bands of guerrillas withdrew to the mountains to rally their forces. The adherents of the Moslem nationalist cause were already prepared to fight back.

There are suitable implications in the fact that some years later, between 1927 and 1928, this stage of the Bolshevik revolution in the Moslem lands was severely criticized by Soviet authorities themselves. It was rightly said that the relentless colonialist and fanatical anti-religious policy of the local Bolsheviks was inimical to the Soviet regime itself and that the harm done during the first months of the revolution was incalculable. Deeply felt alienation from the new regime, not only among the Moslem intelligentsia but also among the Moslem masses, was the result. For this reason, when the Civil War broke out in Soviet Russia in May, 1918, the future of Bolshevik power in the Moslem lands was very uncertain.

The Fourth Stage
The Civil War, 1918–1920

The two and a half years of the Civil War constituted the fourth stage in the Bolshevik conquest of the Moslem territories. This time is perhaps the most tragic period in the history of Russian Islam, with the fighting taking place mostly in Moslem areas—in Central Asia, the Middle Volga-Urals region, the North Caucasus, the Crimea, and Azerbaijan. As soon as the Civil War broke out, in May, 1918, all the Moslem nationalist organizations that had survived the Bolshevik onslaught of the preceding months— even those furthest to the left—went to the side of the Whites. This happened first in Tatar country and in Bashkiria, then in the North Caucasus and Transcaucasia. The general anti-Bolshevik uprising had two distinctive features. In some areas where there was a preponderance of Moslems among the population, for instance in Daghestan and Azerbaijan, the Moslems succeeded in establishing their own governments, which were either of a liberal right-socialist type as in Azerbaijan, or of a clerical conservative orientation as in Daghestan. In other places, where the Moslems lacked sufficient numbers to gain full independence, they sided with the Whites or with the foreign interventionist forces—with the Germans in the Crimea and the Turks or the British in Transcaucasia— against the Red Army. This happened in Bashkiria, in the Crimea, and in the Kazakh Steppe. In the summer of 1918 Soviet power disappeared from almost all Moslem territories except for the city of Tashkent, where the local soviet, even though totally cut off from Moscow, managed to hold out against its surrounding enemies.

This first anti-Bolshevik *volte-face* by the Moslems was due not just to the inequitable policy of the Bolsheviks but also to the initial friendly disposition of the Whites. The first phase of the White struggle was generally directed by centrist-leftist elements (Mensheviks and Right Socialist Revolutionaries), whose attitude towards the Moslems was realistic and favorable. At this time these groups eagerly sought to win the Moslems to their side. But during the second phase of the Civil War, from the autumn of 1918, a political upheaval among the Whites brought right-wing elements to power. Such men as Admiral Kolchak, heading the White offensive in Siberia, and General Denikin, leading the Volunteer Army in South Russia, were fighting for a united, undivided Russia and were strongly hostile towards all non-Russian nationalist movements. This grievous development impelled the Moslems towards a second *volte-face*, and they made overtures to the Soviet side. Their change of front often proved to be a decisive factor in the Civil War because both sides were generally fighting with small armies. The transfer of limited numbers of well-equipped Moslem troops to the side of the Red Army could not help but change the balance of advantage. This occurred when the Bashkirs went over to the Soviet side in February, 1919. They were followed in March by the Kazakh nationalist party, the Alash Orda. In June the nationalist party of the Crimea, the Milli Firka, went underground, allying itself with the Bolshevik guerrillas. This strange turnabout in loyalty by the Moslems is directly attributable to the lack of political insight shown by the leaders of the White forces. The Moslems shifted their allegiance to the cause of bolshevism and deferred to the authority of the Soviet regime only because the Bolsheviks appeared to be a lesser evil than the Whites.

The Fifth Stage

The "Second Takeover," 1920–1924

The fifth stage of the Bolshevik takeover in the Moslem lands began in late 1920, following the victory of the Red Army and the end of the Civil War, and lasted until 1924. It might accurately be called the "second takeover" of the Moslem territories by the Bolsheviks. Unlike the first takeover, which had failed, the second was successful. The first experience had been a brutal, sanguinary struggle, notable for the harsh treatment accorded the Moslems by the Bolsheviks. The second experience was, in contrast, astonishingly liberal. It was the only really favorable, progressive time for Russian Islam during the years from 1920 to 1924.

The pattern of the "second takeover" varied with the degree of resistance in different areas, but two lines of conduct are clearly distinguishable:

(1) In the territories where the Red Army had been fighting the Whites, victory for the Reds brought the re-establishment of contacts with Moscow, and was immediately followed by a purge of Russian colonialist elements from local Party and Soviet organizations. In the Tatar country, the Urals, Bashkiria, the Kazakh country, southern Turkestan, and the central northern Caucasus, these Russian colonialist elements were replaced by Moslems (mostly left-wing nationalists, but sometimes even right-wing conservatives) on the sole condition that they accept the general program of the Communist Party. Occasionally, whole national parties were absorbed by the Communist Party, even though formerly these parties had been adversaries of the Bolsheviks. Such was the case with the Alash Orda party (the rightist organization of Kazakhs), the Milli Firka party in the Crimea, and the Djadidi movement in Turkestan.

(2) In other regions, where power lay in the hands of Moslem nationalist governments, as in Bukhara, Azerbaijan, and Khiva, or where Moslem nationalist organizations had gained control of the area, as in Daghestan or in the parts of Turkestan held by the Basmachis, the Red Army came into conflict with Moslem troops or guerrillas. Sometimes, the clash was long and bloody. In Daghestan, the fighting lasted two years; in Turkestan the Basmachis were not finally crushed until 1928—in some areas, even until 1936. In these areas the Party and Soviet political and administrative apparatuses were introduced in the wake of conquests by the Red Army, and the pattern of the takeover might be compared with the patterns of those in China and Yugoslavia. On the whole, the composition of the local units of the Party and the Soviet government was mixed, with Moslems in the majority. Because of this liberal, pro-native policy, the "second takeover" by the Bolsheviks did not seem to the masses of Moslems to be a dramatic capture of power by an alien Russian government, but rather to be the formation of a kind of native government. Most of the conspicuous positions in the Party and Soviet apparatuses were given to Moslems. The First Secretary of the Communist Party was a Moslem, and the heads of governmental departments for education and the economy were Moslems. Needless to say, this clever policy protected the Soviet regime during the most difficult years of its consolidation of power, from 1924 to 1928. But it was also during this period that throughout the Moslem lands Russian Communists began to occupy the key (but behind-the-scenes) positions of power, such as the posts of Commissar of Internal Affairs (who ran the police) and Second Secretary of the Party (who was responsible for cadres).

The Sixth Stage

The Purge of Moslem Nationalists, 1924–Present

The sixth and last stage of the Bolshevik takeover began at the moment when effective co-operation between the Bolsheviks and the Moslem nationalists had come to an end, which happened at different times in different areas between 1924 and 1928. This last stage was characterized by a purge of natives from the local Party and governmental apparatuses, carried out by Russians who controlled the police and the army. The tragic history of dismissals, arrests, and the physical liquidation of Moslem Communists is outside the scope of the present topic, but it should be pointed out that this is a relatively unknown but highly interesting chapter in Soviet history.

The fight ended sometime between 1936 and 1938 with the defeat of what the Soviet leaders called "bourgeois nationalist deviationists." The new regime, instituted in the late 1930's, was dominated by Russians or by thoroughly russified natives. This was the third and final phase of the takeover of the Moslem lands. However, it might be said that this last phase is not really finished. The Soviet Communist Party is still grappling with the phenomenon of "nationalist deviation" in all the Moslem republics and regions. In fact, nothing is really settled. Soviet power is certainly firmly in place, but just as certainly it is not really accepted.

Soviet Russia and the Red Revolution of 1918 in Finland

C. Jay Smith

Between January and May, 1918, there took place in Finland an armed conflict which the victorious Finnish Whites called a "war of independence," and which the Communists regarded as a "civil war."[1] The historian who makes any claim to objectivity would do well to treat both these definitions with great caution.

The term "war of independence" is intended to imply that the Finnish Reds were in effect agents of the Soviet Russian government and that their seizure of power in the cities of southern Finland on January 27–28, 1918 (in the wake of the proclamation of Finnish independence by a White government on December 6, 1917, and recognition by the Soviet government on December 31, 1917) was a course of action designed not only to impose bolshevism on their country but also to restore the control which Russia had exercised over Finland between 1809 and 1917.

This theory is supported, *inter alia*, by reference to certain undisputed facts. Finns of all political persuasions had been effectively disarmed by the Russians as far back as the first period of russification between 1899 and 1905, and hence could scarcely have fought a serious internecine war without receiving arms from some outside source. Russia was the likeliest source of arms in 1917, since, after the outbreak of the First World War in 1914, Helsinki was the main base of the Russian Baltic Fleet, and considerable Russian ground forces occupied the entire country, primarily to ward

---

[1] The most complete and up-to-date bibliographies of books dealing with the conflict of 1918 in Finland are to be found in the following: John H. Hodgson, *Communism in Finland: A History and Interpretation*, Princeton, N.J., 1967, and V. M. Kholodkovsky, *Revolyutsiya v Finlyandii i germanskaya interventsiya*, Moscow, 1967. Of the books in English, the following may be consulted for the White viewpoint: Erkki Räikkönen, *Svinhufvud, The Builder of Finland: An Adventure in Statecraft*, London, 1938; Joose Olavi Hannula, *Finland's War of Independence*, London, 1939; J. Hampden Jackson, *Finland*, New York, 1940; Carl Gustaf Mannerheim, *The Memoirs of Marshal Mannerheim*, New York, 1954. The book by Hodgson is the best readily available work in English reflecting the Red Finn viewpoint. See also the section on Finland in: Thomas T. Hammond, (ed.), *Soviet Foreign Relations and World Communism. A Selected, Annotated Bibliography of 7,000 Books in 30 Languages*, Princeton, N.J., 1965, especially pp. 334–342.

off any Swedish or German invasion. The Russian soldiers and sailors were still on the scene between March, 1917, and March, 1918, and, reflecting the general mood in the Tsarist armed forces during that year, they were wildly undisciplined, and some at least were ardent supporters of the Bolsheviks.[2]

According to the White version, it was primarily these pro-Bolshevik military forces, acting under orders from Petrograd, who engineered a seizure of power in the industrial cities of southern Finland by the Red Finns on January 27–28, 1918. It is conceded that some two and a half months earlier, the Finnish parliamentary Social Democrats had rejected direct appeals by Lenin, Trotsky, and Stalin that they stage a Finnish "Red October" in the course of a general strike designed to impose a socialist program on the legal White government. But the Whites also point out that during and after these events of November, 1917, the Bolshevik-dominated Russian military forces in the country hampered the efforts of the White government to exercise control, while furnishing arms to an activist para-military group, the Finnish Red Guard, which constituted the extreme left faction of the Social Democrats. Although it was the Red Guard which pushed the rest of the Social Democrats into a seizure of power in late January, 1918, the Guard is said to have received considerable assistance from the Russian military in its subsequent armed conflict with the anti-Communist Finns, at least until the signing of the Treaty of Brest-Litovsk on March 3, 1918. Thereafter, the Whites insist, the Russians continued to furnish "volunteers" to the Finnish Red Forces, even though Soviet Russia had formally relinquished any remaining rights to intervene in Finnish affairs.[3]

---

[2] At the beginning of World War I, Russian forces in Finland included 30,000 to 35,000 troops and 25,000 sailors of the Baltic Fleet. The number of soldiers was increased to 50,000 a year later. At the time of the "July Days" in Petrograd in 1917, Kerensky doubled the size of the Russian garrison, largely because he did not trust the Russian forces already in Finland. See C. Jay Smith, *Finland and the Russian Revolution, 1917–1922*, Athens, Ga., 1958, pp. 9, 18; Hodgson, *op. cit.*, p. 20.

[3] The most detailed and colorful account of Russian military intervention in Finland in 1918 is M. S. Svechnikov's *Revolyutsiya i grazhdanskaya voina v Finlyandii, 1917–1918 gg. (Vospominaniya i materialy)*, Moscow-Leningrad, 1923. It should be noted that the White version of events in Finland during 1917 to 1918 has received uncritical acceptance from some eminent authorities. John W. Wheeler-Bennett referred to the Red Finn seizure of power as a "Bolshevik rising," and to the regime that resulted as the "Soviet Government at Helsingfors" (*Brest-Litovsk: The Forgotten Peace, March 1918*, New York, 1971, pp. 252, 326). As Wheeler-Bennett tells the story, Lenin sent Red Guards, presumably Russian

The proponents of the opposite interpretation, i.e., the idea of a "civil war" in Finland between January and May, 1918, claim that the Red Finns acted as they did not for the purpose of subjecting their country to Soviet Russian control, but to introduce long overdue social and economic reforms, and to ward off a White counter-revolution which, they allege, enjoyed far more outside support than that extended to the Finnish Reds by the Russians. The counter-revolution is said to have started as early as 1914, when some Finns began to promote the idea of a German invasion to drive out the Russians and to defeat the social and economic reform program of the Left, after elections to the democratic Finnish Diet had revealed that a slight majority of the Finns had been won over to Marxist socialism.[4] Later, according to this *Red Finn* version of events, the Finnish Right struck a bargain with Kerensky, agreeing to recognize the sovereignty of the Russian Provisional Government over Finland if Russian troops were used to oust the semi-Red government resulting from the elections of 1916, and to install an all-White administration based on fraudulent new elections in 1917, in which the Social Democrats, who championed Finnish independence, lost their Diet majority. According to this version, the White government in power on November 7, 1917, was actually one installed by Russian troops upon orders from Kerensky. It was therefore the fall of Kerensky which caused the Whites for the first time to demand independence for Finland. This they did while arming another para-military group, the right-wing Protective Corps (established prior to the creation of the Red Guard), with weapons imported from Germany, secretly pleading in Stockholm and Berlin for maximum assistance against Lenin's Russia, and installing as commander of the Protective Corps

---

Red Guards, to Helsinki "to assist in the formation of a 'Finnish Social Republic of Workers'" (p. 271 n.). And as recently as 1965, Adam B. Ulam was evidently under the impression that in 1917 there were large numbers of Finnish "Bolsheviks" in Finland. In his well-known history of the Bolshevik Party we read, for example, that after Lenin fled to Finland following the "July Days" in Petrograd, "Finnish Socialists friendly to the Bolsheviks now occupied important positions in the local government. He [Lenin] used a series of rural hideouts where there was always a Finnish Bolshevik who had a wife or mother . . . overjoyed to shelter Vladimir Ilyich . . . " Adam B. Ulam, *The Bolsheviks : The Intellectual and Political History of the Triumph of Communism in Russia*, New York, 1965, p. 360. William Henry Chamberlin's work, *The Russian Revolution, 1917–1921*, New York, 1935, Vol. I, is a more accurate account, but not without errors.

[4] Despite these Red claims, it is clear that the Germans themselves had no ideological axe to grind with respect to Finland between 1914 and 1918, and that they were not much interested in Finnish independence from Russia *per se*. See Fritz Fischer, *Germany's Aims in the First World War*, New York, 1967, pp. 144 to 154.

General Gustaf Mannerheim (whose thirty years of service in the Imperial Russian Army made him essentially an anti-Bolshevik Russian). Subsequently, the White Finns actually precipitated the fighting by establishing a power base in northern Finland, and then attacking the Russian military forces in several places. The Whites are said to have won the "civil war" because German troops invaded the country in April, capturing Helsinki, and otherwise assisting Mannerheim in the closing days of the fighting.[5]

Examination of certain well-established facts of Finnish history between May, 1918, and October, 1920, when Finland and Soviet Russia signed the Peace Treaty of Tartu, is of some help in reconciling these two rival versions of what took place between January and May, 1918. Whatever may have been the actual intentions of the Finnish Whites immediately after the armed conflict of 1918, their regime was certainly subject to considerable German influence until the Germans surrendered to the Allies in November, 1918. Thereafter the White Finns sought to follow the democratic trends inspired all over Europe by the Allied victory, while eschewing further major military enterprises. It is true that a Finnish government headed by Mannerheim did assist a successful effort during the winter of 1918–1919 to ward off an invasion of Estonia by the Red Army. Otherwise, however, postwar Finland declined to assist directly the general White Russian effort to overthrow Lenin's regime, even when that effort enjoyed maximum Allied support in North Russia and the Baltic region from November, 1918, to November, 1919. The Finns did aid that effort indirectly by persisting in border raids designed to push their eastern frontiers deep into Russian Karelia, in the direction of the Russian railroad connecting Petrograd and Murmansk.[6]

---

[5] The details of the German efforts to assist the Finnish Protective Corps may be found in the following: Johannes Öhquist, *Das Löwenbanner: Des Finnischen Volkes Aufstieg zur Freiheit*, Berlin, 1943, and Gustav Pezold, *Das Waffenschiff. Geheime Waffenfahrten mit S.M.H. "Equity" für Finnlands Freiheitskampf im Herbst 1917*, Hamburg, 1943. Even though written in Nazi Germany during the period when Finland was Hitler's ally, these books make it clear that before mid-February, 1918, a month after the fighting in Finland started, the Germans sent exactly one shipload of weapons to that country, which was scarcely enough to fight a full-scale war! Therefore, during the first month of the war, the White Finns had to be armed principally with captured Russian weapons, and those sent in by the Germans were mainly weapons they had captured from the Russians.

[6] Since the publication of the present writer's book on Finno-Russian relations, half of which deals with the period from the spring of 1918 to the spring of 1922, the following works have appeared in Soviet Russia: V. Petrov, *Finlyandiya v planakh imperialisticheskikh derzhav v 1918–1920 gg.*, Petrozavodsk, 1961, and M. I. Shumilov, *Vo glave oborony severa Rossii v 1918–1920 gg.*, Petrozavodsk, 1967.

At the same time, however, Finland genuinely sought, once the Germans had departed in November, 1918, to heal the wounds of what had been a form of civil war, no matter how great the degree of the Russian and German involvement. Those Red Finns who had not died, either in combat or through maltreatment after the civil war, or who had not emigrated to Soviet Russia (there to establish a Finnish Communist Party, and, for a time, a Soviet-style Finno-Karelian political unit), or who had not emigrated elsewhere, were amnestied and eventually restored to full citizenship in a democratic society. A chastened Social Democratic party was allowed to reappear and later was to support the wars of 1939–1940 and 1941–1944 against Soviet Russia. Of all the "succession" states of East Central Europe between 1918 and 1938, Finland's only serious rival for the honor of having done the most to keep democracy alive between the two world wars was Czechoslovakia, notwithstanding the momentary appearance of the notorious Lapua movement during the 1930's.[7]

However, determination to maintain their democracy in the aftermath of the events of 1944–1948 has clearly confronted the Finns with challenges with which they were not familiar during the inter-war years, since in foreign, if not in domestic, affairs Finland has had to cope with continuous Soviet pressure. As a consequence, the White version of the events of 1917–1918, which had come to be more or less generally accepted in Finland during the inter-war years, has been confronted during the past two decades with a school of revisionism, headed by the historian Juhani Paasivirta, which insists that although the Red revolution of 1918 was Marxist, it was not imported from Russia. The results of Paasivirta's research have only gradually found their way into historical literature in the major Western languages.[8] Up to a few years ago, most of the books in

---

[7] The most balanced account of the way in which the White Finns ultimately responded to their victory is: Leo Harmaja, *Effects of the War on Economic and Social Life in Finland*, New Haven, Conn., 1933. Harmaja leaves little doubt that insofar as socio-economic grievances justified the Red revolution in Finland, they were caused more by the fact that Germany and Russia were fighting the First World War than by White Finn resistance to socio-economic reform. Rintala, a leading supporter of the Red position in the war of 1918, concedes that the socio-economic grievances which are alleged to have caused that war were redressed during the decades 1919–1939. See the sketches of Väinö Tanner and K. J. Ståhlberg in: Marvin Rintala, *Four Finns: Political Profiles*, Berkeley and Los Angeles, Calif., 1969.

[8] Paasivirta's major works are the following: *Suomen itsenäisyyskysymys 1917*, 2 vols., Porvoo, 1947–1949; *Suomen poliittisen työväenliikkeen kehitys*, Porvoo, 1949; *Suomi vuonna 1918*, Porvoo, 1957; *Ensimmäisen maailmansodan voitajat ja Suomi : Englannin, Yhdysvaltain ja Ranskan sekä Suomen suhteita vv. 1918–1919*, Porvoo, 1961 (English translation: *The Victors in World War One and Finland*,

English on the war of 1918 in Finland had a White orientation. Recently, however, there appeared John H. Hodgson's *Communism in Finland: A History and Interpretation*, and Marvin Rintala's *Four Finns: Political Profiles*, which generally follow Paasivirta's line, though Hodgson does not do so blindly.

Despite its ambitious title, the first third of Hodgson's book deals almost exclusively with the events of 1917–1918, after a brief preliminary sketch of the development of the Finnish Social Democratic party prior to those events. Moreover, the author ends his account of the rise of the official Finnish Communist Party with the year 1944, thus missing the opportunity to examine whether any parallels exist between Finno-Soviet relations during 1917–1918, and Finno-Soviet relations during the crucial years between 1944 and 1948. Rintala, on the other hand, in sketches of four important Finnish statesmen—Gustaf Mannerheim, Väinö Tanner, K. J. Ståhlberg, and J. K. Paasikivi—contrives to relate the events of 1917–1918 to all subsequent important periods of Finnish history, and to reach the conclusion that a Finnish statesman's success or lack of success in domestic affairs is less important than his success or lack of success in achieving good relations with Soviet Russia.

Since the present writer as far back as 1955 took the position that the war in Finland in 1918 was a case of "a Russian wolf in Finnish sheep's clothing," it seems only fair at this point to quote extensively the contrary view taken by Hodgson in 1967:

> Finnish workers took arms in what to them was a civil war, whereas the Finnish peasantry went to battle in the belief that they were fighting a War of Independence against a foreign enemy. The eventual triumph of the Finnish Whites was viewed by the bourgeoisie as a military victory against Russia, although scholarly study shows that in actual fact it was a victory of White Finn over Red Finn. ... Russian troops were in Finland for the purpose of defending Petrograd against a possible German attack, but in the interest of achieving an immediate peace with Germany, Lenin was willing by late February to withdraw all forces from Finland. National interest dictated the policy of the Bolshevik government as well as the policy of Finland's revolutionary government.... It is difficult to avoid the conclusion that Russia's role in the Finnish Civil War was negligible. The hands of the Bolshevik government were tied by the struggle for national survival ... One cannot say with any certainty that German aid was the decisive factor in the defeat of the Finnish Reds, but without this aid the struggle would have been longer and much more difficult.[9]

Helsinki, 1965). A major critic of Paasivirta's viewpoint is the Finnish historian L. A. Puntila. See his *Suomen poliittinen historia 1809–1955*, Helsinki, 1963.

[9] Hodgson, *op. cit.*, pp. 71–81, *passim*.

The views of the post-1948 Paasivirta school of Finnish historiography, as reflected in the above quotation, would have a ring of plausibility even if they were not buttressed by extensive research in Finnish documents. Since Tito's defection from Stalin, and more importantly, since the Sino-Soviet split, any analysis of a Communist seizure of power which is based on the notion of "national communism" is apt to enjoy a wide hearing. Moreover, even the most extreme of the White versions of the war of 1918 in Finland has never denied that the Red seizure of power in the country had the support of the great mass of Finnish workers, and that native Red resistance to Mannerheim's White Army and to the Germans was fierce. It is undisputed that fully half of the Finnish electorate voted for Marxian socialism in 1916, that slightly less than half did so in 1917, and that there was a considerable Marxist comeback in the country's politics as early as 1920.

Nevertheless, it can scarcely be disputed: that the fate of Finland had been in the hands of Russia for more than a century when the Finnish Reds seized power in 1918; that an extensive Russian military occupation of the country had existed for nearly four years prior to that time, and continued to exist until the Reds had had six weeks to consolidate their position in southern Finland;[10] that Lenin, Trotsky, and Stalin tried to persuade the Red Finns to seize power, in November, 1917; that remarkably close relations existed between Red Finland and Red Russia between January and May, 1918; or that the leaders of Red Finland went to Soviet Russia and founded a Finnish Communist Party there after May, 1918. Certainly, Soviet Russian historians are as entitled as are Western historians to speak out on the crucial issue of whether a causal relationship existed between the Bolshevik seizure of power in Petrograd on November 7, 1917, and the Red seizure of power in Helsinki less than three months later. In 1967, the same year in which Hodgson offered his modified version of the Paasivirta thesis, V. M. Kholodkovsky published in Moscow his *Revolyutsiya v Finlyandii i germanskaya interventsiya* (The Revolution in Finland and the German Intervention) which sums up the results of extensive research in Soviet Russia over the past two decades on the general subject of what Kholodkovsky describes as the Finnish "civil war." But despite his unwillingness to regard the Russian troops in Finland during 1917–1918

---

[10] Over half of the Russian army in Finland in August, 1917, had melted away by January, 1918, but the remaining 40,000 were either forcibly disarmed and sent home by Mannerheim on and after January 27–28, 1918, or did not begin to leave until the signing of the Treaty of Brest-Litovsk on March 3. A force of at least 1,000 "volunteers" stayed with the Red Finns to the bitter end. Hodgson, *op. cit.* See also Smith, *op. cit.*, pp. 39–45.

as the *deus ex machina* of the Red seizure of power, Kholodkovsky is far from being ready to agree with Hodgson in a belief that "Russia's role in the Finnish Civil War was negligible." He writes, for example:

> That Lenin had in view the possibility of the establishment in Finland of a socialist republic even before the seizure of power by the Russian proletariat is obvious .... Although the Finnish Social Democrats did not follow Lenin's advice about the seizure of power, some mobilization of the forces of the working class was carried out .... The news of the October Revolution acted on the Finnish worker movement like a mighty catalyst, hastening the intensification of the revolutionary crisis.[11]

He goes on to note that Stalin made a trip to Helsinki on November 25, 1917, but failed to persuade the Finnish Social Democrats to seize power. However, some of their leaders were influenced by a visit to Lenin in Petrograd only a month later. Kullervo Manner, one of those leaders, wrote later: "On me at least this encounter with Comrade Lenin exerted such influence that there ripened within me the courage and resolution to make a start on the path of the seizure of power, on which we thereafter set out at the end of January, true, even then with backward looks."[12]

But what of the Russian troops which were in Finland in late January when the fighting broke out? Kholodkovsky vigorously defends their right to be there, on the ground that the approaches to revolutionary Petrograd had to be guarded. Nor does he fail to note that friendly relations had been established between them and the Finnish workers before the seizure of power. He goes on to admit freely the following: "In the circumstances of the ever more impudent attacks by the Protective Corps men, the workers turned to the Russian troops with requests for arms... The leading organs of the Russian troops did not refuse, if the arms were surplus... Simultaneously the Finnish workers turned to Petrograd for arms." Kholodkovsky goes on to relate that on January 20, 1918, Lenin personally arranged that this last request should be honored.[13]

Kholodkovsky finds that it is absurd to try to divorce the struggle in Finland from the events in Russia at the time, and to claim that that struggle was explicable only in terms of Finnish internal developments:

---

[11] V. M. Kholodkovsky, *Revolyutsiya v Finlyandii*, p. 12. Kholodkovsky buttresses his argument with a quotation from the following source, which Hodgson apparently did not use: O. V. Kuusinen, *Izbrannyye proizvedeniya (1918—1964)*, Moscow, 1966.

[12] Kholodkovsky, *op. cit.*, pp. 17, 56.

[13] *Ibid.*, pp. 66—68.

The Finnish revolution was the first of the foreign revolutions which followed on the heels of October. At that time, the very fact that the Bolshevik revolution in Russia did not remain unique, that its initiative was grasped by the workers of another country, that the revolutionary wave began to spread out towards the West, already had overwhelming international significance. The Finnish revolution was the first practical proof of the opinion of the Bolsheviks to the effect that Great October would inaugurate a whole revolutionary age. To some degree it enriched the treasury of the experience of the international worker movement, by emphasizing in its own special way the correctness of the basic fundamentals of the revolutionary tactics worked out by the Bolsheviks.[14]

Kholodkovsky thus reduces to the level of triviality the question of whether the struggle in Finland in 1918 was a "war of independence" or a "civil war." Given the fact that the encouragement and assistance from Petrograd for the Reds was matched by encouragement and assistance from the Swedes and Germans for the Whites, what really needs to be explained, in his view, is why the Red Finns were so slow in taking action, despite the October Revolution in Petrograd, and why they were finally overcome by Mannerheim's White Army. On the first point, Kholodkovsky has the following to say:

The Finnish revolution grew out of conditions different from those in Russia. In terms of her way of life, Finland was closer to the West. . . . Up to 1917, the class struggle between the workers and the bourgeoisie did not assume in Finland such sharp forms as in Russia. Therefore, when the Finnish Social Democrats decided on revolution, they did not copy the tactics of the Bolsheviks, but worked out their own, which they considered more in accord with the conditions of Finland. It would be wrong to condemn each departure of the Finnish revolutionaries from Bolshevik methods. . . . Only in the course of the struggle did the leaders of the revolution become acquainted with Lenin's work, *State and Revolution,* and liberate themselves from the vestiges of Social Democratism. A process of the transformation of the Social Democratic party into a party of a new type was begun.[15]

Finally, Kholodkovsky leaves no doubt that Lenin, if he had had the military strength to do so, would never have permitted the White Finns to drown in blood the Red revolution in Helsinki:

The revolution in Finland would not have suffered destruction if it had had to struggle only against the White Finn army, which could not compare in fighting spirit with the Red Guard. The main factor which guaranteed the preservation in Finland of the bourgeois order was the armed intervention of Imperial Germany. And Soviet Russia was then weak, and could not furnish

---

[14] *Ibid.,* p. 352.

[15] *Ibid.,* pp. 352–353.

revolutionary Finland with the necessary assistance against the interventionists, and save the workers of Finland from the horrors of the White Terror.[16]

None of the above seems to fit exactly with Hodgson's view that "national interest dictated the policy of the Bolshevik government, as well as the policy of Finland's revolutionary government," and that "the hands of the Bolshevik government were tied by the struggle for national survival." Unless, that is, one assumes that even at this early stage Lenin's regime in Russia was essentially a Russian nationalist regime bent on pursuing essentially the same policies towards subject nationalities that Tsarist Russia had pursued, though describing them in different language. One is nevertheless bound, in that case, to ask the question: if Russian national interests were served by having Russian troops in a country which guarded the approaches to Petrograd—threatened as it was by the danger of German attack—were they not even better served if, in addition, Bolshevik Russia demanded of Finland what Tsarist Russia had never demanded—the total conformity of Finnish political and socio-economic institutions with those of Russia?

It is, of course, one thing to discover in the confused and contradictory record of the first six months of the Soviet regime evidence that Lenin and other Bolsheviks incited the Red Finns to action, and quite another thing to assert that the actual behavior patterns of the Red Finns duplicated those of the Russian Bolsheviks between November, 1917, and May, 1918. Kholodkovsky's views on this point are in fact in accord with most White Finn accounts of the Red Finn Government of January–May, 1918; the latter generally stop short of insisting on the absolute identity of Red Finland and Red Russia. A careful, month-by-month survey of simultaneous events in Petrograd and Helsinki between November 7, 1917, and May 5, 1918, does reveal, however, a remarkable degree of identity with respect to the ebb and flow of revolutionary momentum, partly owing to external influences which neither the Russians nor the Finns could control.

---

[16] *Ibid.* The present writer's name was included in a long list of "bourgeois historians" whom Kholodkovsky set out to "unmask" in writing his book. I was denounced for allegedly having cast slurs on Lenin's motives in granting independence to Finland, on the character of Red Finn Finance Minister Edvard Gylling, and on the courage of the Red Finns when the Germans took Helsinki, as well as for being too generous in my estimate of General Mannerheim. It seems probable that I was unfair to Gylling, but my general view of the physical courage of the Red Finns, as presented in my book, is surely very close to that of Kholodkovsky himself. As for Mannerheim, it is perhaps well to note that although Marvin Rintala denounces him in *Four Finns, op. cit.*, for the role which he played during 1917–1919, he feels that the General deserves very high marks for his handling of Finno-Soviet relations after the Second World War.

There is an important point which cannot be made too often with respect to events in Russia during those six months: it is difficult if not impossible to fix upon a precise date when a "Communist seizure of power" actually took place in that country. The very word "Communist" is anachronistic when used with respect to the events of November 7, 1917, in Petrograd. Lenin did propose that the Bolshevik fraction of the Russian Social Democratic Labor Party sever its last links with the Mensheviks and the Second International as early as April, 1917, and adopt the name "Communist."[17] Since a modicum of intra-party democracy still existed, he did not get his way until March, 1918, nearly two months after the Red Finns had taken power in Helsinki, and just as they were on the point of being overthrown.[18] Even then, moreover, the awkward name actually adopted, "All Russian Communist Party (*bolsheviki*)," contained a reminder of the Party's past, and was not replaced by "Communist Party of the Soviet Union" until 1952. Not until March, 1919, did the Party sever its last links with the Second International through the establishment of the Third or Communist International. All that can safely be said about November 7, 1917, in Petrograd is therefore the following: on that date the Bolsheviks and their allies began the process of destroying—in such key places as the Winter Palace in Petrograd, the Moscow Kremlin, and the Stavka in Mogilev—what few shreds of power still remained in the hands of Kerensky's largely phantom government. Moreover, until they ensconced themselves in Moscow in March, 1918, the Bolsheviks themselves were presiding over a largely phantom government.[19]

This being the case, it is perhaps not surprising that Bolshevik revolutionary momentum slowed down considerably towards the end of November, 1917. Lenin and his associates then embarked upon a series of hasty improvisations which, while kept within a broad and hazy ideological framework, were designed mainly to meet concrete situations which had arisen since "Great October." The new regime found its right to rule the former Russian empire challenged, not only in Finland and the area of the Baltic States not yet occupied by the Germans, but also throughout the southern reaches of the country. Its armed opponents included the Petliura regime in the Ukraine, the Cossack communities, the Volunteer Army in the North Caucasus, and the Georgian Menshevik regime in Transcaucasia.[20]

---

[17] Chamberlin, *op. cit.*, Vol. I, p. 118.

[18] Ulam, *op. cit.*, p. 407.

[19] *Ibid.*, pp. 314–382, *passim*.

[20] Apart from Chamberlin, *op. cit.*, the following works are especially notable for their treatment of anti-Bolshevik movements in the southern regions of the Russian empire after November 7, 1917: John S. Reshetar, Jr., *The Ukrainian*

During the dramatic night of November 7–8, Trotsky had consigned the Right Socialist Revolutionaries (SR's) and the Mensheviks to the "dustbin of history." Then, on November 25, there came a great *volte-face*. By starting elections for the Russian Constituent Assembly on that date, the Bolsheviks in effect emptied the contents of the "dustbin" back onto the chessboard of Russian politics, since, as they had anticipated, the SR-Menshevik vote in the elections was twice the size of their own. The risk had to be taken, nevertheless, since armistice negotiations with the Germans started on December 4, and peace negotiations on December 22. Cooperative Left SR's were mustered into the Soviet government, and until midsummer, 1918, they helped maintain the illusion, despite the suppression of the Constituent Assembly on January 18–19, 1918, that at Brest-Litovsk the Germans had been dealing with a coalition government put in office by the votes of the Russian people.[21]

Thus, even though the Finnish Social Democrats during this period were men of the Second rather than the Third International, they were justified in regarding Lenin as to some degree a comrade. Moreover, the leaders of the parliamentary Social Democrats in Helsinki—Kullervo Manner, Yrjö Sirola, Otto Kuusinen, and Edvard Gylling—passed through a phase between November 7 and December 6 which was not poles apart, in terms of revolutionary momentum, from the one through which Lenin and the Bolsheviks were passing in Petrograd during those same four weeks. They started with a considerable degree of revolutionary *élan*, and then, of their own volition, began to apply brakes. The percentage of the Finnish electorate which supported them—and which, through such men as the future leader of the Red Guard, Eero Haapalainen, showed considerable desire for a violent seizure of power—was twice the percentage of the Russian electorate which supported Lenin. On the other hand, the very strength of the future leaders of Red Finland made them more cautious than the Russian Bolsheviks. Moreover, it is clear enough that they were honestly puzzled as to what their attitude towards the new Russian regime in Petrograd, and towards the future relationship of Russia and Finland, ought to be. Lenin's regime might or might not survive very long. It might be replaced by a reactionary one which would try to reimpose the russification of Finland just ended by the Provisional Government. And uncertainty existed as to Lenin's exact relationship to the Marxism of the Second International, hitherto the inspiration of Finnish socialism.

Revolution, 1917–1920: A Study in Nationalism, Princeton, N.J., 1952; Richard Pipes, *The Formation of the Soviet Union: Communism and Nationalism, 1917–1923* (revised edition), New York, 1968.

[21] Ulam, *op. cit.*, pp. 314–382, *passim*.

The future leaders of Red Finland constituted a Central Revolutionary Council on November 8, and endorsed a general strike in the country during November 13–18. Then, alarmed by the excesses committed by their followers while the strike was in progress, they called it off and began to engage in a bitter debate with the leaders of the Red Guard over whether revolutionary violence should be resumed, a debate which finally ended on January 6, 1918, with open defiance of the Party leadership by the Red Guard.[22]

The motives of the Finnish Marxist leaders, who finally surrendered to the Red Guard demands on January 27–28, only when it was clear that otherwise the Guard would take action on its own, were no doubt in many respects admirable. Hodgson portrays them as men pushed along by a juggernaut of worker protest which was simply irresistible, but this was perhaps not the whole story. The Finnish Marxist hierarchy had grasped the essential fact that in a small country like Finland the support of only fifty percent of the population is not enough for drastic socio-economic change, whatever might be the case in nearby Russia.

The tragedy of Finland between November 7 and December 6, 1917, lay in the fact that despite somewhat clumsy efforts by the Social Democratic leadership to use persuasion rather than force to win the support of elements of the "bourgeoisie" for their socio-economic reform program, polarization did set in, and both the Protective Corps and a battalion of Finns then serving in the German Army, as well as a Russian garrison which scarcely understood what was going on in Finland, must share some of the blame with the Red Guard. The general strike produced some socio-economic reforms, though not nearly enough to halt the clamor of the Red Guard. It also produced a White government headed by P. E. Svinhufvud that was stronger than the one which resigned as a result of the general strike. Svinhufvud strode forward more boldly than earlier White leaders, rallying all non-Marxists behind himself, and courting general popularity by ignoring Social Democratic objections to his proclamation of the total independence of Finland on December 6, two days after the Soviet-German armistice negotiations opened. Though he doubtless wanted by this step to disengage Finland from the Russian revolution and the presence of the Russian troops, and also to score points against the Social Democrats, his principal motive probably was a desire to make the independence of Finland a matter of concern at the forthcoming peace conference, and not just a

---

[22] Hodgson, *op. cit.*, pp. 20–50; Smith, *op. cit.*, pp. 19–29.

matter of proclamations by the Finnish Diet and of Finno-Soviet negotiations. He succeeded in this regard only as late as February 25, 1918.

On November 25, 1917, the very day that elections to the Russian
Constituent Assembly began in Petrograd, Lenin dispatched Stalin to
Helsinki to support the Finnish Red Guard in its quarrel with the Social
Democratic leadership over an immediate seizure of power. This action
was in line with other Soviet actions taken over the next three months
against the Petliura regime in the Ukraine, the Cossack communities, and
the Volunteer Army, and, like most of them, it was ineffective. Nevertheless, it scarcely leaves much doubt that Lenin put Svinhufvud in roughly
the same category as Petliura, against whom he was finally able to organize
a Ukrainian Soviet regime in Kharkov. Eventually, however, Lenin extended formal recognition to Svinhufvud's regime—on December 31, 1917.[23]

Does this prove that the loudly trumpeted adherence of Soviet Russia
to the principles of self-determination of nationalities was genuine? Or did
Lenin merely feel confident that in time the Finnish Red Guard, led by
Eero Haapalainen and Adolf Taimi (a Petrograd Finn who had been
dispatched to Helsinki) would, with assistance from the Russian garrison,
move the Social Democratic hierarchy to action and thus overthrow
Svinhufvud and his regime? Clearly, Svinhufvud himself thought during
December, 1917, and January, 1918, that Lenin was planning something
like this, and believed that he who supped with Lenin should carry a long
spoon. Though the White Finn leadership avoided direct clashes with the
Red Guard and the Russian troops as much as possible in December and
most of January, and although Svinhufvud was ready to negotiate with
both Red Finns and Russians as late as January 24, careful preparations
were certainly made by the Whites for what they probably regarded as an
inevitable conflict. Not only was the evacuation of Finland by Russian
forces insistently demanded during that period, but Mannerheim was

---

[23] After forming his government in Helsinki, Svinhufvud preferred to have
no dealings at all with the Soviet Russians except to demand that they remove
their armed forces from Finland. However the Germans, who were not so
particular about whom they negotiated with, advised that Svinhufvud approach
Lenin about independence, and he reluctantly complied. The Finnish Social
Democrats had been even less squeamish than the Germans about approaching
Lenin on the subject. Svinhufvud personally led the Finnish delegation to Petrograd on December 31, but only with difficulty was Lenin persuaded by his
colleagues to meet the Finnish leader. Most of their conversation seems to have
consisted of Lenin's ranting over the fact that the "cowardice" of the Finnish
Social Democrats was forcing him to do business with a "bourgeois" government,
an assertion scarcely reassuring to Svinhufvud.

appointed as early as December 16 to lead the future White Army, and was sent north to establish a power base at Vaasa on January 18.[24]

Nevertheless, it is clear enough that the moves by the principal actors during the month preceding January 27–28, whether in Petrograd or Helsinki, were not caused solely by the polarization in Finland, which made it possible to predict a war between Svinhufvud and Mannerheim, on the one side, and Haapalainen and Taimi, backed by Lenin, on the other. In addition, new momentum was being given to the cause of revolution in both Russia and Finland by the course of the negotiations at Brest-Litovsk between December 22 and February 1.

When these negotiations began, neither side could be sure what the result would be, and they gradually gave rise not only to a rift between the civilians and the military in the German government, but also to the first serious differences among the members of the Bolshevik Central Committee in Petrograd. If the Red Finns had seized power at any point between November 7 and December 22, none of this would have greatly mattered as far as Finland was concerned. In fact, the White Finns finally received help, not so much from the civilian German government as from the German military men who overrode its wishes. Moreover, the nature of the quarrels which broke out among Lenin, Trotsky, and Bukharin after January 18 over the Brest-Litovsk negotiations makes it difficult to say where the Bolsheviks actually stood with respect to the Red seizure of power in Helsinki on January 27–28, 1918.

The Brest negotiations began at a moment when the Soviet Russians, the Central Powers, and the Allied Powers were trying to outdo each other in vague liberal-pacifist rhetoric in an effort to capture the allegiance of a

---

[24] From a strictly military viewpoint, it may be said that the Whites prepared to fight in a far more purposeful fashion than did the Reds between late November and late January, 1918. The Finnish Social Democratic hierarchy was quite unable and unwilling to plan a military seizure of power, and the Red Guard, while full of fight, had no leaders capable of dealing with organized military opposition. The Russians would have been of little help, even if Lenin had not wanted them to remain as invisible as possible. When Trotsky took control of the Red Army and Red Fleet in March, 1918, he found only helpless confusion, and promptly dismissed most of the existing Soviet military leadership. It would therefore be hard to exaggerate the importance of Svinhufvud's discovery of a real professional soldier, Mannerheim, to lead the still badly organized and poorly armed Protective Corps. However, Svinhufvud seems to have been suspicious of Mannerheim from the beginning. If the General was in fact, as the Red Finns later claimed, a White Russian whose real aim was not to free Finland but to restore a White Russian government in Petrograd, into what new dangers might he plunge his native country?

war-weary world for their respective causes. Lenin had already partially disarmed his liberal-pacifist critics by launching the Constituent Assembly elections on November 25, and that body was not finally dissolved until January 18–19. By December 22, Lenin was greatly embarrassing the Allied Powers by making it appear that they were more reluctant than were the Soviet Russians and the Germans to restore peace to mankind. Then, at Brest, Joffe, original head of the Soviet delegation, discovered that the official head of the German delegation, Foreign Secretary Richard von Kühlmann, was surprisingly willing to accede to a program of "no annexations and no indemnities." It is difficult not to believe that Lenin's formal grant of independence to Finland approximately a week later reflected nothing so much as a desire to beat Kühlmann at his own game. After all, protests against the russification of Finland had been a staple item of liberal-pacifist rhetoric since 1899. In addition, Kühlmann had made it clear that he did not regard it as "annexationist" if the Germans recognized and protected nationalist regimes which had sprung up in the border provinces of Russia they already occupied. Lenin may have thought that this line concealed an intention to occupy still more non-Russian border provinces of the former empire; hence the best way to keep the Germans out of Finland was nominally to set it free.[25]

Nevertheless, the Soviets had not gone to Brest to dance a liberal-pacifist minuet with Kühlmann, and Trotsky was dispatched to ferret out the real intentions of the Germans. With the finesse of a toreador handling a raging bull, he finally caused outspoken General Max Hoffmann, who was the real stage-manager on the German side, to admit on January 18 that the Germans intended to annex what they had already conquered, though Hoffmann did not yet ask for additional territory, including Finland.

---

[25] Fritz Fischer's book (cited above) is a major work, but in his eagerness to "unmask" German Chancellor von Bethmann Hollweg, he seems to have given the German civilian bureaucrats of 1917–1918 less credit than they deserved for opposing the "annexationism" of German generals and super-patriots. The Allied blockade was slowly strangling the Germans during the winter of 1917 to 1918, so much so that Hindenburg and Ludendorff, the real rulers of the country, were impatient with the "annexationist" appetites of General Hoffmann and other commanders on the Eastern Front. The important thing for them at Brest-Litovsk was to get control of the food supplies supposed to exist in such great quantities in the Ukraine; the taking of Russian territory per se, whether or not in the form of the liberation of some subject nationality, was a secondary consideration, and the idea of an anti-Communist crusade was not even under discussion. Therefore, the annexationists had to add Finland (and Livonia and Estonia) almost surreptitiously to their lists, long after it had been made clear to the Soviet Russians that Germany wanted the Ukraine.

The Russian Constituent Assembly was forcibly dissolved the next day, and Trotsky was back in Petrograd for new instructions.[26]

A vital turning point in Soviet Russian affairs was now at hand. Insofar as the Bolshevik revolution now became suffused with the patriotic Russian nationalism which Kerensky had tried in vain to arouse in 1917, this was largely the work of Bukharin and his followers, who initially had a majority on the Central Committee. They wished to fight a "revolutionary war" against Hoffmann and his goose-stepping battalions, in marked contrast to Lenin and Stalin, who wanted peace with the Germans at any price. Lenin may have supplied the Red Finns with some arms from the Petrograd arsenals on January 20, but *whether he really welcomed what they did a week later is doubtful.* Certainly their ill-timed acceptance of the advice he had given two months earlier, and had just repeated, scarcely strengthened him in his struggle with Bukharin and the war hawks in Petrograd. In the end, Trotsky had to be sent back to Brest with his "no war–no peace" formula, which merely enraged Hoffmann when it was announced on February 1. At first the Germans responded to it by arranging a separate peace with the Petliura regime in the Ukraine, even though Trotsky produced some Ukrainian Reds from Kharkov who claimed to represent the people of their country. Then, when Trotsky left the conference in high dudgeon, clinging to the "no war–no peace" formula, Hoffmann had his opportunity to resume hostilities (on February 18).[27]

It would, however, be wrong to insist that the Brest negotiations settled the fate of Finland. In fact, the Vyborg (Viipuri) incident of January 19–24 (apparently a purely local affair not planned by any of the protagonists in the coming war in Finland) was decisive; without it the fighting might

---

[26] Soviet Russian diplomatic historians no longer bother to deny that Trotsky represented Soviet Russia at Brest-Litovsk during January and February, 1918, though they fail to name him as the Foreign Commissar. He is introduced into the story of Brest-Litovsk, however, only for the purpose of denouncing the "treason" which he allegedly committed there. He is blamed for not having accepted the terms offered by Hoffmann on January 18, which were in fact milder than the ones finally accepted on March 3. Trotsky is said to have disregarded clear instructions from the Central Committee when, on February 11, he walked out, defying Hoffmann to do his worst.

[27] It is not certain what Svinhufvud, Mannerheim, and the Germans would have done had there been no Red seizure of power in Finland by the time the Germans arrived in Estonia, Narva, and Pskov during the week of February 18–25. Finland had been pregnant with revolution since early November, but it is hard to fight against a revolution still in embryo. Lenin was sophisticated enough to realize in mid-January that the Red Finns, having delayed their revolution so long, might actually serve his cause better by continuing to keep quiet until he had dealt with the Germans.

have been delayed until the final outcome at Brest clarified the situation. The Vyborg clash, involving only the local Protective Corps, Red Guard, and Russian garrison, caused the Social Democratic hierarchy to burn its last bridges to the Svinhufvud regime, to unleash the Red Guard in the industrial cities where it was strong, and to form a Council of People's Plenipotentiaries to rule a Socialist Workers' Republic proclaimed on January 28. In fairness it should be noted that the Whites took so many steps to fight the Russians and the Reds that Mannerheim very nearly managed to take control of northern Finland from the Russians on January 27–28, before the Reds in the south can be said to have really "seized power." Moreover, he almost succeeded in cutting rail communications between Helsinki and Petrograd during the first days of the fighting.[28]

It is useless to speculate as to how the Finnish Socialist Workers' Republic of 1918 might have developed if it had been able, with or without Soviet Russian assistance, at least to hold on to the territory over which it had some control on January 28, 1918. Perhaps it had some chance to survive during its first month of existence, when the Germans sent in the Finnish battalion they had organized as far back as 1915, and supplied Mannerheim with weapons. However, General Hoffmann did not persuade Hindenburg and Ludendorff (the real rulers of Germany) to add Livonia, Estonia, and Finland to the German annexation list until late February, by which time the Finnish Red Guard had proved its capacity, with some Russian help, at least to hold a military line against Mannerheim.

On March 1, the Soviet government signed a treaty with the Helsinki regime. This was on the eve of the military evacuation required of the Russians by the Treaty of Brest-Litovsk, signed two days later.[29] If only because they

---

[28] Since he spent most of 1917 in Russia, Mannerheim had probably worked out in his own mind what he would have done if he had been in charge in Petrograd that year. This, however, would appear to be all there is to the idea, set forth in Marvin Rintala's *Four Finns*, op. cit., that he was interested in Finland mainly as a base from which to stage a Russian counter-revolution. If Rintala had been able to use the Russian documents published by the Soviets pertaining to Mannerheim's career as Regent of Finland during 1918–1919, he would surely be convinced by the record of Mannerheim's dealings with the White Russians, at a time when everyone thought they would win, that there is ample evidence of his transfer of loyalty from Russia to Finland.

[29] As Mannerheim was closing in on Vyborg near the end of the war, the Red Finn leader, Gylling, naïvely sought to negotiate with him. By this time, Red Finland had been reduced to bands of roaming guerrillas, and Mannerheim naturally spurned Gylling's advances. The Soviet government gave a hero's welcome to the Red Finn leaders when they arrived in Petrograd at the end of the war, but tens of thousands of rank-and-file Red Guardsmen left in Finland bore the brunt of the terror unleashed by the Whites.

could not organize an army without Soviet Russian help, the Red Finns can scarcely have had much doubt by March 1 that they had delivered themselves entirely into Lenin's hands, and could only hope that the Swedish, or even the German socialists, would bail them out later. The treaty with Finland created a joint Finno-Russian citizenship and provided that disputes between the parties thereto would be arbitrated by the left wing of the Swedish Social Democratic Party. It is doubtful whether Lenin had much faith in the ability of Red Finland to survive, and the treaty seems to have been intended to pacify those Bukharinites in Petrograd who were accusing Lenin of planning to desert the Finns. Lenin must have felt that it was only a question of time before the Germans, already in possession of Livonia, Estonia, Narva, and Pskov, would be in Helsinki. Indeed, the only hope for the Red Finns was that the Whites would compromise themselves with the Allied Powers by accepting German help. Lenin invited the Allies into Murmansk, very close to the Finnish border, and agreed to accept "bread and potatoes" from the "Anglo-French imperialist bandits." It required considerable effort to hold the White Finns together during March, after Mannerheim discovered that Svinhufvud and the other politicians planned to bring in the Germans, who arrived in early April.[30]

It was at this juncture that Mannerheim succeeded in winning an important victory by capturing the great industrial city of Tampere, and the German intervention speeded up the defeat of the Red Finns. In view of his pro-Allied orientation, the Germans must have feared that a Mannerheim victorious over the Red Finns without their aid might become a dangerous neighbor on the flank of their new possessions in the Baltic States. And the Red Finns themselves had little choice but to throw themselves into the arms of the Soviets during the last month of the war.[31]

The fate of the more responsible leaders of Red Finland was a bitter one: essentially they were the victims, along with the Whites who were

---

[30] The Germans had originally planned to land on the Finnish coast shortly after they arrived in the Åland Islands on March 5, but excuses were found to wait a month longer. Probably the most important reason was that Hindenburg and Ludendorff did not really want so many distractions in the east when they were trying to win the war in the west. In the end, though, the annexationists had their way, probably because it was uncertain what Mannerheim would do after he had dealt with the Red Finns.

[31] In Russia during March and April, 1918, there was some effort by the Bukharinites to blame Lenin for the defeat of the Red Finns. As late as April 20, Lenin was talking wildly of an all-out effort at least to keep the Reds in possession of Vyborg, but the effort was never actually made. After the Red Finn leaders arrived in Soviet Russia, Lenin needed many months to make them understand their mistakes in January, 1918.

casualties of the fighting during January–May, 1918, of great historical forces which they could scarcely hope to comprehend fully, much less control. Comprehension was not faciliated by the war's legacy of blind, emotional hatred which inevitably affected the vanquished far more than the victors. The tide of history which they were powerless to reverse was a manifestation of the great Russo-German duel for control of Eastern Central Europe starting in the time of Nicholas II and William II, and ending under Stalin and Hitler, and of the crisis in international socialism largely created by both that duel and the emergence of the Leninist brand of Marxism. Despite her unique position among the subject nationalities of the Russian empire, Finland belonged to that vast area of Eastern Central Europe embracing Estonia, Latvia, Lithuania, Russian Poland, Byelorussia, the Ukraine, Bessarabia, the Crimea, and Transcaucasia, and also the German and Austrian parts of Poland, the subject nationalities of Austria-Hungary, and the independent Balkan States, which came almost completely under the control of the Central Powers during the First World War. The ultimate fate of this territory was as much the principal issue of the First World War as it was of the Second. The future historian may well conclude that Finland's fate between 1886 and 1919 hinged less upon her evolution in the direction of Marxist socialism of the Second International variety, or Russia's evolution in the direction of Marxist Third International socialism, than it did upon the outcome of the Russo-German struggle for mastery of Eastern Central Europe, which began in the 1880's and did not end until 1945.

There was a military dimension to the Soviet Russian intervention in Finland which both Hodgson and Kholodkovsky all but completely ignore. It is true that the role of the Russian *army* in Finland between November, 1917, and January, 1918, was a minor one. It intimidated the Whites to a degree, but where Mannerheim had only Russian troops to deal with, he had no real difficulties. The Russian army armed the Red Finns, but the latter did most of the actual fighting. In contrast, the role of the Russian Baltic Fleet, actually located in Finland during the crucial days, was a very real one. Contrary to the common supposition, the nerve center of the Baltic Fleet's effective defensive operations during World War I was not Kronstadt, just to the west of Petrograd, but another island fortress, Sveaborg (Suomenlinna), which lies offshore from the central section of Helsinki. Anyone who knows the geography of the Finnish capital will readily appreciate that Sveaborg's guns, and those of any naval vessels stationed there, could at the time dominate Helsinki far more easily than those of Kronstadt could dominate Petrograd. Moreover, between 1914 and 1918, the Russian naval presence at Hanko (Hangö) and in the Åland

Islands (Ahvenanmaa) barred the other maritime approaches to Finland. However loyal to Kerensky, or however neutral, the Russian troops in Finland, Estonia-Livonia, and the Petrograd region may have been during 1917, the Russian Baltic Fleet was unquestionably won over to the Bolshevik cause at a very early stage, and was to a large degree responsible for Lenin's abortive attempt to seize power in July, 1917. Lenin fled afterwards to Finland for refuge from Kerensky less because of a desire for support from the Red Finns than because the Russian fleet headquarters on Sveaborg was still firmly in the hands of his most ardent supporters. As a military venture, the Bolshevik seizure of power in Petrograd on November 7, 1917, was mainly a matter of whether enough armed workers of Trotsky's Red Guard and Lettish riflemen could be found to supplement the already available sailors of the Baltic Fleet. Although the role of the cruiser *Avrora* and of the Kronstadt sailors in the seizure of power is well known, a considerable part of the naval forces taking part in that operation came from Helsinki, both overland and by sea.

Despite their role in the Bolshevik seizure of power in Petrograd, the Baltic Fleet men were still patriotic Russians; only two or three weeks earlier they had fiercely resisted the German occupation of the Moon Sound Islands lying adjacent to their naval base at Tallinn in Estonia, and the Germans had acquired a healthy respect for their ability to defend the Åland Islands, Hanko, and Helsinki. Thus, when Trotsky went to Brest to negotiate with the Germans some two months later, he was not wholly lacking in military assets to improve his bargaining position. If the Germans were slower to espouse the cause of the White Finns than the cause of the White Ukrainians, this probably reflected not only their desire for a quick peace on the Eastern Front but also their recognition that all the maritime approaches to Finland were guarded by a fiercely Bolshevik fleet, which had already proven its capacity to fight effectively. The fleet was, however, vulnerable to natural phenomena: in the dead of winter, the waters of the Gulfs of Bothnia and Finland freeze over, and icebreaker capabilities in 1917–1918 were limited. This may have been a key consideration when Lenin, Trotsky, and Stalin urged that the Finnish Social Democrats act immediately after the Bolsheviks had taken power in Petrograd. By the time the Red Finns did act, the Russian Baltic Fleet units were immobilized, save when icebreakers could clear a path for them. This may have been one reason why the Germans waited until late February, 1918, to advance into Livonia and Estonia, at a time when they knew that the maritime flank of their advancing army could not readily be harried by the Russian fleet units just to the north, across the Gulf of Finland. Moreover, after he was temporarily deprived of this most important military asset, Lenin felt that he had no recourse except to move the Russian capital from Petrograd to Moscow.

The Germans intervened in Finland in 1918 for a number of reasons, but one which is usually missed is that once the ice had melted, their grip on the Baltic States would scarcely have been very secure if Lenin, with the Russian fleet at his disposal in Helsinki, had decided to ignore the Treaty of Brest-Litovsk. It was difficult to suppose that Mannerheim, however strong in the interior, could ever take Helsinki unless the Russian Baltic Fleet was first deprived of Sveaborg. Significantly, the Germans attacked at first only the points in Finland where they knew Russians could be found. Their military objective at the time was not the Red Finn government, but the Russian Baltic Fleet.[32] And it was certainly more vital to Lenin and Trotsky to save their fleet than the Red Finns. Through heroic ice-breaker operations in March and April, most of the fleet made its way safely to Kronstadt from Sveaborg as the Germans moved into Helsinki. Then, as the last of the Red Finns were evacuated into Russia, the ice melted.

Just as the presence of the bulk of the Russian Baltic Fleet in Helsinki between November, 1917, and April, 1918, goes far towards explaining the political happenings in the Finnish capital during that period, so the subsequent history of the same fleet is one explanation why, after November, 1918, Lenin did not accompany his efforts to use the Red Army to establish Red governments in Tallinn, Riga, and Vilna with an attempt to re-establish the Red Finns in Helsinki. It was much easier to plan for Communist seizures of power in Estonia, Latvia, and Lithuania than to plan for a new one in Finland, owing to differences in geographic size and population. In addition, the naval situation suggested a policy of moderation towards the White Finns.[33] If the Russian Baltic Fleet had succeeded in its efforts to regain control of the Gulf of Finland during the winter of 1918–1919, it would have gone far towards preparing the way for a comeback by the Red Finns. The Regent of Finland, Mannerheim, was aware of this and hence eager to help thwart the Soviet reconquest of Estonia. However,

---

[32] As late as March 24, the Russians evidently had the intention of defending Hanko against any German landing, but changed their minds when the Germans actually arrived in April; however, all fleet units and stores were destroyed before the place was yielded without opposition. On the next day, additional Russian fleet units at Sveaborg, including two battleships, two cruisers, and two submarines, began a six-day journey from Helsinki to Kronstadt, with the aid of icebreakers, at the same time that the capital of Red Finland was moved to Vyborg.

[33] Trotsky did threaten the Finns at least once in 1919 with a Soviet invasion, but the rapid emergence of Mannerheim as Finland's political leader in November, 1918, was probably enough to still any enthusiasm in Moscow for giving the Red Finns a second chance.

the appearance of British naval forces in the Baltic and the Gulf of Finland during 1918–1919 relieved the Finns of any need to worry further about Lenin's Baltic Fleet. Meanwhile, in the absence of any indication of a Finnish intent to move on Petrograd, or any indication that the city would be deprived of the protection of the Baltic Fleet, Lenin and Trotsky decided, given the circumstances of the moment, that the fleet would have to serve as a substitute for the re-occupation of Finland, despite the failure to reconquer the Baltic States.

The Finns themselves doubtless deserve much of the credit for the fact that over the last quarter of a century, only their foreign policy, not their domestic policy, has been under Soviet domination, but even more is due to the fact that after May, 1918, the Russians decided, following their third and final attempt at russification of Finland, that their essential objective of securing their Baltic flank could be achieved in some other fashion.

Attempting a Revolution from Without: Poland in 1920

Warren Lerner

The tactic known as *revolyutsiya izvne* or, freely translated, "the revolution from without" has often been practiced by the Soviet Union, although as a specific term or phrase it has long since been excised from the Soviet political lexicon. Half a century ago it was very much part of the Soviet political vocabulary and the avowed cornerstone of a major commitment in Soviet foreign policy. At that time it referred to the use of Soviet power, specifically the Red Army, to export the revolution beyond the borders of Soviet Russia. On a few occasions—in the Baltic countries and Finland—the tactic had been employed prior to 1920, without conspicuous success. Only in the case of Poland did the Soviet regime openly risk its own future as well as the future of world revolution on the validity of "the revolution from without."

Poland in 1920 did not become the target of "the revolution from without" as part of any broadly preconceived strategy, but rather almost by chance, through a series of Bolshevik responses to changing conditions both inside the Soviet realm and in Soviet-Polish relations. The open warfare between the Soviet Union and Poland that erupted in April, 1920, precipitated a chain of events that led to the dramatic westward march of the Red Army, with the Bolshevik leadership openly proclaiming "the revolution from without" and daring Great Power interference.

In the first years of the Bolshevik regime, extension of the revolution into Poland had been the least of Soviet concerns. The cruel struggle for survival, climaxed in mid-1919 by the apparently imminent danger of a Bolshevik defeat in the Russian Civil War, had forced Lenin to pursue a policy of neutralizing Poland. He feared that the entry of an irredentist Poland into the Russian Civil War on the side of the White Armies might well tip the scales against the Bolsheviks. Lenin courted Polish neutrality on two fronts: publicly, he offered all sorts of *de facto* borders favorable to Poland; privately, he empowered the veteran Polish Communist Julian Marchlewski to conduct negotiations with representatives of Josef Pilsudski, then Polish Chief of State. The immediate objective was to convince Pilsudski that a victory of the White Army in the Russian Civil War portended a reconstruction of the old Tsarist Russian empire and hence jeopardized the very independence of the new Polish state.[1] Basically, Marchlewski succeeded in his assignment. Considering the objectives of both sides—Pilsudski's grandiose scheme of a federated Eastern Europe, including the so-called Russian borderlands,[2] and the Bolsheviks' fond belief that the revolution could not survive as a purely Russian affair but had to involve the world proletariat—such a neutralization could at best only be a temporary tactic. In the winter of 1919–1920, as the prospects of the White Armies deteriorated, both the Poles and the Bolsheviks began to re-evaluate their positions and to consider how they might implement their own long-range plans *vis-à-vis* each other. The new circumstances led Pilsudski into a secret agreement with the Ukrainian leader, Simon Petliura, in which Pilsudski pledged Polish support for "liberating" the Ukraine in return for Petliura's acceptance of Polish claims to areas of Eastern Galicia.[3]

In the early months of 1920 the Bolsheviks relaxed their efforts to maintain informal contacts with Pilsudski (who had also lost his zeal in this regard). As various Civil War fronts began to collapse, the White Armies were in disarray and the Bolsheviks began to redeploy troops to the western fronts. Meanwhile the Soviet regime continued to engage in diplomatic correspondence with the Poles on a border settlement. They accused the Poles of not making a serious effort to bring about a *rapprochement*, and complained about Polish insistence on meeting in the town of Borisov, which the Bolsheviks considered unacceptable as a site for talks.[4] There continued to be border incidents—although nothing as serious as the Polish seizure of Vilna in 1919—and various threatening confrontations between Polish and Bolshevik troops, but these fell short of really open warfare. As far as the Bolsheviks were concerned, the Polish question was still unsettled and subject to various forms of resolution.

Did the Bolsheviks have a "plan "early in 1920 for "exporting the revolution" to Poland? It seems highly unlikely, although they still expected,

---

[1] The highly complex issue of Soviet-Polish relations, including Marchlewski's sensitive assignment, is quite well detailed in Piotr S. Wandycz, *Soviet-Polish Relations, 1917–1921*, Cambridge, Mass., 1969.

[2] Pilsudski's scheme, although it lies outside the purview of this study, is worthy of separate inquiry. See M. K. Dziewanowski, *Joseph Pilsudski : A European Federalist, 1918–1922*, Stanford, Calif., 1969.

[3] The agreement actually covered a broader area than just the border issue. For the text of the agreement see Weronika Gostyńska, *et al.* (eds.), *Dokumenty i Materialy do Historii Stosunków Polsko-Radzieckikh*, Vol. II, Warsaw, 1961, pp. 461 to 462.

[4] The Soviet version of this correspondence has been collected in *Krasnaya Kniga*, Moscow, 1920. For a fuller collection of the documents, see Gostynska, *et al.*, *op. cit.*

and in a sense even required, that the Bolshevik revolution become a European revolution. There were a number of precedents for exporting the revolution to states on Soviet Russia's borders. Early in 1918 the Finnish Communists had tried, with Soviet aid, to establish a Soviet regime in Helsinki, but it had collapsed in the face of German-backed resistance. In the Baltic States—Lithuania, Latvia, and Estonia—there had been abortive attempts to use Bolshevik assistance in setting up Soviet govern-ments,[5] but in each country native resistance, reinforced sometimes by the Poles and sometimes by the White Armies, had ended the hopes of these potential Soviet regimes. In virtually all these cases, the commitment of the Bolshevik regime was not and could not be total. Given a fluid situation in 1918, the Bolsheviks had tried and failed to extend the revolution into the Baltic area.

The decision to send the Red Army into Poland in 1920 grew out of the military circumstances of the moment, but it also reflected three years of frustration over the failure of the Bolshevik revolution to evoke more than an ephemeral response in Western Europe. Whether the original act of aggression that triggered the Russo-Polish War of 1920 was perpetrated by the Soviet regime or Poland is a debatable point which can be adequately documented either way.[6] What does appear certain is that peace with Poland was a primary objective of the Soviet government until 1920 (it could hardly have been otherwise given the exigencies of the Russian Civil War), while the eventual decision to march on Warsaw and beyond was reached only after the hostilities commenced and clearly as the result of considerable debate and disagreement among Soviet leaders.

Lenin had spent some of his pre-World War I exile in Poland, but he did not really know the country well. He made no effort to learn the Polish language or acquaint himself with peculiarly Polish conditions, and he did not involve himself in the Polish revolutionary movement except in those instances where disputes might have had some effect on the Russian so-cialist movement. After the Bolshevik revolution of 1917, he tended to entrust the conduct of relations with Poland to various Bolsheviks of Polish origin who were associated with the new Soviet government. Julian

---

[5] As an example of the detailed maneuvering of Soviet forces towards one Baltic state, see Alfred E. Senn, *The Emergence of Modern Lithuania*, New York, 1959.

[6] Most pro-Polish observers would argue that war had existed between the two regimes since at least early 1919 and hence the activities of April, 1920, were a new phase of the war and not the beginning of the war. See Titus Komarnicki, *The Rebirth of the Polish Republic*, London, 1957, p. 446.

Marchlewski, Karl Radek, and Felix Dzerzhinsky were perhaps the major figures in this group. Marchlewski had already proven himself of special value in the negotiations with Pilsudski's representatives in 1919. Even with the Russian Civil War all but over, however, Marchlewski and virtually the entire group of Moscow Poles did not urge any dramatic change in Soviet policy towards Poland, arguing that communism in Poland did not have the indigenous roots necessary to support a Red regime.[7]

Thus, throughout the winter and early spring of 1920, Lenin continued to look upon peaceful coexistence with a capitalist Poland as a fundamentally necessary posture for the Soviet regime, regardless of what the Bolsheviks might really think about the existing rulers of Poland. Leon Trotsky, then Commissar of War, might well have been sincere when he summed up Soviet policy of the time in this way:

> We said to Poland, "What do you demand? The independence of Poland? We recognize it. Do you fear that we will overthrow the bourgeois government of Warsaw? No, we will not meddle in your internal affairs. The Polish working class will overthrow you when it thinks it necessary."[8]

Whether or not one accepts at face value such Soviet declarations—of which there was an ample supply in the spring of 1920—the issue of pursuing peace with Poland no longer applied once Pilsudski's armies opened a "liberation drive" in the Ukraine on April 25, 1920, smashing deeply across the area, and even seizing Kiev, the major city of the Ukraine. The question of whether an invasion of the Ukraine was an invasion of Russia is academic. The Bolsheviks considered that they had been attacked and were now fully at war with Poland. Obviously, the immediate major task for them was to regroup their forces in order to contend with the Polish armies. A more fundamental problem was the need to define a strategy towards Poland.

The Bolshevik press and leadership took the position that Poland had acted treacherously at every point, that the Soviet leadership had in no way—internally or externally—sought to interfere in Poland, that it had bent over backwards to offer Poland the best of diplomatic settlements, and that Poland had reciprocated by becoming a tool of world capitalism's drive to annihilate the base of the proletarian revolution.[9]

---

[7] See, for example, Karl Radek, "Polskiy vopros i internatsional," *Kommunisticheskiy Internatsional*, No. 12, 1920, pp. 2173–2188.

[8] Leon Trotsky, *Sovetskaya Rossiya i burzhuaznaya Polsha*, Moscow, 1920, pp. 5–6.

[9] See Lenin's speech of May 5, 1920, as reported in *Pravda* on May 6, 1920.

So much for public utterances. Privately, the Polish invasion was thought to be as much an opportunity for gain as a threat to security. The Soviet military leaders were reasonably confident that the Poles could not only be stopped but also driven back. Indeed Pilsudski's military successes had all been scored against relatively light resistance and had been largely confined to the initial weeks of fighting. Assuming that the military challenge could be met, the question arose of what Soviet objectives should be. Trotsky argued that the very existence of an anti-Bolshevik Poland posed a threat to the Soviet regime.[10] Other Bolshevik leaders expressed similar sentiments. On May 5, 1920, mass meetings in Moscow were addressed by major Bolshevik leaders, each stating in one way or another that the continued existence of a capitalist Poland could not be tolerated.[11]

Inside the Central Committee of the Bolshevik Party, there was no such unanimity on what to do. Naturally, everyone was in favor of having a Soviet Poland result from the war; what was in dispute was the precise role that the Soviet regime should play in establishing a Red Poland.

The Moscow Poles, Marchlewski, Radek, Dzerzhinsky, Unszlicht, etc., were virtually unanimous in their advice to Lenin not to read the war as an invitation by the Polish proletariat for "liberation" by the Red Army. Although these men were divided among themselves by longstanding disagreements—Marchlewski and Radek had a decade-old feud—all were agreed that any counterinvasion of Poland by the Red Army would be badly received by the Polish population. If there was one factor that bound the Polish people together, it was russophobia, whether directed against Tsarist Russians or Bolshevik Russians.

The Red Army leaders, flushed with their recent successes in the Civil War and confident of their ability to push their armies as far westward as allowed, urged that events demanded a major change in policy. First of all, there was the tantalizing question: since the Poles had never accepted any of the various border proposals and there was no internationally accepted boundary between Poland and Russia, to what line should the Red Army force the Poles to retreat? Others in the Soviet leadership, including Lenin himself, Zinoviev, and Kamenev, seemed to be impressed not only by the military argument but by the possibilities for renewing the drive for world revolution. The idea was advanced that Soviet forces should not waste their energies in futile hopes that the proletariat of the West would rise on its own and strike down capitalism. The correct strategy, it was now argued,

---

[10] Leon Trotsky, *Kak vooruzhalas revolyutsiya*, Vol. II, Moscow, 1925, p. 103.

[11] The theme is extensively reprinted in the coverage of the May 6, 1920, issue of *Pravda*.

was to export "the revolution from without," capitalizing on the prowess of the Red Army. General Mikhail Tukhachevsky, the most prominent of the Red Army commanders—and apparently one of the most ardent advocates of "the revolution from without"—summed up the case for sending the Red Army into Poland when he wrote (at a much later date):

> There is not the least doubt that had we been victorious on the Vistula [the battle of Warsaw] the revolution would have embraced all of Europe in its flames .... A revolution from without was possible. Capitalist Europe had been shaken to its very foundations, and except for our defeat on the field of battle, perhaps the Polish war would have become the link which united the October Revolution [of 1917] and the revolution in Western Europe.[12]

Sometime late in June, 1920, the idea of "the revolution from without" prevailed among the Bolshevik leadership. The first open indication of the new policy came on July 2, 1920, when Tukhachevsky made a highly publicized speech to the Red Army in which he instructed his troops in their new role as the bearers of the revolution to the West:

> Soldiers of the workers revolution! Fix your glance towards the West. In the West will be decided the fate of the world revolution. Across the corpse of White Poland lies the road to world conflagration. On our bayonets we will carry happiness and peace to the working masses of mankind. To the West! Close ranks! Forward march! The hour of attack has arrived. To Vilna, Minsk, and Warsaw—march![13]

Tukhachevsky thus forthrightly proclaimed the decision to use the army to export the revolution. The Moscow Poles were far more cautious and circumspect in adapting to the new policy, a policy about which they obviously had misgivings but which they now had to support. The day before Tukhachevsky's speech, Marchlewski and Dzerzhinsky led a public meeting in Moscow of the "first Independent Conference of Poles Residing in The Moscow Area." They called *inter alia* for a Government of Soviets of Workers and Peasants in Poland, but avoided such aggressive remarks as used by Tukhachevsky.[14]

---

[12] This speech was first printed in Tukhachevsky's book *Pokhod za vislu*, Moscow, 1923, in which chap. viii is specifically entitled "The Revolution from Without." It is also quoted (p. 21) in the work of (General) Boris Shaposhnikov, *Na Visle*, Moscow, 1924, who also freely uses the phrase "revolution from without." However, so disreputable did the term later become that the 1964 reprint of Tukhachevsky's book omits chap. viii entirely rather than have to reprint his references to "the revolution from without."

[13] Quoted in Y. Stepanov (Skvortsov-Stepanov), *S Krasnoy Armii na panskuyu Polshu*, Moscow, 1920, p. 78.

[14] *Pravda*, July 9, 1920. The fact that *Pravda* waited over a week to report the meeting is in itself unusual.

As the Red Army was now pushing westward daily, Tukhachevsky's words could not be dismissed as mere rhetoric. Nor were they so regarded. On July 11, 1920, Lord Curzon, the British Foreign Minister, specifically warned the Red Army not to cross the "ethnic" boundary, following the Bug River, from Grodno in the north to East Galicia in the south. Curzon's statement, which threatened British military intervention, had the effect of establishing a border in an area which had hitherto remained undefined.[15] Now the Soviet regime was forced to commit itself to "the revolution from without." Up to this point, the fighting had taken place on disputed territory. Efforts to intervene in Poland's internal affairs had been merely verbal—and not very effective.

If the Red Army crossed the "Curzon Line," the Soviet Union would in effect be throwing down the gauntlet to the West. Such a move would mark the first outright example of the Soviet regime—marching in the name of world revolution—defying the capitalist West, and risking direct military confrontation. The risks were obviously great. Maybe Curzon was bluffing, but how difficult would it be for the British fleet to bombard Petrograd? To justify such risks the rewards had to be equally great. Lenin was obsessed with the fear, which he repeatedly echoed to Chicherin, his foreign minister, "World capitalism is marching against us."[16] Perhaps Lenin could not resist one last chance to march against world capitalism— via Poland.

Any such move against Poland was still opposed by all the Moscow Poles, but most vehemently by Karl Radek, who had just returned from a year in a Berlin prison after having been witness to the futile martyrdom of the German Communists in the Spartacus uprising of 1919. The latter experience had made him leery of all premature attempts to sponsor revolutions; in addition, his youthful experiences in the Polish revolutionary movement had convinced him that Russian-sponsored revolutions had no chance at all in Poland, regardless of what ideologies might be behind them. Ordinarily, Lenin listened to Radek's advice on Poland with the greatest of respect. Now, however, he found Radek's pessimism intolerable. With the military situation so promising, Lenin found it hard to believe that the revolutionary potential was not equally promising. He dismissed as "defeatism" Radek's warnings that the Polish workers would not rally to the support of the Red Army's revolutionary crusade and forbade Radek

---

[15] The line, inevitably dubbed the "Curzon Line," was to assume even greater importance in the diplomatic conflicts of World War II.

[16] As quoted by Chicherin to Louis Fischer. See Fischer, *The Soviets in World Affairs*, New York, 1960, p. 103.

to write further in the Soviet press on the Polish question.[17] Overruling all other doubters—a group that apparently included Trotsky and Stalin as well as others—orders were issued to the Red Army not to halt at the Curzon Line. On July 24, 1920, Tukhachevsky led his armies across the line and within a few days the Red Army captured its first "Polish" city, the railroad and textile center of Bialystok.

For a period of about four weeks in the summer of 1920, Bialystok became the crux of the entire commitment to "the revolution from without." The center of military action rapidly shifted westward as Tukhachevsky continued to drive towards Warsaw, but the center of political activity—particularly as it concerned "the revolution from without"—remained in Bialystok. In many ways, the city was not an obvious choice for so heavy an assignment as the outpost of world revolution. However, as the only major industrial center west of the Curzon Line captured by the Red Army, it was simply pressed into service. On July 30, 1920, with appropriate fanfare, a delegation of Polish Communists mostly from Moscow, headed by Marchlewski, Dzerzhinsky, and an old Polish revolutionary named Felix Kon, proclaimed a Polish Provisional Revolutionary Committee (*Tymczasowy Komitet Revolucyjny Polski*, known as *Polrevkom* or *Revkom*), as the temporary government of the Polish workers until the "fraternal Red Army" could complete the task of "liberating" all of Poland.[18]

The *Revkom* considered itself as not only the transitional force between Polish "liberation" and the establishment of a Polish revolutionary government but also as the embodiment of socialist revolution for the 100,000 or so people who lived in or near Bialystok. There are on record a number of accounts and pictures of throngs in Bialystok rallying around the *Revkom* and of Marchlewski addressing large and apparently enthusiastic audiences. The diary of the Bolshevik journalist Yuriy Stepanov, who accompanied the *Revkom* into Bialystok, records mass meetings with large numbers of the population singing the *Internationale*.[19] Since Stepanov seems reasonably frank, even if biased, there is little reason to question the reliability of his accounts of popular support for the *Revkom*.

---

[17] Klara Zetkin, *Reminiscences of Lenin*, London, 1929, p. 20. Some later editions of Zetkin's book omit the conversations between her and Lenin on Radek's "defeatism." Up to the summer, Radek had been writing on the Polish question almost every other day in the Soviet press.

[18] Yulian Markhlevskiy (Marchlewski), *Voina i mir mezhdu burzhuaznoy Polshi i proletarskoy Rossii*, Moscow, 1921, p. 22.

[19] Stepanov, *op. cit.*, p. 47. Stepanov noted that the crowd actually sang the *Internationale* rather poorly, but that at least they sang it.

Bialystok was, if nothing else, a proletarian city. As a major railroad juncture between Warsaw and Petrograd in the old Tsarist empire, it had developed extensive workshops for servicing rolling stock. There were also several large textile mills in the city. Most of the town's population found its employment in these two industries. The city itself was then, and is now, a singularly unremarkable worker's city. About the only building of distinction was the Branicki Palace, built over a century earlier. As the largest edifice in town it was quite naturally commandeered by the *Revkom*, who used the building as its headquarters and the extensive grounds for its rallies. Marchlewski could step on the balcony and command a panorama large enough to include almost the entire population of Bialystok. Headquarters in the Branicki Palace afforded the *Revkom* manifold opportunities for displays of public support; it may also have inadvertently contributed to some misplaced confidence in the Polish workers, leading Moscow to believe that the Bialystok experience could be repeated in Warsaw and throughout Poland.[20]

When all the propaganda was stripped aside, the fact remained that Bialystok—an out and out proletarian city—had not offered any serious resistance to the Red Army and that a sizeable proportion of the population —one could argue the exact size—appeared ready and in some cases even eager to support the *Revkom*. This reaction could well be interpreted as a justification for "the revolution from without" and indeed undoubtedly was. The *Revkom* proceeded to issue all sorts of proclamations on nationalization, socialist behavior, etc., but in its brief life span it scarcely had an opportunity to implement any of its decrees. The context of the decrees suggested the establishment of a socialist regime modeled after the Bolshevik state, but they were never really translated into action.[21]

What the *Revkom* and the Soviet leadership overlooked was the simple ethnic fact that Bialystok was not a Polish city; it was a Jewish city, and in 1920 the difference was quite important. The exact number of Jews in the city—as suggested by the census of 1921—is open to debate, but the fact that Jews were a majority is not. The percentage of Jews in the city ranged anywhere from 55 to 75 per cent, depending on who is to be believed. Virtually all these Jews had Yiddish as their primary language and Polish as a secondary language at best. For many Jews in Bialystok, the independence of Poland had not come as a boon. Throughout eastern Poland there

[20] Note the enthusiastic, if scattered, accounts in the Soviet press on the implications of the Bialystok experience for all of Poland. See, for example, "Sovetskaya Polsha," *Izvestiya*, August 19, 1920.

[21] The various decrees by and concerning the *Revkom* have been collected and published as *Tymczasowy Komitet Revolucyjny Polski*, Warsaw, 1955.

had been pogroms "celebrating" Polish independence in the years 1919 to 1920. Bialystok itself, while escaping the worst of the pogroms, had still seen its Jewish community leaders harassed in various ways in 1919.[22] Quite simply, the vested interest of the Jews of Bialystok in an independent Poland was quite small.

Marchlewski was either unaware of the special factors created by the Jews of Bialystok or he paid them no heed. True, one member of his entourage, Felix Kon, was of Jewish descent, but there was no effort to establish rapport with the Bund—the Jewish socialist organization—or to cater to the specific needs of the Jewish community other than to make statements deploring anti-Semitism. On the contrary, Marchlewski, obviously thinking of the future activities of the *Revkom* beyond Bialystok, avoided any special consideration of the Jews. The major Yiddish newspaper of the town, *Dos Naye Lebn*, was closed down, and the old Polish revolutionary newspaper *Czerwony Sztandar* was resurrected in its place. During the severe measures taken against dissident personnel in the city, executions by the Red Army included at least one prominent leader of the Jewish community.[23] Undoubtedly such events vitiated the original feeling of acquiescence with which the Jewish community had met the establishment of the *Revkom*. Yet the *Revkom* could honestly report back to Moscow that the local population had accepted its reign with a reaction ranging from enthusiasm to passiveness, but with little open manifestation of hostility. Did this not portend that if Warsaw were captured by the Red Army a similar reaction would take place?

One writer has reasoned that the choice of the *Revkom* leaders from the ranks of the Moscow Poles, including especially Polish Communists as well known as Marchlewski and Dzerzhinsky, would have led even Polish radicals to oppose a Soviet regime for Poland.[24] There is a small element of exaggeration involved here, but the point is well taken. Poles tended to regard fellow countrymen in the service of other regimes, particularly of Soviet Russia, as traitors. In 1919 there had been an ugly lynching in Warsaw of Poles connected with the Soviet Red Cross mission. Such incidents may have been rare, but implicit public approval of them suggests the underlying attitudes present.

Whatever Polish feelings may have been about Pilsudski or others in the Polish regime, there was no feeling of attachment to the *Revkom* in Bialystok. There the *Revkom* existed primarily because of the Red Army

---

[22] Abraham Shmuel Hersberg, *Pinsk Bialistoker* (in Yiddish), Vol. II, New York, 1950, pp. 272–273.

[23] *Ibid.*, p. 281.

[24] Adam B. Ulam, *Expansion and Coexistence*, New York, 1968, p. 109.

and secondarily because of the non-Polish nature of Bialystok itself. In Warsaw and elsewhere a *Revkom* would have found it difficult to gain even passive public acceptance.

Marchlewski and his comrades never had a chance to find out how they might have been received in Warsaw. By dint of a daring strategy of his own—possibly with the assistance of French military advisers—Pilsudski stopped Tukhachevsky's armies at the very gates of Warsaw. Outflanking the Red Army, Pilsudski inflicted such a severe military defeat on the Russians at Warsaw that they fell into a chaotic retreat across the east Polish plain. As the Red Armies retreated towards Bialystok, the *Revkom* quietly closed its offices and crossed eastward over the Curzon Line. The war itself turned into a stalemate, with neither army having much stomach for a new offensive. An armistice led to protracted border negotiations, the results of which were confirmed by the Treaty of Riga in 1921.

The total span of the *Revkom's* existence was less than a month, and virtually all of its "accomplishments" were on paper. None of its flamboyant decrees had ever been truly implemented. When it retreated with the Red Army, it left virtually no imprint of the fact that it had existed. Today, even in a Communist Poland, the only evidence of the *Revkom's* existence is a hard-to-find plaque high up on the gates of the Branicki Palace and a few flags in the city's museum.

The march into Poland in the summer of 1920 had been the last attempt by Lenin to extend the revolution to the West, unless one takes more seriously than one should the various proclamations of the Comintern (Communist International) through the next several years. Within a few months of the close of the Russo-Polish War, Lenin had to face the revolt of the Kronstadt garrison, a crisis which, together with the problem of the continually deteriorating economy, forced him into a retreat from active pursuit of world revolution. In the spring of 1921 he announced the famous NEP (New Economic Policy)—"one step backwards in order later to take two steps forwards."

Undoubtedly, the failure to export communism to Poland—even with the Red Army camped outside Warsaw—had been a major letdown to Soviet hopes of reviving world revolution in 1920 by means of "the revolution from without." Lenin allowed himself a rambling discourse on what had been at stake in the march on Warsaw and why it had failed:

> If Poland had become Soviet, if the Warsaw workers had received from Russia the aid which they had expected, the Versailles treaty would then have been ruined, and the entire international system built up by the victors would have been destroyed. France would not then have had a buffer state between

Germany and Soviet Russia. It would not have had a battering-ram against the Soviet Republic.

. . . .

Such was the course of the Polish War. That is why we, knowing that war with Poland was closely connected with the position of international imperialism, made the greatest concessions, just so as to keep this burden from the workers and peasants. Then we came into conflict with the Versailles treaty, and it turned out that the bourgeoisie were just as enraged against us as before, but it also turned out that the workers were maturing not daily, but hourly, and that things were moving towards the workers' revolution undeviatingly, *but still too slowly, compared with the rapidity of development in Russia* [italics added].[25]

What Lenin was saying was simply that the workers of Poland, and presumably of the West, had not yet reached the level of class consciousness that would enable them to exploit the efforts of the Red Army to bring about a workers' revolution. Quite the contrary, the evidence should have suggested to Lenin that the workers of Warsaw openly fought against the Red Army.

Lenin himself had been rather careful about his public commitment to "the revolution from without" even during the drive on Warsaw. The specific term "revolution from without" was once used by his generals, but not openly by other Soviet leaders. Though the Second Congress of the Comintern had been almost euphoric about the Red Army's advance,[26] Lenin had not allowed that body to debate openly the options in Poland even if the Red Army should take Warsaw.[27] Even while the *Revkom* existed, Lenin had negotiated with the West, and vicariously with the Polish government as well, on possible peace terms, albeit peace terms hardly likely to be accepted by Poland.[28] Clearly, "the revolution from without" had been a wager, and once the wager was lost, Lenin declined to risk anything else.

Poland was of course to experience a "revolution from without" barely a generation later. The conditions were so different, however, as to defy

---

[25] *Pravda*, October 9 and 10, 1920.

[26] See Zinoviev's grandiose description in his report to the Tenth Congress of the Party, *Desyatyy sezd RKP (B), mart 1921 goda*, Moscow, 1963, p. 500.

[27] Lenin did, however, try to get more of a commitment at the Comintern Congress on what the German Communists could or would do in case of a Red Army triumph at Warsaw. See Willy Brandt and Richard Lowenthal, *Ernst Reuter*, Munich, 1957, p. 138.

[28] Soviet demands at this time included a 200,000 working-man militia—an obvious attempt to undermine the Polish government, so obvious the British were kept in the dark on this provision (Fischer, *op. cit.*, p. 191).

meaningful comparison. Since the major fighting done by the Red Army in 1944 was against the Nazi occupation forces rather than against native armies, the theme of "liberation" was far more plausible. While there were undoubtedly lessons that had been learned from the 1920 experience, few of them contributed to the successful Soviet venture of 1944. Perhaps the Lublin government of 1944 might be regarded as a resurrection of the Bialystok *Revkom* of 1920, but it is not a comparison that will bear detailed analysis. What is comparable and significant is that both in 1920 and 1944, the sovietization of Poland was directly dependent on the success of the Red Army. In 1920 the Red Army lost the war for Poland and turned away from exporting the revolution; in 1944 it won its Polish campaign and in the wake of its victory proceeded to bring "the revolution from without" to all of Eastern Europe.[29]

---

[29] For convenience I have used the term *Revkom* when referring to the central revolutionary committee in Bialystok, although, strictly speaking, the term *Polrevkom* would be more correct, to distinguish the Bialystok committee from the subordinate *Revkoms* that were formed in the villages. Lenin and other Soviet officials often used the term *Revkom* when referring to the Bialystok committee.

The Communist Takeover of Outer Mongolia: Model for Eastern Europe?

Thomas T. Hammond

When the delegates to the First Congress of the Communist International (or Comintern) assembled in March, 1919, they confidently predicted, and undoubtedly believed, that revolutions would soon break out in the advanced countries of Europe, and that eventually the whole world would become Communist. Judged by these expectations, the Comintern proved to be one of the most abject failures in history. In the quarter-century of its existence it carried out *only one* successful revolution, and this was in a primitive, unimportant, and half-forgotten land—Outer Mongolia.[1] The Mongolian revolution went almost unnoticed by Westerners at the time, and even today, with much more information about it available, it is largely ignored by most specialists on the history of world communism.[2]

Nonetheless, for the members of the world Communist movement the Mongolian revolution had a special significance. During the long, frustrating years of the 1920's and 1930's, when revolution failed to materialize elsewhere, Mongolia was the only "proof" of their most cherished hope: that the Bolshevik revolution would prove to be contagious. As one speaker at a Comintern meeting expressed it, "Mongolia is a small country with a population of only 700,000. But it is of exceptional interest and enormous importance."[3] On another occasion a Comintern delegate described the Mongolian People's Revolutionary Party as one that had

---

[1] This is not to say that the Comintern was a failure in the long run. Ironically, its greatest triumphs came after its dissolution, which was announced on May 15, 1943. During the next six years, Communists carried out successful revolutions in eleven countries, and in almost every case the leaders had been trained by the Comintern.

[2] For example, Franz Borkenau's classic, *World Communism*, New York, 1939, does not even mention Outer Mongolia. Similarly, Adam Ulam's excellent history of Soviet foreign policy, *Expansion and Coexistence*, New York, 1968, says nothing about the Soviet takeover in Mongolia.

[3] Comrade Fimm at the Tenth Plenum of the Executive Committee of the Comintern on July 10, 1929. Quoted in *International Press Correspondence*, September 17, 1929, p. 1087. The common abbreviation, *Inprecorr*, will be used in subsequent citations from the official newspaper of the Comintern.

produced "brilliant results," which it was hoped parties in other countries would emulate.[4]

It can be argued, however, that the greatest significance of the Mongolian revolution lies not in the fact that it was the Comintern's only successful revolution, but rather in its role as a model for the tactics used in carrying out revolutions at the end of World War II, after the Comintern had been abolished. Attempts by the Comintern to imitate the Bolshevik revolution in Europe between 1918 and 1923 were a fiasco, but the use of *quite different tactics* in Mongolia succeeded with little difficulty. Therefore it should not be altogether surprising that the methods used in the 1940's to establish "People's Democracies" in Poland, Rumania, North Korea, etc., showed much greater similarity to the Mongolian revolution than to the Russian revolution.

It is conceivable that Stalin himself learned some of his tricks from the Mongolian example, and the same may be true in the case of Georgi Dimitrov, Boleslav Bierut, Mátyás Rákosi, and other Communist strategists of the 1940's. Wolfgang Leonhard, who attended a Comintern school in the Soviet Union during World War II and later helped to install a Communist regime in East Germany, has stated that Comintern personnel were aware of the Mongolian revolution and were expected to be able to derive the proper lessons from it.[5] One might add that if Roosevelt, Churchill, and their advisers had been familiar with Soviet tactics in Outer Mongolia, they would have had a much better idea of what to expect in Eastern Europe and North Korea at the end of World War II.[6]

An examination of the Mongolian takeover is important for still another reason: Communists claim that it shows backward countries how it is possible to jump directly from feudalism to socialism, without passing through capitalism. Lenin himself declared in 1920:

---

[4] Comrade Shagri of Persia at the Sixth Congress of the Comintern on August 20, 1928, *Inprecorr*, November 8, 1928, p. 1470. For a few additional examples of the many Comintern statements regarding the importance of Mongolia, see *Inprecorr*, April 22, 1926, p. 501; April 28, 1928, p. 430; and November 6, 1930, p. 1037.

[5] Personal interview with the author. Leonhard's experiences are described in his fascinating book, *Child of the Revolution*, Chicago, 1958.

[6] The leading (and almost the only) Western expert on Outer Mongolia before World War II was Professor Owen Lattimore, who took a rather benign view of Soviet actions. For two examples of Lattimore's attempts to justify Soviet domination see his article, "Mongolia Enters World Affairs," *Pacific Affairs*, Vancouver, March, 1934, especially pages 16–17, and his introduction to Gerard M. Friters, *Outer Mongolia and Its International Position*, Baltimore, 1949, p. xix.

It would be incorrect to say that the capitalistic stage of development is inevitable for backward peoples.... With the help of the proletariat of the more advanced countries, backward countries can skip over to a Soviet system and arrive at communism through special stages of development, avoiding the capitalist stage of development.[7]

This thesis was reiterated in the 1920's and 1930's by various Comintern officials, who cited Outer Mongolia as an example which other undeveloped colonial peoples should emulate.[8] And many years later, in 1966, Tsedenbal, the present leader of Mongolia, boasted:

The success of the policy of the MPR [Mongolian People's Republic] has exerted a revolutionizing influence on the oppressed peoples, helping to accelerate the world revolutionary process....

In recent years Mongolia has been visited by scores of government, party and other delegations from many Asian and African countries which only a short time ago rid themselves of colonial bondage . and are now searching for the shortest, most effective and painless ways of social progress.[9]

The significance of the Mongolian model for backward countries has also been affirmed by present-day Soviet leaders. For example, Mikhail Suslov, a long-time member of the Politburo, spoke as follows to the Fourteenth Congress of the Mongolian People's Revolutionary Party in 1966:

Elaboration by your Party of the theoretical aspects of the non-capitalist path of development to socialism and the practical experience of building socialism in Mongolia are a valuable contribution to the ideological treasure-store of Marxism-Leninism and enrich the collective experience of the international Communist movement. Mongolia's experience in building socialism is of particularly great practical significance today when the face of Asia, Africa and Latin America is changing, when more and more peoples whose mode of life has been characterized by feudal and even pre-feudal relationships are acquiring national independence and taking the destiny of their countries into their own hands.[10]

---

[7] Speech at the Second Congress of the Comintern, "Doklad Komissii po natsionalnomu i kolonialnomu voprosu," *Sochineniya*, 3rd ed., Vol. XXV, Moscow, 1935, p. 354.

[8] For examples see the following statements in *Inprecorr*: Comrade Bohuslav Šmeral, November 6, 1930, p. 1037; Comrade Sen Katayama, April 22, 1926, p. 501; Comrade Mersi, April 12, 1928, p. 430; Comrade Fimm, September 17, 1929, p. 1088.

[9] Tsedenbal, "The Revolutionary Party and Social Changes," *World Marxist Review*, Toronto, Vol. 9, No. 2, 1966, pp. 10–11. Similar statements by President Modeibo Keita of Mali, Le Duk Tho of Vietnam, and Blas Roca of Cuba are quoted on page 10 of the same article.

[10] *Ibid.*, p. 10. A similar statement by Brezhnev was quoted in the speech by Politburo member Kirilenko at the Sixteenth Congress of the Mongolian People's Revolutionary Party. *Pravda*, June 9, 1971, pp. 1–2.

But while the present or future applicability of Outer Mongolia's experience for underdeveloped countries remains to be demonstrated, there is already much to suggest that the Communist takeover in Mongolia served as a model for the takeovers of the 1940's in Eastern Europe and North Korea. Indeed, the process by which Mongolia became a Soviet satellite is reminiscent of the pattern by which several of the "People's Democracies" were created from 1944 to 1948.[11] At the same time it would be wrong to forget that Communist methods of seizing power have naturally varied from country to country in accordance with local conditions. Among the Communist revolutions of the 1940's, six show the closest resemblance to the Mongolian pattern—those in Poland, East Germany, Bulgaria, Rumania, Hungary, and North Korea. The takeovers in Yugoslavia, Albania, and China were largely the outgrowth of guerrilla wars— something which did not occur in Mongolia. The case of Czechoslovakia is in many ways unique. Nevertheless, all these revolutions display some parallels with the Mongolian takeover, and in the six mentioned they are quite striking.

The purpose of this paper is to examine the steps by which Communist rule was established in Mongolia and to indicate, where appropriate, the degree to which this process was repeated in Eastern Europe and North Korea. Eleven main steps may be distinguished:

1. A revolutionary party is organized with the help of Soviet agents.

2. Foreign (non-Soviet) troops occupy the country, creating dissatisfaction among the population and providing the Soviets with an excuse to invade the country and "liberate" it.

3. A provisional government of the country is formed on Soviet territory, under Soviet direction, and adopts a moderate political program, designed to appeal to a majority of the country's population.

4. A native army is organized, armed, and trained on Soviet soil.

5. The country is invaded by Soviet troops, aided by the native army.

6. The provisional government is reorganized into a broad coalition government, including prominent leaders who are not Communists.

7. Comintern agents, pseudo-natives who were born in Russia, and russified natives who have long resided in Russia are used by the Soviets to help control the new regime.

---

[11] The author is indebted to Professor William B. Ballis for the idea of comparing the Mongolian and East European takeovers, which he suggested in his article, "The Political Evolution of a Soviet Satellite: The Mongolian People's Republic," *The Western Political Quarterly*, Salt Lake City, Utah, June, 1956, pp. 293–328. Professor Ballis mentions briefly (on pages 293 and 327) that there are similarities with Eastern Europe, but does not describe them in detail.

8. Soviet advisers are placed in all the important departments of the government and the party to insure Soviet domination and to aid in the introduction of Soviet methods.

9. The government is later replaced by a "People's Democracy."

10. A series of purges is carried out under Soviet supervision until the remaining leaders are completely subservient to Soviet wishes.

11. The country's political, economic, and cultural institutions are remodeled in imitation of the Soviet pattern.

It is important to note that *camouflage* and *gradualism* are consistently used in taking these steps in order to make them appear democratic and to minimize opposition until Soviet officials and reliable native Communists are in firm control. Camouflage and gradualism are vital to the success of the whole process, since the majority of the population do not want a Communist regime.

The Background to the Soviet Takeover

The goal of transforming Outer Mongolia in accordance with the Soviet model was necessarily a much slower process than in Eastern Europe and North Korea, because the population of this vast territory was so extremely backward and conservative. If Russia in 1917 was not the kind of advanced capitalist state in which Marx had expected proletarian revolutions to occur, this was true ten times over in Mongolia, where no more than a handful of proletarians existed. Most of the population were nomadic herdsmen, and industry was almost non-existent. Owing largely to the influence of Buddhist lamaism, the formerly aggressive sons of Genghis Khan had become a passive, submissive people, content to live in a state of stagnant poverty, and hostile to notions of change and progress.[12]

For centuries Mongolia had been under the domination of the emperors of China, but in 1911 it asserted its autonomy, recognizing as chief of state the head of the church, the Jebtsun Damba Khutukhtu, or Bogdo Gegen, commonly referred to as a "living Buddha."[13] Tsarist Russia recognized Outer Mongolian autonomy and in return received extensive commercial privileges. The Chinese were furious at this Russian meddling, but were powerless to prevent it. Through a series of treaties, combined with economic, cultural, and political penetration, the Tsarist regime was able to establish a *de facto* protectorate over Outer Mongolia while continuing to

---

[12] Serge M. Wolff, "The People's Republic of Mongolia," *Contemporary Review*, London, March, 1929, p. 364.

[13] His title as head of the church was Jebtsun Damba Khutukhtu, while his title as ruler of the Autonomous Outer Mongolian state was Bogdo Gegen.

recognize Chinese sovereignty *de jure*—an imperialist technique later to be imitated by the Soviets.

Mongolian autonomy lasted only from 1911 to 1919, because after the Bolshevik revolution Russia became embroiled in civil war and was unable to defend its protectorate. In 1919 a Chinese army occupied the capital, Urga, and the Mongolian government was forced to "request" that its autonomy be abolished. Since the Chinese rulers were oppressive, many Mongols looked forward to the day when Russia would again help them to end Chinese domination and restore self-government.[14]

This hope of Russian intervention happened to coincide neatly with the policy of the new Bolshevik government in Moscow, which had been expressed by Lenin as early as 1916, before the seizure of power:

> We Great Russian workers must demand from our government that it get out of Mongolia, Turkestan, and Persia.... But does that mean that *we* proletarians *want* to be separated...from the Mongolian, or Turkestani or Indian workers or peasants?... Nothing of the kind.... We shall exert every effort to become friendly and to amalgamate with the Mongolians.... We shall strive to give these nations, which are more backward and more oppressed than we are, "unselfish cultural aid"...i.e., we...shall help them on towards democracy, towards socialism.[15]

Thus, even before the Bolshevik revolution, Lenin had formulated the ideological justification later to be used for the new, Soviet style of imperialism—i.e., on the pretext of helping a backward people to advance "towards democracy and socialism" the Soviets would intervene and "amalgamate" Mongolia with Russia.[16] When Lenin voiced this rationalization for Soviet imperialism, he did not think of it as being in any way similar to the imperialism of capitalist nations, and after the Bolshevik revolution he was at pains to dissociate the Soviet regime from the imperialist policies of its Tsarist predecessor. On August 3, 1919, the Bolshevik government issued a declaration to the Mongolian people which is worth quoting at some length, if only for the contrast it provides between Soviet promises and Soviet deeds:

> The Russian people have renounced all treaties with the Japanese and Chinese governments which deal with Mongolia. Mongolia is henceforth a

---

[14] J. C. Shen, "Outer Mongolia Since 1911," *China Weekly Review*, Shanghai, May 16, 1936, pp. 385–386.

[15] V. I. Lenin, *Polnoye sobraniye sochineniy*, 5th ed., Vol. XXX, Moscow, 1962, pp. 119–120.

[16] Somewhat later, in May, 1919, an article in a Soviet journal suggested that Mongolia might serve another purpose—as a route for Communist penetration "to the rich East and India." Amur Sanai, "Klyuchi k vostoku," *Zhizn natsional-nostey*, Moscow, No. 19 (27), May 26, 1919, p. 2; quoted in Xenia Eudin and Robert North, *Soviet Russia and the East, 1920–1927*, Stanford, Calif., 1957, p. 199.

free country. Russian advisers, Tsarist consuls, bankers, and the rich who have mastered the Mongolian people by means of force and gold, and robbed them of their last possessions, must be driven out of Mongolia.

All institutions of authority and law in Mongolia must henceforth belong to the Mongolian people. Not a single foreigner has the right to interfere with Mongolian affairs.... Mongolia now becomes an independent country and has the right to contact independently all other peoples without any guardianship whatsoever on the part of Peking or Petrograd.

...the Soviet government asks the Mongolian people to enter into diplomatic relations with the Russian people immediately and to send representatives of the Mongolian people to meet the advancing Red Army [which was then pursuing the White armies across Siberia].[17]

Each of these promises was later to be violated by the Soviets, but they may have created a favorable impression on politically conscious Mongolians when they were made, and perhaps were one of the factors which caused the Mongolian leaders to turn to Soviet Russia for assistance.

The establishment of close relations between Russia and Mongolia, as proposed in the declaration, was impossible at the time, since the Bolsheviks were fighting the Whites and Mongolia was controlled by Chinese troops. The most the Soviets could arrange was to send an expedition under the leadership of Ivan Maisky (later to become well known as Soviet ambassador to London). Maisky went to Mongolia ostensibly to investigate the possibilities of trade, but a White Russian who was living in Urga at the time states that Maisky also organized gatherings of Mongolian and Russian revolutionaries.[18] In any event, one result of his visit was the preparation of a most informative book about the country, which provided the Soviet authorities with the latest information on prevailing conditions.[19]

Maisky followed in Lenin's footsteps by also supplying rationalizations for any future Soviet intervention. While granting that Outer Mongolia had the right to "cultural self-determination," he claimed that this did not require "sovereignty." If the country remained under Chinese rule, he asserted, it could expect only "cultural stagnation and economic ruination," whereas with Russia's help it could attain "cultural progress and economic

---

[17] Eudin and North, *op. cit.*, p. 200. Similar generous declarations were made during this period to China, Persia, and Turkey, but were also disregarded in practice.

[18] D. P. Pershin, "Baron Ungern, Urga i Altan-bulak; zapiski ochevidtsa o smutnom vremeni vo Vneshney (Khakhaskoy) Mongolii v pervoy tretiy XX-go veka," (handwritten manuscript in the library of the Hoover Institution, Stanford University), pp. 18–20.

[19] I. M. Maisky, *Sovremennaya Mongoliya; otchet mongolskoy ekspeditsii, snaryazhennoy irkutskoy kontoroy Vserossiiskogo tsentralnogo soyuza potrebitelnykh obshchestv*, Irkutsk, 1921.

prosperity." Nor did he neglect to mention the advantages that Russia might gain in return. Mongolia could provide livestock, fodder, and minerals, and at the same time serve as a buffer between Russia and China. Unconsciously parroting nineteenth-century imperialists, he even declared that Soviet Russia must fulfill "her natural historic mission" of spreading the benefits of European civilization to the backward countries of Asia, and to Mongolia in particular.[20]

The scene was set for the process of takeover to begin. The steps by which this took place (listed above) will now be examined in detail.

Step 1
The Formation of a Revolutionary Party

Whether or not Maisky had anything to do with their formation, by 1919 there were two small revolutionary groups in the Mongolian capital of Urga. One was under the leadership of the twenty-six-year-old Sukhe Bator, who had served in the army, and who after his death came to be known as "the Lenin of the Mongolian Revolution" (which was a gross exaggeration). Sukhe Bator did not learn to read until he was eighteen and never mastered the Russian language. That he ever understood Marxism or could properly be labeled a Communist is dubious. Yet he did lead the small Mongolian "army" that helped to carry out the seizure of power.[21]

The leader of the other revolutionary group was Choibalsan, who was to become Premier of Outer Mongolia from 1939 to 1952, and who is often referred to as "the Stalin of Outer Mongolia" (another dubious comparison). Although younger than Sukhe Bator and less important in the early years of the revolutionary movement, Choibalsan possessed the advantage of having studied at a Russian school in Irkutsk, which meant he could read Bolshevik literature and could serve as a liaison with the Russians. He was perhaps the only native Mongolian in the period from 1919 to 1921 who might accurately be described as a Communist.[22]

In January, 1920, the two small groups of revolutionaries, totaling only about twenty to thirty persons, united to form the "Mongolian People's

[20] Maisky, *op. cit.*, p. 329.

[21] The official biography is given in "Life of Sukebatur," by Sh. Nachukdorji, translated from the Mongol by Owen Lattimore and Urgungge Onon, and published in Owen Lattimore, *Nationalism and Revolution in Mongolia*, New York, 1955, pp. 93–182. Hereafter cited as Nachukdorji.

[22] Robert A. Rupen, *Mongols of the Twentieth Century*, Bloomington, Ind., 1964, Vol. I, pp. 137–138 and 146. This massive work is a virtual encyclopedia of information on modern Mongolia. Volume II is an extensive bibliography of works in many languages. The present author wishes to thank Professor Rupen, who generously agreed to read this essay.

Party." At a meeting in June they adopted a "Party Oath" which demonstrated clearly that they were not Communists, but held views reflecting a combination of Mongolian nationalism, loyalty to the church, hatred of Chinese rule, and some Bolshevik influence. The Oath said in part:

> The purposes of the People's Party of Outer Mongolia are to rid the country of the fierce enemies who threaten the nation and the religion... to recall the lost Mongolian law, to strengthen the State and the religion, inflexibly to defend the Mongolian nation, to revise and change the internal policy of the country, in every way to protect the interests of the *arat* [herder] masses...and put an end to the sufferings of the working people [23]

The conservatism of this "revolutionary" party is also revealed by the fact that several of its members were lamas or nobles. It was revolutionary mainly in its desire to achieve three objectives: to overthrow Chinese rule and achieve autonomy or independence for Mongolia; to modernize the country; and to reduce the powers of the Bogdo Gegen and the princes. Its orientation was thus nationalist and reformist, not Communist.

In the summer of 1920, the Comintern sent one of its agents, S. S. Borisov (an Altai Oirot), together with several other Soviet citizens, to serve as advisers to the Mongolian revolutionaries. Borisov urged the Mongols to send a delegation to the Soviet Union with a request for aid, and, for the reasons explained below, they decided to follow his advice.[24]

It would be a gross mistake to think of the Mongols in 1920 as a people fired with revolutionary zeal and eager to imitate the Bolshevik pattern. As Maisky pointed out in his book, the outstanding characteristic of the Mongols was passivity, and it is doubtful that more than a handful of them had considered the possibility of overthrowing the old feudal-theocratic order. Most of the "revolutionary" leaders were loyal to the church and to its head, the Khutukhtu, and while a few dozen politically conscious individuals wanted to modernize their country, the majority of the population were not just indifferent to change, but actually opposed to it. To the masses the only real cause for complaint lay in the oppressive policies of the Chinese occupying army. It would therefore be quite unwarranted to

---

[23] Rupen, *op. cit.*, pp. 137–138. The name was changed in 1922 to the "Mongolian People's Revolutionary Party."

[24] George G. S. Murphy, *Soviet Mongolia: A Study of the Oldest Political Satellite*, Berkeley and Los Angeles, Calif., 1966, pp. 13–14. This is one of the best books on Outer Mongolia. Professor Murphy was kind enough to read the manuscript of this essay and offer helpful suggestions. Another book of value that has appeared in recent years is C. R. Bawden, *The Modern History of Mongolia*, London, 1968.

say that a revolutionary situation existed in Mongolia in 1919–1921.[25] In this case why, it may be asked, did the Mongol leaders turn to Soviet Russia for help? Facts of geography and demography largely provide the answer. As one of Outer Mongolia's prime ministers later put it, "Our country is surrounded by the territories of Russia and China, and lies in the center, between the two empires.... China has the evil intention of occupying our wide territories and destroying our nation and religion."[26] A similar view was expressed by Rinchino, for several years the top Comintern agent in Mongolia:

> One fact, the number of Mongols, means a great deal. For example, if Russia has 150 millions, Japan has 60 millions, and China in all 400 millions, Mongolia cannot count more than one million inhabitants.
>
> There are too few Mongols. They can at any time be swallowed, but if they are not swallowed, that is only because...next to Mongolia stands Soviet Russia.[27]

As a backward, thinly populated, and militarily weak country, Outer Mongolia was destined to be dominated by either China, Russia, or Japan. Since Russian domination under the Tsarist regime had been rather mild, even benevolent, and since the Russians, unlike the Chinese, had never threatened to engulf the Mongols with colonization, Russia seemed the least of the three possible evils. This is not to say that the Mongolian revolutionaries of 1919 to 1921 wanted their country subjected to Soviet hegemony. On the contrary, they accepted at face value the declaration of August, 1919 (quoted above), in which the Soviet government denounced the Tsarist treaties with Mongolia and asserted that "not a single foreigner has the right to interfere with Mongolian affairs." On the strength of this, they expected the Bolsheviks to help them oust the Chinese and establish Mongolian independence; they did not wish to replace Chinese

---

[25] This point is emphasized by Murphy, *op. cit.*, pp. 2–3, 28, 35, 39, and 68–69. See also Bawden, *op. cit.*, pp. 222, 229, and *passim*.

[26] Tseren Dordji, speaking at the meeting of the First Great Khuraldan in 1924, in: *Novaya Mongoliya; ekonomiko-politicheskoye i kulturnoye sostoyaniye strany. Protokoly pervogo Velikogo khuraldana Mongolskoy narodnoy respubliki*, Ulan-Bator-Khoto, 1925, p. 9. The Hoover Library contains a typewritten English translation by J. Attree, but it is full of errors, some of them serious. The Russian original is cited hereafter as *Novaya Mongoliya*.

[27] Speech by Rinchino, at the Third Congress of the Mongolian People's Party, in: *Tretiy sezd Mongolskoy narodnoy partii*, Urga, 1924, p. 16. This volume, together with the stenographic report of the First Great Khuraldan cited above, constitute two of the richest primary sources available on the early history of the Mongolian revolution. Both are available at the Hoover Institution. Hoover has an English translation also of this one by J. Attree, and it too is unreliable, although it has been widely cited by scholars.

domination with Soviet rule. Indeed, the Mongolian leaders who appealed to Russia for aid nurtured the nationalist dream of not only restoring Outer Mongolian autonomy, but also of uniting all the other territories inhabited by Mongols—Inner Mongolia, Buryat Mongolia, Tannu Tuva, parts of Sinkiang, and other, less important areas.[28]

With these aims in mind, Sukhe Bator, Choibalsan, and their colleagues decided to go to Soviet Russia to seek assistance. In the summer of 1920 they headed north to Siberia, carrying with them an official letter from the Bogdo Gegen that gave an aura of legitimacy to their mission,[29] and were warmly received by the highest Soviet officials in the area.

In August Sukhe Bator addressed an appeal to the Soviets which read in part:

> We, members of the People's Party ..turn to great Russia with a request for aid. We...aspire to restore the Autonomy of Mongolia and to proclaim the Khutukhtu Bogdo as a limited monarch. Then we wish to take necessary measures to limit the hereditary rights of the princes. Having attained the independence of our country, we, profiting by the experience of other countries, will struggle for the rights and interests of our people . Therefore we ask you:
>
> 1. To extend necessary aid to the People's Party of Mongolia, and to assist in restoring Mongolian Autonomy.
>
> 2. To designate a Soviet representative at Kyakhta who will serve as a connecting link between the Soviet Government and the People's Party.[30]

In November, 1920, a Mongolian delegation went to Moscow and attended a special session of the Politburo at which Lenin and Stalin were present.[31] It is possible that, as a result of this meeting, the Politburo decided to invade Mongolia as soon as the necessary preparations could be made. If so, the decision may have been hastened by the news coming from Mongolia about the activities of a certain Baron von Ungern-Sternberg, news that was disturbing in one sense, but quite encouraging in another.

Step 2
Foreign Troops Occupy the Country, Providing the Soviets with an Excuse to Liberate It

Ungern-Sternberg, or "The Mad Baron" as he is sometimes called, was a most bizarre character. A former officer in the Russian Imperial Army, he

---

[28] On the motivation of the Mongol leaders, see also Robert Smith, "Political, Economic and Trade Conditions in Outer Mongolia and Manchuria," pp. 43–44. These typewritten reports, in the library of the Hoover Institution, were apparently written in Manchuria in 1932–1933 and mailed to the Institution.

[29] Nachukdorji, *op. cit.*, p. 134.

[30] Rupen, *op. cit.*, p. 139.

[31] Genkin, quoted in Eudin and North, *op. cit.*, p. 203.

claimed to be the reincarnation of Genghis Khan, and dreamed of recreating the old Mongolian empire, which he would then use as a base for a crusade against the heathen Bolsheviks.[32] In February, 1921, with a force of White Russians, Buryats, Japanese, and miscellaneous other nationalities, he attacked Urga, and the Chinese garrison fled.[33] The independence of Outer Mongolia under the nominal leadership of the Bogdo Gegen was proclaimed, with Ungern assuming the title of Commander in Chief of the armed forces.[34]

Ungern's conquest of Mongolia was a godsend for the Bolsheviks, since it provided them with a justification for doing what they apparently had been planning to do anyway—that is, to invade Outer Mongolia and establish a pro-Soviet government. On November 11, 1920, about a month after Ungern's troops first entered Mongolia, the Soviet Commissar of Foreign Affairs, Chicherin, sent a note to Peking which stated in part:

> The Chinese troops in the Urga region are unable . . to annihilate the White Guardist gangs which operate there; therefore they have turned to our military command and also the command of the Far Eastern Republic asking us to help them combat these gangs of marauders.
>
> The Soviet government...is ready to give aid to the Chinese troops . . . . An appropriate order has been given to our Siberian command. The Soviet government guarantees herewith that its troops dispatched to Mongolia are entering the territory in the capacity of China's friends; and that as soon as the White Guardist gangs in Mongolia are annihilated, the Soviet troops . . will leave Chinese territory immediately.[35]

The Chinese did not appreciate in the least this supposedly generous offer of assistance. Correctly suspecting that the Soviets had objectives beyond the mere defeat of Ungern, the Chinese government replied bluntly that it had never requested help, that it would take all steps necessary to defeat the Whites, and that it did "not need foreign intervention."[36] Fortunately for the Soviets, however, the Chinese did nothing in the succeeding months to drive Ungern out of Urga. Meanwhile, "The Mad Baron" announced his intention to invade Russia and liberate the country from bolshevism—an aim obviously beyond the capacity of his small army and proof in itself of the unbalanced state of his mind. But his proclaimed goal provided a convenient excuse for the Red Army to invade Mongolia.

---

[32] Pershin, *op. cit.*, p. 52–53, 67 and *passim*. Pershin was in Urga when the Baron took the city and had personal dealings with him. While praising Ungern for his courage, Pershin nonetheless found him an erratic, unbalanced person.

[33] Pershin, *op. cit.*, pp. 37, 52, 56.

[34] "Massacre of the Jews at Urga," *The North China Herald*, Shanghai, April 16, 1921, p. 156; Pershin, *op. cit.*, pp. 59, 75.

[35] *Izvestia*, November 14, 1920, quoted in Eudin and North, *op. cit.*, p. 200.

[36] *Izvestia*, January 5, 1921, p. 1.

In this way Ungern played the same role *vis-à-vis* Mongolia as Hitler later played for Eastern Europe: in both cases these avowed enemies of bolshevism provided the Soviets with a justification for invading neighboring states, liberating them from their foreign occupiers, and imposing Communist regimes upon them.

Preparations for the Soviet invasion of Mongolia now moved forward. From March 1 to March 6, 1921, the First Congress of the Mongolian People's Party met in Kyakhta, a Soviet town just north of the frontier. Only about twenty-five delegates attended—hardly a large or a representative sample of the Outer Mongolian population—but with Soviet support they would provide sufficient leadership to carry out the revolution.[37]

Step 3

A Provisional Government in Exile
Is Formed on Soviet Territory

On March 13, 1921, a few days after the Party Congress, the creation of a "Mongol People's Provisional Revolutionary Government" was announced, with Sukhe Bator as Minister of War and Commander in Chief.[38] The new government issued a proclamation calling for the extirpation of feudalism and slavery, the establishment of an equitable tax system, and the formation of a constitutional, parliamentary monarchy under the Bogdo Gegen.[39] Nothing was said about socialism, communism, or the dictatorship of the proletariat; it was a program that might have been inspired by a Western democracy rather than by Soviet Russia. This was the Soviet intention, since at this time Moscow was eager to hide its ultimate aims in order to win the support of the majority of the Mongolian people. The Provisional Government could be used as a rudimentary administration to replace not only Ungern and the Chinese, but also the old Autonomous Government of the Bogdo Gegen. Moreover, since it had been formed on Soviet soil with Soviet aid, and since it would be installed in power by Soviet arms, it presumably would be susceptible to Soviet control.

Twenty-odd years later, Stalin made recourse to this same convenient device when forming provisional governments for Eastern Europe. In the case of Poland the "Union of Polish Patriots" was formed in Russia in 1943, to be replaced the following year, in the Soviet-occupied city of

---

[37] Rupen, *op. cit.*, pp. 141, 155.

[38] Nachukdorji, *op. cit.*, p. 146. Rupen lists the ministers in the government on p. 155 of his book.

[39] The full text of the proclamation is given in: Ma Ho-tien, *Chinese Agent in Mongolia*, Baltimore, 1949, p. 99.

Lublin, by a Communist-dominated "Polish Committee of National Liberation," which in December, 1944, proclaimed itself the Provisional Government of Poland. In Czechoslovakia a somewhat similar role was played by the Košice government, a coalition agreed upon at negotiations held in Moscow. In Hungary it was the Debrecen government, formed with Soviet encouragement after the city of Debrecen was liberated by the Red Army in 1944. In each instance the political programs enunciated by these governments were moderate—designed to appeal to the majority of the population—and carefully avoided all mention of communism, just as in Mongolia decades earlier.

Step 4
Formation of a Native Army on Soviet Soil

With a Mongolian revolutionary party and a provisional government ready for the forthcoming invasion, the next step was the creation of a Mongolian insurrectionary army. A move in this direction had already been taken in 1920, when Sukhe Bator and Choibalsan were given some training at the Red Army officers' school in Irkutsk. Later they organized a "People's Revolutionary Army" consisting of approximately 400 Mongols, who gathered in southern Siberia just north of the Mongolian border.[40] This tiny force obviously was not capable of defeating Ungern, which meant that most of the soldiers needed for the invasion would have to be supplied by the Red Army. It was important, however, to have a Mongol army fighting alongside Soviet troops, in order to give the Russians an aura of legitimacy and to camouflage the fact that the invasion was a case of Soviet aggression against Chinese territory. Therefore Sukhe Bator and his small army were given the honor of striking the first blow. This they did on March 18, 1921, when they crossed the frontier and captured the town of Kyakhta Maimaicheng.[41]

Here the parallel with Soviet tactics in Eastern Europe is evident. It will be remembered that during World War II it was a common practice in the Soviet Union to organize detachments of troops among refugees from countries which the Red Army intended to "liberate." For example, a Polish army was formed in 1943 under the nominal leadership of a Polish general named Berling, although most of its officers were Soviet citizens. Similarly, a Czechoslovak army corps was formed in the Soviet Union under the command of General Ludvik Svoboda, who later co-operated in the Communist takeover of his country.

---

[40] Nachukdorji, *op. cit.*, pp. 141, 144, 147.
[41] Nachukdorji, *op. cit.*, pp. 150–152.

Step 5
The Country Is Invaded by Soviet Troops

When Sukhe Bator's army drove the Chinese out of a small strip of northern Mongolia, the leaders of the Party and the Provisional Government moved over from the Soviet side of the border and proclaimed: "Because throughout our Mongol land the power and authority of the Chinese are no more, the supreme power and authority of our Mongol government have passed entirely into the hands of the Mongols themselves."[42] This claim, of course, had no legitimacy and little popular backing. The vast majority of the population had never heard of the People's Provisional Government, nor had the legitimate ruler, the Bogdo Gegen, given them a mandate for their actions; indeed, he was not even aware of what they were doing.[43] Nevertheless, the Provisional Government issued an appeal to the Soviets for military aid in liberating the country from the forces of Baron Ungern, and, needless to say, the Red Army was happy to comply.[44]

Meanwhile, Ungern behaved in a manner that could only please the Bolsheviks. On May 21, 1921, he issued a proclamation recognizing Grand Duke Michael as the "All-Russian Emperor" and declaring his intention "to exterminate commissars, communists and Jews."[45] He marched his army north towards Kyakhta, but in early June the combined Soviet and Mongol troops defeated him easily. The Baron was eventually captured by the Soviets, tried, and executed.[46] Meanwhile, Soviet diplomats helped by providing camouflage: they informed the Chinese that the Bolsheviks would *not* do the very thing that they *did* plan to do. On June 15, 1921, Foreign Commissar Chicherin dispatched a note which claimed that the Soviet invasion of Chinese territory was really an act of friendship:

> [Ungern's] attacks on the armies of Soviet Russia and of the Far Eastern Republic . forced Russian troops to cross the Mongolian frontier.
>
> Opposition to Ungern is to the interest of China, because by taking this task in hand the Russian Republic at the same time gives support to China, assisting her to crush these bands and maintain her authority.
>
> The Russian Government categorically declares that only with this purpose did it take measures against the traitor Ungern; and likewise declares that when this purpose shall be fulfilled the troops will be withdrawn from

---

[42] Nachukdorji, *op. cit.*, p. 153.

[43] Pershin, *op. cit.*, p. 36.

[44] I. Ia. Zlatkin, *Mongolskaya narodnaya respublika—strana novoy demokratii*, Moscow-Leningrad, 1950, p. 128. The appeal was issued on April 10, 1921.

[45] *Revolyutsiya na Dalnem Vostoke*, Moscow, 1923, pp. 429-432; cited in E. H. Carr, *The Bolshevik Revolution*, Vol. III, New York, 1953, p. 514.

[46] Nachukdorji, *op. cit.*, pp. 159–160; Pershin, *op. cit.*, pp. 108–110.

Mongolia. By taking arms against Ungern the Russian Government confirms its friendly relations with its neighbor, China.[47]

The destruction of Ungern's army as an effective military force eliminated any legitimate justification that the Bolsheviks might have had for intervening in Mongolia, but they had further plans and proceeded to carry them out. Detachments of the Red Army invaded Mongolia again and marched on the capital city of Urga, which they captured on July 6, 1921,[48] thus winning control of the country—a control which has never been relinquished.

If one looks for later parallels with this particular phase of the Mongolian takeover, the best comparison would probably be Finland. When the Soviet Union attacked Finland on November 30, 1939, it proclaimed the establishment of a "Finnish Democratic Republic" headed by Otto Kuusinen, a veteran Finnish Communist who had worked many years for the Comintern in Moscow. This puppet "People's Government" issued an appeal to the Soviets on December 1, 1939, asking for military assistance in liquidating the Helsinki government. The Red Army had already begun its "assistance" the day before by crossing the Finnish frontier.

Step 6
The Provisional Government
Is Reorganized into a Broad Coalition Government

After the capture of Urga, the Provisional Government was replaced by a "People's Revolutionary Government," which, despite its name, was in form a theocratic monarchy, the Bogdo Gegen being retained as a figurehead chief of state.

How can one explain the fact that the Bolsheviks not only refrained from immediately establishing a Soviet regime in Mongolia, but even tolerated a theocratic government? There seem to be two explanations. First, the Bolsheviks realized that they were dealing with an extremely backward, feudal country, which had none of the Marxian prerequisites for a proletarian revolution. Second, the Mongolian leaders, including even the most radical ones, wanted reform and modernization, but not a bloody upheaval like the Bolshevik revolution. Whereas in advanced European countries the Bolsheviks attempted to foment proletarian revolutions, they realized that few if any Asian countries were ripe for revolts of this type—certainly not Mongolia. A Mongolian delegation asked Lenin in November, 1921, if they should transform their People's Party into a Communist Party, and he advised against it:

---

[47] "Moscow's Note to China," *The North China Herald*, July 9, 1921, p. 87.
[48] Nachukdorji, *op. cit.*, pp.159–161; Rupen, *op. cit.*, p. 144; Murphy, *op. cit.*, p.1.

The Mongolian revolutionaries [he said] have much work ahead of them in political, economic, and cultural development before the pastoral population can be called proletarian masses. Once this is achieved, these masses can help in the "transformation" of the People's Revolutionary Party into a communist one. A mere change of signboards is harmful and dangerous.[49]

A Soviet commentator asserted in 1924 that "the Mongolian People's Party is not only not communistic, but is not even a socialistic party."[50] Soviet and Comintern officials seem, however, to have had considerable difficulty in making up their minds just what to call it, and over the years they devised various formulations. One Soviet spokesman declared in 1926 that it was a "united national revolutionary movement,"[51] and in 1934, the Prime Minister of Mongolia referred to his country as follows: "Our republic is a bourgeois, democratic republic of the new type, antifeudalistic and anti-imperialistic, gradually advancing on the road of noncapitalistic development."[52]

"A bourgeois democratic republic of a new type" came to be the standard formulation used in Soviet, Comintern, and Mongolian publications.[53] Only much later, after World War II, did it acquire the designation of a "People's Democracy."

Lenin and the other Soviet leaders apparently realized that it was impossible to introduce socialism into Mongolia except after many years of education, industrialization, and modernization. Another possible reason for the "go-slow" policy, including the retention of the Bogdo Gegen, is that the Mongol revolutionaries may have demanded it, despite Soviet objections. This is the interpretation offered by D. P. Pershin, a former Tsarist official who lived in Urga for some years and was an eyewitness of the events of 1917 to 1921. In describing the plans made by the Bolsheviks and the Mongolian revolutionaries on the eve of the takeover he says:

There was to be formed a new revolutionary government for Urga ..
with the proviso, however, that Bogdo Gegen   was to remain at the head
of this new government. This was done so as to avoid upsetting the Mongo-

---

[49] *IX sezd Mongolskoy narodno-revolyutsionnoy partii,* Ulan Bator, 1934, pp. 32–33, as translated in Eudin and North, *op. cit.,* p. 207.

[50] I. Genkin, "Neskolko slov o sovremennoy Mongolii," which serves as a preface to *Tretiy sezd Mongolskoy narodnoy partii,* pp. xvi–xvii.

[51] Fyodor Raskolnikov at the Fifteenth Congress of the Communist Party of the Soviet Union, as quoted in *Inprecorr,* November 11, 1926, p. 1266.

[52] Prime Minister Gendun at the Seventh Great Khuraldan, as quoted in Yasuo Misshima and Tomio Goto, *A Japanese View of Outer Mongolia,* translated and summarized from the Japanese by Andrew J. Grajdanzev, New York, 1942, p. 13.

[53] For examples, see *Inprecorr,* December 15, 1937, p. 1323; *Bolshaya sovetskaya entsiklopediya,* 1st ed., Vol. XL, Moscow, 1938, p. 68.

lian people, who would feel that no changes had taken place in matters of faith, and that the popular religion would not be infringed upon. . . .

It was said that there was considerable opposition on the part of the Bolsheviks to the placing of a king at the head of the country—and a "living God" at that . . . Jamtsarano [a prominent Mongol revolutionary], so the story goes, categorically insisted that otherwise further negotiations could not proceed.[54]

Elsewhere Pershin writes:

The People's Revolutionary Party. . . acted with great caution, and in important cases even differed with their Bolshevik instructors. . . . The Party followed the principle that a too crude breaking up of old mainstays might arouse among the Mongols. . .serious discontent.[55]

The policy of camouflage and gradualism may have been due to realism on the part of the Bolsheviks. Or the reverse may be true: that impatient, doctrinaire Bolsheviks were forced to move slowly because of opposition from moderate Mongolian revolutionaries. The policy adopted was undoubtedly the correct one, since most Mongolians, and even many of their revolutionary leaders, looked upon the Bogdo Gegen as the legitimate chief of state, and this helped the new regime to establish itself quickly and easily.[56]

Because of the almost total absence of native Marxist revolutionaries in Mongolia, the Bolsheviks at the beginning not only retained the Bogdo Gegen, but also accepted a rather conservative government. Of the seven members of the "People's Revolutionary Government," the Premier and Vice-Premier were both lamas, two were nobles of high rank, and two others had worked for the former Autonomous Government. The only member of this first Urga cabinet who can possibly be labeled a radical— and even his case is debatable—was Sukhe Bator, who retained his posts as Minister of War and Commander in Chief.[57] All these ministers, it should be noted, were natives, i. e., Khalka Mongols; none were Buryats or Soviet citizens. Thus in 1921 there seemed to be little reason for the Mongol people to fear that their country was destined to become a Soviet republic completely subject to Moscow. Therefore opposition to the government or

---

[54] Pershin, op. cit., p. 30.

[55] Ibid., p. 35.

[56] The Bolsheviks generally followed a much more cautious and flexible policy in Asia than in Europe—due, no doubt, to their awareness that Asian countries were not ripe for proletarian revolutions. Thus Soviet tactics in Turkey, Afghanistan, Iran, and China in the decade after 1917 contrasted sharply with the attempts to foment Communist revolutions in Europe. Similarly, the Soviets followed relatively gradual policies in Khiva and Bukhara. However, the Khanate of Khiva and the Emirate of Bukhara were abolished immediately after the Soviets conquered these areas.

[57] Information about the members of the government is given in Murphy, op. cit., pp. 22–24 and 75–76.

to the temporary presence of Soviet troops was almost non-existent. Indeed, the new regime was apparently looked upon as a welcome replacement for the Chinese and Baron Ungern.[58]

But if Outer Mongolia was nominally a monarchy, the leftward direction of its future development was ensured by the continued presence of the Red Army, and when the People's Revolutionary Government requested that these forces remain until the enemy had been entirely defeated, the Soviet government gladly complied. "Soviet troops," said Foreign Commissar Chicherin, "have entered the territory of autonomous Mongolia for one purpose only: to defeat the common enemy, remove the constant danger which threatens Soviet territory, and ensure the self-determination and free development of autonomous Mongolia." The troops would leave, he added, "just as soon as the danger to the free development of Mongolia is removed and the security of the Russian Republic and the Far Eastern Republic assured."[59] In fact, the Soviet troops were there primarily to ensure that Mongolia would again become a Russian protectorate, and they were not removed until this goal had been accomplished.

Whether the "go-slow" policy of 1921, including the retention of the Bogdo, was a clever tactic thought up by the Bolsheviks, or whether it was forced upon them, the Soviets seem to have learned a valuable lesson, because the same tactic of camouflage and gradualism, of appearing to preserve old traditions, old institutions, and even old rulers, was used extensively in the Communist takeovers of the 1940's. The most obvious example is Rumania, where King Michael was allowed to continue as nominal ruler of the country until the Communists were in firm control. In Czechoslovakia, too, the presence of Edward Beneš as President and Jan Masaryk as Foreign Minister in the first postwar governments helped to persuade the people that a Soviet-style regime would not be imposed upon them.

Step 7
Comintern Agents, Pseudo-Natives, and Russified Natives Help Lead the Revolution and the New Regime

Comintern agents played a prominent role in the Mongolian revolutionary movement from the very earliest days. In April, 1920, I. A. Soroko-

---

[58] The initial pleasure of the population of Urga at the Soviet invasion and their friendly attitude towards the Red Army are described in *The North China Herald*, September 10, 1921, p. 760.

[59] *Izvestia*, August 12, 1921, p. 2, as quoted in Eudin and North, *op. cit.*, pp. 204–205. The Mongolian request was published in *Izvestia* on August 10, and is reprinted in Eudin and North, *op. cit.*, p. 204; the two documents are also translated in Leo Pasvolsky, *Russia in the Far East*, New York, 1922, pp. 176–179.

vikov was sent to Urga as the special delegate of the Far Eastern Branch of the Comintern,[60] but the following month was replaced by another Comintern agent, S. S. Borisov (an Altay Oirot), who was active in the events leading up to the revolution of 1921.[61] Some of the Mongols also dealt directly with the head of the Comintern Far Eastern Secretariat, Boris Shumyatskiy.[62]

The Comintern official who played the main part in bringing Mongolia under Communist control, however, was a Buryat Mongol from Russia named Rinchino, who for several years was the most powerful man in Outer Mongolia. As Rinchino himself said:

> I have worked from the beginning of the existence of our People's Party. I went with the representatives of our Party to Moscow. I worked in the Far Eastern Section of the Comintern (Mongolian and Tibetan Section) at Irkutsk. I led Mongolia to the Comintern, which supplied the Mongolian People's Party with instructors and indispensable funds.[63]

Rinchino's "dictatorship" ended with his recall to Moscow in 1928 and replacement as top Comintern representative in Mongolia by Amagaev, another Buryat from Russia. Amagaev acted not only as a Comintern agent, but also as Minister of Finance and Chairman of the Economic Council of Mongolia. Direct management of Mongolian affairs by the Comintern seems to have ceased only in 1931, when Amagaev in turn was ordered back to Moscow.[64]

These two figures, Rinchino and Amagaev, were only the most prominent of the many Comintern agents in Outer Mongolia who might be described as "pseudo-natives" or "sovietized natives." To the first category belong primarily the Buryat Mongols, an ethnic group inhabiting the area to the north of Outer Mongolia, where, in 1923, the Bolsheviks established a Buryat Mongol Autonomous Soviet Republic. Most Mongols within the Russian borders were Buryats, whereas the majority of the inhabitants of Outer Mongolia were Khalka Mongols, whose language is similar but not identical. Many Buryats had been largely russified and spoke the Russian language, while some had even studied at Russian universities. Since few Russians spoke Mongolian and few Khalkas spoke Russian, it was natural

---

[60] Nachukdorji, *op. cit.*, p. 133.

[61] Murphy, *op. cit.*, p. 13.

[62] For biographical data on Shumiatskiy see Eudin and North, *op. cit.*, p.462, and Rupen, *op. cit.*, pp. 146–147.

[63] Speech by Rinchino at the Third Congress of the Mongolian People's Party, as quoted in: *Tretiy sezd Mongolskoy narodnoy partii*, cited also in Rupen, *op. cit.*, p. 143.

[64] Rupen, *op. cit.*, pp. 202, 235. For statements by Amagaev and Danzan on the importance of the Comintern in Mongolia, see Rupen, *op. cit.*, p. 197.

that the Soviets should have used the Buryats as interpreters—and for another purpose as well: the Soviet authorities soon made them the leading element in the new Mongolian government. It was largely Buryats from Russia who served to channel Soviet ideas, methods, and institutions into Outer Mongolia.[65]

This co-operation with Moscow in revolutionizing Outer Mongolia suited the Buryats very well, especially in the early years, since they thought not in terms of subjecting Outer Mongolia to Russian domination, but rather of liberating their brothers from Chinese rule and ultimately creating a strong, independent, progressive nation which would unite all the Mongol peoples (including the Buryats) into a Greater Mongolia. But although motivated by nationalism, the Buryats unwittingly helped to destroy any chances of achieving this nationalist dream. Instead they helped to make Outer Mongolia a satellite of Soviet Russia, while several areas inhabited by Mongols remained or became a part of the USSR.

The degree of Buryat influence in Mongolia may be indicated by the fact that in the 1920's they held the ministries of trade and economy, finance, and education, headed the Central Co-operative organization and the Economic Council, while the trade representative in Moscow and the head of the Mongol Transport Company were also Buryats. They provided the chairman of the Military Council, as well as officers and instructors, thus gaining considerable influence in the army as well.[66] Other nationalities used in Mongolia by the Soviets included Kazakhs, Oirots, and Kalmyks, all of whom, as Asians, were bound, so Moscow doubtless calculated, to be more acceptable to the Mongolians than "white" men such as Russians.

As far as "russified natives" are concerned, the best example is Choibalsan himself, who attended a Russian school in Irkutsk and later received some training at a Red Army officers' academy in the same city. Whether these years in Russia made Choibalsan any less a Mongol cannot be ascertained, but it is clear from his subsequent behavior that he became an obedient servant of Moscow, and this explains in part why he was eventually chosen by Stalin to be ruler of Outer Mongolia.

The career of Choibalsan as a russified (or sovietized) native used by Moscow to further its policies in Mongolia calls to mind a conspicuous example in Eastern Europe after World War II—Marshal Konstantin

---

[65] Pershin, *op. cit.*, pp. 23–24. Rupen, *op. cit.*, on pp. 162–163 gives a list of Buryats who held prominent positions in Outer Mongolia.

[66] Rupen, *op. cit.*, p. 183. See also Walter Kolarz, *The Peoples of the Soviet Far East*, New York, 1954, p. 116. For more information about the Buryats, see the interesting article by Rupen, "The Buriat Intelligentsia," *Far Eastern Quarterly*, Ann Arbor, Michigan, May, 1956, pp. 383–398.

Rokossovsky, who, although of Polish descent, served his entire career in the Soviet army until in 1949 he was appointed Commander in Chief of the Polish armed forces, Minister of Defense, and a member of the Polish Politburo. In this way, Stalin made sure that a pro-Soviet figure stood at the center of the power structure in Communist Poland.

Another instance of this Soviet use of pseudo- or russified natives is provided by North Korea. When the Red Army invaded Korea in 1945, it brought with it as part of the occupying forces about 300 Soviet Koreans, some of whom had been trained at a special school near Khabarovsk in 1942, while others had in all probability attended the Comintern school near Ufa in 1942 and 1943.[67]

In similar fashion pseudo-natives or russified natives helped to establish Communist rule when the Red Army invaded Estonia, Latvia, Lithuania, Western Belorussia, the Western Ukraine, Bukovina, and Moldavia in 1939-1940 and again in 1944-1945. When the Red Army liberated Eastern Europe, it brought in its train groups of native Communists who had lived for years in the Soviet Union, had been thoroughly indoctrinated there, and who in many cases felt their primary allegiance to Moscow. Many of the Communist leaders in Eastern Europe, moreover, were not "natives" in the fullest sense of the word, or at least were not looked upon as such by the local population. To cite only a few examples: Emil Bodnaras (a Ukrainian) in Rumania, Mátyás Rákosi (a Jew) in Hungary, and František Kriegel (a Galician Jew) in Czechoslovakia.

At the beginning of this section (p. 125) it was stated that the Comintern played an important part in the Mongolian revolution; in seeking a parallel with Soviet policy after World War II, the reader may query the legitimacy of any such comparison on the ground that the Comintern was officially abolished in 1943, and could not, therefore, have been involved in the events of 1944–1949. In actual fact, however, the Comintern *did* have a role, just as it had earlier in Mongolia, because the Communist cadres who stage-managed Stalin's takeovers of the late 1940's had been selected and trained by the Comintern before its dissolution. Leaders like Georgi Dimitrov, Walter Ulbricht, Klement Gottwald, Mátyás Rákosi, Ana Pauker, Tito, and Ho-chi-Minh had all worked for the Comintern before World War II, and all of them, except Tito and Ho, spent the war years at Comintern headquarters in Russia. Lesser Communists were trained during the war at a special Comintern school near Ufa, attended by students not

---

[67] Dae-Sook Suh, *The Korean Communist Movement, 1918–1948*, Princeton, N. J., 1967, p. 317; Leonhard, *Child of the Revolution*, pp. 214–215. See also the article on North Korea by Dae-Sook Suh in this volume.

only from Eastern Europe, but also from Germany, Austria, France, Italy, Spain, and Korea (as mentioned above). Although the Comintern was dissolved in 1943, many of its functions continued to be performed by the selfsame persons working in the same building which had served as its headquarters from 1940 to 1941, but which now bore the name "Institute No. 205."[68]

Step 8
Soviet Advisers Are Placed in Important Departments of the Government and the Party

Moscow did not rely entirely on Soviet citizens of Asian stock in establishing its control over Outer Mongolia; Russians also were used extensively. As a foreigner visiting Urga in 1921 commented: "In every office there are three administrative officials—a Mongol, nominally the chief, a Buriat, and a communist Russian. Actually, the Russian is in every instance the chief, the Buriat is his assistant and go-between, and the local Mongol is a figurehead."[69] And an American consul stationed in northern China reported in October, 1921: "There may be a Mongolian Government, but the authority is the Russian Soviet Commandant. He issues orders for the release of men, even if they have been arrested by the Mongols."[70] A Chinese agent who made an extensive trip through Outer Mongolia in 1926–1927 made a similar statement:

> Since Outer Mongolia has become independent all important organs have had Russians as advisers. To put it bluntly, it is the Russians who are directing everything. The Ministry of Finance, for example, has four Russian advisers. The Ministry of War has eight military advisers ... The Secret Police .. has six Russian advisers and is actually headed by one. All the military training officers are Russians . . Even the managers and drivers of the motor company are all Russians. On the surface Outer Mongolia is independent, but in point of fact it is not able to be independent in anything.[71]

---

[68] All of this is described in detail by Wolfgang Leonhard in his autobiographical account, *Child of the Revolution*, chaps. v and vi. Leonhard was a student in the Comintern school until its closing in 1943, then worked for the "National Committee for a Free Germany" in Moscow, and returned to Germany with Walter Ulbricht at the end of the war.

[69] "Russian Affairs As They Interest China," *The North China Herald*, December 10, 1921.

[70] *U.S. Consular Reports*, Kalgan, October 10, 1921; Sokobin, as cited in Ballis, *loc. cit.*, p. 301.

[71] Ma Ho-t'ien, *op. cit.*, p. 95. Rupen, *op. cit.*, on pages 448–451 lists by name and position many of the Soviet citizens occupying important posts in the Mongolian administration.

The Soviets naturally paid special attention to those branches of the administration which controlled armed power. The *secret police* was organized by and at times even headed by Soviet officials.[72] The *army* also was under firm Soviet control, since its original nucleus had been formed on Soviet territory with Soviet equipment and Soviet instructors. After the establishment of the new government in 1921, more Soviet military instructors were sent into the country, with "new and better qualified" personnel arriving as reinforcements in 1923.[73] According to a report by two Japanese observers:

> In each detachment there is a Soviet officer. In general the commander of a cavalry division is a Soviet, but in this case there are two additional Soviet officers. The regiment has only one Soviet officer. The division has a GPU detachment which has police authority over the men in the ranks. The number of Soviet officers in mechanized detachments is greater and the air force consists almost exclusively of Soviet soldiers.[74]

The *economy* was another area where the Russians acquired a dominant influence. This was done by a variety of means, one of the most important being the establishment in 1921 of the Mongolian Central Co-operative, which soon became the country's largest trading organization. In 1924 it was reported that 45 percent of the employees were Russian.[75] In addition, the Russians also operated through Soviet trading companies, which concentrated on exporting Mongolian goods to Russia, while importing little in return.[76] The most effective weapon for gaining influence over the Mongolian economy, however, was the Mongolian Trade and Industrial Bank, formed in 1924 as a joint Soviet-Mongolian company. Most of the staff and all but one of the members of the directorate of the bank were Russian.[77] As the only bank in the country, it had exclusive authority to issue currency (which was minted or printed in Russia), and provided most of the capital needed for trade, co-operatives, industry, and transport.[78] With all of these economic levers at their disposal, and with the government safely under control, the Soviets were able to accomplish what the Tsarist

---

[72] Rupen, *op. cit.*, pp. 198–199; Murphy, *op. cit.*, p. 97. These sources give the names of Soviet citizens known to have been in charge of the police in the 1920's.

[73] Speech by Rinchino at the First Great Khuraldan, in *Novaya Mongoliya*, p. 90.

[74] Misshima and Goto, *op. cit.*, p. 58. Murphy, *op. cit.*, on p. 83 of his book says that this work "is in general highly reliable."

[75] Statement by Gochitskiy, head of the Co-operative, at the First Great Khuraldan. Quoted in *Novaya Mongoliya*, p. 222.

[76] Murphy, *op. cit.*, pp. 90, 199; Rupen, *op. cit.*, p. 199.

[77] Friters, *Outer Mongolia and Its International Position*, p. 128.

[78] Misshima and Goto, *op. cit.*, p. 41.

regime had failed to achieve—the establishment of a monopoly over Mongolian *foreign trade*. Whereas in 1925 the USSR received only 24.1 percent of Mongolian exports, by 1931 the total had grown to 99.2 percent.[79]

In fairness, however, it should be stated that the arrival of Soviet experts in Mongolia brought benefits to the country in the shape of technical "know-how" and ability which had hitherto been completely lacking. The Mongolian Prime Minister cited an example of this in 1924:

> It was long ago time to change the criminal laws from the old Manchu laws . . and to introduce criminal laws modeled after those of the civilized nations of Europe.
>
> Starting in 1921, commissions after commissions were appointed to draft criminal laws, but in general the work did not progress. During the present summer we invited a jurist from Soviet Russia, and under his guidance translations from foreign laws are being prepared, and laws selected from these which are compatible with the laws of our country are being drafted.[80]

Soviet doctors introduced medical services and helped to combat the many widespread diseases, especially syphilis.[81] A Central Veterinary Administration, manned entirely by Russians, was set up to improve the quality of the livestock raised by the nomadic herdsmen.[82]

For these reasons the Mongols had mixed feelings about the hordes of Soviet advisers and experts who descended upon their country. On the one hand, they realized the extreme backwardness of their country, the shortage of capable personnel, and the need to modernize; while on the other hand they resented being bossed by Russians who were often arbitrary, arrogant, or condescending, and they naturally were unhappy over the subordination of Mongolian national interests to those of Moscow. As late as 1924, during the discussions at the Third Congress of the Mongolian People's Party, some delegates were still not afraid to voice criticisms of the Soviet presence. One speaker, for example, demanded to know why all the chauffeurs in the army garage were Russian,[83] while another complained that in his district the branch of the Central Co-operative was staffed entirely by Russians, who were, he said, "unsuitable, very coarse,

---

[79] N. N. Poppe, *Harvard Journal of Asiatic Studies*, December, 1954, p. 475. Poppe is quoting from N. T. Vargin's chapter in *Mongolskaya narodnaya respublika; sbornik statey*, Moscow, 1952.

[80] Prime Minister Tseren-Dorji at the First Great Khuraldan as cited in: *Novaya Mongoliya*, p. 40.

[81] Friters, *op. cit.*, p. 135.

[82] "Mongolians Strive to Attain Real Independence," *China Weekly Review*, November 25, 1933, p. 520.

[83] *Tretiy sezd Mongolskoy narodnoy partii*, p. 101.

and rude."[84] Still another objected (unsuccessfully) to a proposed increase in the salaries of the Soviet military advisers.[85] Such complaints led nowhere, however, as the Mongolian government was in no position to modernize the country without Soviet personnel. The head of the Central Co-operative explained:

> Certain workers raised the question of our not needing foreign instructors. They said we must somehow get along with only Mongols. But in practice this was found to be impossible because: (1) there are no Mongols who know how to run a co-operative, and (2) Mongols knowing general trading matters and bookkeeping could not be found. Therefore we had to employ foreigners, that is, workers from Soviet Russia.[86]

If we turn our attention briefly to Eastern Europe and North Korea in the 1940's, we find numerous analogies. When the Soviet army entered a country, this automatically meant the arrival of a host of Soviet advisers, who assumed important (sometimes dominant) positions in various government and Party departments, and who supervised the reorganization of the latter along Soviet lines. Foreign trade also followed the Mongolian pattern —the new Soviet satellites being forced to drastically reduce trade with capitalist countries and expand trade with the USSR, usually on unfavorable terms. In contrast to the case of Mongolia, the East European satellites were not at an extremely primitive level of development and in desperate need of assistance. Indeed, Czechoslovakia and East Germany and, to a lesser extent, Hungary, already possessed highly sophisticated branches of industry and were in a position to provide the Russians with technical know-how, not vice-versa. In any case, their economies were exploited by the Soviet Union for its own advantage, much as the Mongolian economy had been earlier. Another precedent for later Soviet policy in Eastern Europe may be seen in the formation of the joint Soviet-Mongolian Bank. Similar joint companies were set up by Stalin to gain control of East European airlines, shipping, raw materials, and industrial potential. In the case of Yugoslavia, resistance to Soviet demands for the formation of such companies was one of the causes of the break between Tito and Stalin in 1948.

---

[84] *Ibid.*, p. 204.

[85] *Ibid.*, p. 105. One is reminded of similar complaints voiced by the Yugoslavs in 1945–1948 over the high salaries they were forced to pay Soviet military advisers. In 1933 the Mongolian Revolutionary Youth League passed a resolution asking that Soviet military advisers be removed because of the cost involved. The Soviet government rejected the resolution, sent fifty-four additional advisers, and arrested the leaders of the Youth League. See Misshima and Goto, *op. cit.*, p. 21.

[86] Gochitskiy in *Tretiy sezd Mongolskoy narodnoy partii*, p. 199.

Step 9

The Original Government Is Replaced by a
"People's Democracy"

As we have seen, the regime installed in Mongolia in 1921 was a theocratic monarchy, nominally headed by the Bogdo Gegen, and the first members of the "People's Revolutionary Government" were predominantly lamas, nobles, or middle-class elements. The long-term Soviet aim of making Mongolia a Communist state[87] was facilitated by the death in 1924 of the Bogdo, which came as a great stroke of luck for the Communists. At one and the same time fate rid them of the man who was both head of the church and the head of the state, and when the masses wished to find another "living Buddha" to replace him, they were not permitted to do so. Instead, the First Great Khuraldan (parliament) was convened in November, 1924, and declared Mongolia to be a "People's Republic." A new constitution nationalized the forests, rivers, land, and other natural resources, established a state monopoly of trade, declared the church separated from the state, abolished the titles of the princes and nobles, and ended the ruling rights of the reincarnated saints.[88] It was no accident that this constitution was similar to that of the Soviet Union, since a Soviet citizen, Turar Ryskulov, had a hand in drafting it.[89]

It is interesting to note that the Communist takeover of Mongolia seems to have served as a model for later takeovers even in matters of terminology. When the revolutionary regime was established in 1921, as well as when the monarchy was abolished in 1924, the term "Soviet" was never used. Mongolia became in 1924 a "People's Republic," not a "Soviet Republic." The word "Soviet" may have been avoided partly because the Bolsheviks felt that Mongolia was too backward to be included in the same category as Soviet Russia. A more important reason, however, may have been to

---

[87] In 1924 Rinchino said: "The final aim of the Mongolian People's Party is communism...." *Tretiy sezd Mongolskoy narodnoy partii*, p. 39.

[88] A stenographic record of the proceedings is contained in *Novaya Mongoliya*, cited above. These particular acts are reported on pages 239–242. That some of the delegates were in favor of finding a new living Buddha is indicated by the discussion on p. 254.

[89] Details of the 1924 constitution are given in *Novaya Mongoliya, op. cit.*, pp. 239–249. Ryskulov was a Kazakh and worked for the Comintern. For a biographical sketch see Rupen, *op. cit.*, p. 216. The Mongolian constitution adopted in 1940 was patterned much more closely after the Soviet constitution in force at that time, as is explained by John N. Hazard in "The Constitution of the Mongol People's Republic and Soviet Influences," *Pacific Affairs*, June, 1948, pp. 162–170.

avoid alarming the Mongolian people, most of whom were quite conservative.[90]

During and after World War II the Communists in Eastern Europe and North Korea used similar tactics of camouflage. To minimize opposition and to prevent the people from realizing that their countries were being taken over by Communists, the postwar regimes were careful not to use such labels as "soviet," "socialism," "communism," "the dictatorship of the proletariat," and so on.[91] The term eventually chosen to describe the new regimes was "People's Democracies," but during the early period, from about 1945 to 1948, reference was frequently made to "People's Republics" —just as previously in the case of Outer Mongolia. For example, Georgi Dimitrov, the Communist leader of Bulgaria, declared in 1947: "Bulgaria will not be a Soviet republic but a people's republic."[92] And a Soviet ideologist named Farberov, who played a major role in fitting the new regimes into a Marxist theoretical framework, also referred to the East European states as "People's Republics."[93] That the Mongolian example influenced these formulations of the 1940's is indicated by the fact that Farberov devoted a whole chapter to Mongolia in his book on "Peoples' Democracies." Similarly, Eugene Varga, the Soviet economist, who also

---

[90] It might be noted that the Khorezmi People's *Soviet* Republic and the Bukharan People's *Soviet* Republic, both of which had been established in 1920, were also backward, feudal areas. Perhaps the term "Soviet" was applied to these ostensibly independent republics because the Bolshevik leaders knew that they would annex them to Soviet Russia after a brief interval, whereas the plans for Mongolia did not include annexation. On Bukhara and Khorezm (Khiva) see: Seymor Becker, *Russia's Protectorates in Central Asia : Bukhara and Khiva, 1865–1924*, Cambridge, Mass., 1968, chaps. xv–xvii. The Bukharan and Khivan takeovers were in many ways similar to the Mongolian takeover. The first "People's Republic" seems to have been the "Terek People's Soviet Republic" formed in the northern Caucasus in March, 1918. See Richard Pipes, *The Formation of the Soviet Union*, Cambridge, Mass., 1954, pp. 195–199.

[91] That the use of gradualism and camouflage was a deliberate Soviet strategy is demonstrated by the complaints that Tito received from Moscow during the war for not sufficiently disguising his intention to communize Yugoslavia. For examples, see Vladimir Dedijer, *Tito*, New York, 1953, pp. 174, 180, 209, 233.

[92] Quoted in Z. Brzezinski, *The Soviet Bloc*, Cambridge, Mass., 1967, p. 27.

[93] N. P. Farberov, *Gosudarstvennoye pravo stran narodnoy demokratii*, Moscow, 1949, pp. 297–298. See also the two-part article by Gordon Skilling, " 'People's Democracy' in Soviet Theory," *Soviet Studies*, Glasgow, July and October, 1951. Brzezinski discusses these matters in chap. ii of *The Soviet Bloc*. The term "People's Democracies" does not appear to have become the accepted usage until the appearance in November, 1947, of the Cominform journal, *For a Lasting Peace, for a People's Democracy!* However, Farberov was still using "People's Republics" as late as 1949.

helped to elaborate the theoretical bases for the "democracies of a new type," referred to Mongolia as a predecessor of the East European regimes, pointing out the similarities between Mongolia and its successors.[94] It may be noted, too, that the term "People's Republic" has remained the approved terminology for most Communist countries in Asia. Despite considerable progress along the road to Soviet-style "socialism," Outer Mongolia has retained this title, which it shares in common with North Korea and China. The Communist regime in North Vietnam, however, has remained since its formation in 1945 the "Democratic Republic of Vietnam."

Step 10
A Series of Purges Are Carried Out
Until the Leaders Are Completely Subservient to Soviet Wishes

Whether the Mongolian regime should be presided over by a figurehead "living Buddha" or whether it should be a "People's Republic" was not, of course, the vital issue for the Soviet Union. What mattered was that the rulers of Outer Mongolia take orders from Moscow. This objective was accomplished in part by a succession of purges, apparently directed primarily by Soviet officials stationed in Urga.

Most of the members of the first Urga cabinet, including the Prime Minister (Bodo), were shot in August, 1922, only a year after they had taken office. Sukhe Bator, the Minister of War and Commander in Chief of the Army, died in February, 1923, poisoned by the Soviets, according to one source, although this cannot be proved.[95]

Sukhe Bator's successor as War Minister and Commander in Chief, Danzan, was also Vice-Premier of the government and Chairman of the Central Committee of the Party. As head of the Party he presided at the Third Party Congress in August, 1924, but made the mistake of quarreling with the chief representative of the Comintern, Rinchino, and was even foolhardy enough to oppose a resolution calling for the strengthening of friendship between Mongolia and the USSR.[96] In an astonishing sequence of events Danzan, who started out as chairman of the Congress, had by the end of the Congress been condemned and shot! Witnessing, approving,

---

[94] Skilling in *Soviet Studies*, July, 1951, p. 22. Ballis, *op. cit.*, p. 293, says that "Outer Mongolia . . was the first of the Soviet satellite states to be classed as a people's democracy." However, the present author has been unable to uncover any use of the precise term "people's democracy" prior to the 1940's, whether in reference to Mongolia or any other country.

[95] Murphy, *op. cit.*, p. 78.

[96] *Tretiy sezd Mongolskoy narodnoy partii*, pp. 60–61.

and apparently engineering this purge were Rinchino and the Soviet Minister to Mongolia, Vasilev.[97]

By the end of 1924 about half of the Mongol leaders who had planned and carried out the revolution had been executed, while others were exiled to Russia, eventually to be liquidated in Stalin's Great Purge of the 1930's. Indeed, if one looks at a list of the most prominent figures in the Mongolian Party and government during the 1920's and 1930's, one cannot but be impressed by the number of biographies which end with the phrase "shot in...."[98] Nor did Rinchino escape the fate of his victims; he was ordered to Moscow in 1928 and was later shot in the Great Purge.

The only one of the original revolutionary leaders of 1919–1921 who managed to survive the various purges and retain a position of prominence was Choibalsan, the so-called "Stalin of Mongolia." At the time of the formation of the first revolutionary government in 1921 he was only Deputy Commander in Chief of the Army. But in 1922 he was the key figure in organizing the secret police, in 1924 he became Commander in Chief of the Army, in 1936 he was named Minister of the Interior and First Deputy Prime Minister, and, finally, in 1939, he reached the top as Prime Minister. He remained dictator of Mongolia until 1952 when, unlike most of his colleagues, he apparently died of natural causes.[99]

Why Stalin chose Choibalsan to be his puppet and imitator is a matter of speculation, but two reasons seem logical: Choibalsan was more willing than other native Mongolian leaders to obey Moscow's dictates without question, to give Russian interests priority over those of Mongolia, and to co-operate in purging his friends. Secondly, he had been Commander in Chief of the Army since 1924, and the role which Mongolian armed forces might play in a possible Soviet-Japanese war assumed great importance in 1939, the year in which Choibalsan was named Prime Minister. Perhaps Stalin wanted to be sure that an experienced military man would be in charge in Mongolia in order to help defend the Soviet Union from any Japanese attack.[100]

The fact remains that the purges helped to accomplish the Soviet objective of establishing absolute control over Mongolia, and by the time

---

[97] The quarrels between Danzan and Rinchino, as well as the course of events by which Danzan and his closest supporters were purged, are extensively reported in *Tretiy sezd*, pp. 159–229. Vasilev's statement approving the purge is on p. 225.

[98] Such a list is provided in Rupen, *op. cit.*, Table II, pp. 162–164. See also his useful list of "Former MPR Party and Government Officials" on pages 432–435.

[99] Rupen, *op. cit.*, p. 163; Murphy, *op. cit.*, pp. 77 n., 134.

[100] The second point is presented forcefully by Rupen, *op. cit.*, p. 234.

Choibalsan became Premier, if not before, he and his colleagues had learned that the only key to survival was to co-operate in ensuring total subservience to Moscow, even though this meant economic exploitation and loss of independence in both domestic and foreign policy.

The particular step in the Mongolian takeover described above had a parallel in Eastern Europe so obvious as scarcely to require reiteration—namely, the purges of the 1940's and 1950's. The Polish leader, Gomulka, was removed from power in 1948, apparently because he felt that his country need not blindly follow Soviet methods and orders in every last detail. Similarly, Tito's refusal to subordinate his country's interests to those of the Soviet Union caused Stalin to attempt to bully the Yugoslav Communist Party into purging Tito, but without success. In other instances, East European purges seem to have been ordered by Moscow mainly as an instrument of terror—that is, to demonstrate to the native Communist leaders that the best way to stay alive was to obey Russia's dictates.

Step 11
The Country's Political, Economic and Cultural Institutions are Remodeled Along Soviet Lines

It is reasonable to suppose that when the Soviets invaded Outer Mongolia in 1921, one of their objectives was to establish a Communist regime, thereby fulfilling Lenin's assertion that it was possible for an underdeveloped country like Mongolia to jump directly from feudalism to socialism. At the First Great Khuraldan (parliament) a Soviet official declared: "We must prepare the ground for a gradual transition to the principles of Soviet rule and communism."[101] This transition was rendered inevitable by the presence of Red Army units and numerous Soviet officials in Mongolia, combined with the proximity of the USSR. But the extreme backwardness of the country and the almost total lack of support for communism among the population guaranteed that sovietization would occur very gradually.

Things moved especially slowly from 1921 to 1928, during which time the traditional ruling classes—the nobility and the church officials—retained most of their power and wealth, and the new regime remained weak, except in the capital. Still, even in these early years the first steps in imitating the Soviet pattern were taken. The Mongolian People's Revolutionary Party was organized in the manner of its Soviet counterpart, complete with a Presidium (Politburo), Central Committee, Central Control Commission, and Party Congresses. Soviet-type Party organizations for young people

---

[101] Speech by Erbanov, Chairman of the Council of People's Commissars of the Buryat Soviet Republic, as cited in *Novaya Mongoliya, op. cit.,* p. 22.

included the Revolutionary Union of Youth, or *Revsomol* (equivalent of the Soviet Komsomol), and the Young Pioneers.[102] The constitution adopted in 1924 declared that the supreme organ of government in Mongolia was the Great Khuraldan (which resembled the Congress of Soviets) and it elected a Small Khuraldan (like the Central Executive Committee in the USSR), which in turn chose a Presidium (like the Presidium of the Congress of Soviets). Local khuraldans performed governmental functions on the lower levels in the same way as the local soviets in the USSR.[103]

The formation of a Soviet-style Party and Government in Urga (now Ulan-Bator) had at first little if any effect on the life of the ordinary Mongolian nomad herdsmen, but when, in 1928, Stalin launched his "second revolution" of industrialization and collectivization in Russia, Mongolia was forced to follow suit. "Right-wingers" were ousted from the Party, and a number of radical social and economic policies were adopted, the most important being a Five-Year Plan designed to bring "socialism" to Mongolia. As in the Soviet Union, rapid and forcible collectivization of agriculture brought a drastic decline in the number of livestock, the losses in 1932 alone amounting to more than seven million head out of a former total of about twenty-three million.[104] This hasty and forced collectivization drive was halted and criticized, just as happened in the Soviet Union, but in later years was resumed at a more leisurely pace. "Arat Unions" (comparable to the Soviet *kolkhozes*) were organized, along with state farms (like *sovkhozes*) and hay-cutting stations (similar to the machine tractor stations in the USSR).[105] Private industrial enterprise was banned, along with private trading and transport; the estates of many clerical and lay landlords were confiscated; and a state foreign trade monopoly was established.[106]

The First Five-Year Plan caused such havoc that the population rose up in armed rebellion,[107] whereupon in 1932 the Mongolian leaders officially

---

[102] Ma Ho-tien, *Chinese Agent in Mongolia*, p. 107.

[103] Details of the 1924 constitution are given in *Novaya Mongoliya*, pp. 239–249.

[104] Speech by Choibalsan in 1940, as cited in Rupen, *op. cit.*, p. 233. See also Rupen's comments on p. 232.

[105] Kolarz, *op. cit.*, p. 147.

[106] An eyewitness report of the results of the First Five-Year Plan is given in Misshima and Goto, *A Japanese View of Outer Mongolia*, p. 12. Murphy discusses the Plan in detail in chap. v of his book, while Soviet economic exploitation of Mongolia is described in chap. viii.

[107] According to Professor N. N. Poppe, one of the leading experts on Mongolia, Soviet tanks and planes were sent to Mongolia in 1932 to suppress the widespread rebellion. Cited in Rupen, *op. cit.*, p. 249. Misshima and Goto, *op. cit.*, describe nineteen different rebellions, riots, and plots which they say occurred against the regime between 1921 and 1938.

repudiated the leftist policy, the collective farms were dissolved, and private enterprise was permitted to revive. This was only a tactical retreat, however, and in later years, after the regime had entrenched itself more securely, the process of eliminating the private sector was resumed, but at a slower pace and with more careful planning.

In reality, the chief objective of Soviet economic policy in Mongolia was not the establishment of a socialist economic system, but rather the exploitation of Mongolia for the benefit of Russia. A Soviet official admitted this bluntly in 1929; the Mongolian Five-Year Plan, he said, "must be constructed to permit maximum utilization of the resources of the MPR in the industrialization of the USSR."[108] This policy was effected primarily through control of Mongolian foreign trade. The bulk of Mongolian commerce had traditionally been with China; this was now changed: as mentioned earlier, Mongolia's exports to the USSR jumped from 24.1 percent in 1925 to a remarkable level of 99.2 percent in 1931. Furthermore, poor, underdeveloped Mongolia was compelled to export to Russia more than it imported in return, thereby extending credits to its richer neighbor. It would be untrue to say that the Soviets did nothing to help the Mongolian economy, but as long as Stalin lived their investments "served primarily the interests of the USSR."[110]

Initially, the chief institutions through which Moscow controlled the Mongolian economy were special Soviet companies sent to Mongolia to buy up all commodities that the USSR wished to import. Later, Moscow used a device which was introduced after World War II in Eastern Europe and China—joint companies. These joint companies were ostensibly owned and operated by Russia and Mongolia on an equal basis, but in fact were

---

[108] I. L. Bayevskiy, *Khozyaiystvo Mongolii*, No. 4 (17), 1929, p. 29, as quoted in Murphy, *op. cit.*, p. 120.

[109] N. N. Poppe, *Harvard Journal of Asiatic Studies*, XVII, December, 1954, p. 475.

[110] Murphy, *op. cit.*, p. 202. Murphy provides much detailed information on Mongolian trade, especially on pp. 194–199. See also Friters, *op. cit.*, pp. 136–139, and Violet Connolly, *Soviet Economic Policy in the East*, London, 1933. The ideological justification for such a policy had been provided by Stalin in *Pravda* on October 10, 1920: "Central Russia, that hearth of world revolution, cannot hold out long without the assistance of the border regions, which abound in raw materials, fuel and foodstuffs. The border regions of Russia in their turn would be inevitably doomed to imperialist bondage without the political, military and organizational support of more developed central Russia." See Stalin, *Sochineniya*, Vol. IV, Moscow, 1947, p. 351. Stalin was referring to the border regions that had been legally a part of Tsarist Russia, but he undoubtedly looked upon the Outer Mongolian protectorate in the same light.

dominated by Russians. The first such company was the *Mongolbank*, established in 1924 under a Russian director. Others followed, including *Mongoltrans*, for control of transportation facilities, *Mongolsherst*, which monopolized the trade in wool, and *Mongolstroy*, a construction company.[111]

Cultural life in Mongolia also went through a gradual process of sovietization. Writers were organized into a Union of Mongol Writers, patterned after the Union of Soviet Writers, and were taught to write according to the Soviet principles of "socialist realism." Russian and Soviet authors have predominated among the books translated from foreign languages, while textbooks used in the schools have been mainly Soviet ones. Russification was facilitated by the adoption of the Russian alphabet, and the leading newspapers were modeled on those in the Soviet Union, even to the extent of being given the same names.[112]

This gradual imposition of the Soviet cultural pattern went hand in hand with a drive to destroy the power of the church and eradicate religious belief. In this field, however, the change came about very slowly because of the great wealth and strength of the Buddhist church, the huge number of lamas, and the traditional devotion of the masses. In addition, many of the original Mongolian revolutionary leaders, some of whom were lamas themselves, were sympathetic both to the church and to the Buddhist religion. As described above, the new regime even made the head of the church the nominal chief of state until his death in 1924. In 1928, however, under Soviet pressure the Mongolian Party officially abandoned toleration and came out openly in opposition to the church and religion. A Central Anti-Religious Commission was established as part of the government, and a League of Militant Atheists was organized, just as in the Soviet Union.[113] By the end of the 1930's most of the monasteries had been closed, the number of lamas had declined drastically, the bulk of church property had been confiscated, and many of the clerical leaders had been imprisoned, exiled, or shot. The church as a political and economic force was dead.[114]

One final example of how the Mongols imitated the Soviet model might be mentioned—the creation of a "cult of personality" around the "Lenin" and the "Stalin" of Mongolia, Sukhe Bator and Choibalsan. To compare Sukhe Bator's role in the Mongolian revolution with that of

[111] Murphy, *op. cit.*, pp. 199–200; Rupen, *op. cit.*, p. 199.

[112] Kolarz, *op. cit.*, pp. 149, 151–152; C. Y. W. Meng, "Red Imperialism in Outer Mongolia," *China Weekly Review*, May 30, 1931, p. 470.

[113] *Inprecorr*, May 13, 1931, p. 467. The League joined the International of Proletarian Freethinkers, a subsidiary of the Comintern.

[114] University of Washington, Far Eastern and Russian Institute, *Mongolian People's Republic*, New Haven, Conn., 1956, p. 29; Rupen, *op. cit.*, pp. 200, 244; Murphy, *op. cit.*, pp. 144–145.

Lenin in Russia is the grossest of exaggerations, and it is clear from contemporary records that at the time none of the Mongol revolutionaries
looked upon him as being *the leader* of the movement.[115] But Russia had a
Lenin, so Mongolia had to follow suit, and an elaborate myth was created
about Sukhe Bator, the so-called father of the Mongolian revolution.
Similarly, it is quite an exaggeration to compare Choibalsan with Stalin,
since Choibalsan's role in the revolution was rather minor and he did not
become the leader of Mongolia until 1939. The process of his deification
nevertheless took place. "Choibalsan Prizes" were instituted soon after the
appearance of "Stalin Prizes," and the Mongolian constitution was referred
to as the "Choibalsan Constitution." A mausoleum similar to that in
Moscow was constructed in the central square of Ulan Bator, and today it
displays the mummified remains of Sukhe Bator and Choibalsan.[116]

Outer Mongolia is now as thoroughly sovietized as any of the Central
Asian republics of the USSR; if it were formally annexed to the Soviet
Union, its present situation would not alter in any significant respect. The
Soviet satellites in Eastern Europe and North Korea, by contrast, never
came under such total control of Moscow. Whether Stalin planned to make
them as subservient as Mongolia, or whether he considered this impossible to
achieve in Eastern Europe, is an unanswerable question. As for the imitation of Soviet methods in most aspects of the political, economic, and
cultural life of the East European client states, the details are so familiar
that they need not be repeated here.[117]

Conclusion

It has been the purpose of this paper to point out the elements in the
Soviet takeover of Mongolia which set precedents for later Soviet actions
of this type. There is no way of proving that these precedents were followed
consciously by Stalin in the 1940's, and it is true that few if any of the Soviet
and Comintern officials who directed the Mongolian operation were active
in Eastern Europe or North Korea twenty-odd years later. Stalin himself,
who had the final word in determining the takeover tactics of the 1940's
had, as far as is known, little to do with Mongolia prior to 1928—the
Comintern was the major instrument through which Moscow controlled
Mongolia in the early years, and Stalin was not active in Comintern work

[115] In the discussions at the First Great Khuraldan, held only a year after
Sukhe Bator's death, his name was rarely mentioned and then only with moderate
praise. See: *Novaya Mongoliya.*

[116] Kolarz, *op. cit.*, p. 148. A photograph of the mausoleum is reproduced in
Rupen, *op. cit.*, p. 370.

[117] One of the best accounts is in Brzezinski, *op. cit.*, chaps. iv–vii.

during this period. However, this does not mean that Stalin could not have taken Mongolia as a useful model for his takeover policies in the postwar world. He was well informed at the time about what was going on in Outer Mongolia, since he was present at the Politburo meeting in 1920 which received the delegation of Mongolian revolutionaries. As Commissar of Nationalities he supervised the Buryat Mongolian Soviet Republic, and Buryats, as we have seen, played a major part in the establishment of communism in Outer Mongolia. In addition, as a member of the Politburo and General Secretary of the Party, Stalin must have been familiar with the tactics that were used in staging the revolution and in introducing communism. Certainly he could not have failed to be impressed by the fact that Mongolia was the only country between 1917 and 1940 where the Soviet Union managed to install a Communist regime. In the years immediately after 1917 most of the Bolshevik leaders, as well as Communists in other countries, nourished the illusion that other countries were ripe for revolt and that the "Great October Revolution" would be imitated elsewhere. But attempted revolutions in Germany, Hungary, Poland, Bulgaria, and other places all collapsed. Stalin seems generally to have been less sanguine about the prospects for Communist revolutions in other lands than were Lenin, Trotsky, Zinoviev, or the other leading Bolsheviks, and in the 1930's he made no attempts to promote them. Judging from his policies, he seems to have come to the conclusion that the best way to bring about revolutions was to export them on the bayonets of the Red Army, which he proceeded to do in the 1940's. That he reached this conclusion partly from his knowledge of the Mongolian revolution is well within the bounds of possibility.

In the 1930's Outer Mongolia was bound to draw Stalin's attention. The Japanese invasion of Manchuria in 1931 created fears in Moscow that Japan might be preparing to attempt once more (as she had in 1918–1922) to seize Soviet territories in the Far East. During 1935 a series of Japanese-provoked clashes along the frontier between Mongolia and Manchukuo fed these suspicions, and in 1936 prompted Stalin to issue a public warning that if Mongolia were attacked, the Soviet Union would come to its aid. When the Japanese army moved into northern China in 1937, Stalin responded by sending Soviet troops back into Mongolia. In the spring and summer of 1939 incidents along the Mongolian frontier turned into large-scale conflicts, the most important being the battle of Khalkhin-gol (Nomonkhan), in which a combined Soviet-Mongolian army defeated the Japanese and inflicted 55,000 casualties.[118] Thus the value of Mongolia as a puppet state on the Soviet border and as a buffer against foreign attack was amply demonstrated to Stalin.

[118] Rupen, *op. cit.*, pp. 225–226.

The relevance of this fact to the 1940's is clear. Stalin's policies at the end of World War II were motivated first and foremost by considerations of national security. The Soviet Union required a subservient Eastern Europe to act (like Mongolia in the 1930's) as a *cordon sanitaire* against the capitalist enemies of the socialist Fatherland. Certainly, the tactics of camouflage and gradualism which Stalin decreed for Eastern Europe in the 1940's were remarkably similar to those used in Outer Mongolia (see Steps 1–9, above) but were quite unlike the Bolshevik revolution or the futile attempts to foment revolutions in Europe from 1918 to 1923.[119]

Finally, another interesting possibility deserving of mention is that the takeover of Outer Mongolia influenced Soviet policies in China in the 1920's. Soviet aid to the Kuomintang, (Chinese Nationalist Party), including the dispatch of arms, Red Army officers, and political advisers (especially Mikhail Borodin) may have been based on Stalin's assumption that he could repeat in China what had been done in Outer Mongolia in 1921. In both instances Asian revolutionary nationalists asked the Soviets to give them military assistance in carrying out a revolution and seizing power. Since the Mongolian operation had been so successful, the Soviet leaders may have reasoned that they could stage a similar takeover in China by gaining control of the Chinese revolutionary movement. This was not to be, because in 1927 Chiang Kai-shek turned against his Communist allies and slaughtered them, thereby removing the Communists as a significant force from the Chinese political scene for many years.

There is some circumstantial evidence to link the Chinese revolution of 1926–1927 with Outer Mongolia. For example, it is known that Borodin was in Urga on April 3–7, 1926, and that while there he talked with General Feng Yü-hsiang, one of the most important of the warlords involved in the

---

[119] That Stalin "decreed" the tactics of the 1940's is demonstrated by the accounts of how he attempted (with only moderate success) to force Tito to follow the pattern of tactics used in other East European countries. For examples see Dedijer, *op. cit.*, pp. 174, 180, 209, 233. Wolfgang Leonhard in *Child of the Revolution*, describes how Ulbricht arrived in Germany in 1945 with a plan of operations that had been worked out in advance in Moscow. As in the case of Yugoslavia, the pattern of tactics had to be imposed from above because many of the local Communists wanted to effect the takeover in a more open and revolutionary way, whereas Ulbricht evidently had received orders from Stalin to use camouflage and gradualism.

The existence of a "blueprint" or general tactical line elaborated in Moscow for the takeovers of the 1940's is also indicated by the case of North Korea. Although social and cultural conditions and traditions were markedly different in Korea from those in Eastern Europe, the tactics used (under Soviet supervision) were almost identical with those used in Poland and some of the other East European states. See the article on Korea by Dae-Sook Suh in this volume.

Chinese revolution.[120] Borodin's role was to supervise the Communist takeover of China, and since he is known to have had first-hand knowledge of Outer Mongolian affairs, this could have colored his choice of tactics in China. In addition, there were connections between Outer Mongolia and China through General Feng himself, who is reported to have spent about a year in Russia before returning to China in September, 1926.[121] He received money and arms from the Soviets, and apparently promised to help support Soviet policy in China with regard to the revolution. Feng also co-operated for a time in moves designed to bring about the unification of Inner Mongolia (his center of power) with the Mongolian People's Republic, but he proved to be an unreliable ally of the Soviets, and Inner Mongolia remained a part of China.[122]

---

[120] Rupen, *op. cit.*, pp. 211, 216.

[121] David Dallin, *The Rise of Russia in Asia*, New Haven, Conn., 1949, pp. 225–226; Rupen, *op. cit.*, pp. 187–188, 211–212. The author is indebted to Professor Rupen for pointing out the connections that Borodin and Feng had with Outer Mongolia.

[122] At the same time that the Soviets were intervening in Outer Mongolia, establishing a protectorate over that country, and gradually pushing it in the direction of communism, they were behaving in much the same manner in Tannu Tuva, a small area located on the northwestern border of Outer Mongolia, an area which, in fact, is considered by many Mongols and Tuvans to be part of Outer Mongolia. For further information about Tuva, see the following chapter.

The Absorption of Tuva

Robert A. Rupen

> Tuva, this lost corner of Inner Asia, has a major significance for under-
> standing the reality of Soviet Russia. Soviet Russia is an entirely new, an entirely
> different state, a socialist state. Its foreign policy has and can have nothing in
> common with the cunning, cynical foreign policy of the imperialist powers. So
> say some. Others see in the foreign policy of the Soviets the straight-line con-
> tinuation of the policy pursued by Tsarism. Other words, other methods, the
> same purpose. Scratch a Bolshevik and you find a Russian. What is the truth?
> No one can expect to find the whole truth in Tuva. But one part of the truth,
> perhaps a very important part, *can* be found in Tuva.[1]

Tuva (otherwise known as Tannu Tuva, or Uryanghai), a remote, sparsely populated Soviet Autonomous Republic on the northwestern border of Outer Mongolia, is one of those territories annexed by Stalin during World War II—with the difference that Tuva had already long been virtually colonized by Russia.

The background to the takeover of this small republic, whose indigenous inhabitants are related to the Mongols, embraces the whole history of the longstanding rivalry between China and Russia (whether Tsarist or Soviet) for domination of the Mongol borderlands, revealing the continuity between Imperial Russian pretensions in the area and Soviet policy designed to contain Chinese expansion. The key element in this pre- and post-revolutionary policy has been a determination to prevent Tuvans and Mongolians from uniting on the basis of their ethnic and cultural links, thereby weakening Chinese claims to Tuva.

The story of the actual annexation of Tuva and its incorporation into the Soviet Union as a constituent part of the RSFSR is soon told; the reasons for its seizure are, however, worth examining in some detail, since they provide answers to the question to what extent Soviet policy has been a continuation of that pursued by the Tsars up to 1917 in dealing with the sensitive Asian border regions.

Like the Baltic States in 1940, Tuva "applied for entry" into the USSR on August 17, 1944, certainly in response to Soviet pressure. The request was formally made by the so-called "Little Khural," or people's assembly, of Tuva, at an extraordinary session on August 16, at which the following declaration was unanimously adopted:

> The Tuvan people have gone through the whole 23-year period of free
> revolutionary development with the great Soviet people.

---

[1] Otto Maenchen-Helfen, *Reise ins asiatische Tuwa*, Berlin, 1931, p. 143.

The Soviet State has become mightier under the sun of the Soviet Constitution and has attained the flowering of the material and spiritual strength of large and small peoples in a unified socialist family.

To live and work in this family is the solemn desire of the whole Tuvan people. There is no other route for us than the route of the Soviet Union. Fulfilling the undeviating will and burning desire of the whole Tuvan people, the Extraordinary Seventh Session of the Little Khural of the Workers of the Tuvan People's Republic resolves:

To request the Supreme Soviet of the USSR to take the Tuvan People's Republic into the composition of the USSR.

The Presidium of the USSR Supreme Soviet approved the request, also unanimously, and on October 11, 1944, adopted a law "On the Acceptance of the Tuvan People's Republic into the Composition of the USSR" which reads in part:

The Presidium of the Supreme Soviet of the USSR, taking account of the request of the Little Khural of the Workers of the Tuvan People's Republic concerning the acceptance of the Tuvan People's Republic into the composition of the USSR, resolves:

1. To grant the request of the Little Khural of the Workers of the Tuvan People's Republic and accept the Tuvan People's Republic into the composition of the USSR.

2. To request the Supreme Soviet of the RSFSR to take the Tuvan People's Republic into the composition of the RSFSR with the rights of an Autonomous Oblast.

3. To arrange in accordance with the provisions of Article 35 of the Constitution of the USSR the election of deputies of the Supreme Soviet of the USSR from the Tuvan Autonomous Oblast in April, 1945.[2]

All the evidence points to the fact that Stalin decided to annex Tuva and make it an integral part of the Soviet Union not simply because of the substantial number of Russians permanently settled there,[3] although this was an important reason, but primarily because he wanted a *fait accompli* prior to the impending negotiations with the Western Allies (at Yalta only a few months later, in February, 1945) which were to shape the political map of the postwar Far East. It may seem strange that Stalin did not decide to strengthen the Soviet geopolitical position further by annexing

---

[2] *Istoriya Tuvy*, Vol. II, Moscow, 1964, pp. 235–236.

[3] The population of Tuva in 1944 was 95,400, of whom 80,800 were native Tuvans, most of the rest being Russians. Its area comprises about 66,000 square miles—larger than Belgium, Denmark, Holland, and Switzerland combined. The greatest east-to-west distance is 463 miles and from north to south, 62 to 280 miles. The total area corresponds to that of the state of Washington. The 1970 census gives 231,000 as the total population, of whom 139,000 are native Tuvans. For basic statistical information, see *Narodnoye khozyaystvo Tuvinskoy ASSR: Statisticheskiy sbornik*, Kyzyl, 1967.

the Mongolian People's Republic (Outer Mongolia) at the same time. The answer can only be that Stalin wanted to keep his options open towards both Chiang-Kai-shek and the Chinese Communists led by Mao Tse-tung, and was still uncertain whether the Allies would behave like real or paper tigers, should the Soviet Union swallow Mongolia. At this juncture it was not the Soviet intention to antagonize the United States, since, in the negotiations which followed Yalta, when the Nationalist Chinese and the Russians were drawing up what became the Sino-Soviet treaty of August, 1945, the Nationalists insisted on Soviet recognition of Chinese sovereignty in Outer Mongolia, and only considerable United States pressure persuaded Chiang Kai-shek to accept the Yalta agreement that Outer Mongolia's independent status should remain unaltered. Unilateral Soviet annexation of Mongolia in 1944 would have torpedoed Stalin's expectations for American support in bringing Nationalist China to submit to the Yalta provisions, including recognition of Soviet rights in Manchuria, a strategic area highly desirable to the Russians. It would, therefore, have been foolish to annex Mongolia as well as Tuva—and Stalin was no fool.[4]

Thus, the absorption of Tuva was part of an overall plan to strengthen Moscow's hand in the postwar world. The timing of the annexation was in no way connected with any shift in the situation of the Russian settlers, which had remained unchanged since the nineteenth century. Major economic factors were not involved; no natural resources of strategic value suddenly came to light in Tuva (the uranium deposits were only found in mid-1945[5]), and no construction of important new communication routes took place either just before or after the annexation.

---

[4] The background atmosphere is conveniently rendered in chap. xvi ("China's Hour at Cairo, November-December 1943") of Barbara Tuchman's *Stilwell and the American Experience in China, 1911–1945*, New York, 1971, pp. 396–414. Tuchman indicates that access to Dairen was considered at that time to be a "legitimate demand" on the part of the USSR, and quotes President Roosevelt as having said to Ambassador Bullitt, "I think that if I give him [Stalin] everything I possibly can and ask nothing of him in return, *noblesse oblige*, he won't try to annex anything and will work with me for a world of democracy and peace."

Stalin told Harry Hopkins at the end of May, 1945, that he "proposed no alteration over the sovereignty of Manchuria or any other part of China, either Sinkiang or elsewhere" *(U. S. Relations with China with Special Reference to the Period 1944–1949*, a White Book of the U.S. Department of State, 1949, p. 115).

[5] Although Walter Kolarz, in *The Peoples of the Soviet Far East*, London, 1954, p. 168, states, "It may or may not be a coincidence that Tuva, with its uranium deposits, was annexed to the Soviet Union at a time when atomic research in the western hemisphere was heading towards its climax."

Any discussion of the motives behind the Soviet annexation of Tuva must inevitably throw into relief the similarities between basic Tsarist and Soviet policies *vis-à-vis* the Central Asian borderlands. These similarities greatly outweigh the differences. It might fairly be said at the outset that during the Soviet period Tuva experienced much the same treatment at much the same pace as the rest of the Soviet national minorities—that is to say, the territory was exposed for the first time to deliberate russification, whereas before 1917 events in Russia affected only the Russian settlers in Tuva, not the native population. Tsarist policy directed and shaped the Russian community in Tuva; Soviet actions made an equal impact on both Russians and Tuvans.

The formal Soviet absorption of Tuva in 1944 in itself followed a pre-revolutionary precedent, namely, the establishment of a Tsarist protectorate in 1914.[6] Here, the Soviet leaders emulated their predecessors' methods in minor details as well as in major principles. Imperial Russian nationalist expansionism merged neatly with the peculiar Marxist-Leninist-Stalinist ideological amalgam of the new Russia to play a dominant role in events. On the other hand, as examination of Tuva under Soviet rule will demonstrate, recognition of this very important element—nationalism—does not imply that the Bolshevik ideology played no more than second fiddle to a cynical imperialist policy.

The presence in Tuva from the early nineteenth century onwards of a large and permanent Russian settlement provides the first key to explanation of pre- and post-revolutionary Russian policy. This Slav immigration began as a mainly spontaneous and unofficial, sometimes even illegal, movement, but St. Petersburg finally decided to encourage such settlement, and this led to the establishment of a protectorate in 1914. The bulk of the Russian inhabitants were peasants, but some were engaged in trade and mining. Gold was first mined in Tuva in 1838, but did not develop impressively as an industry, apparently because of the prohibitive costs engendered by the problem of transport over vast distances and a shortage of labor. At first, during the Tsarist period, Chinese merchants controlled most Tuvan trade until challenged by the Russians, and this rivalry came to affect politics, since Russian trading firms called on their government for protection, sometimes with success. It was this established Russian community in Tuva

---

[6] For details of the proclamation of the Tsarist protectorate in 1914, as well as the background for comparing it with the Soviet annexation, see V. I. Dulov, *Sotsialno-ekonomicheskaya istoriya Tuvy (XIX - nachalo XX vv.)*, Moscow, 1956, esp. p. 502; I. J. Korostovets, *Von Ginggis Khan zur Sowjetrepublik*, Berlin, 1926, pp. 189–198; V. M. Iezuitov, *Ot Tuvy feodalnoy k Tuve sotsialisticheskoy*, Kyzyl, 1956, pp. 126–128; and *Istoriya Tuvy*, pp. 235–236.

which caused both the Tsarist and the Soviet governments to exclude the territory as a subject of any international negotiations to determine the status of Outer Mongolia, and to treat Tuva as separate from Mongolia. Tuva was regarded as a non-negotiable area, whereas the fate of Mongolia was submitted to at least some degree of international bargaining. This distinction was always clearly maintained by the Russians, even though obscured by the special interest in Outer Mongolia displayed by both Tsarist and Soviet Russia. Shortly before the revolution, negotiations with China to define the status of Mongolia culminated in the Russo-Chinese-Mongolian Tripartite Treaty of Kyakhta, signed in 1915, and as far as the Soviets were concerned, the matter was settled anew by the Yalta agreements of 1945, from which Tuva was excluded as a subject of negotiation by the pre-emptive annexation in the preceding year, thus banishing the danger of foreign interference.

The weakness and low international prestige of China was another common factor shaping both Russian and Soviet policy with regard to Tuva. Peking could exercise no effective authority in the region, thus providing the Russians with an excuse to "protect their citizens from native attacks and revolts." Russians were able to move in and out of Tuva with impunity without any effective border controls, and this tempted them to decide on annexation. But it was not until China proved incapable of maintaining law and order in the territory that Russia challenged Peking's claim to possession. Any such claim was opposed by Tsarist insistence that no connection, either ethnic or cultural, existed between Tuvans and Mongolians proper. This was also the attitude of the Soviets, and was, of course, traditionally designed to contain Chinese territorial pretensions. It conflicted, however, with the Pan-Mongol aspirations of many Tuvans and Mongols who wanted to unite, and fed the already existing anti-Russian sentiment provoked by the land-grabbing Slav settlers. Cossacks had to be sent into Tuva in 1912 and again in 1916 to protect Russian citizens and stop Tuvans and Mongols from joining forces. For the same reasons, Moscow dispatched Red Army cavalry in 1924 and made plain its determination to repeat such action at any time it considered necessary.[7]

Both Tsarist and Soviet Russia exerted diplomatic and other kinds of pressure on the Mongols to cease making appeals for Tuvans to join Mongolia, and they forced the Tuvans to turn a deaf ear to Mongolian blandishments. Yet when it came to seeking pretexts for establishing dominion over Tuva, both Tsarist and Soviet Russia cynically manipulated "spontaneous requests" from the Tuvans for integration and always

[7] Dulov, *op. cit.*, p. 467; Maenchen-Helfen, *op. cit.*, pp. 74, 149–150, 167.

pretended to act in full accord with the desires of the indigenous peoples, in defiance of opposition from many Tuvans and Mongols.

Perhaps to make it easier for the Chinese to accept Russian actions without obvious loss of face, and to avoid attracting unwelcome attention from the world at large, the protectorate was surreptitiously imposed in 1914 when war was raging (and remained generally unknown for many years), and the Soviet annexation occurred under cover of World War II, not becoming known in the West (at least publicly) until about two years later. The announcement made in the Soviet Union at the time appeared only in the local Tuvan newspaper published in the capital, Kyzyl (formerly Belotsarsk).[8]

Both the Tsarist protectorate and the Soviet annexation acted simply as a "legal" stamp on *de facto* situations; in no important way did they change the existing relationship between Tuva and Russia. Before and after the revolution, Chinese claims were denied, Tuva and Mongolia were differentiated despite strong native objections, and the Soviet authorities, like the Tsarist, sent troops into Tuva whenever Russian citizens appealed for protection. In fact, long before annexation, Tsarist and Soviet Russia maintained what amounted to an "extraterritorial administration" in Tuva for the benefit of the Russian community there, the Tuvans being dealt with separately.[9] Nevertheless, although the pre-1917 protectorate and the 1944 Soviet takeover were largely formalities, they gave a sudden impetus to Russian immigration, the flow of which rose from 2,100 in 1910 to 8,200 in 1916, and leapt from about 12,000 in 1944 to over 30,000 in 1950.

The main *difference* between Tsarist and Soviet policy in Tuva is, as mentioned above, that under Soviet rule the indigenous population is subjected to the impact of the Soviet "nationalities policy" which has so greatly affected all non-Russian national minorities in the Soviet Union. In an all-pervading and deliberate campaign to "sovietize" the population, the main instrument, or "organizational weapon," of Moscow has always been the Tuvan Communist Party, modeled on the Soviet Communist Party and carrying out the latter's program of nationalizing private property, collectivizing agriculture, and uprooting religion, thereby changing Tuvan society in a way never attempted by Imperial Russia. In the early Soviet

---

[8] *Tuvinskaya pravda*, November 2 and 7, 1944. Referred to in *Istoriya Tuvy*, footnote 14, p. 235, and footnote 16, p. 236; also in Iezuitov, *op. cit.*, footnote 1, p. 127. See T. Davletshin, "The Autonomous Republic of Tuva," *Studies on the Soviet Union*, New Series, Vol. V, No. 1, Munich, 1965, pp. 97–104.

[9] S. Shostakovich, "Politicheskiy stroy i mezhdunarodnopravovoye polozhenize Tannu-Tuvy v proshlom i nastoyashchem," *Sbornik trudov professorov Irkutskogo Gosudarstvennogo Universiteta*, Vol. XVI, No. 1, Irkutsk, 1929, p. 178.

period, Buryat Mongols or Altai Oirots (that is, native elements closely related to the Tuvans) were often recruited and trained as Comintern (Communist International) agents executing orders from Moscow, and, unlike the Tsar in World War I, Stalin raised a regular Tuvan army for use against Germany.

This specifically Soviet pattern was not imposed in Tuva until 1929, following almost a decade of rule basically similar to the Tsarist pattern. But from 1929 onwards Stalin began to treat Tuva, the Mongolian People's Republic, and also the Buryat Mongolian Autonomous Republic (ASSR) as "separate but equal." This was the formula applied to the whole Soviet Union, but it is significant that Moscow did not hesitate to pursue the same policy in Tuva (which was still a nominally independent country containing a substantial Russian population) as in the Buryat Mongolian Autonomous Soviet Socialist Republic—an integral part of the USSR—and in a nominally independent Mongolia which had no Russian population.

The radical sovietization policy in Tuva lasted from 1929 to 1933.[10] Its first manifestation was wholly in keeping with Stalin's determination to separate Tuva from Mongolia: Donduk, the ardent Pan-Mongolist leader of the Tuvan Communist Party, was replaced by Solchak Toka, a "new Soviet man" (born in 1901) trained in Moscow at the Communist University of Toilers of the East (KUTV),[11] upon whom Stalin could count to carry out his orders. Toka was Tuva's Choibalsan, and Choibalsan has often been called Mongolia's Stalin. Both he and Choibalsan had far more of a Soviet socialist education and training than did most Tuvans or Mongols, and, in fact, Toka was one of only ten persons eligible for the job of governing Tuva. This change of leadership brought in its train a major purge in Party and government, with other KUTV-trained Tuvans returning from the Soviet Union to fill posts. The same purge occurred in the Mongolian People's Republic, under the direction of Choibalsan and his supporters.

The new hard-liners in power launched an all-out attack on the Buddhist priesthood, as a prelude to sovietization of society. Out of twenty-five monasteries and some 4,000 lamas in 1929, only one monastery and fifteen

---

[10] Much of Maenchen-Helfen, *op. cit.*, deals with Tuva in the midst of this revolutionary change, but see especially pp. 7, 169, 170. Cf. Iezuitov, *op. cit.*, pp. 68–88; *Istoriya Tuvy*, pp. 129–156. See also William B. Ballis, "Soviet Russia's Asiatic Frontier Technique: Tannu Tuva," *Pacific Affairs*, Vancouver, Vol. XIV, March, 1941, pp. 91–96.

[11] This was an important center for training cadres for work in Asia. See Robert A. Rupen, *Mongols of the Twentieth Century*, Vol. I, Bloomington, Indiana, 1964, footnote 136, p. 222.

lamas remained in 1931. The assault on religion was accompanied by collectivization of livestock, which in 1929 embraced only one percent of herds, but which accounted for 45 percent two years later, and, as elsewhere in the Soviet Union, had entailed heavy loss of livestock. The reaction of the Tuvan population was immediate: rebellion flared up throughout the country, for which Soviet sources blame the Mongols living in areas adjacent to Tuva, incited by feudal and religious leaders fighting to retain their privileges. Then suddenly Stalin condemned these extreme policies as "left deviations," and in 1933 in Tuva, Mongolia—and throughout the USSR—a swing to a more conciliatory approach took place, although both Toka and Choibalsan remained firmly in the saddle.

Although the violence of the 1929–1933 sovietization drive in Tuva was not to be repeated, the leitmotif of Soviet policy—i. e., the resolve to prevent Tuvans and Mongolians from making common cause as one nation—was to remain unaltered to this day. To this end, Moscow opposed all manifestations of Pan-Mongolism, for a time a force to be reckoned with, and was unrelenting in its efforts to isolate Tuva from contagion by the movement. But this Soviet (and Tsarist) policy of artificially dividing Tuvans and Mongols ran counter to many facts pointing to the common identity of these peoples. Despite assertions to the contrary by Russian and Soviet authors and politicians, Tuvans and Mongols did in fact share a very similar culture, since both were nomads, lived in yurts and tents, herded livestock, and were bound by a whole range of customs and beliefs which connected areas lying far apart. As Maenchen-Helfen wrote in 1931:

> One would think it only natural for Tuvans to express friendship for neighboring Mongolia, for the Mongolia with which Tuva is culturally so very closely connected. For centuries Tuva was Mongolian territory; the Tuvans never thought of separating themselves from Mongolia. Both countries have the same kind of economy, the same religion. The official language in Tuva was and is Mongolian. Thus it is understandable that the Tuvans, after the collapse of foreign domination, first that of China and then that of Tsarist Russia, considered themselves as part of Mongolia, and the Mongols considered Tuva a Mongolian province.[12]

A major link was, of course, Buddhism, reinforced by a language which, if not identical, at least possessed many common features. Thus, Pan-Mongolism had some substance in the twentieth century, and Tuvans shared its stirrings and ambitions, choosing to follow Khalkha and Buryat leadership, and subscribing in many, if not all, cases to the goal of a unified Central Asian state. This dream was, when it arose in the early twentieth century, a national response to Manchu Chinese and Tsarist Russian pretensions and fed on the widespread antipathy towards both these

---

[12] Maenchen-Helfen, op. cit., p. 18.

powers. When the revolution of 1917 (following hard on the collapse of the Manchu dynasty) swept away Imperial Russia, Tuvans and Mongols hoped for an end to foreign influence and artificial separation. This was a deep-rooted aspiration, as is shown by the numerous anti-Russian demonstrations and revolts which had been occurring over a long period. Between 1917 and 1921 these factors came to a head. Tuvans, anxious to rid their land of both Russians and Chinese, sought to join the Autonomous Outer Mongolian Government in Urga, under the Jebtsun Damba Khutukhtu, but the goal failed because Russia (whether Tsarist or Bolshevik) intended to maintain control over the Russian colony in Tuva, at that time numbering some 8,000. Other historical factors were also at work to thwart Tuvan-Mongol unification. Both peoples were nomadic, with no fixed population concentration; were weakened by tribal feuds which stole energy needed for doing battle with more serious enemies; and contained separatist elements and rivalries which broke vital ethnic and cultural links. For example, shamanism fought Buddhism, corruption spoiled lamas, illiteracy weakened the unifying potential of the language, while the feudal features of the Manchu political hegemony magnified class and status, so that aristocratic privilege often made traitors of potential leaders. The path was smoothed for Moscow still further by the existence of some educated and skillful Buryat Mongol politicians who served the Comintern and the Soviet Communist Party, not, as did others, the cause of Pan-Mongolism. Indeed, to some extent the battle in this part of the world was one between Pan-Mongol and Communist Buryats, with most Tuvans and Khalkhas supporting the losers, i.e., the Pan-Mongolists.[13] Also, being both anti-Russian and anti-Chinese proved to be a luxury Tuvans and Mongols could ill afford, since a third alternative does not exist in Central Asia.

The whole intent behind Tsarist and Soviet treatment of Tuva has been determined by a desire to preserve a Russian settlement and checkmate Chinese ambitions in the area. This accounts for the longstanding Russian insistence on making a distinction between Tuva and Outer Mongolia, a distinction facilitated by the existence of a relatively large Russian population in Tuva and no comparable phenomenon in Outer Mongolia. Because of the Russian settlement factor, both Tsar and commissar have gone to considerable lengths to "prove" that native Tuvans are—in origin, language, and culture—Siberian- and Turkic-oriented rather than Mongol,

---

[13] Cf. Robert A. Rupen, "The Buryat Intelligentsia," *Far Eastern Quarterly*, Vol. XV, No. 3, May, 1956, pp. 383–398. A recent Soviet book by M. I. Golman, *Problemy noveyshey istorii MNR v burzhuaznoy istoriografii SShA*, Moscow, 1970, strongly attacks my views of the Buryats and Pan-Mongolism.

and that Tuva leans geographically to the Russian, not to the Mongolian side.[14]

No such claim could be advanced in the case of Outer Mongolia, where the Chinese presence was always larger and where Manchu control was tighter and more effective, quite apart from the fact that many more Chinese lived there. The Chinese continued to trade in the Mongolian People's Republic even after they had been completely excluded from Tuva.

The thesis that the native population of Tuva differs significantly from that of Mongolia has been a major feature of Russian and Soviet academic studies on the area.[15] It is claimed that the Tuvans are Turkic rather than Mongol; Siberian-tribal rather than Mongol; shamanist rather than Buddhist; mountain and forest dwellers rather than people of the steppe, that is, engaged in hunting as well as herding. And as a further argument it is alleged that Russian influence and russification went much farther much sooner in Tuva than in Mongolia.

There clearly exists some genuine basis for distinguishing Tuvans and Mongols; the former do display far greater Turkic influence, yet it is also true that western Mongols, the Oirots, differ from the predominant Khalkha Mongols in many of the same characteristics that differentiate Tuvans from Khalkhas. Also, some Tuvans are "very Mongol," while others are "very Turkic," so they could be described as constituting an ethnic and cultural bridge between Central Asian Turkic and Central Asian Mongol groups.

---

[14] The sentence in italics in the following quotation from Douglas Carruthers, *Unknown Mongolia*, Vol. I, London, 1913, p. 97, has appeared in practically every Russian and Soviet book dealing in any way with Tuva since 1913:

> This first view of the Upper Yenesei basin left a new impression on me. I realized that this region, although within the limits of the Chinese Empire, is essentially Siberian in character. It is an integral part of Siberia, its drainage flows to Siberia and the Arctic, the conditions (at least so far as we could see them in the northern part of it) as well as the climate, are Siberian rather than Mongolian.... *Physically, politically, and economically the basin should belong to Russia*, and not to Mongolia, and the inevitable absorption of this region by the Siberian element could easily be imagined. Nevertheless, at present the basin remains politically a part of Mongolia, thus showing how absolutely it is shut off and protected from Russian territory. As a result of certain topographical features this region comes more into contact with Mongolia than with Siberia; the influence of a western trade must, however, gradually overcome the natural difficulties of the barrier and eventually bring it into closer relationship with Siberia.

For geography, see, "Prirodnye usloviya Tuvinskoy A. O.," in *Trudy Tuvinskoy kompleksnoy ekspeditsii*, Vol. III, Moscow, 1957; M. M. Glazkov, *Yenisey —velikaya Sibirskaya reka*, Moscow, 1959, pp. 130–153; Werner Leimbach, *Landeskunde von Tuwa : Das Gebiet des Jenessei-Oberlaufes*, Gotha, 1936.

[15] An important work, and the basis for much of this discussion of Tuvans and Mongols, is L. P. Potapov, *Ocherki narodnogo byta Tuvintsev*, Moscow, 1969.

Although this hardly makes Tuvans more naturally suited than Mongols for inclusion within the USSR, both before 1917 and for much (not all) of the time after the revolution, Russians have opposed inclusion of Tuvans in indigenous movements of a Pan-Mongol nature, and forced them to "choose" to develop separately from Mongolia, in conformity with the Russian solution.

The fundamental difference between Tuvans and Mongols, according to Soviet scholars, lies in "forest" versus "steppe" characteristics. Tuvans were semi-nomadic rather than completely nomadic, and displayed more systematic population movements. Hunting was more fundamentally important to their economy and diet. To bolster their argument, Soviet authors dealing with Tuva tend to exaggerate the haphazardness, the frequency, and the range of Mongolian steppe nomadism, ignoring the fact that movement in the open steppe naturally differed from nomadism in mountain and forest areas. This basic difference was said to be reinforced by the considerable Turkic and Uighur influence, connecting Tuvans to Turkestan (Soviet Central Asia and Sinkiang) rather than to the Mongol world. This is true, if not overstressed, but it must be remembered that there were no Moslems in Tuva, and it was Islam which particularly marked Turkestan. Another influence which Soviet scholars allege to derive more from Siberia than from Mongolia was shamanism, and its survival until as late as the 1930's is used as another reason for distinguishing between Tuvans and Mongols. Shamanism is described as being a "Siberian" feature, linking Tuvans with Yakuts, Samoyeds, and others, whereas "Mongol" Buddhism was supposedly always weak and insignificant compared to shamanism. Tribal and clan identification is similarly said to have persisted much longer in Tuva than in Mongolia, and to have been more characteristic of Siberian than of Mongol peoples.

The Russian arguments can, however, equally be opposed by contrary ones showing what Tuvans and Mongols have in common. For example, Buddhism and recognition of the authority of the Jebtsun Damba Khutukhtu in Urga were a strong tradition in Tuva, and it is significant that the Bolshevik partisan commander, Shchetinkin, thought in 1919 that the Jebtsun Damba Khutukhtu could stop Tuvans from harrassing Russian colonists. Also, Toja Tuvans in the east of the country were practically indistinguishable from the Darkhat people near Lake Khubsugul in Outer Mongolia, and Tuvans in the south were very similar to Mongols around Lake Ubsa Nur in northern Outer Mongolia. The separatist Oirots of Outer Mongolia periodically detached their Kobdo District from Outer Mongolia, and in many ways resembled the majority of Tuvans more closely than the Khalkhas. Yet both before and after the revolution, Russians worked to

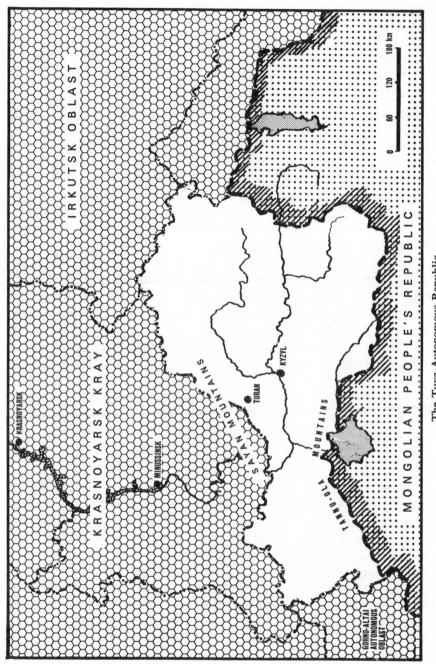

The Tuva Autonomous Republic

manipulate subjection of the Kobdo District and the Oirot Mongols to Urga and Ulan Bator, to include them in a Mongol state.

Compared to the argument that Tuvans are basically different from Mongols and therefore somehow closer to Russia than to Mongolia, the other Russian justification for distinguishing Tuvans from Mongols is more honest, if more difficult to reconcile with Soviet ideology—namely, that Tuvans are more russified.

Rivalry Between Russia and China

At this point it is of interest to examine more closely the traditional Russian-Chinese confrontation in the area, since Soviet policy with regard to Tuva has always been anti-Chinese and anti-Mongol, while in dealing with Outer Mongolia it has been solely anti-Chinese. The anti-Mongol aspect of Soviet Tuvan policy was only a derivation from the predominant concern to frustrate Chinese incursion. The historical evidence and the odds as they appeared in 1944 suggested to the Soviet government that China might play some sort of role in Outer Mongolia, and that if Tuva were connected to Mongolia, China might thereby operate in Tuva as well. This Moscow was determined to prevent.

The inability of Manchu officials to control the Tuvans even before 1911 predisposed the Russians not to consider Chinese sovereignty worth respecting, and strengthened their opinion that the border should in fact be the Tannu-Ola and not the Sayan Mountains. The facts were sufficiently ambiguous to permit this form of wishful self-deception.[16]

Another factor in Manchu vulnerability to the Russian challenge in Tuva was mining. The Soviet resumption of gold-mining in the Sayan Mountains revived an activity begun a hundred years earlier in 1838, and Russian mining of asbestos, begun in the 1890's, brought Russians into the heart of the territory. Climatic, transport, and labor-force problems made the

---

[16] George Kennan assumed in 1886 that Tuva was Mongolian, and not Russian: "The Soyots (Uryanghai, Tuvans)...live a nomadic life in the rugged mountainous region of the upper Yenesei *in northern Mongolia*...Safyanov carried on a trade *across the Mongolian frontier* with the Soyots...." (italics added), George Kennan, *Siberia and the Exile System*, Vol. II, London, 1891, pp. 393–397. The map in Julius Price, *From the Arctic Ocean to the Yellow Sea*, London, 1893, clearly includes Tuva as an integral part of Mongolia.

A very important and detailed discussion of the whole issue, including problems in the wording of the governing treaties, the border-markers on the ground, and many other considerations, appears in: G. E. Grumm-Grzhimailo, *Zapadnaya Mongoliya i Uryankhaiskiy Kray*, Vol. II, Leningrad, 1926, pp. 774–820; and Korostovets, *op. cit.*, pp. 189–198.

mining expensive and thus limited exploitation, but the Chinese carried on no such activity at all. The inability of the rulers in Peking to protect Russians from harassment and attacks by Tuvans forced Russians to protect themselves and call on their government for a change in the administration of Tuva. In his book (quoted above) Korostovets noted that when he spoke with officials in Peking in 1903, they were very poorly informed about conditions in Tuva, and certainly no important work of Chinese scholarship or any scientific expeditions resulted from the very long Manchu Chinese hegemony. In contrast, Russian scholarship and publications accompanied, and often preceded, colonial expansion and activity, and this knowledge sometimes meant power. The Chinese were in no position to resist, since they had no educational system operating in Tuva, nor was the Chinese language in wide use. Manchu prohibition of settlement by Chinese also limited the potential influence of their culture. Since Tuvans were not subject to military service, there was no cultural assimilation by that route. Thus, by 1910 permanent settlement in Tuva by 2,100 Russians, and no permanent settlement at all by Chinese, made the territory Manchu only in form while Russian in content. China's greatest potential advantage over the Russians—the vast number of its "surplus" peasants available for colonization, was never employed, and it is ironic that Russia used that very method of permanent settlement to detach territory from China: no Russian troops entered Tuva until 1912, after the Manchus fell, and no technology or military action had at any time to be deployed against China in the area.

The Manchu ban on permanent settlement by Chinese had the effect of holding the territory open for 150 years, until Russia was ready to move in. The object of the Manchus was to protect the northern nomads from being assimilated by Han Chinese, but the nomads became weak and defenseless, and put up little or no resistance when the Russians arrived on the scene. The Manchu settlement ban was not, however, able to prevent Chinese peasants from moving beyond the Great Wall into Inner Mongolia in the mid-nineteenth century, simply because Mongolia was more accessible than Tuva, which was separated from China by the vast Gobi Desert, all Outer Mongolia, and a mountain barrier. Its geographical position therefore made settlement by Chinese unlikely, and only a vigorous settlement program carried out consistently over a long period of time could have made the outcome any different. But Manchu enforcement of Tuvan isolation was more than token, as Carruthers found in 1910: "We were still within the bounds of the Uryanghai country, which is shut off apart, and kept as a reserve for the Uryanghai tribes; the reservation being so strict that no natives are allowed to pass out of it beyond the line of guardhouses, which decide the southern limit of the native territory on the south of the Tannu-Ola."[17]

To the Russians, on the other hand, the way to Tuva lay invitingly open, and there was unbroken, if often illegal, Russian peasant immigration from Minussinsk along the Yenesei River into Tuva. The Russian community of Turan was founded in 1885, at a time when no Chinese community existed in Tuva, and the 1,200 Russians already equaled the number of natives in the area in and around Turan, providing a nucleus from which further settlement could be based. Meanwhile, the Manchus continued to try to operate from Ulyasutai and Kobdo in Mongolia.

Russian expansion was vigorous, and stimulated by a Western dynamism which contrasted strongly with the passiveness and apathy of the natives and with the negativism of the Manchus. There were no Manchu or Chinese or Tuvan equivalents of a Safyanov, who organized Russian settlers in Tuva, urged new development, argued in the St. Petersburg corridors of power, influenced the press, and constituted a one-man lobby for Tuva. He unceasingly held that Tuva was a land for development, not a preserve, reservation, or museum, as it would remain if the Manchus had their way. By 1910, the Russian unofficial extraterritorial "government" in Tuva was probably larger and more effective than the official Manchu one, and Russian officials probably more active in Tuva than the Chinese, whose influence was exerted through a double screen: the Manchu Emperor was not a Han Chinese and frowned upon Han Chinese settlement north of the Great Wall; and the Manchu administrative system operated indirectly, through Tuvan and Mongol agents, whereas Russian control was more direct and straightforward.

In 1912 a crisis blew up: the Jebtsun Damba Khutukhtu and the Mongols in Urga wanted to include Tuva in their new state, whereupon the Russians insisted that Tuva could not join Mongolia, and sent Cossacks from Kobdo into Tuva to protect Russian colonists from Tuvan attacks. In the following year the Russians began to extend application of Russian law to Tuvans, and a statement by the Imperial Council of Ministers in 1913 put the Russian position as follows:

> Our recent recognition of the Autonomy of Mongolia, the placing of this land under the protectorate of Russia according to the Treaty of October 21, 1912 [Old Style] and the departure of Chinese officials not only from Mongolia but also from Uryanghai, puts the question of the relation of the Russian government towards the latter in a new light. The proclamation of the Republic in China and Mongolian independence, and the departure of the Chinese officials who had been responsible for Uryanghai from Ulyasutai,

---

[17] Carruthers, *op. cit.*, Vol. I, p. 188.

has as a consequence put an end to the dependence of Uryanghai on China; also, Khalkha [Outer Mongolia], now first entered into political life, cannot claim this land. Therefore, His Majesty suggests to Minister Sazonov that Russian policy concerning Uryanghai should take the direction of fixing this land in Russian interests.[18]

A year later, in 1914, the Russian government declared Tuva a protectorate, but in 1918, after the collapse of the tsarist regime, native Tuvans proclaimed their land independent. In fact, however, Tuva became the scene of a struggle between Chinese, White Russian, and Red Russian forces, with the Reds eventually winning out. Red Army units occupied the country, and Comintern agents of Russian, Buriat-Mongol, and Altai-Oirat origin, together with Tuvan "revolutionaries," set up a Soviet-dominated regime. In August, 1921, they proclaimed the formation of an allegedly independent "Tuvan People's Republic." Subsequently there came into being a "People's Revolutionary Party," while the Tuvan constitution was modeled after the Soviet constitution. Thus the Bolsheviks in effect restored the tsarist protectorate over Tuva. However, this did not prevent the Soviet government from issuing a declaration denouncing the tsarist protectorate and proclaiming support for an independent Tuva.[19]

From 1921 to 1926 it was unclear whether Tuva was independent or somehow connected with the Mongolian People's Republic. In May, 1924, the USSR in a treaty with China specifically acknowledged China's sovereignty over the Mongolian People's Republic, thereby abandoning the argument that only the former Manchu suzerainty, rather than Chinese territorial sovereignty, was involved. The Soviet Foreign Office diplomatic list of 1924 indicated the Russian official assigned to Kyzyl as coming under the Russian consulate in the Mongolian People's Republic, thereby suggesting that Tuva was considered as in some way subject or subordinate to the Mongolian People's Republic; and the 1925 list placed the Russian in Kyzyl under the Russian consulate in China. This is as far as recognition of a Tuva-Mongolian People's Republic connection, and China's sovereignty over both, seems to have gone. Late in 1924, the Soviet Commissar of Foreign Affairs, Chicherin, had, however, deprecated the significance of Russia's recognition of Chinese sovereignty over the Mongolian People's Republic,[20] and in the same year, Red Army cavalry invaded Tuva from Minussinsk to suppress a serious Tuvan revolt. In the light of this, no

---

[18] Korostovets, *op. cit.*, p. 196.

[19] X. J. Eudin and R. C. North (eds.), *Soviet Russia and the East, 1920–1927*, Stanford, 1957, pp. 258–259; Allen S. Whiting, *Soviet Policies in China, 1917–1924*, New York, 1954, pp. 171–172; Robert A. Rupen, *Mongols of the Twentieth Century*, Bloomington, Indiana, 1964, Vol. I, pp. 189–191.

[20] Anatoli D. Kallinikov, *Revolyutsionnaya Mongoliya*, Moscow, 1925, p. 95.

more can be said than that Soviet diplomatic from was conciliatory and even generous; and certainly contrasted with Soviet actions, which were tough, aggressive, and decisive. This aggressiveness became more marked in 1926 when a Tuva-Mongolian People's Republic Treaty in July presented Tuva as a fully equal and independent sovereign state, entirely separate from the Mongolian People's Republic. A Tuva-USSR Treaty a month later included provision for exchange of diplomatic representatives, and a Constitution of the Tuvan People's Republic was adopted and promulgated in November, 1926. The Soviet and Tuvan diplomatic representatives in Kyzyl and Moscow were given consular rank in 1926, made "provisional representatives" in 1928, and Ministers in 1929.[21]

In the face of the Soviet decision to keep a firm hold on Tuva the Chinese were powerless: Chiang Kai-shek stated that the incorporation of Tuva into the USSR was formally proclaimed only in a radio announcement on March 17, 1948; and on May 7, 1948, his Nationalist government protested that the annexation violated China's sovereignty, but the protest was ignored. Nationalist China continues to claim Tuva. For example, in delineating the boundaries of China, the *China Yearbook, 1957–1958*, published in Taipei, indicates: "The northernmost point is at Latitude 53°57′N in the Sayan Ridge region of Tannu Tuva."[22] The Russians can never be certain that the rulers of mainland China will not one day assert a claim. As Maenchen-Helfen wrote in 1930: "The Chinese still consider Tuva as part of Mongolia. As they showed in 1918. When will Chinese troops march into Kyzyl again? Russia reckons with a Five-Year-Plan, China with a Fifty-Year-Plan."[23] When Communist Chinese returned to the Mongolian People's Republic to a limited extent in 1953–1957, some echo might have developed in Tuva, but vigorous reassertion of Russian hegemony in Mongolia, the retirement of the Chinese, and the whole developing Sino-Soviet dispute ended any such possibility. Meanwhile the Russian population of Tuva has increased so much (now standing at over 80,000) that Tuva seems firmly anchored in the USSR on demographic grounds, as well as by annexation on paper.

---

[21] See *Godovoy otchet* of *Narodniy Komissariat po Inostrannym Delam* (for various years).

[22] See Chiang Kai-shek, *Soviet Russia in China*, New York, 1958, pp. 104–106, *China Year Book*, Taipei, 1958, p. 20. Cf. Francis Watson, *The Frontiers of China*. New York, 1966, pp. 44–45:

> Chinese Communists apparently accept this loss [of Tuva] but the claim is preserved in maps issued by the Chinese Nationalist Government in Taiwan. Despite the concession of Outer Mongolian independence extracted from Chiang Kai-shek by Stalin in 1945, the Chinese frontiers on these maps enclose Outer Mongolia as a province and Tannu Tuva as a division of it.

[23] Maenchen-Helfen, *op. cit.*, p. 170.

Conclusion

Time after time in the twentieth century, both Tsarist Russia and Soviet Russia have acted vigorously to separate Tuva from Outer Mongolia, and permanent Russian settlement in Tuva has been the principal basis of that separation. The USSR, by recently placing troops and advanced weapons in the Mongolian People's Republic, has made it clear that the Soviet Union's strategic frontier includes this country, but no Russian settlement of any importance has occurred in the Mongolian People's Republic. The *legal* frontier includes areas where Russians live in substantial number, and Tuva is one of those areas. The *strategic* frontier adds the "empty" buffer zone of the Mongolian People's Republic. The future of the Mongolian People's Republic is still negotiable; the future of Tuva is not. Settlement by Russians appears to have been far more important as a motive for annexation than any strategic role for Tuva in protecting the flank of Eastern Siberia—the strategic difference between a Russian border on the Sayan Mountains or at the Tannu-Ola has never been great, since Tuva is a geographical "Switzerland," not likely ever to become an invasion route. He who holds Tuva holds only Tuva. Soviet influence in the Mongolian People's Republic does not result from nor depend upon control of Tuva, since the Selenga Valley southwards to Ulan Bator from the Trans-Siberian Railroad at Ulan Ude is the main Soviet highway to Mongolia. But Moscow is never going to cede this territory to any other power.

The Takeover That Remained in Limbo:
The German Experience, 1918-1923

Werner T. Angress

On October 1, 1918, one month before the German Empire collapsed, Lenin wrote to Trotsky and Sverdlov: "The international revolution has come so close within the course of one week that we may count on its outbreak during the next few days. . . . We shall all stake our lives to help the German workers in expediting the revolution about to begin in Germany."[1] When that revolution did occur early in November, Lenin's high expectations were to be disappointed—a pattern that was to repeat itself until his death in January, 1924. Thereafter, Stalin's rise to power precluded any future Communist revolutions in Germany.

Yet, initially, events in Germany seemed to develop along classic revolutionary lines. The empire of William II collapsed just like that of Nicholas II nineteen months earlier. On November 9, 1918, Germany was proclaimed a republic, and workers' and soldiers' councils—vaguely patterned after the Russian soviets—emerged spontaneously; the following day a Provisional Government was formed by the two rival socialist parties, the Social Democratic Party (Majority Socialists, or SPD) and the Independent Social Democratic Party (Independents, or USPD). For the first time in history the German working class was in control of the government, the old order was apparently vanquished, and red flags flew from public buildings throughout the country.

Encouraging though the picture may have appeared from a distance, on closer inspection it proved to be deceptive. The German revolution, far from having been masterminded by dedicated professionals, came as a result of military defeat and the general war-weariness of a hungry, demoralized people. Triggered by a naval mutiny in Kiel and other northern ports, the revolution spread throughout the country within days, toppling thrones with astonishing ease. But its ideological appeal was weak. Peace, bread, and a return to secure and orderly conditions were the principal desires of the exhausted nation and the objectives to which the new government directed its immediate attention.[2]

---

[1] Hermann Weber, *Lenin in Selbstzeugnissen und Bilddokumenten*, Hamburg, 1970, p. 139.

[2] The literature on the German Revolution of 1918 is too extensive to permit even a selective listing. The following recent publications contain good

In approaching its far from easy task, the Provisional Government followed a political course designed to strengthen and consolidate the achievements of the revolution without frightening those segments of the population that had taken no part in it, notably the urban and rural middle class. This course also recommended itself because it would reassure the Allied victors that Germany was now a democratic state, eager to see order restored and maintained. For these reasons the government appointed a number of non-socialist ministers, secured the co-operation of the army's general staff and officer corps, retained the bulk of public officials, and refrained from introducing such radical measures as the expropriation of aristocratic landholders or the extensive socialization of basic industries. Considering itself a strictly transitional government, it intended to hold elections as soon as possible for a National Assembly that would be entrusted with concluding the peace and drafting a new constitution. Finally, it was determined to suppress all attempts by left-wing extremists to stir up violence and provoke disorders.

The government coalition of Majority Socialists and Independents represented a marriage of necessity. The Independents had been an integral part of the SPD until wartime frictions exacerbated previous ideological conflicts to the extent that the left center and extreme left wing of the SPD seceded in 1916 and founded their own organization, the USPD, the following spring.[3] Yet on November 10, 1918, the Majority Socialist leader Friedrich Ebert, who had become Chancellor the previous day, invited three leading Independents to join him and two fellow Majority Socialists in forming the Provisional Government. Ebert's decision was prompted by tactical considerations. He knew that most of the workers demanded such a coalition, and he also realized that unless the Independents were in the new government, they might be drawn into the extreme left wing of German labor, thereby enhancing the threat of civil war. While the Independents had serious misgivings, they finally accepted Ebert's offer, and until the coalition broke up at the end of December they worked more or

bibliographies: Francis L. Carsten, *Revolution in Central Europe, 1918–1919*, Berkeley and Los Angeles, 1972; Eberhard Kolb (ed.), *Vom Kaiserreich zur Weimarer Republik*, Neue Wissenschaftliche Bibliothek, 49, Geschichte, Cologne, 1972; A. J. Ryder, *The German Revolution of 1918 : A Study of German Socialism in War and Revolt*, Cambridge, England, 1967.

[3] The best account is Carl E. Schorske, *German Social Democracy 1905–1917 : The Development of the Great Schism*, Cambridge, Mass., 1955, especially chaps. x–xii.

less harmoniously with their Majority Socialist colleagues, even though the Majority Socialists tended to set the tone and dominate the proceedings.[4]

From the first day the Provisional Government had to work closely with the workers' and soldiers' councils, which had sprung up in the wake of the naval mutinies and had spread throughout the country, even to the front lines.[5] The councils regarded themselves as the temporary guardians of the revolution. Their main functions consisted in the exercise of local control, the assumption of police duties, and the supervision of transportation, communications, and distribution of food. Contrary to popular legend, only a minority of them had radical aims. Their social and political composition varied widely, especially in the case of the soldiers' councils, which often included men of middle-class background and occasionally even officers. In short, during the first two, crucial months of the revolution the councils "were not a class movement which wanted to impose a 'dictatorship of the proletariat,' but a popular movement [*Volksbewegung*] based primarily on workers and soldiers."[6] Although the government depended on the councils to perform certain functions, relations between the government and the councils were far from harmonious because it

---

[4] For a record of the Provisional Government's daily work and problems see the published minutes of its cabinet meetings: *Die Regierung der Volksbeauftragten 1918–19*, 2 vols., edited by Susanne Miller and Heinrich Potthoff, with an introduction by Erich Matthias, Quellen zur Geschichte des Parlamentarismus und der politischen Parteien, Erste Reihe: Von der konstitutionellen Monarchie zur parlamentarischen Republik, Düsseldorf, 1969.

[5] On the councils see Walter Tormin, *Zwischen Rätediktatur und sozialer Demokratie: Die Geschichte der Rätebewegung in der deutschen Revolution 1918–19*, Beiträge zur Geschichte des Parlamentarismus und der politischen Parteien, Vol. IV, Düsseldorf, 1954; Eberhard Kolb, *Die Arbeiterräte in der deutschen Innenpolitik, 1918–1919*, Beiträge zur Geschichte des Parlamentarismus und der politischen Parteien, Vol. XXIII, Düsseldorf, 1962; Peter von Oertzen, *Betriebsräte in der November-Revolution: Eine politikwissenschaftliche Untersuchung über Ideengehalt und Struktur der betrieblichen und wirtschaftlichen Arbeiterräte in der deutschen Revolution 1918–19*, Beiträge zur Geschichte des Parlamentarismus und der politischen Parteien, Vol. XXV, Düsseldorf, 1963; Reinhard Rürup, *Probleme der Revolution in Deutschland 1918–1919*, Wiesbaden, 1968; Dietrich Schneider and Rudolf Kuda, *Arbeiterräte in der Novemberrevolution: Ideen, Wirkungen, Dokumente*, Frankfort am Main, 1968. On the peasant councils see Heinrich Muth, "Die Entstehung der Bauern- und Landarbeiterräte im November 1918 und die Politik des Bundes der Landwirte," *Vierteljahreshefte für Zeitgeschichte*, XXI, No. 1, January, 1973, pp. 2–38.

[6] Eberhard Kolb, "Rätewirklichkeit und Räte-Ideologie in der deutschen Revolution von 1918–19," *Deutschland und die Russische Revolution*, Helmut Neubauer (ed.), Stuttgart-Berlin-Cologne-Mainz, 1968, p. 96.

remained unclear which had supreme authority. At the same time that the Provisional Government was formed on November 10, an Executive Council of Workers' and Soldiers' Councils was set up in Berlin, but the question of whether it was entitled to speak for and supervise all the councils on a nation-wide basis was left undecided. When as its first political act the Executive Council that day confirmed the Provisional Government in office, it also claimed supremacy over the new government and demanded the right to control it. Without openly disputing the claim of the Executive Council, the Provisional Government insisted on assuming all functions, powers, and responsibilities formerly held by the imperial government. This the Executive Council grudgingly conceded. Since the lines of authority remained blurred and since the Executive Council, although composed of an equal number of members of both parties, was as much dominated by Independent Socialists as the Provisional Government was by Majority Socialists, constant frictions were inevitable. These conflicts lasted until the middle of December, when a National Congress of German Workers' and Soldiers' Councils resolved the contest in favor of the Provisional Government by electing a Central Council composed exclusively of Majority Socialists.[7]

The main reason why Ebert and his two SPD colleagues wanted to curb the influence of the Executive Council was to prevent left-wing extremist factions from turning this body and the local councils into a force that would oppose the government and the Majority Socialists. Of the several radical factions, the most vocal and aggressive was the *Spartakusbund* (Spartacus League). This group had formed during World War I within the SPD, whose "social chauvinism" the Spartacists rejected. Initially known as "*Gruppe Internationale*" until they formally adopted the name Spartacus League on November 11, 1918, the members of the group, under the leadership of Rosa Luxemburg and Karl Liebknecht, spoke out against the war and circulated revolutionary propaganda. But the influence of the Spartacists remained slight, partly because most of the group's leaders, Luxemburg and Liebknecht included, spent the better part of the war in prison. When the SPD split, the Spartacists joined the Independent Social Democratic Party as its extreme left faction; in practice, however, they pursued their own political course under the protective roof of the new party. The outbreak of the revolution in Russia heightened the hopes of the Spartacists that Germany would soon follow the Russian example. Rosa Luxemburg welcomed the events in Russia from her prison cell, but

---

[7] *Die Regierung der Volksbeauftragten*, I, pp. xcii–cvii; Kolb, *Die Arbeiterräte*, pp. 114–137.

her admiration for the Bolsheviks was tempered by severe criticism of many of their political tactics. Impatient though they were, the Spartacists had to wait many months for the German revolution, and when it finally came, in November, 1918, they found it wanting.[8]

When the Provisional Government was formed by Majority Socialists and Independents, the Spartacists continued their customary oppositional stance, though this time in the hope that the masses would support them. Articles in a newly acquired newspaper, *Die Rote Fahne*, branded the revolution a half-measure, called the policies of the government timid, and accused its Majority Socialist members of betraying the workers and its three Independents of acting as lackeys to Ebert and his cohorts. But the brunt of the propaganda turned out by the Spartacists was directed against the promised elections for a National Assembly, which they fought with the slogan: "All power to the workers' and soldiers' councils!" It was the councils, so the argument ran, that could safeguard the German proletariat from renewed enslavement by the capitalists, whose property the government was so eager to protect from the workers—a theme that Rosa Luxemburg expounded in editorial after editorial.[9] Through ceaseless agitation of this kind the Spartacists tried to convince the workers that only by pushing the revolution further to the left could they create a state and a society in which labor would no longer be the victim of exploitation.

The unrestrained tenor of their propaganda, punctuated by sporadic acts of violence and looting on the part of overzealous and undisciplined members of the rank and file, earned the Spartacists an unsavory reputation. They were looked upon as prone to irresponsible extremism, not only by the middle class but also by the majority of the workers, for most Germans believed that the revolution had gone far enough, and they approved as much of the government's efforts to maintain law and order as they disapproved of the noisy Spartacist agitation. Unlike Russia, where the Kerensky government had established neither internal order nor peace, in Germany the Provisional Government took determined steps to secure both objectives. Thus the Spartacists were regarded as public enemies whose attempts to continue the revolution raised the specter of bolshevism,

---

[8] On the Spartacists before the founding of the KPD, see Kolb, *Die Arbeiterräte*, pp. 46–55, 138–157, and *passim*; Ossip K. Flechtheim, *Die KPD in der Weimarer Republik*, Offenbach am Main, 1948, pp. 1–36, reprinted, with an introduction by Hermann Weber, Frankfort am Main, 1969.

[9] A selection of these editorials is in *Rosa Luxemburg: Ausgewählte Reden und Schriften*, 2 vols., edited by the Marx-Engels-Lenin-Stalin-Institut beim ZK der SED, East Berlin, 1955, II, pp. 594–654.

which to the government and the nation alike was anathema. They were seen as a threat both to Germany's internal stability and to its relations with the victorious Entente. Desperately in need of American food and the lifting of the British blockade, and hoping to obtain more favorable peace terms if Germany presented an orderly and democratic profile, the Provisional Government was only too eager to demonstrate to the victors that it would suppress the threat of bolshevism at home and combat it abroad by rejecting Soviet diplomatic overtures. Throughout November, 1918, and beyond, the Bolshevik leaders repeatedly attempted to establish contact with Germany's "revolutionary" government, but the government treated these feelers "in a dilatory manner," refused to readmit the Soviet ambassador (who had been expelled shortly before the revolution broke out), and returned a token shipment of Russian grain.[10]

If the government's anti-Bolshevik posture was intended in part to impress the Allies, it was also prompted by genuine fears that the Spartacists, whom the government and many ordinary Germans associated with bolshevism, represented a real threat to the country. Exaggerated visions of the Spartacus League's numerical strength (recent estimates by historians vary between a few hundred and a few thousand)[11] and of the extent of its public appeal contributed to these fears. Nor was it generally known that Rosa Luxemburg was no blind admirer of Bolshevik political tactics. Her concept of revolution was both more humanitarian and democratic than Lenin's, whose "democratic centralism" she rejected as strongly as she did the Bolshevik practice of terror.[12] She did not approve of a tightly organized, conspiratorial organization—which goes far towards explaining the modicum of control that the Spartacist leaders were able to exercise over the many undisciplined elements of the membership—nor did she believe that a proletarian dictatorship should be imposed by a small revolutionary vanguard alone. Trusting in the political instincts of the masses, who would rise spontaneously once they recognized the proper moment to do so, she expected the Spartacists to prepare the masses for this step by showing them the road to revolution. Only when the masses were ready would the Spartacist vanguard assume the leadership and help them

---

[10] Arno J. Mayer, *Politics and Diplomacy of Peacemaking: Containment and Counterrevolution at Versailles, 1918–1919*, New York, 1967, pp. 229–252; *Die Regierung der Volksbeauftragten*, I, pp. 98–104.

[11] Tormin, *op. cit.*, p. 35, footnote 4; Kolb, *Die Arbeiterräte*, p. 47.

[12] Erich Matthias, "Die Rückwirkung der russischen Oktoberrevolution auf die deutsche Arbeiterbewegung," *Deutschland und die Russische Revolution*, p. 90. For Rosa Luxemburg's views and actions see J. P. Nettl, *Rosa Luxemburg*, London-New York-Toronto, 1966, Vol. II., chaps. xvi–xvii, and *passim*.

establish the proletarian state. In accordance with these views she thus emphasized the slogan "All power to the councils!" because it was the councils rather than the Spartacists themselves who would ultimately express the collective will of the revolutionary working class.[13] Under the circumstances her idealistic vision stood little chance of ever being realized. But the government and the public, exposed as they were to radical slogans, street demonstrations, and scattered acts of violence, came to view "Red Rosa" and her Spartacist "hordes" as harbingers of Bolshevik terror. Acting accordingly, the government treated the Spartacists as outlaws, repulsed Russian attempts to resume diplomatic relations, and adopted a negative attitude towards the councils, although these posed no real threat, as was demonstrated in mid-December by their National Congress, which overwhelmingly endorsed elections for a National Assembly to be held on January 19, 1919.

The isolation of the Spartacists was not relieved by their decision—taken against Rosa Luxemburg's advice—to leave the "protective roof" of the Independents in order to found the German Communist Party (KPD) during the closing days of 1918. The founding congress also failed to heed her warnings not to boycott the upcoming elections for the National Assembly, now that the councils had voted to hold them.[14] A few days later her advice was again ignored when the new party faced its first armed confrontation with the government. The so-called Spartacus Uprising, a misnomer that historians have perpetuated for decades, was not initiated by the KPD, which by itself could not have mobilized sufficient support for such a venture. On January 4, the Provisional Government, which had been composed exclusively of Majority Socialists since December 29, 1918, dismissed the police president of Berlin, an Independent. This step infuriated the Independents and also the Revolutionary Shop Stewards, another left-wing faction loosely connected with the Independents and consisting predominantly of Berlin metal workers. Enraged by the government's action, the two groups secured Communist support through Karl Liebknecht, who acted against the advice of Rosa Luxemburg by committing the KPD to a revolutionary proclamation which the three organizations published on January 6. The details of the ensuing disorders need not detain us here. Protest demonstrations turned into armed clashes in

[13] These ideas emerge clearly from her address to the Founding Congress of the KPD; see Hermann Weber (ed.), *Der Gründungsparteitag der KPD: Protokoll und Materialien*, Frankfort am Main and Vienna, 1969, pp. 172–201.

[14] *Ibid.*, pp. 88–135, describes the discussion and vote on the question. It should also be noted that Karl Radek attended the congress as an emissary of the Russian Bolshevik Party. His address to the congress is in *ibid.*, pp. 67–87.

the heart of the capital, and heavy fighting continued for several days, lasting until January 11, when government forces defeated the insurgents. Although Rosa Luxemburg considered the entire affair a grave mistake, she felt obligated to back it. Once again the slogan "All power to the councils!" reverberated through the streets of the city, and Rosa Luxemburg published incendiary editorials supporting a cause in which she did not believe. On January 15, 1919, four days after the uprising had been crushed, she and Karl Liebknecht were arrested and murdered by government troops.[15]

The January Uprising, rashly undertaken and doomed from the outset, reinforced the negative image that the public had formed about the Spartacists, now the German Communist Party. The Majority Socialists were particularly virulent in their criticism of the Communists, whom they depicted as the principal instigators of this bloody interlude. The adverse reputation which the KPD had acquired in the initial months of the revolution, now further blackened by the January debacle, was to haunt the Communists for the duration of the republican era. Subsequent revolutionary adventures in the course of the next few years—all of them equally futile and disastrous—kept public antagonism alive and erected a lasting barrier of distrust between the KPD and the rest of the German labor movement.

*

Small in numbers and suspect to the authorities, its functionaries subject to arbitrary arrest and its offices frequently raided by the police, the KPD faced a period of severe trials. After the loss of its two most prominent founders, the task of leading the young organization fell to Leo Jogiches, who had been a close personal friend of Rosa Luxemburg. When unrest developed early in 1919 in Bremen, Brunswick, and other cities, with radicalized workers' and soldiers' councils threatening armed resistance if the National Assembly should try to abolish the council system, the KPD was generally blamed for the disturbances. In fact the Party as such had not initiated the protests and did not control them, although local Communist groups generally supported them. A wave of strikes swept through the country in February and reached Berlin early in March.

---

[15] On the January Uprising see Eric Waldman, *The Spartacist Uprising of 1919 and the Crisis of the German Socialist Movement: A Study of the Relation of Political Theory and Party Practice*, Milwaukee, 1958; *Illustrierte Geschichte der deutschen Revolution*, various anonymous authors, Berlin, 1929, reprinted in Frankfort am Main, 1968, pp. 276–308; Kolb, *Die Arbeiterräte*, pp. 223-243; Ryder, *op. cit.*, pp. 200–307.

By March 5 looting, sporadic riots, and the proclamation of a general strike had exploded into fierce street battles in the center of the capital, where left-wing Independents, Revolutionary Shop Stewards, and Communists confronted government troops and police. Three days later, after the general strike had been called off, Leo Jogiches was arrested and killed "while trying to escape," and the KPD lost another experienced and capable leader.[16] Meanwhile, an event of fateful consequences for the KPD took place in Russia. As the German Communists were facing army and police units in Berlin, the Third (Communist) International or Comintern held its founding congress in Moscow.[17] Although this event had no immediate impact upon the battered German Party, the new organization soon came to exert an ever increasing influence on the affairs of German communism.

Early in March, shortly before the fighting erupted in Berlin, the Party had sent Eugen Leviné to Munich, where he was to assume command of the Bavarian Communist Party organization, which was in dire need of firm leadership. Ever since November 8, 1918, when the Independent Socialist Kurt Eisner had staged a bloodless coup, led the overthrow of the Wittelsbach dynasty, and proclaimed Bavaria a republic, that state had been beset by political and economic turmoil. Eisner had tried in vain to strike a balance between the objectives of the Anarchists, Communists, and left-wing Independents, who wanted Bavaria to be governed by the councils, and the objectives of the bulk of the Majority Socialists and middle-class parties, who favored early elections for a new Diet and the establishment of parliamentary democracy. On February 21, 1919, the day when the newly elected Diet was to hold its opening session, Eisner was assassinated by a young nationalist while walking to the parliament building, where he intended to announce his resignation as Minister President.

When Leviné arrived in Munich on March 5, a Central Council of all Bavarian Workers', Soldiers', and Peasants' Councils was acting as an interim government. On March 8, after a number of turbulent debates, the Central Council agreed to convene the Diet for one session in order to allow the election of a new Bavarian government. The election took place on March 17, and Johannes Hoffmann, a Majority Socialist, formed a coalition government with middle-class participation. This outcome met

---

[16] *Illustrierte Geschichte, op. cit.,* pp. 357–367.

[17] Günther Nollau, *Die Internationale: Wurzeln und Erscheinungsformen des proletarischen Internationalismus,* Cologne, 1959, pp. 47–50; *Der I. Kongress der Kommunistischen Internationale: Protokoll der Verhandlungen in Moskau vom 2. bis zum 19. März 1919,* Hamburg, 1919.

with immediate opposition from the Anarchists, Communists, and left-wing Independents, who clamored for a government by the councils rather than by the parliament. To forestall any possible obstruction, the Hoffmann government announced on April 3 that the Diet would reconvene on April 8 and then took the precautionary step of leaving radicalized Munich for the more serene city of Bamberg. But on April 7, the day before the Diet was to meet, a group of politically inexperienced Anarchists and a few Independents, most of them intellectuals, proclaimed Bavaria a Soviet Republic. The domain of the republic, as it turned out, remained largely restricted to the triangle bounded by Augsburg, Rosenheim, and Garmisch. This theatrical coup, partly inspired by Bela Kun's recently established Hungarian Soviet Republic, provoked plans for armed intervention from Berlin, which recognized Hoffmann's government alone as legitimate. While preparations for intervention were under way, the new Bavarian "Soviet regime" employed its collective talents in trying to reform society.[18] In these attempts it was gravely handicapped by its narrow base of popular support. The members of the Munich branch of the Majority Socialists, initially at least half-hearted backers of the coup, had repudiated it at the last minute, and the Communists had refused their co-operation from the outset. Since his arrival in Munich, Leviné had worked hard to revitalize, reorganize, and strengthen the local Party organization, and he was not prepared to join a government that the Communists regarded with disdain and in which they would have been forced to share power. The most that Leviné was willing to concede *after* April 7 was his readiness to defend the regime against outside intervention. Calling the coup a farce and the new state a "pseudo-Soviet Republic" (*Schein-Räterepublik*), the Communists decided to bide their time.[19]

The power and the glory of the First Bavarian Soviet Republic lasted six days. During the night of April 12, the Hoffmann government launched a counter-coup against Munich from Bamberg. It failed, but during the ensuing skirmishes, which lasted through April 13, the Communists exploited the confusion to seize power in their own right. In authorizing

---

[18] The best study of the events in Bavaria is Allan Mitchell, *Revolution in Bavaria, 1918–1919: The Eisner Regime and the Soviet Republic*, Princeton, 1965. See also Karl Bosl (ed.), *Bayern im Umbruch: Die Revolution von 1918, ihre Voraussetzungen, ihr Verlauf und ihre Folgen*, Munich and Vienna, 1969; Tankred Dorst and Helmut Neubauer (eds.), *Die Münchner Räterepublik: Zeugnis und Kommentar*, Frankfort am Main, 1966; and *Revolution und Räterepublik in München 1918–19 in Augenzeugenberichten*, edited by Gerhard Schmolze, with an introduction by Eberhard Kolb, Düsseldorf, 1969.

[19] Mitchell, *op. cit.*, pp. 309, 311–314.

this step, Leviné flagrantly violated instructions from the new chairman of the KPD *Zentrale* in Berlin, Paul Levi.[20] Levi knew—as did Leviné, for that matter—that any radical left-wing regime in Bavaria could not last because of the precarious economic conditions and the certainty of armed intervention by the central government in Berlin. Why, then, did Leviné disobey orders? Why did he permit the Communist seizure of power in the face of what he himself had earlier admitted was a hopeless situation?[21] At his subsequent trial for high treason Leviné stated that while the Communists had not created the chaos to which they fell heir, those responsible—their predecessors—had either been arrested by Hoffmann's raiders on April 13 or else had fled. Anticipating the threat of even more formidable armed intervention, Leviné considered it his duty to provide leadership for the Munich proletariat in its hour of danger and need.[22]

We cannot dwell here on the details of the following two weeks—the life span of the Second Bavarian Soviet Republic. No longer a "pseudo"-regime, it was firmly in the hands of the local Communist organization, which acted independently of the Party *Zentrale* in Berlin and—all claims to

---

[20] *Ibid.*, pp. 308, 319. See also Helmut Gruber, *International Communism in the Era of Lenin: A Documentary History*, Greenwich, Conn., 1967, pp. 170–184. The *Zentrale* consisted of about a dozen or so of the most prominent leaders of the Party, who were elected at each Party Congress. It provided political and ideological guidance and co-ordinated Party activities. The members of the *Zentrale*, as a body, shared all responsibility for Party policy, but it became customary to recognize one member, with the title of Chairman, as the principal leader.

The *Zentrale* must not be confused with the Central Committee (*Zentralausschuss*), composed of delegates from each of the Party's twenty-eight districts, which met with the *Zentrale* when major decisions had to be made and also served as a control agency over the *Zentrale*. To further complicate matters, the term *Zentrale* was replaced by *Zentralkomitee* in the fall of 1925. For more details see Werner T. Angress, *Stillborn Revolution: The Communist Bid for Power in Germany, 1921–1923*, Princeton, 1963, pp. 27–29.

[21] Mitchell, *op. cit.*, p. 309.

[22] Werner T. Angress, "Juden im politischen Leben der Revolutionszeit," *Deutsches Judentum in Krieg und Revolution 1916–1923*, Schriftenreihe Wissenschaftlicher Abhandlungen des Leo Baeck Instituts, 25, Tübingen, 1971, p. 291, including footnote 648; Rosa Meyer-Leviné, *Leviné: Leben und Tod eines Revolutionärs*, Munich, 1972, pp. 262–273 (Leviné's address to the court). To his wife, Leviné stated an additional reason shortly before the battle collapsed. Surrender without resistance, he said, would not change the fate of the fighting Munich proletariat and would not avoid bloodshed. But resistance would heighten the self-respect of the workers and would be the only way to compel the "Whites" to be lenient. *Ibid.*, pp. 181–184.

the contrary notwithstanding—of Moscow as well. Although a few tele-
grams were exchanged between Munich and Moscow via Hungary, "the
Comintern had almost no useful information, not to mention control, of
the soviet regime in Bavaria—no more knowledge than the Bavarian Communists had of actual conditions or Bolshevik tactics in Russia."[23] But
to the government in Berlin it mattered little whether the Bavarian "Reds"
acted independently or on Lenin's orders. Working hand in hand with
Hoffmann's government, Berlin dispatched troops to the Communist-held
region and gradually tightened the noose around Munich. The fighting
lasted for nearly two weeks, though the outcome was never in doubt.
When the Communists were compelled to resign on April 27 over a major
quarrel with the Independents, Munich's "Red Army" command, headed
by a revolutionary sailor, Rudolf Egelhofer, continued to defend the city.
But it was a last-ditch stand. On May 1 government forces entered Munich
and established a reign of terror that proved to be infinitely more bloody
than Leviné's alleged "Red Terror," which had frightened the middle
classes more by threats and the confiscation of arms, food, and homes than
by actual atrocities. The only major act of violence had been the shooting
of ten bourgeois hostages shortly before the conquest of Munich by the
"Whites," a measure ordered not by the Communists but by Egelhofer.
Nevertheless, the Second Bavarian Soviet Republic, which in the popular
mind soon fused with the First and even with Eisner's regime, left a legacy
of bitterness in the country as a whole and in Bavaria in particular. The
fact that Leviné had acted against the instructions from the Party *Zentrale*
was unknown to the public, nor would such knowledge have made any
difference. To the average citizen, the Communists had again demonstrated that they were indeed Bolsheviks. Had they not been led by Russians,
and Russian Jews at that?[24] Were not Russia and Hungary in the hands of
Bolshevik Jews? Thus the already formidable antagonism towards the
KPD grew even stronger, widened the rift between the majority of workers
and the Communists, and created a right-wing backlash in Bavaria that
ultimately benefited Hitler's Nazis.

Not until two years later did German communism become involved
in another revolutionary insurrection. In the intervening period, two
closely related developments affected its fortunes—the increasing intervention of the Comintern in the affairs of the German labor movement and
the growth of the KPD to mass-party status.

---

[23] Mitchell, *op. cit.*, p. 312.

[24] On this issue see Angress, "Juden...," *op. cit.*, pp. 253, 287–289, 297–299,
and *passim*.

When the founding congress of the Communist International met in March, 1919, the German delegate arrived with instructions, issued by Rosa Luxemburg before her death, to vote against the creation of this organization. As mentioned previously, Luxemburg respected the Bolsheviks, but she was exceedingly wary of many of their tactics, and she did not want to see the young KPD become a tool of Russian domestic and foreign interests. Once he was in Moscow, however, the delegate was persuaded to abstain rather than cast a negative vote, and after his return to Germany the KPD became the first Communist Party outside Russia to affiliate with the Comintern.[25] A year later, at the Second Congress of the Comintern, Lenin and his colleagues confronted the assembled delegations with a scheme whereby they "sought to promote the organization of truly Communist parties resting on a mass basis drawn from other left-wing parties by excluding their leaders."[26] To make it impossible for politically unreliable elements to join a member Communist Party and thereby the Comintern, the Bolsheviks formulated the famous "Twenty-one Conditions" for the admission of new members. These conditions were drafted in such a way as to prevent undesirable segments of any labor party, especially their "traitorous" leaders, from joining the Communist camp. Thus the Bolsheviks aimed at splitting potential member parties in order to attract their revolutionary rank and file. The logical party in Germany to raid in this manner was the Independents, whose left wing was restive and resented the "reformist" bent of the Party's leadership. The scheme succeeded when the Independents split in October, 1920, and the left-wing secessionists joined the Communist Party in December. After the influx of these defectors, the KPD emerged as a mass party with roughly 350,000 members.[27]

Party Chairman Levi was well aware that in spite of this growth the KPD was still an isolated minority within the German labor movement. It was small compared with the Majority Socialists, who boasted 1,180,000 members, and it was inferior to the Independents, who still had about 450,000 members after they lost 300,000 to the Communists.[28]

---

[25] Jane Degras (ed.), *The Communist International 1919–1943: Documents*, London-New York-Toronto, 1956, Vol. I, p. 16; Flechtheim, *op. cit.*, p. 57; Nollau, *op. cit.*, p. 48; Gruber, *op. cit.*, pp. 86–89; Herman Weber (ed.), *Der deutsche Kommunismus: Dokumente*, Cologne-Berlin, 1963, pp. 198–201.

[26] Gruber, *op. cit.*, p. 277.

[27] Flechtheim, *op. cit.*, pp. 67–71; Eugen Prager, *Geschichte der USPD*, Berlin, 1921, pp. 191–226. For a discussion of the membership figures see Angress, *Stillborn Revolution*, p. 72, footnote 73.

[28] Tormin, *op. cit.*, p. 115, footnote 3.

Moreover, the Party needed a new image if it wanted to exert influence on the domestic scene and attract additional new members—an essential prerequisite for any serious bid for power in the future. Levi's views conformed closely to the teachings of Rosa Luxemburg, whose disciple he had been for many years. Thus on January 8, 1921, he published an "Open Letter" in *Die Rote Fahne* to both socialist parties and to the labor unions, inviting them to submit a joint set of demands to the government for specific political and economic concessions designed to benefit all German workers. The letter, which had the blessings of the Comintern's German expert, Karl Radek, did not receive a favorable response. But although the Communist offer was rejected, a first step had been taken to bridge the gulf separating the Party from the rest of German labor, and it foreshadowed—if not initiated—the future United Front policy. For Levi had already sensed in the summer of 1919 that the revolutionary wave in Europe was ebbing. Prompted by this realization, and convinced that winning the trust and respect of the non-Communist workers should be the KPD's main objective for the immediate future, Levi was determined to prevent the Party from engaging in any further reckless adventures. He had demonstrated this determination in October, 1919, when he forced the most irresponsible ultra-left extremists out of the Party.[29]

To what extent Levi might have been able to impose such a moderate course upon a party that had just been swamped by radical newcomers will never be known, because by the end of February, 1921, he was no longer chairman of the *Zentrale*. A serious clash with the Comintern over questions affecting not the German but the Italian Communist Party led to a factional struggle within the KPD leadership, and Levi resigned.[30] His place was taken by Heinrich Brandler, who, like Levi, was a former Spartacist, but who, unlike the intellectual Frankfort lawyer, was of genuine working-class background. Among the many problems that Brandler inherited from his predecessor was the question of the KPD's political role in Germany, which since June, 1920, had been ruled by an exclusively middle-class party

---

[29] Charlotte Beradt, *Paul Levi: Ein demokratischer Sozialist in der Weimarer Republik*, Frankfort am Main, 1969, pp. 32–34; Richard Lowenthal, "The Bolshevization of the Spartacus League," *International Communism*, St. Antony's Papers No. 9, edited by David Footman, London, 1960, pp. 30–31. The best account of the *KAPD*, the party formed by the seceding members, is Hans-Manfred Bock, *Syndikalismus und Linkskommunismus von 1918–1923: Zur Geschichte und Soziologie der Freien Arbeiter-Union Deutschlands (Syndikalisten), der Allgemeinen Arbeiter-Union Deutschlands und der Kommunistischen Arbeiter-Partei Deutschlands*, Meisenheim am Glan, 1969, pp. 225–287, and *passim*.

[30] An excellent concise summary, with documents, is in Gruber, *op. cit.*, pp. 280–312.

government. Before long, pressure was put on the Brandler *Zentrale* to follow a bolder political course than Levi had been willing to steer.[31] This pressure came mostly from two quarters—a vocal and ambitious left-wing oppositional faction centered around the Party's Berlin organization and the recently acquired left wing of the Independents. While neither of these groups had any definite plan in mind, both wanted the KPD to demonstrate that it was indeed a revolutionary party that would lead the German proletariat to victory at the first opportunity. Faced by these demands, the new *Zentrale* set out to look for trouble spots that might offer the Communists a chance to take the offensive. The trouble spot they eventually hit upon was the bitter diplomatic struggle between Germany and the Western powers over the question of reparations. This conflict the KPD leaders regarded as explosive; should it blow up, the coveted opportunity for action would be at hand. On March 4, 1921, the Party published an exaggerated report in *Die Rote Fahne* on the international political crisis and called on the workers to demonstrate in the streets, to march in protest against "the dual yoke of foreign and German exploiters," and to demand that the German government conclude a military alliance with Soviet Russia.[32]

The appeal proved to be only a futile exercise in revolutionary rhetoric, but the Party received unexpected "aid" from Moscow. At the beginning of the month, Bela Kun, a functionary of the Comintern since the collapse of the Hungarian Soviet Republic, arrived in Berlin with two fellow emissaries. Although the exact circumstances that led to Kun's mission may never be fully known, the evidence suggests that the plan to "activate" the German Party did not originate at the top level of the Bolshevik hierarchy (i.e., with Lenin or Trotsky)[33] but within the "Little Bureau" of the Executive Committee of the Communist International (ECCI), which, besides Kun, included Grigorii Zinoviev (the Chairman of the Comintern), Karl Radek, and Nikolai Bukharin. Just when Lenin was about to concede that after years of internal upheaval and foreign intervention Russia needed a breathing space, these men still clung to the theory of the world-wide revolutionary offensive, which Bukharin, in particular, propounded in the Comintern press. Convinced that a revolution in Europe would improve Russia's position, they singled out Germany for a Communist rising,

---

[31] The following discussion of the origins, course, and consequences of the March uprising of 1921 is drawn largely from Lowenthal, *op. cit.*, pp. 48–64 and Angress, *Stillborn Revolution*, chaps. iv–vi.

[32] *Die Rote Fahne*, Berlin, No. 105, March 4, 1921.

[33] This is evident from their subsequent reaction at the Third Comintern Congress. For details see Angress, *Stillborn Revolution*, pp. 175–196.

hoping to bring down that country's bourgeois government, to force the succeeding one—whatever its composition—to conclude an alliance with Russia, and incidentally to purge the KPD of those "opportunists" who still supported Levi. Finally, they thought that even a partial success would be a feather in the cap of the Comintern—a powerful argument at least for Zinoviev.[34]

While it is unlikely that Kun was given precise instructions on how to proceed once he reached Berlin, his proverbial revolutionary zeal offered substantial assurance that he would prod the German Communists into action. And Kun lived up to his reputation. He told the *Zentrale* that the Party must take the offensive and demand that the German government form an alliance with Soviet Russia; since the existing government was not likely to oblige, it would have to be overthrown.[35] On March 16 and 17, the matter was debated by a joint session of the *Zentrale* and the Central Committee (*Zentralausschuss*), bringing together delegates from each of the Party's twenty-eight districts. Brandler, well briefed by Kun, who prudently did not attend the meeting, spoke about international tensions and the various counter-revolutionary stratagems in Bavaria and other parts of the country. The situation, he said, clearly called for Communist action. As the combination of international crisis and Communist propaganda was bound to foment widespread unrest, possibly even violence, the KPD would press for a German alliance with Soviet Russia and demand the overthrow of the government. Brandler was confident that these steps would precipitate armed struggles. But in view of the approaching Easter week, which was deemed an unsuitable time for mobilizing workers and calling strikes, action would have to be postponed until the holiday period was over. After a lively discussion, Brandler's proposal carried the day. Yet, before the meeting adjourned, news arrived of an impending police occupation of Germany's central industrial region. Specifically, in the Prussian province of Saxony the Majority Socialist *Oberpräsident* (Governor), Otto Hörsing, had decided to suppress recurring wildcat strikes, thefts, robberies, and other acts of violence.[36] The news confronted the Party leaders with a predicament: the situation in Central Germany looked eminently suitable for unleashing a revolutionary action, but, with Easter

---

[34] Lowenthal, *op. cit.*, pp. 48 (including footnote 85), 49, 57–58, 62–63, and *passim*.

[35] *Ibid.*, p. 59; for a discussion of Kun's role, see Angress, *Stillborn Revolution*, pp. 121–122 ff., including footnotes 42 and 43.

[36] The appeal is reprinted in Peter Wulf (ed.), *Das Kabinett Fehrenbach, 25. Juni 1920 bis 4. Mai 1921*, Akten der Reichskanzlei, Weimarer Republik, Boppard am Rhein, 1972, pp. 584–585.

week coming, the timing for such an action was decidedly unfavorable. The original plan to postpone any action until after Easter Monday was upheld but not for long. All indications as to why the postponement was not adhered to point to Kun, whose argument that this favorable opportunity must be exploited convinced Brandler and most of the other members of the *Zentrale* to change their minds. Whatever the precise circumstances may have been, with the evening edition of March 17 the tone in *Die Rote Fahne* became so aggressive that it amounted to a declaration of war on the government evoking the impression of a party bent on revolution.

During the following days, Communist propaganda grew progressively shriller. However, in the Mansfeld mining district the local workers—mostly miners—did not respond at first to the Communist appeals, in spite of the fact that on March 19 two police contingents had begun the occupation of that region. On Monday, March 21, the Mansfeld organization of the KPD distributed leaflets calling for a general strike in the entire region, but the response was disappointing. Only in the occupied Mansfeld district was the strike appeal moderately effective; elsewhere in the region work continued. Vexed by this setback, the *Zentrale* sent a functionary to Halle to try to persuade the unenthusiastic Party organization in the city to provoke the workers to act, suggesting among other schemes that they dynamite a consumers' co-operative and then put the blame on the police. But the few attempts at sabotage miscarried, and most of the workers in the region still did not rise against the police or follow the example of the striking Mansfeld miners. In the end, it was not the KPD that sparked the fighting—though not for lack of trying—but a notorious revolutionary maverick, Max Hoelz, who was loosely affiliated with a rival Communist organization, the German Communist Workers' Party (KAPD), which had been formed by the left-wing extremists eased out of the KPD by Levi in October, 1919.[37] Taking orders from nobody, but inspiring many of the workers who admired his previous revolutionary exploits, Hoelz succeeded where the KPD had failed. On March 23, the local strike movement turned into an armed insurrection that affected the entire region.

Now that the pot was boiling in Central Germany, on March 24—the Thursday before Easter—the *Zentrale* in Berlin, still coached by Kun and his companions, called for a nation-wide general strike and urged the workers to seize arms, organize themselves, and join the battle against the counter-revolution.[38] At first the prospects looked promising. In the Leuna

---

[37] See above, footnote 29.

[38] *Die Rote Fahne*, Berlin, No. 140, March 24, 1921, as quoted in Marx-Engels-Lenin-Stalin-Institut, *Märzkämpfe 1921*, East Berlin, 1956, pp. 138–141. (This issue was missing from the microfilmed set consulted).

Works, the largest industrial complex in Central Germany, the workers had heeded a regional strike proclamation the previous day and were readying the plant for defense. At the same time the dockers in Hamburg went on strike and demonstrated against the actions of the police in Central Germany, thereby compelling Reich President Ebert to place Hamburg under a state of siege. Strikes, riots, and demonstrations also hit the Rhineland, notably the Ruhr region, where Communist agitation proved to be temporarily effective.

And yet, the nation-wide uprising never materialized. Wherever the Communists were reasonably well represented and organized they scored local successes, but elsewhere—especially in the southern and eastern parts of the country—they failed. The general strike did not spread beyond the few insurgent areas, and even in these it remained sporadic. Factory owners frequently retaliated against striking Communist workers by dismissing them from their jobs. Even in embattled Central Germany the movement suffered from poor leadership and co-ordination, which were exacerbated by constant friction between the KPD and the KAPD. Hoelz meanwhile fought his own battles and co-operated, if at all, only with the KAPD, whose anarcho-syndicalist inclinations he shared. But even he could not prevent ultimate defeat. The great majority of German labor remained aloof, and the government in Berlin did not have to commit the army to action. Except for the loan of an army artillery detachment, which shelled the Leuna Works into submission on March 29, the entire uprising was dealt with by the Prussian police. Hamburg was pacified on the same day, work in the Rhineland was resumed on March 30, and the *Zentrale* had to admit on April 1 that the insurrection was collapsing everywhere. It called off the general strike, and the March Uprising was over.

What had been accomplished? As far as Kun and his mentors in the Comintern's Little Bureau were concerned, they had gambled and lost. If they had hoped that a Communist insurrection might, among other things, force Germany to establish closer relations with Soviet Russia, they had miscalculated.[39] When the two countries did resume diplomatic relations in 1922 at Rapallo, common interest rather than political blackmail was responsible for the rapprochement; nor was it the Comintern that concluded this agreement, but the Russian foreign office. A secondary motive for the insurrection, the purge of the KPD's "right" wing, proved to be more successful, at least for the time being, as Levi was soon expelled from the Party, and most of the other adherents of the Luxemburg tradition of

---

[39] See above, including footnote 34.

independence from Moscow either shared his fate or lost their posts as functionaries.

The immediate effects on the KPD were dismal. Its leadership was split into those who defended the insurrection, which had cost the lives of 145 workers, and those who condemned it as an irresponsible *Putsch*. Aside from Paul Levi, who had publicly criticized the *Zentrale* immediately after the collapse of the uprising[40] and was expelled from the Party for doing so, a number of other leading functionaries, including the venerable Clara Zetkin, shared Levi's sentiments, though not his fate. Roughly 4,000 insurgents were sentenced to long prison terms, Brandler among them, and the Party's membership dropped sharply. When the KPD sent a delegation to Russia in June, 1921, to attend the Third World Congress of the Comintern,[41] its members were deeply divided on how to interpret the recent fiasco. It fell to the Bolshevik leaders to sort out the pieces and restore some semblance of unity to the German Party. Lenin's approach was unequivocal in tone and content. While commending the German workers for their valor, he roundly condemned the Party leadership for having resorted to "putschism," and although he upheld Levi's expulsion for violating Party discipline, Lenin used most of Levi's arguments to chastise the KPD leaders. In the context of Russia's termination of War Communism, the inauguration of the New Economic Policy, and efforts to secure diplomatic recognition and trade treaties in the West, Lenin's position was entirely logical. The part played by Zinoviev, Kun, and company in the uprising was never alluded to, lest it embarrass the Comintern and the Bolshevik leadership. At the sessions of the Congress, Kun remained silent, Zinoviev avoided dangerous subjects, and the ever-flexible Radek, a recent convert to Lenin's viewpoint, condemned the KPD's "wrong" tactics. By far the bluntest speech was delivered by Trotsky, who, in the process of criticizing the March Uprising, stunned his audience by informing them that the world revolution was not just around the corner but still a long way off. The upshot of the Congress was the assignment of a new task to all sections of the Comintern, embodied in the slogan: "To the masses!" The Comintern decreed that while awaiting the return of conditions favorable for world revolution, all Communist Parties were to seek closer contacts with non-Communist

---

[40] The two pamphlets in question were Paul Levi, *Unser Weg: Wider den Putschismus*, 2nd ed., Berlin, 1921, and *Was ist das Verbrechen? Die Märzaktion oder die Kritik daran? Rede auf der Sitzung des Zentralausschusses der V.K.P.D. am 4. Mai 1921*, Berlin, 1921. See also Gruber, *op. cit.*, pp. 313–358, and Beradt, *op. cit.*, pp. 47–60.

[41] For details see *Protokoll des III. Kongresses der Kommunistischen Internationale, Moskau, 22. Juni bis 12. Juli 1921*, Hamburg, 1921, *passim*.

labor and co-operate in the pursuit of common goals, thereby demonstrating to the masses that communism was their best friend. Meanwhile, the red flag of insurrection was to be stored away in moth balls.

*

For the next two years, German communism faithfully pursued the new course, which came to be known as the "United Front policy."[42] The inception of this new course in Germany had in fact preceded the Comintern decision, since Levi's "Open Letter" of January, 1921, had been conceived along similar lines. But the ensuing leadership crisis and the March Uprising had effectively foreclosed Levi's approach, which was only revived after the Third Congress proclaimed it to be official Comintern policy. The responsibility for its execution went first to Ernst Mayer, and after the fall of 1922 to Brandler, who had escaped from prison and gone to Moscow and who eventually returned to Germany under a general amnesty.

For several reasons, the new course proved to be a frustrating experience for the KPD. First of all, Moscow severely restricted the Party's freedom of movement in conducting a United Front policy. Both Meyer and his sucessor Brandler made serious efforts to establish a common basis of co-operation with the Socialists and the trade unions by concentrating on bread-and-butter demands vital to the entire working class. But whenever negotiations on concrete issues appeared to be promising, the Comintern inevitably applied the brakes in order to halt any genuine rapprochement between the KPD and the non-Communist labor organizations. For the Bolsheviks regarded the United Front policy primarily as a tactical device, designed to alienate non-Communist workers from their leadership and lure them into the Communist camp. Moscow did not tolerate close and sincere co-operation with the non-Communist leaders, for fear it might weaken the revolutionary élan of German communism. Every time discussions about joint political or economic steps approached the point of

---

[42] On the United Front policy see Angress, *Stillborn Revolution*, chap. viii, and *passim*, and the detailed East German study by Arnold Reisberg, *An den Quellen der Einheitsfrontpolitik. Der Kampf der KPD um die Aktionseinheit in Deutschland 1921–1922. Ein Beitrag zur Erforschung der Hilfe W. I. Lenins und der Komintern für die KPD*, 2 vols., East Berlin, 1971. While Reisberg shows on the basis of documentary material unavailable to me that the policy was often quite effective in individual plants and even certain localities, he does not disprove my thesis that, overall, the policy was a failure.

agreement, the Comintern would stipulate that all Communist conditions had to be met. Since these conditions were usually too extreme to gain acceptance by the would-be partners, many co-operative ventures never got beyond the stage of negotiations. No wonder that the Party's reputation for obstructionism persisted; although some joint political campaigns were conducted with a fair degree of success on the local level, large-scale attempts to form a United Front were condemned to failure.

Aside from the increasing interference exercised by the Comintern and the continuing isolation and distrust the Party faced at home, a third major problem was factionalism. After the March Uprising the Left Opposition, which had its original stronghold in Berlin, won additional support in other parts of the country, mainly along the northern coast and in the Rhineland.[43] Its chief spokesman was Ruth Fischer, a member of the Berlin organization. The main target of its attacks was the United Front policy, which it rejected as "reformist" and thus harmful to the Party's revolutionary spirit. Until the end of 1922, the *Zentrale* was able to handle this problem with relative success, but in 1923, as tensions increased at home and on the international front, the demands of the Left Opposition for a more activist course became harder to control.

*

The crisis year of 1923 began with the occupation of the Ruhr by French and Belgian troops, a development that considerably intensified Germany's domestic difficulties. The policy of "Passive Resistance" proclaimed by Chancellor Wilhelm Cuno's government in response to the occupation placed additional burdens on the country's already lagging economy, including, in particular, the burden of inflation. A rapid devaluation of the currency led to demands for higher wages, often accompanied by strikes. In addition, the central government quarreled with the right-wing government of Bavaria over the conservative paramilitary organizations in that state and with the left-wing governments of Saxony and Thuringia over the armed proletarian guards (Red Hundreds) in those states. These economic and political stresses created opportunities which the Left Opposition wanted the Party to exploit.

Nevertheless, during the first eight months of 1923 the attitude of the KPD towards the mounting domestic crisis remained erratic, and the

---

[43] For a firsthand but highly subjective and often unreliable picture of the Left Opposition, see Ruth Fischer, *Stalin and German Communism: A Study in the Origins of the State Party*, Cambridge, Mass., 1948, *passim*.

Party lacked any specific plans for a revolutionary rising.[44] While continuing the struggle against the Cuno government, the Communists responded to the Ruhr imbroglio by vowing to "smite" the French Premier Poincaré and his policy of capitalist exploitation of the occupied territory. The *Zentrale* pursued the United Front policy with renewed vigor. Labor unrest was widespread as inflation skyrocketed, wages lagged behind the rising cost of living, and right-wing stirrings in Bavaria and other regions alarmed the workers. But besides their attempts to woo the restive working class, the Communists also devised what might be called a policy of attrition, which was designed to intensify prevailing tensions by means of aggressive slogans, street demonstrations, and related tactics. It was hoped that such tactics would lead to the collapse of the Cuno government and then pave the way for a seizure of power by the proletariat. With these objectives in mind, the KPD took part in strikes and protests, supported the left-wing governments (left Majority Socialists and Independents) in Saxony and Thuringia without actually joining them, and published inflammatory editorials in the Party press.

While these tactics aroused apprehension in the population and the government, the Left Opposition remained dissatisfied, criticized the Brandler *Zentrale's* lack of boldness, and demanded the adoption of a more radical course. But in spite of continuous altercations and mutual recriminations over the Party's policies, Brandler refused to yield to the Left Opposition. He and his colleagues had been badly shaken by the abortive March Uprising and Moscow's criticism of it, and they were loath to embark lightly on another *Putsch*. Moreover, the *Zentrale* had the backing of the Comintern. Karl Radek, the Comintern's German expert, acted as an adviser to the KPD leaders during visits to Berlin or through communications from Moscow, and he supported their policy of limited risks. With Lenin incapacitated after his third stroke (in March, 1923) and the Bolshevik hierarchy preoccupied with a gradually evolving struggle for succession, Moscow wanted—for the moment at least—to maintain the United Front policy in Germany. The Comintern expected the KPD to profit from the United Front policy in view of the country's political and economic difficulties, and the Russian foreign office was eager not to jeopardize its tenuous relations with Germany, which had been gradually improving since the conclusion of the Rapallo Treaty in 1922. A Communist revolution was, there-

---

[44] Unless otherwise indicated, the following account is based on Angress, *Stillborn Revolution*, chaps. x–xiii. For an excellent summary with selected pertinent documents see Gruber, *op. cit.*, pp. 434–470. Exceedingly useful, although written from the vantage point of Soviet Russian policy, is Edward Hallett Carr, *A History of Soviet Russia : The Interregnum 1923–1924*, New York, 1954.

fore, not on the Russian agenda for the first half of 1923. Only in August did Moscow's views on this matter change, and then only because the Comintern misjudged the situation in Germany.

As the domestic crisis grew worse during the summer of 1923, the KPD's public posture became more provocative and the character of the Party press more aggressive.[45] This escalation of Communist agitation was in part a reaction to the progressively deteriorating conditions that marked the last weeks of the hapless Cuno government. But the Party was also trying to use the mounting tensions in the country to gauge the mood of the masses. Were they ready to rally around the red banner? To test the public appeal of the Party, and without concrete plans for a rising, the Communists decided on July 22 to call for nation-wide Anti-Fascist Day demonstrations to be held on July 29. On the advice of the Berlin government, authorities throughout the country, with the exception of those in Saxony, Thuringia, and Baden, responded in the intervening week by banning all outdoor demonstrations. The ban put the Party in a quandary. While the Left Opposition insisted on defying the government, the *Zentrale* compromised by authorizing outdoor demonstrations only in those parts of the country where the Communists could protect them, as in Saxony and Thuringia. Everywhere else the Communists would have to make do with indoor demonstrations. This decision received the blessings of the Comintern by telegraph on July 26. When the crucial day arrived, the turnout was poor. Less than 250,000 persons took part in the demonstrations, a clear indication that the Party's strength was far from overwhelming. To be sure, the KPD had gained 70,000 new members between September, 1922, and the late summer of 1923, but with a total strength of 294,230 members (of whom nearly 33,000 were women), the Party was still a rather small minority in a labor force (male only) of roughly twenty-three million.[46]

The second test came in early August, this time without the Communists taking the initiative. Spearheaded by the printers and supported by the German Confederation of Labor, strikes for higher wages erupted in Berlin on August 8 and soon spread to other occupations, including municipal

---

[45] A particularly crass example is an appeal "To the Party," *Die Rote Fahne*, Berlin, No. 158, July 12, 1923.

[46] *Bericht über die Verhandlungen des III. (8.) Parteitages der KPD (Sektion der K.I.) abgehalten in Leipzig vom 28. Januar bis 1. Februar 1923*, Berlin, 1923, pp. 63–64; *Bericht über die Verhandlungen des IX. Parteitages der KPD (Sektion der K.I.) abgehalten in Frankfurt am Main vom 7. bis 10. April 1924*, Berlin, 1924, pp. 64/73–64/74 (double pagination); *Jahrbuch für Politik, Wirtschaft, Arbeiterbewegung 1922–23*, Hamburg, no date, p. 614.

employees. The KPD took immediate steps to turn the still sporadic movement into a general strike, preferably one that would extend beyond the capital. But on August 14, while the Party was still trying to impose its demands on other labor organizations, the Cuno government resigned. Two days later the strikes collapsed, despite Communist efforts to keep them going. Once again the Party's influence had been found wanting. Far worse, Cuno was replaced by Gustav Stresemann, who formed a Great Coalition government that included the Majority Socialists. This turn of events struck a severe blow to Communist hopes for mass support, since Germany's largest labor party now shared in the responsibilities of government.

These developments, so disastrous for German communism, were seen in a very different light by Russia's leaders, most of whom learned about the situation while away from Moscow on vacation. To them, the Anti-Fascist Day demonstrations and the Cuno strike appeared to indicate that a revolutionary situation was taking shape in Germany. As they followed the news from abroad at their distant vacation spots, they became convinced that the Stresemann government was sitting on a powder keg. And seen from afar, the new government did look vulnerable enough. The occupation of the Ruhr was still in effect. Relations between the central government and Bavaria, Saxony, and Thuringia seemed to be approaching the breaking point. Inflation had reached astronomical proportions, and the Rhineland was threatened by separatist machinations. What could not be detected from abroad, however, were the slowly emerging achievements of the Stresemann government, notably the growing confidence it inspired among the people, including non-Communists workers, by its determined and ultimately successful efforts to deal with Germany's problems.

Stirred by their overly optimistic appraisal of the crisis in Germany and afraid that Stresemann might achieve a detente with France that would endanger the still fragile Russo-German ties, the Bolshevik leaders began to think in terms of a Communist-led revolution in Germany. Zinoviev and Trotsky particularly welcomed the vision of the German proletariat emulating the Russian Revolution of 1917. On August 15, Zinoviev, who was still on vacation, sent word to Moscow that the KPD should be told to take notice of the approaching revolutionary crisis.[47] On August 23 the Politburo met with Radek and several other Bolshevik functionaries to deliberate on measures to be taken. After Radek reported on the German situation in a manner that reflected the enthusiasm of his listeners rather than the skepticism of his own views, it was decided to appoint a committee of four, headed by Radek, to guide the German comrades in the coming struggle.

---

[47] Carr, *op. cit.*, p. 201.

It was also decided to summon Brandler to Moscow for consultation and planning.[48] When Brandler arrived, Moscow was already decked out with slogans in support of the anticipated "German October." Although he had serious misgivings about the projected operations, Brandler was gradually won over by the confident and optimistic Russians. The plan was to prepare for a revolution. It was to be launched from Saxony, where the Communists were supposed to join the government and arm and organize the workers for the impending *Aktion*. The same steps were to be taken in Thuringia. Although Brandler refused to commit himself to a specific target date, he did agree to start the uprising within four to six weeks after his return to Germany. On October 1, Zinoviev wired the gist of these decisions to the *Zentrale* in Berlin. Shortly thereafter, Brandler returned to Germany, where he and two fellow members of the *Zentrale* held brief negotiations with Saxony's unsuspecting Minister President, Erich Zeigner. The Communist trio then joined the Saxon government as ministers on October 12, though without revealing their revolutionary intentions to the non-Communist cabinet members. Four days later, a similar arrangement was worked out with the government of Thuringia.

Between the Cuno Strike early in August and the arrival of Zinoviev's telegram on October 1, Communist propaganda had remained defiantly aggressive, although no plans for action existed as yet. The Party merely continued its policy of attrition, which was now directed against the Stresemann government. It was only after October 1 that active preparations for an armed uprising were begun. Weapons were procured, armed fighting units—the Red Hundreds—were expanded and trained in Saxony and Thuringia, and clandestine maneuvers were conducted in secluded forests. These preparations were directed by the Party's various underground organizations—especially its military-political (M-P) *Apparat*—with the assistance of a small group of Russian "civil war experts" whom the Bolsheviks had dispatched to Germany.[49] Totally absent was any concern for the strength of the potential opposing forces, the military and the police; nor did the Party bother to appraise the attitude of non-Communist labor towards a possible uprising. While Moscow acted on the basis of misinformation about the situation in Germany and demonstrated poor judgment, the KPD, which should have known better, simply followed orders and failed to take into account one factor that is essential to the success of any revolutionary action—mass support.

---

[48] The only known eyewitness account of this meeting is in Boris Bajanov, *Avec Staline dans le Kremlin*, Paris, 1930, pp. 190–198.

[49] On this aspect see Erich Wollenberg, *Der Apparat : Stalins Fünfte Kolonne*, Bonn, 1952, pp. 10–12.

But quite apart from these blunders, the hastily improvised operation was ill-starred from the outset. On October 13, the day after the Communists joined the Saxon government, the district army commander banned all Red Hundreds, and three days later he placed the Saxon police under military control. Minister President Zeigner, who was ignorant of Communist intentions, vigorously protested against this interference and assailed the army and the Stresemann government in an impassioned speech. As a result, the Central government decided to move additional troops into Saxony and Thuringia to forestall any further troubles. If the KPD wanted to act, it had to do so at once. Taken by surprise, the *Zentrale* resolved to make use of a labor conference, which was scheduled to meet in Chemnitz on October 21, to call for a general strike. This was to be the signal for a nation-wide uprising. But when the Communist motion for a general strike was introduced by Brandler at the conference, the assembled delegates of the non-Communist labor organizations greeted his words with icy silence. In crossing the Rubicon, the KPD had suffered a shipwreck. Since Radek and his three Russian colleagues had not yet arrived in Germany to offer guidance, the *Zentrale* decided on its own initiative to call off the planned uprising for lack of support. All the couriers who had stood by to transmit the orders for the start of the uprising to their various local organizations were informed of the change of plans. Only the KPD organization in Hamburg, through a mishap that still puzzles historians,[50] received word to revolt. For several days Communist fighters in that city engaged in the only revolutionary action that Germany was to see during its "Red October" and, for that matter, throughout the remaining years of the Weimar Republic.

*

In analyzing the reasons why the KPD proved unable to seize power, even during the unsettled postwar years, a number of factors that lie beyond the actual attempts at revolution require mention. First of all, the tradition and structure of the German working-class movement militated against radical solutions to political and economic problems. Although the Social Democratic Party started as a revolutionary Marxist movement, under the impact of Eduard Bernstein's revisionist theses it developed along evolutionary lines, placing its hopes for winning control of the state

---

[50] For a cogent appraisal of the various theories on how and why the Hamburg organization received orders to rise, see Hermann Weber's introduction to the reprint of Flechtheim, *op. cit.*, p. 41. A brief account of the rising is in Richard A. Comfort, *Revolutionary Hamburg: Labor Politics in the Early Weimar Republic*, Stanford, 1966, pp. 124–127.

in the electoral process rather than in force and violence. This trend was reinforced by the strong influence that the labor unions, which were comparatively conservative, exerted on the Party leadership. When the Party split during World War I, the revisionist-evolutionary character of the Majority Socialists became even more pronounced, while the cohesiveness of the SPD was strengthened by the secession of its troublesome left wing, which never succeeded in attracting the majority of labor. Nor were the secessionists uniformly radical. Only the left wing of the Independents, with its ultra-extremist appendage, the Spartacists, endorsed outright revolutionary activism.

After the collapse of the old order in November, 1918, when power was thrust upon German Social Democracy, its leaders tried to steer the revolution—which they had not instigated—into moderate channels so as to prevent further turmoil and eliminate the threat of civil war. It was for this reason that the Provisional Government refrained from forcibly changing the existing social structure in Germany, co-operated with the old bureaucracy and the army, and repressed all attempts by left extremists to jeopardize the restoration of law and order.

In contrast to events in Russia in 1917, in Germany the Provisional Government succeeded in meeting the demands of the greater part of the nation and in frustrating all efforts by the radicals to drive the revolution further to the left. In accomplishing these ends it was able to rely on the active assistance of the military and it had the approval of the urban middle classes and also of the peasantry, which, with very few exceptions (e.g., in Bavaria), was not a revolutionary element in Germany. Farm owners, particularly those in the western half of the country, tended to be fairly conservative, and landless farm laborers of the eastern provinces, most of whom were adherents of the Majority Socialist Party, generally remained unaffected by radical propaganda. The few peasants' councils that were formed in these areas behaved with moderation, aside from the fact that they also proved to be rather ineffective, thus making it easy for local landowners to retain firm control over their hired hands.

As the situation in Germany stabilized after the elections to the National Assembly, with the socialist Provisional Government giving way at first to a coalition of middle-class parties and Majority Socialists and then, in June, 1920, to an exclusively bourgeois government, the chances for a successful Communist coup were diminished even further. Moreover, the well-organized and disciplined Majority Socialists not only retained the allegiance of the bulk of German labor, which wanted to improve its lot within the framework of existing institutions, but also eventually reunited with the

Independents in 1922. Throughout this period, most German workers continued to distrust the vehement appeals to violence that came from the extreme left, rejected Bolshevism as an alien force unsuitable for the labor movement in a highly industrialized state, and refused to be swayed by the siren songs of the Communists, whom they referred to derisively as "Moscow's disciples."

Given these circumstances, it is hardly surprising that none of the revolutionary attempts discussed here led to a Communist takeover in Germany. The January Uprising of 1919, unplanned and carried out against the advice of the Party's most prominent leaders, gave the young KPD a notoriety for irresponsible "putschism" that was a lasting liability, thwarting its subsequent bids to win mass support. The fiasco of the Communist Soviet Republic in Bavaria, which was set up by the regional Party organization in violation of instructions from the Zentrale, further tarnished the KPD's reputation. In both cases the German Communists acted independently of Bolshevik Russia, which at that time had virtually no direct contact with the KPD. Only after the founding of the Comintern and the restoration of relatively stable conditions in Germany and Russia did Moscow begin to intervene in the affairs of the German Party. In March, 1921, a few individuals in the Comintern goaded the German Communists into the ill-fated March Uprising, which was later condemned at the behest of Lenin and Trotsky by the Third Congress of the Comintern. This disavowal was prompted partly by Russia's search for ties with the West, but especially by Lenin's awareness that the revolutionary tide on the Continent was ebbing and that most Communist parties, including the KPD, were still isolated minorities within the European labor movement. Ordered to go "To the masses!" the KPD followed the United Front policy—though with little success—until a faulty assessment of the situation in Germany by the men in the Kremlin led to the abortive "German October" of 1923. This debacle proved conclusively that the overwhelming majority of German workers tended towards moderation in politics and refused to be led into reckless adventures by the Communists. As a result of this setback, the Party once again had to face severe criticism from Moscow, this time for having thrown away a "favorable opportunity."[51] But while plans for a future revolution were not abandoned in principle, in practice the chances for a Communist takeover, however illusory these may have been in the past, never returned. Suffering from a steady decline in the quality of its

_____

[51] The "German October" debacle was debated and criticized in Moscow on January 11, 1924, at a joint meeting of the Presidium of the ECCI and a delegation from the KPD. The most detailed source on the meeting is Die Lehren der deutschen Ereignisse, Hamburg, 1924.

leadership, from factional splits that impaired unity of action, and from the abandonment of Rosa Luxemburg's teachings, the KPD became subject to Russian bolshevization and lost whatever freedom of movement it had enjoyed during the first years of its existence. Stalin's accession to power accelerated the growth of Russian influence over the KPD, a development for which Lenin and Trotsky had laid the groundwork. With the policy of "Socialism in One Country" and Stalin's tightening control over the activities of the Comintern, the KPD—until its dissolution in 1933—was condemned to mouthing revolutionary slogans that were never again allowed to culminate in revolutionary action. When communism did come to the eastern part of Germany in 1945, it was brought by the victorious Red Army rather than by the ineffective German Communists.

The Attempted Revolution in China: The First Sino-Soviet Alliance, 1924–1927

Gottfried-Karl Kindermann

Contemporary discussions of the protracted conflict between the partners of the Sino-Soviet alliance often overlook the fact that this is not the first alliance to have been concluded between the Soviet Union and China. Moscow's first alliance with China, entered into in 1924, disintegrated under catastrophic circumstances three and a half years later. The political system of China at that time might be termed a politico-military polycentrism. Following the abdication of the Manchurian Ch'ing dynasty (1644–1912), the tragic failure of China's short-lived experiment with parliamentary democracy, and the collapse of the dictatorship of President Yüan Shih-k'ai (1913–1916), there was no longer any effective central government in the new Republic of China. Actual political power lay in the hands of the military governors, the so-called warlords, who fought each other continually in indecisive civil wars. In accordance with a convenient legal fiction, foreign powers considered the central government of China to be the regime of the warlord who happened to occupy the capital, Peking, at any given moment in the inter-Chinese power struggle. This was so even though control exercised by the warlord did not reach very far beyond the city walls. Under these circumstances a Soviet alliance meant no more than Moscow's political co-operation with one or several of the regional power centers that survived in a state of hostile coexistence. Only one of these regional power centers was led by a political party with a national revolutionary ideology, an anti-imperialist orientation, and a leader who had definite sympathies for some foreign policy objectives of the young Soviet state. This was the Kuomintang or KMT (Chinese Nationalist Party), which was under the leadership of the charismatic Dr. Sun Yat-sen (1866–1925).

Sun Yat-sen was justly considered the "Father of the Chinese Revolution" and the "Founder of the Republic of China." After the failure of parliamentary democracy in China and its replacement by a military dictatorship, he tried to re-establish a constitutional government in Southern China. This government was supported for a time by a number of refugee-parliamentarians who had been expelled from Peking by the new warlord rulers in China's capital.

In spite of his sympathies for the Soviet Union, Sun Yat-sen was not a Marxist. His political ideology was grounded in the so-called "Three People's Principles" (*San-min chu-i*). The first principle (*Min-tsu chu-i*) called for the promotion of Chinese nationalism as the basis for the political reintegration of China and its liberation from imperialism. It comprehended a new way of political thinking no longer focusing loyalty upon the person of an emperor but upon the Chinese nation as a whole. For Sun Yat-sen this kind of nationalism was the psychological precondition for a workable system of republican democracy. The second principle (*Min-ch'üan chu-i*) called for the gradual introduction of parliamentary democracy after a transitional "period of tutelage" in which the national revolutionary party was supposed to organize an educational program to familiarize the Chinese people with the rights and duties of citizens in a modern democratic state. Step by step a system of self-government was to be introduced on different levels, until, prceeding from the smallest to the largest unit, self-government on the national level had been achieved. With this, the "period of tutelage" was to come to an end and to be succeeded by the introduction of a peculiar constitutional system composed of a combination of modern Western and traditional Chinese institutions of government. Sun Yat-sen's third ideological principle (*Min-sheng chu-i*) advocated thoroughgoing but non-violent social changes, including a land reform, the nationalization of basic industries, and the passage of legislation for the protection of wage earners. Judging by his programs and methods, Sun Yat-sen may be regarded as a revolutionary nationalist and a social reformer.

Sun's attempts to destroy the warlord system and establish a modern nationalist government in China were, however, frustrated by his lack of an effective party organization and politically reliable armed forces. He had to rely on the military support of warlords in Southern China who merely wanted to capitalize on the prestige of his name and were not really interested in sharing his long-range national goals. Shortly before he concluded his alliance with the Soviet Union, Sun Yat-sen had been the target of a treacherous *coup d'état* led by one of these warlords. His narrow escape, personally assisted by Chiang Kai-shek, preceded a decisive meeting with the Soviet diplomat, A. Joffe, with whom he concluded what came to be regarded as the founding document of Moscow's alliance with the Kuomintang regime in Southern China. The Sun-Joffe agreement was signed on January 26, 1923.

Sun Yat-sen's motives for entering into an alliance with the Soviet state might be summarized as follows:

1. Sun was influenced by Soviet Russia's voluntary renunciation of former unequal treaties with China, as stated in the Karakhan Manifesto of 1919 (repeated in 1920). This manifesto had created an impression of conspicuous contrast between the Soviet Union's new style of diplomacy and the uncompromising attitude of the colonial powers towards their special privileges in China.

2. Sun's confidence in the possibility of a productive partnership with Moscow had been greatly strengthened by what he saw as ideologically disinterested Soviet assistance to the non-Communist, and even anti-Communist, national-liberation movement of another Asian state, Turkey, in the era of Kemal Ataturk.

3. After many unsuccessful attempts to obtain foreign aid from Japan, the United States, Germany, and the League of Nations, Sun found that the Soviet Union offered his government moral, political, financial, and technical assistance.

4. Moscow seems to have accepted the Kuomintang's claim to hegemonic leadership in the Chinese revolution, a claim on which Sun Yat-sen himself had vigorously insisted. In their joint statement, Sun and Joffe agreed that "the Communist order or even the Soviet system cannot actually be introduced into China, because there do not exist here the conditions for the successful establishment of either Communism or Sovietism."[1] Joffe concurred with Sun that China's most urgent problem was "to achieve national unification and attain full national independence."

Since Sun was not willing to recognize the Chinese Communist Party, a special formula had to be developed permitting the Chinese Communists to maintain their own party while coming under the control of the Kuomintang. Chinese Communists who wanted to participate in the government at Canton had to join the Kuomintang; at the same time, however, they were allowed to retain their membership in the Communist Party. This "dual-membership formula" produced a system of Kuomintang-Communist relations that encouraged close co-operation between the two parties without granting equal status to the Communist Party. Understandably enough, the Chinese Communists protested against this deferential and degrading arrangement, but they were pressured into accepting it by Moscow's emissary, Maring (alias Sneevliet), who threatened them with exclusion from the Comintern (Communist International). What is notable in retrospect is that, though the Chinese Communists gave in, they had had a serious difference of opinion with the Soviet Communists at the very

---

[1] Text of the "Sun-Joffe Joint Statement" in: *China Year Book 1924–1925*, p. 862.

beginning of the first Sino-Soviet alliance. In the eyes of Sun Yat-sen, of course, this was an alliance not between Soviet and Chinese Communists but between Moscow and the Kuomintang.

5. Sun attributed the numerous setbacks of his party to inefficiency in the management of its political, military, and propaganda apparatus. It was his belief that these shortcomings could be overcome by the application of Bolshevik methods that had been successfully tested in the Russian revolution. Sun seemed to see a similarity between the White Russian generals, whom the Bolsheviks had managed to defeat, and the warlords in China. Perhaps he even compared the foreign intervention in Russia after the Bolshevik revolution with the dominant presence of colonial powers in China. In any case, Sun welcomed the arrival of Soviet military and political advisers in Southern China to assist him in his efforts to reform the Kuomintang. The new Party constitution of the Kuomintang was strongly influenced by that of the Soviet Communist Party. With the aid of Soviet arms and money Sun founded the famous Whampoa Military Academy, where future officers of China's revolutionary army were to be trained. Chiang Kai-shek became the first President of the Academy, and Chou En-lai played a leading role in its department of political education. With the aim of ensuring the political reliability of the Kuomintang's new Party army, Chiang Kai-shek introduced a system of political commissars patterned after that in the Soviet Union. To avoid misunderstandings on this point, however, it should be stressed that neither he nor Sun Yat-sen ever intended to accept or imitate the ideological system of Soviet communism. Quite the contrary, Sun's harshest criticism of the theory and practice of Marxism was uttered in August, 1924—i.e., more than half a year after the First National Congress of the Kuomintang had formalized the alliance with the Soviet Union and instituted political and military reforms within the Party.

At the end of 1923, Sun Yat-sen had sent his trusted lieutenant, Chiang Kai-shek, to the Soviet Union as the head of a special study mission. Originally a determined advocate of Sino-Soviet revolutionary co-operation, Chiang returned from the Soviet Union utterly disillusioned with Moscow's intentions regarding its national revolutionary allies in China. As Mao Tse-tung was to do decades later, Chiang had come to believe that the Soviet Union's attitude towards China was essentially imperialistic, regardless of the revolutionary rhetoric of its Bolshevik rulers. Chiang Kai-shek summarized his impressions in a report to Sun Yat-sen in which he warned against placing too much trust in the Russians. The original document seems to have been lost. In its absence the best clue to the specific nature of Chiang's objections may be found in a letter to his friend Liao Chung-k'ai, an outspoken proponent of a Soviet orientation for the Kuomintang.[2] The following passages from this letter can easily be identified with Chiang's previous experiences in Moscow, as described in his partially published diary entries:

> I have to say another word about the problem of the Russian Party. In this matter one ought to distinguish between doctrines and facts. We should not close our eyes to facts just because their doctrines sound credible. According to my observation, the Russian Party is not sincere. Even my previous remark to you that only thirty percent of the Russians' words are trustworthy seems too optimistic. Since you have had so much faith in them, I did not want to disappoint you completely. Those who respect Sun Yat-sen are not Russian Communists but rather international Communists.

Chiang continues:

> As regards the members of the Chinese Communist Party, they have only suspicion and slander but no respect for Mr. Sun. The sole aim of the Russian Party is to make the Chinese Communist Party the ruling party in China. Its members do not believe that they can permanently co-operate with us in order to achieve mutual success.

The last two sentences suggest that while in Moscow Chiang had read the resolution of the Fourth Congress of the Comintern and possibly also that promulgated by the Executive Committee of the Comintern in May, 1923.[3] The first resolution stressed the temporary nature of Communist alliances with national revolutionary parties, and the second referred to Sun Yat-sen in rather disrespectful and distrustful terms.

Further in his letter, Chiang pursued the subject of the Chinese Communist Party, making the following observations:

> ... the Chinese tend to worship foreigners while ignoring the character of their own people. The Chinese Communists in Russia, for instance, only call others slaves of America, England, or Japan. They have not realized that they themselves have become one hundred percent slaves of the Russians....

> When I was urged to join the Communist Party, I replied that in order to do so I would have to obtain Dr. Sun's permission. Thereupon I was ridiculed for being a loyal servant to an individual. I am aware that my character is such that others may laugh at it. But while serving one man I still keep in mind my duty to serve my country and love my compatriots, whereas a traitor sells out his country and betrays his people. I prefer to be considered as the servant of an individual rather than to be honored as a slave of foreigners.

---

[2] The letter is dated March 12, 1924. Chung-cheng Chiango, *Chiang wei-yuan-chang shou-ting ko-ming shu-chien*, Shanghai, 1946, pp. 30–31.

[3] Text of those two resolutions in: X. J. Eudin and R. C. North (eds.), *Soviet Russia and the East, 1920–1927*, Stanford and London, 1957, pp. 343–346.

This temperamental outburst reveals to what extent Chiang's personal and national pride had been hurt in Moscow. He writes in his diary that the Russian Communists had responded with sneers and ridicule each time he tried to explain the ideology of his party. His sense of personal and national humiliation and his feeling of not being looked upon as an equal may be seen as marking Chiang's inner break with the Kuomintang's Soviet partners.

Sun Yat-sen had somehow assumed that the nature of Russia's national interests had been basically changed by the establishment of a new form of government in Russia. Since his mission to Moscow, Chiang Kai-shek had, on the other hand, begun to perceive the fundamental continuity of Russia's national interests in the Far East. Chiang writes:

> Russia's policy aims at making Manchuria, Mongolia, Sinkiang, and Tibet each a part of the Soviet Union. Even with regard to China proper the Russians are not without plans to interfere on behalf of their own interests. In any case, if one relies entirely on the [self-interested] aid of others, he is not likely to succeed. The level of the Chinese is so low and yet they expect others to achieve our aims for us and to carry out the will of heaven while they worship them like gods. How unreasonable this is.
>
> What they call internationalism and world revolution is nothing else but Tsarist imperialism. Only the name is changed in order to mislead people.

Chiang's political realism seems the more remarkable when one considers that his career up to this point had been a purely military one. Almost twenty-five years before his opinion was to become largely accepted by policy-makers in the United States, Chiang expressed the conviction that the objectives of the Soviet Union in the Far East remained essentially the same as those of Tsarist Russia. Contrary to Sun's often illusory expectations of politically disinterested aid from other nations, Chiang had thus begun to regard national interests as an indispensable condition of international politics. All in all one can hardly exaggerate the impact of Chiang's visit to Moscow upon his political views in general and his understanding of Soviet and Chinese Communists in particular. His subsequent role in the Kuomintang-Moscow alliance cannot be evaluated without keeping in mind the lessons he learned at this time.

The first Sino-Soviet alliance was of special importance as a testing ground for Lenin's theories on the role of national liberation movements in world revolution, and the fate of the alliance can be seen as a function of the particular interdependence of political theory and practice in the new Soviet state. In reviewing the international position of the Soviet Union just after the third anniversary of the October Revolution, Lenin said:

Three years ago, when we defined the goals and conditions for the victory of the proletarian revolution in Russia, we always definitely emphasized that this victory could not be considered secure as long as Russia was not supported by a proletarian revolution in the West and that a correct appraisal of our revolution was possible only from the viewpoint of international revolution.

For our victory to be secure it is necessary that the proletarian revolution should be successful in all or at least in several important capitalist countries. Now, after three years of embittered struggle, we see how far our predictions have or have not materialized. They have not come true insofar as there has not been a fast and simple resolution of the matter ... Neither the Russian Soviet Republic nor the entire capitalist world has won or has been defeated. If our predictions have not materialized in a simple, fast, and direct way, they have nevertheless brought about a most important result, which is the maintenance of proletarian power and the Soviet Republic in spite of the postponement of the socialist world revolution.[4]

This admission by Lenin followed the liquidation of the short-lived Soviet republics in Hungary and Bavaria and the suppression of the Spartacus uprising in Berlin. Meanwhile, temporary Soviet regimes in Finland, Latvia, Lithuania, and Estonia had been overthrown by Western-supported independence movements. In the same year in which the Baltic States and Finland won Moscow's recognition of formal secession from the Soviet state, the Red Army suffered severe political and military defeats at the gates of Warsaw. The cumulative impact of these events, which revealed the strength of capitalist power and the weakness of Communist movements in Western, Central, and Eastern Europe, was bound to have a sobering effect upon earlier, more utopian trends of thought among the Bolshevik foreign policy-makers. Doubtless with these experiences in mind, Lenin formulated the following "fundamental rule" of Soviet strategy in international affairs:

We must exploit the antagonisms and contradictions between two capitalist powers—between the two systems of capitalist states—in such a way as to set one against the other. As long as we have not achieved world conquest, and as long as we remain economically and militarily weaker than the capitalist states, we must stick to this rule by learning how to exploit contradictions and antagonisms between the imperialists.[5]

From the Russian as well as the Chinese point of view, the idea of the first Sino-Soviet alliance may be interpreted as a community of interests based upon the existence of common enemies. Utilizing the coincidence of Soviet and Chinese antagonism towards the colonial powers, primarily Great Britain and Japan, Moscow could hope to enlist Chinese forces

---

[4] V. I. Lenin, *Sämtliche Werke*, Wien-Berlin, 1930, Vol. XXV, p. 603.
[5] *Ibid.*, pp. 623–624.

against its opponents in the sphere of international politics. But in view of the existence of an extremely weak Chinese Communist Party, Moscow's negotiators found themselves confronted with a twofold task. First, they had to co-ordinate divergent foreign policy objectives of Soviet and Kuomintang power. Second, they had to find a formula for the coexistence of the Kuomintang and the Chinese Communist Party. Apart from the general intensification of Soviet interests in Chinese affairs, which occurred as a by-product of Russia's re-emergence as a Far Eastern power, and apart from the strategy of attempting to use the Chinese Nationalists as a pawn to checkmate the rulers of Peking, there were other, more important motives for Moscow's interest in Sun Yat-sen's nationalist movement. True enough, China, with its multitude of warring regional parties and centers of power, at the time seemed incapable of constituting a serious challenge to Russia's traditional position in the Far East. Yet in view of this position and by virtue of sharing with China the longest existing land frontier between any two empires, Soviet Russia could not be expected to regard with indifference the question whether any future government of China might be an ally or a foe.

In its search for effective Chinese allies, Moscow had finally come to the conclusion that the Kuomintang was "the only serious national revolutionary movement in China." The historical resolution of the Comintern on Kuomintang-Chinese Communist relations, passed in the same month that the Sun-Joffe agreement was signed, states:

> ... since China's central problem consists in a national revolution against the imperialists and their internal feudal agents (foreign-supported warlords) and furthermore since the working class is ... not yet sufficiently established as a really independent social force, the Executive Committee regards it as necessary to co-ordinate activity between the Kuomintang Party and the young Chinese Communist Party.[6]

Thus, in a way analogous to Moscow's relations with Turkey, the national interests of Soviet Russia were given priority over the independence of the Chinese Communist Party. The nationalist movements of both Mustapha Kemal Pasha and Sun Yat-sen were opposed to the international adversaries of Soviet Russia, and this fact was bound to weigh heavily in the scales of Moscow's foreign policy formulations. In neighboring China, two of Russia's most formidable opponents, Japan and Great Britain, disposed of extended military, political, and cultural spheres of influence. If, given certain conditions, the Kuomintang could be expected to emerge as the victorious and nationally unifying force in China's multifactional

---

[6] Compare Eudin and North, *op. cit.*, p. 344.

Civil War, then it was a postulate of political wisdom to ally with this movement, promote its progress, and preserve it as a safe entente partner.

Apparently with these considerations in mind, the Soviet leaders ordered that "the Chinese Communist Party should exert its influence upon the Kuomintang in order to co-ordinate its efforts with those of Soviet Russia in a common struggle against European, American, and Japanese imperialism." The Chinese Communist Party was further instructed to support the Kuomintang in all united front campaigns "so long as the latter pursues an objectively correct policy." What was meant by an "objectively correct policy" is clear from preceding Comintern resolutions. The *Theses on the Oriental Question* declared, for instance, that "one of the most important tasks of a united anti-imperialist front consists in explaining to the broad laboring masses ... the necessity of an alliance with the Soviet Republic. The demand for a close alliance with the proletarian Soviet Republic is the token of a united anti-imperialist front."[7] The diplomatic objectives of Moscow in seeking an entente with the Chinese Nationalists might thus be summed up as follows:

1. Regardless of the Kuomintang's non-Communist—and even in part explicitly anti-Marxist ideology—Moscow entered into the entente with the basic intention of using the Chinese Nationalist movement as a backstay for its Far Eastern policy.

2. Bolstered by Soviet military and technical assistance, the Kuomintang was expected to become a diplomatic weapon in the revived triangular contest between Russian, Japanese, and British interests in the Far East. While avoiding a direct conflict with the two island empires, Moscow could hope to eliminate or at least weaken their far-reaching influence in neighboring China by promoting a pro-Russian, anti-colonial nationalist movement. In extending political and military power towards the borders of India, Indochina, and Korea, the revolutionary movement in China might serve to ignite anti-colonial revolutions in these countries, or in any event provoke international controversies that would distract Western and Japanese attention from hostile preoccupation with the policies of Soviet Russia.

3. Militarily, the Kuomintang was to be reinforced to enable it to defeat China's foreign-supported warlords, who were operating mainly in the British and Japanese spheres of influence in Central and Northern China. The enlarged military capability of the Kuomintang would mean that China was likely to gain a stronger bargaining position *vis-à-vis* the

---

[7] *Ibid.*

colonial powers and to become less susceptible to the danger of foreign military pressure or intervention. The augmentation of Chinese military power was also bound to diminish the importance of foreign bases on Chinese soil, such as those at Hong Kong and Port Arthur, that served as the strategic backbones of British and Japanese military operations in China.

4. Economically, Chinese nationalism had already demonstrated its effectiveness in disciplined large-scale strikes and boycotts against Great Britain and Japan. In the long run Moscow expected that the collapse of colonial or semi-colonial foreign trade privileges in China and other parts of Asia would accelerate social unrest and hasten proletarian revolutions in the industrialized motherlands of the colonial empires.

5. Politically, Soviet Russia's support for the Kuomintang's interrelated anti-warlord and anti-colonial campaigns was designed to yield twofold dividends: isolation of the Chinese Nationalists from the cultural, diplomatic, and especially ideological influence of Japan and the Western powers, and promotion of a pro-Soviet orientation among the potential civil war victors and unifiers of the neighboring Chinese empire.

6. Temporarily at least, Moscow had instructed the Chinese Communist Party to submit to the political leadership of the Kuomintang in order to prevent the issue of Kuomintang-Communist relations from becoming an obstacle to the conclusion of an alliance. But quite apart from the postulates of Moscow's Marxist-Leninist ideology, the Soviet Union's objective of keeping China a safe ally would conceivably be better served if the Chinese Communists were to succeed in seizing control of the revolutionary movement. Thus, though Chinese Communist power was relegated to a position of only secondary importance, it nevertheless remained one of the basic objectives of Moscow's entente policy.

Besides the resolutions of the Executive Committee of the Comintern governing Chinese Communist policies towards the Kuomintang, one of the most revealing indications of Soviet objectives in China at this time is to be found in the *Statute of the Southern Military Group*, which served as a basic guide for the activities of the Soviet military advisory staff attached to the armed forces of the Kuomintang. Paragraphs one and three of this classified document direct the Soviet advisers:

> 1. To organize and instruct a national revolutionary army in the south of China for the national liberation of China from the yoke of imperialism and for its unification into an independent democratic republic.
>
> . . . .
>
> 3. To popularize the doctrine of Communism and Sovietism, to work towards bringing about a complete reproachement [*sic,* probably *rapproche-*

ment] and a mutual interdependence between China and the U.S.S.R. and to create in the army, in the labor organizations and among the peasantry the resolve for a further revolutionary movement.[8]

From the very beginning, in other words, Moscow pursued the dangerously *ambivalent objectives* of supporting the Kuomintang while simultaneously undermining its domestic Chinese base. Soviet Russia's claim to be the first state to treat the often humiliated Chinese nation on the basis of equality was clearly contradicted by Moscow's efforts to shape and steer the Chinese revolution by means of the Chinese Communist Party. Apart from a skillful psychological appeal to the wounded pride of the Chinese Nationalists, the Soviet Union's most important asset in the beginning was the indifference and outright hostility of Japan and the leading Western powers towards the Kuomintang. Aggravated by the Kuomintang's "foreign aid complex," antagonism and disaffection between the Chinese Nationalists and the Western powers proved to be instrumental in forging a temporary community of interests between the disparate forces of the Kuomintang and the makers of Soviet Far Eastern policy. Moscow's China policy played for high stakes. Paralyzed by domestic stagnation and civil war in the nineteenth and twentieth centuries, China had been mostly condemned to a passive role in Far Eastern international politics. But it stood to reason that an effective revival of China under the auspices of an anti-colonial and pro-Russian regime could hardly fail to produce historically significant changes in the balance of power in the Far East.

The Chinese Communist Comintern delegate Liu Jen-ching presented a classical summary of Chinese Communist objectives in forming an "anti-imperialistic unity front" with the Kuomintang. In the course of an address delivered to the Fourth Congress of the Comintern in Moscow, Liu Jen-ching explained:

> The form of this [Communist-Kuomintang] united front consists in our joining of this Party in our name and as individuals. For this there are two reasons. *First, we want to carry on propaganda among the many organized workers in the national revolutionary party* [the Kuomintang] *and win them over for our side.*
>
> Second, we can struggle against imperialism only if we unite our forces, the forces of the petty bourgeoisie and the proletariat. We intend to compete with this Party where the organization of propaganda among the masses is concerned. If we do not join this Party we shall remain isolated and we shall propagandize a communism consisting of a great and noble ideal, but one which the masses do not follow. The masses certainly would follow the

---

[8] "Statute of the Southern Military Group," translated in M. Mitarevsky, *World Wide Soviet Plots*, Tientsin, n. d., p. 40.

bourgeois Party, which would then use the masses for its purpose. If we join the Party we shall be able to show the masses that we too are in favor of a revolutionary democracy, but that for us revolutionary democracy is only a means to an end. . . . Thus *we shall be in a position to rally the masses around us and split the Kuomintang Party.*[9]

It is important to note that these classical Chinese Communist united front tactics were put into effect on November 23, 1922, that is to say even before the official conclusion of the Soviet-Kuomintang entente at the beginning of 1923, and prior to the death of Sun Yat-sen and Chiang Kai-shek's rise to power. The Chinese Communist objectives as outlined in Liu's address were given official endorsement by Moscow in the resolution on Chinese Communist policy towards the Kuomintang adopted by the Executive Committee of the Comintern on January 12, 1923, in the very same month as the conclusion of the Kuomintang-Soviet alliance.

Li Ta-chao, a prominent member of the Chinese Communist Party and a professor at the Peking National University, became the first Communist who joined the Kuomintang under the new system of dual party membership. When the First National Congress of the Kuomintang formally allowed the Chinese Communists to enter the Kuomintang, Li Ta-chao declared in behalf of the Chinese Communist Party:

> . . . we propose to abide by the Constitution of the Kuomintang and submit to its discipline. If we ever try to make Communist propaganda in the Kuomintang, the Kuomintang is free to punish us according to the rules of the Party.[10]

Officially, the Kuomintang was told by Moscow's chief representative at Canton that the Third International recognized "only the Kuomintang platform" as the program of the Chinese revolution and that Moscow had "ordered" the Chinese Communist Party to join the Kuomintang. Secretly, however, the Comintern instructed the Chinese Communists not to obey but rather to pressure and transform the policies of the Kuomintang in such a way as to achieve two major objectives: subordination of Kuomintang policies to the interests of Soviet Far Eastern diplomacy, and development within the Kuomintang of a Chinese Communist Party that could challenge and annihilate its former ally.

In the second half of 1924 Sun Yat-sen went to Peking to attend a conference on the question of China's political reintegration. In Japan,

---

[9] *Protokoll des Vierten Kongresses der Kommunistischen Internationale*, Hamburg, 1923, p. 615. Italics added.

[10] Leangli T'ang, *The Inner History of the Chinese Revolution*, London, 1930, p. 4.

during a stopover on his journey to Peking, Sun advocated close economic and military co-operation between China and Japan provided that the two culturally related nations could proceed on the basis of full equality, without any hegemonic aspirations on the side of Japan. On condition of a full and equal partnership, Sun had thus offered Japan a much more comprehensive type of co-operation than he had suggested to his Soviet Russian allies. Sun died in Peking shortly after on March 12, 1925, but before his death he signed two documents of special political importance. One of these was a message to the Central Executive Committee of the Soviet Communist Party in which Sun avowed that the Kuomintang would carry on its national revolutionary struggle for the liberation of China from the quasi-colonial fetters imposed on it by the imperialist powers. He instructed his followers to remain "in constant contact" with the Kremlin, which could expect the emergence of a free and mighty China as a friend and ally of the Soviet Union in the course of the common battle for the liberation of the oppressed peoples of the world.[11] The second and more important document signed by Sun on his deathbed was his political legacy. It enumerated those of his writings that were to be regarded as the ideological and programmatic foundations of the Kuomintang's future activities. Without mentioning the Soviet Union or any other state by name, Sun ordered his followers to co-operate "with those peoples of the world who treat us on the basis of equality."[12] This instruction was to become the paramount and most consequential foreign policy maxim of the national revolutionary movement of China.

In the year following Sun's death, the Chinese Communist Party greatly expanded its influence within the ranks of the national revolutionary movement in Southern China. There are several factors that help to explain the rapid rise of Communist power at this time. With the death of its founder and political philosopher, the Kuomintang had lost a leader of almost unchallengeable authority, and its power of decision was considerably weakened by the resulting disunity among various leaders and groups within the Party. This situation provided the Chinese Communists with an opportunity to carry out their plan to extend their own influence through the tactic of promoting conflicts among dissident factions within the Kuomintang. Three groups emerged within the Kuomintang. These might be roughly described as the Right (the so-called "Western Hills group"), the Center (in which Chiang Kai-shek was to become the dominant figure),

---

[11] *The New York Times*, May 24, 1925.

[12] Milton J. T. Shieh, *The Kuomintang, Selected Historical Documents, 1894–1969*, New York, 1970, pp. 108–109.

and the Left (whose leader, Wang Ching-wei, was to become chief of a pro-Japanese quisling government in Eastern China during World War II). One of the most important differences among the three groups lay in their attitudes towards the question of co-operation with the Chinese Communists and the Soviet Union. The Kuomintang Right advocated putting an end to such co-operation at an early date. Chiang Kai-shek and his center group wanted to maintain such co-operation as long as it did not impair the Kuomintang's ideological supremacy within the revolutionary camp. Wang Ching-wei and the Kuomintang Left were increasingly in favor of strengthening co-operation with the Chinese and Russian Communists in order to counterbalance the considerable influence of the right-wing and centrist groups within the Kuomintang. The Chinese Communists skillfully exploited this situation to play one Kuomintang group against the others. At first, they tended to support the left and center groups of the Kuomintang against its right wing. Later, after the expulsion of the right wing from the Party, they co-operated with the left wing in opposing Chiang Kai-shek and his center faction.

The ascendance of Communist influence in Southern China was further promoted by two incidents in 1925 in which British police killed Chinese demonstrators. These massacres led to gigantic anti-British strikes in many provinces of Eastern, Central, and Southern China. In subsequently organizing and directing what were originally spontaneous protests, the Chinese Communists proved to be far superior to their Nationalist counterparts. The number of Communist Party members rose from only 1,000 in May, 1925, to 30,000 in July, 1926, and jumped to 57,963 by April, 1927. The Socialist Youth Corps, a front organization of the Communist Party, increased its membership from 2,000 in 1925 to 35,000 in 1927. As early as 1925, the Chinese Communists had brought an estimated 540,000 organized workers and 400,000 organized farmers under their political control. Within the national revolutionary government in Canton, Communists had been put in charge of the important Organization Bureau (headed by the Comintern delegate T'an P'ing-shan), the Farmers' Bureau (headed by Lin Tsu-han), and the Propaganda Bureau (with Mao Tse-tung as its acting chairman). The 50,000 pickets who had originally been armed and indoctrinated by the Communists for the strike movement began to take over certain functions of the revolutionary government at Canton. Soviet military advisers were actually in command of the general staff, the air force, the navy, and the intelligence section of the Kuomintang's armed forces, while Chou En-lai was in charge of the political education department of the Whampoa Military Academy. The Communists also founded the Military Youth League for the purpose of organizing the Communist and pro-Communist elements among the cadets and young officers of the revolutionary armed forces.

In this situation a clash of opinion arose between Chiang Kai-shek and the Soviet adviser, Michael Borodin (alias Gruzenberg), on the question of when the so-called Great Northern Campaign aimed at conquering Central and Northern China should be started. Borodin vehemently objected to Chiang's urgent appeal to begin the campaign as soon as possible. Years later Borodin confided to Louis Fischer in the course of an interview in Moscow that he had opposed the idea of an early start for that campaign, because he believed that the Communists had a good chance of seizing power in the revolutionary base at Canton before the opening of the campaign. In that case the military offensive for the conquest and reunification of China would have proceeded with the Chinese Communists acting as the factual leaders of a national revolutionary united front movement. Borodin's motives, however, were understood by Chiang Kai-shek, who recognized the Communist intention to bring the Chinese revolutionary movement under the control of the Soviet Union. Though the chances of success were limited, Chiang decided to try to force circumstances in favor of the center group of the Kuomintang by staging his first *coup d'état* on March 20, 1926. In the early morning hours troops loyal to Chiang surrounded the headquarters of the Soviet advisers and kept them under surveillance. At the same time Chiang's men disarmed thousands of Communist-led pickets and arrested a number of leading members of the Chinese Communist Party. Wang Chang-wei, leader of the left wing of the Kuomintang, departed from Canton for "reasons of health," so that Chiang Kai-shek remained as the sole master of the situation.

In a report on Chiang's action, the Soviet adviser Stepanov stated that it had come "as a lightning shock to our comrades as well as the military and civilian population." Stepanov went on to give a self-critical analysis of Soviet and Chinese Communist mistakes leading up to the *coup d'état*.

Our errors may be elaborated as follows:

1. Too rapid centralization of military power. . . .

2. Excessive supervision of the generals and various organs. (Russian advisers often assume leading positions, directly handling all matters.)

3. Inappropriate radical propaganda in the army on problems of imperialism, the peasantry, and communism. . . . We normally pay no attention to Chinese habits, customs, and etiquette. . . . The Chinese Communist Party has also committed many mistakes. . . Its members fail to understand the process of organizing the Kuomintang and then secretly transforming it. They only try, as their primary policy, openly to expand the Chinese Com-

munist Party and to grab complete control over everything everywhere. Thus, they have alienated the KMT and have aroused jealousy on the side of the KMT members.[13]

It is not difficult to see why Chiang's move had come as a complete surprise. How could anyone have expected a Chinese general to rebel against Moscow when it was providing his party with badly needed arms, money, and advisers? The Kuomintang barely held one or two provinces in all of China at the time. Internally divided, the Party faced strong opposition from various regional power centers in the country. In the initial phase of the crisis, Chiang could rely on no more than a small section of the Party to support his move. Yet he won the day by capitalizing on the element of complete surprise as well as the temporary absence of Borodin from Canton. To consolidate his newly won position of political supremacy in the national revolutionary movement, Chiang proposed a number of resolutions to the Central Executive Committee of the Kuomintang. Under the rubric of "Adjustment of Party Affairs," these resolutions were adopted on May 17, 1926. They removed all persons from the chairmanship of Party departments who were members not only of the Kuomintang but also of other parties. The Chinese Communists were thereby ousted from leading positions in the Kuomintang's bureaus for organization, propaganda, and peasant affairs, and were required, moreover, to present to the Chairman of the Kuomintang's Central Executive Committee a complete membership list of their party. The resolutions provided that Kuomintang members could belong to other parties only with the permission of the Central Executive Committee. The Communists were further instructed to cease their criticism of Sun Yat-sen and his ideology of the Three People's Principles. Comintern directives to the Chinese Communist Party and the policy decisions of the latter were made subject to the approval of a joint Kuomintang-Communist conference. Members of the Communist Party were prohibited from holding more than one third of the seats in the central and local decision-making bodies of the Kuomintang, and the Soviet Russian advisers lost their previous power of command over parts of the national revolutionary forces and were limited to strictly advisory functions.

The Soviet Union and the Chinese Communists were thus confronted with a difficult choice. They could have tried to fight Chiang right then and there in Canton, but Chiang had already secured for himself the stronger starting position for such a struggle. A fight between the leftist and centrist forces would also have meant hazarding the self-destruction of an important

---

[13] C. M. Wilbur and J. L. Y. How, *Documents on Communism, Nationalism, and Soviet Advisers in China, 1918–1927*, New York, 1956, pp. 250–251.

potential ally of Moscow's Far Eastern policy, in whom the Russians had already invested a considerable amount of material and technical assistance. Notwithstanding the suggestions of Chinese Communist leaders (possibly including Mao Tse-tung) that the Chinese Communist Party ought to terminate its close co-operation with the Kuomintang, Stalin decided in favor of appeasing Chiang Kai-shek, probably in the belief that continuing co-operation with the Kuomintang might still prove in the interest of Moscow's Far Eastern policy. Chiang's triumph seemed to be complete. In June, 1926, he was elected Chairman of the Central Executive Committee of the Kuomintang and concurrently Commander in Chief of the national revolutionary armed forces. On July 9, 1926, he launched the famous Great Northern Campaign against the regional power centers of the warlords in Central and Northern China. The purpose of the campaign was to destroy the system of politico-military polycentrism and regionalism that had prevailed in China since the death of President Yüan Shih-k'ai in 1916, and to replace it by a new government based on the ideas of Sun Yat-sen for the political and economic reconstruction of China and its liberation from the semi-colonial control of foreign powers.

Within half a year the Nationalist armed forces had conquered most of Central and Eastern China between the Kwangtung Province and the Yangtze River. Towards the end of 1926 the Kuomintang decided to move the seat of its revolutionary government from Canton in Southern China to the Wuhan city-triangle (Wuchang, Hankow, Hanyang) on the Lower Yangtze. A few months later, in the spring of 1927, a new crisis of even greater historical significance sprang up between the Kuomintang, the Soviet Union, and the Chinese Communist Party. The origins of this crisis lay in five developments during the first phase of the Great Northern Campaign:

1. Renewed expansion of the influence of the Chinese Communist Party was accompanied by intensification of its political radicalism. Again, owing to superior political mobilization, organization, and propaganda, the Chinese Communists became extremely powerful in the provinces and regions conquered by the military forces of the Kuomintang. The Chinese Communist Party tried to steer a middle course between ideological inclinations towards social-revolutionary radicalism on the one hand and tactical moderation towards the Kuomintang on the other, but it was increasingly drawn towards open advocacy and violent practice of the tactics of class war that were explicitly condemned by Sun Yat-sen's social reformism. Mao Tse-tung's early writings on the "Analysis of the Classes in Chinese Society" (March, 1926) and even more so his "Report on an

Investigation of the Peasant Movement in Hunan" (March, 1927) define the trend towards greater radicalism and violence in the political tactics of the Chinese Communists.

2. The unilateral hegemony of the Kuomintang, restored by Chiang Kai-shek's first *coup d'état*, was replaced by a leadership condominium consisting of the left wing of the Kuomintang and the Chinese Communist Party. The new leftist coalition unquestionably dominated a meeting of the Central Executive Committee of the Kuomintang that took place in Wuhan between March 10 and March 17, 1927. At this meeting the office of Chairman of the Central Executive Committee—a position held by Chiang Kai-shek—was abolished and supplanted by a Presidium of seven members. The members of the new Presidium included Wang Ching-wei, leader of the Kuomintang's left wing (the same man who had been "exiled" from Canton in 1926), five other Kuomintang leftists, and T'an P'ing-shan, Comintern representative of the Chinese Communist Party. Chiang Kai-shek was not elected to the Presidium and was furthermore deprived of all important executive positions with the exception of his post as Supreme Commander of the military forces. Two Communists were put in charge of ministries in the new Nationalist Government. A "Joint Conference" of the Kuomintang and the Chinese Communist Party was given the task of transforming the national revolutionary regime into a Kuomintang-Communist coalition government at all levels and of harmonizing the strategy and propaganda of the new government with that of the Comintern. The Kuomintang Left had thus discarded the notions held by its center and right-wing groups that the Chinese revolution was to be led by *one* party, the Kuomintang; guided by the will of *one* leader, Sun Yat-sen; and dedicated to *one* ideological system, the Three People's Principles. The practice of subjecting the Chinese Communists holding official positions in the national revolutionary movement to the leadership of the Kuomintang had thus given way to a new system in which the Chinese Communists were to be equal partners in a coalition government bent on co-ordinating its major policies with those of the Comintern.

3. As Chiang Kai-shek's armies, together with the cadres of the Chinese Communist Party, swept over half the country, Great Britain and the United States began to reconsider their policies towards China. Their economic and political interests led them to be apprehensive about a further strengthening of Sino-Soviet ties. At this point, the primary political motive of the advancing revolutionary forces in China was a strongly anti-imperialist nationalism. Frustrated by vain attempts to improve China's international position through peaceful negotiations with other major foreign powers, the Chinese nationalists had sought to achieve

their national objectives by allying themselves with the Soviet Union. Recognizing the potential dangers of the alliance, at the end of 1926 and the beginning of 1927 London and Washington declared their willingness to negotiate the peaceful abrogation of "unequal treaties," the restoration of China's customs autonomy, and the surrender of certain foreign concessions on Chinese territory. Similar though more cautious utterances were also heard from Japan. In other words, the major foreign powers now seemed to be willing to conduct peaceful bilateral negotiations with China precisely on those issues which Sun Yat-sen had sought to resolve for some time before concluding an alliance with the Soviet Union. As a result of the diplomatic initiative of the major foreign powers, the Kuomintang's interest in continued co-operation with the Soviet Union diminished.

4. Paradoxically, not only the possibility of a *rapprochement* between the Great Powers and the Kuomintang but also the acute danger of their military intervention in China was another factor contributing to the new and escalated conflict between the Kuomintang and the Chinese Communist Party. This danger arose as the result of the so-called Nanking incident of March 24, 1927. On that day troops of the national revolutionary army had conquered the city of Nanking. The conquest was unexpectedly followed by apparently systematic assaults against foreign consulates, foreign religious missions, foreign business establishments, and foreign residents. In response to the outrages, the persecuted foreigners asked for the protection of British and American warships on the Yangtze River, and the ships fired on the city. The Nanking incident increased tensions between the Chinese Nationalists and the foreign powers, endangering the chances for a peaceful settlement of the issues between them. With the Boxer Uprising of twenty-six years before still in mind, the incident created a panic among the foreign communities in China and led to an unprecedented concentration of foreign troops at Shanghai, where no less than 30,000 soldiers and 45 warships of various foreign powers were stationed after the incident. Thus, the long-feared specter of joint foreign military intervention was close to becoming a reality when China was still in the throes of civil war between the revolutionary South and the warlord regimes of Central and Northern China. Rightly or wrongly, Chiang Kai-shek took the position that the Nanking incident was a deliberate attempt by the Chinese Communists to drive a wedge between the national revolutionary movement and the conciliatory policies of the major colonial powers, so that China would continue to remain dependent upon the support of the Soviet Union. In his capacity as Supreme Commander of the revolutionary armies, Chiang therefore assumed full responsibility for the settlement of the incident, including the payment of compensations.

5. The final cause of the split between the Kuomintang and Moscow and the Chinese Communists was Chiang Kai-shek's second anti-Communist *coup d'état*, which was carried out in Shanghai. The aforementioned concentration of foreign troops existed side by side in Shanghai with the Communist forces of the Shanghai Commune. The Commune had been established in March, 1927, after an uprising of the local Trade Union Federation drove the mercenary troops of the warlord Sun Ch'uan-fang from the city. The Commune consisted of about 500,000 Communist-led followers, equipped with considerable amounts of arms captured from the arsenals of the defeated warlord. On March 22, 1927, the Commune was hailed in *Pravda* as a force that could shift the Chinese revolutionary movement towards the left, increasing the chances for the Chinese proletariat to become the leader of the revolution. When the spokesmen for the Commune declared that they preferred peaceful methods for regaining foreign-held concessions but might be forced to resort to violence under certain circumstances, Chiang Kai-shek proclaimed martial law in Shanghai. The Commune refused to comply with Chiang's order to lay down arms. (Rumors of an alleged plot by the Commune to storm the foreign-held concessions were circulated, but in fact there was no such plan, at least not at that moment.) Chiang's troops, supported by members of non-Communist trade unions and secret societies, took action against the Commune in the early morning hours of April 12, 1927. With this move, which was aimed at the disarming and suppression of the Shanghai Commune, the first shots were fired in the war between the Kuomintang and the Chinese Communist Party. In one form or another this war has continued to the present day.

A few days after the bloody suppression of the Shanghai Commune, Chiang Kai-shek established a second Nationalist government of China in Nanking composed mainly of centrist elements of the Kuomintang and excluding participation by the Communists. There thus existed two national revolutionary governments in China, the one led by Chiang Kai-shek in Nanking and the coalition government of the Kuomintang Left and the Chinese Communists headed by Wang Ching-wei in Wuhan. The coalition government outlawed Chiang's new regime, but was not able to eliminate it.

For Moscow, Chiang Kai-shek's second *coup d'état* was almost as unexpected as and even more embarrassing than the first, which had taken place little more than a year earlier. Only seven days before Chiang's second coup, Stalin had told a group of Party functionaries in Moscow:

> Chiang Kai-shek is submitting to discipline. The Kuomintang is a bloc, a sort of revolutionary parliament, with the Right, the Left, and the Com-

munists. Why make a *coup d'état*? Why drive away the Right when we have the majority and when the Right listens to us? . . . At present we need the Right. It has capable people, who still direct the army and lead it against the imperialists. Chiang Kai-shek has perhaps no sympathy for the revolution but he is leading the army and cannot do otherwise than lead it against the imperialists.

Besides this, the people of the Right have relations with the generals of Chang Tso-lin [a warlord who was then *de facto* ruler in Peking and in Manchuria] and understand very well how to demoralize them and to induce them to pass over to the side of the revolution, bag and baggage, without striking a blow. Also, they have connections with the rich merchants and can raise money from them. So they have to be utilized to the end, squeezed out like a lemon, and then flung away.[14]

As it turned out, however, it was Chiang Kai-shek who, having utilized Moscow's material and technical assistance to conduct the first phase of the Great Northern Campaign, then flung away the Communists. In retrospect, Chiang's action may be seen as contributing decisively to the postponement of a Communist seizure of power in China for twenty-two years. That a Communist takeover eventually became possible was largely due to the exhaustion and demoralization of the Kuomintang regime from eight years of resistance to Japanese aggression (1937–1945).

With his conquest of Shanghai, China's largest commercial center and most important harbor at the time, Chiang had become materially independent of Moscow. Stalin was quick to recognize that Chiang's second *coup d'état* jeopardized Soviet policy towards China. His response was to insist that the Chinese Communists maintain their co-operation with the Kuomintang Left in Wuhan and that they become the real power in the Wuhan government. To make certain this would happen, on June 1, 1927, Stalin dispatched a now famous cable to Manabendra Nath Roy, the Indian representative of the Comintern in Wuhan, directing him to start an agrarian revolution in the areas under the Wuhan government's control. Roy was instructed to arm 20,000 Communists and 50,000 revolutionary workers and farmers, and to establish revolutionary tribunals for the purpose of purging unreliable elements from the Wuhan government's military forces. A brilliant intellectual though not always a practical politician, Roy was so impressed by Stalin's cable that he naïvely showed it to Wang Ching-wei, the leader of the Kuomintang Left. The result was that on July 17, 1927, all Chinese Communists and Soviet advisers were expelled from the regime of the Kuomintang Left in Wuhan. Greatly alarmed by this new disaster for his China policy, Stalin tried to stem the anti-Communist tide by establishing another armed Commune, this time in Canton. A German

---

[14] Harold Isaacs, *The Tragedy of the Chinese Revolution*, Stanford, Calif., 1951, p. 162. Cf. L. Trotsky, *Problems of the Chinese Revolution*, New York, 1931, pp. 388–390.

Communist, Heinz Neumann, was sent to Canton to stage a Communist seizure of power. Instead of becoming a bridgehead for the Communist movement in China, however, the Canton Commune was drowned in blood as the result of a crushing offensive by the Kuomintang Left. This setback followed the defeat of two Communist uprisings organized by Chou En-lai, Mao Tse-tung, Lin Piao, and others in Central China earlier that year. A last hope for Stalin in China was the seemingly pro-Communist "Christian General" Marshal Feng Yü-hsiang, who had established a military base in Northwest China with the material and technical assistance of the Soviet Union. The question was whether he could be used as a pawn in Stalin's now desperate game for the maintenance of Moscow's influence and political and military investments in China. However, instead of supporting Moscow and the Chinese Communists, Marshal Feng contributed decisively to the negotiations between the Kuomintang Left and Center that led to the reintegration of the Kuomintang at the end of 1927. The resulting Nationalist government in Nanking looked upon the real or alleged involvement of Soviet officials in the Canton uprising as grounds for severing China's diplomatic relations with the Soviet Union. Moscow's first alliance with China thus ended in utter failure.

The Annexation of the Baltic States

Edgar Tomson

Introduction

The fate of the three Baltic States, Estonia, Latvia, and Lithuania, represents an exception to the usual pattern of Soviet takeover tactics insofar as these countries not only had Communist regimes imposed upon them, but suffered annexation to the USSR. Although the other East European states that fell within the Soviet orbit after World War II were usually reduced to satellite status, they never actually lost their national sovereignty, however great their *de facto* dependence on Moscow.

There is also another important difference: whereas elsewhere in Eastern Europe Stalin seized upon the unstable postwar internal situation as the ideal opportunity for intervention, in the Baltic States he was not able to resort to any such pretext. In 1940 Estonia, Latvia, and Lithuania possessed intact political systems; yet this did not save them from being overrun and annexed. The only other occasion when the Soviet Union acted similarly was in Czechoslovakia in 1968, where a legally constituted and fully operative government was overthrown following invasion by Warsaw Pact forces. On the excuse that subversive and anti-revolutionary forces were attempting to detach Czechoslovakia from the Communist bloc and bring it within the Western sphere of influence, Soviet troops marched in and forced the country's leaders to revert to a political course acceptable to Moscow. In the case of Estonia, Latvia, and Lithuania in 1940 the Soviet Union went further and did not shrink from making invasion the prelude to annexation.

The explanation for the Soviet decision to absorb the Baltic States rather than promote within them the emergence of client, yet nominally independent, regimes may well be that the crisis atmosphere of 1939–1940 encouraged Stalin to take speedy and ruthless action. Notwithstanding the Ribbentrop-Molotov pact, Stalin was distrustful of Germany's intentions and believed that in the event of war with Hitler possession of the Baltic States would strengthen the Soviet defensive position, particularly since the Estonian and Latvian governments were not unfavorably disposed towards Germany. It was not enough to forcibly install pro-Soviet Communist regimes in the Baltic States—Soviet security, Stalin probably judged, would be better served by the simple expedient of pushing Soviet frontiers westward to the Baltic borders of the Third Reich. And it *was* a simple expedient to absorb these small nations, which had only been independent from Russia since 1918. They were virtually defenseless, and Stalin had little need to fear that any power would come to their aid. No doubt the erection of a *cordon sanitaire* against eventual German aggression was uppermost in Stalin's mind, since only a few months earlier, in September of 1939, the Red Army had occupied eastern Poland, which was subsequently annexed to the Soviet Union, while Finland also, but for her stubborn resistance in 1939–1940, would probably have forfeited her independence entirely and reverted to Russian rule.

Soviet reasons for annexing the Baltic States on the eve of the German march eastwards are thus patent. It is the actual course of events which led up to this takeover that the present paper attempts to trace, from the moment of the signing of the Nazi-Soviet non-aggression pact on August 23, 1939, up to the final phase of the Soviet takeover a year later, when Estonia, Latvia, and Lithuania were proclaimed "Soviet Republics."[1]

Phase I

The Nazi-Soviet Non-Aggression Pact

On the night of August 23, 1939, in Moscow, Ribbentrop and Molotov signed the non-aggression pact between Germany and the Soviet Union. In the secret protocol appended to the treaty, the two powers declared:

> On the occasion of the signature of the non-aggression treaty between the German Reich and the Union of Soviet Socialist Republics, the undersigned plenipotentiaries of the two parties discussed in strictly confidential conversations the question of the delimitation of their respective spheres of interest in Eastern Europe. These led to the following result:
>
> 1. In the event of a territorial and political transformation in the territories belonging to the Baltic States (Finland, Estonia, Latvia, Lithuania) the northern frontier of Lithuania shall represent the frontier of the spheres of interest both of Germany and the USSR. In this connection the interest of Lithuania in the Vilna territory is recognized by both parties.[2]

In articles 2 and 3, the boundary between the German and Russian spheres of interest, in the event of a territorial transformation in Poland, was to be drawn approximately along the line of the rivers Narev, Vistula, and San, and Germany's complete disinterest in Bessarabia was proclaimed.

---

[1] The author is indebted to Professor Boris Meissner for permission to draw on his book *Die Sowjetunion, die Baltischen Staaten und das Völkerrecht* (Cologne, 1956, 377 pp.), which is a valuable reference work for the diplomatic history of the events under review.

[2] J. Degras (ed.), *Soviet Documents on Foreign Policy*, Vol. III, *1933–1941*, London, 1953, p. 360.

Soviet expansionist designs became clear a month later, on September 25, when Stalin and Molotov disclosed to the German ambassador in Moscow, Graf von der Schulenburg, their desire to retain Lithuania for the Soviet Union in exchange for the provinces of Lublin and Warsaw (up to the River Bug) lying to the east of the demarcation line. Stalin added that the Soviet Union would, provided the Germans agreed, immediately approach the solution of the problem of the Baltic States on the basis of the secret protocol of August 23, 1939, and hoped for the full support of the German government. Stalin spoke specifically of Estonia, Latvia, and Lithuania, but did not mention Finland. At his invitation, Ribbentrop returned to Moscow on September 27 to arrange the final settlement of the German and Soviet spheres of interest. It was agreed that Germany should be left a free hand in dealing with Poland, while the Soviets would make good their claim to the Baltic States. The new demarcation line was drawn according to Stalin's suggestion, although he agreed that some Lithuanian districts in the vicinity of Marijampole should also pass to Germany, so as to render the line "tidier." The secret protocol, dated September 28, 1939, had the following wording:

> The undersigned Plenipotentiaries declare the agreement of the Government of the German Reich and the Government of the USSR upon the following:
> The Secret Additional Protocol signed on 23 August 1939, will be amended in paragraph I, to the effect that the territory of the Lithuanian State falls to the sphere of interest of the USSR, because, on the other hand, the *voivodship* of Lublin and parts of the *voivodship* of Warsaw fall to the sphere of interest of Germany.[3]

In yet another confidential protocol of the same date, the Soviet government declared its assent to the repatriation of all German nationals and *Volksdeutsche*[4] resident in its sphere of interest to Germany proper, or to areas within the German sphere of interest.

Phase II

The Mutual Assistance Pacts Between the Baltic States and the Soviet Union

The secret treaty on the demarcation of spheres of interest was the first step undertaken by the Soviets towards eventual occupation of the Baltic States. Stalin had provided himself with the opportunity to proceed to

---

[3] *Ibid.*, p. 378.

[4] Persons of German origin born or residing abroad, who in many cases had assumed the nationality of their country of adoption.

annexation without Hitler being able to reproach him for intruding into the German sphere of interest. However, further steps were needed before such an invasion and annexation could be carried out, and in planning his course of action Stalin displayed almost Machiavellian skill. When the German-Polish war broke out, the governments of the Baltic States were induced to put into operation the neutrality treaties signed in 1938–1939, and immediately after the entry of the Red Army into Eastern Poland, Molotov assured the envoys of Estonia, Latvia, and Lithuania that peaceful relations with these states would not be harmed by the Soviet action.

Shortly afterwards there occurred an incident which gave Molotov a welcome opportunity to continue his policy along the desired lines. On September 18, 1939, a Polish submarine, the "Orzel," interned in Tallinn (Reval), escaped, causing Molotov to inform the Estonian ambassador that the Soviet Union could no longer recognize Estonia's sovereignty over its coastal waters, and that the Soviet government would therefore itself assume their protection. Soviet naval units appeared in Estonian territorial waters, causing several incidents, and Soviet planes began to violate Estonian air space. Thoroughly alarmed, the Estonian cabinet met to discuss the situation on September 21, in full awareness of its seriousness. It was decided not to mobilize, to refrain from reacting to the provocative Soviet action, and to use the continuing discussions on a new trade agreement to arrive at a clarification of Estonian-Soviet relations. Armed with this policy, the Estonian Foreign Minister, Kaarel Selter, traveled to Moscow on September 23. Molotov intimated that although economic relations between the Soviet Union and Estonia were satisfactory, a new trade treaty could only be considered when political relations, which left much to be desired, had been satisfactorily regulated. The Soviet government demanded cession of bases at several points on the Estonian coast and conclusion of a military alliance in the form of an assistance pact. Tallinn (Reval) and Pärnu were particularly mentioned as naval bases desired by the Russians. Molotov affirmed that they were needed to protect Russia, and that this demand had been agreed upon by the Politburo. In answer to Selter's objection that Estonia had always refused to conclude alliances with Great Powers and above all wished to preserve its neutrality, Molotov retorted that the Soviet Union did not intend to come to terms with the existing situation in the Baltic. Russia had been forced to accept this position in 1919, but was now strong enough to revise it. The Soviet government also knew that there were people in Estonia who would welcome such a pact with the Soviet Union. Although Estonia and the Soviet Union had concluded non-aggression pacts with Germany, the Soviet Union had to be prepared for war and urgently needed bases for the Red Army and Navy on the Estonian coast. Should Estonia attempt to oppose these demands, Moscow would feel obliged to impose its will by force. Estonia could not hope for assistance. England was distant, Germany was involved in the West and was treaty-bound not to interfere.

On September 24, Molotov submitted not only a draft treaty, but also the final draft of a declaration whereby the Soviet government pledged itself, should the assistance pact be signed, to refrain from interfering in the internal affairs of Estonia by attempting to alter its economic and political structure. The Estonian government decided, after lengthy consultation, to accept the Soviet demands in principle, but, if possible, not to consent to a Soviet garrison at more than one place on the mainland, and to reject outright the establishment of a Soviet base in the capital, Tallinn. The Estonian President, Konstantin Päts, regarded the forced renunciation of certain sovereign rights with dismay, but felt it was justified in order to help the Estonian people through a dangerous period, since, in the event of a conflict with the Soviets, the country would inevitably be overrun. On September 27 the Estonian Foreign Minister headed a delegation to Moscow for further discussions, and when it arrived in the Kremlin a TASS report was produced to the effect that an unknown submarine had torpedoed the Soviet steamship "Metallist" in Narva Bay. The Soviets, declaring that a completely new situation had thereby arisen, increased their demands to include the occupation of various nodal transport centers in the interior of Estonia, and the surrender of local police power over wide areas, especially on the coast. Although the "Metallist" incident had been engineered by the Soviets, as Selter was able to establish, the Estonian envoys were hard put to produce a draft treaty the following day in accord with the instructions of their government. The fact that Stalin made concessions to representations by the Estonian Foreign Minister may have been due to the presence in Moscow at the same time of the German Foreign Minister, von Ribbentrop. The non-aggression pact between the USSR and Estonia came into force at 11 p.m. on September 28, 1939.

The main provisions of the pact were contained in Article 3, in which it was stated that the Estonian Republic had granted the Soviet Union the right to lease for a reasonable price naval bases on certain Estonian islands, and in Paldiski, as well as air bases. On these bases the Soviet Union would possess the right to station at its own cost a strictly limited number of army and airborne units, the size of which was to be determined in a special agreement. In Article 5 it was expressly mentioned that the execution of the treaty in no way prejudiced the sovereign rights of the signatory parties, and that the bases and airfields remained Estonian territory.

The Soviet negotiations with the envoys of Latvia and Lithuania followed a course similar to those with Estonia. The Latvian Foreign Minister, Vilhelms Munters, arrived in Moscow on October 2, 1939, at Soviet request, and held two conversations with Stalin and Molotov on the same day and on October 3. He was told by Stalin:

> War is raging, and we have to attend to our safety. Peter the Great made sure that an outlet to the sea was gained. We are now without an exit. We wish to secure the use of ports, roads to these ports, and their defense. I tell you frankly: a division of spheres of interest has already taken place.... As far as Germany is concerned, we could occupy you. However, we want no abuses. Ribbentrop is a sensible person.[5]

Stalin added that Russian troops to be stationed in Latvia would be withdrawn at the end of the war, and Munters endeavored to have their number limited to 20,000. Stalin did not agree to this, saying: "You do not trust us, and we do not quite trust you either. You believe that we wish to seize (*zakhvatit*) you. We could do that now, but we are not doing it. A German attack is possible. We must be prepared in time; others who were not ready paid the price."[6]

Munters had no alternative but to capitulate, and so the assistance treaty between the USSR and Latvia was signed on October 5, 1939, its preamble and the individual articles corresponding almost word for word with the pact made with Estonia. In compliance with the Soviet demand, Article 3 contained a clause granting naval bases at Liepaja and Ventspils (Libau and Windau). After his return to Riga, the Latvian Foreign Minister declared to the nation that a treaty in the form of a mutual assistance pact had been chosen because it was the best way to give expression to the Latvian and Soviet desire to maintain peace and the *status quo* in the Baltic. This, he said, was confirmed by the reference to the peace treaty, to the non-aggression pact between the two states, and to Article 5 of the latest agreement, which made it quite clear that the sovereign rights of both states would not be affected. On October 9, *Moscow News* wrote:

> The Soviet-Latvian mutual assistance pact is a result of the development of friendly relations based on mutual confidence, relations in which the Soviet Union has set an example of respect for the state independence of other countries. The Soviet Union has never availed itself of the advantages which, as a great and strong power, it has over small countries.[7]

---

[5] Meissner, *op. cit.*, p. 62.

[6] *Ibid.*, p. 63.

[7] *Ibid.*

Having dealt with Latvia, Stalin next turned his attention to Lithuania. On October 3 the Lithuanian Foreign Minister, Joseph Urbšys, was summoned to Moscow, where he was confronted by a Soviet demand for the signing of a similar mutual assistance treaty. After Stalin had expressly assured him that the Soviet government did not intend to occupy Lithuania, and after Urbšys had ascertained that Lithuania could expect no help from Germany, he returned with a large delegation to Moscow and, on October 10, 1939, the Soviet-Lithuanian assistance pact was signed. To sweeten the pill, Stalin presented Lithuania with a part of the Vilna region—which in 1920 had been wrested from Lithuania by Poland, and which since September, 1939, had been under Soviet occupation. As in the case of Latvia and Estonia, the treaty (Article 4) granted bases to the Soviet army and air force "to protect the state frontiers of Lithuania." It was emphasized that implementation of the treaty would in no way impair the sovereign rights of the signatory powers, in particular their political structure and economic and social systems. In a speech to the USSR Supreme Soviet on October 31, 1939, Molotov stressed the importance of these assistance pacts for the security of the Soviet Union, and at the same time denied that conjecture concerning an impending sovietization of the Baltic States had any basis in fact. Nervousness about real Soviet intentions was, nevertheless, acute in the Baltic States, and great care was taken to see that there were no incidents during the occupation by the Red Army and Navy of the bases specified in the pacts. It was hoped that neutrality policy might be preserved, in spite of the pacts.

Soviet treatment of Finland was hardly calculated to allay the worst fears of the Baltic States and clearly brought the danger of war nearer. In contrast to the Baltic States, Finland had rejected the Soviet demands for boundary realignment and bases. Fabricated border incidents gave the Kremlin an excuse to rescind the Finnish-Soviet non-aggression pact, break off diplomatic relations and, on November 30, 1939, to order the Red Army to march into Finland.

This Soviet action was branded as aggression by the General Assembly of the League of Nations, which advocated expulsion of the Soviet Union from the League on December 14, 1939. The motion was approved by the League Council, but in a forlorn effort to stave off the impending catastrophe, the Baltic States abstained from voting, hoping that this demonstration of strict neutrality in the Finnish-Soviet conflict would deprive the Soviet Union of any pretext to take aggressive action against them.

News of the conclusion of a peace treaty between the Soviet Union and Finland on March 12, 1940, in Moscow was received with relief by the

Baltic States, and their foreign ministers met in Riga on March 14–15 to reaffirm their policy of neutrality. They also agreed on closer economic and cultural co-operation within the Baltic entente. This was a mistaken move because it aroused Soviet suspicions. The Finns had already exposed themselves by advancing a plan for a Nordic defensive alliance with Sweden and Norway, but had dropped the idea on account of the threatening attitude adopted by the Soviet Union. The Baltic States were less timid, and the blueprint for closer co-operation as a means of reinforcing their neutrality was carefully developed. Although these plans did not have a military character and were not designed to lead to the creation of a Baltic defensive alliance, they were later to provide the Soviet Union with its main pretext for the final takeover of the Baltic States.

Phase III

The Soviet Ultimatums

The German military successes in Denmark, Norway, and Western Europe in April and May of 1940 caused the Soviet government to decide in favor of annexing Estonia, Latvia, and Lithuania, in order to fortify its position, should Hitler decide to attack Russia. Moscow thereupon accused the Lithuanian authorities of having arrested Soviet military personnel in order to extract secrets from them, and of detaining numerous Lithuanian citizens in Soviet employ. In an official Soviet communiqué of May 30, 1940, the Lithuanian government was called upon to put an end to such "provocative" acts, and the findings of a Lithuanian commission of inquiry, which produced no evidence of the alleged offenses, were met with menacing silence. At the same time violent attacks were directed against the Estonian government by the Soviet Party press, which charged it with adopting a pro-British and anti-Soviet attitude.

In the light of this dangerous situation the Lithuanian government decided on May 30, 1940, to send Foreign Minister Urbšys to Moscow to probe Soviet intentions. The Soviet Union acted first, however, by inviting Prime Minister Antanas Merkys to Moscow. Molotov reproached him for failing to ensure the safety of the Soviet garrisons, and maintained that a Red Army soldier, who, according to the Lithuanians, had committed suicide, had in fact been murdered. Molotov went on to allege that a military alliance existed between the three Baltic States, as evidenced by frequent meetings of their chiefs of staff and political leaders. In reply the Lithuanian government formally affirmed its adherence to its treaty obligations with the Soviet Union and promised an immediate investigation of all the Soviet complaints.

It further asserted that Lithuania had not entered into any military alliance with Estonia or Latvia, and even declared its readiness to remove certain cabinet members offensive to the Soviet Union. All this was of no avail: Stalin had made up his mind to strike. On the evening of June 14, the Lithuanian Foreign Minister was summoned to the Kremlin. Molotov received him and read a note from the Soviet government repeating the earlier Soviet accusations, charging the Lithuanian government with deliberately violating the Soviet-Lithuanian assistance pact, and delivering, in the form of an ultimatum, the following demands on the Lithuanian cabinet:

1. The trial of the Minister of the Interior, Kasimiras Skucas, and the chief of the security police, Augustus Povilaitis, as the major offenders in the recent incidents.

2. Immediate formation of a government in Lithuania "able and willing" to put the Soviet-Lithuanian mutual assistance treaty into operation.

3. Agreement to the immediate entry of Soviet troops to occupy the most important centers in Lithuania, in order to guarantee execution of the pact and prevent incidents.

The concluding part of the note contained the comment that the Soviet government expected the Lithuanian government's answer before 10 a.m. on June 15, which left the Foreign Minister only ten hours to obtain instructions. Failure to deliver a reply by the appointed time would, said the note, be regarded as refusal to comply with the demands set forth. Urbšys tried in vain to obtain an extension of this deadline, and sent a brief telegram to his government at 2 a.m. on June 15. President Antanas Smetona immediately summoned the cabinet, Merkys resigned with all his ministers, and General S. Raštikis was entrusted with the formation of a new government. At 9 a.m. Urbšys informed Molotov that Lithuania would comply with the Soviet ultimatum. The Soviet reaction was to reject Raštikis as prime minister and insist on a Lithuanian government composed in agreement with the representative of the Soviet government, Vladimir Dekanozov, who was Deputy Commissar for Foreign Affairs and head of the foreign section of the state security police. This spelled the end for Lithuanian independence. President Smetona fled across the German-Lithuanian border on the same day, and the nation yielded. The way was now open for sovietization. Soviet troops entered Lithuania, and—more in haste than ever to finish off the Baltic States after the news of the fall of Paris—Molotov handed similar ultimatums to the Estonian and Latvian envoys. The note to Estonia read as follows:

... the Soviet government considers it proved that the Estonian government has not only failed to liquidate her military alliance with Latvia, which was concluded before the signing of the Soviet-Estonian mutual assistance pact and directed against the Soviet Union, but has expanded this alliance, drawing Lithuania into it and attempting to attract Finland. Prior to the signing of the Soviet-Estonian mutual assistance pact in the autumn of 1939, the Soviet government was still able to close its eyes to the existence of such a military alliance, although it was essentially inconsistent with the previously concluded Soviet-Estonian non-aggression pact. However, after the conclusion of the Soviet-Estonian mutual assistance pact, the Soviet government considers a military alliance between Estonia, Latvia, and Lithuania, which is directed against the Soviet Union, not only impermissible and intolerable but even extremely dangerous and menacing to the security of the frontiers of the Soviet Union. The Soviet government believed that Estonia would denounce her military alliance with the other Baltic countries after the conclusion of the Soviet-Estonian mutual assistance pact and that the aforesaid military alliance would thus be liquidated. Instead, Estonia, together with the other Baltic countries, began to revive and expand the aforesaid military alliance, which is testified by such facts as the convocation of secret conferences of the three Baltic countries in December, 1939, and March, 1940, in order to organize the amplified military alliance made to include Latvia and Lithuania, the consolidation of the bonds between the Estonian, Latvian, and Lithuanian general staffs kept secret from the Soviet Union, the creation in February, 1940, of a special press organ of the Baltic military entente, the *Revue Baltique* in English, French and German, which is appearing in Tallinn, etc. All these facts indicate that the Estonian government has grossly violated the Soviet-Estonian mutual assistance pact which forbids both parties "to conclude alliances and to take part in coalitions directed against either of the contracting parties." (Article 4 of the Pact.) This gross violation of the mutual assistance pact took place at a time when the Soviet government pursued and continues to pursue an exceptionally amicable and definitely pro-Estonian policy, scrupulously observing all the requirements of the Soviet-Estonian mutual assistance pact.

... The Soviet government considers it absolutely necessary and urgent that:

1. a government be established in Estonia which is able and willing to guarantee the honest execution of the Soviet-Estonian mutual assistance pact;

2. free passage be promptly secured for Soviet troops which are to be stationed in sufficient numbers in the most important centers of Estonia in order to guarantee the fulfilment of the Soviet-Estonian mutual assistance pact and to prevent possible acts of provocation against the Soviet garrisons in Estonia. [8]

The Estonian and Latvian governments immediately decided to comply with the Soviet demands, whereupon Soviet troops moved into Estonia and Latvia on June 17, 1940, and completely occupied the two countries within a few days.

---

[8] *Ibid.*, pp. 75–76.

Phase IV

Formation of "People's Democracies" in the Baltic States

Simultaneous with the handing over of the Soviet ultimatums to the Estonian and Latvian governments, Politburo member Andrei Zhdanov went to Tallinn, while Deputy Foreign Commissar Andrei Vyshinsky proceeded to Riga, where they started, like Dekanozov in Lithuania, to install puppet governments. Zhdanov, who was in charge of the whole operation, set up his headquarters at the Soviet legation in Tallinn. His first move was to appoint as Prime Minister of Estonia the poet Dr. Johannes Vares-Barbarus, assuring him that Estonian sovereignty would be respected and the Soviet troops would later be withdrawn. Vares was unconvinced and voiced his fear that the Soviets would use force. To this Zhdanov solemnly replied:

> Rest assured, Mr. Vares. Be fully reassured. We are not Germans. Everything will be done according to democratic parliamentary rules. We shall ask your President to constitute a new government. Once the present cabinet, which is incapable of solving present problems, is dismissed, the President will have to announce the elections, and you will assume the government by a parliamentary mandate. [9]

The Estonian President, Päts, was allowed to remain in office, and Zhdanov decided that Professor Jüri Uluots, the Prime Minister who had just resigned, was to carry on the government until Soviet arrangements for a new one had been completed. Vares, the Soviet-designated successor to Uluots, dutifully proposed a government made up of Communists and radical left-wing politicians. But President Päts showed spirit and refused to confirm the new cabinet in office. Zhdanov lost patience—Dekanozov and Vyshinsky had already succeeded in forcing through the creation of "People's Democratic Governments" in Lithuania and Latvia, yet Estonian politicians were still having the temerity to put up resistance. So, on Zhdanov's initiative, a Communist "uprising" was staged under the aegis of the Soviet occupation troops. Communist prisoners were liberated from the Tallinn central prison and a demonstration took place in front of the official residence of the President. To prevent bloodshed, President Päts yielded to Soviet pressure and confirmed the cabinet proposed by Vares. Zhdanov could now sit back content.

The Soviet takeover in Latvia under the direction of Vyshinsky was similar. The Latvian government had also resigned immediately after receipt of the Soviet ultimatum, but President Karlis Ulmanis, who had previ-

---

[9] *Ibid.*, p. 78.

ously also held the office of Prime Minister, resigned the latter office, refusing to resume the premiership or to sign the cabinet list proposed by Vyshinsky. His position was hopeless, however, and on June 20, despite his opposition, a "People's Government" was formed with Professor August Kirchensteins at its head, thus violating the provisions of the still-valid Latvian Constitution, according to which only the President was empowered to nominate ministers.

This scant Soviet respect for constitutional forms applied in the case of Lithuania as well. President Smetona had fled the country and Prime Minister Merkys assumed his authority, which was in itself an unconstitutional act. As self-styled acting head of state, Merkys was not entitled to confirm Vyshinsky's nominee, J. Paleckis, as the Prime Minister of a new "People's Government." Paleckis himself, apparently not regarded as sufficiently malleable by Lithuania's new masters, was appointed acting President for a time, and although he nominally remained premier, his deputy, the Foreign Minister, V. Kreve-Mickevičius, assumed the conduct of the government affairs.

To round off this penultimate phase of the takeover in the Baltic States the new puppet governments were made to issue a declaration revoking the Baltic entente treaty of December 12, 1934.

One month later, in July, 1940, the last act was played out.

Phase V

The "United Bloc" Elections and the Annexation of the Baltic States by the USSR

Molotov laid the Soviet cards on the table in a discussion with the Lithuanian Deputy Prime Minister and Foreign Minister, Kreve-Mickevičius. Molotov declared that although the Soviet Union had concluded a friendship pact with the German government, Russia would not fail to take measures to safeguard its security. This, he said, was why his country, although eager to stay out of the World War, had been forced to occupy not only Lithuania, but the other Baltic States. The object was to strengthen the Soviet frontiers. The Russian Tsars since Ivan the Terrible had endeavored to extend their empire as far as the Baltic, not because of personal ambition, but for reasons stemming from the organic development of the Russian state. Molotov declared further that the policy pursued by Smetona and Ulmanis had led the Soviet Union to abandon all considerations but its vital interests. Moreover, small states were destined to disappear in any event, and therefore it was better for Lithuania and its sister states to join the "glorious family of Soviet Republics" than to be swallowed by Germany. Germany was not likely to come to the aid of the Baltic States by declaring war on the Soviet Union, since she already accepted their occupation and could be expected to tolerate their incorporation into the Soviet Union. The population would be consulted in the manner usual in the Soviet Republics, and Molotov added somewhat sinisterly that it would not take four months for the Lithuanian people to declare themselves in favor of unity with the Soviet Union.

The elections ordained by Molotov took place on the same days (July 14, extended into July 15, 1940) in Lithuania, Latvia, and Estonia, and were carried out in such a way as to ensure the desired results. In Estonia, where 81.6 percent of the population went to the polls, 92.9 percent supposedly voted for the electoral list of the Communist-dominated "Union of Working People." In Latvia, where 94.7 percent voted, 97.6 percent of the votes went to the Communist-unified list. And in Lithuania, where 95.5 percent were reported as voting, the Communists obtained 99.2 percent of the votes. How these impressive results were obtained can best be seen by looking at the example of Estonia, where the Communist Party had a particularly small membership. By altering the electoral regulations, which was illegal, since the President did not have the right to effect any change in the electoral law by decree, the Soviet wire-pullers were able to cut short the normal course of preparations for the elections and thereby influence the results: instead of thirty-five days, only nine were scheduled, with no more than four days to nominate candidates. The Soviet occupation authorities had enough influence on the electoral committees to empower them to admit or reject candidates, and such decisions were declared final. Appeals to the Supreme Court were thereby prevented. Most important of all as an intimidation device, was the abolition of the secret ballot: voting slips could only be placed in the urn by a member of the local electoral committee, not by the voter himself. The electoral apparatus was wholly dominated by Estonian Communist Party officials, who also packed the central electoral committee almost to a man. Naturally enough, during the electoral preparations the tendency to eliminate opponents of the "Union of Working People" was evident from the outset. Democratic parties were denied the opportunity to make election propaganda, and applications for registration as candidates made by non-Communists were declared invalid if there were the slightest errors of form, while the candidates of the "Union of Workers" were provided with every facility.

Despite these precautions, at least one opposition candidate on the average managed to stand in every electoral district. So the Vares government once more altered the electoral law by means of a decree dated July 9,

1940, to the effect that all candidates must submit an electoral program no later than 2 p.m. on the following day. This decree was not, however, communicated to the electoral committees until the morning of July 10, which left no more than a few hours within which to send in electoral programs. This was a crude and deliberate move to place the non-Communist or fellow-traveling parties at a hopeless disadvantage, as is shown by the fact that the central electoral committee intimated at the same time that candidates of the "Union of Working People" did not need to submit any electoral program. The reason given was that the basic elements of their program had already been announced in the press.

Notwithstanding this deliberate effort to hamstring their activity, the great majority of opposition candidates contrived to submit programs before the expiry of the time limit. But the Communists were prepared for this eventuality, and, with few exceptions, all the opposition platforms were disqualified on the ground that they consisted of nothing but vague declarations of general intent, or statements designed to mislead the electorate. This argument was advanced even in cases where the platforms were virtually identical with those of the candidates of the "Union of Working People."

Even these thorough measures to stifle free expression of the will of the population and to ensure that only Communists contested the elections were not considered adequate; on July 9 the main electoral committee further ordained that electors must identify themselves by means of an identity card or other official document, and upon voting a mark was to be made on this card. Non-voters were to be treated as "public enemies." Despite all these pressures to ensure maximum casting of votes for officially favored candidates, the percentage of the population which went to the polling booths does not seem to have been as high as the main electoral committee maintained at the time, and it is highly probable that irregularities occurred in the actual counting of votes.

The elections had, however, served their purpose, and the overwhelming victory of the united Communist bloc was followed on July 22 by a "suggestion" to the Soviet plenipotentiary, Zhdanov, from the Vares caretaker government that Estonia should affiliate with the Soviet Union as a constituent republic. The new puppet Communist governments in Latvia and Lithuania, which similarly owed their existence to rigged elections, duly petitioned, too, for admission of their countries to the Soviet Union.

The independence of the Baltic States was finally extinguished the following month, when the three "People's Parliaments" elected delegations to be sent to the USSR Supreme Soviet to make formal application for acceptance as Soviet republics. Lithuania was the first to "seek admission" as the fourteenth Federal Republic of the Soviet Union (on August 3, 1940), and was followed by Latvia on August 5, and Estonia the next day. Stalin, clearly in no mood to lose time in consolidating his hold over the Baltic littoral, preferred that this veneer of legality should adorn an act of Soviet aggression that has to this day not been recognized *de jure* by many Western states, including the United States, Great Britain, France, and the German Federal Republic.[10]

---

[10] Readers interested in studying the subject of this chapter more thoroughly might consult the following works: Alfreds Bilmanis, *A History of Latvia*, Princeton, N.J., 1951; Henry de Chambon, *La Tragedie des nations baltiques*, Paris, 1946; A. Cichners, *Was Europa drohte. Die Bolschewisierung Lettlands, 1940–1941*, Riga, 1943; A. Kaelas, *Human Rights and Genocide in the Baltic States*, Stockholm, 1950; Janis Kalnberzins, *Ten Years of Soviet Latvia*, Moscow, 1951; A. Oras, *Baltic Eclipse*, London, 1948; Frederick W. Pick, *The Baltic Nations: Estonia, Latvia, and Lithuania*, London, 1945; J. Repečka, *Der gegenwärtige völkerrechtliche Status der baltischen Staaten*, Göttingen, 1950; Royal Institute of International Affairs, *The Baltic States: A Survey of the Political and Economic Structure and the Foreign Relations of Estonia, Latvia, and Lithuania*, London 1938; Leonas Sabaliunas, *Lithuania in Crisis: Nationalism to Communism, 1939–1940*, Bloomington, Ind., 1972; A. Spekke, *History of Latvia*, Stockholm, 1951; J. Survel, *Estonia Today: Life in a Soviet-Occupied Country*, London, 1947; J. A. Swettenham, *The Tragedy of the Baltic States*, London, 1952; Albert N. Tarulis, *Soviet Policy Toward the Baltic States, 1918–1940*, Notre Dame, Ind., 1959; V. Stanley Vardys (ed.), *Lithuania under the Soviets: Portrait of a Nation, 1940–1965*, New York, 1965; R. Wittram, *Baltische Geschichte*, Munich, 1954.

Stalin's Policies towards Eastern Europe, 1939–1948: The General Picture

Malcolm Mackintosh

My task is to try to provide general background for the more detailed studies on Eastern Europe in this symposium. What I would like to do is to concentrate on the overall attitude of the Soviet Union towards Eastern Europe during the period from 1939 to 1949 and on Stalin's outlook, personality, and aims as he looked out on Eastern Europe from Moscow. I shall deal briefly with the period before the war, then Stalin's wartime policies, and finally the period after the war, which might be called the years of Stalin's "forward policy" in Europe—roughly from 1944 to 1949.

First of all, a few words about the Soviet Union's attitude towards Europe before 1939. I think that most historians of the Soviet Union would agree that there were two phases of Soviet policy towards Communist expansion in Europe. There was a period of actual encouragement of revolutions, from 1918 to about 1927, during which the Soviet Union either instituted or inspired Communist revolts. This period saw abortive revolts in Germany and Hungary in 1919, the war against Poland in 1920, the attempted revolution in Bulgaria in 1923, and of course the first phase of the Communist revolution in China, which drew to a close in 1927. I may also add that in England in 1926 there was a general strike, in which two distinguished members of the Central Committee of the Soviet Communist Party took a great interest, hoping that it would turn into a Communist revolution.

The years from 1927 to 1939 witnessed the period of "socialism in one country" and the destruction of Trotskyism. Stalin was by this time in full control of the Soviet Union. He found the economy exhausted and the country without industry or defense technology. His instinct and conscious design was to postpone foreign adventures, to put off the encouragement of revolts and direct interferences in the affairs of other countries until the USSR was strong enough economically, and until he felt that other circumstances had upset the Versailles settlement and prepared the way for change. In other words, after 1927 Stalin was not ready to take the initiative in breaking up the Versailles settlement, but when somebody else did—i.e., Hitler—Stalin was glad to step in and exploit the new situation. Almost all Stalin's external involvements during the period 1927 to 1939 were in fact very orthodox, based upon the defense of his country's interests as he saw them. For example, the small-scale invasion of Manchuria in 1929 was held to be a defense of Russia's traditional rights over the Chinese Eastern Railroad. Stalin sent the Red Army into Manchuria to punish the Chinese for having infringed these rights.[1] Also, there were defensive military clashes against the Japanese in Manchuria in 1938 and in Mongolia in 1939. Most of all there was the Spanish Civil War from 1936 to 1939, but I believe that Soviet intervention in Spain was to a large extent a matter of defending the Soviet Union's and Stalin's interests rather than of supporting a Communist or international movement. Stalin went into Spain with the dual object of purging the Spanish left of Trotskyites, anarchists, and so on, and of giving selected officers of the Red Army and Air Force military practice, just as the Germans and Italians were doing.[2]

The second background element which I think is relevant was Stalin's personality and outlook. An understanding of the whole period after 1939 hinges on Stalin's attitude towards Eastern Europe. It is not unimportant that Stalin's personal origins were in a remote area of the Eurasian heartland—in Georgia, which for many centuries had no national status and no national or political sovereignty. Like Napoleon before him, Stalin instinctively fastened onto the nationalism of the nearest great power, which in the case of Napoleon was France, and in the case of Stalin was Russia. Stalin by personality was strong-willed, extremely suspicious, patient, unforgiving, and conspiratorial to an incredible degree. To these traits certain Russian characteristics, including xenophobia, were added, turning him into a leader who was able to exercise such complete domination over the Russian people for so long. It is difficult to describe his fundamental characteristics, but they have something to do with a combination of personal ruthlessness and complete aloofness from the people he was governing. It is important to note that all his life Stalin was bound by Russian nationalism, but driven on and inspired by his incomplete understanding of classical Marxism-Leninism. It is hard to pinpoint exactly what Communist ideology meant to Stalin. But I would submit that a conflict developed for him between the simple and limited horizons which he could easily understand, and the more detailed concepts which a man like Lenin or Trotsky could comprehend. It was not easy for Stalin to understand and develop Marxism, and in many ways, particularly as he grew older, Marxism became confused in his mind with his own conspiratorial outlook and mental make-up. In describing Stalin's personality it is also important to add that his vision was limited by ignorance and distrust of the outside world. And when he did deal with the outside world, he tried to force its

---

[1] *Krasnaya Zvezda*, Moscow, August 6, 1969.

[2] John Erickson, *The Soviet High Command*, London, 1962, pp. 428–431.

problems into a mold applicable to Soviet or European affairs which he understood. And this, as we shall see later, is one of the reasons why he failed. The further he got away from the borders of the Soviet Union, the less likely he was to succeed in carrying out his aims.

Now very briefly let us examine the period from 1939 to 1941. To Stalin this period signified the breakdown of the Versailles system, bringing, as it did, the decision of the Germans in September, 1939, to go to war with Poland. To him it offered chances of change in Europe, and he appears to have been guided by two aims.

The first of these aims was to restore to the Soviet Union its "rightful" territories in Eastern Europe, which implied, naturally, the right to communize them. What Stalin had in mind here was the eastern provinces of Poland, plus the Baltic States, Finland, Bessarabia, and Northern Bukovina. With his roots deep in borrowed Russian nationalism, Stalin felt that these territories should legitimately be returned to their former owner—Russia. Stalin's second aim was to secure a more militarily defensible frontier in the West, against the countries of Europe. To do this he applied the basic policy of allying himself with the strongest power in the area. Hence the Soviet-German pact of August, 1939, a pact which, incidentally, John Erickson shows in his works had been sought by Stalin since the mid-1930's, long before Hitler agreed to make a deal with the Soviet Union.[3] The results of the pact were that the Soviet Union and Germany divided Poland between them, and the eastern provinces of Poland were annexed to the Soviet Union. Characteristic of the Soviet mood at this time was Molotov's remark, after the two armies had met in central Poland, to the effect that Poland, "this ugly offspring of the Versailles settlement," had been destroyed.[4] Then came Stalin's absorption of the Baltic States—Estonia, Latvia, and Lithuania—in 1940. The technique followed here was that first of all Stalin secured military bases from these governments. The next step was political action, whereby a government willing to submit to the Soviet Union was formed, and this in turn led to the actual absorption of the three countries in August 1940.

Next we come to Finland. In the autumn of 1939, when the Soviet demands on Finland were being discussed, Stalin is reported to have said that no other Russian government would have tolerated an independent Finnish state, and therefore the Finns ought to be grateful to Stalin for having done so. But basically the same pattern of tactics that Stalin had used in Poland and the Baltic States was also followed in Finland. There

---

[3] Erickson, *op. cit.*, pp. 432 and 453.
[4] *Pravda*, Moscow, November 1, 1939.

is no doubt in my mind that before the fighting broke out, Stalin intended to absorb Finland within the borders of the Soviet Union, just as he had absorbed the three Baltic States. At the outset he made demands for military bases, some of which the Finns agreed to. He then prepared for political action by forming a Finnish Communist government in exile under Otto Kuusinen,[5] and when this action had no success, he sent the Red Army across the frontier. The invasion failed to overthrow the Finnish government, and no kind of subversion took place inside Finland, so Stalin abandoned his political goals in favor of purely strategic aims. Stalin found it very easy to fall back on national aims, and to put ideological considerations in second place. The settlement with Finland in March, 1940, was a purely military-strategic one, drawing a new frontier, with areas of southeastern and eastern Finland included in the Soviet Union for military reasons.

Then followed the attempt of November, 1940, in which Stalin tried to reach an agreement on spheres of influence with the Germans. There was talk of a division of the world, in which Hitler was to have Europe, the Japanese were to have Asia and the Pacific, and Stalin was to have everything south of the Caucasus, including Iran down to the Persian Gulf. But nothing came of this, mainly because Stalin wanted paramount influence in the Balkans, an area of traditional Russian interest, which Hitler, however, had consigned to Germany.[6]

Turning to the subject of Stalin's wartime plans, the evidence really comes from the three major Allied meetings which were held during the war—Teheran, Yalta, and Potsdam.[7] There is remarkably little internal evidence of Stalin's wartime attitudes towards Eastern Europe except for his plans for Poland, which will be discussed later, and to lesser extent for Czechoslovakia. But these conferences did show a consistent Soviet approach towards Eastern Europe in the postwar period. First, Stalin wished to persuade the Western Allies to accept a spheres of influence agreement whereby Eastern Europe would fall to the Soviet Union. In the course of the three conferences Stalin in effect obtained this objective. Second, Stalin aimed at securing specific international frontiers and zones of occupation in Central Europe, regardless of which areas were actually going to be occupied by Soviet or Western troops. In other words, before

[5] John H. Wuorinen (ed.), *Finland and World War II, 1939–1944*, New York, 1948, p. 66.

[6] R. J. Sontag and J. S. Stuart (eds.), *Nazi-Soviet Relations*, Washington, D. C., 1948, p. 258. See also A. Rossi, *Deux Ans d'Alliance Germano-Soviétique*, Paris, 1949.

[7] Winston S. Churchill, *The Second World War*, London, 1948, Vol. V, pp. 287–360, and Vol. VI, p. 210 and pp. 302–352 and 545–577.

Soviet forces had reached the vital areas in Central and Eastern Europe, Stalin had already insisted on drawing the boundaries of the zones of occupation in Germany, and on arranging the future spheres of influence of the Allied Powers. Third, Stalin used psychological pressure on his Western allies by arranging to have the three Conferences meet shortly after Soviet military victories or Western reverses. For example, the Teheran Conference came soon after the victory at Stalingrad; the Yalta Conference came after the Soviet winter offensive of 1944–1945, when the Western Allies had just suffered a reverse in the Battle of the Bulge; and the Potsdam Conference occurred after the Soviet army had occupied most of Eastern Europe. So in each case Stalin had the psychological advantage.

The development of Soviet policy during the war suggests two further Soviet attitudes towards the postwar settlement. First of all, Stalin showed that he was prepared to exploit situations potentially favorable to the Soviet Union in areas which he had already allocated, on paper, to his Western allies. The best example of this was Greece in December, 1944. This is not meant to suggest that Stalin inspired the Greek Communist attack on Athens in December, 1944, but after the Communist forces rose against the British, Stalin was prepared to take advantage of the situation, even though Greece was theoretically in the Western sphere of influence.

Another of Stalin's attitudes had to do with the wartime resistance movements in Eastern Europe. Stalin made every attempt to control the resistance movements, and to place them under the leadership not just of Communists, but of Communists whose loyalty to the Soviet Union superseded their loyalty to their own country. Stalin's methods of dealing with non-Communist resistance movements are strikingly illustrated by the way in which he destroyed the Polish underground Home Army as Russian troops advanced into Poland and by his refusal to support the Warsaw Uprising of August-September, 1944. He refused to aid the uprising even though Soviet troops were literally a mile to the East of the Vistula River, within easy reach of the Polish underground forces in the city of Warsaw. In fact it was a Soviet citizen of Polish origin, Marshal Konstantin Rokossovsky, who, ironically enough, was in command of the troops opposite Warsaw that might have gone to the help of the Poles had Stalin authorized such action.[8]

Stalin's determination to control resistance movements is also evident from the two Slovak uprisings of 1944. I say *two* Slovak uprisings because

---

[8] For the Polish Home Army viewpoint, see General T. Bor-Komarowski, *The Secret Army*, London, 1950, chap. iv. For the Soviet viewpoint, see *Istoriya Velikoy Otechestvennoy Voiny*, Moscow, 1962, Vol. IV, pp. 244–252.

there was one led by Communists who were to some extent under the control of the Soviet Union, and there was also another one which involved a mutiny by the Slovak national army. Stalin did all he could to prevent the success of the rising of the Slovak national army. He sent his troops on a forced march through the Carpathian passes in the autumn and winter of 1944 in order to reach the Communist units, and he dispatched the Second Czechoslovak Parachute Brigade from the Czechoslovak Corps in the Soviet Union to link up with the Communist rising. But no assistance was given to the Slovak army, which was isolated and crushed by the Germans.[9]

A third case is the partisan movement in Yugoslavia, which started in 1941 and continued until the liberation of the country in 1945. It was a Communist-controlled movement, but as it progressed, Stalin realized that his control over the movement was minimal, and that the Yugoslav partisans were less and less amenable to Soviet dictation. This was due in part to the fact that the Soviet Union gave the partisans relatively little help, although they had a military mission at Tito's headquarters. Stalin was extremely suspicious of the dependence of the partisans on Western aid and of the influence of Western military missions in Yugoslavia. By the time the Red Army reached the borders of Yugoslavia in late 1944, and seized Belgrade in collaboration with the Yugoslav partisans, Tito controlled two-thirds of the country, and the Germans had already started a strategic withdrawal northwards from the Balkans into Hungary. But much more important from Stalin's point of view was the fact that Tito already had his own administrative and police apparatuses. As early as 1944–1945 Stalin tried to penetrate the partisan movement, but was opposed by Tito's own police.[10] This was one of the major reasons for the Tito-Stalin dispute, which broke out into the open in 1948. To some extent this was a battle of two police organizations. Incidentally, and partly to distract their attention, Stalin encouraged the Yugoslavs to assume control over the Albanian Communist partisan movement, which Tito did with conspicuous success, until 1948.

There is good evidence of Stalin's wartime plans towards individual countries only in the case of Poland. His attitude towards Poland is very clear. He would restore Poland after the war if it fulfilled three aims: first, if it agreed to the Soviet annexation of the territories occupied in

[9] For a Soviet view, see Marshal A. A. Grechko, *Cherez Karpaty*, Moscow, 1970, pp. 22–35, which gives the Soviet reasons for discriminating between the two Slovak resistance movements.

[10] Royal Institute of International Affairs, *Documents of International Affairs, 1947–1948*, London, p. 364.

1939; second, if it accepted the role of a buffer state in a protective belt along the western frontier of the Soviet Union; and third, if it supported a political regime obedient to the Soviet leadership. The evidence suggests that Stalin looked on Poland—more than on any other country—through the eyes of a Great Russian, and because of the peculiarity of Russo-Polish historical traditions and relations, quite openly and deliberately set out to impose a Great Russian solution on Poland in the postwar period. It is interesting to note that in December, 1941, at the height of the battle of Moscow, when the Germans were only five or six miles from the gates of the city, Stalin insisted on discussing the Soviet-Polish frontier with the British Foreign Secretary, asking for British recognition of the frontier of June, 1941.[11] Stalin also created a Polish army within the Red Army, transferring to it as military commanders and political advisers many of the Red Army's large pool of officers of Polish descent, such as Generals Swierczewski, Korczyc, and Strazewski. In a word, Stalin accepted quite openly the fact of Polish hatred for Russia, and quite deliberately laid down his conditions for a future Poland, taking this into account.

There is comparatively little evidence of Stalin's attitude towards Czechoslovakia during the war. However, we do know that, unlike Poland, Czechoslovakia had both a pro-Russian and a pro-Soviet tradition, and its government in exile in London was friendly and amenable to Soviet interests and pressures. Consequently, the Soviet Union felt quite confident that it would have little difficulty in dealing with the Czechoslovaks after the war. According to reliable reports, the Soviet intelligence service had penetrated the Czech government apparatus extensively before the war,[12] so presumably the Soviet government had easy access to information about what was going on inside the Czechoslovak government in exile. Frontier changes were easily agreed to by the Czechoslovak government, which ceded Ruthenia or Carpatho-Ukraine to the Soviet Union in 1945 without protest. Partly, no doubt, because of this amicable relationship between the Soviet Union and Czechoslovakia (in marked contrast to Poland), Stalin placed Czechoslovakia in his second group of priorities, with no immediate plans for a takeover.

There is very little direct information about Stalin's attitude towards the ex-enemy states, the allies of Germany—Rumania, Bulgaria, and Hungary—during the war. Of course they had Communist parties in exile. In fact there were two Bulgarian Communist leaderships in being

---

[11] Cordell Hull, *The Memoirs of Cordell Hull*, New York, 1948, Vol. II, pp. 1, 166–67.

[12] Erickson, *op. cit.*, p. 435.

during the war, one in exile in Moscow and one attempting to form a partisan movement in the mountains of Bulgaria. Stalin decided to use his rights of conquest to impose Communist regimes on Rumania, Bulgaria, and Hungary, using in most cases the exiled Communist leaders as the nucleus of future governments.

Stalin had a special interest in Bulgaria. In the first place after Stalin himself, the best known Communist leader in the world was a Bulgarian residing in Russia, Georgi Dimitrov, who was the hero of the Reichstag fire trial in 1933, and later the Secretary of the Comintern (Communist International) until its dissolution in 1943. Stalin looked upon Bulgaria as a counter to Yugoslavia in the Balkans. The fact that Bulgaria bordered on Greece could also be important if possibilities arose in the future for a Communist takeover of Greece, although under the spheres of influence agreement between Stalin and Churchill, Greece was theoretically in the Western camp. Because Bulgaria did not declare war on the Soviet Union when Germany's other allies did, Stalin had to create a crisis through which the Soviet Union could go to war against Bulgaria, thereby giving him the right to occupy the country and exercise the rights of conquest.[13]

In the Soviet zone of Germany Stalin again used the rights of conquest to set the scene for the establishment of a Communist regime, through the Soviet military government, and with the help of German Communist leaders brought back from exile. These men, including Walter Ulbricht, had been engaged in making propaganda among German prisoners of war and had formed an Anti-Fascist Committee of professional soldiers, most of whom became leaders of the East German army when it was founded in 1948.

Stalin seems to have based his policy towards East Germany on three principles: first of all, never again to allow all of Germany to fall under one government, that is, to perpetuate the division of the country into at least two states; second, to use the territory of East Germany as part of the defensive buffer zone that he was building west of the Soviet frontier; and third, to create an alternative German state which could claim to have no connection with previous Reichs. Stalin probably envisaged using the four-power control of Germany to which he had agreed with the Western Allies in order to confirm Soviet domination of his area, and in order to obtain recognition of Soviet claims to intervene in, or at least veto, what was going on in West Germany. To Stalin, the Four-Power Administration was most likely a method of governing which could be

---

[13] An interesting comment on this episode is given in Marshal G. K. Zhukov, *The Memoirs of Marshal Zhukov*, London, 1971, pp. 546–548.

discarded if it failed in either of these two aims; it was, in effect, discarded in 1948 when Stalin decided to try to drive the West out of Berlin.[14]

Stalin's policies towards Finland have always been something of a puzzle, and it is not easy to understand why he treated Poland, Hungary, Bulgaria, and the other countries of Eastern Europe in one way, but left Finland more or less to follow its own path politically. It is an interesting subject, and I would suggest only one possible explanation, namely, that Stalin felt Finland did not need to be forcibly communized at this stage since it was a weak country, and geographically far away from the main line of military attack or defense. Stalin may also have had a sneaking respect for the skillful defense by the Finns in 1939–1940, and decided that the communization of Finland would not be worth the effort required.

Finally, a word about Turkey. It is not generally known that Stalin launched a political offensive against Turkey before the end of the war. In February, 1945, he denounced the Soviet non-aggression pact with Turkey, and the Red Army conducted major maneuvers on the Bulgarian side of the Turkish frontier.[15] An interesting possibility suggests itself: Stalin may have believed that if he took action against Turkey in order to seize the Straits while the war was still on, it would be impossible for the Western Allies to come to the aid of the Turks before Germany was defeated. But if in fact this was what in Stalin's mind, he decided not to pursue the idea.

To turn to the postwar phase,[16] the years immediately following the war were dominated by the Polish settlement, by Soviet use of the rights of conquest in the ex-enemy countries, and by Soviet moves in the Near East and Asia. In Europe, Stalin's first priority was to secure the national frontiers that he wanted. In keeping with this plan, he carried out the annexation of part of East Prussia (assigning the rest to Poland), confirmed the occupation of the Baltic States, and annexed parts of Finland and all of Bessarabia. In the Far East he acquired the southern part of the island of Sakhalin and the Kurile Islands from Japan and rights in Port Arthur from China. This phase developed from Stalin's conviction of Russia's "natural right" to absorb certain territories around its borders, as well as from his concern about requirements for the defense of the Soviet Union. At a banquet in September, 1945, after the operations in the Far East, Stalin

---

[14] Royal Institute of International Affairs, *Documents of International Affairs, 1948–1949*, London, p. 580.

[15] J. Malcolm Mackintosh, *Strategy and Tactics of Soviet Foreign Policy*, London, 1962, p. 10.

[16] Mackintosh, *op. cit.*, chaps. i, ii, and iv, *passim*.

said that the old generation of Russians had waited long for this day of reckoning with the Japanese (he was referring of course to the War of 1904–1905), which is a good illustration of his Russian nationalism.[17]

The next phase could be described as the communization of the primary area, which lay west of the Russian frontier, and included Poland, Rumania, Bulgaria, Hungary, and East Germany. Communization of the area occurred between 1944 and 1947. How this was done is dealt with in detail in the other contributions to this symposium. Very briefly, however, we can say that in most of these countries new Communist leaderships were drawn from exiles who had been living in the USSR. In Poland a special role was given to the Communist Polish army, which was commanded and staffed by Soviet officers of Polish descent after the liquidation of the non-Communist resistance movement, the Polish Home Army. In Rumania, Bulgaria, and Hungary, in the initial phase, control was exercised through the Allied Control Commissions under Soviet chairmen, who were subordinate to the Soviet Ministry of Foreign Affairs and the Central Committee of the Party for policy, and to the Soviet Ministry of Defense for intelligence and security. In East Germany control was exercised through the Soviet military government.

The methods used in these countries were remarkably alike and owed their origin in part to the "Popular Front" techniques which the Soviet Union had practiced in the 1930's. The procedure might be summarized as follows:

(1) First came the establishment of a political coalition called a "National Front," a "Patriotic Front," or something similar, with major Communist Party participation. Communists were placed in control of the Interior Ministry and, if the army was important, the Defense Ministry as well. In some countries, such as Bulgaria, the army was not important; in fact I personally served on a commission which supervised the disbandment of the Bulgarian army in 1945–1946. In this initial phase the defense minister of Bulgaria was a non-Communist army officer.

(2) Second, the Soviets forcibly merged the non-Communist, left-wing, or agrarian parties with the local Communist Party. In Bulgaria, the last party to be forcibly merged was the Agrarian Party, which was the majority party in the country. In East Germany the forcible merging of the Social Democratic Party of that zone with the Communist Party led to the formation of the Socialist Unity Party or SED.

(3) Third came the isolation of the center or right-wing parties. Here the normal procedure was to purge and bring to trial some leaders and to

---

[17] *Bolshevik* (now *Kommunist*), Moscow, No. 16, August, 1945, as quoted in Isaac Deutscher, *Stalin : A Political Biography*, London, 1949, p. 528.

force others into exile. It is interesting that at this stage Stalin followed the pattern established by his treatment of Trotsky, preferring to exile his opponents rather than to execute or imprison them, something that occurred all too often later on.

(4) Fourth, with the political system firmly in the hands of the Communist Party, elections were held on a single list of candidates. In the case of Bulgaria, Dimitrov returned to his homeland from Moscow only after the Communist Party had secured domination of the administration and after elections in which he was the top candidate. The various elections and the formation of Communist governments were followed by pleas for international diplomatic recognition and by the signature of peace treaties with the ex-enemy countries in 1947.

(5) The fifth stage, and the most brutal one, was when Stalin turned upon the "internal" Communist Party opposition in each of these countries, destroyed their resistance leaders, including the people who admired Tito, and indeed all Communist leaders who did not have a "Muscovite" background. Here again there are interesting parallels with earlier Soviet history—the purging from the Spanish left of all non-Stalinist elements during the Civil War, and the great Moscow purges in the 1930's.

It is important to note that during this period Stalin controlled every detailed move by the Communist Parties which were coming to power in these countries, and in many cases the local leaders were caught by surprise when he suddenly changed course. An event which I personally witnessed will illustrate this. In August, 1945, the Allied Control Commission in Bulgaria was discussing the advisability of the Bulgarians holding a general election on a single list. The British and American delegates on the Commission opposed a single list as being "undemocratic," while the Russians supported it as the only "democratic" method of holding an election. Since Stalin always worked at night, all other Soviet officials also had to work at night, so the sessions of the Commission began at 8:00 P.M. and lasted till 4:00 A.M. On this occasion the discussions started on a Wednesday evening and the elections were due to be held the following Sunday. The discussions on Wednesday, Thursday, and Friday proved fruitless, and we assembled again, much dispirited, on Saturday evening at 8:00 P.M. to listen once more to the Soviet argument in favor of a single list. The Russian side of the negotiations was conducted by the Soviet Commander in Chief in Bulgaria, Colonel-General (later Marshal of the Soviet Union) S. S. Biryuzov. He was obviously trying to drag out the discussions until the polling booths opened at 7:00 A.M. on Sunday morning so that nothing could be done about the matter, because the population would already be voting for or against the single list of candidates. But at 1:40 A.M. the telephone rang in the anteroom of the Russian general's office, and he sent his aide, a major, to answer it. When the major lifted the telephone to his ear, he stood there, as though struck dumb. The general thought his aide had become ill, so he strode over in a masterly fashion to the phone and seized it. Immediately he came smartly to attention, and stood upright for about five minutes while we could hear a voice crackling over the line. Then he said, "Yes, Comrade Stalin," and came back to us to declare: "As is well known, the Soviet government has always opposed the holding of general elections on a single list. The elections will be postponed until a more democratic method can be found." The Bulgarian prime minister was then sent for, told that the elections were to be put off, and the polling booths to be closed.

Here was a prime example of the detailed control which Stalin exercised over the communization of Eastern Europe. What was Stalin's motive in acceding to the Western demands in this case? The postponement played into his hands. When the news became known that the elections were off, the Bulgarian population assumed that the Anglo-Americans had won a major political victory over the Soviet Union. They therefore came out into the streets, started to express their opposition openly, and began publishing informal news sheets. This is exactly what Stalin had planned; he was able to identify the opposition elements, the anti-Communist leaders, and those individuals who were against Soviet control. When the time came to clamp down and the elections were held on a single list, it was much easier for the Soviet and Bulgarian police to detect the opposition. This was not an isolated case, but is only one example of how Stalin moved towards total Communist control in Eastern Europe.

Now we come to the next stage during which Stalin extended his activities further afield, in 1947–1949. Some of the disparate moves Stalin made at this time might at first sight appear to be unconnected. First, there was the attempt by penetration to restore Soviet control over Tito's Yugoslavia—the battle between the NKVD (the secret police) in the Soviet Union and the UDBA in Yugoslavia, a battle which Tito won. The NKVD was not able to penetrate the Yugoslav police apparatus, and this paved the way for a major break between the two countries.[18] Second, there was the overthrow of the pro-Russian social-democratic regime in Czechoslovakia in the Communist-led *coup d'état* of February, 1948. Third, there was the blockade of Berlin, which began in April, 1948; the Soviet intention was to drive the West out of Berlin so that the city could be incorporated into

---

[18] Royal Institute of International Affairs, *Documents of International Affairs, 1947–1948*, London, p. 364.

the Eastern Zone, and also become the capital of a future Soviet Germany. Fourth, there was a major increase in East European support for the second Greek Communist rebellion, which had begun in the autumn of 1946. Fifth, there was an attempt to establish a Communist regime in Finland, but the Finns managed to resist; in fact, they secured the dismissal of the Communist Minister of the Interior in May, 1948, without any Soviet reaction. Sixth, in several Asian countries the Soviets encouraged rebellions by Communist-controlled movements, particulary in Indonesia, the Philippines, Malaya, India, and Japan.

What, then, were Stalin's motives for these operations during this second phase from 1947 to 1949? First of all, he was probably motivated by a desire to bring other Communist Parties under more centralized control. The further they were from the frontiers of the Soviet Union and the reach of the Red Army the less firmly these Parties appeared to be under Stalin's control. In particular, Stalin wanted to dispense with the services of Communist leaders who had a background in the national resistance movements or in the Spanish Civil War.[19] An additional step towards greater Soviet control was the formation in 1947 of the Cominform, whose only major action as an institution, however, was to expel Yugoslavia from its ranks in 1948.

A second motive was Stalin's sense of personal and political mission. He would have expressed it somewhat like this: "For twenty-five years I have waited. I have been running the Soviet Union on the basis of socialism in one country; I now have expanded militarily into Eastern and Central Europe; I have gigantic power at my disposal, and I would be a traitor to my whole background if I didn't use these opportunities to spread the benefits of communism to other countries." Although Stalin was basically motivated by the desire to expand the power and influence of his country militarily and politically, and to extend and improve the buffer defense zone which he was building for the protection of the Soviet western frontier, it would be an oversimplification to underestimate the part played by his sense of mission.

Except for the communization of Czechoslovakia, the second stage of Stalin's expansion failed, largely because Stalin was operating in unfamiliar surroundings. He tried to solve problems with methods applicable to the Soviet Union and to areas within easy reach of the Soviet Union that he knew and understood. What he could do in Rumania and Bulgaria he found he could not do in Yugoslavia or Berlin. And it was characteristic of Stalin

---

[19] Among those who suffered were Laszlo Rajk in Hungary, Traicho Kostov in Bulgaria, and Wladyslaw Gomulka in Poland.

that after his first two or three failures he called a halt in Europe in 1949, cut his losses, and turned to the Far East, a decision to which we may attribute the start of the Korean War in 1950.

Could the West have prevented the Soviet occupation of Eastern Central Europe and the communization of these countries? I believe that once the Red Army had survived invasion and put itself in a position to defeat the main forces of the German armies, which had happened by September, 1943, the fate of Eastern Europe was sealed. If the West had tried by political or military means to turn Stalin from his course, there is the distinct possibility that he would have threatened to conclude a separate peace with Germany, provided that a German government would have been willing to offer him Eastern Europe. Stalin would have taken Eastern Europe even if the Western leaders had refused to delineate the zones and boundaries of the future occupation areas in Central and Eastern Europe, and even if the Allies had landed earlier in Western Europe, or had come up through the Balkans and launched a campaign in the Danube Valley. I believe that Stalin would not have agreed to a free-for-all scramble for occupation zones based on the military occupation of territory in the course of the final campaigns. In other words, Churchill's "percentages offer" to Stalin was little more than a rather dramatic expression of the inevitable.[20] In any case, as we have seen, even the "percentages agreement" did not save Greece from two Communist rebellions, one of them, at least, supported from the outside. I do not agree with those who claim that if the Western armies had pushed on into Berlin, Czechoslovakia, and Hungary, or if there had been a Western Adriatic campaign or a Danube Valley campaign, Eastern Europe could have been saved.

To summarize: Stalin was never able to free himself from the bonds of Russian nationalism, with which he identified so strongly. All his policies were related to this loyalty to his concept of Great Russia merged with Soviet power, and this accounted for his preoccupation with such traditional matters as frontiers, buffer zones, and defense problems. But Stalin's belief in Communist ideology and his sense of mission were also deep and lasting. Stalin's motives in Eastern Europe (and beyond) probably included a sense of fulfillment of his and Lenin's destiny to expand communism by one means or another. While he felt loyalty to Russian nationalism, it was from Communist ideology that he got much of his driving force and inspiration. Stalin's limitations became crucial when he was faced with external situations of which he had no experience, i.e., in dealing with such problems as

---

[20] Winston S. Churchill, *The Second World War*, London, 1948, Vol. VI, pp. 201–204.

Berlin, Yugoslavia, and, of course, China in the Far East. Stalin was most successful when he could seal off a country from the outside world and deal with it steadily and in detail, directing all the tactical moves himself. He would then keep the tightest possible hold on events, even to the point of occasionally reversing his previous policies and thereby surprising his own subordinates. But in the face of two or three failures in the areas more remote from Soviet frontiers, he was ready to cut his losses and turn elsewhere. When this happened, Stalin's European policy became one of holding the external line rigidly against the West and continuing the internal counter-offensive against the national communism of Titoism. Finally, it is my belief that Stalin planned the communization of Eastern Europe as soon as he became convinced that the Soviet Union had survived the shock of the German invasion. But by the time the Red Army reached Eastern Europe and was in a position to put his plans into practice, the two motives—nationalism and Communist ideology—were inextricably inter-woven; and this is surely one of the lasting elements of Soviet foreign policy which has survived to the present day.

The Yugoslav Revolution: The First of a New Type
Paul Shoup

The seizure of power in Yugoslavia marked a significant departure in tactics from the Bolshevik revolution. For the first time a rural-based guerrilla movement[1] was able to gain control of a country and set up a Communist government. For the first time, securing the support of the peasantry proved more important than organizing the urban proletariat.

Relying on the peasant was not solely a Yugoslav idea. The Chinese Communists had developed this approach earlier, independently of the Yugoslavs. The guerrilla tactics of the partisans had been utilized before, as the Soviets went to great lengths to point out in their exchange of letters with the Yugoslav Central Committee in 1948:

> The conceit of the Yugoslav leaders goes so far that they even attribute to themselves such merits as can in no way be justified. Take, for example, the questions of military science. The Yugoslav leaders claim that they have improved on the Marxist science of war with a new theory according to which war is regarded as a combined operation with regular troops, partisan units and popular insurrections. However, this so-called theory is as old as the world and is not new to Marxism. As is known, the Bolsheviks applied combined action of regular troops, partisan units and popular insurrections for the entire period of the civil war in Russia (1918–1921), and applied it on a much wider scale than was done in Yugoslavia. However, the Bolsheviks did not say that by applying this method of military activity, they produced anything new in the science of war, because the same method was successfully applied long before the Bolsheviks by Field Marshal Kutuzov in the war against Napoleon's troops in Russia in 1812.
>
> However, even Field Marshal Kutuzov did not claim to be the innovator in applying this method because the Spaniards in 1808 applied it in the war against Napoleon's troops. It thus appears that this science of war is actually 140 years old and this which they claim as their own service is actually the service of the Spaniards.[2]

The Yugoslav Communists, however, were the first to use these tactics successfully to gain power, and under circumstances markedly different from those which existed in Russia in 1917. If—as has been suggested by

---

[1] In the discussion to follow, the terms "guerrilla movement" and "partisan movement" are used interchangeably.

[2] Royal Institute of International Affairs, *The Soviet-Yugoslav Dispute; Text of the Published Correspondence*, London, 1948, pp. 51–52.

Richard Lowenthal[3]—the events in Russia in 1917 marked the last of the great democratic revolutions in European history and the first of the totalitarian revolutions of the twentieth century, then the Yugoslav Communist seizure of power was the first of the twentieth-century revolutions in which a totalitarian party came to power by consciously exploiting conditions of backwardness in a peasant society. So far this strategy has been successfully followed by Albania, China, Cuba, North Vietnam, and the socialist regime in Algeria, as well as being attempted in Greece, Bolivia, and elsewhere.[4]

When examining a successful revolutionary movement, questions naturally arise over which factors were decisive in contributing to the final outcome. The problems which must be considered in this connection never lend themselves to simple analysis, and this is no less true in the Yugoslav case than in the examples of Russia, China, or Cuba. Because of the complex political and military circumstances surrounding the growth of the partisan movement and because of the injection of emotional national issues into the discussion, the Communist takeover in Yugoslavia has been the subject of particularly intense and acrimonious controversy. Debates have raged both over the events themselves and over the reasons for the Communist victory.[5]

In an effort to simplify and isolate the issues, the discussion that follows is divided into three parts. First, consideration is given to the problems

---

[3] Richard Lowenthal, "Three Roads to Power," *Problems of Communism*, Washington, D.C., Vol. V, No. 4, 1956, p. 10.

[4] The Soviet takeover of Mongolia in 1921 also exploited conditions of backwardness, but was not based predominantly on an indigeneous guerrilla movement, as was the case in Yugoslavia.

[5] For the Yugoslav side of the debate with the Soviet Union over the partisan movement, see *Priča o sovjetskoj pomoći za dizanje ustanka u Jugoslaviji*, Belgrade, 1950. There is considerable literature on the collapse of Yugoslavia and who was responsible for it. See Velimir Terzić, *Jugoslavija u aprilskom ratu 1941*, Titograd, 1962; Franjo Tudjman, *Okupacija i revolucija: dvije rasprave*, Zagreb, 1963; Vaso Bogdanov, *Porijeklo i ciljevi šovinističkih teza o držanju Hrvata 1941*, Zagreb, 1961. For the Yugoslav presentation of events related to foreign policy, see Dušan Plenča, *Medjunarodni odnosi Jugoslavije u toku drugog svjetskog rata*, Belgrade, 1962. For émigré writings, see Branko Lazić, *Titov pokret i režim u Jugoslaviji, 1941–1946*, Munich, 1946; Constantine Fotitch, *The War We Lost: Yugoslavia's Tragedy and the Failure of the West*, New York, 1948; Vladko Maček, *In the Struggle for Freedom*, New York, 1957; D. A. Tomasić, *National Communism and Soviet Strategy*, Washington, D. C., 1957; Zivko Topalović, *Pokreti narodnog otpora u Jugoslaviji, 1941–1945*, Paris, 1958. A guide to the vast literature on the resistance movement which appeared in Yugoslavia is: Borivoj Pajović and Milorad Radević, *Bibliografija o ratu i revoluciji u Jugoslaviji*, Belgrade, 1969.

encountered in developing a revolutionary strategy under the conditions that prevailed in Yugoslavia prior to World War II. Next, the tactics which the Communists developed during the war are examined. Finally, an attempt is made to evaluate theories that have been developed to explain the underlying forces at work in the Communist revolution. By raising this last issue, we hope to define more precisely the unique aspect of the Communist seizure of power in Yugoslavia, as well as to illuminate the parallels between the Yugoslav case and the Communist takeovers in other countries.

Problems of Revolutionary Strategy

Any attempt to document the events leading up to World War II in Yugoslavia and the conditions prevailing in the country at the time would raise more issues than can adequately be dealt with here. The same may be said with respect to the history of the Yugoslav Communist Party between the two world wars. A good deal of light can be shed on the problems of the seizure of power in Yugoslavia, however, by a brief discussion of the proposals for carrying out a revolution which were put forth by the Comintern (Communist International) in the prewar period and by a close look at the problems that arose in adapting these tactics to Yugoslav conditions. This approach will also make clear the differences between the Yugoslav Communist revolution as it actually developed during World War II and the Soviet image of how this process was supposed to take place.

Two aspects of the Comintern's policies deserve special attention in respect to Yugoslavia: first, the emphasis on the idea that the revolution might come about as the result of a new war, in which the seizure of power might be "from above," and, second, the attempt on various occasions to link the problem of revolution in Yugoslavia to the role of the peasant question and the national question.

The theory that imperialist wars offer revolutionary opportunities was argued by Lenin and later endorsed by Stalin. In the 1930's, the idea gained its most precise formulation at the Seventh Congress of the Comintern, which urged Communists to be prepared for three types of wars: (1) an imperialist war, in which the task of the Party would be to turn the imperialist struggle into a revolutionary one; (2) a counter-revolutionary war against the USSR, in which the Communist Parties must be subordinated to the Red Army; and (3) a national liberation war, in which the Party must be prepared to co-operate with the bourgeoisie in the struggle for independence.[6] The Congress, while advocating co-operation with non-

---

[6] W. Ercoli [Palmiro Togliatti], *The Fight for Peace*, New York, n.d., p. 83.

Communist groups in the struggle against fascism, also foresaw the possibility that the Communists might seize power in a united front *from above*, using as a pretext the need to take "decisive action" against "fascists and other reactionaries." Since the approach adopted by the Congress touches directly on all aspects of the revolutionary seizure of power in Yugoslavia and the rest of Eastern Europe after World War II, the directives of the Comintern on this matter deserve quotation at length:

> In circumstances of political crises, when the ruling classes are no longer in a position to cope with the powerful sweep of the mass movement, the Communists must advance fundamental revolutionary slogans . . . which lead the working masses right up to the point of revolutionary seizure of power. If . . . it will prove possible, and necessary, in the interests of the proletariat, to create a proletarian united front government, or an anti-fascist people's front government, which is not yet a government of the proletarian dictatorship, but one which undertakes to put into effect decisive measures against fascism and reaction, the Communist Party must see to it that such a government is formed. The following situation is an essential prerequisite for the formation of a united front government: (a) when the state apparatus of the bourgeoisie is seriously paralyzed so that the bourgeoisie is not in a condition to prevent the formation of such a government; (b) when vast masses of the toilers vehemently take action against fascism and reaction, but are not yet ready to rise and fight for Soviet power; (c) when already a considerable proportion of the organizations of the Social Democrats and other parties participating in the united front demand ruthless measures against the fascists and other reactionaries. . . .
>
> In so far as the united front government will really undertake decisive measures against counter-revolutionary financial magnates and their fascist agents, and will in no way restrict the activity of the Communist Party, the Communist Party will support such a government in every way.[7]

The instructions of the Congress are remarkable for their explicitness, and lay to rest the notion that by 1935 the Comintern had given up the idea of revolution. Setting aside the problem of whether the directives of the Seventh Congress were considered binding on Communist Parties during the war—the presumption is that they were not—the predictions made at the Congress confirm that the linkage of war and revolutionary takeover was still part of Communist strategy in the 1930's. The idea of utilizing an "anti-fascist front" as a device for seizing power was also clearly articulated.[8]

---

[7] "The Offensive of Fascism and the Tasks of the Communist International in the Fight for the Unity of the Working Class Against Fascism," *Resolutions, Seventh Congress of the Communist International*, New York, n.d., pp. 30–31.

[8] For an interpretation of the Seventh Congress which parallels that just given, see K. E. McKenzie, "The Soviet Union, the Comintern and World Revolution: 1935," *Political Science Quarterly*, New York, Vol. LXV, No. 2, 1950, pp. 214–37.

A careful examination of the plan for revolution advocated by the Seventh Congress also reveals some of the reasons for the difficulties which were to develop later between the Yugoslavs and Moscow over the tactics to be used in seizing power.[9] The Comintern approach was to seize power from above, either by taking over the levers of control already in existence, or by putting pressure on a front government so that it would not be able to curb the revolutionary activities of the Communists. The concept of a coalition government in which the Social Democrats would be included was also part of the plan. Judging from the types of wars predicted by the Congress and the types of action which the Communist Parties were to take in each case, the Communists were to pursue revolutionary objectives first and foremost in the case of an "imperialist" war—that is, one in which the non-Communist powers of Europe were engaged in combat while the Soviet Union remained a non-belligerent.

This plan, while it departed from the Bolshevik strategy of revolution by calling for the indirect seizure of power in collaboration with the socialists, stressed the importance of the urban revolutionary movement coming to power under conditions of an "imperialist" struggle, conditions which had prevailed in Russia in 1917. Not surprisingly, the plan failed to foresee the possibility of the large-scale occupation of Europe by Germany; the destruction of established authority which occurred in some countries as the result of this development; and the fact that a Communist-led "united front" or "anti-fascist" government, unless organized abroad, might have to be set up outside the major centers of population in which the occupation forces were stationed.

The strategy did foresee that in the case of a "counter-revolutionary war" the duty of the Communist was to obey the orders of the Red Army. In this situation, military considerations relating to the defense of the Soviet Union were to be placed ahead of revolutionary objectives.

It can be seen that during World War II Soviet policy towards the Yugoslav partisans reflected these assumptions. This is especially clear in respect to the Soviet inclination to view the partisan movement in terms of its contribution to the Soviet war effort, and in this connection to place great stress on the effect of Yugoslav Communist operations on friendly relations with the United States and Great Britain. It is also plausible to suggest that the Soviets failed to react more quickly to the rapid spread of the partisan movement because their approach to revolution blinded them to the events in Yugoslavia, where the breakdown of central authority

---

[9] For Soviet relations with Yugoslavia during the war, see Plenča, *loc. cit.*, and Vladimir Dedijer, *Tito*, New York, 1953.

and the paralysis of the political parties as a result of the occupation were playing into the hands of the Communists.

In the 1920's and 1930's the problem of a revolutionary takeover in Yugoslavia arose in still another context. Yugoslavia was an underdeveloped country suffering from deep national divisions. The working class was small, and the non-Communist political parties had great influence among the peasants, who were the overwhelming majority in the country. These facts worked against the spread of Communist influence,[10] and a great deal of discussion took place concerning the possibility that the difficulties of the peasantry and the struggle for national rights could perhaps be used to the advantage of the Communists if only the correct policy could be found.

The basis for this discussion in the mid-1920's was an exchange which took place in 1925 between Stalin and Sima Marković, Secretary of the Yugoslav Communist Party.[11] Stalin, in this famous debate, linked the national question to the role of the peasantry in Yugoslavia. For almost a decade thereafter it was accepted as a truism that "the national question is a peasant question," and that the correct exploitation of both would help create a revolutionary situation. This was especially true in the period between 1928 and 1934, when it was the official goal of the Yugoslav Communist Party to set up a revolutionary workers' and peasants' government.

Since the success of the partisans was due, in a significant measure, to policies adopted towards the national and peasant question, it is logical to see some connection between the Comintern policy of the late 1920's, enunciated by Stalin, and the policies pursued by the Yugoslav Communists during the war. Jozo Tomasevich, in his authoritative account of the war, hints at this connection.[12]

The difficulty of this theory is that Stalin never explained his position clearly, with the result that its exact significance remained obscure, no less to the Yugoslav Communists than to others. While the Communists did have links to the peasantry prior to the war, primarily through students of peasant background, there were few if any Party members who showed the inclination or the ability to organize the peasants against the regime.[13]

---

[10] The Communists did, however, win many peasant votes in Montenegro and Macedonia in the elections for the constituent assembly in 1920.

[11] The exchange appeared in the Soviet journal *Bolshevik*, Moscow, April 15 and June 30, 1925.

[12] See Jozo Tomasevich, "Yugoslavia During the Second World War," in Wayne S. Vucinich (ed.), *Contemporary Yugoslavia*, Berkeley, Calif., 1969, p. 83.

[13] An exception was Vukašin Marković, who led a short-lived peasant revolt in Montenegro in the 1920's, and later fled to the Soviet Union.

Furthermore, attempts to co-operate with nationalist or peasant movements, initiated at Comintern insistence during the 1920's, failed disastrously.[14]

There was therefore nothing in Soviet experience or in the directives of the Comintern which prepared the Yugoslav Communists for the task of organizing a revolutionary movement among the peasantry. The Yugoslav Communist Party enjoyed certain advantages over other parties on the eve of the war—above all, superior organization and discipline, as well as the fact that the Party was not associated with any one nationality in Yugoslavia. But the prospects for revolution were no better at the beginning of 1941, setting aside the possibility of war, than a decade or two earlier. It was the collapse of Yugoslavia under the onslaught of the Axis powers and then the Nazi invasion of the Soviet Union several months later which dramatically altered this situation and led the Communists to form a resistance movement. Once started down this path, contact with the peasant was established, the policy of equal treatment of all nationalities began to have an impact, and the popular anti-fascist front appeals of the mid-1930's were revived.

In closing this section, a cautionary word is in order. The discussion so far has focused largely on revolutionary theory, with the object of showing that the methods adopted by the Yugoslav Communists were the product of special conditions not foreseen by the Comintern on the eve of the war. Nevertheless, the Yugoslav strategy did borrow from the Comintern in certain important respects. The Comintern, contrary to many interpretations, did have clear-cut revolutionary objectives. These revolutionary goals were to be combined, when conditions permitted, with a campaign in support of a popular, anti-fascist front led by the Communists. This blend of anti-fascism, patriotism, and revolution re-emerged in the policies of the Yugoslav Communists during the war, although certain essential elements of the earlier strategy, especially the seizure of power "from above," were abandoned.

Tactics of the Resistance Movement

The methods of partisan warfare developed by the Yugoslav Communists during the war have been described in many eyewitness accounts and are recorded in the copious documentation of the partisan campaigns published in Yugoslavia. Scholarly works which evaluate the partisan

---

[14] In 1924, an alliance was established between Moscow and the Croatian Peasant Party leader Stjepan Radić. At the same time an agreement was reached between the Communists and the Macedonian nationalist organization, IMRO. Both arrangements broke up soon thereafter.

movement in an unbiased fashion are nevertheless rare. As a result, there is still much about certain partisan tactics—the use of terror for example—which remains obscure.[15]

The tactics employed by the Communists were shaped by ideology, by the revolutionary experience of the Party prior to the war, and by the conditions that prevailed in Yugoslavia after the country's occupation. Of these three factors, the last mentioned was in many ways the most important, since it shaped the military side of Communist strategy. At the same time, the Communists showed their mastery of revolutionary tactics by using the resistance movement as a device to facilitate the seizure of power. The methods that the Yugoslavs developed during the course of the war may be considered, in fact, as a combination of military and political moves, the former aimed primarily, although not exclusively, at the occupation authorities, the latter at the London government and the non-Communist political groups still in Yugoslavia.

In the discussion to follow three topics will be considered: (a) utilization of the peasantry and development of techniques of partisan warfare; (b) the application of "Popular Front" tactics; and (c) tactics adopted in dealing with the national question. The purpose of the analysis will be to suggest not only the success of these methods, but also their limitations. In this way false comparisons between Yugoslavia and other countries, based on misunderstandings of the tactics employed in Yugoslavia and their effectiveness, may be avoided.

Utilization of the Peasantry and Techniques of Partisan Warfare. The techniques employed against conventional forces by guerrilla or partisan units drawn largely from the peasantry are well known, and need not be discussed in great detail here. The Yugoslav Communists showed themselves masters at such warfare and fully aware of the principles that underlie it: the advantages of mobility, the importance of gaining the support of the local population, and the need for maintaining discipline.

---

[15] Eyewitness accounts, or accounts based on first-hand experience, include: Stephen Clissold, *Whirlwind*, New York, 1949; Vladimir Dedijer, *Dnevnik*, Belgrade, 1948–1950; Fitzroy Maclean, *Eastern Approaches*, London, 1949; Jasper Rootham, *Miss Fire*, London, 1946; *Četrdeset godina*, Vol. V, *Zbornik sećanja aktivista jugoslovenskog revolucionarnog radničkog pokreta*, Belgrade, 1961. Documents on the resistance movement are contained in: Vojnoistorijski institut, *Zbornik dokumenata i podataka o narodnooslobodilačkom ratu naroda Jugoslavije*, a multi-volume work which has been appearing over the past decade. For an attempt at an analysis of the techniques of partisan warfare and their universal applicability, see Franjo Tudjman, *Rat protiv rata : Partizanski rat u prošlosti i budućnosti*, 2nd ed., Zagreb, 1970.

By contrast, the forces arrayed against the partisans never attained the same degree of discipline and effectiveness. This was particularly true in the case of the Chetniks, whose undoubted bravery did not make up for the high degree of disorganization that prevailed in their ranks and the tendency of Chetnik units to avoid combat, remaining close to the village or locality from which they were recruited. When the main forces of the Chetniks and the partisans clashed during the famous German fourth offensive, the Chetniks were decisively beaten.

The partisans, however, often found that the strong ties of the peasant to his own region led to a stationary type of warfare in which the aim was to defend one's own village or locality. The pressure on the partisan units to remain and fight was especially strong when an enemy column was sent on a punitive expedition against villages which had aided the partisan forces. This problem was especially severe in the early stages of the war, and the formation by the Supreme Command of the Proletarian Brigades in December, 1941, was meant in part to cope with this difficulty. These Brigades were formed mostly from the ranks of the Serbs (many of them workers from Belgrade, Kraguevac, and other towns in Serbia) who had retreated with the Supreme Command from Serbia in the winter of 1941–1942.

While mobility was one of the tactical keys to the success of the partisans, it would be wrong to think of the type of warfare in which they engaged as lacking any relationship to the region in which they fought. On the contrary, it was highly important to the Communists that they identify the partisans with the struggle for liberation, and this was accomplished by forming resistance groups whose task was to challenge the occupation forces in a particular area, and to attempt to remain in that region if at all possible.

This is well illustrated in the case of the Slovenian partisans, who were almost forced to retreat into Croatia but remained, nevertheless, on Slovenian soil, even when threatened with liquidation.[16] The resistance forces in Serbia and Montenegro did, it is true, retreat into Bosnia-Hercegovina and were the core of the forces under Tito and the Supreme Command. The Macedonian partisans, on the other hand, liberated their area without outside help and after fierce battles with the Germans.[17]

Whenever possible the partisans would attempt to consolidate their position, militarily and politically, by forming liberated areas. In these

---

[16] For a detailed description of the partisan struggle in Slovenia, see Metod Mikuž, *Pregled razvoja NOB u Sloveniji*, Belgrade, 1956.

[17] For a recent source dealing with the events in Macedonia during the war, see *Istorija makedonskog naroda*, Belgrade, 1970, Vol. III, chapt. xiv.

areas a Communist administrative structure would be created, based on the National Liberation Committees (*narodnooslobodilački odbori*). These committees had a three-fold purpose: to organize the region in support of the partisan units, mostly through procuring supplies; to serve as a political and propaganda organ in favor of the partisans; and to set up a new power structure in place of the authorities of the old regime, or of the occupation forces.[18]

It was especially characteristic of these organs in the early years of the war that the administrative function and the political function were combined. At one moment the National Liberation Committees would be acting in their capacity as representatives of the NOF, or National Liberation Front; next they would appear as local organs of power carrying out the everyday tasks of administration or gathering supplies for the front. After the second session of AVNOJ (the Anti-Fascist Council of National Liberation of Yugoslavia) in November, 1943, these two functions were separated. Nevertheless, the most striking characteristic of these National Liberation Committees remained the degree to which administration was carried out in a political spirit, and, at the same time, the way the concept of the political front of anti-fascist groups which the committees supposedly represented became identified with the task of consolidating power. This combination made the National Liberation Committees extremely effective instruments in gaining control of the regions in which "liberated territories" were set up. The tactics just alluded to, while extremely important in explaining the ability of the partisans to survive against great odds, did not guarantee military success. Where conditions were not propitious, even the most determined efforts of the Communists to organize a resistance movement failed. This was true above all in areas where national feelings were strongly anti-Yugoslav or anti-Serb, such as the Albanian districts in Kosovo-Metohija. Here the Party was forced, for a time at least, to give up partisan tactics and focus its activities on agitation for better treatment of the population by the occupation authorities.[19] Hostility towards Yugoslavia

---

[18] A good recent summary of the growth of the National Liberation Committees can be found in Dušan Živković, *Postanak i razvitak narodne vlasti u Jugoslaviji, 1941–1942*, Belgrade, 1969. For the development of the committees in the later stages of the war, and the creation of a new administrative structure, see Ferdo Čulinović (ed.), *Stvaranje nove jugoslavenske države*, Zagreb, 1959. A general treatment is Leon Gršković, *Historija narodne vlasti*, Belgrade, 1957. On the problem of the economic activities of the committees, see Djordje Kosanović, *Ekonomska delatnost narodne vlasti u toku NOB*, Zagreb, 1964.

[19] On the partisan movement in Kosovo, see Djoko Sojević, *Zapisi Kosovoskog partizana*, Ljubljana, 1946; *Govori i Članci*, Priština, 1961; and *Kosovo i Metohija, 1943–1963*, Priština, 1963.

played a role in frustrating the efforts of the partisans in Macedonia until 1943, when a resistance movement was organized among the Serb-oriented peasants in the western part of the region. In western Hercegovina the peasants were so hostile that the Communists had to shift their efforts to organizing intellectuals and students in the towns.

The success of partisan tactics was also greatly influenced by the reaction of the population to the policies adopted by the occupation authorities. In Serbia the Germans instituted a harsh policy of reprisals as a way of discouraging attacks on German units. This was one consideration, among others, which led the Chetniks to abandon their attacks on the occupation forces. The partisans, however, adopted the policy of ignoring reprisals, regardless of the cost in lives to non-combatants. The results were sometimes horrifying, as when the Germans executed all the male inhabitants of the town of Kraguevac, in Serbia, following partisan attacks on German troops in the area.

This policy of harsh reprisals on many occasions played into the hands of the partisans, for the population would flee into the hills to avoid punishment, and then would be recruited by the Communists. In Croatia, the influx of Serbs into the partisan ranks resulting from Ustaši massacres was so great that the Ustaši were forced to change their tactics and soften their attitude towards the Serbs.

Later in the discussion we shall see that one theory attempts to explain the success of the Communists in Yugoslavia in terms of the reaction of the peasants to the terror unleashed by the Ustaši and the occupation authorities. It should be borne in mind, however, that there were many cases in which mass reprisals, methodically carried out in response to partisan attacks, discouraged guerrilla activity and even threatened the very existence of partisan forces. In Serbia, German reprisals played an important part in cowing the population and curbing partisan activities. In Slovenia in 1943, reprisals were so severe the partisans expressed apprehension that the Italians might totally annihilate the Slovenian population.

A final point needs to be made in respect to the tactics used by the partisans. Whatever their effectiveness in the rural mountain areas, these tactics were not easy to apply in the plains and around the urban centers, where communications were good and the bulk of the occupation forces were stationed. Partisan troops were even less effective in conventional war involving large numbers of well-equipped troops, as the battles which took place at the end of the war were to prove. More will be said in the conclusions concerning this latter point; for the moment it is enough to note that although the tactics of the partisans were superior to those of their opponents, they did not assure the Communists of ultimate victory.

The Use of Popular Front Tactics and the Struggle for Recognition. The political aspect of the Yugoslav takeover involved tactics aimed at concealing the revolutionary goals of the Communists, while at the same time making it possible for the Communists to pose as the only legitimate government of Yugoslavia. To this end, the Yugoslav Communist Party adopted the technique of speaking through the National Liberation Front, or National Liberation Movement,[20] which in turn was pictured as a broadly based organization representing all the anti-fascist elements in Yugoslavia.[21]

From the outset the Communists, speaking on behalf of the NLF, took the position that no revolutionary changes were intended for Yugoslavia. In the words of Edvard Kardelj, speaking soon after the resistance movement had begun, "the goal of the National Liberation Struggle cannot be other than to achieve national freedom and democratic rights, which will serve the mass of the people to determine freely, after the victory over the occupiers, the form of their internal life."[22] This position was reiterated in the official proclamations of the Anti-Fascist Council of National Liberation

---

[20] Since an official front for all of Yugoslavia was not organized until AVNOJ (*infra*) there is no agreed-upon terminology when referring to the front. Yugoslav writings speak of the National, or People's Front, the National or People's Liberation Front (NOF), and, simply, the National Liberation Movement (NOP). In the early years of the resistance movement, documents issued by the partisans would be signed "National Liberation Partisan Units" (*Narodnooslobodilački partizanski odredi*), or "Volunteer Army" (*Dobrovoljačka Vojska*) or "National Liberation Army" (*Narodnooslobodilačka vojska*). For a recent view of this front organization, in which comparisons are made with other Communist countries, see *Narodni front i komunisti, Jugoslavija, Čehoslovačka, Poljska : 1938–1945*, Belgrade, Prague, Warsaw, 1968.

[21] An example of the complexity of the front organization, in which political and quasi-governmental bodies were formed in rapid succession, is Slovenia. In 1941 a "front" was brought into existence, the "OF" or Liberation Front, which had an Executive Committee (*Izvršni odbor*). The Council of Kočevski, which met in October, 1943, prior to AVNOJ, announced it was the "government" of Slovenia. There came into existence what was known as the "Plenum of the Liberation Front"—the political side of the movement as represented at the Council of Kočevski—and the "Slovenian National Liberation Committee" (*Slovenački narodno-oslobodilački odbor*), which was the executive by virtue of being the highest in a hierarchical structure of National Liberation Committees. The Slovenian National Liberation Committee, meanwhile, turned over its executive functions to the Presidium of the Slovenian National Liberation Committee; this Presidium, in turn, was in fact the Executive Committee of the Plenum of the National Liberation Front. In other words, the two structures, the front and the National Liberation Committees, were merged at the top, with the executive of the former becoming the executive of the latter.

[22] *Put nove Jugoslavije*, Belgrade, 1946, p. 363.

(AVNOJ), and in conversations between Tito and the Allies in the years that followed.[23]

At the same time, it was the position of the Yugoslav Communist Party that the NLF, because it represented all the people of Yugoslavia, was the only legitimate government of the country. This claim was backed up by the creation of an all-Yugoslav national front in 1942—the aforementioned AVNOJ. AVNOJ met twice, first in November of 1942, and then in November of 1943. On the first occasion AVNOJ declared itself the *de facto* government of the country, but because of Soviet pressures refrained from attempting to press this claim on the Great Powers.[24] At its second meeting, in 1943, AVNOJ declared itself the legal government and forbade the return of King Peter until the people, after liberation, had decided upon their own form of government. The London government was denied the right to represent Yugoslavia in any of its dealings with other countries. The claims of AVNOJ, as is known, were finally recognized in principle by a series of agreements made in the fall of 1944 with Šubašić, head of the London government. These were in turn accepted by the Great Powers at the Yalta Conference, which called for the merger of the London government and the government of AVNOJ. In March, 1945, the two governments formally merged, and the provisional government of DFJ—Democratic Federal Yugoslavia—was set up, under Communist control. In this way, the final objective of the Communists—to seize power—was achieved.[25]

In its broad outlines, the approach of the Yugoslav Communist Party towards the question of power resembled that being taken by other Com-

---

[23] For relations with the Allies, see works by Plenča and Dedijer referred to earlier, as well as Milovan Djilas, *Conversations with Stalin*, New York, 1962; and Kiril Mihajlovski, "Mišljenje neprijatelja i saveznika u toku rata o našoj NOB," *Zbornik Historijskog Instituta Jugoslavenske Akademije*, Vol. IV, Zagreb, 1961.

[24] Tito, on the occasion of the first meeting of AVNOJ, said: "We do not have the possibility of forming a legal government, for international relations still do not permit this. But we have the right to one thing: to create a political body in these difficult circumstances.... We have no other type of power on our territory but the power of our National Liberation Committees...." (*Borba za oslobodjenje Jugoslavije, 1941–1945*, Belgrade, 1945, p. 115.) On the proceedings of AVNOJ, see: Prezidium Narodne skupštine FNRJ, *Prvo i drugo zasedanje Antifašističkog veća narodnog oslobodjenja Jugoslavije*, Belgrade, n.d.; Ivan Ribar, *Uspomene iz narodnooslobodilačke borbe*, Belgrade, 1961; Vojislav Simović, *AVNOJ*, Belgrade, 1958; Branko Bokan (ed.), *Bihaćka republika*, Bihać, 1965.

[25] For the Šubašić-Tito agreements, see *United Nations Review*, 1944, *passim*, and *Službeni list Demokratske Federativne Jugoslavije*, Belgrade, 1945. On the consolidation of power, note Branko Petranović, *Političke i pravne prilike za vreme privremene vlade DJF*, Belgrade, 1964, and by the same author, *Politička i ekonomska osnova narodne vlasti u Jugoslaviji za vreme obnove*, Belgrade, 1969.

munist Parties during the war. The revolutionary goals of the Communists were everywhere muted in the call for a coalition of anti-fascist groups to fight the Axis powers. The Yugoslav Communists were nevertheless particularly successful in using this device as a means for forming a political body able to challenge the legitimacy of the government in exile.

To a large degree, this success must be attributed to the mistakes of the Chetniks, the only rival resistance movement of any consequence. By collaborating with the Germans and Italians and by refusing to engage in resistance activities, the Chetniks compelled the Allies to shift their support to the partisans. The London government, which had made Mihailović Minister of Defense, was compromised as a result of the Chetniks' failures. Within Yugoslavia, the tactics of the Chetniks also backfired; collaboration did not result in the destruction of the Communists but did discredit the Chetniks in the eyes of the Yugoslav people.

The success of the Yugoslav Communist Party can also be traced to the fact that by developing a broadly based movement, the Communists were able to present themselves as more representative of the peoples of Yugoslavia than the government in exile, which was continually torn by quarrels among its national factions, and which for most of its life was controlled by Serb elements. The Communists, on the other hand, had by 1943 established National Liberation Fronts throughout Yugoslavia. With the exception of Serbia and Macedonia, meetings of the Anti-Fascist Councils of National Liberation took place in all of the Slav areas of Yugoslavia during the course of 1943. These meetings, claiming to speak for the peoples of the regions in which they met, approved the decisions of AVNOJ and at the same time put themselves forward as the representatives of their own nationality or area.[26] Finally, at the second session of AVNOJ, it was announced that a federal system had been established in Yugoslavia, to go into effect "immediately." The June, 1944, Šubašić-Tito agreement recognized the federal principle. Several months later the London government, completely outmaneuvered by the Communists over the national question, was compelled to accept the federal principle adopted by AVNOJ.

Although the mistakes of the Chetniks and the London government provided the Communists with opportunities not available in other countries in Eastern Europe, popular front tactics played an important role

---

[26] On the meeting of the Anti-Fascist Liberation Council in Croatia in 1943, see Institut za Historiju Radničkog pokreta, *Zemaljsko antifašističko vijeće narodnog oslobodjenja Hrvatske*, Zagreb, 1964. For Macedonia, see *Zbornik na dokumenti ASNOM, 1944–1946*, Skoplje, 1964. Material on the first Serb gathering is found in Narodna Skupština Narodne Republike Srbije, *Zasedanje Velike antifašističke narodnoloboosdilačke skupštine Srbije*, Belgrade, n.d.

in the events which led to the recognition of the Communists. While a detailed analysis of the problem of setting up popular fronts is hardly possible, some of the salient issues of popular front strategy can be examined briefly.

It will be remembered that the strategy for the seizure of power outlined at the Seventh Congress of the Comintern called for a "united front from above" in which the Communists would gradually force out other parties. The possibility of a seizure of power from below was not broached at this time. When the Communists in the occupied countries joined the struggle against the Axis powers, the question of co-operation "from above" or "from below" became acute. In the last analysis, no two approaches to this problem were identical.

For the Yugoslav Communist Party the issue of co-operation with non-Communist groups in some type of coalition was posed very early in the struggle. At first, Mihailović received the lion's share of publicity in the West. At the same time the Soviet Union was pressing the Yugoslav Communist Party for greater co-operation with the non-Communists. In the fall of 1941 Tito and Mihailović began operations in Western Serbia. Negotiations were undertaken in an effort to co-ordinate their efforts against the Germans, but to no avail. The two sides soon clashed, and Chetnik attacks on the partisans played an important part in forcing the Communists to retreat from Serbia in the fall and winter of 1941. While it is clear that Mihailović did not wish the negotiations to succeed, it is equally certain that the Communists were not eager to join in a coalition with the Chetniks. (Tito's assertion to Fitzroy Maclean that he, Tito, was willing to place himself under Mihailović's command in 1941 is hardly credible.)[27]

If the policy of non-collaboration with other resistance groups emerged quite early in the Yugoslav Communist Party's strategy, so did the determination to avoid an opposite extreme, that of projecting revolutionary issues into the anti-fascist struggle. The problem of "sectarian" errors was raised quite early in the war, when partisan units in Montenegro and Hercegovina began taking a revolutionary line. A letter of November, 1941, from the Central Committee of the Yugoslav Communist Party to the Montenegrins showed how sensitive the Party was to political slogans by criticizing the Montenegrins severely for employing the phrase "anti-fascist national liberation *revolution*" to describe their movement.[28] Communist organizations in Montenegro were also accused of raising the red flag in the summer of 1941. The Montenegrins nevertheless persisted in

---

[27] Maclean, *op. cit.*, p. 313.

[28] *Zbornik dokumenata, op. cit.*, Vol. III, Book 1, p. 228.

their ways, for Montenegro was designated a "Soviet Republic" at the "Assembly of Montenegrin and Bokeljski Patriots" held in February, 1942, in the monastery of Ostroga.[29] In Hercegovina the errors committed by the local Party organizations were still more serious. The Communists there called for the sovietization of Hercegovina and began liquidating "potential" as well as "real" enemies.[30] As a result, the entire partisan staff of the region was tried in a military court.

Such deviations were vigorously criticized, and for good reason. The partisan movements in both Montenegro and Hercegovina were seriously undermined by these attempts to inject a revolutionary dimension into the struggle. Partisan strength in these areas did not regain its early levels until the end of the war.

It should, however, be borne in mind that not only revolutionary slogans were responsible for turning many persons against the Communists in Montenegro and Hercegovina. A more important reason was the indiscriminate terror engaged in by the partisans in these areas, a policy for which the Supreme Command itself bears some responsibility.[31]

The Communist understanding of the tactics of the National Liberation Front, as they applied to Yugoslavia, ruled out two options: open pursuit of revolutionary policies on the one hand, and allying with other resistance groups on the other. Between these two extremes there existed many possibilities, ranging from collaboration with the non-Communist political parties within the framework of AVNOJ to token representation of non-Communists in Communist-dominated organizations of the liberation front. Also, bogus parties could have been set up, dominated by the Communists. This last approach was seriously considered in the case of the most politically stubborn opponent of the Communists, the Croatian Peasant Party.

It was the position of the Communists that the Anti-Fascist Councils of National Liberation includ many non-Communists who represented important segments of Yugoslav political life. Tito, for example, in an interview with the foreign press, went to great lengths to emphasize the number and variety of political parties represented by persons in AVNOJ

---

[29] The term Soviet does not appear in Yugoslav documents on the meeting, but is referred to in non-Communist writings on the subject. See especially B. Domazetović, *Revolucija u Crnoj Gori*, Belgrade, 1944.

[30] See *Osnivački kongres Komunističke partije Bosne i Hercegovine*, Sarajevo, 1950, pp. 59–60.

[31] The Supreme Command was in the immediate vicinity at the time these events occurred. While it may not have ordered them, it seems that the excesses could have been quickly halted by orders from above.

and in the regional anti-fascist assemblies.[32] While individuals associated with the non-Communist parties did break away and join AVNOJ, it was rare that an entire group, not to speak of a political party, would associate with the Communists. Slovenia was something of an exception. In this case a liberation front was formed prior to the German attack on Russia, and included groups sympathetic to the Communists. In Serbia, a number of the members of the Independent Democrats joined AVNOJ after the Italian capitulation, as did some of the Agrarians. The refusal of the Croatian Peasant Party to collaborate with the Communists posed a special problem, to which we shall return shortly.

The practice of the Yugoslav Communists was in fact to form a front with the non-Communists "from below," an approach which created some apprehension on the part of Moscow, at least in the early years of the struggle. The Communist position was reflected in the proclamations of the national liberation fronts which stressed that *persons of any social class* were free to join the front. On the other hand, any group which for whatever reason decided not to surrender its identity and merge with the front was almost automatically considered to be in opposition to the national liberation struggle. Thus the alleged all-encompassing nature of the front was, in Communist hands, a two-edged sword. While in theory it was meant to strengthen the resistance movement by bringing together persons of diverse political persuasions, it also permitted the Communists to take the position that "all those who are not for us are against us," and in effect to lay the groundwork for charges of treason and collaboration after the war. This can be illustrated by a statement of Kardelj concerning the OF, or Liberation Front, in Slovenia, in which he said, "The Slovenian national liberation movement, which is represented exclusively by the Liberation Front of the Slovenian People, is an all-peoples national liberation movement."[33] This typical Communist formulation of the significance of the front left little room for real co-operation with non-Communist parties.

Since the political parties of prewar Yugoslavia were unable to function and the London government was ineffective, the Communist tactics of a "front from below" received no real challenge and provided the Party with a veneer of respectability and legitimacy, especially in dealings with the Allied powers. At the end of the war, in an effort to circumvent the Šubašić-Tito agreements, the Chetniks desperately tried to match the political victories of the partisans by calling a congress of Serb, non-Communist parties, which organized a coalition known as the "Yugoslav Democratic Union." The Union issued a proclamation in favor of a federal

---

[32] *Borba za oslobodjenje Jugoslavije, op. cit.*, pp. 194–201.
[33] Gerškovič, *op. cit.*, p. 192.

Yugoslavia and a hereditary monarchy. At the same time a group in the Croatian Peasant Party, led by Košutić, conferred with the Croatian Communists in the hope of gaining some concessions. Košutić proposed to the Croatian Communist Party that a "Supreme Assembly of the Republic of Croatia" be set up with representatives of the Croatian Peasant Party and ZAVNOH, the Croatian Anti-Fascist Council of National Liberation. Needless to say, the offer was rejected. Both the Chetnik plan and the Croatian proposals, conceived as last-minute acts of desperation, revealed the extent to which the non-Communist parties had fallen behind the Communists in political organization.

It would be an error, however, to attribute complete success to the Communists' front tactics. The Communists themselves did not rely solely on the liberation fronts as a means of getting their political message to the people, but from the outset stressed the creation of mass organizations, among the youth and women in particular, which were to act as instruments of indoctrination. In Macedonia the front organization, or Anti-Fascist Council of National Liberation, never really got off the ground owing to the presence of a number of rebellious intellectuals in the organization who opposed the Party's position on the national question.[34]

The failure of the Yugoslav Communist Party to win over members of the Croatian Peasant Party was a particularly serious obstacle to the growth of Communist influence in Croatia. One group, identified with the Croatian Communist Party Secretary, Andrija Hebrang, wished to form an independent Croatian Peasant Party under Communist control. During the time that Hebrang was head of the Croatian Party, attacks on Maček, head of the Peasant Party, were frequent.[35] Some individuals were finally won over to the Communist side, but by and large the Croatian Peasant Party remained free of Communist influence until the end of the war. In the closing months of the conflict, the Communists finally took the step of creating a "Croatian Republican Peasant Party," with Franjo Gazi as president.[36] This group, which disappeared from sight soon thereafter, was probably formed with the intention of providing a propaganda organ for the Communists during the period of the consolidation of power in Croatia.

---

[34] For protests of Skoplje intellectuals against the national policy of the Yugoslav Communist Party, see L. Mojsov, *Bugarska Radnička Partija*, Belgrade, 1948, p. 64.

[35] Hebrang's attacks on Maček can be seen clearly in the proclamations of the first meeting of ZAVNOH, the Croatian Anti-Fascist Council of National Liberation. These attacks were muted in the second session of ZAVNOH, probably on orders from the Supreme Command.

[36] See *Narodna vlada Hrvatske formirana u gradu Splitu dana 14 travnja*, Zagreb, 1945.

As the war drew to a close, the nature of the problem facing the Communists changed. The need for disguise grew less. The main political task became the consolidation of power, utilizing more conventional means. This stage in the Communist takeover in Yugoslavia will be briefly described, but only after first dealing with the extremely important question of Communist policy and tactics towards the national question.

Communist Policy on the National Question. The key to the appeal of the partisan resistance movement lay in its close identification with national and patriotic feelings. These feelings were cultivated among each of the major Slav nationalities through the regional liberation fronts and Anti-Fascist Councils of National Liberation. Each nationality was made to feel that the partisan movement in its region was fighting primarily for the freedom and liberation of that nationality. In the case of the Macedonians, the appeal to national sentiment involved identification with the idea of a Macedonian nationality, a policy which had played only a minor role in the politics of the Macedonian national question up to that time. In its approach to relations among the nationalities, the Party stressed the simple theme of "brotherhood and unity," to which was added, after the second session of AVNOJ, the concept of a federal Yugoslavia. This federation would be based on the recognition of full national rights for the five major nationalities (Serbs, Croats, Slovenes, Macedonians, and Montenegrins), equality and protection of rights for all minorities, and strict prohibition of the expression of national chauvinism or the spread of racial, religious, or national hatreds.[37]

The Communist approach to the national question stood out boldly in a country wracked by national strife. And by and large the partisans lived up to their slogans. Although there were occasional deviations by partisan units from the precept of brotherhood and unity, especially in the first two years of the war, the Communists were successful in controlling national antagonisms within their own ranks,[38] and at the same time were able to

---

[37] In an article appearing in December, 1942, Tito had revived the principles of self-determination and even the right of secession for the republics, about which the Party had remained silent since the mid-1930's. The meetings of the republic or regional Anti-Fascist Councils of National Liberation which accepted the decisions of the second session of AVNOJ were later said to have exercised this right of "self-determination" for the peoples in question.

[38] Hebrang, when he was secretary of the Croatian Party, was accused of encouraging Croatian nationalism at the expense of the Serbs in Croatia. For examples of tensions within partisan ranks, and of excesses against Croatian villages, see Paul Shoup, *Communism and the Yugoslav National Question*, New York, 1968, p. 69.

convince many Croats, Moslems, and Macedonians, as well as Serbs, Montenegrins, and Slovenes, to fight on the side of the partisans.

In dealing with the complex national antagonisms generated by the war, the partisans went to great lengths to avoid provoking hostility based on national grounds. If a Croatian village, for example, was known to be hostile to the partisans, it would simply be avoided, or occupied only after the inhabitants had been convinced they had nothing to fear. Efforts were also made to arrange reconciliations among rival national groups in a locality when that was possible.

These tactics gave the Communists an immense advantage over the Chetniks, whose support was limited to the Serbs and Montenegrins. It also made it possible to create a resistance movement which, while under central direction, could challenge the occupation forces at many points simultaneously. At the same time, the Communist approach to the national question had limitations. The non-Slav minorities, for example, were largely hostile to the Communists and remained so throughout the conflict.[39] In the early years of the war, the majority of the Croatian villages refused to aid the partisans, and there were certain regions, especially in Hercegovina, where the Croatian villages remained supporters of the Independent Croatian State, or NDH, until the end of the war. Macedonia posed special problems for the Communists. Bulgarian national feeling was so strong at the beginning of the war that the Party became infected with pro-Bulgarian sentiment and refused to obey the orders of the Central Committee of the Yugoslav Communist Party. The resulting dispute, in which the Bulgarian Communist Party became involved, was only ended by the intervention of the Comintern. After 1943, the Communists were able to capitalize on the rising tide of Macedonian national feeling which they themselves had helped create. Opposition to the creation of a Macedonian republic which would be part of Yugoslavia was nevertheless widespread among the Macedonians and played a role in delaying the organization of the Macedonian Anti-Fascist Council of National Liberation until 1944.

Despite the Communists' success in gathering recruits from all the Yugoslav nationalities, the fact remains that certain groups, especially the Serbs, made a major contribution to the partisan cause, while others definitely aided the occupation forces. In the latter category, as we have

---

[39] The Slav minorities in the north—the Slovaks and the Czechs—co-operated with the partisans. The German minority in the Vojvodina was a mainstay of the occupation, and the Hungarian minority was bitterly hostile to the partisans as well.

seen, were the non-Slav minorities, especially the Albanians, and also the Slav Moslems.

For the first two years of the war the Yugoslav Communists were almost totally dependent on the Serbs for support. In other words, without Serb participation it is doubtful that the Communists could have launched a successful resistance movement. Most of the Serbs in the partisan ranks were not from Serbia proper, which remained in Chetnik and German hands during the war, but from areas outside Serbia: Bosnia, Hercegovina, Croatia, and Dalmatia. These were the groups which were most ready to respond to the appeals of the Communists to join in the all-Yugoslav resistance struggle.

It can be seen from the foregoing that peculiar conditions were at work which enabled the partisans to gain support where they needed it most—among the dominant nationality. The wisdom of the policy pursued by the Yugoslav Communist Party lay in the realization, from the outset, that this would not be enough. By bringing other nationalities into the struggle the Communists were able to strengthen their hand against the local national movements, and then to make an impressive argument to the Great Powers that they, the Communists, represented all the Yugoslavs, and should therefore be recognized as the legitimate rulers of the country.

The preceding account deals with only the most important tactics employed by the Communists in leading the resistance movement and then gaining recognition from the Great Powers. The description is also incomplete insofar as it does not deal with the Party, which was the key mechanism in instilling discipline, assuring adherence to the principle of "brotherhood and unity," and providing direction to the activities of the National Liberation Committees, the Anti-Fascist Councils of National Liberation, and the mass organizations. The vital role of the political commissar in providing the combination of political and military skills so necessary for guerrilla warfare deserves special mention in this connection.

Having gained recognition from the Great Powers and defeated all domestic rivals, the final assumption of power by the Yugoslav Communists was accomplished without great difficulty. Terror, which had been avoided since 1942, was again used to settle old scores with the Chetniks, Ustaši, and other anti-Communist groups. In one well-documented case, thousands of Chetniks and others turned over to the partisans by the Allies were massacred.[40] A rebellion among the Albanians, which broke out in the fall of

---

[40] See John Prcela and Stanko Guldescu, *Operation Slaughterhouse : Eyewitness Accounts of Postwar Massacres in Yugoslavia*, Philadelphia, 1970.

1944, was put down with great severity.[41] Groups which refused to surrender to the Communists and hid in the mountains were tracked down, a process that took several years.

For a brief time a token opposition operated legally, but during the summer of 1945 its activities were suppressed. The Provisional Government formed in March included Šubašić as Foreign Minister and Milan Grol, of the Serbian Democratic Party, as Vice-Premier. Grol was permitted to publish a weekly newspaper, *Demokratija*, for a brief period. In Zagreb, the widow of Stjepan Radić also attempted to publish an opposition paper. Only one issue appeared. Thirty-six persons who were members of the prewar National Assembly were admitted to the Temporary Assembly (the successor of AVNOJ) in accordance with the Šubašić-Tito agreement that persons from the former parliament who had not collaborated with the occupation forces could participate in AVNOJ. However, even these token concessions to the principles of political democracy were not tolerated for long. Non-Communist leaders were harassed, and their publications were suppressed. Finding it impossible to work under such conditions, Grol resigned his post in August; Šubašić left two months later. In the elections for the Constituent Assembly held in November, 1945, the slate put forth by the Front was uncontested.[42] A new Soviet-style constitution was promulgated in 1946. In this way the Communists completed the final legal steps in their seizure of power.

Theories Explaining the Communist Success

In the introductory remarks it was stressed that many factors contributed to the Communist takeover in Yugoslavia. The revolution was not, however, the result of blind forces in which the efforts of individuals and groups played no part. The Yugoslav Communists clearly took advantage of the situation, and in so doing changed the course of history.

It still remains open to debate why the Communists were able to do so. To put the problem in a slightly different way, it may be asked what forces were at work which made it possible for the Communists, against seemingly great odds, to gain such a dominating position during the resistance struggle.

The question that most frequently arises is whether the Communists really did come to power on their own or whether, on the contrary, it was

---

[41] An account of the Albanian uprising is given in Shoup, *op. cit.*, pp. 104–105.

[42] The National Front was made up of a number of groups, but all were Communist; the only non-Communist elected was Dragoljub Jovanovič.

the entrance of the Soviet armies into Yugoslavia in the closing months of the war that was the decisive factor. We have suggested the difficulty in giving a straightforward answer to this question. The very possibility of revolution was tied to the conditions created by the occupation. Inescapably, therefore, the outcome of the partisan struggle, and thus of the attempt to seize power, depended upon a favorable outcome of the European conflict. During the war the partisans themselves never concealed this fact; their faith in their own victory was inseparable from their faith in the victory of the Soviet Union.

The argument of the Soviets that they liberated Yugoslavia, although clearly politically motivated, also carries some weight if it is remembered that until almost the end of the war, the partisans were still confined to the mountainous areas of Yugoslavia. What might have happened had they attempted to attack the main cities without Soviet or Allied assistance is suggested by the huge losses that the partisans suffered when they met the Germans in conventional combat in the Srem area during the closing phases of the war.

Granting the validity of the above points, the fact remains that the partisans were, by the end of the war, far and away the strongest of the *domestic* groups contending for power, and that they had reached this position almost exclusively through their own efforts. Only the presence of the Germans, after 1943, prevented the Communists from gaining control of the country much earlier than they did. By the same token, only massive intervention by the United States or Britain at the end of the war could have prevented a Communist takeover. This would have been no less true had the Soviet troops never entered Yugoslavia.

If the Yugoslav Communists did not owe their victory to Soviet assistance, it may still be true that the takeover was made possible, in the last analysis, by the greater ruthlessness of the Communists in exploiting the chaotic conditions of the time. To be more specific, it is possible to see the seizure of power as the result of the deliberate use of terror to provoke reprisals; of the utilization of "rootless peasants"[43] to form Communist military contingents; or of the pursuit of a "divide and conquer"[44] policy towards the nationalities in order to break up the opposition. While these arguments all have very different situations in mind, they are in agreement in attributing the success of the Communists to the deliberate use of tech-

[43] Lowenthal, *loc. cit.*

[44] The theory is proposed by Dinko Tomašić, "Nationality Problems and Partisan Yugoslavia," *Journal of Central European Affairs*, Boulder, Colo., Vol. VI, July, 1946, pp. 111–125.

niques which encourage misery and chaos and which are, in essence, totalitarian in character.

This view of the Yugoslav revolution is not entirely without relevance. We have seen that the flow of frightened Serb peasants into the ranks of the partisans was of great importance in providing new recruits. It is true that terror was used early in the war, and quite extensively in the mopping-up operations at the end. One can even find evidence that the leaders of the Yugoslav Communist Party at one point toyed with the idea of deliberately provoking reprisals against unsuspecting villages, with the aim of swinging the peasantry over to the Communist side.[45]

But the anarchic conditions of the occupation in Yugoslavia worked as much against the partisans as for them; we have already seen examples of this fact in the setbacks suffered by the Communists in Montenegro and Hercegovina in 1941 and 1942. The "divide and conquer" interpretation of Communist nationality policy does not deserve serious consideration, although one can understand how it seemed reasonable at the time it was suggested. The image of the "rootless peasant" also exaggerates certain aspects of the partisan campaigns, as our earlier discussion of liberated territories suggests. In sum, while the Communists might have been better prepared to take advantage of the conditions created by the occupation, such conditions were not deliberately encouraged, nor were they *fundamentally* the reason for the spread of the partisan movement.

The Yugoslav Communists, rejecting all theories that the victory of the revolution was the result of "spontaneous" factors[46] or made possible by Soviet intervention, have on one occasion or another emphasized three considerations: (1) the solution of the national question; (2) the development of new tactics of partisan warfare; and (3) the transformation of the partisan struggle into a *revolutionary* movement.

---

[45] There is an interesting statement of Kardelj's dating from early in the war in which he advocates the use of terror. Said Kardelj: "Some comrades fear reprisals ... from the destruction of villages and people and so on. ... But I take the position that just these reprisals will swing the Croatian villages to the side of the Serb villages. In war we need not fear the destruction of whole villages. Terror will inevitably lead to armed action." *Zbornik dokumenata*, Vol. II, Book 2, pp. 31–32.

[46] For an attack on critics who wish to downgrade the achievements of the Yugoslavs, see Ferdo Čulinović, *op. cit.*, p. 21. Čulinović objects to what he calls the "geopolitical" explanation of the Yugoslav revolution, which stresses the importance of the mountainous terrain, the location of Yugoslavia, and the like, and also to the "spontaneity" theory, which makes it appear that the revolution was the result of chance or developed "of its own accord." Čulinović stresses the contribution made by the Party in organizing the revolution and guiding it to victory.

These arguments do not make up a cohesive whole; on the contrary, they have been used at different times and sometimes have been viewed as contending theories rather than complementary explanations. All of them have been touched on, to some degree, in the preceding discussion.

We have commented on the skill with which the partisans developed their guerrilla tactics, and the limitations of this method of warfare; the subject need not be pursued further here. The Yugoslav case reinforces what later experience has shown: that guerrilla warfare will not succeed where the population is hostile, and that the commitment of guerrilla troops to pitched battles with conventional forces can have disastrous results. From a comparative point of view, one may also ask whether the use of guerrilla tactics *necessarily* requires the formation of a resistance army actively engaging the occupation forces from bases in rural areas. We have in mind here the fact that in Greece and Bulgaria the Communists also made great headway during World War II. In the latter case, at least, the tactics used by the Communists were somewhat different (indeed, they bore some resemblance to the unsuccessful strategy of the Chetniks). Finally, it may be asked whether the partisan warfare of the time, notwithstanding the fact that it has been frequently imitated, has become a historical curiosity under present-day conditions. This is a burning question for the Yugoslavs, and we shall return to it shortly.

The contribution of nationalism to the Communist cause is perhaps the most fascinating and complex question to arise in connection with the takeover in Yugoslavia. The Communist position on this issue, developed most fully by Milovan Djilas just after the war,[47] was that the Party had solved the national question *during* the war. As a result, the argument ran, the Yugoslav peoples were united in their support for the new regime. By contrast, the opponents of the Communists were pictured as narrow nationalistic elements lacking in popular support.

There is a twofold difficulty to this theory: it glosses over the depths of national antagonisms in Yugoslavia, and it ignores the fact that while all the Slav nationalities contributed to the partisan movement, it was above all the Serbs whose participation made possible a Communist victory. Viewed in this perspective, the seizure of power in Yugoslavia by the Communists was determined by the outcome of a civil war *among the Serbs*. In determining why so many Serbs opted for the partisans rather than the Chetniks, it is clear that a great deal of weight must be given to factors which go beyond the question of the national policy pursued by

---

[47] "O rješenju nacionalnog pitanja u Jugoslaviji," *Članci. 1941–1946*, Belgrade, 1947, pp. 254–265.

the Communists: the poor showing of the Chetniks, the patriotism and bravery displayed by the partisans in attacking the Germans under great odds, the collapse of the Italian occupation in 1943, and so forth.

The inability of the Chetniks to mobilize sufficient Serb support to check the Communists only points to the broader problem of the paralysis of the non-Communist national parties, on which so much emphasis has been placed here. The reasons for this are complex, and undoubtedly will be debated for some time to come. It may be suggested, nevertheless, that part of the explanation lies in the fact that the occupation of Yugoslavia was also for many persons the collapse of a state and a political system, for which no replacement could be clearly envisaged. This consideration was of course more important for the Croats, especially Maček, than for the Serb politicians.

The Communists, on the other hand, if they did not solve the national question during the war, at least proved they could rule *in the face of the national question.* Since the Great Powers were committed to the existence of a Yugoslav state, this demonstrated capacity to cope with the Yugoslav national problem undoubtedly helped predispose Britain and the United States towards accepting Communist rule in Yugoslavia.

It remains to be asked whether the success of the partisans was not also a reflection of a new dynamic national consciousness brought into being among the peasantry as a result of their mobilization into the resistance movement. Such a process has been suggested in the writings of R. V. Burks[48] and Chalmers A. Johnson.[49] There can also be found in this interpretation the notion that the Communists, in the course of the struggle for power, revealed themselves as fundamentally a nationalist movement. A reasonable conclusion might therefore be that the seizure of power was another manifestation of a *national* revolution, albeit led by the Communists. Johnson, for one, sees in this feature a similarity between the Yugoslav and Chinese revolutions.

This theory has the great merit of focusing attention on the upsurge of patriotism stimulated by the partisan struggle. In certain areas there was indeed something of this awakening of the peasant national consciousness taking place, and at certain moments these national feelings infected the local Party leadership, producing deviations from the Yugoslav Communist Party line on the national question (this was especially true in Macedonia and Croatia). It is important to note nevertheless that in the Yugoslav case

[48] Richard V. Burks, *The Dynamics of Communism in Eastern Europe*, Princeton, N. J., 1961.

[49] Chalmers A. Johnson, *Peasant Nationalism and Communist Power*, Stanford, Calif., 1962.

the peasant already had a highly developed national consciousness, especially in Serbia. National feeling was strong, waiting to be tapped by the partisans. With the exception of the Macedonian peasant, it could not be said that nationalism was the *product* of the struggle and therefore the creation of the Communists.

The theory that the emergence of a *revolutionary* movement made a fundamental contribution to the Communist success appeared first in Yugoslavia in the 1950's, and marked a change in the Yugoslav Communists' thinking.[50] The argument has been presented in pedantic textbook form and does not lend itself to easy summary. Briefly, the position is that the partisan movement was led by the Yugoslav Communist Party and the working class, and achieved basic revolutionary objectives, including the creation of a new form of power in the National Liberation Committees and the partisan military units, as well as a solution of the national question along "revolutionary" lines.

We have noted, in this connection, how careful the Communists were in their statements concerning the form of government which would be organized after the war in Yugoslavia. To argue that the Communists developed revolutionary objectives is to divert attention from the importance of the strategy by which the question of *power* was put before the question of revolutionary political and social change.

Nevertheless, it is clear that one of the advantages the Communists enjoyed during the war lay in the fact that they had a clear-cut set of objectives which went far beyond claiming power in the name of the anti-fascist liberation movement. Furthermore, these objectives were not really concealed. The slogans for taking power—the establishment of *real* democracy, of *real* freedom—were deeply infused with a revolutionary content. Although the Communists were vague about the future form of government, they were very concrete about the need to destroy the old system in its entirety, and were quite direct in dealing with the fact that the war was providing that opportunity.

In this determination to do away with the old system and all the injustices associated with it, we find a powerful force, a motivation in part, for the sacrifices of the partisan fighters, and an explanation for the genuine enthusiasm the partisan movement aroused among large segments of the population.

Finally, one must agree completely with the theory that the Party played a leading role and that its presence was what ultimately insured that the resistance movement would develop along revolutionary lines.

---

[50] Gershković, *op. cit.*, p. 45.

Our discussion of the theories put forward to explain why the Communists came to power in Yugoslavia has not led to the identification of *one* cause as clearly decisive. We see, on the contrary, a coming together of a number of preconditions *and* the presence of a determined, able revolutionary movement ready to take advantage of the opportunity. In this respect Yugoslavia undoubtedly reflects the general situation that has prevailed in other countries where successful Communist revolutions have taken place.

It seems possible to suggest, without undue simplification, several of the main factors which were crucial to Communist success in Yugoslavia. They include: (1) the occupation and the resulting collapse of central authority; (2) the paralysis of the once powerful national political parties; (3) the presence, when the war broke out, of a well-disciplined Communist Party; (4) the ability of the partisans to mobilize the largest nationality—the Serbs—more effectively than did the Chetniks; (5) the support of the Allies for a Yugoslav state; (6) the victory of the Soviet Union (but *not* the presence of Soviet armies in Yugoslavia); and (7) of course, recognition by the Allied powers.

If we broaden the analysis to include consideration of the social forces and conditions under which the revolution took place, it would be necessary to stress that Yugoslavia was a backward country, ideally suited for guerrilla warfare; a country made up primarily of peasants; and, perhaps most important of all, a country where the social, economic, and national problems reflected the strains of a developing state still badly lacking in a sense of national purpose. What the partisans offered, in effect, was a fresh start, utilizing the conditions of backwardness to build up support among the peasantry, and appealing to the most elemental national feelings associated with the desire to expel foreign powers from the homeland.

With all the insights the Yugoslav case affords into the factors which help to determine the outcome of revolutionary movements in developing nations, it can be argued that the Yugoslav situation also was very much a product of its time. This is true in the sense that the victory of the Communists was inseparable from the events of World War II, just as the Bolshevik revolution cannot really be discussed apart from World War I. This brings us a full circle, back to the Bolshevik doctrine that the spread of the revolutionary movement was to take place as the result of a major war. Yugoslavia conformed to this prediction. As we have argued, it was the occupation and the collapse of the existing political system and its parties which were the necessary preconditions for initiating the revolution.

If this is true, it raises the interesting question of whether the type of situation which made possible the revolution in Yugoslavia is likely to be repeated elsewhere, or whether, on the contrary, the events which led to the seizure of power in Yugoslavia are conceivable only under the circumstances created by World War II and its immediate aftermath.

One can argue both sides of this question. On the one hand, the breakdown of authority resulting from armed conflict of some type (civil war or wars against colonial regimes) is a frequent occurrence, and offers great revolutionary possibilities. On the other hand, the idea of an invasion, the creation of "occupation" regimes, and the seizure of power as a result of gaining internal backing *and* Great Power recognition—all this is rather far removed from conditions as they exist today. The Yugoslavs still have great faith in their partisan tactics. They argue, not without reason, that such an approach to war can be utilized even in the nuclear age.[51] But there is little enthusiasm in Yugoslavia today for the Chinese idea of promoting national liberation wars, and little prospect that new revolutionary movements will come to power as the direct result of global conflict. Viewed in this light, the Yugoslav revolution, although the first of a new type, was very much a product of its time, reflecting conditions which had existed in the international arena since World War I, but which are far removed from present-day realities.

---

[51] For a defense of partisan warfare in the nuclear age, see Tudjman, *Rat protiv rata*, Zagreb, 1970.

Ingredients of the Communist Takeover in Albania

Stephen Peters

When Hitler's Germany invaded the Soviet Union in June, 1941, there was no organized Communist movement in Albania. But in November, 1944, a little over three years later, the Albanian Communist Party (ACP), camouflaged as the National Liberation Movement (NLM), became the unchallenged master of the country. And it did so without the benefit of Soviet troops, unlike in the other East European countries, including Yugoslavia, where Communist governments were installed after World War II.

The ingredients for the phenomenal success of the Albanian Communist Party were a combination of ineptness and lack of political acumen on the part of the prewar Albanian ruling élite; the tremendous organizational ability and ideological preparation of Tito's emissaries, who founded the Albanian Communist Party and guided it to success during the war; the skill, fighting spirit, and dogged determination of the Albanian Communists in preparing the ground for the eventual seizure of power, irrespective of the cost in human life and destruction to the country; the advent of the Red Army into the Balkans; and the failure of the Anglo-Americans to formulate a fixed policy for postwar Albania.

The Political, Social, and Economic Climate

The political, social, and economic climate in Albania immediately following the Italian invasion on April 7, 1939, was a primary factor in the character of the resistance movements that developed during the war and the line-up of forces participating in them. A general feeling of frustration, uncertainty, and impotence prevailed in the country, because, with the unannounced flight of King Zog and his entourage on the day of the invasion, the people felt they were left leaderless and defenseless.[1] There was no organized political party of any kind to which the people could look for inspiration and guidance. During his fifteen-year rule King Zog had succeeded in laying the foundations of a modern state, but he had banned all political parties and made no attempt to give the people a sense

---

[1] T. Zavalani, *Histori e Shqipnis, Pjesa e Dytë, 1878–1965*, London, 1966, pp. 223 ff.

of participating in the government. He had shared power with a small élite composed of influential landowners, tribal chieftains, and a few well-to-do merchants. There was thus no affinity between the ruling élite and the people, and no identity between the state and the peasant masses, who composed eighty precent of the country's total population. On the eve of the Italian invasion, the level of education and civil morality was very low.[2]

The wide social and economic gap between the small ruling group of wealthy landowners and rich merchants and the poorly paid workers and poverty-stricken peasants had blocked the development of a cohesive social order that could have withstood the trauma caused by the national catastrophe of April 7, 1939. The people's complete disorientation as a result of the invasion and the sudden flight of the King was further aggravated by the fact that some members of the old ruling class, in contradiction to an evident desire of the people to resist the invaders, considered it prudent either to collaborate directly with the invaders or at least to pay lip service to them in order to salvage what they could, save the country from utter destruction, and avoid possible reprisals and other harsh measures.

Both political immaturity and patriotic zeal seem to have induced even some of the most respected old patriots to counsel prudence towards the Axis. It was their conviction that the country was too small, too poor, and ill prepared to resist the Axis war machine. Hence, the wisest policy, they reasoned, was to lie low, bide their time, and conserve man power and resources in order to resist the Communists should they attempt to seize power at the end of the war. It was indeed the hope and the strong feeling of many leading non-Communist Albanians even as late as the summer of 1944 that the Anglo-Americans could not afford to allow "Slav communism" to prevail just across the Strait of Otranto.

The passive attitude of segments among the old ruling class was of course not shared by all members of that class and much less by the people at large, especially the youth and intellectuals, who were determined to oppose the invaders with all the means at their disposal. Resistance was, accordingly, organized from the first days of the invasion. Originally, it was led by a handful of old and influential patriots, such as Midhat Frasheri, and by intellectuals and youths and a few labor leaders. This resistance gradually developed into organized movements and parties, the most successful of which, as will be seen below, proved to be the National Liberation Movement, which was led by the Communists.

---

[2] Stavro Skendi (ed.), *Albania*, New York, 1956, p. 76; Stavro Skendi, *The Political Evolution of Albania, 1912–1944*, New York, 1954, pp. 11–14.

Yugoslav Leadership and Guidance—A Crucial Factor

It is questionable whether there would have been a Communist Party in Albania had it not been for the initiative taken by the Comintern (Communist International) through the Yugoslav Communist Party. The contacts that the Yugoslav Communist Party, on instructions from the Comintern, made with a few Albanian Communist groups in 1939 and the story of the founding of the Albanian Communist Party on November 8, 1941, by Tito's emissaries, Miladin Popović and Dušan Mugosa, are too well known to repeat here.[3] The point to be stressed is that these two men, aided occasionally by a few other experienced Yugoslav Communist officials who visited Albania from 1942 to 1944, were the architects of the political and military plans that resulted in the Communist seizure of power in Albania in November, 1944. Equipped as they were with the experience of the Yugoslav Communist Party and delegated by the Comintern to lead the Communist movement in Albania, they drafted the program and the first resolution of the fledgling Albanian Communist Party. Their most effective work was done in the organizational field. No sooner had the Albanian Communist Party been created than they issued the first instructions for the formation of Party cells and the recruitment of the first members. It took about six months to form the rudiments of the local organizations, and by April, 1942, Popović and Mugosa felt the Party had gained enough strength and stature, although its total membership did not exceed 200 (mostly students and young intellectuals from the south), to hold its first consultative meeting, chiefly for the purpose of cleaning its ranks of "unreliable" and "disloyal" elements, especially those who were grumbling about the Yugoslav strangle hold on the new Party. It was also about this time that the Party began to form small guerrilla bands, commit terroristic

---

[3] For the official Yugoslav version of the founding of the Albanian Communist Party, see Vladimir Dedijer, *Yugoslav-Albanian Relations, 1939–1948* (translated by U. S. Department of Commerce, Office of Technical Services, Joint Publications Research Service, Washington, D. C., JPRS: 13162, 1962). Although Dedijer's book is somewhat biased in favor of the Yugoslav Communist Party, the account is generally reliable and the documentation is genuine. For the official Albanian version, see *Historia e Partise se Punes te Shqiperise*, Tirana, 1968, pp. 52–80. This official version is extremely biased and incomplete in that it ignores completely the leading role played by Tito's emissaries in the founding of the Albanian Communist Party. See also, Skendi (ed.), *op. cit.*, pp. 80–86, and Vladimir Gsovski and Kazimir Grzybowski (eds.), *Government, Law and Courts in the Soviet Union and Eastern Europe*, Vol. I, New York, 1959, pp. 165–172; "History of the Albanian Communist Party," Parts I and II, *News from Behind the Iron Curtain*, Munich, Vol. IV, No. 11, November, 1955, pp. 3–10, and Vol. V, No. 1, January, 1956, pp. 22–30; and Nicholas C. Pano, *The People's Republic of Albania*, Baltimore, 1968, pp. 39–58.

acts against the local collaborators and pro-fascist elements, stage demonstrations either on its own or in collaboration with nationalist resistance groups, carry on acts of sabotage against the Italian forces, and seize military supplies.

To profit further from the experience of the Yugoslav Communists, Mugosa visited Tito's headquarters in May, 1942, to observe the actual formation and operations of the Yugoslav partisan bands. He also brought with him an appeal from the Albanian Communist Party for formal recognition by the Comintern and for permission to hold the Party's first national conference and elect permanent central organs (the leadership chosen at the founding meeting of the Party was temporary, pending approval by the Comintern.) For several weeks Mugosa was attached to Tito's First Proletarian Brigade to study all facets of its organization and military tactics. Mugosa also carefully studied the functions of the People's Liberation Councils, which the Yugoslav Party had created as local governmental bodies in liberated areas.

According to Yugoslav sources, on September 21, 1942, Tito received a message from the Comintern taking note of the creation of the Albanian Communist Party (but not granting it membership in the Comintern) and authorizing it to hold its first national conference and elect a permanent Central Committee. To prepare for this conference Tito sent to Albania, along with Mugosa, a Yugoslav Party delegation headed by Blazo Jovanović, and including Vojo Todorović, an expert in organizing Party branches and partisan units in the countryside. More important, Jovanović carried with him a long letter from Tito, dated September 22, 1942, to the Central Committee of the Albanian Communist Party. The contents of this letter became the agenda of the conference, which was held in Labinot, a village near Elbasan, in March, 1943, after careful preparation by Jovanović, Popović, Mugosa, and the Albanian Party leaders.

In his letter Tito summarized the message from the Comintern (the message was sent to Tito, not directly to the Albanians), the gist of which was (1) that the Albanians must plan a "careful, conspiratorial" conference so that no *agents provocateurs* might infiltrate it; (2) that the Albanian Party should create a reliable leadership; and (3) that the conference must make concrete moves such as the organization of a "people's liberation struggle" against the Axis forces and the establishment of a national front that would embrace "all Albanian patriots, avoiding for the moment the emphasis on goals which transcend the frame of the national liberation of Albania," and including in the leadership of the partisan formations "as many as possible honest Albanian nationalists and patriots besides Communists."[4]

[4] The complete text of Tito's letter is published in Dedijer, *op. cit.*, pp. 21–24.

For his own part, Tito suggested in his letter that an additional item be included in the conference agenda, namely, the problem of strengthening the Albanian Communist Party by purging all recalcitrant elements. The Party, in Tito's words, could become the leader of the national liberation struggle only if it were unified and monolithic and if its members fulfilled all Party decisions in a disciplined way. He pointed out further that, according to the reports sent to him by the Albanian Party, the basic shortcoming of the Party was the poor work done in organizing the peasantry. He wrote that he could not conceive how the Albanian Communist Party could wage an armed struggle against the invaders without the support of the peasants, for the partisan units had to be composed mostly of young peasants. He also warned that to regard the partisan units, as the Albanian Party actually had, as the armed force of the Party was all wrong, and that they must be looked upon as the armed force of the Albanian people. Another crucial suggestion in Tito's letter was that the Albanian Communists should strive to contact representatives of various bourgeois groups to form with them a united national liberation front, and that they should begin at once to establish the basis for a "people's government" by creating people's liberation councils as governmental organs in all parts of both liberated and occupied territories. This blueprint for action, as contained in the instructions from the Comintern and in Tito's letter, was adopted *in toto* by the conference.

A major decision taken by the conference was the establishment of the Albanian National Liberation Army (ANLA), patterned on Tito's National Liberation Army. To implement this decision, a few days after the conference closed on March 22, 1943, Svetozar Vukmanović-Tempo, then head of Tito's partisan forces in Macedonia, arrived at Labinot and worked out the details for setting up ANLA's General Staff and for organizing the local partisan units. He insisted in particular on the General Staff being organized at once, without waiting for the results of any negotiations that might be held with the nationalist *Balli Kombetar* (BK-National Front) organization, which, Vukmanović-Tempo claimed, was busy forming its own military units. Not to form the General Staff at once, he contended, could mean giving a helping hand to the BK and its "treacherous" plans. According to a report of April 19, 1943, which Popović sent to the Yugoslav Party Central Committee, some leaders of the Albanian Communist Party, including Enver Hoxha, the Party's Secretary General, did not understand the importance of creating the General Staff at once "because of their political immaturity and lack of foresight." They believed, Popović's report added, that they should first conclude the negotiations with the BK and only afterwards begin to establish the General Staff and the shock units of partisans, since if they started doing this immediately the BK would break off negotiations.[5] The Albanians apparently resisted Vukmanović-Tempo's pressure, for they delayed the creation of the General Staff until July 10, and the first shock brigade was not formed until August 15, after an agreement had been reached with the BK on August 2. But the agreement was denounced by the Albanian Communist Party a few days later because of pressure from the Yugoslavs (see below).

The Yugoslav pressure on the Albanian Party, initiated by Vukmanović-Tempo in April, 1943, increased steadily in scope until the eve of Albania's "liberation" in November, 1944, when the Yugoslavs assumed almost complete control of the Party. Vukmanović-Tempo, while on his way back from a visit to the headquarters of the Greek National Liberation Front (EAM) in Greece, visited Albania again in the second half of July, 1943, and reiterated his warning that the Albanian Party was following a wrong course in continuing its negotiations with the BK. He also told the Albanian leaders that he had been disturbed by the infiltration of British officers in the EAM units and by the comradeship that had developed between the British officers and some EAM leaders. Accordingly, he instructed the Albanians to keep a close watch on the British officers attached to the ANLA General Staff and lower echelons. This evoked several secret directives by Hoxha to the local Party committees ordering them to prevent the British officers from interfering in internal political affairs and to send the British to the General Staff headquarters if they disobeyed these orders.[6]

In October, 1943, Vukmanović-Tempo addressed two letters to the Albanian Party ordering it to desist from forming a people's liberation council in Debar, a town just across the border in Yugoslav Macedonia, which had been liberated by an Albanian partisan unit under the command of Haxhi Lleshi, a northern Albanian chieftain who is now President of the People's Republic of Albania. In response to these "insulting" letters, Hoxha sent a communication, dated October 23, 1943, to Vukmanović-Tempo expressing surprise at his bitter tone and rejecting outright his accusations that the members of the Albanian Central Committee were "ultra-chauvinists" and "Albano-megalomaniacs."[7]

---

[5] Dedijer, op. cit., p. 21.

[6] See, for instance, Hoxha's instructions of August 16 and October 1, 1943, in Enver Hoxha, Vepra, Tirana, 1968, pp. 342 and 437–445. See also Historia e Partise se Punes te Shqiperise (hereafter to be referred to as Historia), pp. 145–146.

[7] See text of letter in Hoxha, op. cit., pp. 508–511.

Documents published by the Albanians since 1968, particularly the first two volumes of Hoxha's *Works* and the official *History of the Albanian Workers' Party*, contain a severe indictment of the interference by the Yugoslav representatives in the affairs of the Albanian Party. A section in the Party's history entitled "The Brutal Interference of the Leadership of the Yugoslav Communist Party" charges that the Yugoslav Party exploited and dictated its will on the Albanian Party and attempted to "actuate its chauvinistic aims against Albania."[8] This section also revealed that Vukmanović-Tempo's principal mission during his second visit to Albania in July, 1943, had been to create the "Balkan General Staff," a Tito initiative intended to place under his command the national liberation forces of Greece, Albania, and Bulgaria. According to the Albanian Party history, Titos' initiative came to naught because of the reluctance of the Greek, Albanian, and Bulgarian Communist Parties to place their forces under his direct command.[9]

In 1944 the pressure of the Yugoslav Party on the Albanian Party increased considerably, particularly after Colonel Veljo Stojnic became the Yugoslav Party's official representative to the Central Committee of the Albanian Party. At a crucial plenum of the Central Committee held at Berat in the middle of November, 1944, just two weeks before the complete liberation of the country, Stojnic, according to the minutes of the meeting, launched an assault on the general line of the Albanian Party, characterizing it as a completely mistaken line, demanding that radical changes be made in both the Party line and in its leadership, and branding Hoxha as the "synthesis of all the errors."[10] Stojnic's charges were supported by the majority of the Politburo, to which Koci Xoxe, with Stojnic's backing, had co-opted new members in order to assure a pro-Yugoslav majority. During this plenum Stojnic also raised the problem of future Yugoslav-Albanian relations, stating that Albania did not have the resources to develop its economy independently and therefore there was no other road for it except to tie itself in a confederation with Yugoslavia and "to proceed even further," that is, eventually to merge with Yugoslavia. To achieve this, Stojnic considered it essential for the Albanian Party to prepare the masses and to popularize Tito as the "symbol of the liberation of the Balkan peoples."[11]

A serious attempt was made at this plenum to remove Hoxha from his position as Secretary General, but the majority of the plenum did not

---

[8] *Historia, op. cit.*, p. 177.

[9] *Ibid.*, p. 178, Note 1.

[10] *Ibid.*, p. 181.

[11] *Ibid.*, pp. 179–181; Dedijer, *op. cit.*, pp. 87–90.

support this move, and after an abject self-criticism he was allowed to remain as nominal head of the Party, while the real power was placed in the hands of Xoxe, then Orgburo (Organizational Bureau) Secretary, head of the secret police, and a trusted and loyal friend of the Yugoslavs. The history of the Party itself, most of which was apparently written by Hoxha, states on page 227, while discussing the period 1944–1948: "All the leadership of the Party was concentrated in fact in the hands of Koci Xoxe, Organizational Secretary of the Central Committee." In the interim period between November, 1944, and June, 1948, Xoxe and the Yugoslav representatives in the Albanian Party proceeded to elaborate plans for the final merger of Albania with the Yugoslav federated system, but the Stalin-Tito conflict early in 1948 blocked the fruition of this plan. Xoxe paid with his life in June, 1949, for his support of the plan for a merger and for his opposition to Hoxha.[12]

Resistance Movements and Civil War

The originally passive and active resistance of the Albanians to the Italian invaders had a purely nationalist and patriotic character. It was spearheaded by a few old patriots, young intellectuals, and students, representing all classes and all political beliefs. In anti-Italian demonstrations staged during the first few months of the occupation, a handful of Communists participated as individuals, but after the Soviet-German accord of August, 1939, most of them lay dormant. This early resistance, led by the old, respected patriot Midhat Frasheri, who in the fall of 1942 founded *Balli Kombetar*, aimed at integrating the old nationalist aspirations for an ethnic Albania with the popular demand for the creation of a modern state along democratic patterns. When the BK was formally established, these ideals were expounded in a ten-point program known as the *Decalogue*, which contained the general outlines for the eventual liberation of the country and the reorganization of the social and economic order on genuine

---

[12] For the Yugoslav side of the plan for Yugoslav-Albanian unification, see Milovan Djilas, *Conversations with Stalin*, New York, 1962, pp. 142–147. The most complete account for the Albanian side of the story is given in *Historia*, pp. 241–257. The Yugoslav plan for unification was submitted to the Central Committee of the Albanian Party on December 5, 1947, by Savo Zilatić, then Yugoslav Minister to Tirana. Koci Xoxe then introduced the plan for discussion and approval at the famous Eighth Plenum of the Central Committee in February, 1948, when Mehmet Shehu and several other top Party leaders (but not Hoxha, although marked for eventual elimination) were expelled from the Central Committee. The plan was never consummated, however, because of the Stalin-Tito break. The Yugoslav account of the Eighth Plenum is given in Dedijer, *op. cit.*, pp. 162–165; the Albanian account is given in *Historia*, pp. 247–250.

democratic principles. The question of the political organization of the state was to be decided by the people themselves after the liberation.[13]

The Communists as an organized group did not join the resistance until after Tito's emissaries had created the Albanian Communist Party in November, 1941. Wartime documents published by the Yugoslav government in 1949 attest to the fact that from the Italian invasion in 1939 to November, 1941, the tiny Communist groups played no significant part in the Albanian resistance and consumed most of their time in ideological and personal polemics among themselves.[14] Indeed, up to the founding of the Albanian Communist Party, the number of Communists had been negligible—not more than 150 at most. In their negotiations with some eight disparate and disorganized Communist groups, two of which were Trotskyite, Tito's envoys managed to unite only three, which formed the nucleus of the Albanian Communist Party. But under the skillful guidance of Popović and Mugosa, the newly founded Party engaged in intensive recruiting and indoctrinating in the cities, mostly in the south, concentrating on young intellectuals and youth, chiefly high school students, artisans, small shopkeepers, and a few labor leaders, as well as some riffraff and petty thieves. Backed by these elements and representing itself as a mass patriotic party whose sole purpose allegedly was to free the country from the invaders and to assure democratic freedoms, the Albanian Communist Party began forming small guerrilla bands and conspiratorial groups in the cities. The Party was particularly successful after it formed the National Liberation Movement in September, 1942 (NLM, modeled on the Yugoslav National Liberation Front, was later known as the National Liberation Front and after 1945 as the Democratic Front). The Party used the National Liberation Front as a cloak to conceal its own activities and objectives not only during the war but also as late as 1948. In a frank comment on this situation, the Party's official history states that the Party led "a semi-legal existence even after it seized power...the program of the Party was camouflaged as the program of the Democratic Front, the Party members concealed the fact that they belonged to the Party, and the Party's directives were published as decisions of the Front."[15]

Originally, the National Liberation Front included a few influential nationalist figures, such as Major Abas Kupi, a chieftain from the Kruje region who later abandoned the NLM and created the Nationalist Legality Movement. The NLM quickly became a magnet for many anti-fascist

---

[13] Abas Ermenji, "Shqiperia gjate pesedhjete vjeteve histori," *Albania*, Rome, 1962, p. 165.

[14] Dedijer, *op. cit.*, pp. 9–11.

[15] *Historia*, p. 253.

elements, including in particular a large number of professional people, such as doctors and lawyers, professors and teachers, merchants and artisans. But the rank-and-file followers came from the youth and from the disaffected masses of workers and poor peasants who had been ignored and neglected by the prewar regime and had suffered economic privations. These elements fell easy prey to the NLM's deceptive promises of freedom, land, and economic well-being. In connection with these promises, the NLM (actually the top Communist) consistently and vehemently denied that the movement was Communist or Communist-inspired. At the Congress of Permet in May, 1944, for instance, Hoxha declared that charges that he and his associates intended to bolshevize the country came out of "Dr. Goebbel's kitchen."[16]

In the period from the fall of 1941 to the late summer of 1942 the nationalist resistance groups and the Communists managed to coexist because the latter were in no position to engage in frontal attacks against the nationalists. But once most of the nationalists were organized in the BK, the Communists, considering them a real threat to their movement, began to engage in verbal polemics, accusing the BK of being a tool of reaction. The BK in turn charged the Communists with being nothing else but Tito's lackeys and with working to bring about Yugoslav domination over Albania. The two organizations were particularly at odds with each other over the tactics and extent of resistance to the occupier. It was the tactical policy of the BK to attack the invaders only if they were in no position to take drastic countermeasures that would result in massacres of the population and the destruction of the countryside. Conversely, the NLM advocated constant and relentless warfare against the enemy, irrespective of the consequences to the population. This tactic, which was urged on the Albanian Communist Party leaders by Tito's emissaries, had a twofold objective: first, to persuade the people at home and the anti-Axis coalition abroad that the NLM was the only organized movement fighting the common enemy, and, secondly, to attract to its side those people, especially in the countryside, who had been left destitute by the indiscriminate punitive actions of the enemy and their local collaborators.

Prior to the formation of the Albanian National Liberation Army by the Party's first national conference in March, 1943, the NLM had no organized military units, aside from some scattered guerrilla bands in cities and towns in the south. At the end of 1942, in fact, the NLM had been unable to create any firm bases among the peasantry, the vast majority of whom at this stage of the war supported the BK. Gradually, however, as

---

[16] Skendi, *Albania*, pp. 127–128.

the Italian command in Albania deserted the countryside and concentrated its forces in the cities located along the principal arteries of communication, the NLM began penetrating widely in the villages, recruiting peasant youth and cutting into the strength of the BK. But still, at the end of 1942, in southern and central Albania the largest and most active bands in the countryside were those of the BK.

The situation changed radically, however, in the spring and summer of 1943 because of the weakening of the Italian war potential and the corresponding increase of the partisan formations, especially after the creation of the General Staff of the National Liberation Army on July 10, 1943, and the formation of the First Shock Brigade on August 15, with Dušan Mugosa as *Politruk* (political commissar)[17] and Mehmet Shehu, a brilliant and ruthless military strategist who had headed a battalion in the International Brigade in the Spanish Civil War, as operational commander. At this time the majority of the youth in the populated centers, enticed by the appeals of Communist propaganda and influenced by the victories of the Soviet armies as well as by the widespread anti-fascist spirit created by the Allied informational media, especially the British Broadcasting Corporation and the Voice of America, took to the mountains to join the partisan bands. A pro-NLM climate was thus created all over the country which no BK or other nationalist appeal could counter. Indeed, in the cities in the south, from which nearly all top Communist leaders came, the NLM managed to enlist the support of many influential and well-to-do families whose sons and daughters had joined the partisan bands. It was primarily in the homes of these prominent families that the Communist leaders held their conspiratorial meetings and issued their appeals to the bourgeois classes for material support, which they received in generous quantities.[18]

As the Albanian Communist Party spread its influence and bases in the villages, it also increased the number of cadres among the peasants. With the formation of the first ANLA battalions, the Communists turned their attention more and more to the BK. There were, however, strong elements in the Party's Central Committee, including Enver Hoxha, who believed that some kind of *modus vivendi* could be achieved with the BK, at least for the duration of the war. To this end long sporadic negotiations were held between representatives of the NLM and the BK, the final phase of the

---

[17] *Ibid.*, p. 78.

[18] Enver Hoxha himself often took refuge in the Tirana home of his brother-in-law, Bahri Omari, a well-known patriot and leading member of the BK; he was one of a large group of nationalists who were tried and executed in April, 1945, as "war criminals" or "enemies of the people."

negotiations coinciding with Vukmanović-Tempo's second visit to Albania. As the Party's official history puts it, during this visit Vukmanović-Tempo "unjustly and intolerantly accused the Central Committee of an opportunistic stand towards the BK. This stupid lie was told with the specific purpose of creating the impression that the Albanian Party could not independently do the right thing without the directives from the experienced leadership of the Yugoslav Communist Party."[19] Despite Vukmanović-Tempo's admonitions, however, the NLM continued negotiations with the BK, and on August 2, 1943, an agreement was concluded at Mukaj, a village near Tirana. It provided for the formation of a joint Committee for the Salvation of Albania, whose prime objective was to prosecute the war against the invaders until the country was liberated. Both the ANLA and the BK military units were to struggle for an independent, "ethnic" Albania, that is, an Albania that would retain the Yugoslav provinces of Kosovo and Metohija, which the Axis powers had attached to Albania after the invasion of Yugoslavia in 1941. A few days later the Central Committee of the Albanian Party repudiated the accord on the ground that Dr. Ymet Dishnica and Mustafa Gjinishi, the NLM representatives who signed the accord, had violated the instructions given to them and had accepted the position of the BK delegates.[20]

Actually, the accord was denounced because of the heavy pressure brought to bear by Tito's emissaries, who were reportedly enraged when they realized that the Albanian Party had accepted the premise of an "ethnic" Albania.[21] Soon after the repudiation of the agreement, secret instructions went to the local Party committees and to the ANLA commanders to annihilate the BK units.[22] By the end of September, 1943, the partisan formations, now equipped with large quantities of arms seized from the capitulating Italian armed forces in Albania, had instituted a full-scale civil war, which was fought with tremendous fury for nearly a year and which was won by the Communists.

Since the outcome of the Civil War decided the social order which the Communists imposed on the country after they seized power, it would be fruitful to examine the social composition of the principal contending parties. It should be stressed from the outset that the Communist theory of classes had no relevance either to the make-up of the Albanian Communist

---

[19] *Historia*, p. 178.

[20] Hoxha, *op. cit.*, pp. 335–341.

[21] Dedijer, *op. cit.*, pp. 72–76. The Yugoslavs have never concealed the pressure they brought to bear on the Albanian Party to denounce the Mukaj agreement.

[22] Hoxha, *op. cit.*, pp. 344–379; Skendi, *Albania*, pp. 128–129.

Party or to the nature of the Civil War. The BK originally attracted not only as many workers (actually there was at that time no industrial working class to speak of) as the NLM but also the vast majority of the villagers. Also, while the Communist propaganda media represented the BK as a bourgeois and feudal organization, nearly all the leading Communists derived from bourgeois or petty bourgeois families from the south who were educated in West European schools, and the majority of the teen-age sons and daughters of beys, influential landowners, and other wealthy families, particularly in the south and central Albania, enrolled in the partisan formations, many of them becoming leading Party cadres. And as the military power of the NLM increased in the spring and summer of 1944, large segments of the townspeople in the south, from the simplest artisans to wealthy merchants, intellectuals, and even some clergymen, became active supporters or sympathizers of the NLM.

The BK supporters were more nationalist and democratic in their political beliefs, but their social composition was not different from those who supported the NLM. What determined the outcome of the Civil War, therefore, was the ability of the NLM to enlist large elements of the urban and rural population, especially the youth of all classes, in the partisan formations and in the local people's councils. These people's councils, according to the statute approved by the Second National Liberation Conference held at Labinot on September 4, 1943, represented "the civil authority of the country; they are the political power of the Albanian people."[23]

A primary reason for the success of the NLM in enlisting such large-scale support was owing to the circumstances surrounding the larger war that was being fought outside the Albanian frontiers—specifically, the Anglo-American-Soviet alliance, the rapid penetration of the Soviet armed forces into the Balkans, the successes of the partisan armies in neighboring Yugoslavia and Greece, the refusal of the Anglo-Americans to recognize an Albanian government in exile, and, to a lesser extent, the moral and material assistance that the Anglo-Americans extended to the NLM.[24]

For a brief period in the late summer of 1944 the ANLA units engaged also the poorly trained and ill-equipped nationalist bands of the Legality Movement in the Kruje-Mat area. The demand of Major Abas Kupi for political concessions by the British and his consequent hesitation to take the field against the retreating German forces deprived him of military

---

[23] *Twenty Years of Socialism in Albania*, Tirana, 1964, pp. 15–16.
[24] Zavalani, *op. cit.*, p. 252, and Ermenji, *op. cit.*, pp. 164–176.

supplies he had expected to receive from the British.[25] Faced with superior ANLA units, Kupi's bands were quickly routed, and this, coupled with the utter destruction of the BK forces and the collapse of the German-supported Tirana government in September and October, 1944, created the perfect political and military vacuum which the Communists needed. With a partisan army that by the late summer of 1944 had grown to over 50,000 strong (the Communists claim that the total strength of the eight ANLA divisions in September, 1944, was over 70,000, of whom 5,000 were girls), the Albanian Communist Party was able to seize power as soon as it cleared Tirana of all German forces.

The Stand of the Big Three Towards Albania

During the war the English and Americans did not fully understand the real nature and aims of the NLM and had very little information, if any, on the part played by the Yugoslav Communist Party in manipulating the Communist movement in Albania. Both London and Washington took an active interest in the Albanian resistance against the Axis forces, but this interest was purely military. To encourage the Albanians, irrespective of their political attitudes and motivations, to continue to expand their fight against the common enemy, the American and British governments, in concert with the Soviet Union, issued official statements in December, 1942, promising to restore Albanian sovereignty and independence after the war. The Communists made skillful use of the fact that the Washington and London statements were issued in concert with Moscow and that the British statement, in deference to Greek territorial claims against Albania, included the proviso that Albania's boundaries would be settled at the peace conference.[26] In an effort to enlist popular support the NLM propaganda media gave the statements wide publicity, stressing in particular the implication that the Big Three, issuing the statements in concert, had a common policy towards Albania. Concomitantly, the Communists spread ugly rumors to the effect that the Soviet statement contained no "if's" and "but's" about preserving the territorial integrity of Albania, while the American statement side-stepped the issue and that of Great Britain implied support of the Greek territorial claims. This propaganda on the question of the country's territorial integrity struck a sensitive cord among the people.

---

[25] The story of Abas Kupi and his Legality Movement is told in Major (now Lord) Julian Amery's romantic *Sons of the Eagle—A Study in Guerilla Warfare*, London, 1948. The book makes fascinating reading, but it grossly exaggerates the war potential and the following of Major Abas Kupi, the only officer in King Zog's gendarmerie who had the courage to fire on the Italians when they landed at the port of Durres in the early hours of April 7, 1939.

[26] Skendi, *Albania, op. cit.*, pp. 20–21; Zavalani, *op. cit.*, pp. 252–257.

In an attempt to give more direct aid to the resistance groups, in the spring of 1943 the British infiltrated liaison officers into Albania who made contact with both the BK and the NLM, and in the fall of the same year American officers from the Office of Strategic Services (OSS) joined their British colleagues in some of the BK and NLM guerrilla bands. The general tasks of both the American and British officers were to commit sabotage against the Axis troops, to collect intelligence on their movements and on the activities of the resistance groups, and to render assistance only to those guerrilla bands actively engaged against the common enemy. In brief, their mission dealt purely with military and intelligence matters; they had no guidance and no authority to deal with political matters. By the spring of 1944 most of the British and American missions were attached to the ANLA General Staff and its lower commands, presumably because the ANLA units were the most aggressive against the Axis troops. During this period the British also sent a high-level mission to Abas Kupi in the Kruje-Mat region, but this mission, despite its persistent efforts, failed to muster Kupi's forces against the retreating Germans. Its failure was in part due to an apparent decision in London in the spring of 1944 to give help only to the NLM forces. In fact, in the summer of 1944 an official ANLA mission was attached to the British Balkan Command in Bari, and a high-level ANLA delegation was invited to Italy to negotiate an agreement with the Balkan Command for increased deliveries of arms and foodstuffs to the partisan units. As a result of this agreement, considerable quantities of war supplies were dropped by planes or unloaded along the southern coast, which had already been liberated by the partisans. By the summer of 1944, therefore, the Anglo-Americans had definitely cast their die, at least militarily, in favor of the Communist-dominated NLM. And this they did not because of any pressure from Moscow but because it was obvious by then that the NLM was the principal force fighting the Germans. The Anglo-Americans still hoped, however, that a democratic regime could be established after the war.

Aside from the Comintern's delegation of authority to the Yugoslav Communist Party to found a Communist Party in Albania, the Soviet Union took no direct part in the development of the Communist resistance movement in Albania. Moscow never dispatched any supplies to the Albanian partisans, and no Soviet liaison officers were attached to the ANLA units. The first Soviet military mission, composed of an officer and a few ranks, reached the ANLA General Staff from the headquarters of the National Liberation Front in Greece only in August, 1944, and it was sent in response to an invitation by the Congress of Permet, held in May of that year, to the Big Three to attach official military missions to the ANLA

General Staff. (The British and American liaison officers who had been operating in Albania since the spring of 1943 had no official standing; they represented the intelligence services of the two countries).

The Soviets have revealed precious little about Stalin's wartime attitude towards the Albanian Communists, but judging by the disparaging remarks he made on several occasions to Yugoslav Party officials, he apparently had no high regard for the Albanian people or the Albanian Communist leaders.[27] Until late 1947 Stalin apparently was content to let Tito handle the Albanian problem and prepare the groundwork for an eventual federation—under Stalin's domination, of course—of Yugoslavia, Bulgaria, and Albania. But when Soviet-Yugoslav relations deteriorated late in 1947, Stalin used Yugoslavia's behavior towards Albania as the pretext for requesting a high-level Yugoslav delegation to visit Moscow in January, 1948.[28] However, even during the discussion that followed between Stalin and Milovan Djilas, Stalin said that the Soviet government had no special interest in Albania and that Yugoslavia was free to "swallow" Albania any time it wished to do so.[29] There is no reason to think that Stalin did not mean what he said, but the Yugoslavia that was to be allowed to swallow Albania had to be one that was completely dominated by him.

An examination of the published documents dealing with Teheran (November, 1943) and Yalta (February, 1945) shows that Albania was never mentioned specifically at either conference. More important, Prime Minister Churchill, either by commission or omission, failed to list Albania on the piece of paper he shoved across the table to Stalin in the Kremlin on the evening of October 9, 1944, when he indicated the degree of Soviet and Western influence to be exercised during the war in Hungary, Rumania, Bulgaria, Yugoslavia, and Greece.[30] In all probability Churchill did not think Albania was of sufficient importance to be made a subject of discussion with Stalin. It would be idle speculation now to try to guess what Stalin's reaction would have been if Churchill had included Albania and indicated a ninety percent British influence, as he did in the case of Greece. By that time the Albanian Communists had eliminated all internal opposition and were in the process of clearing the country of the last retreating German units. Stalin was no doubt aware of this, as he was of the fact that ELAS (the Communist-dominated Greek Army of National Liberation) had obtained the upper hand in Greece. Nevertheless, he gave Churchill a free

[27] Vladimir Dedijer, *Tito*, New York, 1953, p. 303; Djilas, *op. cit.*, pp. 79, 143.

[28] Djilas, *op. cit.*, p. 133.

[29] Dedijer, *Tito, op. cit.*, p. 311; Djilas, *op. cit.*, p. 143.

[30] Winston S. Churchill, *The Second World War :* Vol. VI, *Triumph and Tragedy*, Cambridge, 1953, p. 227; John Lukacs, "The Night Stalin and Churchill Divided Europe," *The New York Times Magazine*, October 9, 1969, pp. 36–50.

hand in that country. The question arises, therefore, as to whether Stalin would have objected to a British landing in Albania, simultaneous with the landings in Greece. The fact is that the Albanian Communists, from the capitulation of Italy in September, 1943, until late in 1944, lived in deadly fear of Anglo-American landings.[31] This was due to the fact that no assurances of any kind had been given to them by Stalin that such landings would not occur. Tito apparently feared for the fate of Albania, for in the middle of October, 1944, he sent an urgent message to the Albanian Party to convene at once the Anti-Fascist Liberation Council of Albania (created at the Congress of Permet in May, 1944, and patterned on the Anti-Fascist Council of National Liberation of Yugoslavia—AVNOJ), in order to convert the Albanian Anti-Fascist Committee (also founded at Permet as the executive branch of the Anti-Fascist Council and patterned on the Yugoslav National Committee) into the Provisional Democratic Government of Albania.[32] The purpose of this move was to confront the Anglo-Americans with an accomplished fact when Albania was fully freed of German troops. The Albanians complied promptly, convened what is known as the Congress of Berat, or the Second Conference of the Anti-Fascist Liberation Council of Albania (it corresponded to the second session of AVNOJ held at Jajce on November 29, 1943, which created the Yugoslav National Committee), and transformed the Albanian Anti-Fascist Committee into the provisional government, with Enver Hoxha as prime minister.

The official history of the Albanian Party, commenting on these fateful days just before the seizure of power, admits that the final plans of ANLA's General Staff for the "liberation" of the country were formulated with a view to forestall any "attempt by the Mediterranean Anglo-American Command to deter the National Liberation Army from engaging in a final assault...and to destroy the forces of internal reaction." The strategic plans, adds the Party's history as an afterthought, "provided also for the pursuit of the German forces across the state borders."[33] Even as late as February, 1945, several months after they had obtained control of the country, the Albanian Communists were by no means sure that Stalin would not give a free hand to the British with regard to Albania, as he had done in the case of Greece. The deep concern of the Albanian leaders was particularly evident during the Yalta meeting when Enver Hoxha, apparently in the dark as to what was being discussed by the Big Three, personally visited for the first and last time the American Military Mission (OSS) in Tirana, in an

---

[31] Hoxha, *op. cit.*, p. 369.

[32] Dedijer, *Yugoslav-Albanian Relations*, p. 79.

[33] *Historia, op. cit.*, pp. 169–170, 173–174.

obvious effort to ascertain whether the question of Albania was being raised at the conference.[34] But once the conference was over and its general decisions and agreements announced to the press, Hoxha and his colleagues felt secure, and soon after launched their program for communizing the country.

In the meantime, the Hoxha regime was tacitly accepted by the British and American governments. In May, 1945, the State Department dispatched an "unofficial" mission to Tirana to investigate the situation and report on the possibility of recognizing the Hoxha regime, and the British sent a high-level military mission for the same purpose. On December 10 of the same year the American and British governments, again in concert with the Soviet government, addressed separate notes to the Hoxha government offering to establish diplomatic relations with it, but the Americans and the British included certain minor conditions which the Albanians did not accept.[35] As a consequence, Washington and London have not, to this day, established diplomatic relations with the Albanian Communist regime.

Conclusions

The advent of communism in Albania, like that in the other countries of Eastern Europe, was not the result of a spontaneous popular revolution aimed at the destruction of the old order and the creation of a new, socialist society. It was rather the product of the Axis aggression and the assumption by the Communists of the leading role in the resistance movement. Once Churchill and Roosevelt concluded at the Second Quebec Conference (September, 1944) that "as long as the battle in Italy continues there will be no forces available in the Mediterranean to employ in the Balkans," except for small British landings in Greece,[36] the fate of Albania was sealed. While it is true that communism in Albania did not arrive "on the wings of the Red Army," as Ana Pauker phrased it in the case of Rumania, the penetration of the Soviet army into the Balkans encouraged the

---

[34] The author was at that time a member of the American Military Mission in Tirana and was in personal contact with Hoxha.

[35] The Yugoslavs take the credit for preventing the Albanian government from accepting the American condition that it accept the validity of bilateral treaties and agreements concluded between the two countries prior to April 7, 1939. In his *Yugoslav-Albanian Relations*, which is actually a Yugoslav White Book, Dedijer cites Josep Djerda as maintaining that "the Albanian government was even ready to accept the conditions of the American government . [but] with the outside influence it was possible to dissuade the government in time not to accept American conditions" (p. 118).

[36] Churchill, *op. cit.*, p. 159.

Albanian Communists to intensify their efforts in the summer and fall of 1944 to eliminate all nationalist opposition.[37]

Nor would Albania have gone Communist if the British landings in Greece had been extended to Albania as well. Under the circumstances, the only thing Stalin could have done would have been to send Churchill a formal note of protest. Indeed, Churchill might have met more opposition from Washington than from Moscow.

Within the country, the Communists were the only group that, with the firm and experienced guiding hand of Tito's emissaries, had the vision to establish a well-organized and disciplined political party with the unalterable goal of seizing power. The various nationalist groups and tribal chieftains did not have the foresight to create political parties; they established only loose or personal resistance movements which lacked strong and disciplined leadership. Above all, these movements were unable to gauge either the people's sentiments for relentless resistance to the foreign invaders, or the desires of the Anglo-Americans, whose primary concern was military rather than political and who accordingly were willing to make common cause only with those elements in the occupied countries who pinned down as many enemy divisions as possible. Additionally, the nationalist groups did not possess the unscrupulousness, the fighting ability, the sense of self-sacrifice, and the conviction of the Communists that power could be won by continuous struggle, not only against the foreign invaders and their collaborators but also against anyone who would threaten to block their ultimate objective, the seizure of political control. While the guidance and the ideology came from abroad, therefore, the people who fought and won the war against both the invaders and the nationalists were the native Communists and their local sympathizers.

The non-existence of a government in exile and the elimination of all organized internal opposition before the seizure of power enabled the Albanian Communists to by-pass the process of going through various stages of coalition governments, unlike the other East European countries. There was no need for the Albanian Party to share power with other political parties or groups, for they did not exist. The conversion in

---

[37] The rapid penetration of the Soviet armies in the Balkans was one of the reasons that induced Churchill to visit Moscow in October, 1944. As he phrased it in his *Triumph and Tragedy*: "The Russian armies were now pressing heavily upon the Balkan scene, and Rumania and Bulgaria were in their power. As the victory of the Grand Alliance became only a matter of time it was natural that Russian ambitions should grow. Communism raised its head behind the thundering Russian battle-front. Russia was the Deliverer, and Communism the gospel she brought" (p. 208).

October, 1944, of the Anti-Fascist National Liberation Committee into a provisional government and subsequently into a permanent government did not involve changes of program or leadership. From the outset the Party created a monolithic, authoritarian police state. A few nationalists who had remained to the end with the NLM and who were presented by the Democratic Front as candidates in the first postwar national elections held in December, 1945 were ruthlessly purged as "enemies of the people" as soon as they began agitating for free debate in the People's Assembly.

Finally, it should be re-emphasized that the Communist takeover in Albania was in one respect unique. It had no parallel in the other East European countries where Communist governments were installed, since Albania was not "liberated" either by the Red Army directly or by Tito's partisan formations, none of whom set foot on Albanian soil either during the war or immediately after the seizure of power. Neither Stalin nor Tito supplied any war material to the Albanian National Liberation Army, although, as has been demonstrated above, it was Tito's emissaries who supplied the ideological and technical advice and direction. The Communist seizure of power in Albania, therefore was the most indigenous of all the Communist takeovers in Eastern Europe, because the Albanian Communist Party was the only one to seize power without direct military aid from foreign Communists. In this respect Albania differs from Yugoslavia, Czechoslovakia, and China, for in each of these countries the local Communists received substantial aid from the Red Army.

The Greek Communists Tried Three Times— and Failed

D. George Kousoulas

In the short span of less than eight years, from 1942 to 1949, the Greek Communist Party (KKE) made three major attempts to seize power by force. All failed. The reasons behind each failure, when examined closely and without the distorting effect of preconceived assumptions, offer valuable insights into Communist-led movements aimed at the forcible takeover of state power.

Each of these attempts was different in its form of execution, its configuration of forces, its strategy and tactics, and its relationship to non-Greek factors of power. The first attempt took place during the country's occupation by the Axis. Using patriotic slogans to mobilize the people in a resistance organization, EAM (the National Liberation Front), and in its guerrilla force, ELAS (the Greek Popular Liberation Army), the Greek Communists succeeded in establishing the strongest resistance movement in Greece. ELAS then tried to eliminate all other resistance organizations, so that at the crucial moment of German withdrawal it would be the only significant politico-military force in the country. Its efforts largely succeeded. By the time the Germans left Greece in October, 1944, EAM/ELAS was indeed the major force in Greece. Only one other important guerrilla force existed at the time—EDES (the National Democratic Greek Army). Under the leadership of Napoleon Zervas, it was isolated in remote Epirus in northwestern Greece. The efforts of the Greek Communists were of course aided by the preoccupation of the British with military considerations and by British disregard, until 1944, of the political repercussions of Communist advances in Greece.[1] The Greek Communists might easily have consummated control over Greece in October, 1944, since with the departure of the Germans there were no barriers to a takeover left at the time. Why they did not is one of the questions to be explored in this essay.

The second attempt to seize power took place in December, 1944, in the form of a popular uprising supported by Communist-led guerrilla units. This effort was of relatively short duration, lasting only forty-one days and unfolding primarily in a small but vital geographic area, the Greek

---

[1] E. C. W. Myers, *Greek Entanglement*, London, 1955, p. 230.

capital. While the Communists continued to use the guise of the National Liberation Front and the Greek Popular Liberation Army, the old resistance coalition had crumbled, and the December "revolution" was clearly a Communist Party show. This second attempt was encouraged by Tito, but received no material assistance from him; nor did it receive any endorsement or open support from Moscow. It employed the traditional tactics of barricades, house-to-house and street fighting, and the storming of isolated outposts of the government forces. At the outset of the fighting, the Communists enjoyed a large measure of superiority over their opponents in military prowess. The attempt failed in the end, and the reasons why point to some of the factors determining the fate of "popular uprisings" in the twentieth century.

The third attempt differed from the other two in a number of ways. It took the form of a protracted guerrilla campaign which lasted almost three years; was materially supported by Yugoslavia, Bulgaria, and Albania; and was clearly led by the Communist Party, without the deceptive veil of patriotic motivations. It, too, failed, and the reasons why afford a better understanding of the cohesiveness of the Communist movement and the "laws" of guerrilla and counter-guerrilla strategy and tactics.

In all three attempts, the Greek Communists did not act as Moscow's "puppets," but largely as self-propelled "technicians of revolution," mostly interested in seizing power for themselves. They acquiesced to Moscow's instructions only once—in October, 1944—and this they did rather reluctantly and simply because the overall circumstances of the time allowed little room for independent action. Moscow's role in the first two attempts was extremely limited and largely negative. Moscow initially exploited the third attempt for propaganda, but eventually took a strongly hostile attitude towards the Greek guerrillas for reasons to be discussed in the following pages.

The First Attempt
A Popular Resistance Movement

With the country's occupation by the Axis in the spring of 1941, the fabric of the Greek state as fashioned by the dictatorial Metaxas regime (the "Fourth of August" regime) was completely shattered. Four years of intensive propaganda by the regime had left no lasting mark on the people. Not even the courageous stand of I. Metaxas against the Italian ultimatum of October 28, 1940, seemed to imprint any sense of loyalty to the regime of the "Fourth of August" on the national consciousness. On the other hand, the democratic political leaders, discredited in the public eye for their petty quarrels in the days before the dictatorship, and with their ties to the people cut off for four years, failed to grasp the historic significance of the moment and spent themselves in reviving old controversies over the fate of the throne. The Greek Communist Party had been extensively disassembled during the dictatorship, with most of its leaders imprisoned or exiled. Many had denounced their ties with the Party, while three rival "leaderships," one of them created by the Ministry of Public Security itself, claimed to speak for the Communists. All this changed radically as the German tanks rolled into the country. Most of the loyal and experienced cadres of the Greek Communist Party escaped from their places of detention. In the absence of effective national leadership, the Communists provided the most knowledgeable leadership group in the country, and were the best suited to lead the resistance movement. Such a movement could draw easily on the people's patriotic feelings, love of freedom, and indignation against the brutalities of the occupation forces. The Communist Party did not identify itself as such openly.[2] Acting behind the guise of a patriotic organization known as the National Liberation Front (EAM) and using almost exclusively patriotic slogans to mobilize public support, it soon formed the largest resistance organization in the country.

While focusing public statements on the nation's desire to regain its freedom and independence, the Greek Communist Party actually planned a forcible takeover of state power in Greece. From the outset, it viewed the resistance movement as a means for seizing power after the liberation of the country. As early as December, 1942, George Siantos, then Secretary of the Central Committee of the Greek Communist Party, in addressing the Party's first major meeting during the occupation, stated:

> The immediate objective of our Party today is the expulsion of the foreign conquerors. This is the immediate objective of the Communist Party of Greece. Yes; but do we forget the ultimate strategic objective of our Party, namely, the struggle for Socialism and the final liberation of our people from every political yoke and exploitation of man by man? Not only do we not forget this objective but, on the contrary, our present policy will open up the way for the realization of our ultimate strategic objectives.[3]

To achieve these "ultimate strategic objectives," the Greek Communist Party, using ELAS as its instrument, sought to eliminate all other resistance organizations in Greece and to infiltrate the military forces being organized

---

[2] Svetozar Vukmanović-Tempo, in *Le Parti communiste de Grèce dans la lutte de libération nationale* (mimeographed copy), writes: "In general the Party concealed its identity from the broad masses of the Greek people."

[3] *Dheka Khronia Agones, 1935–1945*, Athens, 1946, p. 146.

by the Greek government in exile in the Middle East.[4] By the end of the occupation it had largely accomplished both these ends. Yet, when the Germans began to evacuate the country and ELAS held effective control over most of Greece, the Greek Communists did not move to seize power. "Thus, although we had decided on armed insurrection, beginning in September, 1944, instead of going ahead, instead of organizing the struggle for power, instead of seizing power, we capitulated and kept order!"[5] Why?

In August, 1944, Colonel Gregory Popov landed on a mountain air strip in Thessaly and established the first direct liaison between the Greek Communists and Moscow. The directive he brought to the Greek Communist Party reflected the tentative understanding between Churchill and Stalin on the division of responsibility in the Balkans. With Greece assigned to the British sphere of influence, the Greek Communist Party was instructed in no uncertain terms to co-operate with the Government of National Unity being formed in the Middle East under the premiership of George Papandreou. The leaders of the Party who were privy to this "advice" had their reservations about the wisdom of such co-operation. They could see quite clearly that with the withdrawal of the Germans the road would be open to seize power by using the 20,000 members of the underground ELAS in Athens. But they could not entirely ignore the first direct instruction from the Kremlin in many years; nor could they be sure that the British would not land in Greece with substantial forces accompanying the returning Government of National Unity. Could they withstand a clash with the British under such conditions and in the face of Soviet disapproval? Clearly not.

From the perspective of a quarter century, with much of the pertinent evidence at hand, we can say with a reasonable degree of certainty that Greece failed to fall under Communist rule in October, 1944, only because of the Stalin-Churchill agreement, which put Greece entirely under British control at the crucial moment. In this regard, Yugoslavia presented a different case because the Stalin-Churchill agreement provided for a fifty-fifty share of influence there, and the British had no way of imposing their half of the bargain. Belgrade was entered by the Red Army, not by British troops, and the Red Army was joined by Tito's partisans in a common political front. By contrast, the agreement kept the Russians out of Greece.

---

[4] Those interested may find a detailed account of the events and more extensive documentation in D. George Kousoulas, *Revolution and Defeat : The Story of the Greek Communist Party*, London, 1965.

[5] Vassilis Bartzotas, *I Politiki Stelekhon tou KKE sta Teleutea Dheka Khronia*, Central Committee of KKE, 1950, p. 49.

However, it might be argued that for purely military reasons Stalin would have rejected an expedition into Greece in any event as a time-wasting diversion from the main thrust into Central Europe.

The Second Attempt
A Popular Uprising

The same Communist leaders who accepted the Soviet instructions in October, 1944, and thereby lost their best chance to seize power, launched a violent uprising in December and made their second major bid for a forcible seizure of power. There is no indication that Stalin encouraged this uprising in violation of his agreement with Churchill. The opposite appears to be true. When Churchill came to Athens on Christmas Day, in the midst of the fighting, and declared during a conference with the Communists (and in the presence of Colonel Popov) that the British troops were in Greece with the approval of President Roosevelt and Marshal Stalin, the Soviet representative indicated clearly that this was indeed the case. The point was made even more dramatically a few days later, when, on December 30, Moscow announced the appointment of an ambassador to the very Greek government the Greek Communists were trying to overthrow.

Why did the Communist leaders ignore Soviet wishes in December? In October they had deferred to Soviet instructions because they had found it difficult to react negatively to the sudden appearance of a Soviet representative and to reject his first directive, but also because they expected substantial British forces to enter the country together with the Greek government. When the latter did not happen, they felt that the chance they had missed in October was not totally lost and that they could take advantage of it now. They reasoned that Stalin would hardly complain if they succeeded, especially since he could not be held responsible for the outcome, or be accused of perfidy by the British. They were encouraged in their belief by Tito, who was not bound by any agreement similar to that of Stalin and Churchill, and who could only view with apprehension the re-establishment of "capitalist" control in Athens.[6]

One must acknowledge that the Communist leaders acted on fairly sound grounds in deciding to launch the December "revolution," at least as far as Communist prescriptions for a forcible takeover were concerned. Stalin, amplifying Lenin's instructions, wrote in *Problems of Leninism* that Communists "should never play with insurrection, but when [they] begin one [they] must go to the end." His further instructions were quite explicit:

---

[6] For a detailed account, see D. George Kousoulas, *op. cit.*, pp. 197–218.

You must concentrate a great superiority of forces at the decisive point at the decisive moment. ... You must take the offensive [because] "the defensive is the death of every armed uprising"; you must take the enemy by surprise and seize the moment when his forces are scattered. You must strive for daily successes, even if small, (one might say hourly, if it is the case of one town). The selection of the moment .. must coincide with the moment when the crisis has reached its climax .. the vanguard is prepared to fight to the end, the reserves are prepared to support the vanguard, the maximum consternation reigns in the ranks of the enemy.[7]

Lenin had already supplied a note of warning: "The history of insurrections teaches us that the oppressed masses have never won a fight to the death without being reduced to despair by long sufferings and acute crises of every kind."[8]

With almost the entire country under control of the National Liberation Front and the Greek Popular Liberation Army (EAM/ELAS) the Communists could "concentrate a great superiority of forces at the decisive point," namely the Greek capital. Meanwhile, the forces of the "enemy" were indeed "scattered." Zervas' National Democratic Greek Army (EDES) was isolated more than 300 miles away from Athens, in remote Epirus; the Greek forces from the Middle East were too small to present a truly effective challenge; and the British forces which had landed in Greece in October were not only small in number but also dispersed in the major cities through Greece "in a manner which suited the administrative task for which they had come to Greece, and was not adapted to fighting." It was the "prevalent assumption of the British military authorities...that EAM/ELAS did not intend to precipitate a fight."[9] The "prevalent assumption" of the British flowed from the Western belief in the monolithic nature of the Communist movement. Confident that Stalin was sincere in his agreement with Churchill, they assumed that the Greek Communist Party would simply follow orders as an obedient agent.

Another condition set by Leninist prescriptions for insurrection is the "neutralization of the middle segments of the population." This, too, had been largely achieved. In many instances, the most vocal anti-Communists had been members of the Security Batallions organized by the collaborationist government of Ioannis Rallis in 1944, and were discredited for their co-operation with the Germans. After the country's liberation, many of them were imprisoned, for the most part by EAM/ELAS, with the approval and in the name of the Government of National Unity. The majority of

---

[7] J. V. Stalin, *Problems of Leninism*, Moscow, 1947, pp. 72–73.

[8] V. I. Lenin, *Preparing for Revolt*, London, 1929, p. 289.

[9] C. M. Woodhouse, *Apple of Discord*, London, 1951, p. 211.

those who could be considered as "middle segments of the population" were in the towns and cities controlled by EAM/ELAS and therefore were unable to render effective assistance to the national government. Besides, since the Communists and their allies participated in this government as members of a coalition, they could precipitate a crisis at any time by withdrawing from its ranks. Moreover, the "bourgeois" politicians who made up the roster of the government had been at loggerheads over the constitutional issue (the return of the King) until recently; a major crisis could easily revive the old quarrels and precipitate a disintegration of the anti-Communist camp from within.

In the weeks prior to the December uprising, continuous demonstrations gave the impression that "the vanguard was prepared to fight to the end, and that the reserves were prepared to support the vanguard." The morale of the ELAS men was high, and the Communist leadership had largely succeeded in convincing them that the British and the Government of National Unity (its "bourgeois" segment) were trying first to disarm ELAS and then to push the country back into the throes of "capitalist exploitation." Finally, a bloody demonstration on December 3 served as the "acute crisis" needed to reduce "the masses to despair." The demonstration is often pictured by some commentators as the event which sparked the uprising. In truth, the orders for the attack on the Greek capital were issued at least three days earlier.[10]

From a Marxist-Leninist point of view, the conditions for a successful insurrection had appeared to be present. Yet the insurrection failed. Why? The Communists made two tactical mistakes which certainly did not help their cause. They spent too much time pursuing "daily" successes by attacking isolated outposts of outlying police stations in the capital and other small strongholds of resistance, and they diverted a considerable ELAS force against Zervas' EDES in Epirus. This last move made little sense, since a Communist victory in Athens would have spelled the end of Zervas anyway.[11] These two tactical mistakes were not enough by them-

---

[10] The following operational orders were dispatched by the Central Committee of ELAS re-established on November 28: Secret Order No. 25/1 December, 1944, of the First Army Corps of ELAS; Operational Order No. 791/2 December, 1944, of the II Division of ELAS; Secret Order No. 52/3 December, 1944, from the Army Corps to the II Division of ELAS.

[11] There have been two explanations offered for this unnecessary military operation. One was that Siantos wanted to remain sole master of activities in the capital; the second that the Yugoslavs were planning, under the pretext of helping ELAS, to move their troops into Macedonia and Epirus and attack EDES, the implication being that Siantos acted with patriotic motives.

selves to bring about a Communist defeat, but they gave the British time to add their weight to the scales. This spelled the doom of the uprising.

The British began to move substantial military forces into the Athens region towards the end of December. Their superior fire power eventually forced ELAS to withdraw from the capital and, with its major forces virtually destroyed, to accept a truce, followed by the Varkiza agreement, which restored the control of the national government over the entire country. Although the agreement allowed the Greek Communist Party to remain as a legitimate political party and the National Liberation Front to continue as a major political organization, the Greek Popular Liberation Army was disarmed.

The intervention of the British and their eventual success in crushing the Communist rebellion showed that popular uprisings in the twentieth century have little hope of success if they face a well-organized, well-equipped, and well-disciplined army under the control of a cohesive and determined government. In the case of Greece, this counterweight was added primarily by foreign forces—British troops—in the absence of adequate domestic forces. Later, in East Germany in 1953 and in Hungary in 1956, foreign forces—the Red Army—would just as effectively suppress popular uprisings on the other side of the fence. Today, a popular uprising may succeed only if a government fails to use the devastating fire power of its military establishment against the insurrectionists. (This applies primarily to an uprising which takes place in an urban setting, a well-defined territory, and with the main forces made up of armed civilians using small arms. A long guerrilla war presents entirely different problems, as we shall see in the following pages.)

The Third Attempt
A Guerrilla Campaign

An uprising is, of course, a form of violent revolutionary activity entirely different from a protracted guerrilla campaign. The Greek Communist Party's third attempt to seize power took the form of an extended guerrilla operation. Its failure tells a great deal about the prerequisites for a successful anti-guerrilla campaign.

Even as they were negotiating at Varkiza for the agreement which ended the December uprising, the Greek Communist leaders were contemplating the possibility of another armed attempt to seize power. In January, 1945, they packed and concealed stores of weapons in mountain caves, and in highly orchestrated collusion, they "accepted" a partial amnesty which left the ordinary members of ELAS exposed to prosecution and therefore more amenable to Party control and eventual mobilization for a new armed confrontation.[12] The entire strategy of the Greek Communist Party at this time centered around preparations for a third try for power. N. Zakhariadis himself,[13] then head of the Greek Communist Party, stated in 1950: "What was the strategy of KKE in the post-Varkiza period? It was the strategy which has as its objective 'to gain time, to undermine the opponent, and to gather forces, to pass then on to the attack' (Stalin). It was the strategy of retreat—maneuver to preserve and regroup the main forces and the reserves, to pass to the new attack."[14]

Was the Greek Communist Party acting as a proxy for the Soviet Union in preparing the ground for a new armed confrontation? The prevailing view then, which is the most widely accepted view even today, was that the moves of the Greek Communists were part of a wider scheme on the part of the Soviet Union to spread its influence into the Eastern Mediterranean and the Middle East. There were several converging events to support this view. Moscow was putting pressure on Turkey to cede Kars and Ardahan to the Soviet Union and to accept Soviet military bases on the Straits. It was also pushing to gain control of Iranian Azerbaijan and Kurdistan. In the United Nations in January, 1946, the Soviet Union charged that the presence of British troops in Greece threatened international peace and security.[15] The standard interpretation of these developments was that the brewing armed conflict in Greece was directed by Moscow as part of a renewed thrust towards the Mediterranean. Even President Truman in his *Memoirs* writes: "*Under Soviet direction*, the [intelligence] reports said, Greece's northern neighbors—Yugoslavia, Bulgaria, and Albania—were conducting a drive to establish a Communist Greece."[16] The available evidence today seems to indicate that such a conclusion was oversimplified and only partially correct. As often happens in human affairs, "the obscurest epoch is today," to use Robert Louis Stevenson's aphorism.

It appears that Moscow exerted pressure on Turkey and Iran in 1945 and 1946 for the purpose of testing the resistance quotient of the Western

---

[12] The British and the two "rightist" members of the government delegation at Varkiza offered full amnesty, but I. Sofianopoulos, Foreign Minister and an old friend of KKE, objected to such general amnesty on the grounds that it would open the way to personal revenge by removing criminal cases from the realm of the courts. In reality he was playing KKE's card. For more details, see D. George Kousoulas, *op. cit.*, p. 224.

[13] Since 1934, he had been the Secretary General of KKE.

[14] N. Zakhariadis, *Provlimata Kathothigisis* (mimeographed copy), 1950, p. 87.

[15] Security Council Official Records, First Year, Supplement No. 1, Annex 3, p. 73.

[16] Harry S. Truman, *Memoirs*, Vol. II, New York, p. 121. Italics added.

powers, and primarily that of Britain. As soon as Stalin met with determined opposition from the British, which was reinforced by the policies of a new American administration under Truman, he did not pursue the matter. Apparently his major preoccupation at the time was structuring a protective shield of loyal satellites in Eastern Europe against a possible revival of German militarism. In this context, the verbal attacks on the British presence in Greece were a useful diversionary maneuver which could detract public attention from Soviet activities in Eastern Europe. Moscow, however, was not particularly eager to see a re-opening of the campaign of violence which the Greek Communists had lost in the streets of Athens in December, 1944. In fact, at the very same moment that Moscow was raising the question of the British presence in Greece in the United Nations, Molotov and Zhdanov were advising Dimitrios Partsalides, the Greek Communist Party's emissary to Moscow, that the Greek Party should participate in the elections in Greece scheduled for March 31, 1946. As Partsalides told the Politburo of the Greek Communist Party on February 21, the two Soviet leaders had indicated to him that the Soviet government was committed to recognizing the results of the elections. The Soviet leaders did not explain the reasons for this commitment, but what lay behind it is fairly obvious in retrospect. Moscow was about to embark on a series of controlled elections in Eastern Europe and wanted to establish grounds for reciprocal non-interference on the part of the Western powers.

Partsalides' report to the Politbureau threw the Party leadership into confusion, because the decision had already been made on February 12 to abstain from the elections. In fact, the Party leaders had taken a more fateful decision: "After weighing the domestic factors, and the Balkan and international situation, the Plenum *decided to go ahead with the organization of the new armed struggle.*"[17] Under further probing, Partsalides admitted that he was not certain whether the Soviet "advice" was a directive, or merely a suggestion leaving the final decision to the Greek Communist Party, which was in a better position to determine the "objective conditions" in the country. Finally, "the Party Central Committee, starting from the assumption that a revolutionary situation existed in the country, decided to abstain from the elections and *turned towards the armed struggle.*"[18] It is worth noting that the first assertion that it was the Greek Communist Party's own decision to launch the "armed struggle" was made by Zakhar-

---

[17] N. Zakhariadis, *Kenourghia Katastasi, Kenourghia Kathikonta*, Nicosia, 1950, p. 38.

[18] This statement was made by Kostas Kolliyiannis, the present leader of KKE at the Party's Eighth Congress in September, 1961 (text from Kolliyiannis' report).

iadis in 1950, and the second was made ten years later by Kolliyannis, who in 1956 had deposed Zakhariadis in the wake of de-Stalinization. These two statements by the previous and present leader of the Greek Communist Party leave no room for doubt that the decision to launch a third bid for power was made mostly on the Party's own initiative and even in the face of Soviet reservations. The myth of "persecuted democrats" taking to the mountains (repeated in a recent book)[19] is refuted by the testimony of the Communist leaders who initiated the operation. The abstention from the elections of 1946 was later referred to by both Zakhariadis and Kolliyiannis as a "tactical error."

The evidence is rather conclusive that in launching the third attempt to seize power the Greek Communist Party was encouraged by Tito. Zakhariadis himself, writing at a later day (1950), after the collapse of the guerrilla campaign, stated: "Tito and his clique promised us the most substantial aid. This played a decisive role in our decision [to go ahead with the new armed struggle], because in Yugoslavia, the main factor in the Balkans at that time, our new revolutionary move did not have an opponent who could pose insurmountable obstacles." In fact, Yugoslavia's role went much further than just not posing any obstacles. Tito provided extensive material assistance and offered Yugoslav territory for the training and regrouping of guerrillas.[20]

In supporting a Communist-led guerrilla operation in Greece, Tito was acting in accord with a traditional axiom of Greek-Yugoslav relations predicated on the security needs of the two countries. Simply stated, the axiom holds that Greece, without sufficient space to the north, needs the Yugoslav land mass as a shield against potential aggressors from the north. Yugoslavia, on the other hand, can better withstand pressures from the Germanic or the Slavic colossi if it can count on assistance from the maritime powers operating through a friendly Greece. In 1946 Tito was apparently worried that London, to better protect Greece against possible encroachments from the north, thereby securing British lines of communication in the Mediterranean, might try to undermine and possibly overthrow his government and re-establish a pro-Western regime in Belgrade, thus restoring the Belgrade-Athens axis. The guerrilla operation being planned by the Greek Communist Party could only create problems for Athens, avert any action against Tito, and even in case of ultimate failure

---

[19] Andreas Papandreou, *Democracy at Gunpoint : The Greek Front*, New York, 1970, p. 65.

[20] N. Zakhariadis, *Provlimata Kathothigisis*, p. 38. Also *Report* by KKE Politbureau member Vassilis Bartzotas to the Sixth Plenum of the Central Committee, October 9, 1949.

give him time to consolidate his own regime in Yugoslavia. Thus, in March, 1946, Zakhariadis, on his way back from Prague, stopped in Yugoslavia and was promised "all-out help."

The Greek Communist Party was being used by both the Soviet Union and Yugoslavia for different purposes. The Party leaders, probably not fully aware of their role, went ahead with their armed struggle, because they erroneously thought that a revolutionary situation existed in the country and because they apparently interpreted Soviet moves at this time as part of a major thrust towards the Mediterranean (accepting in this the prevailing assumption in the West). They were wrong on both accounts, and they paid for their false assumptions with the defeat of their armed struggle.

Zakhariadis, in his book *Dheka Khronia Palis*, wrote: "We all agreed that [domestically] the situation was ripe, that we should take up arms and fight."[21] That the situation was "ripe" for revolution was purely wishful thinking. If anything, the opposite was true. With the first general elections and later, on September 1, 1946, with the plebiscite that returned King George II to his throne, putting an end to the irksome "constitutional question," the ranks of the democratic politicians were closing, while at the same time the disintegration of the National Liberation Front coalition pushed the Greek Communist Party more and more into a corner of political and moral isolation. The country was beset with a host of problems, and the people were not interested in a new round of fighting but in the enormous task of reconstruction and normalization after the long years of war, occupation, and civil strife. Furthermore, a new Greek army was being organized with British assistance, providing the Greek government with a real source of power. The expectation of the Greek Communists that the British would remain aloof from a new confrontation could not be substantiated by past experience. Why should the British allow a Communist takeover in 1946 when they had prevented one in 1945, with a less favorable international climate and at great cost to themselves?

While the conditions in Greece could hardly justify the optimism displayed by the Communist leaders, the tactical advantages of a guerrilla operation seemed to provide the grounds for their decision to renew the armed conflict. Guerrilla warfare gives the insurgents a power advantage over their opponents in a ratio of almost ten to one. This is because the number of regular and special troops required to fight effectively against the guerrillas is not determined by the numerical strength of the guerrillas but by the size and nature of the area that must be protected against hit-and-run guerrilla attacks (defense) or saturated with personnel for "seize-and-

---

[21] N. Zakhariadis, *Dheka Khronia Palis*, Athens, 1946, p. 40.

hold" operations (offense). The Communist leadership concluded that with twenty-five major mountain ranges in Greece and "a total front line of 3,000 kilometers...huge forces [would] be required on the part of the enemy."[22] Yet, in spite of these tactical advantages, a guerrilla operation suffers from a basic strategic weakness; it can hardly expect to achieve a decisive and lasting success as long as it remains a host of bands roaming the countryside without permanent bases, unable to establish continuous control over populated areas in the target country. To bring the campaign to a successful end, a guerrilla movement must eventually turn to conventional warfare. But once it does, the guerrillas lose their tactical advantage, since they face the opposing regular army on more or less equal terms. If at the moment of transition, the government forces are well organized, well equipped, and in good fighting spirit, the guerrilla movement is in serious trouble. The Greek Communists failed to take into account these strategic considerations.

The Greek Communists also were wrong in assuming that their armed struggle would receive Moscow's blessing as part of a broad move to expand Soviet control into the Mediterranean. Stalin exploited the Greek guerrilla operation for its propaganda value as long as it did not interfere with his strategic objectives at that time, namely the consolidation of Soviet control in Eastern Europe. Stalin's attitude towards the Greek operation changed radically following the enunciation of the Truman Doctrine in March, 1947, and the realization by the end of the year that Washington was discarding its traditional isolationism in favor of a more active role in world politics. The guerrilla operation in Greece, a somewhat secondary activity in Stalin's eyes up to that time, suddenly became a problem of momentous import. At a time when Stalin was hard at work to set up a system of reliable satellites in Eastern Europe, the Greek guerrillas were providing the Americans with an excuse to enter Greece and potentially checkmate Stalin's advances in Eastern Europe.

Knowing that the Greek operation was primarily a Yugoslav-supported affair, Stalin summoned a Yugoslav delegation to Moscow in February, 1948, and insisted that "the uprising in Greece [had] to fold up (he used the word *svernut* which means literally to *roll up*).[23] Musing many years later over Stalin's almost savage opposition to the Greek guerrilla operation, Milovan Djilas, who was present at the meeting, wrote:

> Not even today am I clear on the motives that caused Stalin to be against the uprising in Greece. Perhaps he reasoned that the creation in the Balkans

---

[22] *Komep*, Athens, May, 1947.
[23] Milovan Djilas, *Conversations with Stalin*, New York, 1962, p. 181.

of still another Communist state—Greece—in circumstances when not even
the others were reliable and subservient could hardly have been in his interest,
*not to speak of possible international complications which were assuming an increasingly
threatening shape and could, if not drag him into war, then endanger his already-won
positions.*[24]

The part of the statement emphasized in this text is particularly revealing.
Stalin was indeed worried about the "international complications," namely,
United States involvement in Europe and in particular the establishment
of an American presence in Greece. He had reason to be apprehensive that
these "developments" could "endanger" his "already-won positions"—in
Eastern Europe.

Stalin's strong misgivings over Yugoslav policies were revealed during
the same talks with the Yugoslav delegates by his insistence on bringing
Yugoslav foreign policy under Soviet control. The incident with Kardelj
—who was summoned at midnight by Molotov to sign an agreement of
"mutual" consultation on foreign policy matters—is particularly telling.
Equally revealing is Stalin's opposition to the Yugoslav-Bulgarian designs
for a Communist federation in the Balkans that would eventually include
Greece.

In Stalin's eyes, Tito was the prime mover of Yugoslav policy, and as
long as Tito remained in power, Stalin could not be assured of Yugoslavia's
compliance regardless of any midnight agreements. Thus, he launched a
determined campaign to remove Tito and his immediate lieutenants from
power and replace them with more pliable "comrades." His effort eventually
failed because Tito, familiar with the rules of the game, outpaced Stalin's
moves at every step. However, Stalin in failure achieved exactly what he
hoped to achieve by his initial counteraction against Tito. Following once
again the traditional axiom of Greek-Yugoslav relations, Tito gradually
withdrew his support to the Greek guerrillas and sought to improve his
relations with the maritime powers to better withstand the pressure of a
now hostile Soviet Union.

Yugoslavia's gradual withdrawal of material support for the Greek
guerrillas was certainly a contributing factor to the eventual demise of the
Communists' third try for power, but not a decisive one since aid continued
to come from Albania and Bulgaria.[25] Other important factors which
should not be ignored include the cohesiveness of the national front against

---

[24] *Ibid.*, pp. 182–183. Italics added.

[25] In view of Stalin's opposition to the Greek guerrilla movement, this may
indicate either faulty communications with Moscow, or that the Communist
governments of these two Balkan states deliberately by-passed Soviet objections
because the war served their interests by helping them to consolidate their rule.

the Communist assault. The political leadership representing the over-whelming majority of the Greek people stood steadfastly together and provided guidance and inspiration for a successful anti-guerrilla campaign. Because of this unity, the Greek Communist Party and its military arm, DSE (the Democratic Army of Greece), remained isolated and failed to attract a broad popular following. In fact, Markos, the leader of DSE, stated that since the middle of 1947 recruiting had been achieved "almost entirely by force."[26] This inability to attract popular support would have probably spelled the defeat of the Democratic Army of Greece with or without a cut-off in supplies from Yugoslavia.

While the Greek Communist Party was unable to attract volunteers "and find a decisive solution to our problem of reserves,"[27] the Greek armed forces were growing in number and adopting effective anti-guerrilla tactics. With the expansion of their ranks and an increase in armaments, the Greek armed forces discarded the self-defeating and frustrating tactics of "search and destroy," and passed on to the strategy and tactics of "seize and hold." What this meant was the gradual extension of government control over well-defined territories. It involved the selection of a target area, the concentration of regular and special forces in superior numbers, continuous offensive operations, the extermination or capture of guerrilla forces in the area, the destruction of guerrilla spy networks in the villages, mopping-up operations by auxiliary units, the organization of local units for static defense, measures to prevent reinfiltration of the area, exercise of effective government control over the cleared territory, and then the selection of another suitable region for repeating the process. By employing this strategy and tactics, the Greek army succeeded in securing and holding large areas in 1948 and 1949 and pushing the DSE to the strongholds of Grammos and Vitsi along the Albanian frontier. A decision of the Greek Communist Party to pass on to conventional warfare (imposed by Zakhar-iadis against Markos' advice) merely sped up the end, which came in August, 1949, with the Greek army's final assault on Grammos and Vitsi.[28] The remnants of the DSE sought refuge in Albania.

---

[26] This was revealed by Markos in 1948 in his "platform," in which he registered his misgivings on the conduct of the war and disagreed with Zakhariadis on the wisdom of passing on to the conventional type of warfare. See, *Neos Kosmos*, Vol. VIII, August, 1950, pp. 476–483.

[27] N. Zakhariadis, *Pros tin III Synthiaskepsi tou KKE*, Central Committee of KKE, 1950, p. 117.

[28] The decision of the Yugoslav government to disarm any guerrillas crossing into Yugoslavia (the so-called closing of the frontier) was taken in late July, a few days before the final assault on Grammos and Vitsi. Since most of Vitsi and all of Grammos are geographically adjacent to Albania, not to Yugoslavia, the decision had only limited effect on the final outcome.

Conclusions

Bearing in mind that the Greek Communist Party's revolutionary ventures and its ultimate failure were at least partly shaped by local factors, the following generalizations are offered:

(1) The assumption that Communist revolutionary movements throughout the world are centrally co-ordinated and tightly orchestrated by a definable "center" appears to be overdrawn. If this assumption was not valid during the days of Stalinism and Moscow's unassailable position as the citadel of Marxism-Leninism, it must be much less so today, with the fragmentation of the Communist "camp."

(2) The Soviet Union and Communist governments in general seem to be much more motivated by their particular interests (the consolidation and preservation of their rule, the security of their state, the pursuit of what they regard as their national interests) than by the promotion of the Communist movement as an unqualified and overriding goal. "Fraternal" parties may well be sacrificed in the process, as the Greek Communists must have discovered.

(3) The leaders of local revolutionary movements appear to be primarily concerned with imposing their own rule and gaining power for themselves. This applies just as much to Marxist-Leninist "technicians of revolution" as it does to other varieties of revolutionaries, even when they start as "proxies."

(4) A popular uprising faces serious disadvantages today because of the deadly effectiveness of the state security apparatus.

(5) A guerrilla operation is most vulnerable in its early stages, before the bands take roots and impose their hold on the villages, but the government of the target country must bring maximum pressure to bear as soon as the bands appear and until their complete extermination. Small-scale, spasmodic measures work in favor of the guerrillas.

(6) A counter-guerrilla strategy of "seize and hold" is decidedly more effective than a strategy of "search and destroy," which is both time-wasting and frustrating to the loyal troops.

(7) A counter-guerrilla operation is at least partly political in nature and therefore cannot succeed unless the government wins the allegiance of the people.

(8) While an uprising, such as the Communist action in Athens in 1944, may be crushed by either foreign or domestic troops, a rural-based, protracted guerilla campaign cannot be easily suppressed by foreign troops, because even the presence of such troops tends to discredit the government and give a moral advantage to the guerrillas.

(9) A guerrilla force cannot consummate its victory unless it progresses to conventional warfare. But this deprives it of its tactical advantages and exposes it to deadly dangers if the loyal troops of the target country are in a high state of morale and preparedness.

The Communist Takeover of Rumania: A Function of Soviet Power

Stephen Fischer-Galati

The Communist takeover of Rumania was a protracted process, and in this respect bears striking similarities to the Communist takeovers of Bulgaria, Hungary, and Poland. This common element aside, the seizure of political power by the Communists in Rumania had unique characteristics that foreshadowed the "Rumanian independent course" adopted in later years. It might be said that the "ideological bases" for the Rumanian independent course are rooted in the "objective conditions" of the takeover.

It has generally been assumed that the installation of the Groza regime in March, 1945, was the turning point in the process by which the Communists came to power in Rumania. That date has received the sanction of the present leaders of the Rumanian Communist Party, and elaborate speeches were made on March 6, 1970, in celebration of the twenty-fifth anniversary of the "installation of the democratic government."[1] In fact, however, power was assigned to the Rumanian Communists by the Soviet Union as early as the fall of 1943, and a blueprint for the actual seizure of power was worked out by the Kremlin at that time. The original plan called for the outright assumption of political power in Rumania by the "liberating Soviet armies" through the instrumentality of the Rumanian Communist contingent comprising the so-called Tudor Vladimirescu Brigade. The plan also contemplated the "liquidation" of the Rumanian Communists incarcerated by the Antonescu regime, so as to prevent the formation of any coalition government prior to the arrival of the Red Army and of the "Moscow" Communists headed by Ana Pauker, Vasile Luca, and other Rumanian expatriates who had spent the war years in Russia, and who were picked by the Soviets as the future rulers of Rumania. Had this linear plan been realized, the takeover would have been simple and direct and probably

---

[1] See, in particular, the issue of *Scinteia*, the daily newspaper of the Central Committee of the Rumanian Workers' Party (i.e., Communist Party), for March 7, 1970.

would have served as a prototype for seizures of power in other countries about to be liberated by the Soviet Union.[2]

The change in tactics was in part caused by certain conditions common to all Eastern Europe at the time, but more so by conditions peculiar to Rumania. It is unlikely that fear of confrontation with its wartime allies would have prevented the Kremlin from following through with its plan, particularly since both Britain and the United States were in agreement "that the USSR should temporarily regard Rumanian affairs as mainly its concern." At least the British position was restated later, in 1944, in the well-known Stalin-Churchill agreement on the delineation of spheres of influence in Eastern Europe, whereby *carte blanche* was given to Moscow in dealing with Rumania. Instead, the Kremlin's plans for the outright installation of a Communist regime in a nation about to be conquered were frustrated by the royal *coup d'état* of August 23, 1944.[3]

The coup is to be viewed as unique in the history of Communist take-overs in that it removed the rationale for a seizure of power by the Red Army in behalf of its political clients, the members of the Moscow contingent of the Rumanian Communist Party. Inasmuch as King Michael removed Marshal Antonescu from power, disavowed ties with Hitler's Germany, and joined the side of the victorious allies, the liberation of the new Rumanian cobelligerent in the manner contemplated by Stalin became impossible. The Kremlin had to accept that reality. It also had to accept another reality, in turn unique to Rumania. This was the participation of a Communist group alien to Moscow in the regime established immediately after the coup. The participants in the so-called armed uprising, which led to the replacement of the Antonescu regime, the reversal of alliances, and the admission of Communist representatives to the new Sanatescu government, were Rumanians remote from the Kremlin, men whose political fate had been ignored by Moscow both before and during the war, and whose political and perhaps even physical extermination had been proffered by the Kremlin to Antonescu as the price for Rumania's unconditional surrender to the USSR. Thus, when the Russian armed forces and their political stooges appeared in Bucharest late in August, new "objective conditions"

---

[2] The most comprehensive account of the preliminaries to the takeover in Rumania is by Ghita Ionescu, *Communism in Rumania, 1944–1962*, London, 1964, pp. 71–93. Among other things, Ionescu reviews the entire question of Stalin's wartime plans for postwar Rumania on the basis of official Rumanian materials and other data (pp. 79–81). Ionescu's data, brought up to date, have been further analyzed in: Stephen Fischer-Galati, *The New Rumania : From People's Democracy to Socialist Republic*, Cambridge, Mass., 1967, pp. 16–25.

[3] Details in Ionescu, *op. cit.*, pp. 83–86.

for the outright installation of a Communist regime had to be taken into account.

The Soviet armies of liberation, which by that time had become co-belligerents with those of Rumania, could not remove the newly installed Sanatescu regime by force. Instead, the Soviet military and political forces in Rumania formally agreed to the maintenance of a hastily formed coalition government which included as Minister of Justice the Rumanian Communist Lucretiu Patrascanu. Covertly, however, the Russians were preparing for the removal of both the coalition government and of Patrascanu and lesser Communist officials in the Sanatescu cabinet. In fact, the Russians trusted the Rumanian Communists in the coalition almost as little as they did the non-Communist members of the government. It is only in this context that the actual seizure of power occurred.

Details of this process have been discussed elsewhere.[4] Suffice it to say that the Soviet High Command in Rumania assumed *de facto* control of the country's military forces and internal security early in September by virtue of the Rumanian Armistice Convention of September 12, 1944. Correspondingly, through invocation of explicit and implicit provisions directed against "fascism," the Russians began the systematic removal of regional and local officials and their replacement by pro-Moscow Communists, while concurrently condemning the non-Communist members of the Sanatescu government for harboring fascists. Thus, Soviet in-filtration of the governmental machinery and continued military presence in Rumania—both in the name of protecting the interests of all cobelliger-ents against fascism—provided the Russians with the power needed to rule Rumania without outright installation of a Communist regime. The authority of the government was in fact pre-empted while Sanatescu was formally in power.

Under the circumstances, the Russians were in a position to bide their time until the "objective conditions" for securing formal control through a Communist-led government of their liking could be attained. By October, 1944, consolidation of Communist power, particularly in the countryside, neutralization of the political opposition, completion of the "liberation" of Eastern Europe, and avoidance of any action that would have jeopardized the Soviet Union's plans through a confrontation with the United States and Britain were of paramount importance to the Kremlin. Fear of Western opposition to its action in Rumania was of less importance to the Kremlin in the fall of 1944, however, than apprehension over internal popular

---

[4] See Stephen Fischer-Galati, *Twentieth Century Rumania*, New York, 1970, pp. 70–90.

resistance to an externally dictated formal change in the political order. The Western Allies had in effect written off Rumania, provided that no bloodshed would mar the consolidation of Communist power in the country. With this assurance, the Russians were able to concentrate on immobilizing the Rumanian people by identifying the Soviet Union's interests with Rumanian national aspirations, all the while accelerating the process of securing political power for the servants and clients of the USSR in Rumania. This sub-phase of the takeover began early in December when the Sanatescu regime was replaced, at the Soviet Union's demand, with a government headed by General Radescu.

The significance of the shift from Sanatescu to Radescu rests both in the expansion of the Communist power base and in the character of the Communist representation in the new government. The much-heralded appointment of Teohari Georgescu as undersecretary of the Ministry of the Interior was symbolic of the growing power of the Communists. More important was the fact that Georgescu and the other members of the new cabinet were Rumanians, identified with the Rumanian masses and at least theoretically with Rumanian national interests—in juxtaposition to the predominantly Jewish and other non-Rumanian "Muscovites," who held key positions in the infiltrated governmental structure and in the Party. The same Rumanian character was evident in the leadership of the so-called National Democratic Front set up in October for the purpose of identifying the Communist, Rumanian, and Soviet cause with that of all "anti-fascist" Rumanians. By this time, these tactics were not unique to Rumania; they were becoming the pattern for the eventual outright seizure of power by Soviet-backed Communists everywhere in "liberated" Eastern Europe. The main difference between the case of Rumania and that of Bulgaria or Hungary, for instance, consists in the fact that the adjustment of Soviet tactics in Rumania in the period immediately prior to the more formal takeover of March, 1945, was a direct result of the Rumanian shift in alliances in August, 1944.

It is worth noting that in Rumania the "Popular Front" was not an indispensable tool for the seizure of power by the Communists. Rather, the coalition of organizations comprising the National Democratic Front—i.e., the Communists, Social Democrats, Union of Patriots, Ploughmen's Front, and united trade unions—provided a convenient organization that could be propelled into power by the Russians at a moment of the Kremlin's choice.[5] The National Democratic Front, as such, performed no political

---

[5] The functions of the Front and its activities are discussed at some length in Ionescu, *op. cit.*, pp. 94–106.

activities which could have substantially altered the "objective conditions" for the takeover. Internally, these conditions were determined by the subversion of the police and security forces through the forcible inclusion into the state security apparatus of trained agents approved by the NKVD (the Soviet secret police), and by the continuing reinforcement of the "Muscovite" cadres in regional and provincial administrative units, particularly in Moldavia. Externally, the *de facto* acceptance by the Western powers at the Yalta Conference of the Soviet Union's dominant rights in Rumania facilitated the removal of the Radescu government in March, 1945, and the installation of the "popular democratic" regime led by Petru Groza. The decision of March, like all previous ones related to the takeover, was clearly a function of Soviet policy.

The principal contribution made by the National Democratic Front during the Radescu period was to make propaganda for the identification of Rumanian national interests with Communist interests and, as significantly, of Rumanian interests with those of the Kremlin. Unquestionably, the denunciation of "fascists" trumpeted by the Communists throughout Rumania's industrial centers, to the intellectuals in Bucharest, and even to the peasant masses, and the corollary identification of the "traditional" political parties with "fascism" gained adherents to the Communist cause. The extravagant promises of a better future under socialism were apparently less persuasive; however, the assurances that the interests of all the victorious allies were the same as Rumania's, and that only the Front could facilitate the attainment of Rumania's historic aspirations owing to its special ties with the people and the Kremlin were believed by many Rumanians.

There can be no doubt that the removal of the Radescu regime, on the direct intervention of Andrei Vyshinsky, was dictated by Moscow's appraisal of a variety of factors at work in March, 1945. But it would be erroneous to assume, as has been done by many students of Rumanian and Soviet politics, that the so-called ultimatum was given without any consideration of the internal "objective conditions" in Rumania. The ultimatum was, in fact, delivered at a time propitious for a Communist takeover because the premises and promises of the Communists were plausible and were at least superficially capable of being fulfilled by the Soviet-favored Groza regime.[6]

The widespread acceptance of the simplistic explanation that King Michael succumbed to the ultimatum issued by Vyshinsky, deferring in favor of Petru Groza because the alternative would have been military

---

[6] Details in Fischer-Galati, *Twentieth Century Rumania*, pp. 91 ff.

intervention by the Red Army units stationed in Rumania, only reflects the naïveté of students of Communist takeovers in Eastern Europe. Granted that the Yalta Conference facilitated Soviet plans for "democratization" in Rumania, it did not provide any basis for direct intervention in Rumanian affairs. The crisis preceding the ultimatum was precipitated by Communist *agents provocateurs* and by irresponsible supporters of the Radescu cabinet. Radescu's decision to disperse by military force a demonstration planned by the National Democratic Front, plus his own intemperate denunciation of the "foreign" occupiers of Rumania, provided the Russians and their intermediaries with the *raison d'état* for removing the "fascist Radescu clique."

The evidence tends to show that Vyshinsky's action became possible only because of Radescu's response to the "provocation" of the Front, and that the Kremlin's decision was not premeditated except to the extent that it fell within the framework of long-range Soviet determination eventually to install a puppet government in Rumania. The opportunity to exploit the "objective conditions" in Rumania in February and March was not to be missed by the Kremlin, but those conditions did not permit even Vyshinsky simply to commandeer and achieve a final solution to the Rumanian question. In March, 1945, the Kremlin and the Rumanian Communists in fact scored only a partial victory; the so-called takeover at this time was by no means complete.

Ghita Ionescu's characterization of the Groza regime as one element in a "duality of power" is an accurate assessment of the extent of the takeover.[7] The choice of Groza by the Kremlin indicates the Soviet Union's inability (or unwillingness) to force a showdown with the Western powers and with the Rumanian population, since the preferable Soviet solution would have been the installation of a "Muscovite"-dominated regime. The exclusion of Ana Pauker, Vasile Luca, and other non-Rumanian Communists from visible positions of power, and the inclusion in the Groza regime of native Communists such as Gheorghiu-Dej, Lucretiu Patrascanu, and Teohari Georgescu points to the continuing need for identification with Rumanian democratic interests. The Groza government was officially regarded by the Soviets as a "progressive" and representative Rumanian regime for a "democratic" Rumania. The fact that its very existence was guaranteed by the presence of Soviet armed forces in Rumania was to be ascribed to Soviet determination to enforce the provisions of the Armistice Convention on "fascism" in Rumania, a position presumably subscribed to by the Soviet Union's Western allies. Officially, the coalition regime of

---

[7] Ionescu, *op. cit.*, pp. 107 ff.

Groza stood for "democracy" and Rumanian interests. Soviet backing guaranteed its continuance in power.

If we were to accept the view that the Yalta Conference sanctioned, at least tacitly, the Soviet Union's *de facto* domination of Rumania in 1945, it would be necessary to agree with the widespread idea that power was actually seized by the Rumanian Communists in March, 1945. The Soviet Union's prudence in the handling of Rumanian affairs would suggest, however, that Stalin did not regard the decisions of Yalta as providing unconditional authority for an outright Communist seizure of power in Rumania. Otherwise, it would be difficult to explain why the Kremlin deliberately sought to win over the Rumanian population to the policies of Groza and to associate the Groza regime with Soviet friendship for Rumania and the Rumanian people. Indeed, the Russians acted as the executors of the Armistice Convention and covertly displayed greater generosity towards Rumania than their Western cosignatories. Stalin recognized the validity of Rumania's claims to Northern Transylvania earlier than his allies; in fact, he unilaterally guaranteed the return of the coveted portion of that province to Rumania a few days after the installation of the Groza regime. And Groza's cabinet itself, acting in accord with the Russians, followed Stalin's action with a massive agrarian reform designed to satisfy the land hunger of the poorer peasantry. In sum, then, the initial actions of the Groza regime were reconcilable with traditional Rumanian goals far more than with those of communism—Rumanian or Russian. This is not to say that there were any loopholes left in the political system that would have allowed its alteration through domestic forces acting independently of Moscow's wishes. The Red Army and Communist functionaries guaranteed the security of the Groza government.[8] Thus, we need not concern ourselves with the reasons for the prolongation of the Groza phase in the process of the total seizure of power by the Communists in Rumania except in the context of Soviet policy in Rumania. That policy, after March, 1945, was essentially a function of the Cold War.

Soviet economic penetration, primarily through the establishment of the infamous "Sovroms" (joint Soviet-Rumanian companies), was intensified after March, 1945, and the onslaught of Communist propaganda and organized political activity increased markedly after the installation of Groza. The process of consolidating Communist power in the regional and central apparatus of the government also went on at an accelerated pace. However, the Kremlin shied away from excessive displays of power.

---

[8] Details in Fischer-Galati, *The New Rumania*, pp. 29 ff., and in Ionescu, *op. cit.*, pp. 109 ff.

The caution of the Russians and their deliberate attempt to retain the image of guarantors of a democratic order in accord with the wishes of the Western Allies coincided with the Kremlin's efforts to carry out the provisions of the Potsdam Conference, whereby peace treaties were to be concluded with "recognized democratic governments." The entire political effort in Rumania was adjusted to the "spirit of Potsdam" even at the price of allowing members of the "traditional" political parties to retain posts in the Groza cabinet, and of issuing guarantees to the West with respect to the continuation of democratic rule by the Groza government. The desire to maintain the fiction of democracy in Rumania was shared by the Soviet Union and the West alike, and was found unsatisfactory only by politically conscious Rumanians in the traditional political parties. The power play within Rumania became potentially explosive after Potsdam, as the West was not prepared to lend support to the traditional parties, which sought a showdown with the Soviet Union and its disciples in Rumania. The Russians and their clients were, on the other hand, unwilling to risk a direct confrontation with the political opposition for fear of possible Western intervention in behalf of democracy.

The tactical procedure of the Soviet Union, adapted to post-Potsdam conditions, was to discredit the traditional political organizations of Rumania by stigmatizing them as "fascist" and to pose as the champion of democracy by defining democracy as a universal struggle against fascism. It was in this spirit that Marshal Ion Antonescu and his closest associates were tried and executed in the spring of 1945 and that those who sought a showdown between true, traditional' democracy and Groza-Kremlin democracy were attacked by the Russians. In the last analysis frustration of the Kremlin's obvious plan for Rumania could have been achieved only through overt support by the West for the traditional parties or, failing that, through refusal to abide by the provisions of the Potsdam Conference and the supplementary Moscow accord of 1946 in the face of continuing violations of the spirit of those provisions by Stalin and his agents.[9] In the absence of positive action by the United States and Britain, the Russians were free to discredit and intimidate the supporters of the democratic parties, while setting the stage for the "free elections" which were to ratify the validity of the mandate assumed by Groza in March, 1945, and to provide the basis for the conclusion of a Rumanian peace treaty in conformity with the international agreements in force in 1946. Ultimately, then, two events need to be examined with respect to the question of the actual

---

[9] A most persuasive argument, amply documented, is contained in Ionescu, *op. cit.*, pp. 113 ff.

seizure of power: the elections of November, 1946, and the conclusion of the Rumanian peace treaty in February, 1947.

The elections of 1946 were intended to legitimize the "democratic" order represented by the Groza regime, and the peace treaty was meant to secure a final ratification of that order. It is evident that only the refusal of the United States and its Western allies to recognize the validity of the elections or to conclude a peace treaty with Rumania would have prevented a total seizure of power by the Communists, and that only an uprising led by the opposition identified with the traditional political parties—that is, a revolution commanding the support of the masses—could have forced the hand of the West and upset the plans of the Kremlin.

On the assumption that the masses were profoundly dissatisfied with the Groza regime and the Russian presence in Rumania, students of Rumanian politics have suggested the possibility of such drastic action. They have proclaimed that the results of the elections of November, 1946, were totally false and obtained through fraud and intimidation of the electorate by the Communists and the Red Army.[10] It is doubtful that this interpretation of the elections of 1946 is quite accurate. The fact is that because of the continuing policies of moderation and identification of the Rumanian people's interests with the policies of the Groza government and the Soviet Union, the Communists were able to persuade most people to vote for the candidates of the National Democratic Front, and by control of the electoral machinery were in a position, if necessary, to falsify the results. To assume that any regime could have secured a majority of 347 seats—against 33 for the National Peasant Party and 3 for the National Liberal Party—by sheer intimidation of the electorate and by manipulating the results and to suppose that such falsification would have been accepted passively by the "cheated" population and the leaders of the opposition would in turn presume total control by the Communists and total indifference by the West.

The latter presumption would in fact be accurate, but not the former. The Communists and their electoral allies were quite successful in discrediting their opponents by pre-empting the political platforms of the National Peasant and National Liberal Parties and promising the voters more than these parties could. Moreover, the Communists could easily demonstrate the futility of voting for the traditional parties since the Russians were backing the National Democratic Front, and since the West

---

[10] See, in particular, Robert L. Wolff, *The Balkans in Our Time*, Cambridge, Mass., 1956, pp. 287–288, and Ionescu, *op. cit.*, pp. 123–125. A reappraisal of the electoral results is contained in Fischer-Galati, *Twentieth Century Rumania*, pp. 104–106.

tolerated the Russians' activities and lent no visible support to the demand of the traditional parties for properly supervised free elections. From this point of view, the casting of votes for the traditional parties would have been useless, and for many of the voters risky, the more so since the Front advocated the pursuit of internal and foreign policies which were not incompatible with the broad interests of the population. The politically conscious citizens of Rumania anticipated the terror to come; the masses were generally apolitical and pragmatic.

Legalization of the internal order in Rumania through the elections, with the indirect support and post-electoral validation of the results by the West, marked the immediate prelude to the actual and irrevocable seizure of power by the Communists. The final action was the signing of the peace treaty.[11] The formal recognition of the boundaries and political order of postwar Rumania and, most significantly, of the military presence of the Red Army was the act whereby the Communist seizure of power was consummated. For, in the last analysis, the seizure of power in Rumania was entirely a function of Soviet power and the acceptance by the United States and its Western allies of the Russian occupation of Rumania and rule through a puppet government.

No matter what arguments may have been presented by the Rumanian Communists, by the Soviet Union, by the West, by political refugees, by students of Rumanian politics, or by anyone else who has found it necessary to appraise the reasons for the establishment of communism in Rumania, the fact remains that it was the Soviet Union that desired the establishment of a Communist regime in Rumania, and that the Red Army, acting as an instrument of Russian policy, provided the power base for the seizure of control by the Communists. It would indeed be fallacious to assume, as has been done by contemporary observers of Rumanian politics, or to assert, as has been done by Communist ideologists, that the *gradual* nature of the takeover was a function, at least in part, of the Communist desire to obtain genuine mass support between 1944 and 1947. While it is true that the Party's power increased during that period mostly through Soviet support, it also increased through spontaneous (sincere or opportunistic) joining of its ranks by the politically naïve and the politically conscious. But whether the Party was weak or strong mattered little to Moscow in terms of execution of the Kremlin's plans and policies. At the right moment, when the formal abandonment of Rumania by the Western powers occurred, as it did in 1946 and early 1947, the Kremlin was able to use its clients in

---

[11] A sensitive discussion of the preliminaries and of the actual provisions of the treaty itself will be found in Ionescu, *op. cit.,* pp. 126–131.

Rumania to secure another part of Stalin's empire. Any client could have been used as effectively as Groza and his team once the peace treaty had been signed by the Western powers.

Thus, the Soviet Union's goals were realized only because the United States and its allies condoned Soviet actions in Rumania. Without the Soviet military presence in Rumania and without a United States policy that reflected indifference towards Soviet actions in that country, the Communists could not have seized power *de facto* in March, 1945, and *de jure* in February, 1947. In this respect the case of Rumania bears striking similarities to the cases of Bulgaria, Hungary, Poland, and East Germany. But the prevention of the outright Soviet conquest of Rumania by the *coup d'état* of August, 1944, and the subsequent need for procrastination in the process of seizing power granted the Rumanian Communists the necessary respite which, in later years, allowed them in turn to assert their independence from the Soviet occupiers.

A Revolution Administered: The Sovietization of Bulgaria

Nissan Oren

Strictly speaking, the sovietization of Bulgaria commenced with the entry of the Red Army on September 8, 1944. The process ended in the latter part of 1947 when the Red Army departed from the country and the peace treaty was ratified. By that time, Bulgaria had been successfully insulated against the influence of the West, the domestic anti-Communist opposition had been effectively crushed, and the monopoly of the Bulgarian Communist Party had been assured. While the transformation of society still lay ahead, and massive collectivization had not yet been started, the contours of the new order had already become clearly visible.

The purpose of the present study is to provide an analytic overview of the basic processes at work during these first three years. The chronology of major events is readily available and need not be repeated.[1] The approach chosen in these pages is one of functional scrutiny of the forces in operation on the various levels of development and their interaction. This procedure is deemed justified in view of the fact that both the fund of factual knowledge and the perspective of time appear adequate from the vantage point of the present-day observer.

Not unlike other complex situations, a vertical incision of Bulgarian politics reveals a multilevel phenomenon. While ultimately the total political experience emerges as a synthesis of the various forces at work, the

---

[1] Robert Lee Wolff, *The Balkans in Our Time*, Cambridge, Mass., 1956; Hugh Seton-Watson, *The East European Revolution*, 2nd ed., New York, 1954; Elisabeth Barker, *Truce in the Balkans*, London, 1948; Stephen D. Kertesz, (ed.), *The Fate of East Central Europe*, Notre Dame, Ind., 1956, and *East Central Europe and the World: Developments in the Post-Stalin Era*, Notre Dame, Ind., 1962; L. A. D. Dellin, (ed.), *Bulgaria*, New York, 1957; J. F. Brown, *Bulgaria under Communist Rule*, New York, 1970; Herbert Feis, *Between War and Peace: The Potsdam Conference*, Princeton, N. J., 1960; and *From Trust to Terror: The Onset of the Cold War, 1945–1950*, New York, 1970, represent but a selection of works in English in which Bulgarian domestic and international affairs in the post-World War II period occupy important or major parts. The number of books in Bulgarian is enormous. Here they are represented only by an official history and a major collection of documents covering the first stage of sovietization: *Istoriia na Bulgariia*, Vol. 3, 2nd ed., Sofia, 1964; *Ustanoviavane i ukrepvane na narodnodemo-kraticheskata vlast. Septemvrii 1944–Mai 1945*, Sofia, 1969.

particular sequences unfold separately, and often distinctly from each other. Being a small country situated in the midst of great and small power rivalries, the impact of international politics on Bulgaria was bound to be of paramount importance. Not unlike the case of other small states, Bulgarian domestic politics were, in many respects, the product of events outside the country. Domestic realities had their own significance. In the final analysis, however, international politics took precedence over domestic politics. Ultimately, developments at home were molded by the will of the mighty and by the actions of their protégés within the country.

From its inception, the modern Bulgarian state could not do without the active support of at least one big power. This was and remains a permanent feature of Bulgaria's international position. The primary reason for this dependence has lain in Bulgaria's unfulfilled national aspirations. Repeatedly, the Bulgarians have tried but failed to enclose within their political boundaries the areas and peoples whom they considered to be an integral part of the "Bulgarian tribe." In the early years the choice of patron alternated between the Austro-Hungarian empire and Tsarist Russia. In the 1920's, when Austria had become irrelevant, Germany lay prostrate, and Russia had succumbed to Bolshevik rule, the Bulgarians tried their hand at maintaining an entente with Mussolini's Italy. France and the West were committed to Bulgaria's rivals and were thus out of reach. In the 1930's, Germany became the only acceptable alternative.[2] When Hitler mastered the Balkans, the Bulgarians were rewarded for their collaboration by receiving Macedonia and Thrace as their bounty. They declared war on the Western Allies, hoping to make themselves nominal belligerents. The Bulgarians did not declare war on Soviet Russia, partly because there was nothing to be gained from military participation in Hitler's invasion of Russia, and partly because of a certain pro-Russian sentiment prevalent among the Bulgarian people.

The reckoning came in 1944. Engulfed by the German military presence in the Balkans, yet realizing that Germany was bound to lose the war, the statesmen of the day contemplated a policy of disengagement, but failed to pursue an active diplomacy towards this end. They clung to the newly acquired territories in the hope that the German armies would evacuate the country and that the Red Army would stop its advance on the northern bank of the Danube. From the start, however, the game was largely out of

---

[2] See Marin V. Pundeff's "Bulgaria's Place in Axis Policy, 1936–1944," unpublished dissertation, University of Southern California, 1958, and the particular treatments in C. A. Macartney and A. W. Palmer, *Independent Eastern Europe*, London, 1962, and John A. Lukacs, *The Great Powers and Eastern Europe*, New York, 1953.

their hands. While new destinies were born on the various battlefields, the final verdict was read in the conference rooms of the big powers.

The record of inter-Allied diplomacy is complete and can hardly be improved upon by the addition of new evidence.[3] To salvage Greece, Churchill was prepared to pay a high price to the Soviet ally. Stalin's designs for Bulgaria were quietly but forcefully presented, and were accepted without retort. In the extensive Anglo-Soviet diplomatic exchanges which commenced in the early spring of 1944, and which ultimately led to the "percentages agreement" between Churchill and Stalin in October of the same year, the question of Bulgaria was only incidental.[4] At best, Bulgaria could command Churchill's complete disinterest; at worst, his strong feeling of repugnance. By having joined the Central Powers in World War I and thus having contributed to, if not caused, the failure of Churchill's favorite campaign in the Dardanelles, Bulgaria had won his lasting hatred. These, however, were subjective, if not unimportant, considerations. Churchill's assessment that the Russians would not be appeased unless Bulgaria were added to their bag of spoils must have played an important role in determining his attitude towards the disposition of Bulgaria. Not even the slightest attempt was ever made to bargain over Bulgaria. The consequences were crucial for Bulgaria as well as for the entire Balkan Peninsula. The placement of the lines of delineation between the wartime partners along the Bulgarian-Greek frontier rather than along the Danube brought about an irrevocable transformation of the geopolitical setting in the Balkans.

The spilling over of Soviet might into Bulgaria affected the future of Turkey and much more so the turbulent history of postwar Greece. The interest of the Turkish government not to see the Red Army established along its European frontier harmonized closely with the interests of the wartime regime in Bulgaria. To the last, the Turks believed that the Russians would not cross the Danube. They desisted from making meaningful representations to the Western powers aimed at assuring that the Russians

---

[3] *Foreign Relations of the United States. Diplomatic Papers, 1944*, Vol. 3, Washington, D. C., 1965, pp. 300–554, as well as entries in selected volumes of the same series, provides a comprehensive record.

[4] Hull, who opposed the British scheme from the start, could not fail to observe in June of 1944 the casualness with which Churchill had added Bulgaria to the list of countries "to be dealt with by Russia"; Cordell Hull, *Memoirs*, Vol. 2, New York, 1948, p. 1454. On Bulgaria and the Balkans in Anglo-Soviet wartime relations, see various entries in Winston S. Churchill, *The Second World War*, Vol. 6, Boston, 1953; Herbert Feis, *Churchill, Roosevelt, Stalin*, Princeton, N. J., 1957; and D. F. Fleming, *The Cold War and Its Origins*, Vol. 1, Garden City, N. Y., 1961.

would stay at a distance. As far as Turkey was concerned, this was a blunder in a wartime diplomacy that was otherwise brilliantly executed.[5] The Greek government in exile went far beyond this. Blinded by hatred towards the Bulgarians for their occupation of Greek Thrace, its leaders failed to see the long-range advantage of having their neighbor to the north neutralized, if unpunished. They insisted on frontier rectifications, failing to see the futility of such rearrangements if Bulgaria were to succumb to Soviet rule.[6] The Yugoslav government in exile did much the same. The sum total of these activities, or the lack of them, meant that the possibility— slight as it might have been—of establishing Bulgaria as a neutralized buffer in the Balkans was never contemplated. The fleeting chance of having Bulgaria set up along the lines of the Finnish example—i.e., friendly to the Soviet Union but unoccupied by the Red Army—remained unexplored.

At home, the wartime regime formulated a diplomacy both insufficient and ineffective. The death of King Boris in August, 1943, transferred governmental power into the hands of a group of second-rate politicians. Their inclination was to play for time, when only resolute action could have proved significant. From the start, they were inhibited by their own records of close collaboration with Nazi Germany. Led by Professor Filov, the senior man in the Regency Council set up after the death of the King, the regime remained ill-informed of the major developments in wartime diplomacy. The line of action that it pursued was to reason with the Germans and appease the Russians, with whom diplomatic relations had been consistently maintained.[7] Tentative contacts established with the Western powers via Istanbul were at a low level and thus of little use.[8] While incapable of formulating a decisive diplomacy, the regime remained power-

---

[5] Turkish-Bulgarian relations during the last year of the war are traced in some detail by Nikola Balabanov, Bulgaria's Minister to Ankara, in his "A Year in Ankara," serialized in *Bulgarian Review*, Vols. 4–7, Rio de Janeiro, 1964–1967. The Turks were clearly inhibited in their dealings with Britain and the United States largely because of their refusal to enter the war against Germany actively.

[6] D. G. Kousoulas' *The Price of Freedom : Greece in World Affairs, 1939–1953*, Syracuse, N. Y., 1953, and his *Revolution and Defeat : The Story of the Greek Communist Party*, London, 1965, as well as Stephen G. Xydis' *Greece and the Great Powers, 1944–1947*, Thessaloniki, Greece, 1963, have important information on the subject. For a contemporary Bulgarian Communist view on the same, see Pantelei Shterev, *Obshti borbi na bulgarskiia i grutskiia narod sreshtu khitlerofashistkata okupatsiia*, Sofia, 1966.

[7] Voin Bozhinov, *Politicheskata kriza v Bulgariia prez 1943–1944*, Sofia, 1957. This monograph sums up Bulgaria's diplomacy from a Communist viewpoint.

[8] Stoicho Moshanov, *Vunshnata politika na Demokraticheskata partiia*, Sofia, 1946. This is a brief account of the Bulgarian mission to Cairo given by Moshanov himself, the chief Bulgarian delegate.

ful enough to contain the oppositionist elements at home that might have brought about a change in Bulgaria's wartime orientations.[9]

Judgments made in retrospect constitute all too easy a way of apportioning blame. The fact remains that the developments which converged on Bulgaria in the late summer of 1944 considerably narrowed the margins of a more favorable outcome. These developments can be enumerated briefly. First, there stood the agreement of the British government to recognize that Bulgaria rightfully belonged to the Soviet sphere of military activity. This acknowledgement was the direct, if not the inevitable, outcome of a decision taken much earlier by the Western powers not to invade the Balkans. The result was that the British claim over Greece was to become effective only when the German armies had already started to evacuate Greek territory. Furthermore, the collapse of Rumania on August 23, 1944, came suddenly and much before it was expected. Overnight, as it were, the Red Army found itself on the banks of the Danube. The military position of the Germans thus became untenable. Yet, their evacuation of Greece was delayed. In view of this, it was difficult to see how the Russians could continue their advance westward without securing their left flank. In early September, therefore, the crossing of the armies of the Second Ukrainian Front into Bulgaria had become a military necessity which complemented and harmonized with Soviet political designs.

The Russians declared war on Bulgaria on September 5. The British and American ambassadors in Moscow expressed surprise, but did not protest the act.[10] Thus reassured, the Red Army crossed into the country on September 8. This sealed the fate of the Muraviev government, which was made up of respectable, democratic Bulgarian leaders who had assumed office on September 2.[11] It also cleared the way for the *coup d'état* which Moscow's protégés carried out during the night of September 8–9. The fact that the Bulgarians had officially proclaimed war on Nazi Germany a few hours before the coup changed little. With their masterful maneuver, the Russians gained possession of the country as well as the juridic right to

---

[9] The stand and activities of the various opposition groups during the war are described and analyzed in the present author's *Bulgarian Communism: The Road to Power, 1934–1944*, New York, 1971, chap. viii. There are numerous books and monographs on the subject produced by Bulgarian Communist authors; of the lot, by far the best is, Ilcho Dimitrov's *Burzhoazanata opozitsiia v Bulgariia, 1939–1944*, Sofia, 1969.

[10] Instead, they inquired from Molotov whether Soviet troops would enter Bulgaria; see Feis, *Churchill, Roosevelt, Stalin*, p. 418.

[11] On the fate of the short-lived Muraviev cabinet, see Oren, *op. cit.*, pp. 247–251; also, *Istoricheski pregled*, No. 5, Sofia, 1964, pp. 3–33.

formal belligerence. The ill-started negotiations between Bulgarian representatives and representatives of the Western powers in Cairo were brought to an abrupt end. Soviet insistence that negotiations for an armistice be shifted to Moscow was duly honored. The road to tutelage was now wide open.

It is difficult to see at what point in time and how the Bulgarians could have changed the above-described sequences of events. Paradoxically, the ultimate national interest could have been served only by an act of irresponsibility. Had the Bulgarians perceived the future and become formally and actively engaged in military activities against the Germans in the Balkans immediately after the collapse of Rumania, they conceivably could have foreclosed the necessity, or the excuse, for the Red Army's crossing. Such perceptions were not easily forthcoming, however. Nor was a forceful and imaginative leadership readily at hand. Whether or not the late King could have lifted his country out of the abyss by emulating his colleague in Bucharest remains a moot question. The people of Zveno, who had twice before taken power by the force of conspiracy, were largely committed to the Communists, and thus unavailable to carry out a maneuver aimed against Soviet interests.[12] None would have found the Bulgarian army readily responsive in view of its well-established pro-German officer corps. The fear of German military reprisals, which the Germans indeed contemplated, would have constituted a powerful deterrent in any case.[13] The Bulgarian maze was thus intricate and escapes were few, if any.

The *Putsch* of September 9, 1944, which brought to power the Fatherland Front, requires no detailed recounting. It was carried out and cast in a typical Balkan fashion. The Ministry of War was captured with the aid of a few junior officers who unlocked the doors from within and allowed the revolutionaries-to-be to enter unopposed. The Minister of War had been forewarned and indeed recruited beforehand. He was duly rewarded by

---

[12] Even though the link between Zveno and the Communists dating back to the 1930's was long suspected, it is only in the last few years that it has become possible to document the matter on the basis of a number of memoirs of old Communist functionaries as well as other sources; for details, see Oren, *op. cit.*, pp. 131–132.

[13] Department of the Army, *German Antiguerrilla Operations in the Balkans (1941–1944)*, Department of the Army Pamphlet No. 20–243, Washington, D.C., August, 1954. This is a disinterested account of the German army in the Balkans during the war, based on captured German military documents. While references to Bulgaria are many, the relatively good relations between the Bulgarian and German officers, as well as the German plan to strike at the Bulgarians in case they went over to the Russians and possibly occupy Sofia, are related in pp. 60–62.

being posted as commander in chief of the Bulgarian army. Having sensed the way the winds were blowing, the command of the police in the capital and other well-placed bureaucrats had come to terms with the Fatherland Front and stayed aloof, when not actively collaborating. The ministers of the Muraviev Cabinet were rounded up without opposition. The services of the few Communist contingents which were brought to the capital on the eve of the coup were not required. The capital as well as the provinces complied without resistance. The opening shot of what was to be the beginning of the most radical transformation in Bulgaria's modern history amounted to no more than a banal changeover, strikingly devoid of ecstasy or glory.[14]

Once established, the Red Army garrisons came to constitute the single overriding factor in the sovietization of Bulgaria. The active use of Soviet bayonets was not required. The Soviet high command intervened only occasionally to put right those things they disliked or feared. In the main, however, the sheer presence of the new overlords sufficed to maintain the new authority.[15] While this was a fixed and given element in the making of Communist rule, the reordering of the Bulgarian setting was a function of resources which sprang from within. The story unfolded around four major problems: communism, collaborationism, oppositionism, and Western interventionism.

When the Bulgarian Communists were called upon to master the politics of Bulgaria, their strength and influence was somewhat less than it had been a decade earlier and considerably less than twenty years before. In the context of European communism this was a major exception. Towards the end of the war radicalism was on the upsurge in most West European countries, as were their respective Communist parties. In Eastern Europe the contexts varied, but in none of the countries did the position of the Communist Party resemble that of the Bulgarians. Under the impact of foreign occupation, Yugoslavia, Albania, and Greece underwent civil wars. The Communists in these three countries were at the pinnacle of their

---

[14] The Communist literature on the September coup is legion, though not too reliable. The course of events leading to the *Putsch* and the takeover of the capital and the provinces are traced in Oren, *op. cit.*, pp. 251–258. Years later, the Minister of War, General Marinov, wrote his own account, which substantially confirmed his early collaboration with Zveno and the Communists; on this, see his article in *Istoricheski pregled*, No. 3, Sofia, 1968.

[15] The memoirs of the late Marshal (at the time Colonel-General) Biryuzov, the commanding general of the Red Army in Bulgaria who also represented his government at the Allied Control Commission in Bulgaria, offer valuable evidence on many aspects relevant to the takeover; see S. S. Biryuzov, *Sovetskiy soldat na Balkanakh*, Moscow, 1963, chaps. iv—viii.

prestige when liberation came. In Rumania, communism had always been weak, and the minute Communist Party was made up largely of the nationals of the many ethnic minorities. When the Russians came, the Communist Party of Rumania had to be almost reinvented. In the Czech and Slovak lands the Communists were more influential in 1945 than they had ever been. The occupation and resistance in Poland did not reinforce the native Communists. The relative circumstances in Hungary are more difficult to judge, as the Communists there were few and weak and had never been held in very high esteem, the Béla Kun regime notwithstanding.

Communism in Bulgaria stands apart as a political and socio-economic phenomenon and cannot easily be compared with that of other countries. Despite a meager urban working class, and possibly because of it, the impact of communism on the national life of the country was highly significant. In many ways communism was a direct continuation of the latent nationalist revolutionism which characterized Bulgarian politics in the years after the liberation from the Turks. The repeated failures to resolve the national problem, as the Bulgarians saw it, promoted existing radical tendencies, and this in turn strengthened the extreme left. Bulgaria came very close to the brink of revolution at the end of the First World War. The revolutionary potentials of 1918 were not effectively harnessed, largely because of the lack of a capable leadership. Still, the Bulgarian Communist Party in the postwar years became the strongest organized political force, second only to that of the Agrarians. Since the latter were populists, while the Communists remained orthodox Marxists, and since the Bulgarians did not produce their own Lenin, the two movements competed with each other until they were separately crushed. When the Agrarian regime was overturned in June of 1923, the Communists proclaimed their neutrality. The Comintern (Communist International) was enraged and ordered an armed revolution. In September of the same year, when circumstances had changed and the opportunity had been missed, the Communists carried out Moscow's decree somewhat half-heartedly. The revolution-to-be became nothing but a sporadic rebellion which was cruelly suppressed. The abortive attempt degenerated into Communist terrorism, which remained a practice for a number of years. Despite these aberrations and the constant need to readjust to the ever-changing line of the Comintern, Communist influence continued to gain momentum until 1934, when once again an opportunity was missed. In May of that year, parliamentarianism was brought to an end in the aftermath of a military takeover. Moscow had not yet formulated its policy of the "Popular Front," and the Communists found themselves driven underground once again, together with all other political groups in the country. In the second half of the 1930's, Communist fortunes witnessed a relative decline. With the rise of authoritarianism guided by the Court and its entourage, Bulgaria underwent a period of relative stability.[16]

The bulk of Communist energies in the period between 1934 and the entry of the German army in March of 1941 was consumed by intra-Party struggles. Party ranks were decimated by two concurrent purges which, at the time, remained largely invisible to the outside world. First, there were the upheavals generated by right and left factionalism, which had been aggravated by the defeat in the abortive uprising of 1923. The second purge was directly linked to Stalin's Great Purge, which depleted the ranks of the Bulgarian Communists in Soviet exile. Since the end of 1923 a few thousand Bulgarian Communists had found their way into exile in the Soviet Union. They came to constitute one of the largest political emigrations on Soviet soil. It was inevitable that the crushing defeat at home would produce a barrage of charges and countercharges among them. The Party's Old Guard, made up of Kolarov and Dimitrov, came under fire from younger leftist elements who vehemently castigated the veterans for their ineptness in the conduct and execution of the disastrous uprising. The leftists prevailed and by the late 1920's were able to capture control of the Party apparatus in exile. The left sectarians, as they came to be called later, gained control over the Party underground organization at home as well. By 1933, when the Gestapo arrested Dimitrov, who was soon to be charged with primary responsibility for the famous Reichstag fire, he was an outcast as far as the Bulgarian Communists in exile were concerned. What was all too little known at the time is that Dimitrov had found himself in Berlin, heading the Comintern branch in Western Europe on the insistence of his younger Bulgarian detractors, who wanted him removed from the Comintern headquarters in Moscow. The courage of his stand at the Leipzig trial made Dimitrov famous. His newly acquired reputation, however, would not have sufficed to secure him a first-rank career in the Comintern had not Moscow shifted, in the meantime, away from the policies of extreme leftism and onto the new tactics of the Popular Front. Once established as the General Secretary of the Comintern, Dimitrov undertook to revenge himself upon his detractors. The Bulgarian Party organization in Soviet exile was ruthlessly cleansed of leftists who were now termed Trotskyites. The

---

[16] For the origins and early development of communism in Bulgaria, as well as for the abortive uprising of 1923, there is no substitute for Joseph Rothschild's *The Communist Party of Bulgaria*, New York, 1959. Since 1944, the Bulgarians have never tired of analyzing over and over the reasons for their failure in 1923. The works produced on the subject would fill a small library. D. Kosev's *Septemvriiskoto vustanie 1923 godina*, Sofia, 1954, remains the single best work published in Bulgaria.

organization at home was likewise purged of leftists by Dimitrov's hench-
men, who were dispatched to the home country to reorganize the Party
organization along the new Dimitrov line. Inevitably, this purge merged
with Stalin's Great Purge. Accused of all conceivable crimes, the leadership
of the left sectarians in exile, together with several hundred rank-and-file
Bulgarian Communist émigrés, were shot or perished in Siberian concentration camps.[17]

The Bulgarian Communist Party, which a decade earlier claimed a
membership of about 35,000, with several thousand more in the youth
Party organization, possessed but a fraction of its previous organized
membership when the Germans entered the country in March of 1941.
Still, it was not the diminished numbers of organized Communists that
made the wartime Communist record a meager one. The objective wartime
circumstances stood firm against the interests of the Communists, who
throughout the war tried but failed to make their program comply with
what the overwhelming majority of Bulgarians considered in the national
interest. Bulgaria was not an occupied country, after all, but a willing ally
of Nazi Germany. While in the past Bulgaria had fought and lost, this time
she gained all she wanted without fighting.[18] On the whole, the intellectual
leadership of the Party at home saw little sense in participating in armed
resistance. Rather than fight, they were concerned about ensuring that the
underground Communist organizations in newly annexed Macedonia and
Thrace be integrated within the Bulgarian Party, instead of within the
respective Communist parties of Yugoslavia and Greece.[19] Only the young

[17] The intricate history of "left" and "right" in the Bulgarian Party and more
particularly in the Bulgarian political emigration in the Soviet Union, as well as the
position of Dimitrov *vis-à-vis* the massacre of a few hundred Bulgarian exiles at
the hands of Stalin's police, are traced in detail in Oren, *op. cit.*, chaps. ii—iii;
see also the present author's "Popular Front in the Balkans: Bulgaria," *Journal
of Contemporary History*, Vol. V, No. 3, London, 1970, pp. 69–82.

[18] See Traicho Kostov, *Politicheskoto polozhenie i zadachite na partiiata*, Sofia,
1945. This is a singularly important document in the form of a detailed report by
Kostov, then the Communist Party's Secretary General. It relates with some
honesty the difficult position in which the Party found itself throughout the war.
Published immediately after it was delivered at the first postwar Party plenum,
the report has never been reprinted since. (It was not included in Kostov's
collected works published after his rehabilitation.) It has been generally disregarded
by the historians of the resistance.

[19] The single most important documentary source on Bulgarian-Yugoslav
Communist relations during the war and immediately after is *Istorijski arhiv
KPJ*, Vol. VII, Belgrade, 1951. For obvious reasons, the Bulgarians have been
hesitant to part with their own information on this painful subject. On the issues
of Macedonia and Thrace, the Bulgarian Communists have proved no different
than most, if not all, Bulgarian political parties of various colorings.

and the relatively new recruits to the Party contributed to the underground resistance, which was established largely on Moscow's insistence. The armed effort did not amount to very much, and it was never able to attain popular support of any size. The few irregular contingents which succeeded in maintaining themselves did so thanks to the active support extended to them by Tito's partisans.[20]

The war experience in Bulgaria confirmed what has by now become common knowledge: that the influence and strength of communism is a correlative of national rather than class dissatisfaction. For those fanatically devoted to the Communist cause, this was a bitter lesson which, nevertheless, had to be learned. The fact that they had performed better than their comrades in any one of the countries allied with Germany offered them scant consolation. What mattered most to them was what they saw across their frontiers. While their own might had shrunk, the Yugoslav Communists, whom the Bulgarian Party had patronized somewhat disdainfully during the inter-war period, had grown to formidable proportions in a few years. These were facts which no amount of history-rewriting could obliterate. After 1944 the Bulgarians found themselves on the defensive *vis-à-vis* Belgrade and adhered to the Russians for protection and reassurance.

If the comparative international position of the Bulgarian Communists was not too favorable, their relative position on the home front was substantially better. The principal factors which operated in their favor can be briefly enumerated. First, the Communists had succeeded in preserving a semblance of organized political life throughout the war. Their political rivals, on the other hand, being ill-equipped to maintain underground organizations, re-emerged politically scattered. Second, after 1944 the Bulgarian political spectrum as it had existed before 1934 was drastically curtailed. From the center all the way to the extreme right, the political groups of the past were not allowed to reorganize because of their past affiliations with authoritarian and, later, crypto-fascist regimes. As a result, the relative weight of the Communist Party increased correspondingly. Third, the Communists were reinforced by the return from the Soviet Union of surviving Communist exiles, who strengthened the ranks of the Party, adding substantially to its political and administrative capabilities. Fourth, the Communists increased their membership more rapidly than

---

[20] On the Communist wartime resistance, see various entries in Oren, *Bulgarian Communism*. The standard official work published in Bulgaria is Nikifor Gornenski's *Vuoruzhenata borba na bulgarskiia narod* . . ., Sofia, 1958. On the support given by Tito's partisans, the best testimony is given by Bulgaria's most successful and best known partisan leader, in Slavcho Trunski, *Neotdavna*, Sofia, 1965.

any other group. Only three months after the coup of September, 1944, they could count on a membership of nearly a quarter of a million. This spectacular increment was to be explained by the addition of Communist dropouts, who were now permitted to re-enlist, but above all by the inclusion of marginal and often opportunist elements quick to perceive that the future belonged to communism. Finally, but not least important, the fact that the Ministries of the Interior and Justice were headed by Communist functionaries gave the Party an enormous advantage, a circumstance that needs no amplification to those familiar with East European politics.[21]

Many new techniques and new forms of political action were imposed from above. On the national as well as on the provincial level, the Fatherland Front was superimposed on the existing governmental and administrative organs. The Front, as such, was a Communist invention. The Communists were overrepresented in the various Fatherland Front Committees which sprang up overnight. Political and administrative decisions had to be cleared first with the respective Fatherland Front Committees before being executed by the existing governmental bodies.[22] A newly fashioned Institute of Military Advisers was established within the general staff of the army. Military political commissars were, in all cases, Communist appointees. They supervised the professional officer corps and reported directly to the Party Politburo. Strategically placed Communist functionaries throughout the civil administration were given high officers' ranks, which provided them with immunity and additional authority.[23]

Police terror was, of course, not a Communist innovation. The newly instituted People's Militia, which replaced the old police force, intervened everywhere in the daily conduct of civilian life, representing an immediate threat and an effective deterrent to those who failed to comply. Those voluntary public associations which were allowed to be re-established were

---

[21] On the reorganization of the Communist Party during the first few months after the coup, see the survey in *Istoricheski pregled*, No. 2, Sofia, 1965, pp. 3–31.

[22] There exists a very large volume of literature, some of it quite objective, on the role of the Fatherland Front committees as political and administrative instruments. The use made of the Fatherland Front by the Communists during the first few months after the September coup is reported in some detail by its General Secretary, Tsola Dragoicheva, *Politicheska, organizatsionna i stopanska deinost na Natsionalniia komitet . . .*, Sofia, 1945.

[23] *Otechestvenata voina na Bulgariia, 1944–1945*, 3 Vols., Sofia, 1961–66; this is a basic source on the reorganization of the army and the initial purge of the officers corps. Also important are Shteriu Atanasov, *et al.*, *Kratka istoriia na Otechestvenata voina*, Sofia, 1958, and Shteriu Atanasov, *Pokhodut na zapad*, Sofia, 1966. Atanasov was an old Communist functionary who had returned from Soviet exile and was made a senior political commissar of the reorganized army.

infiltrated and, failing this, were taken over by police license. Strict censorship, noisy public mass meetings, new styles of agitation and mass propaganda, and insistence that progress and the future belonged to socialism were all included in and fostered by the new political style.

In more than one way, the above-described patterns of action were not original to the Bulgarian Communists. They were applied with slight variations in the sovietization of all East European countries. Peculiar to Bulgaria were the advantages that the Communists derived from the ideals of slavophilism and, especially, from the insistence that Bulgaria's territorial integrity would best be protected by the Soviet Union. It is undeniable that Pan-Slavic appeal and love for Russia had always been potent forces among the Bulgarian masses. For reasons that need no elucidation, it was only the Bolshevik revolution which gave the Communists the exclusive claim on Pan-Slavism, whereas for all the others the aversion to bolshevism took precedence over love for Russia. While the influence of Slavic sentiment is not measurable, the Communists could and did exploit it, not without positive effect. At the same time, their claim that they alone could protect Bulgaria's national interests was a dubious asset. No one could reasonably dispute the Communist assertion that only Russia could assure Bulgaria's territorial integrity in the face of Greek revanchism. To a lesser extent, the same was true in relation to Turkey. The position of Britain in these two cases was clearly anti-Bulgarian. Although not as strongly pronounced, the stand of the United States could hardly be judged favorable.

While all this could be counted as a Communist asset, the fact that Yugoslavia had turned Communist was to prove a lasting liability. For the first time in history, the Macedonians in Yugoslavia were given political autonomy. Marshal Tito wanted a federation in which Bulgaria would become one of seven Yugoslav republics. This grand design was not to the liking of the Bulgarian Communists, and they did all they could to sabotage, or at least delay, its realization. Their position was significantly weakened when they came face to face with Tito's stubborn insistence that the Macedonian Federal Republic incorporate that part of Macedonia which lay within Bulgaria's political frontiers. Once again, Macedonia posed a dilemma to which the Bulgarian Communists could not give a clear-cut answer. They were forced to make concessions while employing dilatory tactics as best they could. Not until 1948, when the break between Tito and the Cominform became final, could the Communists in Sofia relax. On balance, however, the threat emanating from Athens was always judged greater than that represented by Belgrade, thus giving the Communists an advantage which outweighed the disadvantage. Until the peace treaty was ratified, the Communists could claim with a degree of justification that they alone had become the true guardians of Bulgaria's national integrity. It was a powerful argument which weakened the anti-Communist opposition and strengthened those who were inclined to collaborate.

Collaboration with the Communists and opposition to them represent two distinct counterparts of a single whole. Given the setting of the times, both collaboration and opposition represent a source of dismay and fascination for the observer who is writing a full generation later. Taken seriously, as they should be, the two phenomena must be treated with extra care and sensitivity. The tasks of analysis are formidable. Moral judgments have to be made and considerations of motive taken into account. Those who chose the road of expediency at the time must not be allowed to gain acceptance of their claim to wisdom years later. In this matter, more than in all others, one must separate the retrospective judgments from the specific acts of the various participants, which were executed in the context of the knowledge available to them at the time. The pitfalls of relativism must be avoided as well. The collaborationists can and do claim absolution on the ground that by having collaborated they helped salvage what little there was to salvage from the Communist avalanche. For them, this is possibly the best defense available. On the other hand, the few oppositionists who survived can assert with justice that by opposing sovietization they, at the very least, taught the younger generation of Bulgarians an object lesson in political pluralism, a subject of which younger generations had been ignorant in the past and were to remain so in the future.

A distinction must be drawn between collaboration with the Communists before September of 1944 and after. As early as 1942, at Moscow's instigation, Communist functionaries sought political partnership with the leaders of the democratic camp. This was the origin of the Fatherland Front. The small Democratic Party, headed by Mushanov, remained resolute in its refusal to enter the Front. The leadership of the tiny but respectable Social Democratic Party split, a few going over to the Fatherland Front, while the veteran Pastukhov remained aloof. The realignment within the former Agrarian movement followed along the lines of the schisms which had taken place much earlier. The majority, headed by Gichev, refused co-operation, while the so-called Pladne group, which was led by Nikola Petkov and had split off from the main body of the Agrarians in the early thirties, joined hands in the Fatherland Front. The small but influential Zveno group, which was not a political party but a small faction of people holding influence in professional military circles, went over to the Communists. Their liaison with the Communists dated from the second half of the 1930's and had been firm throughout the war. The tiny group of Radicals, who opposed the wartime regime but believed that Germany would win the war, remained unallied.[24]

The first Fatherland Front government, therefore, was made up of the Communists, the Pladne Agrarians, one part of the Social Democrats, the Zveno group, and a number of unaffiliated individuals. Despite their outstanding anti-fascist record, Mushanov (Social Democrat) and Gichev (Agrarian) were arrested and eventually tried in the so-called People's Court. Their followers were not allowed to organize. The Pladne group, now in power, endeavored to amalgamate within its ranks the followers of Gichev. Relations among the various partners of the Fatherland Front were tense from the outset, but the coalition survived for a time. Headed by Georgiev as Prime Minister and Velchev as the Minister of War, Zveno suffered insult and intimidation at the hands of the Communists, but adhered firmly to the partnership. The Russians were concerned that the Bulgarian army be fit and able to fight the Germans, and Zveno was useful in providing the cement which kept together the non-political professional officer corps. Petkov believed that the alliance of forces on the international scene would have to be mirrored in Bulgaria if the integrity of the country were to be secured. In January of 1945, the Soviet high command in Bulgaria forced him to expel from Agrarian ranks Dr. G. M. Dimitrov, who had spent the war years as a political exile in Cairo and had returned to Bulgaria after the entry of the Red Army. This was to prove a significant act which signaled the beginning of the end for the coalition. The Communists were set on holding early general elections which were to formalize the existing government and confirm their dominant position. Even though Kolarov and Dimitrov had not been allowed to return to their home country from Moscow, the Communists, led by Kostov, were confident of carrying their partners and avoiding a crisis. Gradually, however, the terroristic outrages which the People's Militia conducted unabatedly

---

[24] Kiril Dramaliev, *Istoriia na Otechestveniia front*, Sofia, 1947, tells the Communist side of the story on the inter-party wartime negotiations. The best Communist account is found in Ilcho Dimitrov, *Burzhoaznata opozitsiia v Bulgariia*, already cited. On the history of the Democratic Party, see the memoirs of its founder, Aleksandur Malinov, *Stranichki ot nashata nova politicheska istoriia*, Sofia, 1938. On the Agrarians of the 1930's and the war years, there are two important monographs with a great deal of factual information, namely, D. V. Petrova, *BZNS i narodniiat front, 1934–1939*, Sofia, 1967, and *BZNS v kraiia na burzhoaznoto gospodstvo v Bulgariia, 1939–1944*. The memoirs of the founder of Pladne are naturally subjective but informative: Kosta Todorov, *Balkan Firebrand*, New York, 1943. On the Zveno group, see Dimo Kazasov, *Zveno bez grim*, Sofia, 1936, and selective entries in his *Burni godini, 1918–1944*, Sofia, 1949. The respective positions of all the above factions in relation to the Communists are treated in Oren, *Bulgarian Communism*.

throughout the country caused a revulsion which soon gathered momentum. The massive People's Trials, which were aimed against the leaders of the old regime, engulfed many who were politically innocent but for their anti-Communist position. From the outset, the Communists cultivated doubtful elements within the parties which were their nominal partners, and in the spring of 1945 they endeavored to install them at the top of their respective organizations. This brought about a break which, in turn, gave rise to a formally organized and united anti-Communist opposition. While the victorious Allies were gathering at Potsdam, Petkov and his friends from the Social Democrats prepared a memorandum which called on the Allied governments to use their prerogatives to prevent the forthcoming elections which the Communists were certain to stampede.[25]

Given the specific international and domestic contexts, the publication of this document represented a significant development in the course of sovietization. Moved by considerations of high policy, the Russians yielded and the elections were postponed in the face of Western protestations. Throughout the upheaval, the ministers of Zveno remained true to their Communist overlords. This served to give the government of the Fatherland Front, from which the democratic leaders had exited, a degree of badly needed legitimacy. Yet, without any doubt, the postponement of the elections compelled the Communists to retrench, while the opposition was allowed to organize openly. There were now two parallel and identically named Agrarian and Social Democratic Parties. Sizeable majorities of each joined the opposition, while the minorities remained within the Fatherland Front and the government. The Bulgarian peasants were not fooled by the schism, and the overwhelming majority gave their trust and support to the opposition headed by Petkov. The new situation represented a turnabout in the traditional political positions of the past. For the first time in their history, the Communists found themselves a ruling party faced with an audacious and vocal opposition. Radically different from the past, however, was the fact that this time the country was occupied by a foreign power determined to maintain its grip. Dimitrov and Kolarov were now brought back from Moscow to reinforce the cadres at home and boost their morale. The opposition in Bulgaria was a genuine force which did not require Western backing. Had the terms of the game been equal, the opposition

---

[25] The full text of the memorandum is reproduced in *Foreign Relations of the United States, Diplomatic Papers, The Conference in Berlin, 1945*, Vol. 2, Washington, D.C., pp. 724–725. The same volume contains important information on all aspects of the domestic upheavals as reported by the United States representative in Sofia. The full story, however, must be pieced together from the Bulgarian press of the time, Communist and anti-Communist.

would have prevailed over the Communists by the force of the ballot. This could have become a reality only if the Western powers had contained and, in some way, balanced the Russian presence.

Bulgaria always remained a very small component in the complex of inter-power relationships which were about to degenerate into the Cold War. Even though the United States was not a party to the Anglo-Soviet "percentages agreement," it could not alter the *de facto* division of military zones as they had become fixed at the end of the war. The American minister in Sofia, supported by the representative on the Allied Control Commission, begged his government to stand fast and not allow the loss of the little that had been gained after the postponement of the scheduled elections. He was a man of character who knew Bulgarian conditions intimately. His perceptive dispatches were infused with an almost prophetic sense of things to come. They were of no avail, however. A commission of inquiry dispatched by President Truman to the Balkans reported back the facts as they stood. This did not change the underlying tendencies within the American government, which were aimed at working out a *modus vivendi* with the Soviet Union. A few months after the postponement, the elections were indeed held. The opposition leaders decided to boycott the ballot. The outcome was thus preset, and the Communists proceeded to convene a parliament packed with their followers and their stooges. The opposition refused to carry out the recommendation made jointly by Secretary Byrnes and Molotov that two opposition leaders be included in the Fatherland Front government. On their part, the Communists proceeded to complete the purge within the professional army through the early retirement of a few hundred officers. The purge put the final stamp on Zveno, bringing about its complete emasculation.[26]

Still, there was one more card to be played in the Bulgarian political game. As long as the peace treaty with Bulgaria had not been signed, the Russians and the Communists were obliged to tolerate the domestic opposition. A new election was set with the opposition taking part. Despite police outrages, the elections of 1946 proved to the Bulgarians at home and to the world—or the part of it still willing to listen—that these peasant people continued to hope for political freedom in the face of all odds. The opposition gained more than a million votes and elected 101 deputies to the

---

[26] See James F. Byrnes, *Speaking Frankly*, New York, 1947, on the meetings of the Foreign Ministers. There is much material on the 1946 purge of the army; see, for example, Damian Velchev, *Statii, rechi i zapovedi* ..., Sofia, 1946; Georgi Dimitrov, *Za bulgarskata narodna armiia*, Sofia, 1959; and selected entries from the writings of the purge's architect himself, namely, Traicho Kostov, *Izbrani statii, dokladi, rechi*, Sofia, 1964.

new parliament. Even though they remained a minority, they set themselves a record unrivaled in any other country within the Soviet domain. For a few months the voice of the opposition in parliament was heard loudly and clearly. Although Soviet Russia could not be directly attacked, communism was. The fact that Bulgaria's future borders were being fixed at the Paris Peace Conference did not inhibit the Bulgarian opposition from condemning their oppressors at home. This left them open to charges of treason. It was to the credit of the Bulgarian opposition that, despite the cruel dilemma which faced it throughout, it continued to assault political tyranny and, by so doing, proved that it was capable of aspiring to a high plane, where the true interests of the people lay. But the moment the peace treaty was signed, the fate of the opposition was sealed. The subsequent record of Petkov's arrest and eventual trial is all too well known. His execution was followed by the removal and imprisonment of his collaborators and followers. In the years to come, the jails and the labor camps became the only forums where views other than those of the Communists could have a hearing.[27]

Since 1947, Bulgaria has remained one of the most compliant of the countries engulfed by the vast Soviet domain. The high pitch of the struggle ending in sovietization contrasts sharply with the uninterrupted silence of the last generation. For those who perceive history as a cyclic phenomenon, Bulgaria's docility in the last twenty-five years can be seen as a period of exhaustion counterposed to the permanent upheaval and turmoil of an earlier era. More basic are the objective circumstances which once again have closed in on this besieged country. The perpetual need for at least one mighty protector has not been modified or altered.

---

[27] On the peace treaty with Bulgaria and the respective positions at the Paris Peace Conference, see entries in *Foreign Relations of the United States, 1946*, Vol. 4, Washington, D.C., 1970. For a Communist view of Bulgaria's international position, see Voin Bozhinov, *Zashtitata na natsionalnata nezavisimost na Bulgariia, 1944–1947*, Sofia, 1962.

The Communist Takeover in Poland

Susanne S. Lotarski

Although wars generally accelerate the forces of socio-political change, it is conscious political decisions and actions which channel these forces and determine the particular scope and nature of postwar transformations. World War I speeded up change in Russian society, but it was the determined action of the small band of Bolsheviks which launched Russia on its particular path of development. In the same way, World War II opened the way for the transformation of Poland by altering the social structure and radicalizing political opinion. The socio-political system which emerged in Poland after the war was not, however, an inevitable consequence of these changes, but a result of a conscious effort by the Communists to seize political power and impose their particular program. To do this they had to engage in a difficult and bitter struggle.

Neither their earlier history nor their wartime record provided a basis for the Communists' takeover. In the interwar period, the Polish Communist Party was among the weakest in Europe and operated outside the mainstream of Polish politics. The Party's anti-national stand, its radical program, and its association with the Soviet Union repelled most Poles. The Party was forced to operate clandestinely, and many of its members were arrested. As if these handicaps were not enough, the Communist Party was dealt a stunning blow by Stalin himself, who in 1938 dissolved the Party and imprisoned or executed many of its leaders. Although the Party was revived after the German attack on the Soviet Union, it played only a minor and divisive role in the resistance movement. Since the largest of the underground armies were anti-Communist, the resistance hindered rather than helped the Communists in their takeover of Poland.

Even the social changes that occurred in Poland during the war proved but moderately helpful to the Communists. The long war and the oppressive occupation had a shattering impact on Polish society, altering both social structure and political opinion. The landowning class disappeared almost completely, the lower-upper and middle classes were largely destroyed, and some thirty-five percent of the intelligentsia perished. Thousands more from these classes were scattered around the world in exile. Thus the strength of the traditionally most active and politically most sophisticated strata of Polish society was greatly diminished. Political opinion was also affected by the war. The prewar regime of "colonels" was largely discredited, and support grew for the introduction of far-reaching socio-political reforms.

Communist historians stress the importance of these social and political changes and argue that they opened the way for a radical transformation of the Polish system. There is little evidence, however, to support the contention that these changes created any considerable support for communism. Perhaps the best evidence against such arguments is the pains that the Communists took to eschew Communist terminology and to present their programs in a reformist cast. Well aware of their unpopularity, they camouflaged their activities through various front organizations and chose to call themselves the "Polish Workers' Party" rather than the "Polish Communist Party." The war had contributed to a blurring of party differences and the growth of reformist sentiment, but at the end of the war, as at its start, political opinion in Poland was overwhelmingly opposed to the creation of a Communist system.

The anti-Russian and anti-Soviet sentiments of the Polish population were an additional liability faced by the Communists. Attitudes towards the Soviet Union colored attitudes towards communism, Communist Parties, and Communist programs, and in Poland these attitudes had long been negative. Tsarist Russia had been the chief culprit in the partitioning of the Polish state in the eighteenth century and had ruled most of Poland until 1918. Soviet Russia replaced Tsarist Russia, but ill will between the neighbors was inflamed by territorial disputes, by the Polish-Soviet War of 1920–1921, and by conflicting ideologies. In 1939 Stalin's pact with Hitler cleared the way for the German attack on Poland and provided for the Soviet Union's absorption of half of Poland's territory. Thus, despite the Communists' repeated declarations that they desired a truly independent Poland and were not subordinate to the Soviet Communist Party, they continued to be identified as agents of an aggressive foreign power and supporters of its territorial claims.

Communism was also identified with such unpalatable policies as collectivization and militant atheism. These were serious handicaps in a country where there was deep attachment to the land and where Catholicism was identified with patriotism and national survival. In the post-Stalinist period, Polish communism has achieved a measure of accommodation with both the peasantry and the Catholic Church. At the time of the postwar struggle for power, however, the Polish Communists' willingness or ability to make compromises on such issues as private farms and freedom of religion was not apparent, especially in view of the Soviet Union's policies of forced collectivization and religious persecution.

The key to the Communist takeover in Poland was Soviet military, diplomatic, and tactical support. Even with Soviet assistance, however, the Polish Communists faced an inordinately difficult challenge. Their small party was composed of disparate wings and was confronted with popular hostility and a political opposition of considerable strength. To consolidate their power, the Communists had to wage a civil war which lasted more than two years and resulted in the loss of over 17,000 lives. Despite these difficulties, or perhaps because of them, the actual takeover was quite rapid. For all practical purposes, the Communists had gotten control of the key levers of power by the end of the European war in May, 1945. The speed of their offensive enabled the Communists to utilize the authority and power of the Soviet armed forces to support their takeover. It also enabled them to take advantage of the dislocations and fluid political situations of a war zone and to establish their presence before other political parties had a chance to reorganize themselves. Such a rapid takeover was also advantageous diplomatically, as it presented the Allied conferences negotiating the future of Poland with a *fait accompli*. Gradualism in the Polish case would have increased the difficulties of taking power.

The Communists were able to take power as quickly as they did for a number of reasons other than the aid they received from the Red Army. Of great importance were the Polish military and police units that the Communists organized with Soviet assistance and supervision. These forces were used not only to fight underground guerrilla detachments, but also to arrest political opponents, implement decrees, oversee the operation of institutions and organizations, gather information, and disseminate propaganda. Of equal importance was the advance planning and preparation that the Communists carried out during the years 1942 and 1943. The core of the future leadership was trained at Comintern schools in Marxist-Leninist theory and in techniques for agitation and infiltration.[1] Political programs were painstakingly drafted, and detailed evaluations of their

---

[1] The Initiative Group of Polish Communists was established under Comintern auspices and prepared its programs with the advice of the head of the Comintern, Georgi Dimitrov. The Communists who parachuted into Poland in the spring of 1942 had all been students in the second course of the Comintern School at Kushnarenkovo, near Ufa, in the USSR. Marian Malinowski, "Powstani Polskiej Partii Robotniczej," in W. Gora and J. Golebiowski (eds.), *Z najonwszych dziejow Polski, 1939–1947*, Warsaw, 1961, pp. 106–109.

[2] For instance, in May, 1943, Hilary Minc, head of the Economic Research Bureau of the Executive Committee of the Union of Polish Patriots, prepared a memorandum concerning land reform which outlined plans for the seizure of estates, including livestock, buildings, and equipment. Andrzej Korbonski, *The Politics of Socialist Agriculture in Poland, 1945–1960*, New York, 1965, p. 58.

political implications were made.[2] Organizations purporting to be broad fronts of progressive citizens were created and controlled by the Communists in both the Soviet Union and Poland.[3] Extensive political and military training was carried out in the Polish detachments of the Soviet Army.[4] These plans, implemented with considerable flexibility and pragmatism, complemented the military and diplomatic efforts by the Soviet Union to ensure a Communist victory in Poland.

Soviet Diplomacy

The crucial role of the Red Army should not obscure the valuable part played by Soviet diplomacy in easing the Communist path to power. The military and political decisions made by the Allies during World War II helped considerably to improve the position of the Communists *vis-à-vis* the other political groups in Poland. The future of Poland was a frequent subject of discussion in Allied wartime negotiations and provoked numerous acrimonious exchanges. The history of these negotiations has been documented extensively, and it will suffice here to review the major problems and to see how their resolution contributed to the Communist takeover.[5]

Two issues dominated the Allied disputes over Poland that took place from 1941 to 1945: (1) the postwar frontiers of Poland, and (2) the composition and nature of a postwar Polish government. In both cases, the solution advanced by the Soviet Union was finally adopted.

From the time it joined the Allies in June, 1941, the Soviet Union insisted that the boundaries of postwar Poland should correspond with Polish ethnicity. This meant that Russia would retain all the territories

---

[3] A similar program of training, planning, and the formation of preliminary governmental organizations among German Communists in the USSR during the war is described by Wolfgang Leonhard in *Child of the Revolution*, Chicago, 1958.

[4] For this reason, the First Polish Army, which was trained on Soviet soil, was considered more reliable politically than the Second Polish Army, which was created within Poland. Fryderyk Zbiniewicz in *Sesja naukowa poswiecona wojnie wyzwolenczej narodu Polskiego 1939–1945*, Warsaw, 1959, p. 272.

[5] Among the many books on the diplomatic negotiations regarding Poland, see especially the following: Edward J. Rozek, *Allied Wartime Diplomacy: A Pattern in Poland*, New York, 1958; Wlodzimierz T. Kowalski, *Walka dyplomatyczna o miejsce Polski w Europie 1939–45*, Warsaw, 1966; John A. Lukacs, *The Great Powers and Eastern Europe*, New York, 1953; Herbert Feis, *Churchill, Roosevelt, Stalin*, Princeton, 1957.

it had occupied as a result of the Nazi-Soviet Pact of 1939.[6] The Polish Government-in-Exile, at first supported by Britain and the United States, strongly opposed the transfer of its eastern territories to the Soviet Union and held out for the restoration of the Russo-Polish border set by the Treaty of Riga in 1912. At the Teheran Conference of 1943, however, Churchill proposed that Poland be moved westward so that it would be situated between the Curzon Line and the Oder-Neisse rivers. Roosevelt did not object, and of course Stalin did not either. By the time the Yalta Conference took place in February, 1945, the question of the eastern frontier was almost a dead issue, and it was the western boundary which became the source of conflict. The "Big Three" had agreed at Teheran to the Oder-Neisse line, but had not specified which branch of the Neisse, east or west. The Soviets held out for the Western Neisse, which would give Poland more territory, including the city of Wroclaw. Since no agreement was reached, the subject was not mentioned in the final Yalta communiqué.

The stand-off on the western frontier question continued at the Potsdam conference of July, 1945, and the most the Allies were able to decide was to place the former German territories "under the control of the Polish state."[7] The permanency of this frontier and of Poland's control of these territories became a hostage of the Cold War. Until the agreement concluded between West Germany and Poland in 1970, Poland's right to these territories continued to be disputed, with the West considering the Potsdam formula a temporary decision, valid only until the signing of a German peace treaty.

The frontier agreements, on the whole, contributed to the consolidation of Communist power in Poland. Although the retention by Russia of the eastern territories hurt the Communists, most Poles realized that the western territories were considerably more valuable economically. Furthermore, the Soviet Union endorsed the Polish claim to the western

---

[6] These territories comprised almost half of Poland's territory and one-third of its population, forty percent of which was ethnically Polish. The area was rich in natural resources, providing sixty-three percent of Poland's oil output, ninety percent of its natural gas production, forty-two percent of its water power, and substantial yields of potassium, phosphates, tobacco, flax, hemp, and maize. See Rozek, *op. cit.*, p. 37.

[7] Z. Jordan, *The Oder-Neisse Line: A Study of the Political, Economic and European Significance of Poland's Western Frontier*, London, 1952; S. L. Sharp, *The Polish-German Frontier*, New York, 1947; W. Wagner, *The Genesis of the Oder-Neisse Line: A Study of Diplomatic Negotiations during World War II*, Stuttgart, 1957; E. Wiskemann, *Germany's Eastern Neighbors*, London, 1956.

lands, while the United States and England refused to do so. This meant that only Russia could be counted on to defend Poland from any future attempts by Germany to recover its lost territories. For this reason alone, the postwar foreign policy of any Polish government would be heavily dependent upon Soviet support. Thus the unresolved question of the western frontier cast the Communist Party in the role of a defender of Polish territorial rights and national interests, thereby contributing to the achievement of an accommodation between the Party and the Polish people.[8] In addition, the acquisition of the western lands gave the Communists many farms with which to buy peasant votes.

On the issue of the postwar Polish government, Soviet aims became apparent more gradually and were pursued more covertly. In November, 1941, Stalin told the new Polish ambassador in Moscow, Stanislaw Kot, that he was in favor "of rebuilding a free and independent Polish State, irrespective of its internal political system,"[9] but the sincerity of this statement may well be doubted. In any case, at the Teheran Conference two years later, Stalin was demanding a Poland "friendly to the Soviet Union." Two events had occurred in the meantime which were to have a profound impact on the Polish problem. First, the severance of diplomatic relations between the USSR and the London Government-in-Exile freed Stalin to make preparations for his own, Soviet-sponsored Polish government. Second, by the time the Allied leaders met at Yalta in February, 1945, almost all of Poland had been occupied by Soviet troops, and a Provisional Government had been installed and recognized by the Soviet Union.

At Yalta the Western powers refused to accept this puppet regime, but insisted that a new, respresentative government be formed. After much contention, they accepted the Soviet proposal that the Provisional Government be the nucleus of the new government. The agreement said that "the Provisional Government which is now functioning in Poland should ... be reorganized on a broader democratic basis with the inclusion of democratic leaders from Poland itself and from Poles abroad."[10] The Communists made no commitment to include any specific non-Communist leaders, and no safeguards were enacted to ensure that the agreement concerning "free and unfettered elections as soon as possible" would be carried out.[11] After

---

[8] Adam Bromke, "Nationalism and Communism in Poland," *Foreign Affairs*, New York, July, 1962, pp. 635–643.

[9] Stanislaw Kot, *Listy z Rosji do gen. Sikorskiego*, London, 1955, p. 178.

[10] U. S. Department of State, *Foreign Relations of the United States ; Diplomatic Papers : The Conferences at Malta and Yalta*, Washington, D.C., 1955, p. 973.

[11] *Ibid.*

months of haggling, the Soviets finally agreed to admit Stanislaw Mikolaj-czyk and four other non-Communist Poles to what was now called the Provisional Government of National Unity. The new government was still dominated by Communists and fellow travelers, however. Despite this fact, it received full diplomatic recognition from the United States and Great Britain on July 5, 1945. Soviet military force had installed the Communist government in power, but it was Soviet diplomacy that won it international acceptance.

The Americans, concerned above all with winning the war and establishing a durable peace, gave top priority to maintaining good relations with the Soviet Union. They realized the importance of Poland to Russian security, and they knew that American interests in Poland were not really vital. The Americans were also reluctant to assume responsibilities in Eastern Europe. The British were conscious of their commitments to the Poles, but they became frustrated at being caught between the antipodal positions of their Soviet and Polish allies, and this increased their willing-ness to compromise with the Soviet Union, which was contributing so much to the winning of the war. The London Poles strove to defend the interests of their country and people. They refused to compromise on such issues as the Curzon Line and the murder of their officers at Katyn, thus exasperating the British and provoking the Soviets. The case of Czechoslovakia suggests, however, that greater consciousness of geopoli-tical realities and less intransigence on the part of the London Poles would not have averted a Communist takeover. The Soviet Union was vitally concerned about the borders and the government of Poland, and its interest in the Polish question was far greater than that of Britain or the United States. The Soviet Union had clearly defined goals, and in contrast to Britain and America, it had the power to realize them.

The Revival of the Polish Communist Party

The Communist Party that came to power in Poland developed from two nuclei. The "Moscow" nucleus was created from among those Polish Communists who in 1939 found themselves in the eastern Polish provinces incorporated into the Soviet Union. The cities of Bialystok and Lwow be-came the main centers of Polish Communist activity. A few Polish Com-munists took part in Soviet institutions in the newly annexed parts of the Ukrainian and Belorussian Republics, and some obtained jobs with the

Soviet administration.[12] In mid-1941, after the German attack on the Soviet Union, an "Initiative Group" of Polish Communists, recruited from among the Lwow and Bialystok activists, was created by the Comintern. Polish Communists, under Comintern tutelage, underwent intensive training and prepared position papers and programs for future use. The majority of Polish Communists in the Soviet Union, however, operated in a front organization, the Union of Polish Patriots, until the creation of the Central Bureau of Polish Communists in the USSR in January, 1944.[13]

The Initiative Group played a major role in organizing the "native" nucleus of Communists, who had maintained informal contacts with one another in the German-occupied territories through various small groups such as the Union of Friends of the USSR and Hammer and Sickle. Ideological differences divided these groups, and Gestapo raids destroyed several of them.[14] Comintern blessing for a reorganization of the Communist Party came at the end of December, 1941, when members of the Initiative Group were parachuted into Poland behind German lines. There, in accordance with previously made plans, they helped to create the Polish Workers' Party (the new name for the Communist Party) and issued its first appeal. Although created by the Moscow group, the native nucleus gradually took on a life of its own, especially after the execution of the two Moscow Communists who served in turn as First Secretary, the subsequent loss of radio contact with Moscow, and the election of a native Communist, Wladyslaw Gomulka, as First Secretary. The bifurcated development of the Party between "Muscovites" and "natives" caused differences in orientation which continued to plague it for many years after it assumed power, especially in the intraparty struggles of 1948 and 1956.[15]

The Polish Workers' Party entered upon a new and different stage of existence when Soviet troops entered Poland and previously made plans

---

[12] For example, Wanda Wasilewska (a leading organizer of Polish Communist activities in the Soviet Union), Stefan Jedrychowski (later a minister in the Polish Government), and Jan Turlejski were members of the Supreme Soviet of the USSR; Marceli Nowotko (the first Secretary of the Polish Workers' Party) was a deputy to the Bialystok District Soviet; Wladyslaw Gomulka worked in Lwow as a junior administrator in a factory; Hilary Minc taught economics in Samarkand.

[13] For a scholarly account of the activities of the Communist Party during this period and later, see: M. K. Dziewanowski, *The Communist Party of Poland*, Cambridge, Mass., 1959, pp. 157–182.

[14] Malinowski, *op. cit.*, pp. 93–105.

[15] The differences between "Muscovites" and "natives" as well as the intraparty struggles are discussed in: Adam Bromke, *Poland's Politics: Idealism vs. Realism*, Cambridge, Mass., 1967; Hansjakob Stehle, *The Independent Satellite*, London, 1965; and Adam Ulam, *Titoism and the Cominform*, Cambridge, Mass., 1962.

were put into operation. Party membership grew very rapidly, as indicated below:

Membership in the Polish Workers' Party

June, 1942	4,000
January, 1943	8,000
July, 1944	20,000
January, 1945	30,000
December, 1945	210,000
January, 1947	500,000—plus

SOURCE: Nicholas Bethell, *Gomulka*, New York, 1969, p. 70

As different parts of the country were liberated, Communists who had been trained at Comintern schools were immediately sent in to organize Party units, oversee the establishment of local government, and implement the land reform. Others were assigned to publishing newspapers and propaganda materials. Party schools were established to train new members of the *apparat*, and the first graduates of the Central Party School in Lublin were sent to direct Party organizations in areas being liberated further west. Relaxation of its rigid admissions procedures and the granting of various privileges (jobs, food, clothing, housing) enabled the Party to expand its membership rapidly. Recruits came primarily from among workers desiring industrial recovery, poor peasants who wanted more land, opportunists, careerists, unemployed civil servants, and those who saw Communist rule as inevitable and Communist Party membership as the only way in which to participate in reconstructing the country. After the reorganization of the Provisional Government in July, 1945, and the reconstitution of the Polish Peasant Party and the Socialist Party, the Communists suffered some reverses, especially in factory council elections and in rural areas, where Party cells had to go underground to avoid reprisals. Nevertheless, the very fact of power enabled the Party to grow, so that by the elections of January, 1947, it had over a half-million members.[16]

The Formation of a Communist Government

From the beginning of the war Poland had its own Government-in-Exile, based in London and recognized by the Allies. Its backbone was within Poland, where resistance to the Germans was carried out by the "Underground State" and the Home Army. Most of the wartime leaders, both in London and Poland, came from the traditional political parties

---

[16] Richard F. Staar, *Poland, 1944–1962*, Baton Rouge, Louisiana, 1962, p.167.

(i.e., the Peasant Party, the National Democratic Party, the Socialist Party, and the Labor Party), which had been emaciated during the Pilsudski era from 1926 to 1929. These parties, which were leading the nation in its struggle for survival, assumed that after the war they would be entrusted with the leadership of Poland and that their wartime coalition would provide the basis for the future government.[17]

The attitude of the Communists towards the London Government vacillated between restrained criticism and outright condemnation, and relations with it were one cause of controversy within the Communist Party. In February, 1943, during the period of diplomatic relations between the London Government and Moscow (August, 1941, to April, 1943), the Communists made a bid to be included in the wartime underground coalition.[18] With the failure of this bid and the rupture of diplomatic relations between the London Poles and Moscow (on April 26, 1943), the Communists adopted a completely hostile position towards both the London Government and the Home Army. At the same time, the Communists began to stress the need to form a "broad national front" and set about creating their own rival institutions. At the end of December, 1943, they announced the creation in Warsaw of the National Council for the Homeland (*Krajowa Rada Narodowa*, or *KRN*), which they claimed was "the only democratic representation of the Polish nation and its sole spokesman."

The National Council was far from being a broad or representative coalition. Despite prolonged negotiations with the Peasant Party and with left-wing Socialists, the Communists had not succeeded in bringing the mainstream of these parties into their coalition. The manifesto announcing the Council's creation was signed only by Communists, by splinter elements from the Socialist Party and the Peasant Party, and by smaller groups which the Communists had sponsored among intellectual and trade-union circles. The National Council nonetheless provided a useful base from which to issue manifestos and decrees and to advance Communist goals. Leadership positions were retained by trusted Communists, including Boleslaw Bierut, a long-time Comintern agent, who was chairman. In one of its earliest

---

[17] Among memoirs about the London Government, see: Edward Raczynski, *In Allied London*, London, 1962; Stanislaw Mikolajczyk, *The Rape of Poland*, New York, 1948; and Jan Ciechanowski, *Defeat in Victory*, Garden City, 1947. On the underground, see: Stefan Korbonski, *Fighting Warsaw*, London, 1956; Jan Karski, *The Story of a Secret State*, Boston, 1943; and Zbigniew Stypulkowski, *Invitation to Moscow*, New York, 1951.

[18] Bethell, *op. cit.*, pp. 57–60; Dziewanowski, *op. cit.*, pp. 173–174; Andrzej Korbonski, *op. cit.*, pp. 55–56.

decrees, the Council declared itself the supreme authority over all Polish military units, whether in Poland, Russia, or the West.[19]

Aside from the National Council inside Poland, another Communist center claiming to speak for Polish interests, the Union of Polish Patriots, was created early in 1943 in the Soviet Union. Founded and controlled by Communists, the Union was supposedly a united front of all Poles living in the USSR, regardless of party affiliation. The Union got considerable support from Soviet authorities. Among other things it was given the use of a radio station, known as "Radio Kosciuszko," which made broadcasts from Russia to the people in Poland. The Union was also formally put in charge of the Polish army being organized in the Soviet Union. The Union of Polish Patriots became the Moscow counterpart of the Polish Government in London.[20]

As the battlefront moved westward towards Polish territories, both the National Council for the Homeland and the Union of Polish Patriots realized the urgency of making provisions for the future administration of Poland. In the latter half of 1943 and early 1944, the Union of Polish Patriots apparently made several requests to the Soviet government for permission to begin preparing, from among Poles living in the Soviet Union, an apparatus which would be ready to take over the administration of Polish territories behind the lines of the Soviet Army.[21] In mid-May, 1944, a delegation from the National Council for the Homeland arrived in Moscow and requested permission to set up a provisional government of Poland. During the next two months of extended conversations in Moscow among the National Council delegation, the Union of Polish Patriots, and Soviet representatives, the future government of Poland was forged from the two Communists centers. The Union of Polish Patriots recogized the National Council for the Homeland as "the sole representative of the Polish Nation" and formally subordinated itself to the Council.[22]

On July 22, 1944, immediately after Soviet troops crossed the new Polish-Soviet frontier, the National Council announced the creation of the "Polish Committee of National Liberation," which was to be the temporary government. The next day, July 22, this Committee made public

---

[19] Dziewanowski, *op. cit.*, pp. 170–173; Jerzy Pawlowicz, "Ksztaltowanie sie demokratycznego frontu narodowego," in Gora and Golebiowski, *op. cit.*, pp. 245–251.

[20] Malinowski, *op. cit.*, pp. 107–109; Andrzej Korbonski, *op. cit.*, p. 55.

[21] Wlodzimierz T. Kowalski, *Walka dyplomatyczna o miejsce Polski w Europie*, Warsaw, 1966, p. 390.

[22] Bethell, *op. cit.*, pp. 76–78.

its "Manifesto" or program, and made Lublin the temporary Polish capital, thus gaining its popular name, the "Lublin Committee." The Committee was composed of representatives of the National Council for the Homeland, the Union of Polish Patriots, and the Central Bureau of Polish Communists. All of the Committee's fifteen members were Communists or fellow travelers.[23]

The Lublin Committee immediately set about strengthening its position. On July 26, agreements were signed between the Committee and the Soviet Union concerning the boundaries of Poland (the Committee formally accepting Soviet claims to the eastern territories) and the transfer of civil administration from the Soviet Army to the Committee. It also began publishing newspapers, enacted a land reform, initiated nationalization measures, and established courts for the trial of "war criminals." The Underground State and Home Army were now considered by the Lublin Committee and the Soviet Army as illegal organizations, their leaders, who in accordance with instructions from the London Government presented themselves to the Russians, were arrested and in some cases executed. On December 31, 1944, the Lublin Committee moved one step closer to ultimate takeover by declaring itself to be the Provisional Government of Poland and naming its President, Edward Osobka-Morawski, as the new Prime Minister. The Secretary of the Polish Workers' Party, Wladyslaw Gomulka, became one of the two vice-premiers. Despite protests from the Anglo-American Allies, the Soviet Union granted official recognition to the Provisional Government in early January, 1945.[24] There were now two governments claiming the right to rule Poland. The arbiter between them was the Soviet Union.

The London Government, the Lublin Government, and the Allies

Relations between the London Government and Moscow had always been strained, even in the period when formal diplomatic relations existed between them. The eastern frontier question and the London Poles' attempts to create a Polish-Czechoslovak confederation were but two issues of contention.[25] In April, 1943, the request by the London Government that the International Red Cross investigate the mass graves of Polish officers discovered at Katyn provided the Soviets with an excuse for severing diplo-

23 For a list of members of the Lublin Committee and information about them, see Rozek, *op. cit.*, pp. 452–455.

24 Bethell, *op. cit.*, pp. 78–82; Rozek, *op. cit.*, pp. 229–233, and 326–328.

25 Piotr Wandycz, *Czechoslovak-Polish Confederation and the Great Powers, 1940–1945*, Bloomington, Indiana, 1956.

matic relations.[26] Relations were never re-established, despite prolonged negotiations and several visits by Premier Stanislaw Mikolajczyk to Moscow. In addition to demanding the withdrawal of the anti-Soviet accusations concerning Katyn, Stalin was by then demanding a Polish government "friendly to the Soviet Union."

Soviet support was crucial in gaining Allied acceptance of the Lublin government. On Stalin's insistence, it was the Communist Provisional Government which became the nucleus to which "democratic leaders from Poland itself and from Poles abroad" would be added. The broadening of this nucleus was delayed for several months—to Communist advantage—by Soviet procrastinations and objections, and only those persons were added who were acceptable to the Soviet Union. The circle of leaders available to represent the Underground Government was seriously reduced in March, 1945, when sixteen of its foremost members were lured from hiding and spirited away to Moscow by the Soviet secret police. There they were brought to trial on charges of running an illegal organization (the Home Army), an illegal pseudo-government, "drawing up plans for military action in a bloc with Germany against the USSR," and hence of being guilty of criminal actions endangering the security of the Soviet Union. The defendants comprised the top leadership of the resistance movement, including the head of the Underground Government and the Commander-in-Chief of the Home Army.[27] This Soviet move was intended not only to discredit the resistance in the eyes of the nation and the world, but also to deprive the resistance of its most experienced men at the very time when the reorganization of the Provisional Government was being negotiated and the political situation within the country was reaching a crisis.

When negotiations for the inclusion in the government of "democratic leaders from Poland itself and from Poles abroad" were finally concluded on June 21, 1945, one of the major prewar parties, the National Democratic Party, was completely excluded, while the Peasant Party was promised (but not actually given) only one-third of the posts. Mikolajczyk obtained two positions, as Second Deputy Prime Minister and Minister of Agriculture,

---

[26] On April 5, 1943, the Germans announced that they had uncovered mass graves of over 10,000 Polish officers killed by the Russians in the area of Katyn and Smolensk. These men were only part of the estimated total of 12,000 to 15,000 Polish officers who disappeared after the occupation of eastern Poland by the USSR in 1939. Those not found in the graves at Katyn presumably were killed by Soviet authorities elsewhere. See J. K. Zawodny, *Death in the Forest : The Story of the Katyn Massacre*, Notre Dame, 1962; Rozek, *op. cit.*, pp. 123–133.

[27] Zbigniew Stypulkowski, *Invitation to Moscow*, New York, 1951, pp. 211–340. The author was one of the sixteen leaders who were taken to the Soviet Union and put on trial.

but he was completely outnumbered by Communists and those who were taking orders from the Communists. Fourteen of the twenty-two government positions were filled by Lublin Poles. While this new government was nominally a coalition of five parties, the Communists controlled the armed forces, the police, and other levers of power, and they could count on complete Soviet support.

Still, the reconstituted Provisional Government was, in a sense, a temporary step backwards for the Communists. In Mikolajczyk and his Peasant Party a new force of considerable independent organizational strength and popular support was added to the governmental coalition, and the Communists would now have to defend the gains they had made. By the time this occurred, however, the Communists were already firmly in control of the government, and they were able to set the rules of the game. If the original intention in creating institutions such as the National Council for the Homeland had been to gain as favorable as possible a representation for the Communists in the postwar government, by June, 1945, it was rather a question of how much representation would be allowed the London parties in the Communist-created coalition.[28]

The Referendum of 1946 and the Elections of 1947

The next step towards consolidating Communist rule was in the arena of electoral politics. The Yalta agreement had called for "free and unfettered elections as soon as possible." The Communists pressed for an electoral coalition in which each party's share on the single list would be determined beforehand. Mikolajczyk's Peasant Party refused to join a coalition that would give it only one-fourth of the parliamentary seats, so the Communists maneuvered to postpone the elections by first holding a referendum on three constitutional issues. The issues were formulated by the Communists in such a way as to place their opponents in the awkward position of either supporting the Communists or disavowing their own principles. The Peasant Party favored all three measures, but to preserve its identity in the face of Communist pressure for fusion, it advocated a "no" vote on the question of abolishing the Senate. The referendum campaign was a

---

[28] Gomulka told Mikolajczyk and others in Moscow in June, 1945: "Do not take offence, gentlemen, that we only offer you as many places in the government as we think possible. Because we are the hosts here.... We desire an understanding with all our hearts. But do not think it is a condition of our existence. Once we have attained power we shall never give it up." Quoted in Bethell, *op. cit.*, p. 102.

foretaste of things to come: branches of the Polish Peasant Party were closed down, its paper allocation was cut, and many of its members were arrested.[29] Army units were ordered to distribute Communist electoral propaganda, electoral commissions were packed with Communist supporters, and ballot boxes were seized by the secret police to prevent recounting. The official results, disputed by Mikolajczyk, claimed a Communist victory, with only thirty-two percent "no" votes.

Despite Stalin's promise at Yalta that elections would be held in Poland "in about one month," the elections were delayed for almost two years, until January, 1947. Perhaps Stalin's promise was completely insincere, or perhaps the poor showing of the Communists in the Austrian and Hungarian elections of 1945 contributed to his decision to postpone the Polish vote. In any case, the two years were well used by the Communists to make sure that the elections, when finally held, would produce the desired results. The campaign for the parliamentary elections of January 19, 1947, was a repeat performance of the referendum campaign, except that it was more intense and perfected. The Communists and their allies put up a single bloc of candidates, but two minor parties were created and allowed to put up additional candidates in order to confuse the voters. Decrees were enacted that made it difficult for candidates of the Peasant Party to qualify, and "anti-fascist" measures were employed to bar many people from taking part in political activities. Thousands of Peasant Party members were arrested, including 142 of its candidates. Agitation units in the army aided the Communist cause by spreading propaganda, organizing meetings, and using intimidation and force.[30] Electoral districts were gerrymandered, Peasant Party lists were disqualified, and "voluntary open voting" was imposed in many districts. The vote tallying process was also irregular. Peasant Party representatives were barred from witnessing the tallying, and ballots were confiscated. The official results gave the Peasant Party only ten percent of

[29] Mikolajczyk claimed at the end of June, 1946, that 1,200 members of his party were under arrest. For his account of the referendum and elections, see his *The Rape of Poland*, New York, 1948, pp. 161–202.

[30] At a symposium in 1958, General Ignacy Blum reported that following the November, 1946, order commanding active participation of the Army in the election campaign, 2,614 "Protection-Propaganda Brigades" composed of 56,510 officers and soldiers were dispatched to political work. He also admitted to the use of force: "The conditions in which the soldiers worked .. in many cases were the cause of various sectarian deviations, even including administrative pressure on the civilian population." "Udzial Wojska Polskiego w obronie narodowych i spolecznych interesow ludu polskiego oraz w umacnianiu wladzy ludowej w latach 1945–1948," in *Sesja naukowa poswiecona wojnie wyzwolenczej narodu Polskiego 1939–1945*, Warsaw, 1959, p. 251.

the parliamentary seats, while the Communist bloc got eighty percent.[31] The Peasant Party was thus eliminated from participation in the government, and the Communists were thenceforth "legally" in full control.

The Achievement of Community Party Hegemony

In their drive for power, the Communists destroyed the multiparty system of Poland and established their own hegemony. As their strength grew, thanks to Soviet support, the Communists became increasingly belligerent in their tactics towards the other parties. Initially the Communists tried to take advantage of the differences of opinion in the London Government, hoping to split it by distinguishing between its "progressive" forces (the Peasant and Socialist Parties) and "reactionary" forces (the National Democrats and Pilsudskiites). The Communists tried to persuade the leaders of the "progressive" parties to abandon the London Government's underground institutions and to join the Communists in a left-of-center coalition.[32] These attempts to create a coalition "from the top" failed because the Communists were somewhat pretentious in their claims and set conditions for co-operation befitting a much stronger force, while the leaders of the Peasant and Socialist Parties suspected Communist motives.[33]

Even while they were approaching the leaders of the "progressive" parties, and attempting to achieve a coalition "from the top," the Communists were already trying to create a coalition "from the bottom." This was an effort to split each of the "progressive" parties by appealing to

[31] Mikolajczyk, *op. cit.*, pp. 180–202; Arthur Bliss Lane, *I Saw Poland Betrayed*, Indianapolis, 1946, pp. 240–245, 276–288. Lane was the US Ambassador to Warsaw at that time. See the US note citing specific violations of pledges in *Department of State Bulletin*, XVI, No. 394, January 19, 1947. Maria Turlejska, in *Zapis pierwszej dekady 1945–1954*, Warsaw, 1972, admits that police measures were used against the Polish Peasant Party and that the results of the 1947 elections were falsified.

[32] For a review of Communist overtures to the underground Peasant Party, based upon correspondence with Peasant Party leaders, see Andrzej Korbonski, *op. cit.*, pp. 55–66.

[33] The negotiations between the Communist and non-Communist undergrounds merit investigation. An agreement between them could have significantly altered the course of Polish politics. The underground that was loyal to London would undoubtedly have been split, but given the divisions within the Communist movement, it is not impossible that it too would have been split, or the relative strength of the two factions altered. Success in establishing a broad left-center coalition before the entry of Soviet forces into Poland would have strengthened the position of the "natives" *vis-à-vis* the "Muscovites." For an interesting account of the negotiations, see M. Turlejska, *O wojnie i podziemiu*, Warsaw, 1959, pp. 106–136.

disaffected elements among their local leaders and members. Within both the Peasant and Socialist Parties there were differences of opinion concerning co-operation with the Communists, which the Communists attempted to exploit. The clandestine nature of underground activity during the war—based as it was on personal contacts, co-optation, and imperfect communication—facilitated factional attempts to gain control of a party. For instance, left-wing elements in both the Socialist and Peasant Parties in early 1944 called party congresses at which, while claiming to speak for a majority of members, they condemned the policies of the party leaders and altered the composition of the executive committees in favor of the leftists.

The Socialist Party, which was already divided over a variety of issues, was particularly vulnerable to such tactics. It was split between a right wing and a left wing, and the left wing in turn was split between a minority which supported co-operation with the Communists and a majority which did not. Through various intraparty maneuvers and with help from the Communists, the "united front" minority succeeded in seizing control of the Socialist Party and bringing it into the Communist coalition.[34]

In the case of the Peasant Party, factionalism was induced artificially by people who had led a short-lived Communist-sponsored peasant party in the 1920's. In February, 1944, aided by a handful of the Peasant Party's radical members, they convened a congress at which the Party's leaders were condemned and a new executive committee was elected. This group eventually became known as *Wola Luda* (People's Will). In May, 1944, the Communists called upon their local members to help the People's Will take over the Peasant Party's organizations throughout the country.[35] The mainstream of the Peasant Party continued, however, to adhere to the London orientation.

The most open and violent struggle of the Communists against the political opposition began after the formation of the Provisional Government of National Unity in June, 1945. By this time, most of the anti-Communists were centered around Mikolajczyk and his Polish Peasant Party, and it was this party which therefore bore the brunt of the Communist

---

[34] Antoni Przygonski, "Polityka i dzialalnosc lewicy socjalistycznej w latach 1939–1944," in Gora and Golebiowski, *op. cit.*, pp. 155–185; Antoni Reiss, *Z problemow odbudowy i rozwoju organizacyjnego PPS, 1944–46*, Warsaw, 1971. The loss of its foremost leaders contributed significantly to the disorganization of the Polish Socialist Party. M. Niedzialkowski and S. Dubois were executed by the Gestapo; H. Ehrlich and W. Alter were executed in the Soviet Union in 1943.

[35] Andrzej Korbonski, *op. cit.*, p. 61. The Polish Workers' Party also helped distribute the literature of the left-wing socialists. Przygonski, *op. cit.*, p. 183.

offensive. In order to deal effectively with the opposition, the Communists first had to control their own agrarian and socialist collaborators, and especially had to prevent these groups from reaching an understanding with Mikolajczyk's forces. The Peasant Party-People's Will, which had been given four posts in the Lublin Committee, first experienced Communist disciplinary methods when differences emerged between it and the Communists over land reform policies and relations with the London group. Its leader, the Minister of Agriculture, Andzej Witos, was forced to resign from the Lublin Committee, and the Party was induced to dismiss him, the chairman of its executive committee, and many other Party officials. In the spring of 1945, several officials of People's Will were arrested. People's Will was subjected to another purge later in 1945, after some of its leaders negotiated a merger with Mikolajczyk's Peasant Party. Communist sympathizers within People's Will forced the Party to disavow the contracting leaders and the merger. The dissidents and their followers joined Mikolajczyk's party, which now for clarity called itself the Polish Peasant Party. The Peasant Party-People's Will, although seriously weakened in the process and reduced to an obviously bogus organization, was henceforth a compliant partner in the Communist coalition.[36]

Independent stirrings within the Socialist Party were similarly restricted, though not entirely quelled. Socialist politics during 1945 and 1946 were marked by a confrontation between the Party's two major orientations. The left wing favored close co-operation with the Communists and supported their policies, while the right wing preferred a much more independent role for the Party. Fearing that the right wing would gain dominance and attempt to reach an agreement with Mikolajczyk, the Communists lent their assistance to the left wing. As in the People's Will, recalcitrant elements were gradually eased out of leadership positions.[37]

The Socialist Party and the Peasant Party-People's Will had an important role to play in the Communist political scheme. They served to broaden support for the new regime and to isolate its opposition. Their presence gave the Communist-dominated government, people's councils, electoral bloc, and other institutions an appearance of being genuine coalitions and helped to secure support from persons who would not have supported the

---

[36] Andrzej Korbonski, *op. cit.*, pp. 102–103, 111–112.

[37] Bronislaw Syzdek, "Powstanie odrodzonej PPS i jej dzialalnosc w pierwszych latach Polski Ludowej," in Gora and Golebiowski, *op. cit.*, pp. 378–392. Zygmunt Zaremba provides an account of the underground Polish Socialist Party immediately after the war, including his meeting with the future Prime Minister, Jozef Cyrankiewicz, in *Wojna i konspiracja*, London, 1957, pp. 298–336.

Communists alone. The willingness of these parties to co-operate with the Communists seemed to justify Communist claims that Mikolajczyk's Polish Peasant Party was sectarian and unco-operative at a period when national recovery required unity. People's Will could, in addition, create confusion among the peasantry and divert support from Mikolajczyk's Polish Peasant Party. People's Will was also used to reduce the Polish Peasant Party's strength in the government and in the National Council for the Homeland. The agreement establishing the Provisional Government of National Unity had specified that one-third of the positions in the government would be assigned to the Peasant Party. With the split of the peasant movement into two parties, this allocation was divided between them, thus further reducing the already limited access of the opposition to the levers of power.

Having isolated the Polish Peasant Party, the Communists launched an all-out campaign to eliminate it as an independent force. The Party's cadres were reduced through assassinations, arrests of Party leaders, dismissal of local government officials belonging to the Party, and harassment of Party adherents. The Party's ability to communicate with its supporters was diminished through such tactics as the packing and disruption of meetings, with police agents shouting down the speakers. Access to radio broadcasting was denied to the Party, while its newspapers were censored and their circulation restricted. Party offices were raided, and local Party branches were closed. The terror against the Polish Peasant Party increased through-out 1946 and became particularly intense just prior to the parliamentary elections of January, 1947.[38] (The tactics used in the election campaign have been described earlier.)

The electoral defeat of the Polish Peasant Party had a doubly debilitating effect. It not only removed the Party from positions of power, but created a crisis of confidence within the Party and facilitated its fractionalization. Within months of the elections, those favoring accommodation with the Communists broke with the Party and established a separate group, the Polish Peasant Party-Left. When, in the face of increasing pressures and imminent arrest, three of the top Party leaders, including Mikolajczyk, escaped abroad, the way was open for the Left to take over the Party which it had deserted. Shortly thereafter a merger was negotiated with the Communist-sponsored People's Will Peasant Party. The merger permitted the explusion of unreliable leaders within both parties, many of whom were subsequently arrested for alleged espionage, economic sabotage, and collaboration with the Germans.

---

[38] Mikolajczyk, *op. cit.*, pp. 145–179; Stefan Korbonski, *Fighting Warsaw*, London, 1956, pp. 240–269.

This completed the subordination of the peasant movement and signalized the establishment of Communist hegemony in Polish politics.

The Defeat of Armed Resistance

At the time the Communists began their drive to power, Poland was under German occupation and various resistance movements were operating throughout the country. Until the latter part of the war, when the Red Army and its Polish detachments entered Poland, the bulk of Polish military forces and supplies were in non-Communist hands. The largest resistance unit was the Home Army, the official heir of the prewar Polish Army, loyal to the London Government and directed from Warsaw. Its strength in mid-1944 was about 250,000 persons. The next largest group, the Peasant Battalions, was subordinate to the Home Army but operated somewhat autonomously and had 158,000 troops. The Nationalist Armed Forces numbered about 72,000 men. The Communist resistance movement, the People's Guard, later called the People's Army, was the smallest of the groups, commanding only about 40,000 persons or 5 percent of the resistance forces.[39] Since 95 percent of the resistance troops were non-Communist, they posed a real threat to Communist plans to take power, and the potential for civil war was great. The leaders of the resistance movements were well aware that their forces could play an important role in shaping postwar political arrangements, and each group jockeyed to improve its position. For instance, both the Home Army and the People's Army sought to attract the Peasant Battalions to their side.

With the arrival of Soviet troops in Poland, the Communists' small resistance force was augmented by the "Berling Army." This army, known by the name of its commander, General Zygmunt Berling, was first formed in the Soviet Union in April, 1943, as the Kosciuszko Division of the Red Army. In January, 1944, it was enlarged to become the First Corps of the Polish Armed Forces in the USSR, and in March it was transformed into the First Polish Army. Upon entering Polish territory, it was put under the formal authority of the National Council for the Homeland, and the People's Army was merged with it, the combined unit being named the Polish Army. At the same time, in July, 1944, all armed clandestine organizations on liberated territories were ordered dissolved and their members

---

[39] *Polskie Siły Zbrojne—Armia Krajowa*, London, 1950, Vol. III, p. 119; *Materiały zrodlowe do historii polskiego ruchu ludowego*, Warsaw, 1966, Vol. LV, p. 484; *Podzial administracyjny i terenowy ZJ i NSZ*, *Zeszyty do Historii Narodowych Sil Zbrojnych*, Chicago, 1961 (No. 1), p. 30; Tadeusz Bor-Komorowski, *The Secret Army*, London, 1951, pp. 196–197.

were urged to join the Polish Army. The Polish Army operated in conjunction with the Soviet Army, and a majority of its officers were Soviet citizens. It played a major role in fighting the anti-Communist resistance.[40]

Since it was the strongest of the resistance groups and was formally linked with the London Government-in-Exile, the Home Army bore the brunt of the Communist attacks. During the Home Army's official existence, that is until July, 1945, the Communists sought to undermine it in various ways. They conducted a propaganda campaign against it, accusing it of passivity in the struggle against the Germans and of concentrating its actions against Soviet partisans who operated behind German lines. These accusations were broadcast from the Soviet Union into Poland in an attempt to diminish the Home Army's support among the population. The charges were also repeatedly made by the Soviet Union to the Anglo-American Allies in the hope of severing their support for the Home Army. The 1944 offensive against the Germans, when the Home Army emerged above ground, provided the Communists and their Soviet allies an opportunity to deal the Home Army a serious blow. Units of the Home Army participated in the offensive, and in the process co-operated with and made themselves known to the commanders of Soviet units. They had in fact been ordered to do so as part of the Home Army's "Operation Tempest" (an action designed to harass German communication lines and incite armed uprisings). Shortly after the conclusion of each operation, however, the Soviet Army forced the Home Army units to dissolve. They were offered the alternative of either disarming and disbanding or being integrated into the Berling Army with complete loss of autonomy. In some cases the leaders of these units, under the pretext of an invitation to confer with the Soviets about future operations, were arrested and deported or executed. As a result, thousands of officers of the Home Army found themselves in prisons freshly vacated by the Germans. In the light of these experiences, the Home Army Command in October, 1944, ordered its "Operation Tempest" discontinued. The Lublin regime required that all groups abandon their allegiance to the London Government and recognize the Lublin Committee as the sole legal government. Thus the Home Army was again driven underground.[41]

---

[40] The importance of the Berling Army as a recruitment and training ground for political leaders has diminished with the passage of time, but not disappeared. At least 11 out of 115 full members and 8 out of 93 syndidate members of the Central Committee of the Polish United Workers' Party elected in 1971 previously served in the Berling Army.

[41] Bor-Komorowski, *op. cit.*, pp. 196–197; Dziewanwoski, *op. cit.*, pp. 174–176.

The Warsaw Uprising also contributed decisively to the weakening of the Home Army. Begun on August 1, 1944, under the leadership of the Home Army, the uprising lasted sixty-three days. It was a struggle for survival in which every man, woman, and child took part. At the end, almost 200,000 inhabitants were dead and the city lay in ruins. About 18,000 to 20,000 members of the Home Army lost their lives, and another 16,000 were taken prisoner by the Germans. The uprising, its purpose and wisdom, still evokes bitter and partisan disputes, and many questions about it remain unanswered. There is evidence to suggest that the uprising was undertaken in order to re-establish the London Government in the capital prior to the entrance of Soviet forces and the Lublin Committee. Did the Home Army leaders seriously miscalculate the military situation, or did the Soviet Army deliberately sit on the other side of the Vistula and wait for the non-Communist Poles to be slaughtered? On July 24 and 25, Radio Moscow and Radio Kosciuszko had broadcast appeals for an uprising in Warsaw in support of the Soviet forces, yet when the uprising occurred no help was forthcoming from the Red Army. Units of the Communist underground in Warsaw did participate in the uprising, and General Berling independently directed a division of his Polish Army to head for Warsaw, an act for which he was apparently relieved of his post. As in the similar case of the uprising in Slovakia, which occurred at about the same time, no direct aid was received from the Soviet Army. Furthermore, Stalin refused to grant Churchill's request that British and American planes dropping supplies to the beleaguered city be permitted to land behind Soviet lines for refueling. Aiding the Warsaw Uprising would not have been to the Soviet Union's advantage, for a Warsaw victory would have undermined the "friendly" Lublin Committee. As great as were the physical losses of the uprising to the non-Communist resistance, the psychological blow was equally severe. It created a feeling of despair and diminished the will to fight.[42] The Home Army was officially dissolved in July, 1945, with the creation of the Provisional Government of National Unity; however, an armed underground of considerable proportions continued to operate.

The Communist campaign against the underground forces began in earnest in the fall of 1945. Although supposedly 44,000 persons had taken

---

[42] For a recent evaluation of the impact of the Warsaw Uprising and an examination of the continuing controversies and disagreements concerning the event, see Andrzej Korbonski, "The Warsaw Uprising Revised," *Survey*, Summer, 1970, pp. 82–98. Adam Bromke, in *Poland's Politics: Idealism vs. Realism, op. cit.*, argues that the uprising marked a turning point in Polish political culture from romanticism and idealism to prudence and realism.

advantage of the amnesty announced on August 2, 1945, it is estimated that in the fall of 1945 there were still about 32,000 to 35,000 people actively engaged in underground units, of whom 6,000 to 8,000 were members of the Ukrainian Independence Army.[43] The hard core of the Home Army transformed itself into a group called "Freedom and Independence," while other groups such as the National Armed Forces and the National Military Organization retained their old identities. Initially they were grouped in units as large as 600 to 800 persons, equipped with machine guns, light field artillery, mortars, and transport vehicles. Smaller units of twenty to thirty persons also existed, and from mid-1946 most groups operated in units of this size. Aided by considerable popular support, these armed detachments acted to protect persons who had been associated with the resistance, to retaliate for specific acts of violence, and to disrupt Communist authority.[44] The underground particularly attacked activists of the Polish Workers' Party, officials of the Communist administrative and land reform agencies, policemen, security officers, and Soviet agents. In some regions the resistance forces were so powerful that the Communist Party itself had to go underground, lest its members be assassinated.

The intensity and ferocity of the civil war varied according to region and time. The largest conflict occurred in the eastern provinces of Lublin, Bialystok, and Rzeszow, and in the eastern part of the Warsaw province, while the western territories experienced almost no fighting. The warfare was most intense between November, 1945, and July, 1946, that is, in the period preceding the referendum. According to figures published by the Historical Section of the Central Committee of the Polish Workers' Party, 7,963 civilian supporters of the new regime were killed by the underground, while 2,400 members of the army and the police died in the same way. The majority of the civilians killed were functionaries of the People's Militia and the organs of public security (4,028 persons, or more than 50 percent), while about half of the civilians killed were members of the Polish Workers' Party (3,945, including 245 full-time apparatchiks). The vast

---

[43] Blum, *op. cit.*, p. 242. The Ukrainian resistance was separate from that of the Polish and lasted for some time longer. It appears that the majority of losses among Polish and Soviet Army personnel were incurred in actions against the Ukrainian organization. See *Polegli w walce o wladce ludowa*, Warsaw, 1970.

[44] According to an official Polish Communist history, "The people's government was opposed not only by individuals, but also by the organized forces of the reaction, enjoying the support of a considerable portion of the population, and having at their disposal armed detachments whose numbers ranged to several tens of thousands." *Polegli w walce o wladze ludowa*, p. 24. This book was prepared by the Historical Section of the Central Committee of the Polish Workers' Party.

majority of the underground's victims, some 75 percent, died in 1945–1946.[45]

By 1948, the anti-Communist underground had been virtually wiped out. It is estimated that 7,500 underground fighters were killed and 2,000 were wounded between June, 1945, and April, 1948.[46] Additional thousands were taken prisoner and their civilian supporters arrested. The armed struggle had required the commitment of a large portion of the new regime's resources. A special Internal Security Corps had to be created because the regular security organs and the People's Militia did not have enough strength to deal with the underground. Five infantry divisions of the Army, almost half of the Army's personnel, also had to be detailed to this task.[47] Thus it appears obvious that, although a Communist victory in Poland had been assured from the start, it was nonetheless a costly operation. Except for Yugoslavia, no other country taken over by the Communists experienced armed resistance as great as in Poland. The bitterness and cleavages generated by this conflict survived long after the fighting had ended, and even to this day they color the interpretation of this period of Poland's history.

Control of Local Government

While establishing their mastery over the central apparatus of the state, the Communists also had to extend their authority over the regions and localities. Local government came under their control through the establishment of local soviets. Before the war, regional and local government was dual in nature, consisting of centrally appointed administrators and local self-government bodies. These local institutions were not abolished immediately by the Communists, but their functioning was placed under the control of a new institution which the Communists created, the people's councils (*rady narodowe*). These councils, patterned after the soviets in

---

[45] *Polegli w walce o wladze ludowa*, pp. 28–29. These figures are the result of the Historical Section's attempt to verify all casualties attributed to the struggle to establish Communist power. This volume contains not only tabulated data, but also a listing of the verified casualties by name, with place and date of birth, occupation, party membership, and the perpetrator of the death. No figures or no Party membership information was available for 3,318 persons, and many of them may have been Communist Party members. The Peasant Party lost 191 men and the Socialist Party lost 1,972.

[46] Blum, *op. cit.*, p. 260.

[47] *Ibid.* p. 263.

Russia, were first established in February, 1944, in Lublin and Warsaw, but they were not formed on a nation-wide scale until September, 1944.

Like their national counterpart, the local people's councils were supposed to be representative coalitions of various organizations. In fact, however, their membership was carefully co-opted by the Communists. They were composed not of elected representatives, but of delegates appointed by various political and social organizations. Both the organizations which could send delegates to the councils and the persons who could represent these organizations on the councils were restricted by the organic statute. "Clearly the purpose was to bring into the people's councils, which had been assigned an important role in building the framework of the new system, such persons who decidedly supported the building of such a system—and only such persons, excluding the internal enemies of People's Poland."[48] The people's councils were given the right to control the activities not only of the state administrators and self-government bodies, but also of all other institutions and organizations operating locally. The councils played an important role in the struggle for power, for they determined which organizations would be allowed to function locally and which persons could lead them. They also exerted an influence on the administrative decisions affecting localities and individuals, decisions through which support could be bought or opposition punished.[49]

The western territories, which Poland acquired from Germany as compensation for the losses to the Soviet Union in the east, were also used by the Communists to consolidate their power. At the end of 1945, a separate Ministry of Recovered Territories was created and placed in the care of Gomulka. The departure of most of the German population from this agriculturally rich and industrially developed area and its subsequent resettlement by Polish refugees from the east provided the Communists with many opportunities for patronage. Special agricultural brigades of the army were detailed to operate agricultural estates, and 200,400 soldiers of the Berling Army and their families were settled on farms in this area.[50] The western territories became a special domain of the Communists, a state within a state. It was here that collective farms were first introduced in Poland.

---

[48] Maurycy Jaronszynski, *Zagadnienia rad narodowych*, Warsaw, 1961, p. 19.

[49] Susanne S. Lotarski, "Political Culture of Local Politics in Poland," Unpublished Ph. D. Dissertation, Columbia University, 1973.

[50] Blum, *op. cit.*, p. 262. The Deputy Inspector responsible for military resettlement in this area was Piotr Jaroszewicz, who had been a political instructor in the Berling Army, and who, since December, 1970, has been the Prime Minister of Poland.

Economic Reforms

As in other East European countries, the process of obtaining power in Poland was linked to a series of popularly supported reform programs. Of the two sets of economic reforms—agrarian reform and the nationalization of industry, banking, and commerce—land reform was the more important in the takeover stage, while the industrial reforms played a more important role in the consolidation of Communist power. Both reforms not only destroyed the economic strength of the conservative forces, but also undermined the moderate liberal parties, depriving them of issues by which they could maintain their identities and compete for influence.

Land reform, which was accepted by all but the most conservative parties, became one of the focal points in the struggle for power. Since the substance of the Communists' land reform program differed little from that of other parties, the main question was who would actually direct the reform and derive the political benefits. The Communists were determined that land reform would be carried out by them, and according to their timetable and their guidelines, so as to gain maximum support for their cause.

The land reform was distinguished by extreme haste. Decrees establishing reform institutions and procedures were promulgated within days of the creation of the Lublin Committee. In the territories east of the Vistula, Communist plans called for the division of estates and the granting of property titles to new owners by early December, 1944, that is, even before the Lublin Committee transformed itself into the Provisional Government. In areas where German forces were expelled in early 1945, land reform was scheduled to take place before the spring sowing. Land reform in Poland was, in fact, near completion when initial reform decrees were just being enacted in neighboring countries.

Political considerations determined confiscation and distribution policies. The Catholic Church, a strong political force in Poland, was allowed to retain its estates. Poland was also the only country in Eastern Europe where middle peasants (owners of five to twenty hectares, some thirty-five percent of all landowners) were entitled in principle to receive land. Given the shortage of distributable land and their desire to maximize the number of beneficiaries, the Communists chose to allocate small parcels of land (two to three hectares) to a large number of people, even though it meant creation of many farms that were too small to be economically viable.[51]

---

[51] Henryk Slabek, *Polityka agrarna PPR*, Warsaw, 1967, p. 205. For an evaluation of the land reform, see Andrzej Korbonski, *The Politics of Socialist Agriculture, op. cit.*, pp. 68, 72, 89–98.

The methods of implementing the reform were adjusted when necessary to assure the achievement of Communist goals. The original conception of a carefully administered reform was abandoned in favor of a more revolutionary approach which circumvented established procedures and lines of command.[52] Workers' and soldiers' brigades were organized and sent into each county to mobilize the peasantry and carry out the land distribution.[53] The Polish Army, on orders from the land reform commissioners, carried out propaganda campaigns against opponents of the Lublin Committee, explained provisions of the land reform, organized elections to communal committees, surveyed land, and intervened with unco-operative authorities.[54] Adherence to Party guidelines was considered so important that even the Party's own agents were rebuked and punished for deviations from specific provisions.[55]

The land reform brought considerable benefits to the Communists. Through it the Communists managed to gain, if not the support, at least the neutralization of the peasantry, who constituted over half of the population. At the same time, the Communists were able to complete the destruction of the influential, anti-Communist landowning class. More important, however, the success of the land reform undermined the only effective opposition group, the Peasant Party, and laid the groundwork for its eventual destruction. Coincidentally, the land reform diverted attention from the Warsaw Uprising, increased the Lublin Committee's prestige abroad, and reduced its reliance on the Red Army.

---

[52] During September, 1944, less than forty percent of the estates were taken under state control, and no land was distributed. On October 9, Gomulka told the Party that it would be able to conduct the land reform only if it mobilized its entire strength and the reform assumed the character of a social revolution. Slabek, *op. cit.*, pp. 119, 124.

[53] About 1,500 persons participated in the workers' brigades in 1944, over 60 percent of them drawn from the Polish Workers Party. The army, in addition, assigned about 6,000 officers and soldiers to similar brigades. In 1945 such brigades were organized in much larger numbers. About two-thirds of the brigades operated in Lublin province, the birthplace of the new regime. These brigades provided the motive force for the redistribution of land. They assisted the special commissioners in removing estate owners and administrators, organized village meetings, helped establish communal committees for land confiscation and land distribution, compiled lists of peasants entitled to receive land, and helped to divide the land. Communal committees appeared and land was distributed in direct relationship to the presence of these brigades. Slabek, *op. cit.*, pp. 20, 225–227, 235–236; *Sesja naukowa poswiecona wojnie wyzwolenczej narodu Polskiego 1939–1945*, Warsaw, 1959, p. 272.

[54] Slabek, *op. cit.*, pp. 226–227.

[55] *Ibid.*, pp. 233, 270.

Nationalization of industry and banking encountered little opposition, especially since Gomulka, the Secretary of the Party, and Hilary Minc, the Minister of Industry and Commerce, said that the new regime would follow a specific Polish way to socialism, in which state, co-operative, and private sectors could co-exist. Even before the war many of the country's largest industries and most of the banks had been state- or foreign-owned. During the war most enterprises came under German control, and their owners in many cases were deported or executed. Except for some of the extreme conservative groups, there was a general consensus that key branches of the national economy should be directed by the state. The only points of controversy between the Communist and non-Communist parties, therefore, were the scope of nationalization and the question of compensation.

The arrival of Soviet troops and of the Lublin Committee in Poland was followed by a hasty and sometimes violent confiscation by the state of all large and medium-sized industrial, banking, and foreign trade enterprises. This confiscation was carried out by "operational groups," which were charged with "taking over the factories into the hands of the democratic state and creating a new system of economic management."[56] The formal Nationalization Decree, adopted on January 3, 1946, nationalized all industrial establishments capable of employing more than fifty workers per shift. By the end of 1946, 91.2 percent of industrial production was being produced by the socialist sector. Nationalization of industry and banking contributed greatly to the consolidation of Communist power, giving the new regime control over both resources and jobs. At the same time, it enabled the Communists to take credit for industrial reconstruction and to win support from workers and technicians. Nationalization, which was carried out with considerable help from the Socialist Party and its trade unions, also strengthened the Communists' argument for a merger of the two workers' movements.

Many of the problems which the Polish United Workers' Party has encountered in governing Poland can be traced to the conditions under which it gained control of the country. The Party commanded the support of only a small minority of the population, and came to power only after a fierce and bloody struggle.[57] The bitter resistance to the Communist

---

[56] Janusz Golebiowski, "Walka obozu demokratycznego o przejecie i nacjonalizacje przemyslu," in Gora and Golebiowski, *op. cit.*, p. 270.

[57] In 1956 Gomulka himself admitted that in the immediate postwar years the Polish Workers' Party had not commanded the support of the nation. *Przemowienia 1946–47*, Warsaw, 1958, pp. 197–198.

regime was essentially nationalist rather than anti-socialist in nature. The Communists, however, were not immediately able to benefit from the reforms which they introduced. Having triumphed with Soviet assistance, they thereby forfeited the freedom to deal with national and Party problems in ways that could have bridged the gap between Party and society. The "Polish road to socialism" promised by Gomulka was abandoned, and Poland, like other states in Eastern Europe, was subjected to a collectivization drive and to "Stalinist methods of governing," as they are euphemistically referred to today. The Party itself was caught up in a series of purges and became a victim of its own system. Even after 1956, when a considerable measure of accommodation was achieved between the people and the Communist government, problems dating to the period of the takeover persisted. The agricultural economy, for instance, continued to be plagued by dwarf, uneconomical farms, many of which had been created during the land reform, when the Communists were more concerned with winning support than with creating strong family farms. Thus the Polish case demonstrates that the way in which power is attained has ineluctable consequences for the subsequent exercise of that power, even in a Communist dictatorship.[58]

---

[58] For an interesting analysis of the problems faced by the new political order in the postwar period, see Jan Szczepanski, *Polish Society*, New York, 1970, pp. 34–42.

The Partition of Germany and the Neutralization of Austria

Hans W. Schoenberg

In addition to examining the Soviet creation of present-day East Germany, this study will briefly recount the fate of Austria and the former German provinces east of the Oder-Neisse Line following World War II. In doing so, it will seek answers to these questions: Did the takeovers of the German areas differ from the other takeovers in Eastern Europe? In what respect did they resemble them? Did they fit into a general Soviet plan for takeovers in the postwar period? Could the takeover of East Germany have been frustrated? Why was the West able successfully to oppose the Communist takeover of Austria and all of Berlin?[1]

Hitler's invasion of Poland on September 1, 1939, not only precipitated World War II but also opened the door for Stalin to the heart of Europe. At the Potsdam Conference in 1945, Averell Harriman said that Hitler's

[1] For the most pertinent, autobiographical account of the takeover of East Germany, see Wolfgang Leonhard, *Die Revolution entlässt ihre Kinder*, Berlin, 1955 (in English, *Child of the Revolution*, London, 1963). Quotations cited are from the German edition. Among numerous books on the conferences of the Allies, see Herbert Feis's two comprehensive works *Churchill, Roosevelt, Stalin: The War They Waged and the Peace They Sought*, Princeton, 1957, which deals with the Yalta Conference, and *Between War and Peace: The Potsdam Conference*, Princeton, 1960. For more specialized treatment of the diplomatic preparations leading to the Communist takeover of Germany's eastern provinces, see Wolfgang Wagner, *Die Entstehung der Oder-Neisse Linie in den diplomatischen Verhandlungen während des Zweiten Weltkrieges*, Stuttgart, 1953 (3rd ed., 1964) (in English, *The Genesis of the Oder-Neisse Line—A Study in the Diplomatic Negotiations during World War II*, Stuttgart, 1967). See also, by the same author, *Die Teilung Europas—Geschichte der sowjetischen Expansion: 1918–1945*, Stuttgart, 1959, a valuable survey of Soviet political activities in Europe through the close of World War II. On population expulsions as a means to facilitate the takeovers of the German areas and on the internal and international political tensions to which these gave rise, see Hans W. Schoenberg, "Germans from the East: A Study of Their Migrations, Resettlement, and Subsequent Group History, 1945 to 1961," Ph.D. dissertation, School of Advanced International Studies, The Johns Hopkins University, Washington, D.C., 1968 (published with additions, in particular on West Germany's *Ostpolitik* through 1968, as *Germans from the East: A Study of Their Migration, Resettlement, and Subsequent Group History since 1945*, The Hague, 1970). Quotations cited are from the latter.

Other useful studies of the events in East Germany include: Walther Hubatsch, *Die Deutsche Frage*, Würzburg, 1961; Arthur M. Hanhardt, Jr., *The German Democratic Republic*, Baltimore, 1968; and Norbert Mattedi, *Gründung und Entwicklung der Parteien in der Sowjetischen Besatzungszone Deutschlands, 1945–1949*,

greatest crime was leaving Europe prostrate.[2] In retrospect, of course, it is easy enough to see a direct historical line proceeding from the Hitler-Stalin non-aggression pact of 1939 (to which was appended a secret treaty dividing Eastern Europe into spheres of influence and partitioning Poland) to the events of the postwar period. The connections are clear: Hitler's subsequent decision to extend his empire eastward, his eventual defeat, the truncation of Germany and consequent division of Europe, and the emergence of a new European political structure resting on an uneasy balance of power between two superstates. A chief distinction of the Communist takeovers of the German areas is, then, that unlike the smaller East European states, Hitler's Germany was itself a major aggressive power. By invading the Soviet Union on June 22, 1941, Hitler provoked the massive Soviet counteroffensive which eventually led to the Communist takeover of Germany's eastern parts. At the same time, the invasion rendered almost automatic the takeovers of the East European states, for in order to push back and defeat Germany the Red Army had to cross their territories, giving the Soviet Union the unique chance to bring them under its control. In the event, the westward extension of Soviet power in the 1940's was slowed down only by particularly courageous or traditionally mature nations such as Finland in the north, some of the Balkan states in the south, and (for reasons to be explored later) Austria in the middle.

Hitler's attack on the Soviet Union came at a time when Moscow had been well-nigh inactive since the early 1920's in its European revolutionary ventures. A ruthless, hypomanic giant, Hitler had convinced himself of the need for German expansion eastward and of the threat of Soviet ambitions. In setting out to crush the Soviet Union, he stirred an equally ruthless but far shrewder giant, Stalin, who had been temporarily resting, to launch an all-out Pan-Slavic campaign that drew the entire Soviet nation into an unprecedented patriotic and imperialist effort. Hitler's invasion of Russia also led the United States, Great Britain, and France, into an alliance

---

Bonn, 1966. For the background to the developments in Austria, see Kurt L. Shell, *The Transformation of Austrian Socialism*, New York, 1962.

For general introductory reading on developments in Weimar Germany, putting Soviet-German relations in historical perspective, the following two works are indispensable: Karl D. Bracher, *Die Auflösung der Weimarer Republik*, Villingen, 1964; and Walter Laqueur, *Russia and Germany: A Century of Conflict*, London, 1965. For Soviet concepts of self-determination, see the excellent study by Boris Meissner, *Sowjetunion und Selbstbestimmungsrecht*, Cologne, 1962. Finally, for a better understanding of events in postwar Germany, see the memoirs of Winston Churchill, Lucius D. Clay, Dwight D. Eisenhower, and Harry S. Truman.

[2] His remarks, made at Potsdam on July 29, 1945, are quoted in Wagner, *op. cit.*, p. 27.

with the Soviet Union that was unnatural both politically and ideologically. The common resolution of the Soviet Union and the three capitalist powers to defeat Nazi Germany—and even, initially, to dismember it—is another aspect of the Communist takeovers of the German areas that is peculiar to them alone.

The catalogue of methods used by the Soviet Union to extend its political power into the middle of Europe is impressive, ranging from the outright annexation of the northern part of East Prussia (without the face-saving exercises used earlier in the Baltic States and in spite of the fact that this province had never been a part of Russia) to the holding of nearly free elections in Berlin and Austria. To the list of methods also belongs the unadorned incorporation into Poland of the former German territories east of the Oder and Neisse rivers (including Pomerania, Silesia, and the southern part of East Prussia) as well as the former free city of Danzig. These territorial rearrangements meant that the area of Germany, as constituted by the treaty of Versailles, was reduced by twenty-three percent.

In support of its expansionist aims, the Soviet Union relied heavily on economic exhaustion, exploiting its role as military victor to carry out extensive dismantling in the remaining German areas. Some of its techniques for gaining control resembled those used elsewhere: the seizure of power took place behind the camouflage of the Soviet military occupation, and Moscow-trained politicians played an important role in the process of sovietization. (Such Soviet-trained leaders were not used to any great extent in Austria.) The most unusual measure taken by the Soviet Union was, however, the mass expulsion of German populations from Eastern Europe, in retaliation for the near success of the Nazi invasion and the extent of the devastation, cruelty, and toll in human lives that had accompanied it.

But while a pro-Soviet Communist government seized and consolidated its power in East Germany, a formal and final peace remained to be achieved. The most important Communist takeover in Europe in terms of the motivations behind it and the size and strategic value of the area under control created a major source of international tension in the postwar period. As the actual and symbolic focus of the Cold War, the continuing division of Germany and Berlin, more than any other Communist incursion, constantly threatened to upset the uncertain, provisory equilibrium of East-West relations. Not until twenty-seven years after Germany's total defeat in 1945 was the takeover of East Germany and the Oder-Neisse provinces recognized *de facto* by West Germany and the three Western Allies. It is this function as a protracted, unresolved international problem that is perhaps the most important aspect of the Communist takeovers of the German areas.

To take a closer look at the historical background, when Soviet-supported revolutionary fervor sparked unrest and revolts in Germany after World War I, Moscow hoped that the outcome would be a powerful block of 200 million Russians and Germans "able to resist any and all imperialist encroachments."[3] As it turned out, this part of the world did not fall to the Communists in 1919, and they had to wait for another chance. Two decades later Hitler's territorial plans for *Lebensraum* in the East far exceeded the ambitions of the German imperial government. In Hitler's scheme the Polish, Czech, and Baltic peoples of Eastern Europe were to be Germanized or dispersed. The indigenous populations of Russia proper, Belorussia, the Ukraine, and Transcaucasia were to be kept at the lowest possible levels of economic and cultural development by German administrators. Except for Finland, the East European states were to remain wholly dependent upon Germany and Italy. It is not altogether surprising, therefore, that the Soviet Union, prompted by almost visceral fear of another German revival, called for the mass uprooting of German populations in Eastern Europe after World War II. These population transfers played an important part in the westward shift of the Polish frontiers and in the absorption of the East German provinces by Poland and the Soviet Union. They also came to impose a special image of revenge and punishment on the postwar treatment of Germany, and for over two decades the resentment they engendered complicated the political scene in Europe. Parallel to the forceful consolidation of the Soviet Union's overlordship in Eastern Europe, an irredentist political faction of refugees grew up in West Germany and exercised both overt and covert influence on the Bonn government.[4]

With the unconditional surrender, Hitler's Germany ceased to exist, *de facto*, and the government of the German people became the responsibility of the four occupying powers: France, Great Britain, the United States, and the Soviet Union. The Potsdam Conference (July 17 to August 2, 1945) provided for "the transfer to Germany of German populations, or elements thereof, remaining in Poland, Czechoslovakia, and Hungary." In keeping with this provision the four powers subsequently agreed on a plan to move the entire German populations of Poland (including Germans in the areas east of the Oder-Neisse Line), Czechoslovakia, and Hungary to the Soviet, American, British, and French zones. Under this plan, some 6,650,000 Germans were to be transferred to the four zones of occupation in 1945 and

---

[3] William H. Chamberlain, *The Russian Revolution 1917–1921*, 2 Vols., 3rd ed., New York, 1954. See Wagner, *Die Teilung Europas*, p. 15.

[4] For a detailed account, see Schoenberg, *op. cit.*, chap. vi and pp. 314 ff.

1946. Eventually, they joined nearly 5,000,000 other Germans who had fled westward from Eastern Europe before the advancing Red Army.

The wholesale transfer of populations was not without precedent, having been practiced in Tsarist Russia as early as the fifteenth century.[5] But as a subterfuge for expansionist policy it was brought to perfection by the Soviet Union in the aftermath of World War II. The circumstances surrounding both the flight of East Germans from the advancing Red Army and the expulsion of German minorities from Eastern Europe were disastrous owing to the speed of the Soviet westward thrust, the lack of evacuation plans, and the absence of any international interest or supervision (see Table 1). All the better was the Soviet Union able to achieve its larger strategic and political aims.[6]

Table 1

Diminution of East and Ethnic German Population
(Excluding Germans from the Soviet Union)

	Reich Germans Oder-Neisse Territories[1]	Sudeten Germans Czechoslovakia	Ethnic Germans East Europe[2]	Total
Germans Present, 1939—1945:				
German Population, May 1939	9,575,200	3,477,000	3,946,300	16,998,500
Plus Natural Growth to End of War	382,000	156,000	108,400	646,400
Subtotal	9,957,200	3,633,000	4,054,700	17,644,900
Less War Casualties[3]	667,500	180,000	252,000	1,099,500
Total German Population at End of War	9,289,700	3,453,000	3,802,700	16,545,400
Germans Accounted for, 1945—1950:				
Number Removed	6,817,000	2,921,400	1,865,000	11,603,400 [4]
Number Retained[5]	1,134,000	258,700	1,324,300	2,717,000
Total Germans Accounted for	7,951,000	3,180,100	3,189,300	14,320,400
Germans not Accounted for, 1945—1950	1,338,700	272,900	613,400	2,225,000

[1] East Prussia, East Pomerania, East Brandenburg, and Silesia.

[2] Baltic Area including Memel, Danzig, Poland, Hungary, Rumania, and Yugoslavia.

[3] Civilians and Armed Forces.

[4] To the Federal Republic (the earlier US, British, and French Zones) and West Berlin 7,900,000 (68 percent); to the Soviet Occupied Zone 3,200,000 (27 percent); to Austria and other Western countries 500,000 (5 percent).

[5] Including POW's and other detained Germans.

SOURCES: Statistisches Bundesamt, *Die deutschen Vertreibungsverluste—Bevölkerungsbilanz für die deutschen Vertreibungsgebiete 1939—1950* (Mainz: Kohlhammer, 1958) in Schoenberg, *op. cit.*, p. 33.

[5] Expulsion, eviction (*vyseleniye*), and transplantation or dispersion (*razdrobleniye*) were used as a political tool in Tsarist Russia. The Tsarist government would move allegedly hostile groups of landowners from territories added to its domain to the interior or to remote borderlands. It would then settle trusted subjects in their stead. The first such compulsory migrations occurred during the reign of Ivan III (1462–1505). The practice was continued under the Romanovs (from 1613) into modern times. The virtual westward physical shift of Poland in 1945 was brought about in exactly the same way.

[6] In all, including ethnic Germans in the Soviet Union, a total of eighteen million East Germans were moved. See Schoenberg, *op. cit.*, chaps. i and iii and Figure 2, chap. iii, p. 37.

Initially, the plans of the Allies called for the actual dismemberment of Germany to destroy the basis of its military and industrial power. Subdivision into three or more states was proposed. But the Western powers could not reach an agreement with the Soviet Union on just how this was to be accomplished. At the Yalta Conference (February 4 to 12, 1945) the Allies had discussed the removal of German minorities from Eastern Europe and come to an understanding on the delimitation of zones of occupation in Germany. In a declaration called "Instruments on the Initial Occupation and Control of Germany" published in Berlin on June 5, 1945, the four zones of occupation and the area to be placed under Polish administration were delineated within Germany's 1937 boundaries. The four powers also stated that their governments would "hereafter determine the boundaries of Germany or of any area at present being part of Germany."[7] Though located in the Soviet zone, Berlin was to be occupied by all four powers and governed by a special inter-Allied authority under an Allied Control Council.

Notwithstanding these formal arrangements, the Soviet Union had been at work at least since the beginning of its last major offensive in January, 1945, to confront the Western powers with a *fait accompli*: a completed territorial and population change in Poland and East Germany. By the time of the Yalta Conference, the Polish Provisional Government (Communist) had already begun to prepare for the administration of the Oder-Neisse lands, which it looked upon as "recovered Western [Polish] territories," as did the Soviet Union. On March 14, 1945, the Soviet leadership officially transferred administrative control of these territories to Poland. Contrary to previous understandings, Stalin had in fact created a fifth zone of occupation. In addition, he annexed the northern half of East Prussia (including Königsberg) to the Soviet Union. At the Potsdam Conference four months later Truman and Churchill (succeeded by Attlee) protested these unilateral actions in vain. Despite the fact that millions of Germans (those who had been unable to flee or who had been overtaken by the Red Army) were still under the control of the Soviet and Polish governments, Stalin argued that while on paper the Oder-Neisse lands constituted German territory, "for all practical purposes they were actually Polish... since there was no German population [left]."[8] Nothing short of joint United States and British military action could have changed this situation.

[7] U.S. Department of State, *A Decade of American Foreign Policy: Basic Documents, 1941–49*, Washington, D.C., 1950, pp. 506–522.

[8] To this Admiral William D. Leahy remarked to President Truman: "Of course not...the Bolshies have killed all of them!" (Harry S. Truman, *Memoirs*, New York, 1955, Vol. I, pp. 368 f.). Cf. Feis, *The Potsdam Conference*, *op. cit.*, pp. 226 f.

The expulsions of Germans from Eastern Europe thus served the interests of the Soviet Union in three interrelated ways. First, they partially accommodated a sense of revenge for the cruelty of the Nazi aggression and to some extent helped to lessen the fear of another German revival. The protective cordon between the Soviet Union and Western Europe was to be free and clear of German habitation and influence. Second, they facilitated the Communist takeover of Germany's eastern provinces and helped to consolidate it by decisively eliminating the justification for an alternative arrangement. Third, they added substantially to the administrative and social burdens of postwar Germany. Given the dislocation of communications, famine, a desperate shortage of housing, an unstable currency, and a rampant black market in the vanquished country, the Soviet Union hoped that the influx of millions of refugees from Eastern Europe would put the finishing touch on conditions for a Communist takeover of all of Germany. Such hopes were exaggerated. A Communist regime was only slowly, if inevitably, set up in the Soviet-occupied zone, and West Germany remained steadfastly independent of it.

In contrast to the heavy-handed treatment of the Oder-Neisse territories, the subsequent takeover of East (central) Germany[9] was an imaginative exercise in Communist tactics, reflecting a high degree of flexibility and patient determination. Basically, the steps taken were the same as elsewhere in Eastern Europe. A Soviet-trained group of exiles returned to East Germany and assumed control of its regional administration, occupying key positions in local government such as chief of police, superintendent of education, director of civil service, etc. These Soviet-trained functionaries closely managed the conduct of public affairs and meticulously guided the organization of political activities.[10] Gradually, but relentlessly, the Communist Party absorbed all rival political groups and under one pretext or another ousted their leaders. The Communists then called for the holding of single-list elections, and ultimately a "People's Democracy" was proclaimed.

Of these steps, the training of German exiles in the Soviet Union merits close attention, as it suggests the scope of Soviet expansionist aims and underlines the explicitness of Soviet subversive tactics. Even before

---

[9] Until changed by the liberal government of Willy Brandt, in 1971, the official West German designation of Communist East Germany was "Soviet Occupied Zone," or "Central Germany," while the German provinces east of the Oder-Neisse Line were referred to as "East Germany."

[10] For details on Soviet training of German Communist functionaries, see Leonhard, *op. cit.*, and Hubatsch, *op. cit.*

World War II, the Soviet Union had taken an inventory of German political émigrés on its territory to determine which of them were reliable Communists. After the dissolution of the German Communist Party in 1933, most German Communists had either gone underground or left the country to avoid arrest. Among others, Walter Ulbricht fled to the Soviet Union by way of Sweden. In the Soviet Union these German Communists were trained to take part in an "invisible government" that would bring them to power in Germany under the guise of democratic procedures. During World War II, the Soviet Union also formed a group of selected prisoners of war, mostly military officers, who were charged with the task of accelerating Germany's defeat. When this group failed to produce the desired results, the Soviet Union concentrated its efforts on priming the civilian exiles for immediate use.

Such treatment differed notably from that given to German exiles in the West during World War II. The Western Allies backed the Polish government in exile in London and also backed General de Gaulle, who had fled to London after the French armistice in 1940, but they almost entirely neglected the German political émigrés who might well have formed the nucleus of a democratic government for all of Germany. Exercising considerably more far-sightedness, if not cunning, the Soviet Union succeeded in creating a circle of highly indoctrinated, thoroughly reliable German agents to assist its scheme for the subjugation of Germany. Unlike the Soviet-trained Poles in the Communist-dominated Lublin government, moreover, the Soviet-trained Germans remained largely in the background and did not as quickly become the subject of an international controversy.

Two groups of German exiles moved west from the Soviet Union during the final phase of World War II, the Ulbricht group and the Ackermann group. The Ulbricht group was singled out for the takeover of the Berlin area. Flown to a location near Berlin on April 30, 1945, the day on which Hitler committed suicide, the Ulbricht group began its work—appropriately enough—on May 1. Its activities were highly systematic. Ulbricht began by rounding up local German Communists, most of whom he had known personally before the war. With his phenomenal memory of people, he was soon able to put together a trustworthy following, bound together not only by its Communist convictions, but also by its experience of Nazi persecution. Simultaneously, control over all the administrative districts of the Berlin area was established. In Berlin itself, for example, some twenty administrative districts were placed under the direction of magistrates who were little more than front men. Respectable, bourgeois citizens, they were chosen because their political orientation faithfully reflected that of the district population. But behind each of them invariably stood a deputy who was a dependable Communist. As already mentioned, other key administrative officials were also Soviet-sponsored Communists, including in particular the heads of police. A classic statement by Ulbricht best describes the technique: "It's got to look democratic, but we must have everything in our control."[11]

The Communists were thus able to bring the Berlin area under their administrative control about a month before the armies of the Western Allies reached it. The central government of the city of Berlin was set up in much the same way, with the appointment of a mayor who was a reputable conservative and of a deputy who was a Moscow-trained Communist. In general, this pattern was followed throughout the Soviet zone of occupation, always with the backing of the Soviet armed forces. Helped by the advice of his associates, Ulbricht would decide on the composition of the administration to be installed in a given area and make his recommendation to the Soviet military commander who had jurisdiction over that area. The officials appointed were allowed to hold office as long as they adhered to the policies of the Soviet military government.

After administrative control had been established, the Communists turned their attention to the direction of political activities. In war-torn urban areas citizens aid committees and anti-fascist groups had sprung up spontaneously. But irrespective of how constructive their work was, they were immediately disbanded if they could be shown to have the least anti-Soviet inclination. It was clear from the outset, therefore, that the Soviet occupation forces were going to do what they could to minimize political opposition. The Soviet zone was the first of the four zones of occupation to permit the organization of political parties and the last to allow elections to take place. The Communist Party was, of course, the first political party to be established. Working hand in hand with the Soviet military administration, Ulbricht knew of the date set for the decree on founding political parties, and he had his entire party program and hierarchy of officials already prepared. A brief recapitulation of the timetable will suffice to illustrate the built-in advantage of the Communists. On June 10, 1945, little over a month after the unconditional surrender, the decree authorizing the formation of political parties was issued by General Zhukov, head of the Soviet military administration. On June 11, the newspapers carried an appeal signed by sixteen German Communists, of whom thirteen were Soviet-trained. On June 12, a constituent assembly met to proclaim the revival of the German Communist Party. The other parties—the

---

[11] See Leonhard, *op. cit.*, pp. 357 f., verbatim: "Es ist doch ganz klar: es muss demokratisch aussehen, aber wir müssen alles in der Hand haben."

Social Democrats, the Christian Democrats, and the Liberal Democrats—were not founded until a month later.

The next phase of the political takeover saw the creation of an anti-fascist "Popular Front" and the subsequent drive towards the formation of the Socialist (Communist) Unity Party. The Communists again seized the initiative. They brought the four political parties in East Germany together in an informal coalition pledged towards rooting out remnants of fascist influence. Under this arrangement, socialism was never mentioned, and no controversial ideological problems were ever discussed. At the inter-party meetings ideas that would be readily acceptable to all political elements in the coalition were welcome. Some examples are: formulating an anti-fascist policy (naturally in those days everyone was anti-fascist); constructing a truly democratic government for Germany, with civil liberties guaranteed for all; and enunciating continuing support for the Soviet military administration.

This last undertaking had special importance inasmuch as certain Communists inside and outside the Ulbricht group had come to espouse the Leninist theory of a country's own road to socialism, which was directly at odds with the policies of the Soviet military administration. What is more, under the direction of the Soviet occupying forces, a number of extremely unpopular measures had already been put into effect. About one-third of the agricultural land in East Germany had been parceled out in small peasant holdings under a far-reaching reform calling for the expropriation without compensation of all large farms and estates. The collection of reparations, for which a total of $10 billion was demanded, had begun. Factories, mining equipment, overhead electricity wires, rolling stock, and sometimes the rails themselves had been—also by way of reparation—dismantled and removed to the Soviet Union. Full-scale socialization of the manufacturing industries was under way. Under these circumstances, support for the Soviet military government was, clearly, of more than nominal importance.

The outcome of the free elections held in Austria in late 1945 flashed a warning to the Soviet administrators in East Germany. The defeat of the Communists was particularly heavy in Vienna, where the Social Democrats won strong backing. Acting quickly, the Communists in East Germany launched a determined drive for the formation of a single, unified party. On April 22, 1946, after four months of campaigning and enforced negotiations, the Communists and the Social Democrats were fused into the Socialist Unity Party (*Sozialistische Einheitspartei Deutschlands* or SED). But despite this last effort to clinch an electoral victory behind the façade of democratic procedures, the first municipal and regional elections held in East Germany did not bring the Communists the results they expected. The SED turned out to be the strongest single party everywhere in East Germany except Berlin, but it barely won fifty percent of the vote in almost all the districts (see Table 2).[12] In Berlin, where the Soviet military government had to compete with the influence of the Western Allies, the SED won close to thirty percent of the vote in the Soviet sector and much less in the Western sectors of the city. A comparison with the last free elections that had taken place in Berlin, shortly before the collapse of the Weimar Republic in 1933, shows a substantial decline in Communist support, no doubt largely attributable to the encounter of Berliners with the Red Army at the close of World War II.

Table 2

Municipal and Provincial Elections, in September and on October 20, 1946
(Percentages of Valid Votes Cast by Parties and Provinces)

| | — SED — | | Christian — Democrats — | | — Liberals — | | — Others — |
	Sept.	Oct.	Sept.	Oct.	Sept.	Oct.	September
Saxony	48.4	49.1	19.7	23.3	20.2	24.8	1.6
Saxony-Anhalt	49.5	45.8	13.3	21.9	19.8	29.8	1.8
Thuringia	46.4	49.3	16.7	18.9	23.7	28.5	5.1
Brandenburg	54.3	43.5	15.6	30.3	17.2	20.5	3.4
Mecklenburg	63.2	49.5	15.2	34.1	9.5	12.5	2.8

Elections in Greater Berlin, October 20, 1946 and in West Berlin 1948 to 1954
(Percentages of Valid Votes Cast by Parties and Sectors)

Sector and Year	Social Democrats	SED	Liberal Democrats	Christian Democrats
Soviet 1946	43.6	29.8	7.9	18.7
American 1946	52.1	12.6	10.6	24.7
British 1946	50.7	10.3	11.9	27.1
French 1946	52.5	21.2	7.2	19.1
Total	48.7	19.7	9.4	22.2
West only, 1948	64.5	NR	16.1	19.4
West only, 1950	44.7	NR	23.0	24.6
West only, 1954	44.6	2.7	12.8	30.4

NR = Not running.

Comparison With 1928 and 1932 Elections
By Selected City Districts Representing Approximately Half of the Berlin Population. In Percentages of Total Votes Cast)

| Berlin | — SPD — | | — KPD — | | — Center — | | — Right — | |
	1928	1932	1928	1932	1928	1932	1928	1932
Wedding	34	23	40	47	7	4	7	24
Center	31	22	26	34	13	6	25	37
Zehlendorf	23	18	6	10	14	9	50	61

NOTE: The remaining percentages are attributable to other organizations or not valid.

SOURCES: See Table 3.

[12] These elections were intentionally scheduled to begin in industrial Saxony in the hope that an absolute SED majority there might spread to the agricultural regions.

Until the first Berlin crisis in 1948 and the establishment of the Pankow government in 1949, the Communists continued to concentrate their efforts on the political education of the East German population. No more municipal or regional elections were held in this period, though normally they would have taken place. Instead, the Soviet military administration and the SED prepared for the first national elections, which were to take place in 1950. A network of training centers was set up throughout East Germany to enable the Communists to influence the entire population at the local level. Nearly two hundred thousand Party members, both adults and youths, were actively engaged in disseminating information and drumming up support for the Communist cause. The culmination of this effort was the successful outcome of Germany's first Communist-organized, single-list elections held in October, 1950. With an affirmative vote of 99.7 percent, the Ulbricht group of Soviet-trained politicians, already firmly in control, had achieved the decorum they sought for their takeover of East Germany.[13] The failure of the quadripartite Allied Control Council, the blockade of Berlin, and the founding of the Federal Republic of Germany (West Germany) had preceded this final phase of the takeover of East Germany, mirroring the deep split between the Soviet Union and the Western Allies. Germany and Berlin were to remain divided.

Under the protection of the Western Allies, the western sectors of Berlin maintained their independent status, working in close association with the Federal Republic of Germany. As an aperture through which refugees from East Germany could escape to the West, Berlin was a particularly grave problem for the Communists. The economy of East Germany was seriously weakened by the mass exodus of refugees. It is estimated that by 1961, when West Berlin was sealed off by a concrete wall topped with barbed wire, about 5,800,000 inhabitants of East Germany had fled to the West, mainly by way of West Berlin.[14] Even after the erection of the wall, West Berlin continued to be a major problem by its very existence as an independent enclave in Communist East Germany.

In the south, Austria escaped the fate of East Germany, and the case of Austria is of interest for this reason. In contrast to the postwar administrative arrangements in Germany, the policy of the Allies called for the treatment of Austria as a liberated country. This meant that Austria was allowed to form its own central government, which would take direct responsibility for the administration of the country. The Red Army had occupied the eastern part of Austria, including Vienna, in the spring of

---

[13] Hubatsch, *op. cit.*, pp. 71–76.
[14] See Figure 10 in Schoenberg, *op. cit.*, p. 61.

1945, and initially prevented the United States and Great Britain from occupying the sectors of Vienna earmarked for British and American control by prior agreement with the Soviet Union. As indicated earlier, no important Soviet-trained exiles returned to Austria with the Red Army to participate in the reconstruction of the government. A famous Austrian socialist, Karl Renner, was designated as head of the Austrian government, and political parties quickly grew up. With the entire country as well as Vienna still under quadripartite control, the first postwar elections took place on November 25, 1945, amid considerable socio-political tensions. The results were emphatically disappointing to the Austrian Communists, and as pointed out above, were looked upon by the Ulbricht group in East Germany as symptomatic.

Subsequent national elections in Austria in 1949 and 1953 were to confirm the failure of the Austrian Communists (see Table 3). Unlike the German socialists, the Austrian socialists were consistently able to sustain their popularity in times of crisis, as the comparison with the national elections in 1930 suggests. In the Soviet sector of Vienna, the Communists secured only eleven percent of the votes cast in the elections of 1945, while the socialists continued to hold an absolute majority throughout the city, as in the elections of 1930. On the national level, the socialists won a plurality of over forty percent of the votes as they had in 1930, while the Communists were able to win only five percent of the poll.

Table 3

Austrian Elections
National Election Results (1945 Through 1953)
(In Percentages of Valid Votes Cast)

Date	SPOE (Socialist)	KPOE (Communist)	VdU (Independent)	OEVP (Peoples Party)
November 25, 1945	45	5	—	50
1949	39	5	12	44
1953	42	5	11	42

Results in Vienna: November 25, 1945 (By Electoral Districts)

	SPOE (Socialist)	KPOE (Communist)	VdU (Independent)	OEVP (Peoples Party)
Soviet Sector (IV and V)	63	11	—	26
Other Sectors:				
(I, II and III)	47	5	—	48
(VI and VII)	60	8	—	32

Comparison With 1930 National Elections

	SPOE (Socialist)	KPOE (Communist)	VdU (Independent)	OEVP (Peoples Party)
Vienna	60	—	14	26
Austria	43	—	12	45

SOURCES: Karl D. Bracher, *Die Auflösung der Weimarer Republik*, Villingen, 1964; Kurt L. Shell, *The Transformation of Austrian Socialism*, New York, 1962; Norbert Mattedi, *Gründung und Entwicklung der Parteien in der Sowjetischen Besatzungszone Deutschlands, 1945—1949*, Bonn, 1966.

The lack of support for the Austrian Communists as evidenced by the elections was probably one reason for the eventual withdrawal of the Soviet occupation forces, but there were also other important considerations. Hitler had annexed Austria in 1938, proclaiming its *Anschluss* (Union) with the Third Reich. As "Greater Germans," the Austrian people had fought in the German armies in World War II, and their encounter with the Red Army had left them with pronounced anti-Russian feelings. An efficient central government with sound domestic policies was quickly established in Austria following World War II, and the country as a whole made steady economic progress. (This was in part attributable to the European Recovery Program, which was implemented in Austria in the face of strong Soviet protests.) The Soviet zone of occupation was too small for it to be a viable state. If the Communists had been able to control all of Austria, it might have been worth taking over, but the eastern zone by itself was not.

For all these reasons, Austria was able to conclude a treaty with the Soviet Union and the other occupying powers on May 15, 1955, whereby it regained its independence. Austria's declaration of permanent neutrality at this time was important to the Soviet Union as an assurance against another *Anschluss* with Germany. As a neutral state, Austria serves as a buffer between Eastern Europe and the West and as an obstruction between the Federal Republic of Germany and Italy, members of NATO. When the Soviet occupation forces withdrew from Austria in 1955, Western troops also had to withdraw, thereby giving up the strategic alpine passes located in the western zones of occupation. Finally, the granting of independence to Austria was not without a certain amount of propaganda value for the Soviet Union.

The setback in Austria was not the only challenge to Soviet hegemony in Europe. In the north, Finland retained its independence in the face of Soviet encroachments. In the south, Yugoslavia asserted its autonomy from the Soviet Union in 1948. Yugoslavia's defiance of Moscow evoked caustic official criticism from East Germany. It was said: "The errors committed by the Yugoslav Communist Party show us that a clear and unequivocal pro-Soviet policy is today the only possible policy for a socialist party.... the presidium of the SED finds that certain false theories about Germany's own road to socialism exist. The attempt to construct a special German way would lead to disrespect for the great Soviet example."[15] Such increased emphasis on pro-Soviet sentiments, coupled with political

---

[15] Leonhard, *op. cit.*, pp. 510 f.

purges before and after the elections of 1950, helped to create the uniformity of public thought and the unanimity of public assent that went into the making of a "People's Democracy" in East Germany.

In its accession to hegemonic control over Central Europe, the Soviet Union violated several important principles of international law, including the right of a nation to self-determination. Also disregarded were Lenin's views on the "national road to socialism" and the theories of Marx and Engels on the equality of Communist Parties. The term "self-determination" had been coined by the First International in 1865 in support of Poland, and in 1896 the Second International had proclaimed the right of self-determination for all workers suffering "under the yoke of a military, national, or other despotism."[16] In 1882 Engels wrote to Kautsky: "The victorious proletariat cannot force its achievements on a foreign people without undermining its own victory." At the Eighth Soviet Communist Party Congress in 1919 Lenin declared: "We must not govern by decree from Moscow." At a meeting of the Communist International in 1921, he said: "We will never ask you to imitate us like slaves." Lenin even ridiculed foreign Communist Party officials who "hang Soviet resolutions in a corner like icons and pray in front of them."[17] Yet Ulbricht and the German Communists found just such a slavish approach effective in getting along with their Moscow bosses. This conflict between Communist theory and practice had severe consequences for the Germans. The popular uprising in East Germany in 1953, the stream of refugees to the West until 1961, and the many suicidal attempts to cross the Berlin wall from East to West since 1961 suggest the extent of the difficulties.[18]

Could the Communist takeover of East Germany have been avoided? As in the rest of Eastern Europe (except in parts of the Balkans), the Red Army brought the Communist revolution to East Germany, and nothing short of a Western military counteroffensive could have prevented it. Such a move by the Western Allies was unfeasible, given the continuing war in the Pacific. Other possibilities for the Western Allies were to advance on Germany through Italy and the Balkans, pushing as far as possible into Southeastern Europe. But having decided on the English Channel as the most favorable route of invasion, the main determinants of Germany's fate became questions of timing and strategy. Had the Western forces begun

---

[16] V. I. Lenin, *Selected Works*, Vol. I, Moscow, 1946, p. 705. See Meissner, *op. cit.*, p. 13.

[17] Leonhard, *op. cit.*, pp. 489 f.

[18] Since the erection of the wall, beginning in August, 1961, thousands have tried to escape to the West, hundreds have succeeded, and some seventy have been killed in the attempt by East German border guards.

their offensive sooner and driven further east, more of Germany might have remained under their control instead of falling to the Soviet Union. But even given actual events, United States troops did not need to withdraw from Saxony, where they first met with the Red Army. Occupation of this territory by U.S. forces would have contradicted the initial understanding between the Western Allies and the Soviet Union, and the Red Army might well have denied the Western Allies access to Berlin, but trading entry into Berlin for Saxony's industry would have rendered East Germany less capable of existing as a separate state.

Perhaps greater stress should have been placed on politico-military (rather than just military) actions in order to sidetrack or limit Soviet ambitions. Closer relations with resistance groups inside Germany and even sponsorship of a German anti-Communist exile government would have made sense, provided of course that such groups and such a government would have worked hand in hand with Western military forces at the close of the war. When Soviet expansionist designs became more apparent in late 1944 and early 1945, collaboration with enlightened factions of the German military may have been called for. During the final phase of the war, the Dönitz government showed a desire to stem the Russian tide, rescue millions of German civilians and troops from the East, and sue for partial capitulation. This willingness could have been utilized by the Western Allies to effect a swifter advance eastwards in Germany.[19] Such a step would have been a departure from the Allies' policy of unconditional surrender, but viewed in light of later developments this policy may have been unwise in any event. It would seem, in other words, that a judicious combination of military and political strategies might have led to an expanded Western presence in Germany and elsewhere in Eastern Europe. As the case of West Berlin demonstrates, a resolute political posture based on a credible military capability can forestall a final Communist takeover, and it is on the basis of this concept of deterrent force that an uneasy peace has been maintained in Europe for over two decades.

The treaties between West Germany and the Soviet Union and West Germany and Poland concluded in 1970 and ratified in 1972, as well as the concomitant Big Four and East-West German Berlin agreements, leave open the question of the motivation of the Soviet Union. To be sure, the Communists have finally won some recognition of their takeovers of the German areas. But are they now interested in ensuring a "Pax Sovietica" in Central and Eastern Europe? Would this include a continuation of ideological

---

[19] See especially W. Lüdde-Neurath, *Regierung Dönitz: Die letzten Tage des Dritten Reiches*, Göttingen, 1964, pp. 73 ff.; and Cajus Bekker, *Flucht übers Meer: Ostsee deutsches Schicksal, 1945*, Oldenburg, 1959.

warfare, another era of "peace as war by other means"? Can Soviet acceptance of West Germany's new eastern policy be compared with the Soviet
withdrawal from Austria? Or does it constitute an effort to neutralize West
Germany as a prelude to further attempts at aggrandizement?

After the Red Army withdrew from Austria, the U.S. Secretary of State,
John Foster Dulles, optimistically declared that "the Soviet leaders are
scrapping thirty years of policy based on violence and intolerance."[20] About
the same time, Nikita Khrushchev warned that no one should think that
the Soviet Union had forgotten about Marx, Engels, or Lenin.[21] The Soviet
leadership has planned and acted with a rhythm, a "high and low tide of
revolution."[22] The takeover of the German areas, seen in the context of the
recent East-West gestures of reconciliation, may have marked the beginning
of a phase of low tide in the Soviet Union's revolutionary efforts in
Europe.

Yet, two Germanies, a divided Europe, and the East-West schism
remain—a result of Nazi aggression, Soviet imperialism, and the Western
Allies' initial co-operation and bungling. *Quidquid delirant reges, plectuntur
populi* (Where kings err, people suffer).

---

[20] See Henry A. Kissinger, *Nuclear Weapons and Foreign Policy*, New York,
1969, abridged edition, p. 48.

[21] He added that this would happen "when shrimps learn to whistle." See
Denis Healey, "When Shrimps Learn to Whistle," *International Affairs*, London,
January, 1950, p. 2.

[22] Joseph Stalin, *Fragen des Leninismus*, Moscow, 1947, pp. 74 f. See Wagner,
op. cit., p. 27.

The First Two Communist Takeovers of Hungary: 1919 and 1948

Paul Ignotus

It is possible to speak of three Communist takeovers in Hungary. The first took place in 1919, soon after World War I; the second in 1944–1945, or rather from 1944 to 1949, as five years went by before the Stalinists consolidated their power; and the third in 1956. Since the repression in 1956 belongs to a different chapter of history, to the post-Stalin period of development in Communist countries, this article will concentrate on the first two takeovers, the one that followed World War I and the one that followed World War II.

During World War I, nobody in Hungary really knew much about communism, and if someone thought he did know something, his concepts of it were usually very simple. The Hungarians, together with the Austrians, fought on the side of the German Reich in the war against the Triple Entente. An alliance with the Germans was by no means an attractive proposition to the average Hungarian, but his attitude towards the Allies was perhaps even less enthusiastic. Leftist Hungarians were inclined to be pacifistic and naturally tended to dislike the Germans even more than they did the French or British. But in nationalist and right-wing circles the emphasis of dislikes was the opposite. Surely the revolution in Russia, which had nothing to do with German imperial tyranny though it served to weaken the Entente, must have appealed to practically all Hungarians. What a wonderful turn of events it must have seemed: the Russia of the Romanovs, the most backward and despotic empire in Europe and indeed in the world of the twentieth century, transformed into a spearhead of socialism and world peace! When a dithyrambic poem glorifying Lenin appeared in *Az Est*, the most popular of the Hungarian daily newspapers, at the time of the Bolshevik victory, no one thought of objecting. To Hungarians, Leninism seemed to be a trump card against the national enemy as well as a promise for a bright future of pacifism.[1]

---

[1] For further details on the revolutionary events of 1918–1919, one might consult the following accounts in English: Rudolf Tökes, *Béla Kun and the Hungarian Soviet Republic*, New York, 1967; Frank Eckelt, "The Rise and Fall of the Béla Kun Regime in 1919," Ph. D. Dissertation, New York University, 1965; David T. Cattell, "Soviet Russia and the Hungarian Revolution of 1919," M.A.

By October, 1918, the Central Powers had been beaten. The Hapsburg monarchy disintegrated almost overnight, and was transformed into a group of national states, a development which was both a dream and a nightmare for Hungarians. Full independence with democratic rule (universal suffrage and the secret ballot, which until then had not existed) was the dream; the secession of the non-Magyar nationalities from Hungary was the nightmare. Hungary's non-Magyar peoples made up slightly more than fifty percent of the country's total population. Liberal-minded Hungarians had been trying to tie the non-Magyar nationalities to Hungary by granting them equal rights; their leading spokesman, Professor Oszkár Jászi, an expert on the nationalities, agitated for an "Eastern Switzerland."[2] This idea was indignantly rejected by the Hungarian rulers, who wanted "Magyarization" of the nationalities. It was these same leaders who were responsible for pushing Hungary into the World War almost as if it had been a satellite of the German Reich. With the collapse of the whole German-Hungarian militarist scheme, it was natural for Hungary to try another way. Hungary now embraced liberalism in all aspects of its life as well as in its relations with the outside world. It embarked on a land reform which was to distribute the feudal estates among the peasantry; put democratic self-government to work; progressed towards what is today called the welfare state; and sought friendly relations with the neighboring nationalities (Slavs of various denomination—Slovaks, Ukrainians, Serbs, Croats—and also the Rumanians). The response of the Entente, and even more so of the neighboring nationalities, was to snub Hungary, treating it harshly and, indeed, cruelly.

Hungary was now under the leadership of people who had wholeheartedly opposed the oppressive, pro-German tendencies during the war, but their efforts were to prove ineffectual. The elected leader of the government was Count Mihály Károlyi.[3] Professor Jászi was a member of his cabinet, along with representatives of the Social Democratic Party, which

Thesis, Columbia University, 1949; Istvan Deak, "Budapest and the Hungarian Revolution of 1918–1919," *The Slavonic and East European Review*, London, January, 1968; Ferenc T. Zsuppan, "The Early Activities of the Hungarian Communist Party, 1918–1919," *The Slavonic and East European Review*, June, 1965. Many additional references are listed in two bibliographies: Ivan Völgyes, *The Hungarian Soviet Republic : 1919. An Evaluation and a Bibliography*, Stanford, 1971, and Thomas T. Hammond (ed.), *Soviet Foreign Relations and World Communism. A Selected, Annotated, Bibliography of 7,000 Books in 30 Languages*, second printing, with revisions, Princeton, 1966.

[2] See Oszkár Jászi, *Revolution and Counterrevolution in Hungary*, London, 1924.

[3] Count Károlyi has given his version of the Hungarian drama in Mihály Károlyi, *Memoirs : Faith Without Illusions*, London, 1956.

until this time had been excluded from parliament. The most important socialist leaders, Ernest Gerami and Sigismund Kunfi, were both appointed ministers in the first Károlyi cabinet. A group of intelligent but inexperienced idealists, the Károlyi leadership made one gesture after another to reassure the victorious Allies and their East European protégés of the peaceful intentions and democratic desires of the Magyars, but the more it went out of its way to do so, the more cruelly Hungary was treated by the victors. While the victorious Great Powers (France, Britain, Italy, and the United States), notwithstanding their supposedly humanitarian outlook, seemed to be completely insensitive to the fate of the Magyars, the Rumanian and Slav succession states springing up around Hungary after World War I proved to be rapacious and vengeful. Practically half of Hungary was occupied by combined forces of French, Senegalese, Czechoslovak, Rumanian, and other soldiers, and that part of the Hungarian population located in the rump country suffered many hardships as a result of being cut off from coal supplies and trade routes. Trainloads of refugees arrived in the capital from the occupied territories. Most of these people were forced, for lack of accommodations, to live in railroad cars throughout the winter months of 1918–1919.

It hardly needs to be said that for a regime believing in a liberal order and friendly ties with a humanitarian victor, these conditions were insupportable. Bitterness engendered extreme passion. Rightist elements were inclined to vest their hopes in armed resistance, and many were planning nationalist guerrilla warfare against the occupation forces. But the great power which might have given its protection to such a venture no longer existed, for there was no more German Reich. On the other hand, the existence of the Soviet Union, with its aura of revolutionary triumph, was impossible to ignore. Following World War I, a further boost was given to Soviet prestige in Hungary by the thousands of prisoners of war returning from Russia. They talked a lot about the Red Army. Certainly, their stories were not always attractive; horror stories were mixed with tales of sturdy, valiant Red soldiers appropriating homes of the rich and helping proletarians to find decent overnight accommodations. People of course believed what they were preconditioned to believe. The myths and counter-myths would have been inconclusive if other circumstances had not intervened.

Of the former prisoners of war, the most important was a man called Béla Kun, who had been something like an insurance clerk and a journalist in prewar Hungary. He was quite a clever man, though not particularly imaginative. His main faculty was to produce Marxist slogans with overwhelming fluency so that they impressed even those unable to understand them. In Russia he had been in touch with Lenin and trained by the Leninists, and it was his task in Hungary to prepare the way for a takeover. Other malcontents with leftist political ideas rallied around him, and the Party of Communists in Hungary was formed. It published a newspaper bearing on its front page the slogan "Workers of the World Unite!" Class-conscious and internationalist as this catch phrase sounded, the workers failed to show much inclination to join the Party, and if they did, they still did not betray any particular enthusiasm for an internationalism quite so doctrinaire. It was young intellectuals and quasi-intellectuals who crammed the premises of the newly founded Communist Party, and if these ideologists now and then found a peasant or an unskilled worker whom they could put on display with his mispronunciation of technical terms, they were quite proud of it. Nonetheless, in isolated places there seems to have been some response to the Communist propaganda. Communists succeeded in foiling the drive to split up the big estates by declaring each estate to be the property of a co-operative, which was to be run like a commune. Communists agitated for the cessation of payment of rents in the capital, a popular proposition that worked to their advantage in gaining allies. Ultimately, however, the workers took part in a great march against the Communists, and those Communist leaders (including Kun) who had done the most to upset the public order were imprisoned.

Then came the bombshell. On March 20, 1919, the Károlyi government was presented with a *démarche* by a French colonel acting on behalf of the victorious allies.[4] This demand further restricted the territory which could be held by Hungary until the peace settlement. More territory inhabited by Magyars (to say nothing of areas occupied primarily by Slavs and Rumanians) was to be surrendered to the succession states, which had proved to be hostile not only towards the Hungarian government but also towards the Magyar people as a whole. Even before this, the hope had been spreading that Russia would be the instrument of salvation. Such hope was grounded in a mixture of patriotic enthusiasm and revolutionary crystalgazing. There was speculation that the whole western world was on the verge of revolution, and some journalists in Budapest started propagating the idea that Hungary should not be left out. Among the leading Social Democrats, the highly intelligent Kunfi, who disliked the Bolsheviks for the way that they had treated the Mensheviks, nevertheless started telling his friends that Hungary would have to rely on Lenin's help because all other hopes had collapsed.

---

[4] See Peter Pastor, "The Vix Mission in Hungary, 1918–1919: A Re-examination," *Slavic Review*, New York, September, 1970; and Arno J. Mayer, *Politics and Diplomacy of Peacemaking: Containment and Counterrevolution at Versailles, 1918–1919*, New York, 1967.

Confronted with the *démarche* calling for further territorial concessions, Count Károlyi felt that it was impossible to go on trying to carry out the principles summed up in Wilson's Fourteen Points. He did not, however, intend to hand the country over to the Communists. His idea was to create a socialist government, based on the support of workers and peasants within the country, and he hoped to enlist the good will of the Communists by showing his readiness to rely on Russian aid. Some of the socialists (Gerami, for instance) looked upon this approach as unrealistic and withdrew. Kunfi, on the other hand, thought that it must be not only accepted but also enlarged upon. Social Democratic leaders went to see Béla Kun in prison and concluded an agreement according to which the United Socialist Party, combining both Socialists and Communists, was to be founded and a dictatorship of the proletariat proclaimed. In the new government created on March 21, 1919, the only full-fledged People's Commissar coming from the Communist Party was Béla Kun himself, who was given the portfolio of Foreign Affairs to enable him to keep in touch with Lenin. The other leaders of the government came from the Social Democratic Party, with an old-fashioned ex-bricklayer, Garbei, being appointed as President. The new government was not intended to be a purely Communist regime. But once tied to the Soviet Union, it provoked the hostility of the major powers in the West, and there was no way for it to stop short of transforming Hungary into a Leninist province. Paradoxically, at a time when internationalism was even banning the display of national colors, Hungary turned Communist for avowed nationalistic reasons. Béla Kun was at first astonished by his quick rise to power, but he soon convinced himself that this was due to his own genius.

Under Kun it was not long before it became clear that the Entente and its allies in Eastern Europe (Czechoslovakia, Rumania, and Yugoslavia) were not prepared to tolerate the existence of a Communist state in the Danube basin. Nothing fails like failure: the Kun regime became unpopular as quickly and easily as it had come to power. It was a target of jokes as well as an object of hatred. The feeling that it was doomed induced the black-marketeers to hoard their wares, the peasants to hide their goods, and the variety show actors to hint at the imminent downfall of the Hungarian Soviet Republic. The military cadets organized an armed counter-revolution, as did even the farmers.

The downfall of the Kun regime was precipitated by the resistance of the whole population, and among the elements of society conspicuous for their resistance was the peasantry, who made up the majority of the total population. But, even so, the strength of the internal resistance must not be overrated. Descriptions of peasant resistance as the main factor in the overthrow of the Kun regime are misleading. Such resistance contributed to the overthrow, but the really decisive factor was the defeat of the Hungarian Red Army by Rumanian forces attacking from the east. Just before the Rumanians entered Budapest an interim government was formed by right-wing Social Democrats. It did not last long, however, for with the military assistance of the Rumanians a purely reactionary clique of White armed forces overthrew the caretaker government and paved the way for a White terror. Admiral Miklós Horthy, who was later to head the regime, had initially organized his White gangs under the protection of the French occupying forces in the south of Hungary. Some of the occupying forces had found the raging White terror too harsh, the more so because it was directed not only against Communists but also against other social, political, and religious elements: Jews, Freemasons, organized labor, and peasants who had been agitating for land reform. But once the Whites were established in power the prospect of displacing them seemed quite formidable. Moreover, the victorious powers were content to see a White regime in the place of the Red one, even though they disapproved of many of the Whites' policies. Hungary was ruled from 1919 until 1944 by this White regime with Admiral Horthy as Regent, and though there were a number of variations in the political posture of the Horthy government, a consistent feature of it was its hostility to communism.[5]

In World War II, the Horthy government fought on the side of Nazi Germany. There is no doubt that Admiral Horthy and the reactionaries whose advice he followed at the time disliked the Nazis and were convinced that Germany could not win the war. But Hungary was definitely not pro-Allied in any sense that might be understood in London or Washington, let alone in Moscow. What Horthy and his advisers would have liked to see was a limited German victory, possibly without Hitler as the head of state and probably without prejudice to American and British world influence. When it became clear by the end of 1944 that such an eventuality was out of the question, Admiral Horthy ironically turned about and asked the invading Soviet forces for an armistice. Horthy was then removed from power by the Hungarian Nazis, who established their own regime of terror, which was bloodier and more cruel and devastating than anything yet witnessed in Hungary. The Nazis accused Horthy of betraying his country to the Bolsheviks. Far from it, in the quarter of a century of his rule, Horthy, like those who deposed and imprisoned him, consistently

---

[5] *The Confidential Papers of Admiral Horthy*, Budapest, 1965; C. A. Macartney, *October Fifteenth. A History of Modern Hungary, 1929—1945*, Edinburgh, 1961; Paul Ignotus, *Hungary*, Washington, D.C., 1972.

relied on the widespread unpopularity of the Communists, which stemmed from the four months of chaotic Communist rule in 1919.

This is not to say that there were no pro-Communist elements in Hungary under Horthy. People opposed to the Horthy regime itself (and needless to say there were many) at the same time had a good deal of sympathetic interest in the Communists. The very fact of official disapprobation made communism an attractive proposition to many. To this was added the circumstance that it was the Red Army which after all liberated Hungary from the Nazis. In this context the word "liberated" is often set within quotation marks, but despite the very unpleasant experiences of the Russian military occupation and Communist dictatorship I feel that it is correct to speak of liberation, for the Red Army kept an already ravaged Hungary from ultimate enslavement and destruction, and saved the lives of about a quarter of a million Jews who were earmarked for extermination by the Nazis. It is true that the Red Army could hardly have achieved this victory without the help of the Western Allies, and that the Soviet Union tried to conceal and belittle Western assistance. It is also true that the Soviet occupation of Hungary unleased an orgy of rape, looting, and exile of people to Siberia, and that economic relief to the Hungarian population came only from the West, mainly from the United States. But all this does not alter the circumstance that the brunt of the German war was borne by the Red Army and that in liberating the peoples of Eastern Europe from Nazi slave and death camps, the Soviet Union sacrificed more lives than any other power. As a result, in Hungary, fear of the Red Army was mixed with a sense of gratitude towards it.

With the Russian army came many Communist émigrés. At the end of 1944, when the first large slice of Hungarian territory was captured by the Red Army, a Hungarian anti-Nazi government was formed. This first provisional government was repellent to the Hungarian Democrats not because it included a few Communists (it was taken for granted that this would happen), but because the most conspicuous posts in the government were filled by former high officials of the Horthy regime. It seemed opportunistic to set up a government so obviously calculated to please the Whites. Subsequent events vindicated these feelings. The Communists had included high White officials only to remove them later when it was convenient. In the end, the Communists treated even more harshly the liberals, agrarians, and social democrats; the Whites were merely displaced, but the democrats were imprisoned and tortured. The "suspects" in a third category—Communists who were rightly or wrongly imagined to be guilty of deviations—were usually executed; at any rate, their "leaders" were.

The Communist takeover which began in Hungary in the winter of 1944–1945 and evolved into full-fledged Stalinization by the autumn of 1949 was in many respects different from the takeover of 1919. In 1919 the Communists had stumbled into power, hardly realizing how they had got there. In 1945 their slogans concerned themselves with patriotism, democracy, reconstruction, and unity with the forces of peaceful progress. The very memory of the Kun regime was anathema to the Communists. Anyone who said a favorable word about it was energetically rebuked for rubbing salt in the wounds of the population. This attitude was only partly due to the fact that Béla Kun had been murdered in Russia as a "Trotskyite," as had been many other Hungarian Communist refugees. More important, the Communists wished to efface the unpopularity they had inherited from the Kun regime. They strongly denied planning to establish any sort of dictatorship.

The leader of the Communists in Hungary was a former Deputy People's Commissar under Kun, Mátyás Rákosi.[6] Rákosi seems to have had a respectable career, judging by the standards of anybody who values sacrifices made and risks taken for personal convictions. Sent from Russia in the inter-war period to organize illegal work, Rákosi was arrested and kept prisoner in Hungary for sixteen years. In 1940, however, the Soviet government made a special agreement with the Hungarian authorities providing that Rákosi be released and returned to Russia. Long confinement in prison affects different people in different ways. It is hard to say what Rákosi would have been like had he not spent sixteen years in prison, but if the ordeal had any impact on his character, it was to make him not more, but less sensitive to suffering similar to his own. Many called him, disapprovingly, dogmatic. He was nothing like that. He simply had no use for ideology. He might have been an idealist in the beginning, but all that he was interested in later was power. He was not unlike a traveling salesman of the greediest and most mendacious type. His commodity was revolution, and he sold it because he was convinced that it would pay. True, he was capable of taking many risks. But any foolhardy speculator on the stock exchange can take risks. It is also true that he cared for money less than he cared for power. But this was quite natural in a world in which property seemed less secure than offices based on arms. People are used to thinking that the only contrast to unselfishness is greed expressed in terms of money, but Rákosi had greed for power. Rákosi had another deceptive feature. He was a quick-witted conversationalist, prepared to show not only good will but even sentimental attachment to a single person or a category of

---

[6] For Rákosi's career before World War II, see the two Communist accounts, Mátyás Rákosi, *Face au tribunal fasciste*, Paris, 1952, and G. Szamuelly, *Matias Rakoshi; zhizn i borba geroya mezhdunarodnoy proletarskoy revoliyutsii*, Moscow, 1935.

people. But his loyalties were all self-serving, and he kept his "friends" only as long as they could be of use to him in his drive for power.

Rákosi did not set himself up as a dogmatist after the liberation. In fact he liked to pose as a mediator, as the wise man of the country. He leaked the gossip that the "Eye of Moscow" in the Hungarian Communist Party, secretly supervising even him, was his second-in-command, Ernö Gerö. Rákosi was a jovial-looking, squat, baldheaded man, not at all impressive, but friendly enough in appearance to inspire confidence. Gerö was a lanky, ascetic-looking man, something of a successful cross between an inquisitor and a cash register; his was the job of controlling economic policy and seeing that the Russians be perfectly served. Rákosi informally complained that he himself would be much more open to non-Communist Hungarian patriots "if only that dogmatic Gerö and that violent Rajk didn't force our path." Rajk was a nice young man although really a fanatic; in the Communist set-up he was the most important among the non-Muscovites. Rákosi deliberately gave him the most controversial jobs to do, those most likely to provoke widespread resentment.

There is no doubt that from the beginning in 1945, Rákosi aimed at achieving absolute power. But he played cautiously. A coalition government was formed. General elections, genuinely free and democratic, were held. The Communists had to share power—at least nominally—with three other parties: the Independent Smallholders Party, the Social Democratic Party, and the National Peasant Party. Of these, the so-called Smallholders Party became the gathering place of, among others, all right-wing elements, from conservative clergymen to moderate liberals. Practically everybody who disavowed communism but did not believe in democratic socialism gravitated towards this party. The agrarian orientation implied by the name Smallholders Party is deceptive. Although smallholding peasants actually did support the Party, its character was distinctly bourgeois or middle class. The Social Democrats represented predominantly the skilled workers in the manufacturing industries, but also took in those other segments of the population—whether farmers, proletarians, or bourgeoisie—who believed that the middle road between capitalism and communism was the one on which Europe and Hungary should embark. The National Peasant Party, although it could boast of some outstanding members (several prominent poets, for example), was to all intents and purposes a branch of the Communist Party. It was Communist bait put out for the poor peasants and nationalist middle-classes; its anti-Communist wing was quickly silenced, partly driven into exile.

As the general mood of the country was rather conservative, the first elections brought the Smallholders a majority of the votes. They won really more than they would liked to have won, for the extent of their success was regarded as an indication of the deep resentment felt by most Hungarians for the occupying Russian army. As the responsible parties knew that they had to make an attempt at amicable relations with the victorious Soviet forces, this evidence of a generally anti-Soviet mood was not welcomed. The Reverend Zoltan Tildy, leader of the Smallholders Party, had done his very best to be on good terms with the Russians, and after the elections he seemed to be embarrassed. It was said about him that he was like a man who has won a lion in a lottery and does not dare to take it home. But his problems were solved by his becoming first the Premier and then, following the proclamation of the Republic, its President, while the Communists, like the Social Democrats and the small National Peasant Party, went on serving in the coalition government.

Despite the many acts of violence which made the Soviet military forces unpopular, it would be a mistake to think that either their raping or their stealing (they were particularly fond of wrist watches) had anything to do with Communist ideology. In fact many Hungarians assumed that the Soviet military mission had a policy different from that of the Moscow-trained Communists and that it sought to build links with the orthodox capitalist forces in Hungary. The interference of the Red Army in the internal affairs of Hungary was very sporadic at that time. In sum, the Hungarian people did not hesitate to show their dislike of communism, and the occupying army refrained from overruling their behavior; the Hungarian Communists were, in other words, just one of four coalition partners, in strength numerically far behind the Smallholders, and in working-class support far weaker than the Social Democrats. How then did they achieve their absolute power by the autumn of 1949?

The answer was given by Rákosi himself in a moment of captivating sincerity when he boasted that he had "sliced off" the non-Communist partners in the coalition "like pieces of salami." Indeed these "salami tactics" of his were most effective, and little else was needed to insure his success except perhaps a lack of scruples and a "knife" to cut the "salami." The political police, used from the outset by the Moscow-trained Communists, served as the "knife." People broadly fitting the description of "democrats" and "patriots" could be seen in prominent positions in the government in almost the same proportion as they were chosen by the elections. But the political police was strictly Rákosi's stronghold. A sort of moral justification seemed to exist for this arrangement: under the Horthy regime the Communists were the group that had suffered the most from political persecution, and they felt more capable than any other party of judging where the fascist danger might still lie. In any event, this was one point on which the Communists were unwilling to bargain and could count on being backed up by the occupying forces. It remained only for Rákosi to decide when this "knife" in his hands should be put to work.

Rákosi did not fail to take advantage of the disunity and mutual distrust which existed among his non-Communist partners. The Social Democrats looked upon the Smallholders with suspicion. They did so not only because they found the Smallholders Party a refuge for those wanting to restore the prewar, semi-fascist system of government, but also because they felt that as a party with vague goals, it lent itself most easily to Communist infiltration. It is true that crypto-Communists of seemingly high respectability could be found among the Smallholders. Particularly irritating to the Socialists were public figures such as the amusing Roman Catholic, Abbé Stephen Belogh, who was a favorite of the Soviet generals and got along quite well with the Communist leaders but snubbed the non-Communist left-wingers.

The first great "slicing-off" operation started with a campaign organized by the Communists against what they termed the right wing of the Small-holder's Party. The darkest side of this campaign was that its target was not really the reactionary or semi-fascist caucus whose connection with the Smallholders was a convenient subterfuge, but simply those of its members who were most outspoken about Communist malpractices. With the consent first of the Social Democrats and the National Peasant Party and later of the Smallholders Party itself, Rákosi began to eliminate these "right-wing" Smallholders.

The next "slice" was that segment of the Social Democrats which could be termed its right-wing faction because of its activities during the war, when under the pressure of semi-fascism it had to make accommodations, at least nominally, with the government in power. The former leader of the Social Democrats, Charles Peyer, was a brave and sound but extremely vain man, who could not understand that in the changed circumstances he should accept his subordinate position in the Party leadership, quietly playing second fiddle until things calmed down sufficiently to speak openly about the wartime arrangements. Peyer's emotionalism and vanity played into the hands of Rákosi, who maneuvered the Social Democrats into "slicing off" part of their right wing.[7]

Possibly the most brash "slicing-off" maneuver was the one in which the bulk of the Smallholders Party was liquidated. The political police

---

[7] The story of one Social Democrat who was arrested and sentenced to fifteen years at hard labor is contained in Paul Ignotus, *Political Prisoner*, New York, 1960.

exposed a "conspiracy" based mostly on trumped-up charges. As some of those involved were of right-wing authoritarian outlook, however, the charges could be made to seem credible. Furthermore, a leader of the Smallholders Party, Bela Kovács, was accused of collaborating with the conspirators, and the Communist Minister of Interior, Rajk, asked the National Assembly to suspend his parliamentary immunity and turn him over to the police. Debate on the fate of Kovács was going on, marked by a good deal of dissension, when suddenly the Soviet military police seized him on the grounds that he had been plotting against the occupying forces. This was one of the very few instances when the Russians openly, with unlawful exercise of force, interfered in Hungarian political affairs. But one such blow was enough to create a panic. In a short time, another leader of the Smallholders Party, Prime Minister Ferenc Nagy, was intimidated into going into exile with many of his followers.[8] The same happened in the case of Peyer, the ex-leader of the Social Democrats. A number of Smallholders such as the Reverend Tildy were tolerated for a while, but during their short reprieve their actions were prompted and controlled by the Communists.

Following the rout of the Smallholders Party, the Social Democrats, led by Anna Kéthly and Antal Bán, had their turn in the Communist salami slicer. In the second general elections, held in 1947, Rajk went out of his way to organize the means for falsifying votes, mainly in an attempt to reduce the number of Social Democrats in the coalition. In reaction there was an anti-Communist uproar among the Social Democrats, who sought to get rid of their nominal leader, the very weak Arpad Szakasits, as the person responsible for such malpractices. Szakasits, panic-stricken, accepted the help of the crypto-Communists or fellow travelers in his party. This brought the interference of the political police, which made it impossible for groups within the Social Democratic Party to side with their real leaders, Kéthly and Bán. The rest of the country was stunned by this constraint, but most people did not feel they could interfere in the disputes between the two Marxist parties. As a result, by early 1948 "unity" among the workers had been achieved, meaning the Social Democrats had been absorbed by the Communist Party. Bán went into exile, and Kéthly was put under house arrest and later imprisoned; more appropriately, so was Szakasits, together with his fellow-traveling abettors.

The year 1948 has been recorded in Hungarian history as the year of the "Turning Point," the time when Hungary was transformed into a "People's

---

[8] Ferenc Nagy tells of his fight with the Communists in *The Struggle Behind the Iron Curtain*, New York, 1948.

Democracy," which, according to Rákosi's definition, meant "a dictatorship of the proletariat without the Soviet form." From 1948, there was no pretense about Hungary's accepting Soviet rule, in fact if not in name. Yet it took another year before Rákosi's power was made total and his system streamlined to Stalinist requirements.

The larger industrial plants in Hungary were nationalized by government decree in the spring of 1948. At the same time, a drive against the kulaks, or well-to-do peasants, was begun as a preliminary move towards confiscating their plots and forcing them to join the state-controlled collective farms. Then came the drive against the Church. József Cardinal Mindszenty, the Roman Catholic primate, played into the hands of the Communists by being rather rigid and diehard. He had stood up valiantly against the Nazis, but he did not properly understand the changed circumstances once the Nazi danger was over. He refused to see that the position and power of the hereditary authorities such as the Roman Catholic Church could not remain unaltered, and he therefore became an easy target for attacks against himself as a reactionary, which in a way he was. Towards the end of 1948 Mindszenty made some conciliatory gestures towards the "People's Democracy," but it was already too late then, and it is doubtful whether he could have achieved more with an elastic, less doctrinaire approach. In the winter of 1948–1949 he was sentenced to life imprisonment on contrived charges, as were his main associates. The same treatment lay in store for those Roman Catholics who had sought to replace Mindszenty's rigid policy with a more flexible, more progressive one.[9]

Neutralization of the Protestant Churches—Lutheran, Calvinist, and Unitarian—followed in the wake of the assault on the Catholic Church, as did the persecution of small sects such as the Jehovah's Witnesses. The Jews, who were often accused of Zionism, were treated even more harshly. This came as a surprise to many, since the Moscow-trained Communist leaders—Rákosi, Gerö, etc.—were of Jewish origin almost to a man. For them, however, their Jewish blood was an additional reason for singling out other Jews for the pillory and the torture chambers, since in doing so they hoped to gain the confidence of the former Nazis who were their chief supporters against the Social Democrats. They hoped at the same time to win the trust of Stalin, who was known to have anti-Semitic feelings, notwithstanding his reliance on Jewish sympathies in the fight against Hitler during World War II.

---

[9] See Jozsef Cardinal Mindszenty, *Cardinal Mindszenty Speaks: Authorized White Book Published by Order of Joseph Cardinal Mindszenty*, New York and London, 1949; *The Trial of Jozsef Mindszenty*, Budapest, 1949.

Meanwhile, an external political development contributed to making the Stalinist terror in Hungary impervious to restraint and bloodier than perhaps even its planners had foreseen. This was the conflict between Stalin and Tito, culminating in the withdrawal of Yugoslavia from the Soviet Communist fold. Rákosi put himself at the head of the anti-Tito campaign, and Hungary outstripped all the other Communist satellites in its vilification of Yugoslavia. These efforts were reinforced by troop concentrations on the Yugoslav border, and by halting the delivery of goods destined for Yugoslavia. Then in the early summer of 1949 came the great shock: the leader of the non-Muscovite Communists, the fanatic Rajk, was branded a "Hungarian Tito" and arrested. Whether Rákosi took this step merely to please Stalin or whether he used the Tito scare as an excuse to get rid of a rival has never been made clear. The fact is that Rajk, together with masses of non-Muscovite Communists, was tortured into "confessing" crimes he never committed. That Rajk had fought in Spain in the International Brigade was only one more reason for treating him as a suspect. Communists who had traveled anywhere in the West—to Spain, France, or Britain—were looked upon as potential breeders of discontent. In the coming years, in fact until Stalin's death, more Communists were executed in Hungary than under Admiral Horthy. (Incidentally, the Minister of Interior who had Rajk arrested on Rákosi's orders was an ex-worker named Janos Kádár whose turn for arrest and torture came some two years later.) On August 20 (which is Saint Stephens' Day in memory of the first king of Hungary), 1949, Rákosi with his rubber stamp parliament adopted a constitution which consummated Hungary's bondage not only to Communist ideas but also—and more emphatically—to Soviet interests. A country's coat of arms may not be of very great importance, but there were suitable symbolic implications in the circumstance that Hungary was provided with a new coat of arms at the same time that it was given a new constitution. With its sickle and hammer and five-pronged star, this coat of arms is hardly distinguishable from that of any Soviet republic. But Hungary called itself a sovereign state, and its Moscow-trained leaders recited nationalist cant. That all this would have been despised by the unconsciously patriotic Communists of 1919 is the great difference between the two Communist takeovers in Hungary.[10]

---

[10] An account of the takeover in Hungary from the point of view of a member of the Smallholders Party is: Peter Horvath, "Communist Tactics in Hungary Between June 1944 and June 1947," Ph. D. Dissertation, New York University, 1956.

The Prague Coup of 1948: The Elegant Takeover

Pavel Tigrid

Nearly a quarter of a century has gone by since the "February victory" of the Communists in Czechoslovakia, and one might imagine that the details of the takeover are now familiar and the ground well worked over by historians. But a closer look shows that this is not so. There are still large gaps in the record of this event, which marked the beginning of the full-scale Cold War and the process leading straight to the Soviet invasion of Czechoslovakia on August 21, 1968. Documents on some of the international links are missing, the testimony of participants is often conflicting, and the sediment of ideological verbiage on the Communist side requires the attention of more than forty maids with forty mops.

There are several studies by Czech émigrés[1] which on the whole stand up to critical analysis quite well, though sometimes they are marred by political or personal defensiveness: after all, politicians always have to explain away their defeats. There are also books by Western writers which, though not free of factual errors, wrong names, dates, and the like, are particularly useful in setting the events in a broad international context.[2]

[1] Hubert Ripka, *Le Coup de Prague*, Paris, 1949 (in English as *Czechoslovakia Enslaved*, London, 1950); Josef Korbel, *The Communist Subversion of Czechoslovakia*, Princeton, 1959; Vratislav Bušek, *Poučení z únorového převratu*, New York, 1954; Edward Táborský, *Communism in Czechoslovakia 1948–1960*, Princeton, 1961; Ivo Ducháček, *The Strategy of Communist Infiltration: The Case of Czechoslovakia*, New Haven, 1949; Jozef Lettrich, *History of Modern Slovakia*, New York, 1955; Josef Josten, *Oh my Country*, London, 1949; Ivan Gadourek, *The Political Control of Czechoslovakia*, Leyden, 1950; Václav Chalupa, *Rise and Development of a Totalitarian State*, Leyden, 1959; Otto Friedman, *The Breakup of Czech Democracy*, London, 1950; Jan Stránský, *East Wind over Prague*, New York, 1951; Ferdinand Peroutka, *Byl E. Beneš vinen?*, London, 1950; Lev Sychrava, *Svědectví a úvahy o pražském převratu*, London, 1951; Bohumil Laušman, *Kdo byl vinen?*, Vienna, 1953; Jaromír Smutný, *Únorový převrat*, London, 1954; L. K. Feierabend, *Pod vládou Národní fronty*, Washington, 1968; Miloslav J. Brouček, *Československá tragedie*, New York, 1956; and Pavel Tigrid, *Marx na Hradcanech*, New York, 1960.

[2] Dana A. Schmidt, *Anatomy of a Satellite*, Boston, 1962; Paul E. Zinner, *Communist Strategy and Tactics in Czechoslovakia, 1918–1948*, London, 1963; William E. Griffith (ed.), *Communism in Europe*, Cambridge, Mass., 1966; Francois Fejtö, *Histoire des Démocraties populaires*, Paris, 1952; U.S. Department of State, *Moscow's European Satellites*, Washington, D.C., 1955; Stephen D. Kertesz (ed.), *The Fate of East Central Europe*, Notre Dame, Ind., 1958; John Brown, *Who's Next?*, London, 1951; and Morton A. Kaplan, *The Communist Coup in Czechoslovakia*, Princeton, N.J., 1960.

The Czech and Slovak Communist literature written in the 1950's and early 1960's is by contrast feeble in its analysis, evaluation, and conclusions.[3] Thick layers of propaganda are daubed over the most innocent historical fact lest it cast any shadow on the policies, tactics, or leaders of the Czechoslovak Communist Party, which is regularly described in terms of almost erotic enthusiasm. The younger generation of Czech historians makes no bones about this. "In many cases," says one of them, "books were written about the February events purely for propaganda and, accordingly, depicted them to a large extent in a one-sided and distorted light....It would be interesting to trace the mutual influence of émigré writing and of the various propaganda tracts about February that appeared in the 1950's."[4] General Josef Pavel, Commander of the People's Militia during the coup, stated on the radio twenty years later (February 16, 1968) that "the majority of things published in our country from February, 1948, up to 1965, are not to be taken seriously." One active Communist participant in the Prague coup was to remark:

> We gave a distorted picture of the February story... The true history of February, I feel, has never been faithfully narrated; only now are conditions ripening in which a critical study, among other things, could and should be made of the errors and half-truths and untruths uttered about February, 1948, both at home and abroad. This would be a valuable contribution to Marxist historical science . and would give previous historians of those events a chance to exercise self-criticism.[5]

The chance, alas, was very short-lived; it lasted for exactly eight months, months packed with events so dramatic and fast-flowing that even the historians were dazzled, and their nervous energy was in any case taken up with such immediate tasks as the preparation of the "Black Book" on the

---

[3] G. Bareš, *Naše cesta k socialismu*, Prague, 1948; *Dejiny KSČ*, Prague, 1960; Klement Gottwald, *Spisy*, Prague, 1955–1958, Volumes XI–XIV; Svoboda, Tučková, Svobodová, *Jak to bylo v únoru*, Prague, 1949; Zdenek Fierlinger, *Ve službách ČSR*, Prague, 1947; V. Kopecký, *ČSR a KSČ*, Prague, 1960; J. Opat, *O novou demokracii 1945–1948*, Prague, 1966; *Otázky národní a demokratické revoluce*, Prague, 1955; G. Spurný, *Unorové dny*, Prague, 1958; *Unor 1948*, Prague, 1958; *Vítezny únor 1948*, Prague, 1959; J. Veselý, *Kronika únorovych dnu*, Prague, 1959; *Ze čtyriceti let zápasú KSČ*, Prague, 1960; J. Kozák, *K nekterym otázkám strategie a taktiky KSČ v období prerustáné národní a demokratické revoluce v revoluci socialistickou*, Prague, 1955; V. Král, *Cestou k únoru*, Prague, 1963; *Spiknutí proti republice*, Prague, 1947; M. Vartíková, A. Lantay, *Február rozhodol*, Bratislava, 1963; J. Nedved, *Cesta ke sloučení sociální demokracie s komunistickou stranou v roce 1948*, Prague, 1968; H. Kračmárová, P. Lesjuk, B. Pelikán, Z. Snítl, *K únoru 1948*, Prague, 1958; and Ružena Krízenecká, Zdenek Sel, Jirí Zeman, *Československo 1945–1948*, Prague, 1968.

[4] Václav Pavlíček, "Unor 1948," in *Právník*, Prague, No. 3, 1968.

[5] *Kulturní noviny*, Prague, No. 7, 1968.

first week of the invasion. Nevertheless, a few books and articles did appear in that period which serve to correct and supplement our knowledge of the February crisis and its inner mechanism. The following paragraphs, then, are an attempt to summarize what Czech historiography during the Prague Spring of 1968 has contributed to our understanding of the events of February, 1948.

It is a small contribution, though by no means negligible. And if it is small, the Prague historians are not themselves to blame. Not only was time short, but there were several other difficulties. Even during the Prague Spring, Party and state archives were not completely accessible to scholars. This applied particularly to the "Confidential" and "Secret" categories of the Communist Party archives. The records of non-Communist parties, such as the Czech National Socialist and People's Parties and the Slovak Democratic Party, were thrown open, but for the most part these revealed only the behavior of Party leaders during the critical days, so that their historical value is secondary. Indeed almost all the studies on February, 1948, published twenty years later complain that important details have been withheld, that "the inadequacy of source-material prevents a really scholarly analysis,"[6] and that consequently "the Czechoslovak revolution is still a subject of endless dispute among the country's historians; not even today are they in agreement about what it amounted to."[7] Soviet sources are entirely inaccessible, and there is great argument about the little that has been quarried and published from them. One Czech historian cautiously notes, in reference to the years 1947 and 1948, that "a number of Soviet political positions taken at that time need more thorough study and scientific treatment—particularly by Soviet historians—based on close acquaintance with primary documents."[8]

A further difficulty is hinted at here. Not even during the brief interlude of the Prague Spring was it possible to give Soviet studies of the February crisis the names they broadly deserve—mere fabrications and propaganda. On the contrary, it appeared to Czech historians to be their civic and patriotic duty to avoid any such exposure or at least to postpone it lest it be exploited to aggravate the pressure of power politics upon Czechoslovakia. Any of the available publications about February, 1948, which appeared during the Prague Spring reveal the self-imposed discipline of the historians.

---

[6] Pavlíček, *op. cit.*, p. 177.

[7] Pavlíček, *op. cit.*, p. 178.

[8] M. Bouček and M. Klimeš, "Unor v československé revoluci," *Nová mysl*, Prague, No. 2, 1968, p. 141.

But considerable enlightenment can be gained by reading the passages in these publications dealing with the following four themes: the international background to the Communist takeover in Czechoslovakia; the domestic reasons for the takeover and the political management of power that made it feasible; the constitutional aspects of the takeover; and the moral to be drawn from all these fresh insights and admissions.

February and Its International Setting

The literature of the Prague Spring all concurs with the somewhat unreliable studies of the 1950's in insisting that the rapid deterioration of relations between the victors of World War II had a direct and, evidently, paramount role in determining that the Communist seizure of power in Czechoslovakia should take place no earlier, and no later, than February, 1948. The Czech Marxist historians agree in seeing 1947 as the time when a decisive break occurred in those relations. They cite the declaration of the Truman Doctrine in March, the failure of the Moscow talks between the four Foreign Ministers in April, the exclusion of Communists during the same spring from the government coalitions of France and Italy; the dispatching of the U.S. Sixth Fleet to the eastern Mediterranean in May; formulation in the same month of the policy of "containing" communism; and the announcement of the Marshall Plan in June. There is a striking unanimity among the Czech historians that Moscow judged a new world war to be almost imminent at this time. A long document drawn up by a special commission of the Czech Communist Party on instructions from the Central Committee states that a military conflict in Europe was expected by the mid-1950's, and hence

> the arms race was intensified on both sides of the divided world. The Cold War spirit engendered a war psychosis, encouraged fears that a clash was threatening and raised tensions not only between the countries of the two blocs, but also within the countries at whose head stand the two superpowers, the Soviet Union and the USA.[9]

The outstanding Czech Marxist writer Karel Kaplan dates anxieties over a new world war from the second half of 1947, when he sees the Russians and Americans preparing for it *inter alia* by reinforcing their positions in their respective spheres of interest.[10]

There is an interesting distinction here, however. Though the new analyses in 1968 continue to regard the United States as the main culprit,

---

[9] *Zpráva komise UV KSČ o politickych procesech a rehabilitacích v Československu 1949–68*, Vienna, 1970, p. 6.

[10] *Nová mysl*, Prague, No. 6, 1968.

and sometimes as the instigator of the Cold War, they do lay some of the blame on the Soviet Union. For example, the Central Committee study mentioned above states specifically that "the intensification of international tension came about not only through the actions of the capitalist world, and especially of the United States, but also through acts of foreign policy committed by the socialist camp."[11] This report quotes Mikoyan's observation at the Soviet Communist Party's Twentieth Congress that "in foreign policy we have made this and that mistake in the past and have sometimes been to blame for the aggravation of relations."[12] One Czech historian cautiously, but quite unequivocally, states that even the Marshall Plan and Czechoslovakia's attitude towards it must be judged in the light of "dubious measures in Soviet foreign policy."[13]

The Truman Doctrine and its later amplification in the Marshall Plan evidently produced serious and sometimes frantic fears lest

> a world-wide conflict break out in a short space of time... The USSR realized the vast economic preponderance of the United States, and realized that such a preponderance could quite speedily upset in radical fashion the existing military balance, especially if—as must be considered likely—the West German forces, then being revived, were integrated into the military potential of the West. The USSR sought to forestall American war preparations by taking sound measures in good time, using not only the Soviets' own domestic resources but the duly concentrated and centralized strength of the entire socialist community.[14]

In a round-table discussion organized by the periodical, *Reportér*, for the twentieth anniversary of February, Karel Kaplan asserted that

> the roots of February are to be found back in the middle of 1947... when the world was beginning to split into two, of which the Marshall Plan was the most striking demonstration. Or to put it in more general terms, it was the entry of the USA into European politics .. Naturally this brought an immediate confrontation between the interests of the two World Powers. The Soviet Union had to safeguard the victory she had achieved in World War II.[15]

As Pavlíček has put it, Soviet foreign policy when faced with this situation "had to react, and to try to respond adequately."[16]

---

[11] *Zpráva komise UV KSČ o politických procesech a rehabilitacích v Československu 1949–68*, Vienna, 1970, p. 6.

[12] *Loc. cit.*

[13] Pavlíček, *op. cit.*, p. 178.

[14] *Zpráva komise UV KSČ o politických procesech a rehabilitacích v Československu 1949–68*, Vienna, 1970, p. 7.

[15] *Reportér*, Prague, No. 7, 1968, p. II.

[16] Pavlíček, *op. cit.*, p. 178.

One of its responses was certainly the final political, economic, and military fusion of Czechoslovakia into the Soviet bloc. It also follows with equal certainty from an examination of the Czech material that the Marshall Plan affair confirmed the view of Stalin and his advisers not only that Dr. Eduard Beneš and the National Front system were unreliable, but that the Gottwald group at the head of the Communist Party was not wholly reliable either.

Klement Gottwald and the other Communist members of the Czechoslovak cabinet had, of course, originally voted in favor of their country's participation in the Marshall Plan. The reasons for this surprising decision had never been clear. Not until 1968 was it possible to publish an illuminating interview with Prokop Drtina, former non-Communist Minister of Justice and a member of the government delegation which discussed the Marshall Plan with Stalin in Moscow. Drtina explains in this interview that Gottwald favored participating in the Marshall Plan, since "even the Communists appreciated the economic advantage for Czechoslovakia of such a policy."[17] Gottwald, moreover, had twice sought Moscow's view through "Party channels" prior to the Czechoslovak cabinet session. Receiving no answer, he evidently construed this as consent, even though he was "extremely embarrassed" during the cabinet meeting. Drtina continues:

> When we reached Moscow we discovered that the main point [of our visit] was to consider our attitude towards the Marshall Plan. Stalin was categorically opposed. But I am puzzled to this day why they had not made this clear before. Stalin told us in so many words that the whole thing was aimed against the USSR, who had not even been invited to the preliminary talks organized by the Western powers, but only at a later stage. Anyone lending themselves to this operation would have to be considered by the Soviet Union as participating in an operation hostile to itself. This was a surprise for the Czechoslovak delegation. All this time Stalin spoke calmly and quietly with no excitement or table-thumping. We had our treaty of alliance with the Soviets, obliging both sides to refrain from taking part in any action directed against the other partner's interests. Stalin chose his words so as to correspond to the treaty language.
>
> In the discussion on this subject Masaryk argued that he could see nothing incompatible with Soviet interests and that he had gathered nothing of the kind in his talks with foreign ministers in the West. I took a similar line, trying to find out why we had had no answer earlier. Stalin did not react to this; he left my arguments unanswered, as well as the proposal to send an observer who could leave later on.

---

[17] *Ibid.*, p. 179. The interview with Drtina took place on January 31, 1967, and the text was authorized by the former minister before publication.

Stalin reinforced his own argument by saying we were the only people's democratic state to agree to take part in the Plan (a statement to that effect had already been published before we reached Moscow), and that he had learned that the Polish government had decided against taking part. This was the first time we had heard of it.

In the discussion Stalin referred to Czechoslovakia's strategic position surrounded by Germany, and how much the Russian alliance meant for her.

Right from the start Gottwald made clear that we would fall into line. He was evidently influenced by his preceding conversation with Stalin.

It seems that Gottwald and the other leaders of the Czechoslovak Communist Party had finally acknowledged that the Soviet presence in the heart of Europe had to be taken into account whenever direct or indirect Soviet interests were at stake. At the same time it was obvious now that the Czechoslovak Communist Party "would in view of the exacerbated international situation...[have to] safeguard the people's democratic system and decide the issue of power once and for all in favor of the working class."[18]

Josef Pavel, who will be remembered as Minister of the Interior during the Dubček era and who was commander of the illegal working-class People's Militia at the time of the coup in February, 1948, declared early in the Prague Spring that the Marshall Plan had

> contributed to the economic division of Europe as well as to the economic expansion of the western part. The Americans were not so stupid [as to overlook the fact that] a prosperous Europe might take the wind out of the Communist sails, especially in France and Italy. It was the object of American policy to localize communism within its current limits   The Soviet Union had a prime interest at this time in consolidating its home front and consolidating its bloc of allies.. In that divided world Czechoslovakia, too, had to cast a clear vote.[19]

Some Prague historians assert that the main point of interest in the Marshall Plan affair was the *way* in which the Czechoslovak government was forced to change its original decision on direct instructions from Stalin. The incident afforded quite clear evidence even then of the "limited sovereignty" enjoyed by the Czechoslovak state. For this country, obviously, there existed "no other option but the Soviet one. The only subject for discussion was not *whether* to adopt pro-Soviet policies but *which* pro-Soviet policies to adopt."[20] And true enough, "by the second half of 1947 the Czechoslovak Communist Party was beginning, in accordance with the

---

[18] Bouček and Klimeš, *op. cit.*, p. 145.

[19] From a statement made on Czechoslovak television on February 24, 1968.

[20] Pavlíček, *op. cit.*, p. 180.

altered international situation...to refine its plans, especially the preparation of tactics for use in various contingencies."[21]

The exclusion of Italian and French Communists from their governments was undoubtedly a distress signal in Moscow's eyes, and served as an argument for those extremists in the Czechoslovak Party leadership who had long been demanding a tough line against their non-Communist partners in the National Front. The extremists started asserting that plans were brewing in non-Communist circles "to throw the Communists out of the government just as [had been done] in France,"[22] or in the Stalinist jargon of the day "to repeat in Czechoslovakia what international imperialism had managed to achieve in Italy and France—to break the wave of revolution."[23] One group of Czech historians writing during the Prague Spring says unequivocally: "Following the elimination of Communist representatives from the French and Italian governments, the Czechoslovak Communists were afraid of a similar attempt being made in their country."[24]

The Cominform and the Putsch of February, 1948

Viewing the Marshall Plan as an "American move aimed at grouping together all the Western capitalist states," the Communist movement responded to "the final splitting of Europe," the division of the Continent into "two antithetic and implacably hostile political blocs," by "setting up the Information Bureau of Communist and Workers' Parties."[25] At the inaugural meeting of the Cominform, held in September, 1947, in the little town of Szklarska Poreba in Polish Silesia, the Czechoslovak Communist Party's policy was severely attacked from the outset by the Soviet delegates. Its representatives, Rudolf Slánský and S. Baštovanský, were given to understand that they had failed to appreciate the consequences of the new situation, described by Zhdanov at Szklarska Poreba as follows: "The world is divided into two camps: the anti-democratic, imperialist camp on the one hand, and the anti-imperialist, democratic camp on the other."[26]

This first Cominform meeting at the same time expressed approval of the "huge and revolutionary changes" that had followed the last war. The

---

[21] Bouček and Klimeš, op. cit., p. 146.

[22] J. Hendrych in the Czechoslovak Communist Party's Central Committee organ, Život strany, Prague, No. 4, 1968, p. 1.

[23] J. Dolanský in Rudé právo, February 25, 1968.

[24] J. Belda, et al., Na rozhraní dvou epoch, Prague, 1968.

[25] Bouček and Klimeš, op. cit., p. 145.

[26] Quoted in Frederick C. Barghoorn, "The Soviet Critique of American Foreign Policy," Columbia Journal of International Affairs, New York, Winter, 1951, pp. 5–15.

balance of power "between capitalism and socialism had shifted radically in the direction of socialism, thanks to the historic victory of the Soviet Union over fascist Germany."[27] The list of political consequences attributed to this Soviet triumph was headed by "the complete victory of the working class over the bourgeoisie in every East European land except Czechoslovakia, where the power contest still remains undecided at the end of 1947."[28] It is obvious that the focus of attention at Szklarska Poreba was the Soviet delegation. Unfortunately, the records of this meeting, fateful as it was for Czechoslovakia, remained inaccessible even during the Prague Spring.[29] But the basic line is clear:

> The progressive unification of the socialist camp was being carried out with a view to applying Soviet methods of organization and social management in all the People's Democracies. This was in conflict with the earlier theory of separate ways to socialism, a theory now condemned by the Cominform and declared by the leaders of Communist Parties in the socialist countries to be "enemy doctrine." The process of forming the socialist camp revealed features which violated the principles of proletarian internationalism as applied to relations between socialist states.[30]

From published material and other known facts it may be concluded that the exclusion of the French and Italian Communists from their governments was a topic of heated discussion at the meeting, though the Soviet representatives and their East European partners seem to have looked upon what happened as a much worse blow than did the Italian and French delegates themselves.[31] In any case the fate of the Italian and French Communists was used as a warning to the Czechoslovak Communist Party. The historian Kaplan reports as follows:

---

[27] Miroslav Bouček, *Praha v únoru 1948, Prague,* 1963, p. 16.

[28] *Ibid.*

[29] In an article in *Nová mysl,* Prague, No. 6, 1968, Karel Kaplan remarks that he was not able to inspect the records of the first Cominform session and therefore could only deduce the course of the discussion from the published speeches and detached comments of Czechoslovak participants, as well as from their reactions to the debate.

[30] *Zpráva komise UV KSČ o politických procesech a rehabilitacích v Československu 1949–68,* Vienna, 1970, p. 7.

[31] There is interesting evidence in an interview with Fierlinger at that time. "I spoke to Thorez," he said, "when I was going through Paris after the Communists were thrown out of the government. It never occurred to Thorez that this state of affairs would last and that the Communists would not get back into the cabinet." (Quoted by Pavlíček, *op. cit.,* p. 178. Transcript authorized by Fierlinger on January 2, 1968.)

Criticism of the policies of the French and Italian Parties, which had been forced out of government, led to the rejection of the parliamentary road to socialism, and also to an extremely distrustful attitude on the part of several other parties. Among these was the Czechoslovak Communist Party, whose political orientation aroused in others anxiety about the fate of the revolution.

The Cominform interpreted the international situation and outlined the tasks of the Communist parties. Among the main factors in world affairs A. A. Zhdanov included the preparations by the imperialists, led by the USA, for a world war. Part of these preparations took the form of political and ideological attacks on the People's Democracies and the USSR. Therefore, in his view, the primary task of the Communist movement was to fight against American imperialism as the main enemy of peace and socialism, and especially against its "invasion of Europe." This struggle was to permeate all spheres of social activity in every country. All the Cominform members agreed with Zhdanov's evaluation and tried to project it into the policies of their own parties. So the inaugural meeting of the Cominform achieved, among other things, ideological unification of Communist and socialist countries under the leadership of the Soviet Communist Party, thus laying the groundwork for the creation of the socialist camp.[32]

It is hard, then, to contest the view expressed by another Czech writing twenty years after the event, that in looking back, from the moment the Cominform was set up "one can see not only a much intensified drive towards central management of the People's Democracies, but an aversion to the theory of specific roads to socialism and pressure for a faster solution to the *power question* in the last remaining People's Democracy where it had not been settled: Czechoslovakia."[33] Some Czech historians have concluded that the *international* scene was auspicious for a takeover in Czechoslovakia in early 1948.[34] The Soviet Union and the Cominform had made it obvious that they intended to reinforce their own bloc politically, and the Western powers, in particular the United States, were doing likewise. At the same time the Soviet bloc countries were expending "a great deal of resources and energy on developing modern military techniques and preparing themselves for war. They had a huge land force equipped with conventional arms and partly deployed in Europe, where there was as yet no equivalent

---

[32] Kaplan, *op. cit.*, p. 5.

[33] Pavlíček, *op. cit.*, p. 182 (italics added). Pavlíček enumerates a number of factors "marking a new situation." One was the sharp reaction of *Pravda* (January, 1948) to Dimitrov's published talk on the prospects for closer collaboration between the "People's Democracies." Dimitrov's plan to form a strong economic and political entity, independent of the USSR, was even at that time—as the Prague historian relates—"completely at odds with the trend of policy among the Soviet leaders towards the People's Democracies."

[34] E.g., Bouček, Klimeš, and Fiala.

counterforce in existence."[35] Be that as it may, the consensus of Czech historians in 1968 was that "the way the international scene was going in 1947 would probably have frustrated any compromise settlement (between Communists and non-Communists in Czechoslovakia) even if the domestic situation had made it possible."[36]

So all that remained was for the Communists to prepare the ground for a coup and to find the domestically suitable moment for it in the last country of the Soviet bloc where the question of power, Lenin's *Kto kogo?*, had still to be answered.

By a series of coincidences it turned out to be the leaders of the non-Communist parties who played into the Communists' hands, earlier and in a different way than the Communists had expected.[37] But neither side had any reason to delay the contest any longer, and besides the Czechoslovak Communist Party had made its promise to the Cominform. As nearly always happens in a democratic state when a single party or an alliance of parties wants to seize power, in Czechoslovakia the Communist Party "radicalized" the situation by making demands and presenting bills in parliament that were politically or economically impractical but had a demagogic impact by being socially attractive. When such bills were rejected by the National Front—as usually happened—or when they were voted down in parliament, the Communist Party would launch an intensive campaign, reproaching the opposition for breaking up the Front or favoring the rich. At the same time an hysterical clamor would be created

---

[35] We read elsewhere on the other hand that the Czechoslovak armed forces "had no military doctrine of their own. From the very start the [Czechoslovak] Communists argued for the acceptance of Soviet doctrine. Yet at this time Soviet military theorists were still developing their own ideas." Quoted from a remarkable address by Dr. J. Hodic given at a seminar of the Marx-Lenin Institute, November 9 to 11, 1967, and summarized in the periodical *Právník*, Prague, No. 4, 1968. Dr. Hodic noted that from 1949 on a sharp increase of military expenditure had occurred in Czechoslovakia, greater than in Britain, France, or even the USA. The increase in military investment—often wasted through continuously changing production plans—was at the cost of living standards. Dr. Hodic notes that there was even "a certain militarization of political life."

[36] Belda, *op. cit.*, p. 105.

[37] This is not to say that the Communists did not definitely expect a confrontation and were busy making preparations for it. At a Central Committee session in November, 1947, it was, for example, concluded that a "government crisis" would occur in 1948 (see Bouček, *op. cit.*, p. 20). This same session, according to Pavlíček (*op. cit.*, p. 184), played a decisive role in "shaping the new Communist Party line," while Bouček (*op. cit.*, p. 29) avers that it "inaugurated a new phase for the whole Party—the final round in the struggle to win an absolute majority of the public for the Party's policy."

about growing threats to the state "from without and within," represented by vague "forces of reaction" and their "agents." There was talk of anti-state conspiracies, of intrigues and assassination bids. All this was somewhat disturbing to the non-Communist parties and their leaders, who saw that the only way of forestalling mob rule was to hasten the general elections and find out how much strength the Communist Party really enjoyed.

A number of samplings of opinion had seemed to suggest that properly run elections would give the Communist Party considerably fewer votes than in 1946.[38] The Communist leaders were themselves aware of this, and as early as November gave out instructions, as we shall see, for "new-style elections" to be prepared. Any public proposal for "new-style elections" would be bound to break up the government coalition and cause a crisis. The Communists were, indeed, relying on such a crisis to occur sometime in the spring of 1948, and there is new evidence to show that Gottwald and his friends counted on provoking a crisis through the election proposals, rather than on the elections actually being held. As one Prague historian has said, then, in November, 1947, it was already "crystal clear that a decision had to be reached as to who held power. It only remained to settle when the critical moment was to be chosen, who would choose it, and how the choice would be made."[39]

The Home Front on the Eve of the Crisis

The outlook was bad in many ways. In their more recent writings Prague historians have depicted an array of problems causing tensions within the governing coalition, and have evaluated the impact of these problems on the Communist Party and on Party policy up to February. All the writers agree in estimating the seriousness of the economic difficulties, especially the supply of food, which plagued the country in the second half of 1947. The harvest was bad—with yields forty percent lower than the average of those for 1934–1938; rations had to be cut appreciably, especially bread rations; and the black market grew apace. The poorest segments of the population felt the shortage the most. Displays of public anger proliferated, with almost all the demonstrations opposing the Communist Party and its economic policy. In Slovakia, always the weakest

---

[38] In 1946, the Communist Party won 38 percent of the votes and the Social Democrats 12 percent, so that together these parties had a small but definite majority.

[39] Pavlíček, op. cit., p. 185. Another historian, describing conditions in the National Front in late 1947, writes that "Every issue discussed ended up with the power question: who could beat whom" (Zd. Deyl, "Jednání Národní fronty Čechu a Slováku v únoru 1948," in Dejiny a současnost, Prague, No. 1, 1968, p. 1).

link in the chain of Czechoslovak communism, rumors spread among the godfearing: "His wrath had at last overflowed and He was about to smite the Communists, for he could no longer...bear the sight of so much injustice."[40] Or as a Marxist historian put it in 1968: "In the eyes of the public it was the Communists who were most to blame for the way the economy was going. ...Every policy is judged by its objective results."[41]

To distract attention from a situation that was awkward for them, the Communist Party leaders came out late in August, 1947, with their demagogic demand for a "millionaires' tax." The proposal was a clever appeal to ordinary human envy, but of the political parties, even the Social Democrats opposed it, so that in early September the Communists were outvoted in the cabinet and thus suffered their first defeat since the war.[42] This setback was followed by two more defeats in parliament itself, namely in the voting (on September 10 and 12) on proposals to raise the salaries of public employees and to introduce a new land reform.[43] The unity of the National Front was clearly a thing of the past.

The Communist Party compensated for these failures, however, by using its power in a police-state fashion to reverse the unfavorable situation in Slovakia. Ever since the war had ended, the Czechoslovak Communist Party and its centralist leadership in Prague had been whittling down the rights of the autonomous Slovak bodies, as these were defined in the Košice program, and had even sought to hamper the work of its sister organization, the Slovak Communist Party. The latter had in any case been suspected from the first of "bourgeois nationalism," that cardinal sin which was to lead, soon after February, to the persecution, imprisonment, and even execution of leading Slovak Communists. In the previous

---

[40] Vl. Mináč, *Zvony zvoní na den*, Prague, 1963, p. 173.

[41] Belda, *et al.*, *op. cit.*, p. 151.

[42] The Communists were shocked by this vote. Their main paper published the names of the ministers who had voted against the Communist Party's proposal, and so deserved the pillory according to the political practices of that time.

[43] In this question too the Communist Party was mainly concerned to see "irresistible pressure" exerted on the non-Communist partners in the National Front. This emerges clearly from the records made partially accessible in 1968. The Communist Minister of Agriculture, J. Ďuriš, for example, suggested holding a congress of peasants' commissions to "push through the new land reform by sitting in permanent session until the National Front agreed to it. The proposal amounted to the creation of a kind of diarchy calculated to cause an immediate government crisis." (Belda, *et al.*, *op. cit.*, p. 199.) The Central Trade Union Council similarly reacted to the February 10 vote by summoning "on the initiative of the Communist Party" a congress of representatives of works' councils and trade unions, with the aim of "putting right...the government's incorrect decision!" (*ibid.*, p. 222).

year, the Prague Communists had attributed a spurious "anti-state conspiracy" to top men in the same Slovak Democratic Party which had
inflicted such a stinging defeat on the Communists in the 1946 elections.[44]
"The people," as the Communist papers said at the time, thereupon
demanded "in no uncertain terms that the conspiracy be liquidated." What
was in fact liquidated was the remains of the autonomous authority of the
Slovak government—the Board of Commissioners in which the Democratic Party held the absolute majority. This was accomplished by a whole
series of unconstitutional tricks and intimidations (including police-backed
strong-arm measures) organized by the Communist-run Ministry of the
Interior in Prague.[45] Fraudulent demonstrations and congresses were
staged, and even a one-hour strike during which "workers" demonstrated
against the "hegemony" of the Democrats, of all things. In these ways the
Czechoslovak Communist Party attained what it had been really aiming at
from the start: the elimination of Slovakia as a potential political force. In
doing so, it removed what might have proved to be a source of weakness and
vulnerability in the event of a fateful contest for power such as was becoming imminent.

The Social Democrats Tilt the Balance

A further warning of a shift in strength inside the National Front—a
shift once again to the disadvantage of the Communists—came in November,
1947, when the Social Democratic Party held its congress at Brno and
Zdenek Fierlinger and his left wing were defeated. The man who now
came to the fore, Bohumil Laušman, had co-operated with the Communists for years; but in the recent past he had several times voted with other
parties in the National Front and conducted secret talks with one or
another of them.[46] What was more important, the machinery of the Social

---

[44] The Democratic Party won 62 percent of the vote, the Communists
30 percent.

[45] The historian Kaplan stated quite clearly in 1968 that the February crisis
saw "the Slovak Democratic Party set largely at odds with its own leaders
by police action" (*Reportér*, No. 7, 1968, p. VI). Bouček and Klimeš are
more precise still: "The victory of the Democratic Party in the elections
created a widespread potential danger for the socialist forces in the whole country.
This forced the Communist Party to try to secure a radical improvement in the
balance of strength, to the advantage of the revolutionary side." (Bouček and
Klimeš, *op. cit.*, p. 146). Pavlíček also mentions "intervention by the security
forces" in the Slovak crisis (*op. cit.*, p. 184).

[46] In the end he fell between two stools, emigrated to the West but was
kidnapped in Austria by Czechoslovak agents and brought back to Prague.
There he died in unexplained circumstances, probably being murdered in prison.

Democratic Party now passed into the hands of officials who, unlike Fierlinger or Evzen Erban, were not fellow travelers.

The proceedings of the congress at Brno, the story of the behind-the-scenes activities of the Party's leading men and their inconclusiveness and indecision even at the height of the February crisis, are on the whole well documented; the Prague historians writing more recently have little to add to our knowledge here. Evzen Erban, then a member of the Fierlinger group and today on the Presidium of the Central Committee, confirmed in 1968 that there was "a close connection between the Brno congress and the political crisis of 1948."[47] He went on to say: "The line that gained acceptance at Brno was that the Communists should be eliminated from the government as they had been in France and Italy, or at least driven from their leading position in the National Front and isolated."

Eyewitnesses and historians are in any case agreed that the Social Democrats, though they had emerged as the smallest party from the 1946 elections, held the key to domestic political developments. And this was especially true during the third year after the war ended. As Professor Ducháček has put it:

> The weakest of the Czechoslovak parties, the Social Democrats, was the focus of political activity right from May, 1946, up to February, 1948. It was on them, too, that the Western socialist parties concentrated their attention; and so did the non-Marxist parties inside Czechoslovakia, and the Communists on their side as well. So it happened that the party which had been most heavily defeated in the elections . . . was solicited and cajoled by all the others.[48]

Although Communist fears of "isolation" in the National Front, such as Gottwald spoke of on November 17, 1948, must, as we shall see, have been allayed by and large long before February, they were genuine enough after the Brno congress and led the Communist Party to speed up its "mobilization schedule." Recent disclosures from the archives of the Slovak Communist Party show that soon after Brno, in early December, 1947, the Slovak Communist official Karol Šmidke proposed that "the National Front should be immediately regenerated from below by the creation, in every district and parish, of National Front Committees containing representatives of the mass organizations as well of as the political parties."[49]

---

[47] *Kulturní noviny*, Prague, No. 7, 1968.

[48] Yale Institute of International Studies, "The Strategy of Communist Infiltration: the Case of Czechoslovakia," New Haven, Connecticut, July, 1949, p. 30.

[49] Quoted by Belda, *et al.*, *op. cit.*, p. 197, from the Archives of the Institute for the History of the Slovak Communist Party, Central Committee Session of May 4, 1947.

In other words, a formal proposal to set up soviets was made nearly three months before they came into being. It was rejected. A straightforward explanation of these tactics was provided by the Communist Minister of Information, Václav Kopecký, at the session of the Czechoslovak Communist Party's Central Committee held in November, 1947. He said: "We possess great power. If we used it directly this might be called dictatorship. So we shall choose a moment to apply this strength when no one can accuse us of abandoning democratic methods."[50]

The Fifty-one Percent Theory

"Democratic methods" were held to include the "new-style elections" set for the spring of 1948. These had been under intensive preparation by the Communist Party since the previous autumn, both through the public campaign to secure the support of "the majority of the nation" and by way of winning over reliable fellow travelers among the other parties. One is compelled to ask in the first place why this new brand of elections, with a single list of candidates, had been chosen at all. The answer is, however, quite simple: the Communists knew that a repetititon of the democratic elections held by secret ballot in 1946 would inflict heavy losses on them.

Though Czech historical writings of the Stalin era of course firmly deny that there was any such danger, those of 1968 view the situation somewhat differently. Writing in 1968, Kaplan sees that "in this country it would be hard for anyone to get fifty-two percent of the vote with four parties in the field,"[51] that is, under the very system the Communists were proposing to replace by a "unified" one. Pavlíček quotes Gottwald himself as having told Laušman in confidence, in December, 1947, or the following month, that he "did not rule out the possibility of an electoral setback."[52] A poll taken by the Czechoslovak Student's Union in the autumn at the universities of Prague and Brno gave the Communists and Social Democrats together a mere 25 percent, with a crushing 75 percent majority for the National Socialists and People's Party. At the end of 1947 the Social Democrats cautiously anticipated that "the Czechoslovak Communist Party will remain the largest, but forfeit some of its votes."[53] In January, 1948, the Prague Institute of Public Opinion calculated that in the forthcoming elections the Communists would win only 28 percent of the votes,

---

[50] Quoted by Belda, et al., op. cit., from the Archives of the Central Committee of the Czechoslovak Communist Party, Vol. 01, Part 4, Entry 15.

[51] Reportér, Prague, No. 7, 1968, p. IV.

[52] Pavlíček, op. cit., p. 185.

[53] As recorded by Belda, et al., op. cit., p. 206.

or 10 percent less than in 1946.[54] A loss of this size would not only damage the prestige of the "leading" party but entail the loss of one or two of those ministries—the Interior, Agriculture, or even the premiership—which the Communists rightly considered essential for preserving their position of power. A vision of the French and Italian situations now haunted Communist Party headquarters. And it was this which led to the massive campaign for a single-ticket election instead of separate Communist candidatures.

Too little attention has been given to this campaign by historians at home and abroad, though it was highly significant for it meant the following three things: *First*, the Communist Party had been seriously preparing for elections with the hope of gaining what, only two months later, they were to attain without any voting at all through the February takeover. *Second*, the Communists had been conducting secret negotiations with certain leading figures in the other parties who were prepared to go along with them and betray their colleagues. *Third*, the very pattern proposed for these "unified elections" would have amounted either to a bloodless coup or to the deliberate provocation of a violent struggle for power.

It was at the November session of the Party Central Committee that Gottwald first mentioned steps to draw up a common list of candidates. "Our list," he said, "...must go beyond the framework of the Party and bring together everything that is really progressive and democratic in the country."[55] The Communists proposed, in other words, to enter the elections arm-in-arm with the collaborators from the other National Front parties, men rightly regarded by their own parties as turncoats and informers, but later described in Communist Party jargon as "representatives of opposition groups in the reactionary parties and among public figures."[56] The Communist Party was thus obliged to "fight the critical battle during the *pre-electoral period*, "so that the elections themselves, set for May, 1948, could "award a clear victory to the progressive forces,"[57] i. e., the Communists.

The chief instrument of success was not, then, intended to be the "gigantic rallying of Communist forces," as the Stalinist historians enthusiastically call it. More important than that, the Party Central Committee was advising members "to co-operate closely with opposition-minded and left-wing

---

[54] *Ibid.* The findings of the poll were published in *Anatomy of a Satellite*, Boston, 1952, p. 106, by the former Prague correspondent of the *New York Times*, Dana Adams Schmidt. Belda, *et al.* question the accuracy of this on the grounds that the poll had not been completed before the February events interrupted it.

[55] Klement Gottwald, *Spisy*, Vol. XIV, Prague, 1958, p. 192.

[56] Bouček and Klimeš, *op. cit.*, p. 143.

[57] *Ibid.*, p. 147, italics added.

circles in the other parties and so make sure that at the right moment all the National Front components could be purged of their right-wingers."[58] During the Prague Spring some highly intriguing and hitherto unpublished details came to light about this "co-operation." A special Department for Work within the Non-Communist Parties was set up in the apparatus of the Communists' own Central Committee. The man then in charge of it, O. Hromádko, was to describe his experiences at a specialist seminar in November, 1967, at which he made a great impression on his listerners. It was not until the Prague Spring that publication of a summary of his reminiscences was allowed, and then only in a little-known legal periodical, *Právník*, from which it is worth quoting in detail:

> [Hromádko's reminiscences] were mainly devoted to the period following the Brno congress, when the need appeared to embark on a policy of subverting the non-Communist Czech parties. He first described the phase immediately prior to the congress, when it was assumed that the right wing [of the Social Democratic Party] would support F. Tymeš in place of Zdenek Fierlinger, and the Communist plans to help the left wing maintain its position. When it became clear that B. Laušman had joined the right, a left-wing statement was drafted by agreement between Fierlinger, J. Štastný, and R. Slánský and read out next day at the congress. This laid the foundation for a new political grouping and for the concept of a list of candidates for the next elections comprising Communists and representatives of the mass organizations and opposition circles in the other parties. After the plenum of the Communist Party Central Committee in November, 1947, a department was set up in the Committee to deal with non-Communist parties, and its main job was to subvert the National Socialist Party... Contacts were made with various groups and individuals who for one motive or another had been at loggerheads with the new Party leadership, men such Koktán, Mátl, Jíše, Dr. Pátková, and the National Socialist co-operative farmers. Contact was even made indirectly with Dr. Richter, whom the National Socialist leaders had boycotted because of his progressive activities. All these groups and persons were gradually brought into mutual connection by conspiratorial methods. Dr. Šlechta had already co-operated with the Communist Party before the war.

> At the same time the Party began a campaign to win new members and from time to time published in *Rudé právo* the names of notable National Socialist officials who had joined the Communists. There was also a campaign to win support from National Socialist deputies in parliament for a possible united left-wing list of candidates, which, though not successful in every case (such as with Bolen, or when Koktán tried to solicit Ripka's agreement), increased the general nervousness among the National Socialist leaders. The same end was served by the proposal to call a nation-wide conference of opposition groups in the National Socialist Party, by the issue of a single

---

[58] Belda, *et al., op. cit.*, pp. 196–197.

edition of an illegal National Socialist opposition periodical, and so on. . . . This kind of splitting activity, which the Communists had practiced even before the war, was the only line that promised success.[59]

The idea of subverting the other parties arose in the higher echelons of the Czechoslovak Communist Party some time in the summer of 1947,[60] and implementation of the idea was begun in the autumn.[61] There are various records to confirm what was always suspected—namely, that the basic method was simply corruption. Ministerial positions were promised to any third-rate politician in the other parties who was ambitious and venal enough to allow the Communists to use his name at the appropriate moment in support of the united list of candidates, and to keep them informed of what his own party was planning to do. It was the assistance of these informers that enabled the Communist Party, when the February crisis came, not only to be accurately apprised of its rivals' intentions but swiftly to present to the President, when the non-Communist ministers unexpectedly resigned, a ready-made list of nominees for an "augmented" Gottwald cabinet. The additional members were simply National Socialist, People's Party, and Social Democratic politicians who had been suborned in this way.

Among the Social Democrats there was no secret about these maneuvers. Fierlinger himself has written as follows:

> The initiative came from Comrade Gottwald, who had the idea of a new National Front to include some officials of the other parties. The scheme was to have a common list of candidates with the names of prominent figures from all our political parties, and this would be published on the eve of the elections. We agreed to the proposal and started to prepare the operation. Unfortunately, the negotiations with some of the parties were not kept altogether secret. People began to talk about it, names leaked out, and in those cases where we could not publicly admit to everything we were in a very awkward position.[62]

Bitter quarreling and intrigues developed among these Social Democrats during the February events, for Gottwald had had talks not only with reliable fellow travelers like Fierlinger, Erban, Tymeš, and Koušova-Petránková but also with the middle-of-the-roader, Laušman. As a result, when the Social Democratic left wing approached Laušman on February 20

[59] *Právník*, Prague, No. 4, 1968, p. 365.

[60] According to a record by J. Linek dated March 7, 1966, and quoted by V. Pavlíček in *Politické strany po Únoru*, Prague, 1966, p. 100.

[61] Král, *op. cit.*, p. 68.

[62] Quoted by Belda, *et al.*, *op. cit.*, p. 198, from the Archives of the Central Committee of the Czechoslovak Communist Party, "On the History of the Struggle for Unity of the Working Class Camp in the Czechoslovak Republic."

—the very day the non-Communist ministers resigned—and asked him to set up a "left-inclined majority" based on "co-operation between Social Democrats and Communists," Laušman turned a deaf ear.[63] It must have caused him some quiet amusement when, three days later, his own party's left wing under Fierlinger walked out of a top-level meeting in protest at the rejection of the Communist proposals, for "while the left wing of the Social Democrats was announcing its disapproval of its party's policy, Laušman had meanwhile come to terms with Gottwald for the whole party to join his government."[64]

The other non-Communist parties paid little attention to the Communist antics in their ranks, and they paid heavily for this. They imagined that the activities of the Communists were designed simply to procure informers, rather than to lay the groundwork for a new system of power.[65] Thus, when the February crisis occurred, Gottwald was able to offer cabinet seats to prominent members of non-Communist parties, men duly appointed and duly exercising their offices. And he was able to present a list of these men to the President as spokesmen of parties now suddenly "regenerated."

The National Socialist deputy, A. Neumann, for example, was approached by a special messenger from Gottwald and told that the Communists counted on his support; the terms of the arrangement would be settled with Gottwald himself. On the night of February 22 the terms were indeed settled; Neumann was offered, and accepted, the post of Minister of Justice in place of the National Socialist minister, Drtina, who had just resigned.[66] About the same time Gottwald secretly conferred in his Prague villa with two confidants from the People's Party, Deputies J. Plojhar (a Catholic priest) and A. Petr. The conversation took the following course:

> Gottwald began by explaining the situation to us and telling us the Communist Party had decided to prevent a reactionary *Putsch*. At the same time he told us they intended that the National Front coalition should continue in the government, but there was no question of accepting any of the ministers who had abdicated. The National Front could only be regenerated with the help of honest people who had stood by the side of the working class. Finally, Gottwald told us he had discussed things and that the two of us could be

---

[63] Erban, *op. cit.*, p. 3.

[64] Pavlíček, *op. cit.*, p. 193. The writer adds that Laušman's intriguing somewhat upset the Fierlinger wing's relationship with the Communists.

[65] Cf., Julius Firt's essay "Záznamy" in *Svedectví*, Paris, No. 40, 1971.

[66] Neumann's statement was authorized by him on February 2, 1968. See Pavlíček, *op. cit.*, p. 191.

included in the next cabinet. He said he had seven portfolios to dispose of and we could choose whichever we liked. Petr chose Transport, and I asked if I could have Justice to look after. [67]

The most oppressive problem for President Beneš, however, and an extremely important one for the outcome of the crisis, was the web of intrigue in the armed forces. The roots of it went far back into the past, to the negotiations in Moscow over ministerial appointments to the first postwar Czechoslovak government and to the wording and implementation of the principle of heading certain ministries with "above-party personalities." This label was fastened by the Communists—with the accord of the other parties—on such men as General Ludvík Svoboda, who was appointed Minister of Defense (and was one day to become President of the Republic). Though the non-Communists never had any illusions about Svoboda's integrity, it was not until 1969 that the full extent of his perfidy in February, 1948, was revealed—by Svoboda himself. At a plenary session of the Party Central Committee in September, 1969, or over a year after the invasion of the country by the Five Powers, Svoboda made the following admission:

> In April, 1945, I was again summoned to Moscow, where a government had been put together. I was included and given the post of Defense Minister...I said to Gottwald: "Tell me, Clem, why don't you have me as a Party member now?" Clem was smoking his little pipe; now he took it out and said with a laugh: "Ludvík, d'you know what parity means?" (Laughter in the hall.) "Yes, I know what parity is, but what has it got to do with me?" He took his pipe out again and said: "It's got a lot to do with you!" Then he explained just what would happen if they took me into the Party, how every time they had a 'militant vote' in the cabinet they would lose one vote, mine, and a second one, Nejedlý's. Then there was Hasal, who was a Beneš man; but the Party had proposed him for the Ministry of Railways. Then there was Jan Masaryk; some comrades here will back me when I recall that he never took part in a militant vote. Whenever one took place he'd say: "Come along chaps, don't get into a fight," and go off ... So that's how the Party got four extra votes—as Comrade Gottwald explained to me.
>
> It was in May, 1945, that we came back to Czechoslovakia and finished this struggle successfully. And at that time Gottwald said to me: "Don't apply to join the Party any more now. When the time comes we'll invite you in, but meanwhile we shall be counting on you."
>
> I was a faithful and well-disciplined member of the Party. And when February, 1948, came along I was in a better position to help the Party and the

---

[67] *Ibid.* Plojhar's statement was authorized on February 16, 1968. In Slovakia, similarly, the then Chairman of the Board of Commissioners, Dr. Husák, simply nominated men loyal to himself in place of commissioners of the Democratic Party who had resigned.

state than I ever was with one battalion or one brigade, or with my own body come to that. Now it was the whole brand-new Czechoslovak army.

Some of you who were at the extraordinary session of the regenerated National Front may know that a lot of people complained we turned up late. Some people said: "Svoboda only joined in at a late stage because he'd been having dealings with the Social Democrats" and so on. Oh no, not at all. That was all done at Klement Gottwald's request—Zorin and Slánský were there at the time, when Gottwald said to me: "Well, Ludvík, will you be coming?" And I said "Yes, but I shan't be alone, another couple of generals will be coming too." "All right, but come along about eight or ten minutes after the start—it'll be more effective." What I said to that was "Now look here, Clem, we're soldiers, we can't turn up late." "No, you come eight to ten minutes later." All this was in his flat, and in the afternoon or evening there was a reception at the Soviet embassy. It was to celebrate the anniversary of the creation of the Soviet army. I saw Clem again there and he said to me, "You be here at the telephone, or get someone to wait at the telephone for you; we'll go on ahead and ring you from there." And that's what happened. It took us eight or ten minutes to drive there, so we arrived late. And when we opened the door we realized what Gottwald had meant by "effective." They'd never seen the army there before. And suddenly there we were, three generals. Well, naturally, it was a pleasant surprise.

When I spoke at that session I said the army was marching with the people. And not because anyone had ordered it to. I was practically in a position to do whatever I wanted, but strictly speaking I wasn't authorized to announce that the army was marching with the people, because there was a President and a Commander in Chief and I made this declaration without Dr. Eduard Beneš' consent. So I thought I should get into a lot of trouble. The next day Hasal rang me up and said the President wanted to talk to me. So I went to the telephone full of misgivings and heard Beneš saying: "I fully approve of your having gone to the session of the regenerated National Front and made the statement you did. I was particularly pleased at your saying that the army was on the side of the people." Naturally I was very bucked about this. And he went on to say: "I fully agree with the order you gave out in your capacity as Minister of Defense." That was an order in which I called on the army to follow my instructions unconditionally and made the individual commanders of local garrisons responsible for seeing they were obeyed. And I'd added: "At this difficult time, men, we must rally round more than ever, rally round our Commander in Chief, President Beneš, who represents the greatest force for unity at this moment." Beneš liked that bit. I could have put whatever I'd liked into my orders. Remember how lots of you criticized me and said, What's this idiot Svoboda doing? What's he saying these things for? We *had* to say these things so as to get the support of the unreliable elements that we had in the army. Well, judge for yourselves whether we were right or not. [68]

---

[68] From the official record—never published in Czechoslovakia—of the plenary session of the Czechoslovak Communist Party's Central Committee from September 24 to 25, 1969. Quoted in *Svedectví*, Paris, No. 38, 1970, pp. 293–294.

The spokesmen of the non-Communist parties were certainly in a very precarious position at the beginning of February. It is less certain, however, that they realized it themselves. As we have seen, the drift of international events was unpropitious, and no one had any illusions of help coming from "outside," that is, from the West. On the domestic scene, the non-Communist parties were now faced with further Communist challenges in the shape of another wave of nationalization, another bout of land reform to be forced on the country by a huge pressure campaign culminating in a congress of "peasants' commissions," and—as a parallel piece of black-mail—by a congress of works councils and trade unions. For all this the Communists required the support of the Social Democrats in order to secure majorities in the National Front, the cabinet, and parliament; but such support was a doubtful prospect, particularly in economic and social matters. Nevertheless, the Communists' preparations for a "unified" list of electoral candidates were now in full swing, and their splitting activities among the other parties promised favorable results. But this only confirmed the decision of the leaders of the National Socialist Party (prompted by its shrewdest spokesman, Hubert Ripka), and later of the leaders of the People's Party and to some extent those of the Social Democrats and Slovak Democrats, to bring things to a head. All the documents that came to light during the Prague Spring confirm what the Stalinist historians had averred, that this decision and its timing caught the Communist Party leaders by surprise. Yet once events had reached this point the Communists exploited them energetically; for it gave them an opportunity they would otherwise have had to seek or manufacture for themselves.[69]

---

[69] The background is well known. The Communists had long been boosting their positions in the secret police and other organizations controlled by the Ministry of the Interior and its Communist minister, Václav Nosek. The Prague Spring writers do not deny that "the Communist Party's influence in the executive bodies and departments of the Ministry of the Interior showed an upward trend," to quote Belda, *et al.*, *op. cit.*, p. 220. At a National Front meeting on February 5, 1948, the National Socialists proposed that a special commission be appointed to look into the situation in the police force. The Communists interpreted this as a move to curtail ministerial authority in this important sector and decided "not to give way an inch in the question of the security forces," as Gottwald told Ripka on February 9 (see J. Smutný, *Unorovy prevrat*, Vol. II, London, 1954, p. 3). At the cabinet session on February 13 the Communists again found themselves outvoted in a decision to instruct the Minister of the Interior to dismiss eight urban district police chiefs who had just been appoined in place of non-Communists. The Prime Minister's Office was to notify the government by February 24 that this instruction had been carried out. The next cabinet meeting, on February 17, broke up when it was ascertained that the decision about the police chiefs had not been imple-mented; it seemed pointless to go on when an individual minister was ignoring or

The Elegant Takeover

More recent information has added little to what is already known about the mechanics of the February takeover. However, it does cast some light on the frequently debated question whether the Communist Party achieved absolute power by methods that could be called constitutional, parliamentary, and peaceful, or whether it carried out an unconstitutional, illegal, violent *Putsch*.

For many years Stalinist historians had painted the episode as the model of a bloodless takeover in a fully developed industrial country. Scholars writing in 1968, even if highly critical of the Party's policies, confirm the tactical brilliance of its leaders in contrast to the pathetically amateurish showing of their rivals. In the words of one commentator:

> February was...an elegant performance. Everything had been masterfully prepared, nothing forgotten...Additional means of applying pressure, including the armed forces, had been kept in reserve, but everything went off beautifully without need of them...The Communist Party had managed to devise a superbly functioning mechanism for solving the basic political contest...it held all the prime levers of power.[70]

Hubert Ripka has described in detail what the non-Communist ministers proposed to do.[71] The weaknesses of their plan have been quite objectively analyzed by the Marxist historians of 1968. Kaplan writes:

> The National Socialist leaders had had no prior discussion of the steps leading up to the resignations—either with the Social Democrats or with the non-Party ministers. It was assumed they would automatically agree; simply because the main ground for resignation was the state of affairs in the security police, it was inferred that everyone who had voted for the National Socialist proposal on February 13 would resign too... But what in fact was the scene after the resignations had been handed in? Out of a cabinet of twenty-six, fourteen ministers were still in office. That being so, the Gottwald govern-

---

sabotaging a government decision. But the National Socialists had already made up their minds the previous night about the resignation of their ministers. Though their meeting was a secret one the Communists "were aware of the Opposition leaders' decision immediately after February 16." (See Jaroslav Šedivý's contribution to the symposium *Československá revoluce v letech 1944–1948*, Prague, 1966, p. 222.) The extraordinary cabinet meeting called by Gottwald for February 20 never took place, for on the same day the National Socialist, People's Party and (Slovak) Democratic ministers handed in their resignations to the President, and the crisis was on.

[70] *Reportér*, Prague, No. 7, 1968.

[71] In Hubert Ripka, *Czechoslovakia Enslaved*, London, p. 150. As early as February 23, Ripka sent a message to Gottwald saying he "realized that as a politician" he had lost the battle, and would "retire from political life now" (from the Central Committee archives, quoted by Belda, *et al.*, *op. cit.*, p. 233).

ment was still able to operate on the principle that it was competent to reach decisions as long as one half or more of its members, in addition to the prime minister, were present. This conclusion had been reached, moreover, by the Communist Party Presidium, which had abandoned the essence of the coalition's, and of the National Front's, political program. They had become forces of opposition, and since the country's system, People's Democracy, did not allow an Opposition they had ruled themselves out of political life.

To the Communists, the answer appeared to be to replace the ministers . . . and then to throw all their weight behind a single demand: that the resignations should be accepted and that the cabinet should be made up again with representatives of the regenerated National Front.

From the very moment that the government crisis broke out the Communist Party went vigorously on the offensive. It placed chief reliance on the Revolutionary Trade Union Movement, the Peasants' Commissions, and all the other organizations it controlled, and started setting up Action Committees as the actual instrument for mobilizing the masses.[72]

Kaplan adds his view that the non-Communist ministers were naïve to think the crisis of their resignation would be settled "by the old procedures of the pre-Munich Republic," by negotiation, that is, between the President, the Prime Minister, and the political circles as a closed system. But believing this, they threw the whole burden of responsibility onto Beneš. "And that," observed one writer in 1968, "is why they all lashed out at Beneš after February had happened, accusing him of leaving them in the lurch."[73]

The critical move in the six-day "February battle" was without doubt the lightning creation throughout the whole country of "Action Committees of the National Front." These were in fact soviets: new organs of government at all levels, from which any non-Communists were barred whom the Party cared to label as renegades, opposition forces, or traitors.[74]

The device was so effective that the Communists never needed to step up the pressure by staging the general strike they had been planning, let alone to call upon the armed forces they had standing ready.[75] The Action Committees, as the new historians remind us, played the "decisive role" in February, as they were set up "outside the existing structure of power and government." They arose "by a process of revolution" and wrested for themselves "wide-ranging authotity"; they became "an instrument of power which in each area brought about, by revolutionary means, changes

---

[72] Belda, *et al., op. cit.*, pp. 230–232.

[73] *Reportér*, Prague, No. 7, 1968.

[74] See J. Mlýnský, "Uloha akčních výborů Národní fronty pri zajištování únorového vítezství," in *Sborník historicky*, Prague, No. 12, 1964. Also see Pavlíček, *op. cit.*, p. 128 ff.

[75] Belda, *et al., op. cit.*, p. 236.

in the composition of the National Committees, of the political parties, and of the whole machinery of government."[76]

To all this the non-Communist parties had no means of reply—not even of verbal reply, for the Communist Minister of Information had effectively barred them from the radio. Their own newspapers were sabotaged from the first day of the crisis by Communist Party cells in the printing shops and distributing agencies. What is harder to believe, however, is that the non-Communist parties had made no contingency plans in case President Beneš should fail, as he ultimately did, to stand up to Communist pressure and break his promise by accepting the resignation of the ministers. Stalinist historians in the 1950's wrote about "preparations for a *Putsch*" by the non-Communist parties, about "armed commandos" under National Socialist orders, and about "the dark aims of reaction" bent on overthrowing the state. Their successors in 1968 completely ignore these *a posteriori* Party myths, or they allude to them with faint irony.[77] They find it still hard to explain, however, what it was that induced the non-Communist leaders to cause a crisis so suddenly and improvidently. They speak of "the unexpected resignation of the ministers, which for their opponents was of course a welcome windfall."[78] The only chance of success the non-Communists had was that the President would refuse their resignation and that the National Front coalition would be renewed in some new form or that elections would be called. But even here the Communist Party leaders turned the situation to their own advantage, concentrating "all their efforts"[79] on urging Beneš to solve the crisis their way and assuring him continually that they favored "a legal, constitutional, and parliamentary procedure."[80]

---

[76] *Ibid.*, pp. 238–239.

[77] "The leaders of the right-wing parties underestimated the effectiveness of campaigns among the masses... This partly explains the lack of effort that these parties put into such exercises themselves .. and hence a certain complacency on their part." (Belda, *et al., op. cit.*, p. 244.) (Or from *Reportér*, Prague, No. 7, 1968, p. V):

> The National Socialists were soldiers without a general, and the leaders of that party were generals without an army... During the most critical days Dr. Zenkl went off to Olomouc... to receive the freedom of Lanškroun... There he was told "Mr. Chairman, we shall not be giving you the freedom of Lanškroun..." They turned their backs on him, to his great perplexity... By the time he had got back from his weekend it was all over.

[78] Bouček and Klimeš, *op. cit.*, p. 150.

[79] *Ibid.*, p. 149.

[80] Pavlíček, *op. cit.*, p. 43. It is worth a passing remark that neither the Communists nor, more surprisingly, their opponents appealed to parliament throughout the crisis. Surprisingly at first blush, that is ; but in practice it was the National

Thus arose the thesis, so often quoted in Communist textbooks inside and outside Czechoslovakia, that the course of events demonstrated the possibility of a Communist Party acquiring absolute power by perfectly parliamentary and non-violent means in a state where a number of parties

---

Front, not parliament, which ever since the war had been "the alpha and omega of the new pluralist system" (*Dějiny a současnost*, Prague, No. 1, 1968, p. 2). Parliament was either obviated or else merely rubber-stamped whatever had been agreed in the National Front. Since during the February crisis there were no such agreements, but only dissension, nobody was sure how a parliamentary vote would actually turn out. Hence at the very height of the crisis the Speaker's Committee of the National Assembly decided *unanimously* that the plenary assembly for the following day should be canceled.

As one Prague historian was to write twenty years later: "At a time when the further course of the crisis was still hard to discern, none of the parties involved in the crisis evidently desired a full meeting of parliament" (Pavlíček, *op. cit.*, p. 192). And again: "Throughout the whole crisis...the thoughts of the right-wing parties never turned to parliament" (*ibid.*, p. 196). Pavlíček has analyzed in detail the options available to the non-Communist parties of achieving a genuinely parliamentary, constitutional settlement of the crisis. He concludes that "the National Assembly's decision was crucial for the fate of the government." If the democratic parties had insisted on the National Assembly being convened, the dice must clearly have fallen against the Communists (*ibid.*, p. 197). The non-Communist ministers, far from considering this solution, went out of their way to help Gottwald fulfill his role as premier. For as soon as parliament had been pushed out of the picture "the mere proposal to fill the empty ministerial seats was enough to enable the government to start functioning again" (*ibid.*, p. 198). The non-Communists were themselves to rue their frequent resort to undemocratic methods. Drtina, the former Minister of Justice, explained this as follows in an interview with Pavlíček:

> It was a feature of public life in the First Republic that votes of confidence were never held; everything always depended on agreement and support in parliament—if these were lacking, a crisis was on the way. A large role in this was played by the Petka, the Big Five, who had no constitutional authority at all, but did enjoy real authority...So none of the non-Communist parties now spared a thought for parliament; they all regarded the National Front as a kind of coalition (albeit with a different structure and way of acting) in which the Communists held preponderant power.

Belda, *et al.* (*op. cit.*, p. 261) make a similar point:

> The course of the February crisis in the government might have been greatly affected by the National Assembly. That it was not is due less to Communist policy than to the lack of prior planning by the non-Communist parties and to their general amateurishness. For the National Assembly was in a position to express non-confidence in the government and this would probably have led, in the circumstances of the day, to the election date being advanced...The position in the Assembly was very complex...A diffuse debate would probably have resulted, which might have made the crisis both more complicated and far longer. But some of the spokesmen of the non-Communist parties, including sections of their leadership, preferred to put off a National Assembly session in the expectation of a decision coming primarily from the President.

had previously shared that power democratically. As late as 1960, Minister of Information Kopecky was writing that "...the way our people settled accounts with the forces of reaction in February was conformable with democratic procedures, legal methods, and constitutional and parliamentary requirements."[81] The Marxist historians of 1968, be it noted, took a considerably different view, and this is their most signal contribution to a juster assessment of the events of twenty years before.

Negotiation If Possible—Force If Necessary

What the non-Communist parties were banking on in the February showdown was not so much a constitutional as a presidential solution. In this respect the Communists agreed with them, but in contrast had alternative plans in readiness, such as forcing Beneš himself to resign if he were unprepared to approve the new "regenerated" National Front cabinet, or such as resorting to armed conflict. In the Communist Party's deliberations about whether to negotiate or, as some radicals like Duriš and Kopecký were suggesting, to "fight it out," the personal prestige of President Beneš with the Czechoslovak public played an important role. The Communists realized that his prestige was "exceptional,"[82] and to persuade him to accept their solution would itself be a triumph. During the critical days, Gottwald accordingly visited Beneš at least six times, flanked by the Trade Union Chairman, Zápotocký (who described for Beneš' benefit the "deep dissatisfaction of the workers"), and by the Minister of the Interior, Nosek (who intimidated the President with accounts of the revolutionary mood among the "broad masses of the public"). Each time they asked Beneš to accept the resignations and sign his approval of the new government, and in the end they backed their request with threats.

At this point the lineaments of the alternative—violence—become visible. The Communists did not resort to force, but they made ample play with the threat of it. That, in the given situation, proved to be perfectly adequate. The convocation of the Congress of Works Councils and the Congress of Peasants' Commissions was the first step towards setting up extra-parliamentary pressure groups. The mob was now expected to coerce the National Front into ruling in a style which it had already voted against; the creation of "National Front Action Committees" through the length and breadth of the country conferred a pattern of organization and authority upon what was completely illegal activity. Other extra-parliamentary activities by the Communists included the passing of "spontaneous"

---

[81] Kopecký, *op. cit.*, p. 422.
[82] Pavlíček, *op. cit.*, p. 198.

resolutions and the dispatching of alleged workers' delegations to confer with the government or the National Front. In Slovakia, an illegal Slovak Partisans' Headquarters was set up as the "steering body" of the auxiliary police forces. In some of the larger factories the ranks of the militia were strengthened, and distribution of weapons began.

There is little mystery today about the issuing of arms, first to the Factory Militia and then to the new and extra-legal People's Militia, whose "General Staff" was set up under a Communist commander, J. Pavel, on the morning of February 20. As one of his many acts of indiscretion, Minister Kopecký wrote in 1960 that on February 25, 1948, "tens of thousands of brand-new rifles and automatics were sent by the arms factory workers in beautiful crates with all accessories, and within a few hours these had been handed out to the working-class elements of the newly created People's Militia."[83] Pavel himself was to add further details later:

> When the crisis had been going on for four days, ten thousand rifles and two thousand automatics were brought up on seven lorries from the Brno arms factory through Šling's good offices. Was it fear or caution that made us leave the automatics...in their cases and only hand out the rifles to the workers—practically without ammunition—on the last day of the crisis? Why did we let the Militia out onto the streets only when the new government had been practically confirmed?[84]

In a radio interview dating from the same period Pavel admitted that the creation of the People's Militia was "not entirely in accord with our legal code." However, the Communist leaders had not wanted to use the police against the "people." "In no circumstances were we prepared to disperse crowds with rifle-butts, or in fact to use force. That is why we did not want to use the police; but equally we could not let the situation get out of hand. We had to use workers, the People's Militia in fact."[85]

Other commentators agree that the formation of the Militia "went beyond the authority of the police." To quote one of them: "As armed units the People's Militia had no precedent in Czechoslovakia.... Their total strength in the February crisis amounted to between fifteen thousand and eighteen thousand workers, the largest units being in Prague where the Militia was 6,650 strong."[86]

There is plenty of evidence for the generalization of one Prague historian who writes that in February, 1948, the Communists "used both parlia-

[83] Kopecký, *op. cit.*, p. 412.
[84] *Mladá fronta*, Prague, February 25, 1968.
[85] In a talk on Czechoslovak radio, February 16, 1968.
[86] Belda, *et al.*, *op. cit.*, p. 251.

mentary and extra-parliamentary methods to reach an immediate and final solution of the power question."[87] He points out that

> ...each component of the armed forces—Militia, police, and army—contributed to the final issue of the February confrontation...Basically, the government crisis was settled in accordance with constitutional methods. But in some respects of course the constitutional and parliamentary framework of those days was broken through, notably by the Action Committees in purging the lower Party levels and state and governmental bodies, and again by the establishment and arming of the People's Militia...It was the work of the National Front Action Committees and the appearance of the People's Militia that represented the element of revolutionary violence in the February events. Nevertheless, recourse to force was not planned ahead by the Party (despite sectarian voices that had been calling for a solution by force ever since the war ended); it merely arose in February, 1948, from the actual situation at hand and from the methods of struggle chosen by the reactionaries.

As this writer, Pavlíček, insists, it would be wrong, then, to exaggerate the legal, constitutional, and parliamentary aspects of the crisis settlement:

> The largest role was that of the political operations organized by the Communist Party: the creation of the Action Committees, the existence of the People's Militia, and the enormous enthusiasm of the great majority of the working class and the masses of the people...February was the true watershed of the revolution...It was February that decided in principle which of the two paths Stalin had spoken of in 1946 Czechoslovakia would now pursue. She had chosen the Soviet path.[88]

Or as Belda, writing twenty years later, after the Soviet invasion, still had the courage to put it: "The February confrontation cannot be reduced to a struggle solely between capitalism and socialism. For at the same time a battle was in progress between two concepts of socialism."[89]

In their re-evaluation of the February takeover, most Marxist historians described the mode of its execution in such terms as "a constitutional settlement of a government crisis, and at the same time a revolutionary settlement of a general political crisis throughout the country...a shift of power... through a contest outside the electoral field."[90]

At the same time, writers of this camp declare that "in countries of the western European kind, a socialist revolution obviously cannot be a single act.... The struggle for leadership in such countries makes it needful to win the support of the masses for any proposed steps before complete power is assumed."[91]

---

[87] Pavlíček, *op. cit.*, p. 150.
[88] *Ibid.*, p. 200.
[89] *Reportér*, Prague, No. 7, 1968.
[90] Belda, *et al.*, *op. cit.*, p. 271.
[91] Bouček and Klimeš, *op. cit.*, p. 152.

It remains to say something about Soviet involvement in the February events. There was much excited talk about this at one time, especially in connection with the sudden visit to Prague of the Soviet Deputy Minister of Foreign Affairs, Valerian Zorin, on February 19. But there was no proof of direct Soviet intervention then, nor is there any today. This is not to say there was no pressure from Moscow—political, diplomatic, ideological, and above all psychological—in favor of the Czechoslovak Communist Party. Recent Marxist writings admit this quite clearly. One of them, for example, quotes with approval the verdict of Sir Robert Bruce Lockhart that Russia "neither provoked [the February crisis] nor decided upon its timing, though there was no doubt that she could have forced a decision one way or another whenever she wished."[92]

When he came to Prague, Zorin held numerous consultations with non-Communist as well as Communist ministers. The fiction was maintained that he had come to check on Soviet grain deliveries to Czechoslovakia. In fact, he came to check on the crisis and, if need be, to alert the Soviet leaders. Not until twenty years had passed was it publicly stated that Zorin had discussed the domestic front in Czechoslovakia with Gottwald, that "Soviet political leaders had long been restive over anti-Soviet trends in some areas of Czechoslovak public life," and that Zorin had promised Gottwald "the Soviet Union would not allow the West to interfere in Czechoslovakia's internal affairs."[93] There was, of course, no such threat from the West. Zorin's wording, reiterated in *Pravda* of February 22, 1948, ominously foreshadowed the pre-invasion menaces of 1968.

The February crisis developed so rapidly, and so favorably for the Communist side, that Stalin had no reason to intervene directly. The Soviet Union, in the terminology of the day, wished to see "a further reinforcement of Czechoslovakia's character as a People's Democracy."[94] That wish was granted in February. So one can in principle accept the view of the 1968 historians that "no open, external interference in Czechoslovakia's domestic affairs took place during the February events."[95] As one of the Prague Marxists points out, of course, "the chief interest in settling matters was felt on the other side," that is, in Moscow and in the Cominform, a fact of which "the revolutionary forces inside Czechoslovakia were well

---

[92] "The Czechoslovak Revolution," *Foreign Affairs*, New York, July, 1948. (Quoted by Belda, *et al., op. cit.,* p. 268.)

[93] Belda, *et al., op. cit.,* pp. 264–265.

[94] *Ibid.,* p. 265.

[95] *Ibid.,* p. 268.

aware."[96] As another writer puts it, "a showdown with the bourgeoisie...
had to come, and so did a power-political clarification of the Czechoslovak
scene."[97] No matter how the showdown might have materialized, we read
elsewhere, "the final result would have been the same."[98]

Conclusions

Recent Marxist accounts of the events in Czechoslovakia in 1948 hold
in common that the deterioration of relations between the victors of World
War II played a crucial part in the Communist takeover. The promulgation
of the Marshall Plan and the setting up of the Cominform are often cited as
milestones along the road to the protracted Cold War, which Stalin and his
entourage seriously expected to turn at any moment into a shooting war.
By the end of 1947 Czechoslovakia was the only "People's Democracy" in
the Soviet sphere where the Communist Party had not yet acquired absolute
power. This situation, given the international context, was untenable.
Moscow and the Cominform accordingly put constant pressure on the
Czechoslovak Communists to change the balance of power inside the
country for once and for all to the Party's advantage.

This pressure, and the flat commands which were presumably given
towards the end, were not to be resisted. They even ruled out a compromise
between the Communist and non-Communist parties; the non-Communist
parties of course tried hard to achieve a compromise, but the Communists
in Prague would not accept such an arrangement because it was unacceptable to Moscow. To the surprise of the Czechoslovak Communist Party it
was the leaders of the *other* parties who brought things to a head. They
imagined that in the cabinet crisis which they themselves provoked they
would enjoy the critical support not only of the small Social Democratic
Party, but also of the "specialist" ministers with no affiliation, and, above
all, of the President. Almost from the very first hours it was clear that none
of these assumptions had come true. And the non-Communists had no
alternative plan in their pockets.

For their part, the Communists were justified in fearing that in consequence of the failure of government policies in several fields they would
lose hundreds of thousands of votes in any fair election and so forfeit their
claim to the "leading role" in Czechoslovakia. For this reason, they started

---

[96] Jaroslav Šedivý, "Ješte jednou k únoru 1948," *Príspévky k dejinám KSČ*,
Prague, No. 4, 1966, p. 513.

[97] Jaroslav Kladiva, "Uvodní referát konference historiku k 20. výročí
osvobození ČSSR," in the symposium *Československá revoluce v letech 1944–1948*,
op. cit., p. 42.

[98] Bouček and Klimeš, *op. cit.*, p. 150.

preparing a "unified" list of candidates—an electoral fraud familiar in every Communist-dominated country. At the same time the Communist Party systematically used corruption to gain a foothold in the non-Communist Parties and win collaborators within their ranks. These collaborators proceeded to prove their value not only in the February *Putsch* but throughout the twenty years to follow.

The Stalinist historians' claim that the Communist Party reached power in 1948 by non-violent and constitutional means is basically false. The government crisis was settled in accordance with constitutional forms thanks to the democratic principles and intentions of the non-Communist coalition partners, and to the Communists' own preference for a bloodless takeover. But apart from that, everything the Czechoslovak Communist leaders did and planned to do in aid of a "constitutional solution" was unconstitutional, illegal, and based on force. It was only the fact that the Communists achieved a quick and easy victory that made an armed *Putsch* superfluous. Weapons had already been distributed and further supplies made ready; militia units had been formed in the factories; the generals were on call. If anything had gone wrong, Zorin was in Prague to recommend that the Red Army intervene, and there is no reason to doubt that if Stalin received such a recommendation he would have acted on it. Czech Marxists writing recently are quite clear on this.

It follows from all this that in 1948 the non-Communist leaders in Prague had only a choice between various roads to defeat. Their long-term strategy, and even their tactics in starting and ending the crisis, were patently improvised, defensive, ill thought out, and lacking planning for a contingency. The faith they, as democrats, had in a constitutional outcome was in a sense touching; their political amateurishness was unforgivable. President Beneš' behavior may be partly excused on grounds of serious ill health; all the same, it must be said that his conduct was smart rather than statesmanlike. What was worse, he and his political followers did not always adhere to the spirit or the provisions of the constitution, while on the other hand Beneš never found the nerve to frustrate Communist maneuvers by calling upon the police or the armed forces, as the constitution not merely allowed but directed him to do if a *Putsch* threatened.

Such were the wages of the continuous postwar undermining of democracy—encouraged, among other things, by a "closed" coalition and consequent formation of all policy behind closed doors, by the ban on forming new parties or reviving certain old ones, by the habit of by-passing parliament, and by the establishment of "mass" organizations to exert pressure. In this way, totalitarian or pseudo-revolutionary principles penetrated into the very foundations of the parliamentary system. The spokesmen of the democratic parties did not simply tolerate these radically undemocratic features of "Peoples' Democracy" but formally incorporated them in the government's initial postwar program and in numerous decrees and draft bills over the following three years.

In their recent writings Czech historians show that it was these anti-democratic saplings which grew up into the hideous jungle of Stalinism that overshadowed the next twenty years. The same writers discern the links between February, 1948, and the stormy period of the Prague Spring, with is tragic sequel in August, 1968. And they even suggest between the lines that the "February victory" was the forerunner of a great defeat: the defeat alike of democracy and the Democrats, and of the Communists and their own ideals too.

Finland in 1948: The Lesson of a Crisis

Kevin Devlin

In this series of studies of Communist takeovers I have to discuss one of the interesting and possibly instructive cases of a takeover which failed to take place. Within the general framework of a survey of Communist techniques for the seizure of power I have to examine the reasons why a strong and well-organized Communist Party, in very favorable geopolitical circumstances, did not seize power in Finland in the early postwar years.

What happened in Finland in the spring of 1948—and what *might* have happened—is still to a considerable extent a matter of speculation and controversy, as we shall see. It is also a matter of more than academic interest. If Finland, an outpost of Nordic democracy, was in danger of falling under Communist rule through a minority coup or Soviet intervention, then it is clearly important to find out, if we can, just why Finland escaped that fate. This inquiry will help us to understand better the complex phenomenon called the Cold War, which has been the dominant factor in international life for the past generation. It may lead us to the conclusion that Finland's postwar experience is of wider, and neglected, relevance; and it will certainly lead us, I think, to re-examine some of the postulates on which our world-view is based.

In the years after 1948 we heard a good deal about "the lesson of Czechoslovakia" (though whether that lesson was correctly interpreted is another matter). But in those years of East-West polarization and Manichean loyalties the Western public heard comparatively little about the contemporary lesson of Finland. This neglect was understandable, if regrettable. At a time of such historic confrontations as the Berlin blockade and Tito's defiance of Stalin, a short-lived crisis in a minor North European country was of peripheral concern. Moreover, for linguistic as well as geographical reasons, Western political scientists and journalists paid, and have continued to pay, relatively little attention to Finnish developments in general and the fortunes of Finnish communism in particular.[1] However, this relative neg-

---

[1] Among the few good works in English on this subject are: John H. Hodgson, *Communism in Finland*, Princeton, N. J., 1967; Bengt Matti, "Finland," in W. E. Griffith, (ed.), *Communism in Europe : Continuity, Change and the Sino-Soviet Dispute*, Cambridge, Mass., 1966, Vol. II, pp. 371–410; and James H. Billington, "Finland," in C. E. Black and T. P. Thornton, *Communism and Revolution : The Strategic Uses of Political Violence*, Princeton, N. J., 1964, pp. 117–144.

lect is to be regretted because, notwithstanding the country's unique geopolitical situation, even today we do have something to learn from the Finnish story. But before we ponder that lesson—before trying to find out just
what happened in Finland in the spring of 1948—we must glance briefly at
the background: at the history of Finno-Soviet relations and that of the
Finnish Communist movement over the past half-century.

Finnish communism began in blood and bitterness. The country's declaration of independence in December, 1917 (after seven centuries of Swedish rule and a century as a Tsarist province), was followed within weeks by
the outbreak of a short but savage civil war, pitting bourgeois-nationalist
forces against a Red Guard fired by the Leninist example. With the help of
a small but effective expeditionary force sent by the embattled Germans,
General Mannerheim's nationalist army decisively defeated the Red Guard.
Tens of thousands of the defeated revolutionaries were placed in concentration camps (of the British Boer-War type, not the Nazi type), where more
of the insurgents perished through neglect and ill-treatment than had
died in the actual fighting. Others, including most of the Red leadership,
fled to Russia; and there the Communist Party of Finland (SKP—*Suomen
kommunistinen puolue*) was founded in exile—a fact of more than symbolic
significance. From the first, and apart from the hierarchical discipline of the
Comintern (Communist International), a special relationship existed between the SKP and the Communist Party of the Soviet Union (CPSU)—it
was more than historical accident that led Otto Kuusinen, the father of
Finnish communism, to end his long life as a member of the top Soviet
leadership.

Defeat in the Civil War left the "domestic" Communists facing a bitter,
uphill struggle, during which they repeatedly attempted to form and dominate alliances with left-socialist forces. In 1928 police raids largely broke
up the clandestine *apparat* set up in accordance with Comintern instructions. Two years later, following an anti-Communist campaign by the right-
wing nationalist "Lapua movement," the SKP was formally banned. On
the level of domestic politics, then, the prewar story was one of class
militance and bitter antagonisms—a record of repeated failure which nevertheless laid the foundation for the SKP's future strength as the party of
social protest.

While the SKP struggled through semi-legality into clandestinity, the
new Finnish state was meeting the problem of relations with its powerful
neighbor to the east through a policy of what might be termed anti-Soviet
neutralism. Two wars within a few years put an end to that policy. The
attack launched against Finland by the Soviet Union at the end of Novem-

ber, 1939, was not aimed at annexation: its primary purpose evidently was to strengthen the USSR's defensive position on the Leningrad front, and the Finns could almost certainly have obtained peace by acceding to the Kremlin's limited territorial demands. However, a secondary and more tentative purpose—the restoration of suzerainty over the former Tsarist province—was indicated by the installation of a puppet Communist government under Otto Kuusinen at Terijoki on the Karelian Isthmus. It appears that an important factor in this secondary, political plan was the belief of the SKP leadership—a belief they impressed upon Stalin—that a substantial part of the Finnish working class would rally to the Terijoki government and refuse to support the war effort.

A number of factors contributing to the drama of the Winter War were to exercise a decisive influence on the postwar developments that are our main concern. First, there was the immensurable but extremely important element of national character: during those critical years the Finns proved themselves to be a tough, patriotic, stubborn and, finally, realistic folk. Receiving much admiration but little practical help from the Western democracies, they fought back with skill and valor at the Mannerheim Line, in the forests and on the frozen lakes.

At the same time the Winter War brought proof that Finnish Communists and the working class they aspired to lead were not immune to the virus of militant patriotism: far from it. Despite a tradition of class struggle, Finnish workers rallied to the anti-Soviet war effort as wholeheartedly as the farmers and the bourgeoisie—and so did thousands of individual Communists. The most important of these was Arvo Tuominen, the Secretary-General of the SKP. A veteran of the Comintern, and apparently steeled in loyalty to Stalin, whom he had actually served for a time as personal secretary, Tuominen was to have headed the puppet government at Terijoki. In reaction to the shock of the invasion, however, Tuominen not only refused to accept the Terijoki Premiership (which then went to Otto Kuusinen) but also defected from the Communist Party and called on Finnish workers to fight the Soviet invaders. Subsequently, he put his polemical gifts at the disposal of Väinö Tanner's Social Democrats—in the anti-Communist cause. His defection was a lesson the Russians, and the Finnish Communist leaders, would not forget.

A third important factor was the caution which Stalin brought to his exercises in international *Realpolitik*, and which in this case was accentuated by his desire to avoid a conflict with the Nazi regime. The settlement that the Soviet Union imposed on the outmatched but unconquered Finns at the end of the Winter War in 1940 could not be called punitive: it consisted mainly of the annexation of the Karelian Isthmus and other territories around Lake Ladoga, with the obvious aim of guarding the Leningrad marches.

What is worth noting is that the Russians did not insist—as they clearly could have done—on the relegalization of the Finnish Communist Party as part of the 1940 peace settlement. Similarly, Stalin lost interest in Otto Kuusinen's puppet government as soon as it became clear that it had virtually no support within Finland. Here we come upon another of the important and enduring factors: the Soviet leadership's tendency to subordinate the interests of the SKP (and of other foreign Communist parties) to its own *raison d'état*.

If the Finns, defeated but certainly not humiliated, had remained neutral for the rest of the war, it would have been better for the country—and worse for the SKP. However, the destiny of the SKP and the course of Finno-Soviet relations were both fatefully changed in the summer of 1941, when, following Hitler's invasion of the Soviet Union, the Finnish government (or, rather, a majority faction of the government) seized the chance to wage what was essentially a revanchist war as "cobelligerent"—not, strictly speaking, an ally—of the Third Reich. The Winter War had been waged by a nation united in patriotism, but this was by no means true of the so-called Continuation War (1941–1944). Discontent over the virtual alliance with Nazi Germany was perhaps the most important factor in preparing the way for the political strength of the SKP and its left-socialist allies during the postwar period.

The effects of what must be reckoned a strategic error were, however, tempered by the tough realism of the Finns. In 1944 they once again admitted defeat. They then had to fight their third war within four years, to expel the German expeditionary troops in accordance with the new peace settlement imposed by the Russians, and they did so in somber acceptance of a profoundly changed situation. For the defeat in the Continuation War, within the wider context of the impending Allied victory over the Third Reich and the advance of the Red Army into Central Europe, had transformed Finland's geopolitical situation. Premier (later President) Paasikivi summed it up in late 1944 when he observed that henceforth the first principle of Finnish foreign policy would have to be to avoid anything prejudicial to Soviet interests. It is worth recalling that when Churchill and Stalin reached their agreement in November, 1944, whereby postwar "spheres of influence" in various East-Central European countries were expressed in percentage terms, Finland was not among the countries considered. At the end of World War II there can have been little doubt in the mind of any statesman, East or West, that Finland lay within the Soviet sphere of interest. An important corollary was that if Finland was to maintain its status as an independent, pluralistic democracy within the geopolitical shadow of the Soviet Union, it would have to rely upon its own efforts and resources to do so.

This was to be a crucial factor in the developments of 1948. But it was balanced by an even more important circumstance: if Finland lay within the Soviet sphere of influence, this affected mainly its international policies and not (or at least very much less) its domestic affairs. The Soviet victors made no attempt to weaken, let alone dig up, the roots of Nordic democracy, which already ran deep in Finland. If they had, they would certainly have had trouble on their hands: remembering the anti-Communist populism of the up-country Lapua movement and the nationalist fervor of the Winter War, they might also have noted that the Finnish coat of arms features a brandished crusader's sword.

Of course, the Russians, acting through the Soviet-dominated Allied Control Commission, did exert influence on domestic Finnish affairs in the early postwar years. But when they did so, it was mainly in order to promote the political fortunes of the now relegalized SKP or to hinder those of Väinö Tanner's social-democratic party (SSP). Apart from this limited but useful Soviet assistance, the ascendant SKP had other sources of strength in the immediate postwar period. One was the tradition of working-class radicalism already noted. Another was the fact that Tanner's Socialist Party was not only deeply divided but also, in the eyes of many Finns, discredited because of the virtual alliance with the Third Reich during the Continuation War. In this situation the Communists reverted to Kuusinen's Leftist Front strategy.

In late 1944 the Communists joined a strong grouping of secessionist left-wing socialists to form a new electoral front organization, the SKDL—the Finnish People's Democratic League. From the first, the Communists dominated the SKDL and its ancillary organizations. They held the great majority of the League's Diet seats; they provided its Secretary-General, while a non-Communist held the less important post of Chairman. There was no doubt that the SKDL functioned as an instrument of Communist policies. Nevertheless, this political strength was to some extent deceptive. The Communists dominated the SKDL organizationally and politically, but they constituted only about one-third of the League's membership and a still smaller minority—perhaps between one-sixth and one-eighth—of the SKDL electorate. This was another important limitation on their ability (assuming that they so desired) to move outside the framework of constitutional democracy.

In the 1945 elections the Communists, acting through the SKDL, became one of the four major forces in Finnish political life—the others being the Agrarian (later Centrist) Party, the social-democratic SSP, and the Conservatives. In these elections the SKDL won 23.5 percent of the total vote and one-quarter of the Diet seats. The SKP thus became, and has remained, one of the "Big Three" of West European communism. Like the Italian and French Communist Parties, it can count upon getting between one-fifth and one-quarter of the national vote, and its electoral strength has been more stable than that of the other two.

The Communists now not only were in the government but also occupied some very important posts in it. On the eve of the 1948 crisis, they or their left-socialist allies in the SKDL held the Premiership and the portfolios of the Interior, Defense, Social Welfare, Public Works, and Transportation, as well as controlling some key trade unions and the national radio system. The most important of these Communist office-holders, for our story, was the Minister of the Interior, Yrhö Leino, who was to play a central, if still obscure, role in the events from February to April, 1948. His ministry directed what amounted to a para-military force, the 1,000-strong mobile police. In addition, a new state police force of some 400 men—later abolished after an investigation into its activities—was under the control of a tougher Communist leader, Aimo Aaltonen, who was to be Chairman of the SKP for nearly two decades.

The domestic and historical facts and factors outlined above form only part of the complex backdrop to the Finnish drama of 1948. A more adequate study would demand consideration of wider contemporary developments—notably the onset of the Cold War, the Marshall Plan for the economic reconstruction of Western Europe, the civil war in Greece, and the consolidation of Soviet hegemony in the "people's democracies" of Eastern Europe. It might be said in fact that the Finnish drama consisted of three acts with a prologue; the prologue was the Communist seizure of power in Czechoslovakia in February, 1948. This was an event that had profound repercussions in all the Scandinavian countries (thus, it had much to do with Norway's decision to join the emergent North Atlantic alliance, after initial hesitation).

The takeover of Czechoslovakia was still going on when Stalin sent the Finnish President, J. K. Paasikivi, a note, dated February 22, calling for a Soviet-Finnish "treaty of friendship, co-operation and mutual assistance analogous to the Hungarian-Soviet and Rumanian-Soviet Treaties" that had just been concluded. This was an ominous reference, for the latter treaties were obviously part of a Stalinist *Gleichschaltung*, a consolidation of

Communist power and Soviet hegemony in Eastern Europe. Did Stalin's *démarche* represent a comparable attempt to absorb Finland into the Communist bloc? If it did, the Finns would have to meet the threat on their own—they would get little or no practical help from the Western powers, any more than the luckless champions of Czechoslovak democracy had done. The first act ended on a somber note.

President Paasikivi's first response to Stalin's demand was one of masterly inactivity: he simply stalled for time, for a full month. Developments on the domestic front during this outwardly undramatic "second act" can be considered a little later. Here, if we can uncover them, lie the answers to our two basic questions: why the Communists failed to seize power in Finland in the spring of 1948; and whether they really tried to do so.

Meanwhile, we pass on to Act III, and its unexpected *dénouement*. On February 20, a seven-man mission with three "moderate" SKDL members, including Premier Pekkala and Interior Minister Leino, left for Moscow to enter into negotiations with the Soviets on Stalin's demand for a friendship treaty. Instructed by Paasikivi, who exercised his wide presidential powers to the full during the crisis, the members of the mission were presumably prepared for tough bargaining; they can hardly have anticipated what actually happened.

In the course of the negotiations the Soviet line changed, suddenly and magnanimously. Stalin settled for a friendship treaty which was based largely upon the draft Paasikivi had prepared as a bargaining position, and which certainly was *not* "analogous to" the treaties just concluded with Hungary and Rumania. Finland did not have to enter into a military alliance with the Soviet Union, as had seemed inevitable a few weeks earlier; its neutrality was explicitly recognized. True, it was a modified neutrality: Finland bound herself to resist aggression by (West) Germany or its allies directed *through* Finland against either Finland or the Soviet Union. But the Finns would fight only within their own country, and only after "mutual consultations" with the Soviet government. In short, the treaty confirmed the status quo. It gave the Soviet Union what amounted to a veto right on Finnish *foreign* policy—a situation that since 1944 had already been a fact of geopolitical life for the Finns—but it left Finland's domestic sovereignty and its Western-Nordic democracy intact.

Why did Stalin, after an initial show of pressure, grant the Finns a friendship treaty on what almost amounted to their terms? Why did he let them off so lightly, when he was obviously in a position to turn the screws tighter if he had so desired? One explanation advanced at the time can be dismissed: namely, that Stalin had a soft spot in his heart for Finland because he had once found asylum there in Tsarist days. We need not scan the historical record to conclude that it was not a question of a soft spot in Stalin's heart, but rather of a hard spot in his head.

Here we must glance, however briefly and inadequately, at the wider contemporary background, at the early years of the Cold War in Europe.[2] Reducing the matter to its simplest and quite unargued terms, what happened in 1946–1947 was that Stalin (partly in response to Western moves and counter-moves) was consolidating the political positions which the Red Army had won for him in Eastern Europe. He was building a great defensive glacis from the Baltic to the Mediterranean that was essentially to be a territorial extension of the Soviet system. In 1947 the Truman Doctrine (foreshadowing NATO) and the Marshall Plan represented the negative and positive poles of United States reaction to the growth of this East European empire. The Russians in turn met this American reaction by tightening inter-party discipline with the formation of the Cominform in September, 1947, at the same time launching the so-called "Zhdanov offensive"—the sovietization of Eastern Europe, a harder line on the part of the West European Communist Parties, and diversionary insurrections in Asia.

Instead of pausing to substantiate this broad-stroke outline of complex, epochal developments, I shall proceed to offer, with equal lack of analytical foundation, some conclusions bearing upon our more limited theme:

1. The postwar consolidation of satellite Communist regimes in East Central Europe was primarily an expression of traditional Russian expansionism and of Soviet *raison d'état*—not of the Leninist drive towards world revolution.

2. So far as it lay within the Kremlin's power, the political interests of foreign Communist Parties, whether ruling or non-ruling, were almost consistently sacrificed to those of the Soviet regime.

3. The postwar years brought an important qualitative change in the character and role of "Western" Communist Parties—those operating in economically advanced societies of pluralistic democracy. The change con-

---

[2] If space permitted, it would be relevant to discuss at this point the work of the American "revisionist" historians, such as D. F. Fleming, William Appleman Williams, Gar Alperovitz, and David Horowitz, who in recent years have challenged accepted views by arguing that their own country was primarily responsible for the outbreak of the Cold War. Certainly, there was a large measure of reciprocal misunderstanding involved in the onset of the Cold War; to some extent, as Arthur Schlesinger, Jr. has remarked, it was "the product not of a decision but of a dilemma." My own view, however, is that, while the revisionist historians have performed a useful function by challenging the dualistic simplicities and selective approach of some earlier Western accounts, they have tended to make the pendulum swing too far to the other side. Correction is not refutation.

sisted in the abandonment by these parties, at first in practice and much later also in theory, of the revolutionary substance of Leninism: that is, in adapting to environmental realities (in truly Marxist fashion), they gave up any attempt to overthrow the existing socio-political order by frontal assault or subversive violence. This assertion could be substantiated by many examples; but for our purposes the point is that despite special circumstances this general tendency applied also to Finland.

We can now return to the question posed earlier, setting it against this wider contemporary background. Why did Stalin not try to coerce Finland into the status of a satellite or semi-satellite in the spring of 1948? The shortest answer is that it was not in his interests, as he perceived them, to do so. Strategically, the Soviet Union had little to gain and a lot to lose by attempting to incorporate Finland into the Eastern bloc.

Little to gain: Soviet security on the northern flank was already assured by geopolitical realities, by Finnish acceptance of a "special relationship," and by the bulwark of a neutral Sweden beyond. The spread of Communist rule for its own sake was *not* one of Stalin's dominant priorities; nobody familiar with the history of the international Communist movement will be disposed to argue the point. On the other hand, potentially the Soviet Union had something to gain by maintaining a special relationship with a bourgeois-democratic Finland. Stalin could use it to influence developments in the other Scandinavian countries; and it could be extremely useful in the event of a shift towards a posture of East-West *détente*. (The fact that during these years of Cold War polarization the Russians abided by the four-power occupation system in Austria, and made no attempt to impose Communist rule in their zone, is surely relevant.)

More important, the Soviet Union stood to lose a lot from any serious move to incorporate Finland into the bloc. Given the temper of the Finns, their history, and their constitutional-democratic system, a Communist regime could have been imposed, in my opinion, only through armed intervention; and this would have been ruled out for many reasons. In the first place, it would have meant, if not war, certainly a large-scale movement of national resistance, active and passive, which might well have led to a wider international conflict, and which at the least would have proved to be a sore and enduring embarrassment to the USSR. Second, such intervention would have jeopardized the sovietization of Eastern Europe, which was Stalin's primary goal at that time.[3] It would have consolidated the emergent Western

---

[3] It is worth stressing again that, in strategic and geopolitical terms, Finland was, quite literally, of peripheral concern to the Soviet leadership; if it had been a Central European or even a Middle Eastern country, Stalin would certainly not have treated it with such magnanimous forbearance.

alliance, which Stalin was then trying to disrupt through a generally ineffective campaign by the West European Communist Parties. Finally, direct Soviet intervention in Finland might well have driven neutral Sweden, with its industrial strength, into that alliance.

My conclusion will already be evident: that the Soviet Union made no real attempt to impose the status of a satellite or a Communist-dominated regime on Finland in 1948. As we shall see, the sequel to the artificial crisis— a political disaster for the Finnish Communist Party—makes this abundantly clear. Stalin's concern, as always, was to extend Soviet power and promote Soviet interests, not to add another country to the camp, and still less to further Leninist revolution. It may be that one of his main purposes was to create a diversionary crisis, to distract some attention from what was happening in Czechoslovakia. In the process, no doubt, he was prepared to make what political gains he could from a position of strength in this "border country" (as he had been taking cautiously vicarious risks for the sake of possible strategic gains in the other border country of Greece). But he would not have confused his priorities. What is certain is that the political fortunes of the Finnish Communist Party took a notably low place on his list of priorities. And with this factor—the role the SKP played in the crisis, and the effect upon its future—we are back to what I have called Act II: the period between Stalin's demand for a friendship treaty and the departure of the Finnish delegation for Moscow four weeks later.

The first point to make is that for a week or two after the reception of Stalin's note Communist activity did not go much beyond pro-Soviet and anti-rightist propaganda: the SKP did not behave like a party preparing to seize hegemonic power with the help of Soviet pressure. Subsequently, however, the Party stepped up its campaign against the alleged threat of right-wing forces to Finnish democracy; and at the same time Communist-inspired disturbances broke out in Helsinki, Tampere, and other centers. Did these ominous activities represent preparations for an attempt at a coup? Despite the categorical assertions of some writers, we move, I think, into an area of speculation and uncertainty, partly because many of the relevant facts are still obscure or unknown. Most accounts of what is said to have been the crucial episode are based, ultimately, upon the writings of two former Communist leaders, Arvo Tuominen and Yrhö Leino. Tuominen we have met before: the Secretary-General who defected from the Party at the time of the Winter War and became a mordant critic of the SKP; his objectivity and authority as a witness to the Party's covert postwar activities might be questioned by some. About the contribution of Leino, newly appointed Communist Minister of the Interior at the time of the crisis, there is a special difficulty to which I shall return in a moment.

The version commonly accepted in the West is given by Professor James H. Billington:

> [On] March 19, 1948, the day before he was scheduled to leave for the Moscow negotiating sessions, Leino, the Communist minister of the interior, took the dramatic step which may well have turned the tide of Finnish history. He paid a secret evening visit to the army chief-of-staff, Aarne Sihvo, and warned him of the forthcoming campaign of violence. Thus alerted, the strongly anti-communist 30,000-man army cancelled all leaves, quietly increased garrison strengths near the big cities, and simply took over the arsenal of Leino's own mobile police force. The badly outnumbered police force was afraid to act; and the possibility of a forcible coup was out of the question.[4]

Although sources are not specified, one presumes this passage to be based upon the book of memoirs, *Kommunisti sisä-ministerinä* (Communist Minister of the Interior), which Leino completed ten years later. Note that I say "completed," not "published." For in fact the book was suppressed by the Finnish authorities on the eve of publication—a fact that commentators who refer to the work generally neglect to mention. The suppression was reportedly due to the intervention of the Soviet Embassy in Helsinki. It is known, however, that some pre-publication copies survived. Professor Billington, Professor Hodgson, and other authorities who cite the book (although understandably never giving direct quotations) have evidently had access to one of these surviving copies; I have not.

Nevertheless, I still have doubts about Leino averting a Communist coup through his secret visit to the army leader. One piece of evidence supporting these doubts was provided by the Copenhagen newspaper *Information*, which on February 22, 1962, published a translation, with facsimile of the Finnish original, of what were said to be excerpts from the relevant chapter of the suppressed memoirs. According to this, Leino did not give General Sihvo any secret warning of an impending coup—although he *was* opposed to the Communist Party's policies during the crisis.

There is another serious weakness to the "secret warning" story, although, again, it is usually ignored in accounts of the crisis. Two months later, in May, 1948, the Diet passed a vote of non-confidence in Leino, mainly on the ground that he had handed Finnish refugees of Soviet citizenship back to the Russians. President Paasikivi, invoking an article of the Constitution (as he need not have done) then called upon Leino to resign.

---

[4] Billington, *op. cit.*, p. 129. According to other accounts, Leino warned that there was serious unrest in both right-wing and left-wing circles. A more cautious account of the entire episode ("Leino was instrumental in thwarting what may have been an attempt to overthrow the Finnish government") is given by Hodgson, *op. cit.*, p. 205, footnote.

The latter—backed by all Communist and left-socialist deputies—refused to do so, whereupon the President dismissed him. It was only later that Leino was expelled from the Party (and divorced by his wife, Hertta Kuusinen).[5] This sequel is hardly in harmony with the story of the secret warning.

It is, of course, possible, or even probable, that the SKP leadership was planning to intensify the anti-rightist demonstrations and disturbances that had already begun—and that the "moderate" Communist Leino let General Sihvo understand something of the sort was in the offing. But plans that could be effectively blocked by firm but unspectacular anti-riot measures would surely have had as their objective not a necessarily bloody and extremely problematical attempt to seize power but a more limited exercise of political influence.

Disturbances timed to coincide with the Finno-Soviet negotiations over the friendship treaty would have had an obvious aim: to bring supplementary pressure to bear upon the non-Communist majority of the cabinet, and thereby make it easier for Stalin to impose his will upon the Finnish delegation—his will, whatever it might be, for the unexpected outcome of the Moscow talks indicates that the SKP leaders were not privy to the Soviet dictator's devious counsels. They nevertheless would have been aware that riots that got out of control might well provoke his wrath—another argument against the hypothesis of a planned coup.

If there is one constant factor in the history of Finno-Soviet relations, it is the readiness of the Soviet regime to sacrifice the interests of the Finnish Communist Party to other considerations. For the SKP, 1948 was a year of political disaster. In the elections that took place shortly after the crisis, in July, the Communists and their allies lost a quarter of their Diet seats. Worse followed: they were excluded from the government because they tried to insist on having certain key ministries that the new social-democratic Premier, Fagerholm, refused to give them.[6] They were to remain out of office for 18 years, while the other three major parties rang the changes on

---

[5] It might be noted that another ex-husband of Hertta Kuusinen was obscurely involved in the 1948 crisis. This was Tuure Lehén, whom she divorced to marry Leino. Lehén, a Soviet citizen and Red Army general, came to Helsinki from the USSR in January, 1948, and was later said to have been training Communist "barricade squads." The Communists denied this charge; and if any barricade squads did exist, they never went into action. After divorcing Leino, Miss Kuusinen—daughter of Otto and a leading figure in the SKP throughout the postwar period—married yet another prominent Communist.

[6] Characteristically, the reaction of the Stalinist SKP leadership to the setback of 1948 was to institute a purge during which more than ten percent of the members were expelled, or excluded by the withholding of new Party cards.

coalition combinations, at an average rate of one a year. During that long period the Soviets several times intervened in Finnish political life—notably in 1958, when they brought about the fall of Fagerholm's second government, and in 1961, when they effectively blocked the presidential candidature of the socialist-backed independent, Honka. But these so-called "night frosts" were primarily directed against the Social Democrats and other "unfriendly" elements. The Soviets did not at any time intervene, by invoking the 1948 treaty or otherwise, to obtain the re-entry of the Finnish Communists into government, although they obviously could have done so.[7]

I think it is clear that the Soviet Union made no serious effort to incorporate Finland into the Communist bloc in 1948; and I have argued the proposition that the Finnish Communists themselves made no serious effort to seize power. Granting that, and taking into account the unique geopolitical situation, what can we learn from the Finnish experience in 1948? One lesson surely is that we should take a more skeptical view of allegedly "inevitable" historical tendencies, and give more weight to the often unpredictable human element. The collective temper of the Finnish people— their determination to maintain their freedom and their way of life—may not have been the decisive factor in the resolution of the 1948 crisis; but it was certainly one of extreme importance. The relevance of this consideration to other situations (such as the successful Communist coup in Czechoslovakia in 1948, as well as the Vietnamese War) hardly needs elaboration.

In other ways, too, the crisis offers a significant contrast to other contemporary developments. At a time of intense East-West polarization the non-Communist leaders of Finland managed their own affairs shrewdly and

---

[7] It is worth noting that when the Communists finally did get back into government, in May, 1966, it was not the result of any help from the Soviets, but was rather due to the growth of progressive-revisionist tendencies within the SKDL and the SKP, combined with changes in Social-Democratic attitudes towards the Communists and the Soviet Union. Nor did they return to anything like the power and influence they enjoyed in early 1948: in the socialist-centrist-Communist coalition formed in 1966 two Communists held minor ministries, while a non-Communist SKDL leader was a deputy minister—and each of the three had to share control of his department with a deputy minister from another party. In March, 1971, five years after their return to government, the Communists found themselves again out of office. Under pressure from the conservative faction led by Taisto Sinisalo, now Vice-Chairman of the precariously reunited SKP, the SKDL deputies voted against the government's program of economic stabilization—whereupon Social Democratic Premier Karjalainen implemented his threat to resign, and subsequently formed a new coalition without the Communists.

resolutely, seeking no help from outside. The crisis and its outcome thus foreshadowed a shift back towards a more complex, polycentric system of international relations, in which neutral or unaligned states, as well as dissident members of both the main power blocs, would play a more active role.

Perhaps the most important lesson to be drawn from Finland in 1948 is that of the societal strength of economically advanced, pluralistic democracies of the North European type. After a quarter-century of the "special relationship" with the Soviet Union, Finns accept it calmly, facing its occasional challenges with merited self-confidence. And, while Finns tranquilly expose themselves to Soviet politico-cultural influences, the reverse is decidedly not true. As Europe moves into the post-Cold War era, historical experience suggests that in a genuine dialogue the balance of persuasion would lie with the social-democratic West and not with the authoritarian East.

It is in large measure this societal strength that has imposed on "Western" Communist parties the need to adapt to their environments—a process in which the Italian Communist Party had played a sophisticated, vanguard role. This in turn has meant the virtual abandonment (except by extremist factions) of the goal of Leninist revolution. The contradictions between dogma and reality lay at the root of the SKP's inability to exploit the 1948 crisis. The refusal of a conservative leadership to face this dilemma meant that when the currents of adaptive change finally began to move within the SKP during the latter half of the 1960's, the ultimate result was a profound split within the Party, which has merely been alleviated, and not ended, by the Extraordinary Congress held in February, 1970.[8]

A final lesson of the 1948 crisis has already been noted. It demonstrated the pragmatic opportunism of Soviet foreign policies, and the consistent tendency to subordinate *raison révolutionnaire* to *raison d'état*. Just as the subversive capabilities of Communist movements in Western societies have often been exaggerated, so we have often tended to ascribe to the Soviet regime an evangelistic drive which it does not commonly manifest. The economic and political advantages to the USSR of the special relationship with bourgeois-democratic Finland have become clearer in the course of the past two decades. (Khrushchev's magnanimous evacuation of the Porkkalla naval base in September, 1955, was one notable demonstration of this.) But already in 1948 Stalin had his priorities coldly listed. If the Finns preserved

---

[8] See the author's study, "Finnish Communism," in *Survey*, London, Nos. 74–75, Winter-Spring, 1970, pp. 49–69. It may be noted that the Finnish elections of March, 1970, brought Communist electoral strength to its lowest postwar level, leaving the SKDL with only 36 Diet seats out of 200.

their democratic system, it was, in the last analysis, because the Soviet dictator saw little profit and considerable loss in any attempt to overthrow it.

It is ironic but fitting that the fiftieth anniversary celebrations of the Finnish Communist Party, held in September, 1968, had to be postponed because of the invasion of Czechoslovakia, which was criticized by the SKP's progressive faction and approved by the conservative Communists, while the centrists unhappily equivocated. Over the quarter-century following the end of the World War II the destinies of Czechoslovakia and Finland offer a recurrent contrast rich in significance.

Thus, in 1945 the Red Army liberated Czechoslovakia, simultaneously earning the gratitude of the people and laying the iron foundations of Stalinist rule; whereas the twice defeated Finns, manfully shouldering a formidable burden of reparations, were able to rebuild their democratic polity without enduring Soviet occupation. In 1948 the Czechoslovak Communists seized power in the country which under Masaryk's leadership had given Central Europe a luminous model of liberal democracy. In the same year, as we have seen, Finland's democratic leaders shrewdly faced and boldly survived an apparent Soviet threat to their liberties, while the discomfited Finnish Communists lost their governmental posts. In 1968 the overwhelming majority of Czechoslovak Communists united behind the Dubček leadership in an unprecedented—and, fatefully, infectious—experiment in "socialist democratization"; while the Finnish Communists, bearing the burdens without particularly enjoying the profits of governmental responsibility, were engaged in a bitter factional struggle.

The Autonomous Republic of Azerbaijan and the Kurdish People's Republic: Their Rise and Fall

Rouhollah K. Ramazani

World War II and the fight against the Axis powers provided the Soviet Union with an unprecedented opportunity to invade a number of countries on its periphery—in Eastern Europe, the Middle East, and the Far East. In each of these countries (except Austria) the Red Army took advantage of this opportunity to help establish Communist regimes patterned after the Soviet model, and almost all of these regimes have survived to date. Only in Iran did the Soviets, under the protection of the Red Army, establish Communist regimes which they later abandoned.

Having witnessed earlier Soviet actions in Bulgaria, Poland, North Korea, and other areas where the Red Army had penetrated, observers in the West expected that Iran had lost its Azeri and Kurdish areas permanently when they were similarly occupied. But in 1946 the Red Army withdrew from Iran, and six months later Iranian troops moved into the northern areas, overthrowing the Azeri and Kurdish republics. Why did the Soviet Union relinquish the establishment of two Communist regimes in a neighboring country? Why did it choose this course of action in Iran while it was doing just the opposite in other countries?

The Azeri and Kurdish regimes also represent cases of insurgency. What contributed to the rebellion of these two communal groups in Iranian society? Were these insurrections wholly created by the Soviets, or were they also influenced by conditions indigenous to the Iranian situation? What factors, on the other hand, contributed to the dramatic collapse of the two rebel regimes? Did they break up simply because the Red Army eventually withdrew, or were there also internal causes at work?[1]

Soviet support of the Azeri and Kurdish insurrections in 1945 was primarily intended to maximize Soviet power and ultimately to gain control in Iran by means of what George Kennan aptly called the "fissionist technique," which implies exploitation of minority or nationality problems for

[1] This paper draws in part on research for a larger study of Iran's postwar foreign policy supported by the Social Science Research Council. Responsibility for the facts and interpretations appearing here is solely the author's.

Soviet ends.[2] In the period from 1941 to 1945, the adoption of this technique represented the boldest Soviet bid for control in Iran. The last indication of Soviet ambitions in Iran before the Anglo-Russian invasion on August 25, 1941, was given in the Soviet negotiations with Germany in 1940. At that time V. M. Molotov, Chairman of the USSR Council of People's Commissars, demanded bases on the Bosporus and the Dardanelles and recognition of Soviet aspirations in the "area south of Batum and Baku in the general direction of the Persian Gulf."[3] The German attack on the Soviet Union on June 22, 1941, did not alter these ambitions; on the contrary, it eventually lent the opportunity to realize them. The German attack on the Soviet Union was central to the Allied decision to invade Iran, and the decision was made, according to Churchill, in order to open "the fullest communication with Russia."[4] Nonetheless, both Britain and the Soviet Union explained their joint attack on Iran solely in terms of the German aggression. The Soviet Union claimed that German agents in Iran had organized "terrorist groups," which were to be smuggled into Soviet Azerbaijan, "above all into the principal Soviet oil district of Baku— and into Soviet Turkmenistan."[5]

The occupation of northern Iran by the Red Army made it possible for the Soviet Union to realize its objectives in Iran in a number of ways, such as by supporting insurrections in Azerbaijan and Kurdistan. In examining Soviet behavior towards Iran two interrelated considerations should be borne in mind. First, the Soviet invasion of northern Iran did not destroy the Iranian political order, in contrast with Poland, for example, where the

---

[2] Iran is a country of minorities, the Azeri and the Kurdish peoples being two of the major communal groups. Their vulnerability to Soviet manipulation, however, did not simply derive from their minority status. Their geographic proximity to the Soviet Union and their cultural and linguistic ties with similar peoples across the Soviet border rendered them susceptible to the Soviet fissionist technique. Accurate population figures for these areas are difficult to obtain, but the Azeris of Iran probably number over three million people. They speak Turkic and share cultural ties with an approximately equal number of Azeris in the Azerbaijan Soviet Socialist Republic. The Kurds, like the Azeris, speak a language different from Persian; Kurdish has its own vocabulary, grammar, and phonetic system. The Kurds in the USSR number, according to Soviet statistics, some 89,000, as compared with roughly two million in Iran.

[3] See U.S. Department of State, *Nazi-Soviet Relations, 1939–1941*, Washington, D.C., 1948, p. 259.

[4] Winston S. Churchill, *The Second World War*, Vol. III: *The Grand Alliance*, Boston, 1950, pp. 476–477.

[5] For the text of the Soviet note, see Leland M. Goodrich (ed.), *Documents on American Foreign Relations*, Vol. IV, Boston, 1942, pp. 676–681.

Soviet Union and Germany smashed the existing government, after which the Red Army and its Polish sympathizers moved into the resulting vacuum.[6] Second, to a large extent the survival of the Iranian political order was due to the fact that the Soviet occupation in the north was counterbalanced by the British presence in the south; despite the wartime alliance, Britain was not only Russia's traditional rival in Iran, but also possessed strategic and oil interests in the southwestern part of the country. With the entry of United States forces in 1942, Soviet activities were further hampered. The Soviet-Western alliance in Iran became strained as early as 1941, and the wartime origins of the Cold War are clearly shown in this situation. The Soviet Union's failure to control Western-supported Iran from 1941 to 1945 goes a long way towards explaining its barefaced resort to open support of the Azeri and Kurdish insurrections at the end of the war.

The earliest concrete signs of Soviet objectives and methods in Iran occurred in the wake of the Anglo-Russian invasion. On August 25, 1941, the Russian forces poured into the northwest, pushing towards Tabriz (the capital of Azerbaijan) and Pahlavi, and advancing in the northeast towards Meshed, while the British forces were striking from the Persian Gulf and Iraq. Three days after the cease-fire, on August 31, 1941, Soviet planes simultaneously bombed civilian areas near Teheran, causing panic, and dropped propaganda leaflets extolling the life of peasants and workers in the Soviet Union as contrasted with the sorry fate of their counterparts in Iran.[7] At the diplomatic level, the earliest concrete manifestations of Soviet intentions and methods also occurred in the wake of the invasion. Iranian requests for changes in the Soviet zone of occupation were refused, and compensation was denied those who suffered losses after the cease-fire had gone into effect.[8] More important, just over a month after the invasion, Soviet interference in the occupied north reached such proportions that U.S. Secretary of State Cordell Hull became "extremely apprehensive" about it and British Foreign Minister Anthony Eden called it "harmful and unwarranted."[9]

---

[6] The statement on Poland is based on a reading of Hugh Seton-Watson, *The East European Revolution*, London, 1950.

[7] See U.S. Department of State, *Foreign Relations of the United States, 1941*, Vol. III : *The British Commonwealth, the Near East and Africa*, Washington, D.C., p. 444. Hereafter cited as *Foreign Relations, 1941*, with appropriate volumes indicated.

[8] These attitudes were revealed in the Soviet note of September 6, 1941. For the text, see Husain Kuhi Kermani, *Az Shahrivar 1320 ta Faj'ah-ye Azerbaijan va Zanjan*, Vol. I, Teheran, n. d., pp. 99–101.

[9] *Foreign Relations, 1941*, Vol. III, pp. 466–467.

The instances of Soviet intimidation, interference, and propaganda added to the American and British desire to extract solemn commitments from the Soviet Union reiterating Iran's independence and clarifying the status of Soviet troops there. Britain and the United States thus hoped to check the aggrandizement of Soviet power in Iran. The chances for reaching an agreement were extremely favorable at the time because of the Kremlin's desperate need for British and Iranian co-operation in facilitating the transport of supplies to the Soviet Union. The slowness of the Iranian response to the proposed tripartite treaty between Iran, Great Britain, and the Soviet Union was mainly a reflection of the continuing pro-German sentiment in the country, but the statesmanlike efforts of Prime Minister Mohammad Ali Foroughi eventually overcame the vociferous opposition of the pro-German elements in the Majlis (the national assembly). The treaty was finally signed on January 29, 1942, granting the Allies the unrestricted right to use, and in case of military necessity even to control, all means of communication through Iran. In return the Allies committed themselves to the principle that the presence of their troops in Iran did not constitute occupation, and undertook to "respect the territorial integrity and political independence of Iran."[10] The Soviet Union and Britain also promised to withdraw their forces from Iran not later than six months after all hostilities between the Allied powers and Germany had been suspended.

These solemn assertions, in retrospect, did little to check the Soviet drive towards ultimate control in Iran. The obligation to withdraw the Allied forces did not become operative until later, but the commitment to respect Iran's territorial integrity and political independence was soon clearly breached. Acts of Soviet interference in Iranian affairs reached such proportions by 1943 that they were regarded by Americans in Iran as directed towards "exploitation" and "domination" of the country. In Azerbaijan, where the Red Army had complete control, an American representative of the Food and Supply Adviser and the American Consul at Tabriz were both forced to leave, and permission to enter the Soviet zone of occupation was denied an American adviser sent to organize the Iranian Gendarmerie (rural police).[11] The Soviet Union's activities extended far beyond efforts to isolate Azerbaijan from the rest of the country; the central government itself was pressured into the signing of unfavorable

---

[10] For the text of the Treaty and the related annexes see Goodrich, *op. cit.*, pp. 681–686.

[11] See U.S. Department of State, *Foreign Relations of the United States, 1943*, Vol. IV: *The Near East and Africa*, Washington, D.C., 1964, pp. 345–346, 349 and 360. Hereafter cited as *Foreign Relations, 1943*.

agreements with the USSR, such as the arms agreement of January 23, 1943, the financial agreement of March 18, 1943, and the rice and cotton piece-goods agreement of November 4, 1943. Under the arms agreement Iran was forced to finance the manufacture of certain small arms and ammunition in Iranian plants for delivery to the Soviet Union. Under the financial agreement it had to advance the rials needed by the Soviet Union for its operations in Iran. And under the rice and cotton piece-goods agreement, the Iranian public had, in the last analysis, to subsidize the export of rice to the Soviet Union.[12]

The mounting evidence of Soviet expansionist aims led Britain and the United States to seek further guarantees of non-interference by the Soviet Union in Iran. By late 1943 Iran was in a far better position to receive the backing of the Allies in its bid for independence, since the persistent problem of German nationals had been resolved, and Iran had finally declared war on Germany (on September 9, 1943). Iran's hopes for self-government were also strengthened by the success of the Allied powers in the North African campaign, the Russian defense of Stalingrad, and the British capture of the so-called "Meyer documents," exposing the activities of German agents and a number of their Iranian sympathizers. The idea of adopting a declaration confirming the guarantee of Iran's independence in return for facilitating Allied war efforts was first proposed by Britain and supported by the United States at the Foreign Ministers Conference in Moscow on October 23, 1943. But the Soviet Union adopted "a negative attitude" towards the proposal, claiming that the Iranian people and government were content with respect to the intentions of the three powers, and that the proposed declaration would simply repeat the assurances already given Iran under the tripartite treaty. The members of the Soviet delegation "answered evasively or ignored questions designed to draw out any specific objections they might have to the policies set forth in the British and American draft texts. They showed no disposition to compromise or to put forward alternative proposals."[13] The proposed declaration "ran aground," to borrow Secretary Hull's words, "on the rocks of Soviet opposition."[14]

---

[12] See U.S. Department of State, *Foreign Relations of the United States, 1944*, Vol. V : *The Near East, South Asia, and Africa ; the Far East*, Washington, D.C., 1965, pp. 311–316. Hereafter cited as *Foreign Relations, 1944*.

[13] *Foreign Relations, 1943*, Vol. III, p. 731 ; *Foreign Relations, 1944*, Vol. IV, pp. 400–405.

[14] Cordell Hull, *The Memoirs of Cordell Hull*, Vol. II, New York, 1948, p. 1506.

The matter of a declaration was taken up again in the negotiations between Churchill, Roosevelt, and Stalin at the Teheran Conference. There is no evidence that the Soviet Union had ever seriously considered the proposal, but Stalin's approval of the American draft was obtained as the result of Roosevelt's personal intercession.[15] The declaration was signed by the three Allied leaders on December 1, 1943, and a copy of it was initialed by Mohammad Saed, Foreign Minister of Iran, indicating Iran's acceptance. In addition to agreeing on the maintenance of Iran's independence, sovereignty, and territorial integrity, the Allied leaders recognized Iran's economic difficulties, and in view of Iran's assistance in the prosecution of the war, agreed to give "full consideration" to its economic problems upon the cessation of hostilities. To Iran, the most important aspect of the declaration was the official support of the United States (at the highest level) for these principles, as it had sought such support in one way or another since 1941.

Nonetheless, the tripartite declaration, like the tripartite treaty of 1942, placed no real check on Soviet interference in Iranian affairs; the boldest instances of intervention, in fact, occurred after its adoption. In September, 1944, Sergey Kavtaradze, Soviet Deputy Commissar for Foreign Affairs, suddenly arrived in Teheran, with the aim of obtaining oil concessions. The Iranian government canceled negotiations with the Deputy Commissar as well as with American and British firms because of the presence of foreign troops on its territory. The incident caused the downfall of the government of Mohammad Saed, who was accused by *Trud*, the organ of the Soviet trade unions, of tolerating and even encouraging "pro-fascist elements in Iran" that were bent on sabotaging the flow of supplies to the Soviet Union. The bitter denunciation of the Iranian government in its own capital by a high-ranking Soviet official crowned all previous Soviet interventionary acts. The failure to gain oil concessions, which were part of larger Soviet objectives, was followed by resort to more obtrusive means. In recounting a most revealing discussion with M. A. Maximov, the Soviet Ambassador at Teheran, Averell Harriman stated that Maximov "intended to take aggressive measures to attain the Soviet objectives."[16] As Harriman put it, these objectives appeared to be much more far-reaching than simply gaining oil and mineral concessions and appeared to include the overthrow of the government, which Maximov described as representing five percent

---

[15] See Don Lohbeck, *Patrick J. Hurley*, Chicago, 1956. Even if the President's personal role were not as crucial as it would seem from this source, the role of the United States government was indeed decisive in the light of all other available evidence.

[16] *Foreign Relations, 1944*, Vol. V, p. 355.

of the Iranian population. In Harriman's words, Maximov used the extraordinary argument that because the Soviet government knew what the Iranian people wanted, it was proper for the Soviet government to see that the opinion of the Iranian people found political expression.

Within a few months, the Soviet Union—true to the intentions expressed by its ambassador—had helped to establish two insurgent regimes in northern Iran, under the protective wing of the Red Army. For some ten months prior to the rise of these rebel republics, the Soviet Union managed through diplomatic means to defy Iranian, British, and American pressure calling for the withdrawal of the Red Army troops, which were being employed to help the Azeris and the Kurds seize power. This assistance took three major, related forms: infiltration of Kurdish and Azeri parties, interception of central government forces, and the protection of local rebels.

Soviet control of political parties proved to be the most important instrument for seizing power. Infiltration of the parties insured both a successful rebellion and the subservience of the rebel governments to Moscow after their establishment in power. From the beginning, the lion's share of Soviet support went to the Azeris. The first manifesto of their party (which is paraphrased below) received generous Soviet press coverage on September 14, 1945. In reporting this, George F. Kennan, the American *chargé d'affaires* in Moscow at the time, saw parallels between the nationality problem in Azerbaijan and in Eastern Poland, Sinkiang, Turkish Armenia, and other areas, believing that in Azerbaijan as "in these other areas, Soviet fissionist technique seems to be based on racial affinities transcending the Soviet border."[17] The "fissionist technique" was put into effect in Azerbaijan by the Soviet Consul General in Tabriz, who master-minded the rebellion. The military arm of the rebellion had been strengthened by the import of a large number of "refugees" from Soviet Azerbaijan into Iran. On November 15, 1945, the Soviets began the wholesale distribution of arms to the rebels, and on the following day the "revolution" was launched.[18]

The process of infiltrating the Kurdish Nationalist Party, known as Komala, had also been completed by mid-November, 1945. At Mahabad, as in Tabriz, the Soviet Union nurtured open rebellion against the central

---

[17] See U.S. Department of State, *Foreign Relations of the United States, 1945,* Vol. VIII: *The Near East and Africa,* Washington, D.C., 1969, pp. 400 and 424. Hereafter cited as *Foreign Relations, 1945.*

[18] Robert Rossow, Jr., "The Battle of Azerbaijan," *The Middle East Journal,* Washington, D.C., Vol. X, No. 1, 1956, p. 18.

government; Soviet agents circulated among the tribes, told them to mobilize for the coming struggle for independence, and armed the "democrats" of Kurdistan, many of whom were from Soviet Azerbaijan. Insurrections had begun, but if the Iranian armed forces had been bolstered with troops from Teheran, and if the Iranian government officials who were on the spot had acted decisively, the uprisings could have been quelled. However, the Soviet Union saw to it that neither of these elements of the central government was able to act.

The second way in which the Soviets assisted the rebels was by intercepting Iranian government armed forces, an interventionary practice that had been rehearsed in two instances a few months before. The first instance took place when Soviet authorities prevented the Iranian commander at Meshed from acting against thirty-seven deserters, concomitantly refusing to permit reinforcement of the gendarmes at Gunabad and prohibiting the landing of Iranian army planes there. The second incident took place at Firuzkuh, when 200 gendarmes, dispatched from Teheran and heading for Shahi, were stopped by the Russians and ordered to return to the capital.[19] Following these precedents, on November 20, 1945, a Soviet military force halted an Iranian relief column at Qazvin while on its way to aid the beleaguered garrisons in Azerbaijan;[20] a commander of the Soviet force also threatened to open fire if the Iranian force moved further.[21] The outrage of Iran over this blatant violation of its sovereignty led to a complaint to the nascent United Nations, with the full support of the United States and Great Britain. The Soviet Union replied to Iran's first protest by claiming that the sending of Iranian forces to Azerbaijan was not "expedient," and would lead to "disturbances and bloodshed."[22] The Soviet Union also threatened the further use of force, stating that if the central government sent troops to the north, it would be compelled "to bring in new reinforcements of its own."[23] Thus by intercepting the government army, and by threatening further reprisals through diplomatic channels, the Soviet Union prevented the Iranian forces from reaching the north to put down the insurgents of Azerbaijan and Kurdistan.

---

[19] See Muhammad Khan Malek (Yazdi), *Ghoghay-e Takhlieh-ye Iran*, Teheran, 1947–1948, pp. 42–43 ; *Foreign Relations, 1945*, Vol. VIII, pp. 447–448.

[20] For eyewitness accounts by American officials, see *Foreign Relations, 1945*, Vol. VIII, pp. 447–448.

[21] See Rossow, *op. cit.*, p. 17.

[22] See Malek, *op. cit.*, pp. 54–60 ; and *Foreign Relations, 1945*, Vol. VIII, pp. 470–471.

[23] *Foreign Relations, 1945*, Vol. VIII, pp. 470–471.

The third way in which the Soviets supported the seizure of power was to protect rebel forces against any adverse move by agents of the central government who happened to be on the sites of rebellion. Before the fall of Tabriz, the Azeri rebels seized control of the main Azerbaijan communications arteries by capturing the principal towns on the major routes to the province. The rebels took over the main towns by cutting telegraph links with Teheran and Tabriz, occupying post office buildings, terrorizing the civilian population, and—most important of all—disarming government soldiers, police, and the gendarmerie. The Red Army troops intervened in favor of the rebel forces in most towns, and prevented the free movement of government units.[24] Once most of the major towns had been captured, the primary routes blocked, and communications with Teheran effectively severed, the rebels attacked the garrison in Tabriz, forcing the capital of Azerbaijan to surrender. The establishment of the "Autonomous Republic of Azerbaijan" on December 12, 1945, was the cue for the Kurds to proclaim the "Kurdish People's Republic" on December 15, 1945, at a meeting at Mahabad attended by tribal leaders and "three Soviet officers in a jeep and armed with tommy-guns."[25]

The ability of the Soviet Union to assist in the creation of these republics derived only in part from the Red Army's presence in northern Iran. The character of the Iranian political system in general and the party system in particular served to enhance the favorable opportunity that the presence of Soviet troops provided.[26] With the abdication of Reza Shah in the wake of the Anglo-Russian invasion of 1941, the governmental stability insured by the authoritarian regime of the "Patriot King" collapsed, with drastic results. His programs of modernization over the preceding two decades had exacerbated communal conflicts on the one hand and accelerated the rise of new social and economic groups on the other. The Azeri community had been generally neglected by the central government, and

---

[24] For the texts of reports from government forces to Teheran and related accounts in Persian on the role of the Red Army troops, see Najafqoli Pesyan, *Marg Bood Bazgasht Ham Bood*, Teheran, 1948–1949, pp. 46–61; see also *Foreign Relations, 1945*, Vol. VIII, pp. 480–483, 490–491, and 430–431.

[25] For details, see Archie Roosevelt, Jr., "The Kurdish Republic of Mahabad," *The Middle East Journal*, Vol. I, No. 3, 1947, p. 257. See also William Eagleton, Jr., *The Kurdish Republic of 1946*, London, 1963; and Hassan Arfa, *The Kurds: An Historical and Political Study*, London, 1966.

[26] For theoretical discussions on the relationship between political development and party politics and between modernization and communal politics, see (respectively) Samuel P. Huntington, *Political Order in Changing Societies*, New Haven, Conn., 1968; and Robert Melson and Howard Wolpe, "Modernization and the Politics of Communalism: A Theoretical Perspective," *The American Political Science Review*, Washington, D.C., Vol. LXIV, No. 4, 1970, pp. 1112–1130.

the Kurds had been subjected to a ruthless policy of detribalization. The policy of centralization, which aimed at the creation of a national political community corresponding to the formal political boundaries of the Iranian state, had been for all practical purposes the objective of the Persian-speaking political élite. The programs of modernization had been attended not only by forcible administrative centralization but also by repression of political participation through parliamentary manipulation and denial of opportunities for organization of political parties.

The Anglo-Russian invasion and the Shah's abdication were followed by new social, economic, and political circumstances which contributed directly to the eventual rise of the two republics. Demands for more goods and services continued in the face of scarce resources, while wartime conditions and the Allied occupation weakened the ability of the central government to improve the situation. All the Shah's large-scale activities ceased; the number of livestock decreased; and the conditions of the railways deteriorated, mostly because of the transportation of some four million tons of American and British war matériel to the Soviet Union.[27] A shortage of food, at times verging on famine, caused serious bread riots, and grave economic conditions engulfed all communal groups, including the Azeris and the Kurds. The food shortage also widened the gap between the rich and the poor, between the peasants and the wealthy landowners, who continued to dominate the parliament and the government. In the chaos of the post-invasion period the Kurds and the Azeris fared no better than under Reza Shah's economic and administrative regimentation. The sense of insecurity accompanying the processes of modernization and increasing centralization was now compounded by the removal of the central government's forces as a result of the invasion; in response the Azeris and the Kurds sought even closer identity with their own communal groups as a means of insuring greater security.

With the removal of the Shah's authoritarian rule, unprecedented political activities, including party politics, burst forth with explosive energy. The Shah's perception of the requirements for building a modern, independent, and stable state had led him to be preoccupied with strengthening the army and the bureaucracy as the basic pillars of his regime. The participation of the people in the government suffered in two major ways: parliament served chiefly as an instrument for legitimizing royal policies, and party politics were suppressed or prevented completely. After his abdication, the factional, cliquish, and personalistic features of pre-Reza Shah party politics, with all their susceptibility to foreign manipulation,

---

[27] See: United Nations, *Economic Development in the Middle East, 1945 to 1954*, New York, 1955, pp. 59–60.

were regenerated, but in the context of new social and economic classes and alienated communal groups.

The best organized and financed political party that emerged was the Soviet-supported Tudeh ("Masses") Party. Many of the Shah's political prisoners were freed after his abdication, including some who had been jailed in 1937 as suspects of Socialist-Communist persuasion. The leading member of a group of fifty-three suspected Communists, Dr. Taqi Arani, had died in prison, but his colleagues formed the Tudeh Party after their release in 1941. This group consisted of four Iranian intellectuals—a surgeon, a lawyer, a university professor, and a writer. The Party hoped to win the confidence of the masses. It espoused the Leninist principle of "democratic centralism," and patterned its organization after a hierarchy of party congresses, provincial committees, local committees, and cells. In terms of its leadership and programs, however, the Tudeh Party reflected the predominant influence of the Persian-speaking community. The Party was formed and led primarily by persons who were Marxist members of the Persian and the persianized intelligentsia residing in Teheran and who tended to underestimate the regional conflicts between the capital and the provinces. As such they viewed their society through a class perspective, scorned the communal dimension, and ignored linguistic and regional issues.[28]

In contrast, such issues constituted the core of the grievances held by the Democratic Party of Azerbaijan, which was established in 1945. The leader of this party, Ja'far Pishehvari, was also released from Reza Shah's prison, but did not belong to the group that formed the Tudeh Party. He was a Turkish-speaking Azeri who had been born in Tabriz in 1893. He had emigrated to Russian Azerbaijan at the age of twelve, had assisted in the formation of the first Iranian Communist organization in Baku (in 1920), and had been a member of the Executive Committee of the Soviet Socialist Republic of Gilan (in 1920–1921). Pishehvari had belonged to the Tudeh Party for a short time, and he published articles in his own newspaper, *Azhir*, criticizing the Tudeh Party for its class orientation in a non-indus-

---

[28] Ervand Abrahamian also argues (successfully) that the Tudeh and the Azeri parties "were not simply two sides of the same coin." He points out:

> On the contrary, they were separated from each other by contrasting social bases, conflicting interests, and at times, clashing policies. The former was organized by Persian intellectuals who had come to communism through the Marxism of Western Europe. The latter was formed by Azeri patriots who had reached the same destination through Leninism [and] the Bolshevik Party in the Caucasus.

See his "Communism and Communalism in Iran : The Tudah and the Firqah-e Dimukrat," *International Journal of Middle East Studies*, London, Vol. I, No. 4, 1970, p. 315.

trial society such as Iran.[29] He is quoted as saying in his memoirs that at the time of formation of the Democratic Party of Azerbaijan no party other than the Tudeh existed in Azerbaijan, and the Tudeh had become "weakened and discredited as the result of years of struggle."[30] He is also quoted as saying that in three long days of discussions with two fellow Azeris they decided to establish their own party, and he instructed one of his colleagues to get the Tudeh leaders to join them.[31] On the day that Pishehvari announced the formation of the Democratic Party of Azerbaijan (September 3, 1945), he issued its first manifesto, which received the backing of the Soviet Union. The manifesto demanded, *inter alia*, the adoption of Turkish as the official language of Azerbaijan and autonomy for the people of the province within the Iranian state.

With the previously mentioned aid of Soviet arms distributed to the rebels on November 15 and the interception of Iranian forces by the Red Army at Qazvin on November 20, the Democrats gained control of most of Azerbaijan by November 21. They then called a national congress to declare the separation of the province from the central government in Teheran. The congress claimed for the people of Azerbaijan "distinct national, linguistic, cultural, and traditional characteristics"; denied the Azeri desire for separation from Iran; supported a democratic, constitutional government in Iran; expressed the determination of the Azeri people to "base their autonomy on the firm foundation of democracy"; and declared that the people of Azerbaijan had the right to form their own government and to administer "their internal and national affairs." In conclusion, the congress declared that in seeking to implement these objectives it would resort only to "indoctrination and organization" (*tabliq va tashkilat*) and would avoid internal war and fratricide. But, the congress further declared: "if the central government should attempt to destroy the legitimate rights of the [Azeri] people by means of resort to arms and invasion it will defend its rights at any cost and will fight for its autonomy to the last Azeri national."[32]

With the establishment of the "Autonomous Republic of Azerbaijan" on December 12, 1945, Pishehvari became premier, and Ali Shabastari, another veteran Azeri Communist, was elected speaker of the Azeri national assembly, which elected a nine-member cabinet. Pishehvari was also

---

[29] *Ibid.*, pp. 306–307.

[30] See Pesyan, *op. cit.*, p. 21.

[31] Pishehvari's own memoirs as quoted in Pesyan, *loc. cit.*, claim that the Tudeh in Azerbaijan joined his party as a result of negotiations, but other accounts indicate that the Tudeh was cavalierly absorbed.

[32] For the text of the Proclamation, see Pesyan, *op. cit.*, pp. 61–64.

chosen as the provisional minister of labor.[33] The immediate objective of the rebel government was the creation of an effective army out of a motley force of volunteers (*fada'ian*), immigrants (*muhajerin*), and new recruits (*qizilbash*). By the time of the downfall of the regime, over 10,000 men were carrying arms, and between 70,000 and 100,000 could be mobilized. The rebel army, although formally autonomous, was under the control of the Democratic Party. The Party organization, which resembled that of the Tudeh Party, consisted of a central committee in Tabriz, provincial committees, district committees, and local committees. The most important links between the Party and the army were the political officers, who numbered thirty by the time of the downfall of the regime. Generally, these men arrived in Iran from Soviet Azerbaijan and performed two main functions: supervision of the military commanders and political indoctrination of the rank and file. The principal military cadres consisted of the volunteers who were initially placed under a committee headed by Pishehvari himself. The regime also established primary and secondary military schools, a military and police college, and a political study program. The political officers were required to pass examinations in political economy, the history of social evolution, dialectical materialism, the history of the "world's great liberating parties," psychology, and military science.[34]

The degree of popular support for the regime during its existence is difficult to assess, but whatever appeal it may have had just before or soon after the formation of the government diminished rather rapidly afterwards. The factors underlying the decline of the regime's initial appeal included inadequate fulfillment of promises such as those concerning land distribution. This was left undone owing to the regime's short duration or its sheer inability to undertake such a complicated program, or else because the Communist rebels were more interested in confiscating the land of their "enemies" than in distributing it to the landless peasants. The regime earned hostility among the younger people by pressing hard for conscription.[35] The disenchantment with the regime also became widespread

---

[33] *Ibid.*, p. 124.

[34] For details, see *ibid.*, pp. 126–148.

[35] The American Vice Consul at Tabriz (Robert Rossow, Jr.) reported on February 11, 1946, to the Secretary of State, that the only support of the regime was from its own active members, estimated at not over "five percent of the population excluding those under duress." He added that disagreement over extremist terrorism, the economic situation, and the Kurdish problem had weakened the internal organization of the government and the Party directorate "to the reported annoyance of Soviet mentors." See U.S. Department of State, *Foreign Relations of the United States, 1946*, Vol. VII, *The Near East and Africa*, Washington, D.C., 1969, pp. 332–334. Hereafter cited as *Foreign Relations, 1946.*

in the rank and file of the military, particularly after the Red Army withdrew from Azerbaijan without leaving behind adequate military equipment for the Communist insurgents.[36]

As mentioned above, the establishment of the Azerbaijan regime was a cue for the formation of the Kurdish People's Republic on December 15, 1945.[37] Although the situations of the two republics appeared to be much alike, there were vast differences between them. The single important similarity was the pre-eminent role of the Soviet Union, but Soviet tactics were different in the two cases, largely because there were great disparities in the size, the social structure, and the general characteristics of the Azeri and Kurdish communities. At Mahabad, as in Tabriz, the vehicle for the creation of the rebel regime was a Soviet-supported party, but the Kurdish Democratic Party was created at the expense of the Kurdish Nationalist Party, or Komala ("Committee"), which had existed secretly since 1943. Founded by a dozen young Kurdish nationalists, the Komala basically resembled Western liberal democratic models in its organization and functioning, while the Soviet-engineered Democratic Party was led single-handedly by Qazi Muhammad, hereditary judge and religious leader of Mahabad, and a member of its most respected family. He announced the formation of the Party shortly after his return from a brief trip to Baku, arranged by the Soviets, in September, 1945. The Kurdish Party's manifesto, signed by Qazi and over one hundred leading Kurds, complained of Reza Shah's denial of their human and constitutional rights; demanded Kurdish autonomy within the Iranian state; declared Kurdish as the official language; and professed the intention to achieve unity and complete fraternity with the people of Azerbaijan.

The state apparatus created by the Kurds, like that of the Azeris, was accomplished through a party mechanism, but the operations of the Kurds were on a much smaller scale than those of the Azeris, and were marked by the personal and familial characteristics of Kurdish tribal society. In contrast to the Azeri Democratic Party, the role of the Kurdish Democratic Party in distributing seats of power was much less important. Although most of the cabinet ministers belonged to the Kurdish Party, the criteria for the assignment of posts derived primarily from tribal considerations. Qazi himself became the President of the republic, and his cousin was selected as both Minister of War and Vice-President. Other important posts were distributed to prominent families and rival tribes. For example, the post of the Prime Minister was given to a popular religious leader from

---

[36] See Pesyan, *op. cit.*, pp. 137–141.

[37] The factual information on the Kurds here is based principally on Eagleton, *op. cit.*, and Pesyan, *op. cit.*

another family, and the Ministry of Foreign Affairs and Ministry of Roads were placed under the leadership of two members of an influential faction of the same tribe (Dehbokri), which rivaled the Qazis politically.

Tribal characteristics were also reflected in the structure of the army. Given tribal opposition to communism, Qazi Muhammad's obvious reliance on the Soviets would probably have been challenged soon after the formation of the Party, had it not been for the fortuitous arrival of the armed Barazanis from Iraq.[38] But the regime decided to create a Kurdish army instead of relying on the Barazani forces. Because the tribal structure could not be revamped overnight, the commissioned officers of the new army had to be drawn mainly from the town of Mahabad, and the tribal chiefs took honorary ranks and remained with their tribes. The Mahabad army had at most some seventy officers and over one thousand enlisted men, which made it about one-tenth the size of the Azeri army in both categories. The Kurdish officers not only dressed in Soviet-style uniforms, but were organized and trained by a Soviet fellow-officer, Captain Salhaddin Kazimov, who came to Mahabad solely for this purpose.[39]

The Kurdish regime was a puppet regime, engineered by the Soviets. This state of affairs was compounded by the primitive conditions of Kurdish society, and by the difficulties of trying to create a state out of a tribal people in a matter of months. Observers have often emphasized the anti-Russian and anti-Communist feelings of the Kurds as a factor in the eventual downfall of the regime. But regardless of these sentiments, the collapse of both the Azeri and Kurdish puppet regimes must be attributed in part to the extremely low levels of social, economic, and particularly political development in the two communities.[40] Notwithstanding its instability, the central government in Teheran was superior in every respect to the insurgent regimes at Tabriz and Mahabad.

Only a year and a day after it came into existence the Autonomous Republic of Azerbaijan collapsed. "The pall is lifted," said the American Consul in Tabriz in a dispatch to the Department of State. "I have never seen so many smiling faces since I came to Azerbaijan."[41] Just a year from the day of its establishment, the Kurdish People's Republic also collapsed. It is generally assumed that the fall of the two rebel regimes occurred simply and only because of the withdrawal of Soviet forces. There is no doubt that the withdrawal contributed directly to the disintegration of the two puppet governments, but this does not mean that there were no other

---

[38] See Roosevelt, *op. cit.*, p. 257.
[39] See Pesyan, *op. cit.*; Eagleton, *op. cit.*; and Roosevelt, *op. cit.*
[40] These points are further discussed in the following section.
[41] See *Foreign Relations, 1946*, Vol. VII, p. 561.

considerations. Some understanding of these considerations may be gained by examining why the Soviet Union decided to withdraw its forces in the first place, and why the two Republics did *not* crumble *immediately* after the departure of the Red Army. After all, Soviet forces were evacuated on May 6, 1946, and the two rebel regimes lasted another half year.

The eventual withdrawal of the Soviet forces from Iran may be attributed to persistent Iranian, British, and American diplomatic efforts, but pressure from the United States, possibly including a personal ultimatum from President Truman to Stalin, played the decisive role. This pressure falls into two consecutive phases, before and after March 2, 1946, the magic date of evacuation under the tripartite treaty. As early as February 1, 1945, Foreign Secretary Anthony Eden and Secretary of State Edward Stettinius agreed at Malta on the importance of getting Soviet concurrence on the principle of gradual withdrawal *pari passu*. Mr. Eden raised the question with Molotov at a meeting of the Foreign Ministers at Yalta on February 11, 1945, but Molotov opposed Eden's suggestion for evacuation of the Allied troops before the end of hostilities.[42] Little more than a week after V-E Day, in identical notes to the three powers, Iran demanded the withdrawal of all Allied forces, reflecting its concern over the continued presence of the Russian, and to a lesser extent the British, forces.[43] Iran admitted that under the tripartite treaty the Allied forces could remain until six months after the end of the Japanese war, but felt that the spirit of the treaty called for immediate withdrawal, since the presence of Allied troops in Iran could contribute nothing to the war against Japan.

Neither the end of the war with Germany nor the Japanese defeat produced any notable change in Soviet resistance to Anglo-American and Iranian pressures for withdrawal. Although at Potsdam, on August 1, 1945, the Soviet Union did agree to the British proposal for withdrawal of forces from Teheran, Stalin opposed total and immediate withdrawal. He told Churchill that although Britain felt that the term of the Allied troops in Iran had expired, the Soviet Union did not, and that it would consider withdrawal only after the termination of the war against Japan.[44] The Japanese defeat occasioned Iran's second major diplomatic demand, on

---

[42] For details, see U.S. Department of State, *The Conferences at Malta and Yalta, 1945*, Washington, D.C., 1955, pp. 500–501, and 877; see also *Foreign Relations, 1945*, Vol. VIII, pp. 363–364.

[43] For the text of the Iranian note to the Soviet Union, see Malek, *op. cit.*, p. 24; see also *Foreign Relations, 1945*, Vol. VIII, p. 371.

[44] See U.S. Department of State, *The Conference of Berlin (The Potsdam Conference), 1945*, Vol. I, Washington, D.C., 1960, pp. 949–958.

September 11, 1945;[45] British Foreign Minister Ernest Bevin then informed Molotov that the American and British forces would be completing their withdrawal from Iran by March 2, 1946, that is, six months after the Japanese surrender.[46] Molotov's reply proved vague and noncommittal; he insisted that there was no need, contrary to Bevin's suggestion, to set a specific date for evacuation at the forthcoming meeting of the Council of Foreign Ministers. Bevin and Harriman raised the question of withdrawal with Stalin separately on December 19, 1945, but Stalin told Harriman that the Iranian government was "hostile" to the Soviet Union and therefore it was necessary for the Soviet Union to decide whether Soviet troops could be withdrawn under the terms of the tripartite treaty of 1942 or must be retained under the Soviet-Iranian treaty of 1921.[47] In an informal discussion of the Iranian question in Moscow on December 13, 1945, Secretary Byrnes expressed fear that the dispute would be raised at the January meeting of the United Nations, but Stalin replied that the Soviet Union was not afraid of having the Iranian question raised at the United Nations meeting and "no one need blush if it should come up."[48]

Not only did the Soviet Union not seem to blush when Iran charged the Soviet "officials and armed forces" with interference in its internal affairs,[49] but it even committed new acts of "aggression." It moved fresh troops and heavy equipment into northern Iran, accompanied by unusual troop movements towards Teheran after the Iranian complaint had been placed before the United Nations and the evacuation deadline had expired. The problem thus entered its second phase. In the opinion of Secretary James Byrnes, it seemed clear that the USSR was adding military invasion to political subversion in Iran, and as he told his colleagues in the Department of State: "Now we'll give it to them with both barrels."[50] Mr. Dean Acheson, then Undersecretary of State, believed that the United States ought to let the USSR know emphatically that it was aware of the Soviet moves, but "leave a graceful way out" if it desired to avoid a showdown.[51] In a long note to Molotov, dated March 6, 1946, the United States asserted that it was informed of the Soviet Union's decision to retain troops in Iran

---

[45] For the text of the Iranian note, see Malek, *op. cit.*, pp. 47–48.

[46] For Bevin's note, see *Foreign Relations, 1945*, Vol. VIII, pp. 413–414; Malek, *op. cit.*, p. 37.

[47] *Foreign Relations, 1945*, Vol. VIII, pp. 510–511.

[48] *Ibid.*, pp. 517–519.

[49] For the text of the Iranian letter containing these charges, see United Nations, *Security Council, Official Records*, First Year, First Series, Supplement No. 1, New York, pp. 16–17.

[50] *Foreign Relations, 1946*, Vol. VII, p. 347.

[51] *Ibid.*

after March 2, 1946, without the consent of the Iranian government. The note also referred to the Soviet commitment under the tripartite treaty and expressed an earnest hope that the Soviet Union would immediately withdraw all its forces from the territory of Iran.[52] In a stronger message, dated March 8, Secretary Byrnes said that the United States wished "to learn whether the Soviet Government, instead of withdrawing Soviet troops from Iran ... is bringing additional forces into Iran. In case Soviet forces in Iran are being increased, this Government would welcome information at once regarding the purpose thereof."[53]

Two more recent pieces of evidence raise the crucial question of whether the United States did not, in fact, go beyond diplomatic pressure in order to bring about the eventual withdrawal of Soviet forces. First, in a press and radio conference on April 24, 1952, President Truman stated that in 1945 [*sic*] he had to send an ultimatum to the Soviets to get out of Persia. The President said that "they got out because we were in a position to meet a situation of that kind."[54] Second, former President Truman wrote in 1957 in an article in *The New York Times*:

> From my experience with the Russians, I have learned that they are bound to move where we fail to make clear our intentions.
>
> For example, shortly after the end of World War II, Stalin and Molotov brazenly refused to keep their agreement to withdraw from Iran. They persisted in keeping their troops in Azerbaijan in northern Iran. Formal steps were taken through diplomatic channels and the United Nations to get the Russians to withdraw. The Soviet Union persisted in its occupation until I personally saw to it that *Stalin was informed that I had given orders to our military chiefs to prepare for the movement of our ground, sea and air forces*. Stalin then did what I knew he would do. He moved his troops out.[55]

What significance can be attached to these two pieces of evidence is at best difficult to say. Former President Truman's statement of April 24, 1952, was explained on the same day by a White House spokesman. He told the press that "the President was using the term ultimatum in a non-technical layman sense," and that "the President was referring to United States leadership in the United Nations, particularly in the Security Council and through diplomatic channels, in the spring of 1946, which was the major

---

[52] For the text of the note, see *ibid.*, pp. 340–341.

[53] The text of the note is to be found in *ibid.*, p. 348.

[54] *Ibid.*, pp. 348–349.

[55] I should like to thank the North American Newspaper Alliance for permission to quote this passage. It is taken from an article written by the former President himself and published in *The New York Times*, August 25, 1957. The italics are added.

factor in bringing about Soviet withdrawal from Iran."[56] In an editorial note appearing in the publication of the Department of State where this information is provided it is stated: "No documentation on the sending of an ultimatum to the Soviet Union has been found in the Department files or in the files of the Department of Defense, nor have several highest officers of the Department in 1946 been able to affirm the sending of an ultimatum."[57]

Assuming that this statement as well as that of the White House spokesman show convincingly that no "ultimatum" had in fact been sent, the former President's own article of August 25, 1957, raises the question once again. The article was concerned with the Middle East crisis, particularly the Syrian situation at the time, and the role of the United States *vis-a-vis* the Soviet Union. But neither the fact that the article does not deal exclusively with Iran nor the circumstance that in it a former Democratic President is criticizing a Republican administration would seem to provide sufficient ground for discounting its unequivocal assertion of direct communication with Stalin over the issue of withdrawing Soviet forces from Iran. This more recent statement of the President has, for whatever reason, gone unnoticed by the Department of State document which mentions President Truman's radio and press conference of April 24, 1952. It has also gone unnoticed by two eminent scholars. Professor Herbert Druks, in his book, *Harry S. Truman and the Russians, 1945–1953* (New York, 1966), page 125, writes, on the basis of his interviews with Harriman and Truman, that the former President wrote Stalin directly, warning that unless the Russians withdrew their forces within six weeks he would "move the fleet as far as the Persian Gulf." Professor Druks's account seems to corroborate the former President's article in *The New York Times*, but it makes no reference to that article. Herbert Feis, in *From Trust to Terror: The Onset of the Cold War, 1945–1950* (New York, 1970) page 84, quotes Loy Henderson, Chief of the Division of Eastern European Affairs in 1946, as telling him that, as far as he knows, "Truman never sent an admonitory message to Stalin." Feis cites Druks's account, but he, too, seems unaware of the former President's article in *The New York Times*; he wrote some thirteen years after the article that he had seen: "No other reference [namely, other than Druks's] to such a personal message from Truman."

Neither the President's own memoirs nor those of Secretary Byrnes make any mention of an "ultimatum." The President does mention in his memoirs the United States note of March 6, 1946, which, as we have seen,

---

[56] See *Foreign Relations, 1946*, Vol. VII, pp. 348–349.
[57] *Ibid.*, pp. 348–349.

contained no ultimatum, but he also states that he told Secretary Byrnes to send a "blunt message" to Premier Stalin.[58] It would be tempting to surmise that this was what the President was referring to in his article quoted above. On the other hand, the "blunt message" could refer to the Secretary's message of March 8, 1946, which was indeed stronger than the note of March 6, but it does not help clarify the problem. First, the Secretary's message of March 8 was sent to "the People's Commissar for Foreign Affairs," rather than to Premier Stalin, who is specifically named in both the President's memoirs and in his article quoted above. Second, although the Secretary's message of March 8 followed the United States note of March 6 and preceded the Soviet announcement of withdrawal on March 24, there is nothing in the text of the message resembling the contents of the passage quoted above; not even a hint of military action can be found in the message of March 8.

Ultimatum or no ultimatum, there is little doubt that the United States played the decisive role in bringing about the withdrawal of Soviet forces from Iran. To say this, however, is not to discount the importance of the Soviet Union's reaction to the discussion of the problem at the United Nations or to minimize the roles of Iran and Great Britain. The British diplomatic role has already been discussed, and it may be added that Britain's position was consistently expressed throughout the debate of the question in the United Nations. But the concern of the Soviet Union with the debate in the United Nations requires closer examination, as does the role played by Iran itself.

If it can be shown that the Soviet Union *was* concerned about the public discussion at the United Nations of its behavior in Iran, it would then be reasonable to assume that this concern was influential in shaping the Soviet decision to withdraw. Emphasizing such concern would seem to contradict an earlier sign of Soviet nonchalance, as it will be recalled that Stalin told Secretary Byrnes informally at the Moscow Conference that the Soviet Union would not "blush" if the question was raised at the United Nations. However, later, on the morning of January 28, 1946, just before the question was first discussed at the United Nations, Bevin told Stettinius that Vyshinsky "had shown considerable nervousness,"[59] and had said he was ready to drop the Russian charges regarding Greece and Indonesia if Britain would make satisfactory concessions with respect to the Balkan situation. Bevin had "flatly" told Vyshinsky that "he would not allow the

---

[58] See Harry S. Truman, *Memoirs by Harry S. Truman*, Vol. II: *Years of Trial and Hope, 1946–1952*, Garden City, New York, 1956, p. 94.

[59] For the relevant report, see *Foreign Relations, 1946*, Vol. VII, p. 320.

Iranian situation to be dropped by the Security Council."[60] Soviet concern over the debate in the United Nations continued even after the issue was taken up by the Security Council. This concern may be inferred from repeated Soviet attempts to block the debate by a variety of tactics.

One tactic was insisting on bilateral negotiations between the Soviet Union and Iran. In reply to Iran's first complaint to the United Nations, contained in its letter of January 19, 1946, Vyshinsky stated that the Soviet Union and its neighbor, Iran, "can and should" settle the questions which affect their relations "by means of bilateral negotiations."[61] On January 28, when the question was discussed in the Security Council, the Soviet Union again insisted on bilateral negotiations, stating that it would not consider any other approach to a solution.[62] In pursuance of the Security Council resolution of January 30, the Soviet Union and Iran entered into direct negotiations, but without results. Nevertheless, when the Iranian complaint was taken up again on March 25, the Soviet Union claimed (without success) that negotiations were still going on and that it would therefore be contrary to the Council's own resolution of January 30 to bring the matter before it again.[63]

The most favored Soviet tactic, however, was to keep the Iranian question off the agenda. In the early discussions leading to the resolution favoring bilateral negotiations, the Soviet Union wanted to remove the question from the agenda, and towards this end suggested that if the negotiations failed any member might bring the question up again.[64] On March 26, Gromyko again argued against the inclusion of the question on the agenda, claiming that the withdrawal of Soviet forces had already begun.[65] Iran nonetheless continued to retain the question on the agenda with the diplomatic encouragement of the United States. But in April a seemingly curious change occurred in Iran's position. On April 9, 1946, Husain Ala, Iran's representative, advised the Security Council that his country still wished to discuss the question of withdrawal, but on April 15, he informed the Council that his government "withdraws its complaint from the Security Council." This shift has been explained by the serious

---

[60] *Ibid.*

[61] For the French translation of the Soviet note, see United Nations, *Security Council, Official Records, op. cit.,* pp. 17–19.

[62] For the full text of Vyshinsky's statement reproduced in English after the meeting, see *ibid.,* pp. 39–44.

[63] *Ibid.,* No. 2, pp. 12–13.

[64] See Vyshinsky's remarks in *ibid.,* No. 1, pp. 65–67.

[65] He said the evacuation was generally begun on March 2, and the evacuation of troops from remaining districts on March 24; see *ibid.,* No. 2, p. 11.

illness and resignation of the American Ambassador, Mr. Wallace Murray,[66] but in light of more recent evidence, it may be suggested that the shift was primarily the result of Soviet pressures on Iran. The Soviet Ambassador I. V. Sadchikov, pressured Prime Minister Ahmad Qavam to instruct Ala to withdraw Iran's complaint. Sadchikov told Qavam that Iran's insistence on retaining the case before the Security Council was an insult to the USSR and would not be tolerated, and Qavam promised Sadchikov to telegraph Ala to withdraw the complaint.[67] Having secretly pressured Iran to make this move, the Soviet Union then openly attacked the retention of the question on the agenda, contending that to leave a question on the agenda after a state had withdrawn its complaint amounted to a violation of the Charter.[68]

Apart from the decisive influence of the United States and the importance of Soviet concern over the United Nations debate, Iran's own role in effecting the withdrawal of Soviet troops was by no means a small one. Briefly stated, Iran adopted three diplomatic means. First, it leaned almost completely on American support. This Iranian technique had its roots in what the present writer has elsewhere called "third-power policy," that is, the pattern of repeated reliance in the modern diplomatic history of Iran on a third power as a counterweight to traditional Anglo-Russian rivalry there.[69] Faced with a Soviet bid for maximum power, Iran relied primarily, although not exclusively, on the United States in resisting it. The second technique of Iran's diplomacy was exposure of Soviet behavior in the limelight of the United Nations, as has already been seen. The third major technique was direct negotiations with the Soviet Union. From the start of his premiership on January 27, 1946, Qavam believed that the immediate objective of the Soviet Union in northern Iran was the acquisition of an oil concession. The validity of his view was borne out in the course of his trip to Moscow, which took place between February 19 and March 11, 1946. During the negotiations between an Iranian mission, headed by Qavam, and Stalin and Molotov, the Soviet leaders took the harder line, and no agreement was reached. But it became abundantly clear that the Soviet leaders wished to discuss separately the evacuation of Soviet forces, the

---

[66] See Richard W. Van Wagenen (in consultation with T. Cuyler Young), *The Iranian Case, 1946*, New York, 1952, p. 67, footnote.

[67] *Foreign Relations, 1946*, Vol. VII, p. 417.

[68] For the relevant discussion in the United Nations, see *United Nations, Security Council, Official Records*, New York, First Year, First Series, No. 2, pp. 123–126.

[69] See Rouhollah K. Ramazani, *The Foreign Policy of Iran, 1500–1941 : A Developing Nation in World Affairs*, Charlottesville, Va., 1966, pp. 277–300.

problem of Azerbaijan, and the question of an oil agreement, while Qavam subtly, but unequivocally, made the agreement on oil contingent on the evacuation of Soviet forces.[70] When finally signed, Qavam's oil agreement with Sadchikov did not explicitly link the question of withdrawing forces with ratification by the Majlis. But in fact, the agreement was a major inducement to Soviet withdrawal. More important, Soviet anxiety over its ratification was used later by Qavam as the principal wedge to bring down the two rebel regimes. And in the end the Majlis refused to ratify the agreement.

This brings us to the last, crucial question: what caused the painless collapse of the two puppet regimes? It would be tempting to suppose that since the presence of the Red Army was the main factor underlying their establishment, the withdrawal of the Red Army was the only reason for their demise. If this were the case the two rebel regimes should have crumbled immediately after the Soviet evacuation, but they survived for half a year after the Red Army's departure. There is little doubt that the evacuation of Soviet forces was the necessary condition for the downfall of the two insurgent republics, but in itself it was not sufficient to bring about their collapse. Since we have already mentioned the conditions of the Azeri and Kurdish regimes as a contributory factor, it remains to examine the impact of the role played by the central government.

With the evacuation of the Red Army troops, Qavam was able to concentrate his efforts on the problem of the rebel regimes. But his policy must be understood in the light of the way his predecessor, Premier Ibrahim Hakimi, had approached the problem at the very outbreak of the insurrections. It has been suggested that the initial decisions of a government threatened by internal war "are usually the most fateful and long-lasting of any it will be called upon to make throughout an insurrection."[71] These decisions generally define the issues at stake, the presumed character of the struggle, and the legitimate basis for its termination. Hakimi's decision to send troops northward in mid-November, 1945, showed that he viewed the upheavals as spurious and unlawful and that he intended to crush them at an appropriate time. Qavam at first pursued a tactical policy of reconciliation with the insurgents, negotiating with the Azeri leaders through the well-known pro-Soviet figure, Muzaffar Firuz; conceding much of the autonomy desired by Pishehvari, including the appointment of three Tudeh members to his cabinet; and promoting Firuz to a major post in the central

---

[70] This important point was made in the second *aide-memoire* of the Iranian Mission during the course of discussions at Moscow. See Qasem Masoodi, *Mesyon-e 'E'zamy-e Iran be Mosko*, Teheran, 1946–1947, p. 71.

[71] See Lucian W. Pye, *Aspects of Political Development*, Boston, 1966, p. 139.

government. Owing to pressures from the Shah, and because of British troop movements in the southwest (in response to a Tudeh-sponsored general strike), Qavam's conciliatory attitude was soon reversed. Qavam still hoped to placate the Tudeh in view of the coming elections of the Majlis, which he wanted to control, thereby steering the government towards the center.[72] To blunt the propaganda campaign of the Tudeh and the Azeri insurgents, he also decreed the distribution of state lands to peasants, and to steal the thunder of the "Democrats of Azerbaijan," he created almost overnight his own "Democratic Party of Iran."[73]

Taking the position that the uprisings in Azerbaijan and Kurdistan were basically illegitimate and rebellious, Qavam decided, with the support of the Shah, to bring down the rebel regimes by means of force. On the one hand, he calculated that by keeping the Iranian complaint before the Security Council he would make it difficult for the Soviet Union to send troops back to Iran.[74] On the other hand, he counted on the strong Soviet desire for early parliamentary elections in Iran in anticipation of expediting the ratification of an oil agreement, and felt that for this reason the Soviet Union would hesitate to take forceful action against the dispatch of government forces to the rebel-held provinces. The Soviet ambassador vehemently opposed Qavam's decision to send troops and resorted to threats, declaring that the Soviet government would not remain passive in the face of the disturbances that might result from the Iranian operation near the Soviet frontier.[75] But Qavam's calculated steadfastness brought the desired results; the government troops crossed the Azerbaijan frontier on December 10, 1946, and upon their arrival the two republics collapsed almost overnight.

Why did the insurgent regimes crumble without any significant resistance? The Iranian Communist rebels, like the Polish Communists, relied primarily on the Soviet army, and in the absence of Soviet forces no resistance was possible. The Iranian Communist rebels, unlike the Yugoslav Communists, enjoyed little popular support, and could not mobilize the

---

[72] See *Foreign Relations, 1946*, Vol. VII, pp. 490–491.

[73] *Ibid.*, p. 505.

[74] Despite differences between Premier Qavam and Husain Ala, it is clear that both wished to keep the question before the Security Council as long as possible. We have already indicated that Qavam's previous instruction to Ala to withdraw the complaint had been the result of Soviet pressures at Teheran. After the evacuation of Soviet forces, Iran maintained successfully that its complaint had been withdrawn only insofar as it referred to the presence of those forces, and not as it applied to the matter of Soviet interference, which had been a question from the beginning of the difficulties.

[75] *Foreign Relations, 1946*, Vol. VII, p. 560.

civilian population to fight a guerrilla war. The Azeri and Kurdish party machineries and governmental structures suffered from serious organizational shortcomings. The low levels of socio-economic and political development of the Azeri and Kurdish people placed the rebel governments at a considerable disadvantage in relation to the central government. It was not possible for the two regimes to join hands in resisting the forces of the central government, as communal antagonism got in the way. Modernization had not only intensified the conflict between the Persian-speaking community on the one hand and the Azeri and Kurdish communities on the other, but had also increased antagonism between the Azeri and Kurdish communities themselves.

The ancient communal antagonism between the Azeris and the Kurds had been largely suppressed as a result of the centralization and detribalization policies of Reza Shah. At the same time, in Iran, as in other societies,[76] modernization in its early phases tended to exacerbate communal differences. The Anglo-Russian invasion removed the restraint of the armed forces over the Azeri and Kurdish communities; the Kurds of the Shakkak and Herki tribes, for example, attacked and looted Azeri villages.[77] The socio-economic changes of the inter-war period had intensified, rather than diminished, the sense of parochial identity in both communities. The emergence of two separate political parties, and finally of two governments, seemed to institutionalize the communal conflicts, despite the façade of similarity between the two regimes. The Soviet Union itself was at times forced to mediate between the two insurgent groups in order to forge a united front against the central government.[78] Neither group came to the aid of the other in the fight against the government forces, even when their common survival was at stake.

In light of the foregoing discussion, what conclusions can be drawn about the role of the Soviet Union in the rise of the Azeri and Kurdish republics in 1945–1946? The initial Soviet objective in invading northern Iran was to aid the war effort against Germany, but later this objective began to give way to the overriding goal of increasing Soviet power and ultimately controlling Iran. In pursuing this aim, the Soviet Union resorted to intimidation, propaganda, and acts of interference, and showed great reluctance, long before the establishment of the rebel regimes, to comply with Iranian, British, and American demands for the early withdrawal of

---

[76] The relationship between modernization and communalism is far more complicated than this brief statement would seem to suggest. For a theoretical study of the subject and numerous references, see Melson and Wolpe, *op. cit.*

[77] See Arfa, *op. cit.*, p. 72.

[78] Roosevelt, *op. cit.*, p. 258.

troops. The frustration of the Soviet Union in the face of Iranian as well as Anglo-American resistance to its ambitions from 1941 to 1943 was crowned by its dramatic failure to wrest an oil concession from Iran in 1944. Overt aid to the Azeri and Kurdish rebels in their seizure of power, interception of the central government forces, and protection of the local rebels in 1945 represented the boldest moves of the Soviet Union in its drive for control in Iran. The collapse of the rebel regimes did not automatically result from the withdrawal of Soviet forces, but this was the determining factor in their dissolution. The central question, then, is what finally prompted he withdrawal of the Red Army. The persistent diplomatic pressures of the United States as evidenced at Yalta, Potsdam, Moscow, and the United Nations proved decisive in this regard, whether or not President Trumtan actually threatened Stalin with military intervention. Assuming an ultimatum was indeed delivered, it provides no comforting evidence for a "revisionist" interpretation of the origins of the Cold War. If anything, the evidence in this study points out that within a month after the invasion of Iran in 1941 the Soviet Union sought increasingly and persistently to maximize its power there. If any ultimatum was delivered to Moscow in 1946, it came only after some five years of aggressive Soviet acts.

To suggest that the United States played the dominant role in bringing about the withdrawal of Soviet forces from Iran is not to deny the influence of other factors. Great Britain at times proved even more alert to Soviet designs than the United States, took the initiative in several instances in checkmating Soviet moves, and fully supported American and Iranian diplomacy. Iran's own role was also an important one. Iran masterfully employed diplomatic techniques, such as relying on the United States to act as a counterforce, exposing Soviet behavior in the United Nations, linking the conclusion of an oil agreement to the withdrawal of Soviet forces, and finally refusing to ratify the oil agreement. The firmness of President Truman and Secretary Byrnes was matched, if not surpassed, by the courage of Qavam, Ala, and the young Shah. Little Iran, like Finland, showed how far skillful diplomacy can go in compensating for a lack of military power.

Finally, the Azeri and Kurdish insurrections were neither purely the creation of the Soviet Union, nor doomed simply because of the withdrawal of Soviet forces. Indigenous circumstances also had their effect. The legacy of twenty years of Reza Shah's repressive rule thwarted all chances for channeling the claims of emerging socio-economic groups to the polity. The Shah's policy of centralized modernization was not accompanied by the development of commensurate political institutions, and tended to reinforce traditional communal antagonism, whether between the Persian-speaking élite and the Azeri and Kurdish leaders, or between the Azeris and the Kurds themselves. Just as the former antagonism lay in part at the root of the insurrections launched against the central government in Teheran, the latter antagonism rendered any attempt at co-operation between the two rebel regimes unattainable, even in the interest of survival.

A Preconceived Formula for Sovietization: The Communist Takeover of North Korea

Dae-Sook Suh

Whatever may have been their initial and ultimate objectives in liberating the northern half of Korea, the Soviet troops that occupied the country for three years and four months beginning in August, 1945, implanted a viable Communist regime that has proven to be stable and friendly towards the Soviet Union. The importance of such a regime cannot be overstated. Not only was it the first Communist system of government to be instituted in Korea, but also it divided Korea politically and was alien to the people and culture of the country. Furthermore, less than two years after the Soviet occupation, the regime in the North launched a fraticidal war to communize all of Korea. The rapid consolidation of power by the Communists and the rigid regimentation they were able to enforce to assure political stability would seem to attest to the efficiency of the techniques they employed for the takeover of North Korea. However, a closer and more careful analysis reveals that the Communists did not make detailed preliminary preparations, did not possess a plan designed solely for the takeover, and did not have the mass support of the Korean people. Instead, the takeover was a haphazard application of the practices used in Soviet-occupied territories in Eastern Europe, particularly in East Germany, Poland, and Rumania.

This study will attempt to examine the Soviet techniques used in the takeover of North Korea and to compare them with those used in the East European countries and East Germany. No effort is made here to treat the Soviet occupation of Korea comprehensively or to give a systematic exposition of Soviet occupation policy in Korea. The study is rather intended to be a comparative analysis of the strategies of the Soviet occupation authorities in installing a Communist regime in North Korea.

One classification of Communist takeovers in Eastern Europe distinguishes three kinds of seizures of power: a successful guerrilla struggle, assumption of control through popular support and parliamentary means, and the outright imposition of a Soviet-backed regime, which is sometimes called a baggage-train government.[1] In this scheme, the Korean case might

---

[1] R. V. Burks, "Eastern Europe," in C. E. Black and T. P. Thornton (eds.), *Communism and Revolution*, Princeton, N. J., 1964, pp. 86–93.

be classified as a variant of the third category, but the baggage-train government that traveled on the Trans-Siberian railway to North Korea seems to have lost much in transit. Whatever finesse was used to set up the Communist regimes in Eastern Europe gave way to the rudeness and rigor of a military takeover in Korea that relied on little if any knowledge of the local situation.

The tactics used in the Soviet takeovers of East Germany and Poland have much in common with those used in North Korea. In both areas the military and the security police gained firm control; efforts were made to create popular front governments; and a forced fusion of the Socialist and Communist Parties took place, as exemplified by the creation of the Socialist Unity Party in East Germany and the Workers' Party in Korea. Moreover, the Home Army in Poland and the Korean Volunteer Corps in North Korea were both disarmed, and there were attempts to de-nazify the bureaucracy in East Germany and to eliminate the Japanese influence over the leaders of North Korea. Another aspect common to both the East European and Korean situations is the relative weakness of the local Communist Parties. Indeed, some puzzling developments in Korea can be better understood when compared and analyzed under the general rubric of Soviet occupation policy.

The takeover of North Korea might also be explained in terms of three stages of sovietization, evolving from (1) the formation of a genuine coalition through (2) the establishment of a bogus, Communist-dominated coalition, to (3) the creation of a monolithic Communist regime. However, there are other aspects of the Korean takeover that are unique, such as the relative ignorance of Korean affairs on the part of the Soviets, the rigid indifference towards the North on the part of the old Korean Communists, the special problems of the trusteeship and partition of Korea, and the singularly important role played by the Soviet-trained Koreans who were working with the occupation forces.

Had it been given a zone of occupation in Korea, Nationalist China would probably have proved to be the best prepared of the victorious Allies to establish a regime representative of the Korean revolutionary movement and readily acceptable to the Korean people as a whole. Nationalist China had nurtured a Korean government in exile for almost two and a half decades. Regardless of its shortcomings, the Korean Provisional Government in Chungking was the center of the Korean independence movement. In retrospect, it is ironic that Syngman Rhee, an American-trained Korean (although not American-sponsored) emerged as the leader in the South, for his "rapid realization of Korean independence" turned instead into the permanent division of Korea, and this division greatly facilitated the Communist takeover of the North.

Before the entry of the Red Army into Eastern Europe, the Soviet Communists were well informed about the various Polish underground leaders and their groups, most of whom were as anti-Soviet as they were anti-German; and although Hitler was successful in extirpating most of the German Communists living in Germany, the Soviets supported a contingent of exiled German Communists in the Soviet Union. In Korea, the Japanese were successful in curbing the Communists and reducing them to miniscule groups of slight importance, but the Soviets were generally ignorant of who the Korean Communist leaders were and of who among them might be identified with the Korean liberation movement and command its respect.

Two groups of Koreans, both unrelated and unknown to the Korean independence movement, were enlisted by the Soviets for the Korean takeover; one was a Korean minority living in Uzbekistan and Kazakhstan, while the other was a contingent of Koreans who had fought with the Soviet army during World War II, first in Europe and later in Manchuria and North Korea. The first group consisted of second- and third-generation Koreans and numbered over 300,000 persons; many of the Soviet-Koreans in this group were called on to manage the initial takeover in the North— e.g., Ho Ka-i, Nam Il, Pak Ui-wan (Ivan Pak), and Ki Sok-bok, to mention only a few.[2] The second group consisted of Koreans who either had been taken into the Soviet army when oriental minorities in Siberia were enlisted for combat in Europe[3] or else had been secretly trained by the Russians. No evidence is available to substantiate the allegation that the Soviet Union secretly trained Koreans specifically for the future occupation of Korea, but there are many reports of political and military training being given to Koreans in the Soviet Union.[4] Kim Il-song, Premier of the Democratic People's Republic and head of the Korean Workers' (Communist) Party,

---

[2] For a description of minority groups in the Soviet Far East, which includes the Koreans, see Walter Kolarz, *The Peoples of the Soviet Far East*, New York, 1954. For accounts of the Korean minority groups in the Soviet Maritime Province and Siberia, see, among others, Syn-khva Kim, *Ocherki po istorii Sovetskikh Koreytsev*, Alma-Alta, 1965; Chong-sik Lee and Ki-wan Oh, "The Russian Faction in North Korea," *Asian Survey*, Vol. VIII, No. 4, April, 1968, 270–88.

[3] There is a description of the Siberian soldiers in Alan Clark, *Barbarossa, the German-Russian Conflict, 1941–1945*, New York, 1965, pp. 149–150, 170–172, 196–199; and a Russian account of the Siberian soldiers in *Stalingrad*, Moscow, 1943, pp. 74–76.

[4] See, for example, Kazama Jokichi, *Mosko kyosan daigaku no omoite*, Tokyo, 1949, p. 109; or Wolfgang Leonhard, *Child of the Revolution*, Chicago, 1958, p. 178.

relates that when the Soviet Union declared war against Japan, his partisans co-ordinated their efforts with the Red Army in the struggle against the Japanese for the liberation of Korea.[5]

Claims that Kim Il-song was trained by the Soviet army and held the rank of a field officer have not yet been verified.[6] The most commonly accepted story is that he was trained somewhere near Khabarovsk and joined the Soviet campaign in the battle of Stalingrad, fighting under General Ivan M. Chistiakov. General Chistiakov led the 21st Division of the Red Army in the battle of Stalingrad and later commanded the 25th Division in the occupation of North Korea. As late as November, 1944, Japanese intelligence reported that Kim was trained at the Okeanskaya Field School near Vladivostok, and that he worked for the Soviets, making two trips to Moscow to help co-ordinate the efforts of the Allies in Manchuria.[7] Assuming that Kim did fight under General Chistiakov and that he did become a friend of General P. L. Romanenko, who later assisted him in North Korea, it would seem that the Russians had known Kim for only four years at the most,[8] and that his involvement with them was primarily of a military nature. It is known that Kim cannot speak Russian, although he is fluent in Chinese.

Compared with the Communist leaders sponsored by the Soviet Union in Poland and East Germany, Kim was a relative newcomer as a collaborator. For example, Boleslaw Bierut of Poland had been a Comintern agent in Berlin, Vienna, and Prague, while Wilhelm Pieck of Germany had worked for the Comintern since the 1920's. Furthermore, Bierut stayed in Russia after his release from prison in 1938, and Walter Ulbricht of Germany spent many years in the Soviet Union preparing for his return with the Russians. Probably all the Russians had from Kim was his pledge of loyalty to the Soviet Union. But this may have been all that was required of him, for he did not have the support of the Korean Communists or of the Korean people, and so could only be considered tentatively as a leader. He did

---

[5] P'yongyang hyangt'osa p'yonch'an wiwon-hoe, *P'yong yang chi*, P'yongyang, 1957, pp. 410–414.

[6] Most of the accounts by the South Koreans allege that Kim returned to Korea as a major in the Soviet Army. There is a most vituperative eyewitness account in Han Chae-dok, *Kongsan chui iron kwa hyonsil pip'an chonso*, che ogwon, Seoul, 1965, pp. 129–130.

[7] "Kin Nichi-sei no katsudo jokyo," *Tokko gaiji geppo*, November, 1944, pp. 76–78.

[8] See the account of Generals Chistiakov and Romanenko in the Stalingrad campaign in A. I. Evemenko, *Stalingrad*, Moscow, 1961, pp. 387–426. See also A. M. Samsonov, *Stalingradskaya bitva*, Moscow, 1968, pp. 379–381, 437–441, and 526–527.

command a small contingent of partisans who had supported him faithfully since the guerrilla campaign in Manchuria, and who had shared his experiences under the Chinese and Soviet Communists.

If the process of sovietization in North Korea is viewed in terms of the stages previously described as characteristic of Soviet takeovers in the East European countries, the constituent events fall roughly into three periods.[9] The first stage, a period of genuine co-operation, lasted from August, 1945, to January, 1946, coinciding with the brief career of the Five Provinces Administration Bureau. It has been suggested that the Soviet authorities ordered the nationalist and Communist leaders to join in administering North Korea through the Bureau.[10] This coalition ended when an irreconcilable rift developed between the Soviet-Koreans and the non-Communist leaders in the North over the question of a Korean trusteeship. Many nationalist leaders, including the chairman of the Bureau, Cho Man-sik, were arrested and imprisoned, while those who escaped arrest fled to the South.

The second stage, a period of bogus coalition, can be said to have begun in February, 1946, with the formation of the North Korean Provisional People's Committee headed by Kim Il-song. A major step towards this coalition was the merging of the New People's Party and the North Korean Branch Bureau of the Korean Communist Party, which was reportedly ordered by the Russians in August, 1946, to set up the Workers' Party of North Korea. A similar merger of three leftist parties in the South, including the Korean Communist Party, was also carried out in November, 1946, creating the Workers' Party of South Korea.

The emergence of a monolithic regime, the third stage in the takeover, could be detected as early as February, 1948, when the People's Army of Korea was formally established and the Workers' Party of North Korea held its second congress. And by April, 1948, when the North-South

---

[9] The pattern of takeovers in Eastern Europe is described in: H. Seton-Watson, *The East European Revolution*, New York, 1961, pp. 169–171. Also in H. Seton-Watson, *From Lenin to Malenkov: The History of World Communism*, New York, 1955, pp. 248–249. A somewhat different analysis of the Korean process, but using the same formula, is in Ho-min Yang, *Puk-han ui ideorogi wa chongchi'i*, Seoul, 1967, pp. 79–109.

[10] Han Chae-dok, one of the thirty-two members of the Five Provinces Administration Bureau, reported that the first meeting on August 26, 1945, was presided over by General Romanenko, and that the thirty-two members of the Bureau were equally represented, sixteen each, by the nationalists and the Communists. Han, who later defected to the South, related that he was a member of the Communist group. See Han Chae-dok, *op. cit.*, pp. 171–188. See also an eyewitness account in Anna Louise Strong, *In North Korea*, New York, 1949, pp. 10–25.

Consultative Conference was held, the existence of a Communist dictatorship was undeniable. It was a mere formality to proclaim the establishment
of a government in the North in September, 1948; soon after, in December,
the Soviet army withdrew from Korea.[11]

In Eastern Europe similar techniques of sovietization were used in those
countries where comparatively few fundamental changes had occurred
between prewar and postwar conditions; this necessitated the forming of
coalition governments at the outset as a transitional phase. The obvious
examples are Czechoslovakia, Hungary, and Bulgaria. In Korea, however,
there was a marked social change after the war, with the uprooting of Japanese influence and the revitalization of Korean tradition representing major
undertakings. Thus the Soviet military takeover in North Korea was relatively easier than in Eastern Europe. For the Soviet Union, the task in Korea
was simply to implant communism, rather than to form a coalition with
nationalist elements as one step towards the ultimate creation of a Communist regime.

When they first occupied the North, the Soviets were unaware of the
political and social setting of Korea, and unequivocally disavowed any intention either to administer Korea militarily or to implant a Communist system.
However, it seems clear that the Soviet Union resolved to institute a Communist regime in the North as early as December, 1945, when the Koreans
opposed the Allied plan for a trusteeship of Korea. The Soviet Union was
aided in this resolve by the indifference of the Korean nationalists and the
old Communist leaders, who hoped only for the speedy withdrawal of
Soviet forces from Korea. In contrast to the Polish government in exile in
London, whose leaders were arrested when they approached the Russians
in Poland, the Korean Provisional Government in Chungking had no intention of establishing relations with or even contacting the Russians. Almost
all the prominent Korean leaders, including the old-guard Communists,
were in the South, trying to establish a national government by negotiating
with the Americans.

The sovietization of North Korea was effected through the seizure of
three key organizations: the military, the party, and the administrative
mechanism. The specific tactics used were similar to those employed in

---

[11] For postwar political developments in Korea, see, among others, Kim
Chong-bom and Kim Tong-un, *Haebang chon-hu ui Choson chinsang*, Seoul, 1945;
a South Korean government account in *Hyondae-sa wa kongsan chui, che iljip*,
Seoul, 1968; a North Korean official account in *Choson chung-ang yon'gam, 1949*,
P'yongyang, 1950; and a Russian account in F. I. Shabshina, *Ocherki noveyshey
istorii Korei, 1945–53*, Moscow, 1958.

Eastern Europe. There was the actual presence of the Red Army, and no domestic forces were allowed to emerge—nor were any Korean nationalist forces permitted to return—to compete with the Soviet-Koreans and Kim Il-song's partisans. Although there was no attempt by the Koreans to challenge the Soviet military presence, as was the case in Warsaw, and no incident to poison relations with the Soviet Union, such as the massacre of Polish officers in the Katyn Forest, the Soviets did take steps to disband the Korean Volunteer Corps returning from Yenan. Estimates place the number of soldiers in the Corps, which was a military arm of the Korean Independence League or the Yenan Communists, at 2,000. When contacted by the Corps, which wanted to cross the border between China and Korea at Antu-Shinuiju, the Soviet occupation forces, in co-operation with the Soviet-Koreans and Kim's partisans, completely disarmed it and allegedly deported some of its members to Manchuria in a move reminiscent of the treatment of the Polish Home Army.[12] This was an important step in shaping the distribution of the contenders for power in the North at the time. After the incident at the Antu-Shinuiju border, the Yenan Communists, who had had a popular following in Korea, lost much of their strength and came to represent a negligible force in comparison with the Russian-sponsored contingent of Soviet-Koreans. The number of Koreans who accompanied the Soviet occupation forces when they entered North Korea is thought to be approximately 300, but to this number must be added the group of non-military Soviet-Koreans brought in from Uzbekistan and Kazakhstan.

The Soviet-Koreans and Kim's partisans played a dominant role in the sovietization of the North, and were particularly conspicuous in controlling the internal security police and the North Korean army. (In much the same way, manipulation of the police and the army was a source of Communist strength in the countries of Eastern Europe.) A Soviet-Korean, Pang Hak-se, headed the Political Security Bureau of the Ministry of Internal Affairs and played the same role in Korea as Stanislaw Radkiewicz did in the Security Office in Poland. Pang was born and raised in the Soviet Union and was said to have worked for the NKVD (the Soviet secret police) in Uzbekistan prior to his return to Korea as a captain in the Red Army. Pang and Kim P'a, another Soviet-Korean, who was a boss in the Security Bureau,

---

[12] Marian K. Dziewanowski, *The Communist Party of Poland. An Outline History*, Cambridge, 1959, pp. 174–175. Kim Ch'ang-sun, *Puk-han ship-o-nyon-sa*, Seoul, 1961, pp. 61–65. Tsuboe Senji, a former Japanese police officer, reported that there were only 400 men, in his book *Chosen minzoku tokuritsu undo hishi*, Tokyo, 1959, pp. 468–469.

were said to have been the two most feared men in the North during the Soviet occupation.

The military forces were likewise controlled from the very beginning by partisan comrades of Kim Il-song, including An Kil, Kim Ch'aek, and Ch'oe Yong-gon. The first groups to appear in uniform in Korea were the Red Security Corps, the Peace Preservation Corps, the Border Constabulary, and the Railroad Guards; all the senior officers in these groups were followers of Kim or else Soviet-Koreans. A number of military training schools were established and directed exclusively by the Soviet-Koreans and Kim's partisans.[13] Apart from controlling the military forces in Korea through their Soviet-Korean collaborators, the Soviet occupation forces initiated a program to train Korean soldiers in Siberia. Under this program, begun in late 1945, some 10,000 North Korean soldiers received military and technical training in Khabarovsk and Chita.[14] Ch'oe Yong-gon, the Minister of Defense in North Korea, had an impeccable Communist military record, and was totally dedicated to the Communist cause. In sum, just as in Eastern Europe, Communist strength in North Korea relied on a close hold over the security police and the military.

The takeover of the Party machine by the Communists in the North also largely followed the pattern set in Eastern Europe. For example, the common Soviet policy of choosing local Communist leaders who had few domestic ties is glaringly apparent in the case of Korea, for Kim was unaffiliated with any Korean organization and was unknown to the Korean people. He had to be introduced to them as a hero of the Korean revolution by the Russians, and even then many doubted the authenticity of his meager record in the partisan struggle in Manchuria.[15] Although he did participate in the anti-Japanese campaign, he played no part in the Korean Communist movement before the Soviet occupation. In contrast to some of the Communist leaders in Eastern Europe who had well-known names in their native countries before World War II, such as Dimitrov in Bulgaria and Gottwald

---

[13] The North Korean army is discussed by V. A. Matsulenko in *Koreyskaya narodnaya armiya*, Moscow, 1959; Roy E. Appleman, *United States Army in the Korean War: South to Nakton, North to Yalu*, Washington, D.C., 1961, pp. 7–18; Ki-won Chung, "The North Korean People's Army and Party," *The China Quarterly*, London, No. 14, April–June, 1963, pp. 105–124.

[14] Department of State, *North Korea. A Case Study in the Technique of Takeover*, Washington, D.C., 1961, pp. 85–86; Malcolm Mackintosh, *Strategy and Tactics of Soviet Foreign Policy*, London, 1962, pp. 33–45.

[15] For the record of Kim's participation in the anti-Japanese struggle in Manchuria, there is his own account, Baik Bong, *Kim Il Sung, Biography 1*, Tokyo, 1969. See a more realistic account in my book, *The Korean Communist Movement, 1918–1948*, Princeton, N. J., 1967.

in Czechoslovakia, Kim was a stranger even to most Korean Communists. It was not until after the murder of Hyon Chun-hyok (a native Communist leader who represented the Korean Communist Party in the North) and the death of Kim Yong-bom (chairman of the North Korean Branch Bureau of the Korean Communist Party) that Kim and his group took control of the Communist Party in the North. Surrounded by his armed partisans, Kim assumed the chairmanship of the Branch Bureau at its third enlarged plenum in December, 1945. His takeover was facilitated by the absence of potential "Titoist groups," for most of the prominent Communist leaders were in the South, and they made no effort to contest Kim.

Thus, in contrast to Eastern Europe, where popular support aided such native Communists as Dimitrov, Gottwald, and Tito, in North Korea Kim came to power without any popular following. The coercive fusion of political parties which underlay the creation of the Workers' Party of North Korea corresponded with the creation of the Socialist Unity Party in East Germany and the forceful merger of Communists and Social Democrats in Eastern Europe. The merger of the North Korean Branch Bureau of the Korean Communist Party and the New People's Party must have been ordered by the Soviets, for it would seem that without their directives such a merger could not have happened so smoothly or so soon after the liberation.[16]

The tactic of merger, or the strategy of "unity from below," was an attempt to join the supporters of the Yenan Communists with the Workers' Party of North Korea, in much the same way as the Soviets tried to split the German Social Democratic membership from its leaders. In North Korea the merger was attained at the cost of having Kim Il-song yield the chairmanship of the united party to a leader of the Yenan Communists, Kim Tubong, while accepting only the vice-chairmanship for himself. A parallel merger of the three leftist parties in the South was carried out with the creation of the Workers' Party of South Korea and had a devastating effect on the main forces of the Korean Communist Party in the South. This strategy of forceful fusion was successful in Korea, for it not only split the membership of the Korean Communist Party in the South on the issue of the merger, but also contributed significantly to the weakening of the Communist forces in the South, thus enhancing indirectly the influence of the Soviet-Korean forces in the North.

At the time of the founding congress of the Workers' Party of North Korea in August, 1946, it claimed a membership of 366,000 or about

---

[16] John P. Nettl, *The Eastern Zone and Soviet Policy in Germany, 1945–1950*, London, 1951, pp. 88–90; Pang In-hu, *Puk-han Choson nodong-dang ui hyongsong kwa paljon*, Seoul, 1967, pp. 81–110.

four percent of the population. As in most of Eastern Europe, virtually every member of the Party had joined after the war. Four months after
the merger, the Party membership had almost doubled, reaching 600,000 in
December, 1946. As in East Germany, most of the members were either
opportunist or were unable to flee to the other part of the country and
therefore decided to co-operate with the Communists.

The reshaping of the Party was quickly undertaken. By 1948, approximately ten percent of its members had been purged. The shuffling and
reshuffling of the Party membership by utilizing the device of issuing new
identity cards resulted in the emergence of a very youthful group, not
unlike in the Communist Parties in Eastern Europe. In 1948, nearly
seventy percent of the Party membership was under thirty-five years of age
and more than fifty percent was under thirty.[17] The control exercised over
the Party by the Soviet-Koreans and Kim's partisans was so strict that internal disagreements were few, and such disputes never reached the level of
intensity that they did under Gomulka in Poland, Kostov in Bulgaria, and
Clementis in Czechoslovakia.[18] O Ki-sop, a native Communist, at times
voiced his dissatisfaction publicly, but his opposition was patiently put down,
eventually curbed, and later condemned, thus judiciously avoiding a direct
confrontation within the Party. By eliminating channels for dissent in this
way, the Party in North Korea assured its place, much as the Socialist Unity
Party in East Germany did. In both countries Communist power derived
not from the Party organizations or from popular support, but from the
ubiquitous presence of the occupation authorities.

A merger in the style of the United Polish Workers' Party did not occur
in Korea until after the withdrawal of Soviet forces, but when it did it was
more like an absorption of the Workers' Party of South Korea by the North.
The coalition was finalized in June, 1949, and Kim Il-song formally assumed
chairmanship of the Workers' Party of all Korea, which included the old
Communist revolutionaries who had fled to the North from the American-
sponsored, anti-Communist regime in the South.[19]

Only two splinter parties were allowed to function in the North. These
were the North Korean Democratic Party and the Ch'ondo-gyo Friends
Party. The latter was the party of an old Korean religious sect, and although
peasant-oriented, it had little political importance. On the other hand, the

---

[17] Department of State, *North Korea*, pp. 19–20.

[18] Dziewanowski, *op. cit.*, p. 213. Seton-Watson, *The East European Revolution*,
pp. 307 and 316.

[19] On the United Polish Workers' Party, see Dziewanowski, *op. cit.*, pp.
225–240. For the Workers' Party of Korea, see Pang In-hu, *op. cit.*, pp. 125–138.

Democratic Party, a nationalist group, was led by Cho Man-sik, who was perhaps the only man in the North who commanded significant popular support. The extent to which the Communists infiltrated the Democratic Party is not known, but two important leaders of Kim Il-song's partisans, Ch'oe Yong-gon and Kim Ch'aek, were members. As with certain peasant parties in Eastern Europe, which were secretly managed by the Communists to confuse the people, Kim's partisans were able to wield strong influence in the Democratic Party, and eventually the Soviet-Koreans, together with the partisans, took it over completely.

The Soviet Union took considerable care to inflate its role as the liberator of an oppressed people in Korea. In fact, in direct contrast to its policy in East Germany, it did not set up an overt Soviet military administration in the North.[20] This was particularly appealing to the Koreans, especially in light of the United States military government in the South, which denied the legality of any local authorities, including the Korean Provisional Government returning from China. In Eastern Europe the first postwar administrations were either created by the Soviets, as was the Lublin Committee in Poland, or else were Soviet-sponsored, as was the Provisional Government of General Miklos in Hungary. In the absence of a native civilian government and without a Soviet military administration in Korea, a coalition was hastily formed, consisting of nationalist and Communist leaders. But the revolutionary credentials of both groups were not very impressive, and the coalition, the Five Provinces Administration Bureau, proved to be ineffective.

Although the Soviet occupation authorities did not set up a direct military administration in Korea, this in no way meant that they relinquished tight military control over the country. One account relates that during the period of the Five Provinces Administration Bureau, the Soviet army, under General P. L. Romanenko, created a committee consisting solely of Soviet-Koreans and Kim's partisans to carry out the wishes of the Soviet occupation forces.[21] Little is known about the committee except that every one of its forty-three representatives was either a card-carrying member of the Soviet Communist Party or a trained recruit of the Soviet occupation forces. The most conspicuous counterpart of this group in Eastern Europe was the Lublin Committee in Poland. But the Soviets were more secretive in Korea, where their regulatory committee was in existence for a very short period of time and did not provide the basis for the People's Committee that was

---

[20] Franz L. Neumann, "Soviet Policy in Germany," *The Annals*, Philadelphia, Pa., No. 263, May, 1949, pp. 165–179. The Russian proclamation of October 12 is given in *Choson chungang yon'gam, 1949, op. cit.*, pp. 58–59.

[21] Kim Ch'ang-sun, *op. cit.*, pp. 53–54.

formed later. Furthermore, the Korean group was not as influential as the Lublin Committee, nor is it known whether it was imported from the Soviet Union in a "baggage train," or was hastily put together by the Soviet forces after the occupation.

The issue of a trusteeship for Korea brought a decisive change in the political climate.[22] The Soviet directive to the Communists was to acquiesce and even support the plan for a five-year trusteeship, but the proposal was resisted by all Koreans. For the Korean Communists, the question was perhaps as unpopular as that of the German-Polish border or reparations was for the German Communists. The Korean Communists dutifully supported the plan for a trusteeship, but unlike the question of Germany's Polish border, the idea of a trusteeship was never worked out because of the overwhelming repugnance to it on the part of the Korean people in the South. When it became obvious that the American military authorities were yielding to popular pressure in the South, there was a period of rapid sovietization in the North. Purges of non-Communist leaders who had opposed the trusteeship in the North took place in much the same way as the elimination of non-Communist leaders in Eastern Europe.

Shortly after, in February, 1946, the formation of the Provisional People's Committee of North Korea was proclaimed, with Kim Il-song as chairman, and a year later the People's Committee of North Korea was organized. The People's Committee was to rule the North until the establishment of a formal government on September 9, 1948. In setting up these committees and the government in general, the Soviets attempted to preserve the appearance of a broad popular front. Many leaders of the Democratic Party and the Ch'ondo-gyo Friends Party, as well as leaders of the Yenan Communists and domestic groups within the Workers' Party of North Korea, were placed in ministerial positions. One study contends that positions of prominence were differentiated from positions of power in the North Korean governmental structure, and that most of the positions of authority were entrusted to Soviet-Koreans. The Soviets are said to have exercised control through vice-ministers who were either Soviet-Koreans or members of Kim's partisans, and it is claimed that the actual power was held by these men.[23] The extent to which the Soviets managed these committees is difficult to ascertain, but close analysis of the committees reveals

---

[22] There are numerous accounts of the question of the trusteeship in Korea. The details of the negotiations are to be found in Soon Sung Cho, *Korea in World Politics, 1940–50: An Evaluation of American Responsibility*, Berkeley, Calif., 1967. See also George M. McCune, *Korea Today*, Cambridge, Mass., 1950.

[23] Yi Hong-gun, *Soryon kunjong ui simal*, Seoul, 1950, pp. 4–10; Department of State, *North Korea, op. cit.*, pp. 18–54.

two important factors which suggest that the degree of Soviet influence in North Korea bears comparison with the situation in the East European countries.

The first of these factors is the background of the leaders who collaborated with the Soviet military. Though there is little doubt that the People's Committees represented a wide range of popular groups, their leaders resembled closely the types of people who co-operated with the Soviets in Poland—professional army men, prewar civil servants, returning émigré politicians, politicians with totalitarian proclivities, and leftist leaders won over by the Polish Workers' Party.[24] All of these types were present in North Korea, but none matched the Soviet-Koreans and the partisans in strength. Kim Il-song and his partisans used different types of people at different times. Together with the Soviet-Koreans, they were able to manipulate these groups by means of the de-japanization campaigns in the North. Under Japanese rule, the majority of Korean revolutionaries who operated in or near Korea were subdued. Indeed, there were very few Koreans who kept alive the anti-Japanese struggle, except for those who fled and lived abroad, such as the Soviet-Koreans, the Yenan Koreans, and Kim's partisans. As a result, in the postwar period many Koreans could easily be accused of having collaborated with the Japanese, and these men held their positions at the whim of the Soviet-Koreans and the partisans. Ultimately, all those who could be said to have collaborated with the Japanese in any way at all were eliminated. Much like the de-nazification of the bureacracy in East Germany, the de-japanization campaign was gradually carried out not only among true collaborators, but among innocent anti-Communists as well.

The second factor attesting to the extent of Soviet control is the rapidity with which reform measures were inaugurated and completed. The Provisional People's Committee undertook six major reforms in the North in less than six months.[25] More than fifty percent of the farm land was redistributed in a sweeping land reform inaugurated in March, 1946. An eight-hour workday was established for the first time by a decree promulgated in June, 1946. These steps were quickly followed by the nationalization of virtually all heavy industries in the North, the regulation of a system of tax-in-kind in agriculture, the declaration of the equality of the sexes, and the formulation of an elect on code. The effort to win the support of the people by championing reforms was a common characteristic of the Com-

---

[24] Dziewanowski, *op. cit.*, pp. 188–189.

[25] Ch'ian-guk t'ukbyol chongbo-kwa, *Puk-han kongsan koeroe chong-kwon e taehan koch'al*, Seoul, 1958, pp. 31–53; Pak Tong-un, *Puk-han t'ongch'i kiguron*, Seoul, 1964, pp. 3–16.

munist administrations in Eastern Europe, but the rapidity with which these reforms were proclaimed and executed in Korea was most unusual. In Korea, such measures seem to have represented the implementation of a preconceived formula for sovietization rather than the application of a program of action to win popular support. Aside from these reform measures, the creation of a monolithic regime and the institution of a stable control mechanism in the North seems to have been secured when the North Korean Communists announced the creation of the Korean People's Army in February, 1948, even before the formation of their government. In March, 1948, when the nationally prominent leaders from the South, Kim Ku and Kim Kyu-sik, met with the Communist leaders of the North at the North-South Political Consultative Conference, the Communists displayed a solid front, and the two leaders from the South could not help but recognize the rapid polarization of Korea.

It has been asserted that the Soviet zone in Germany provided a climate favorable to the advancement of the Socialist Unity Party there.[26] In Korea, the North was perhaps less amenable to a Communist takeover than the South was. However, the takeovers in both Korea and Germany did not depend on the popularity of the Communists or on the reforms they carried out or promised. The takeovers in both countries were effected by a small segment of cadres that the Soviet forces had either brought with them or trained in these countries and then superimposed on their societies.

A major purpose of the Soviet occupation and control of East Germany —apart from a desire to protect Soviet territory from the potential threat of a united, re-armed Germany—was to obtain reparations.[27] Initially, some Japanese industries in Korea and Manchuria were stripped by the Soviets, but the takeover of North Korea seems to have reflected more a desire on the part of the Soviet Union to improve its strategic position in the Far East, especially in the face of United States influence in both South Korea and Japan. In Korea, as well as in the ring of states along the European border of the Soviet Union, Stalin's chief motive in establishing Communist regimes was to protect and promote the national interests of the Soviet Union. Just as the creation of the East German government was tactically deferred until after the proclamation of the West German government in Bonn, the North Koreans waited until after the government in the South was established to announce the formation of the Democratic People's Republic of Korea. The popularity of the regime in North Korea has been as dubious

---

[26] *The Soviet Zone of Germany*, Human Relations Area File No. 34, Harvard-1, pp. 5–6.

[27] Nettl, *op. cit.*, p. 305.

as that of East Germany, with both countries subject to declining populations, as large numbers of people flee whenever the opportunity arises.

In general, then, many characteristics common to other Communist takeovers are also to be found in the events that took place in North Korea. The Communists introduced a number of reforms in North Korea, and they brought about a coalition of Communist and Socialist Parties to increase their strength. The similarity in the choice of labels which are not obviously Communist to designate the newly created parties—for example, the Polish Workers' Party and the Korean Workers' Party—is indeed striking. Many opportunists and Communist sympathizers were admitted to the parties to confuse the people. In Korea, the strategy of unity from below was an efficient means of eliminating the leaders of other parties and enlisting their followers. Control of the security police and the military, purges and political murders, exploitation of prominent nationalist leaders, and the fashioning and installing of a Communist dictator—all these were strategies employed in Korea that followed closely the usual formula of Communist takeovers elsewhere. The Soviet-Koreans and Kim Il-song's partisans were "Muscovites" compared with the native Koreans, and even to the Korean Communists they were Manchurian "bandits," non-Koreans serving a foreign master.

Some facets unique to the Korean situation turned out to be in the Communists' favor. In the North, being an unpopular "Muscovite" was not a problem, because popularity was irrelevant to the situation. Simple military control was the primary consideration, with the Soviet-Koreans and the partisans ruling the North irrespective of their popularity among the people. Ignorance of Korea on the part of the Soviet Union was compensated for by indifference towards the North on the part of the prominent native Communists in the South. The division of Korea and the perpetuation of this division were, perhaps, the keys to the ease with which the sovietization of North Korea took place, just as the division of Germany made possible the establishment of a Communist regime there. In these two countries, as well as in the rest of Eastern Europe, Communist and Soviet tactics display remarkable similarities.

Vietnam: From Bolshevism to People's War

Dennis J. Duncanson

Forty years have passed since the Indochinese Communist Party made its first bid for power. Today, as the Vietnam Workers' Party (North) and the People's Revolutionary Party (South), it rules half the territory of all three countries that formerly constituted French Indochina, controlling a third of the nationals in Laos and Cambodia and 20 million out of 38 million of the nationals in Vietnam. But its takeover of the remainder of Vietnam, and perhaps of Laos and Cambodia—as predicted by Prince Sihanouk[1]—is still an unfulfilled Party "task." Neither the later, nor even the middle, stages of such a protracted struggle for power were foreseeable at the outset, and the Party's history is less the gradual unfolding of any long-range plan than the tale of exploiting opportunities presented by the initiatives of other political forces. "Imbued with Marxism-Leninism," it has "changed its orientation in complex and difficult situations in order to lead the revolution to success, like an ocean liner weathering storms and avoiding reefs to reach its destination."[2] The now ageing comrades in the Party assert that, behind all their contrasting "fronts," they have never swerved from the purpose of bringing their people under the Party's absolute rule.[3]

If we did not know before, the Sino-Soviet dispute has taught us that Marxism-Leninism means different Party lines to different Communists. The question continually being reframed is whether the Vietnamese Communists' policies have been learned (or dictated) from the Soviet Union and China, or have been worked out independently, from local circumstance and experience. The Indochinese Communist Party has acknowledged its indebtedness to China and Russia many times, but has always added that adaptation to "the concrete situation" in Indochina has been necessary as "new boulders have blocked the path." The list of persons Ho-chi-Minh has emulated—first Lenin, later Mao Tse-tung—is a long one; the Viet-

---

[1] Articles in *Preuves*, Paris, April, 1970, and elsewhere before his dismissal.

[2] Truong Chinh, *March Ahead under the Party's Banner*, Hanoi, 1963, p. 44; elsewhere (Truong Chinh, *The August Revolution*, Hanoi, 1962), he attributes the idea to Stalin.

[3] E.g., Premier Pham-van-Dong explaining "front" tactics (*Nhan Dan*, Hanoi, September 13, 1960). The "comrades" number fewer than ten now, for the rank and file have been recruited and discarded, generation by generation, purpose by purpose.

namese revolution has, at different stages, followed both the pattern of *coup d'état* that was characteristic of bolshevism and the pattern of the "steady-state" that is characteristic of "people's" (earlier called "protracted") war. The Indochinese Communist Party at first constituted as intimate a branch of the Comintern (the Communist International) as any other Communist Party,[4] and up to 1945 its decisions on when and how to act were taken in unison with parties in other Southeast Asian countries, if not further afield. Since those days, both the Soviet Union and China have played an essential role, as "fraternal" states, in the self-directed struggle of the Indochinese Communist Party, going beyond ideological example and revolutionary or administrative method. China has been "the great rear base area" from which the Indochinese Communist Party has set out to win power in Indo-china, and both patrons have continued to remain as indispensable to the Party's progress, in their different ways, as they were in 1931; there is no Sino-Soviet dispute over support for the Democratic Republic of Vietnam and "the fraternal peoples of Indochina."[5] The adaptation of Marxism-Leninism to Vietnamese society, whether as a tactic of revolution or as a system of government, has been a process inseparable from the territorial expansion of Communist power; ideology was at its purest when Ho-chi-Minh first crossed into Vietnam on his return from Moscow and Yenan, and it underwent modifications as he advanced southwards, to acquire—or, anyway, lay claim to—state power.

The progress of the Indochinese Communist Party has been barred by Western powers—first by France, and later by the United States. But it is an error to view these two powers simply as obstacles to Communist expansion in Indochina, and a greater error still to portray them as entrenched forces whose eviction has been the purpose of the Party's struggle. On the contrary, both of them made positive contributions to the Party's early strength, without which its further growth would have been improbable; both were exploited as allies before they were turned upon as enemies. Furthermore, even as enemies, both continued to be vital sources of strength, logistically and politically, against the other contenders for power—who were the Party's real enemies—in a form of psychological warfare with first principles traceable to Lenin's bolshevism.

---

[4] *Outline History of the Vietnam Workers Party*, Hanoi, 1970, pp. 24–25, confirmed in many similar publications. The Fourth Congress of the Comintern in 1922 laid down the rule that all national parties were branches of the International (Lenin's "our Party"), which "directed their struggle" and kept them under "international discipline" (*Quatre premiers congrès mondiaux de l'Internationale communiste*, Paris, 1934, p. 159).

[5] For a detailed study of this point, see Harry Harding and Melvin Gurtov, *The Purge of Lo Jui-ch'ing*, Santa Monica, Calif., 1971.

Thus, three strands of tactics can be discerned, however intertwined, running through the history of the Indochinese Communist Party: the *coup d'etat*, guerrilla warfare, and "psywar," which has aimed at disarming foreign support for the intended victims of the Party's takeover. A different external interest has been associated with each strand, so that the development of a nucleus of Communist power in Indochina should be seen not as a yearning to be free from foreign entanglements, but as the skillful orchestration and manipulation of those entanglements.

Comintern Beginnings

Almost universally, Ho-chi-Minh is pictured as a Garibaldi: "led to Marxism-Leninism through nationalism" is the way he described himself later on.[6] But his early career was that of a Communist of his times—of a class-warfare internationalist, preferring "living socialism" (in Lenin's phrase) to "dead chauvinism."[7] After serving an apprenticeship subverting colonial laborers against the war effort[8] for "agitprop" in France in 1917, Ho turned up as a Communist journalist in Paris in 1920, displaying an interest in "oppressed races" that was not specially focused on Indochina.[9] For both Lenin and Stalin, agitation among the "oppressed races" was a means of disrupting supplies of raw materials to world markets with the hope of causing widespread unemployment in Europe and America and facilitating revolution in the centers of capitalism. Borodin's mission to Sun Yat-sen's republic in 1924 was intended to cast China in that role by bringing the Kuomintang (or Chinese Nationalist Party) under the influence of the Comintern; Ho-chi-Minh went along on this mission as a Chinese interpreter under the alias Sung Man-chüeh.[10]

---

[6] Ho-chi-Minh commemorating Lenin's centenary in *Echo du Vietnam*, Paris, 1960.

[7] V. I. Lenin, *Selected Works*, Vol. III, Moscow, 1961, pp. 126–27. Ho's earlier name, "Nguyen-ai-Quac" (later "Quoc"), meaning "patriotic," began as a pen name for a group of Communists (*Nhan Dan*, May 16, 1960); it had been chosen in order to attract the attention of President Wilson at Versailles, among all the other candidates for power-through-Balkanization wooing Wilson in Wilsonian terms (*Our President—Ho-chi-Minh*, Hanoi, 1970, p. 67.)

[8] German agents were active against the Allies throughout the Far East, and especially in Indochina (see Nguyen-phut-Tan, *A Modern History of Vietnam, 1802–1954*, Saigon, 1964, p. 320), but there is not evidence that Ho, like Lenin, was in touch with them.

[9] His name appears in the international agitation over the Memphis lynchings, and he is reported by those who knew him to have been much interested in Latin America.

[10] S. R. Mohan Das, *Ho-chi-Minh*, Bombay, 1950, p. 3, quotes the Indian Communist M. N. Roy as saying he was already using "Ho-chi-Minh" as well.

At that time Canton was the Mecca of discontented students from all the colonial territories of Southeast Asia. Especially numerous were the Vietnamese, who were not physically distinguishable from the Cantonese and were conscious of belonging to the same cultural empire. All through the nineteenth century, the "southern court" at Hué had co-ordinated its external policy with that of its suzerain, the "northern court" at Peking, in the face of Western encroachment—in particular that of France. Both China and Vietnam had been similarly torn at the time by rebellions of superstitious sects and secret societies linked across the frontier. The most devastating rebellion was that of the Taiping in China; now favored, now opposed by the West, its survivors, who became known as the Black Flag "pirates," moved into the border hill country with the joint approval of Peking and Hué, and harried the French forces annexing Tonkin. Their territory became the fief of the warlord De Tham, and remained unsubdued by France for thirty years.

On another social plane, Japan, modernized without Western domination, had become—both by its example and through its wealth—a haven for Chinese intellectuals moved by feelings of vindicating the East against the bullying West, and many of them (most famous was Liang Ch'i-ch'ao) periodically took refuge in Tokyo. Among the Vietnamese who benefited from membership in Liang's coterie was Phan-boi-Chau; when Borodin and Ho reached China, Phan was head of a secret organization there which recruited students in Vietnam for training at the Canton military academy as native cadres for a Chinese-manned army which, with diplomatic support from Japan, would one day win Indochina back for "orientalism."[11] One of Ho's tasks under Borodin was to take over this organization for the Comintern and redirect the best recruits, along with Chinese comrades, to the Sun Yat-sen Academy in Moscow. Ho stepped into Phan's shoes when the latter was betrayed to the French police during a visit to Shanghai—a betrayal procured, some believed, at Ho's instigation.[12] When Ho encouraged his followers to address him as *ong cu* (euphoniously translated, for Western ears, as "uncle"), he was assuming the style of Phan.

---

[11] According, that is, to Liang Ch'i-ch'ao's program as expounded in Phan-boi-Chau's autobiography in Georges Boudarel, "Mémoires de Phan-boi-Chau," *France-Asie*, No. 194, Paris, 1970, p. 49. "Orientalism" had received a fillip in China around 1921 from the visits of John Dewey, Bertrand Russell, and (most persuasive) Rabindranath Tagore—inventor of the "spiritual East versus materialistic West" configuration.

[12] Reasons for not believing this treachery are argued in Boudarel, *op. cit.*, p. 197. For how Ho benefited from Phan's arrest, see *Contribution à l'histoire des mouvements politiques de l'Indochine française*, Hanoi, 1933–34, Vol. III, p. 2.

The *coup d'état* led by Chiang Kai-shek in 1927 against the Communists inside the Kuomintang, including Borodin and Ho, precipitated a parallel Vietnamese schism among the heirs to Phan-boi-Chau. For the next few years Ho concentrated on organizing the Nanyang (Southeast Asia) Communist Party (otherwise known as the League of the Oppressed Peoples of the East). This body was recruited among Chinese youngsters overseas, as a rival to the Kuomintang, which was likewise expanding in Southeast Asia, and as an instrument for carrying on trade-union agitation among Chinese coolies with the aim of disrupting world supplies of raw materials. There was in this no intention to promote the nation-statehood of colonial peoples, and the Party organ, *Pan-Pacific Worker*, denounced out of hand "all racial and national barriers," "national capitalism" and "patriarchal and nationalistic phraseology" standing in the way of "a single united Trade Union International."[13] Meanwhile, other Vietnamese followers of Phan formed a Nationalist Party (VNQDD) at Hanoi to fulfill the project of Liang and Phan and began to subvert the *Garde indochinoise* who policed the frontier provinces. In opposition to them Ho early in 1930 negotiated a pact at Hong Kong, in the name of the Comintern, between his own Communist recruits and the little home-based Stalinist and Trotskyist study groups, centered mainly on Saigon; this was the origin of the Indochinese Communist Party. Both the VNQDD and the Indochinese Communist Party—the latter in line with the Comintern's world-wide *Putsch*—expected great things from the economic depression in 1930.[14] The VNQDD rashly hazarded its arm in a *coup d'état* in Tonkin in support of a "provisional government in exile" at Canton. But no military aid was forthcoming from Chiang, while the intended suppliers of cash, the Vietnamese colony in Siam, were found to be dominated by Ho's Nanyang Communist Party.[15] The VNQDD was crushed by the French authorities, and so was the Indochinese Communist Party when, in 1931, in the wake of the VNQDD, it

---

[13] Statutes in issue No. 1, pp. 4–5. Ho himself had written in *L'Humanité*, Paris, May 25, 1922, that nationalism was a "dangerous" sentiment among colonial peoples.

[14] For the Comintern directive giving this reason for having a unified "proletarian" Indochinese Communist Party at that moment, see *Nhan Dan*, May 17, 1960.

[15] Peter A. Poole, *The Vietnamese in Thailand*, Ithaca, 1970, p. 20; also Hoai Thanh, *Days with Ho chi Minh*, Hanoi, 1963, pp. 119 ff. They had been mobilized to subscribe money for agitation first by Phan-boi-Chau (see Poole, *op. cit.*, p. 70). According to a recent Vietnamese authority, Dong Tung, in his "Viet-kieu tai Thai-lan," *Su Dia*, No. 16, Saigon, 1969, p. 34, the conflict between the Indochinese Communist Party and the VNQDD left them "divided and perplexed."

tried to set up soviets in Annam (contemporary with those in southeast China). This was an immediate setback, but a useful experience in persuading peasants, even if at pistol point, to destroy the plantations and crops they lived off and so deepen their own hardships and discontents (and dependence on the leadership), recalling St. Petersburg in 1905.[16]

Ho's personal involvement in the Comintern *Putsch* resulted in his arrest at Hong Kong and in the threat that he would be deported to Indochina. The Comintern secured his release, to fight another day against capitalism, by winning the sympathetic ear of the British "capitalist" press and thereby bringing to bear the weight of "capitalist" democracy and "capitalist" justice, and successfully neutralizing the Hong Kong government's collaboration with the French Sûreté—another useful lesson, this time in psywar.[17] Numbers of cadres in both the VNQDD and the Indochinese Communist Party were executed in Indochina for murdering their fellow countrymen, but the majority were set free after an amnesty campaign in France based on press reports of excesses committed by the harassed and provoked security forces.[18] The VNQDD lived on in China; some of its members joined the Chinese army. Ho, along with the Comintern's Far East Bureau, was likewise mothballed, after the Long March, at Mao Tse-tung's headquarters at Yenan,[19] while another Comintern representative, Le-hong-Phong, rebuilt the Indochinese Communist Party's fortunes at home in accordance with Stalin's next "line," the "united front." Ironically, economic hardship favored the growth of Taiping-like religious brotherhoods, especially the Cao Dai, and also improved recruiting for government para-military forces, because "the petty bourgeoisie had little confidence in the revolution," as the Party historians complain, "and a number of them fostered an adventurous spirit or became superstitious."[20] It was economic recovery which made industrial agitation possible again for the Indochinese Communist Party[21] and brought opportunities to finance it out of "capital-

---

[16] Andrée Viollis [Andrée Tizac], *Indochine S.O.S.*, Paris, 1935/1949, p. 90; René Vanlande, *L'Indochine sous la menace communiste*, Paris, 1930, pp. 140–42 and 213; Tran-huy-Lieu, *Les Soviets de Nghe-Tinh*, Hanoi, 1960, *passim*.

[17] Cf. his defense counsel, D. N. Pritt Q.C., in *The Times*, London, September 6, 1969.

[18] *Contribution à l'histoire des mouvements politiques de l'Indochine française*, Hanoi, 1933–1934, Vol. III, p. 5.

[19] Pham-van-Dong, writing in the official biography, *President Ho chi Minh*, Hanoi, 1966, p. 14.

[20] *Thirty Years of the History of the Party's Struggle*, Hanoi, 1960, p. 40.

[21] *Etudes vietnamiennes*, No. 23, Hanoi, p. 207. In dating recovery to the Seventh Comintern Congress in 1935, this passage emphasizes Stalin's change of policy to the "united front."

ist" rivalries over distribution of profits between well-to-do Vietnamese and the greedy Banque de l'Indochine.[22] Stalinist united-front participation in parliamentary politics, in conjunction with a few French Communists in Saigon, exposed the Communist Party to Trotskyism and other ungovernable schisms,[23] but also shielded the secret core of the Party as it moved about the country infiltrating public offices and substituting Party trade unions where previously there had been VNQDD "protection."[24] A few supporters of the Indochinese Communist Party waited for their "Red October" among the Vietnamese communities in Siam or Laos or, like the VNQDD, in south China.

The Second World War

The European war and the collapse of France boded well for a change of fortune. Indochina escaped Japanese occupation at first, because the Vichy government allowed Tokyo to use Saigon as a military headquarters for other colonial dependencies in Southeast Asia and to use Haiphong as a route for extricating troops encircled by Chiang Kai-shek in China. Communists throughout the region aligned themselves with the Allies as soon as the Nazi-Soviet pact broke down; their "resistance" to Japan was sufficient to justify secret shipments of British or American arms, but they kept a clear eye on the target of succession to the colonial powers if Japan should lose. With an interest in stability, non-Communists accepted the *fait accompli* of Japanese supremacy for the time being; in Indochina, where Japanese subversion had profited from partial demobilization of the Sûreté in Front-populaire days,[25] the Cao Dai and Hoa Hao brotherhoods in the south flourished in the Japanese sun, while intellectuals and bourgeoisie in the center

---

[22] *Etudes vietnamiennes*, No. 24, p. 112.

[23] *Outline History, op. cit.*, p. 27.

[24] On resort to extortion in the name of Phan, see Georges Coulet, *Sociétés secrètes en terre d'Annam*, Saigon, 1926, p. 138. On the VNQDD, see *Contribution à l'histoire des mouvements politiques de l'Indochine française*, Vol. II. On the Indochina Communist Party see Jean Dorsenne, *Faudra-t-il évacuer l'Indochine?*, Paris, 1932, p. 106. The VNQDD also lived by hold-ups and "squeeze" on the Haiphong-Kunming railway, with Kuomintang connivance (see Department of State, *Foreign Relations of the U.S.*, O.I.R. Report No. 3708, "Political Alignments of Vietnamese Nationalists," Washington, D.C., 1949, pp. 25–27). The Sûreté observed that information about people found in the pockets of Indochinese Communist Party cadres was not concerned with their politics, but with their rating for contributions (*Contribution à l'histoire des mouvements politiques de l'Indochine française*, Vol. IV, p. 165).

[25] Egbert Haas, *Frans Indo-china en de Japaanse expansiepolitiek 1939–1945*, Leiden, 1956, p. 184.

and north, together with VNQDD-supporters of anti-Chiang and pro-Wang Ching-wei persuasion, joined the new "Dai Viet"—a third successor to Phan-boi-Chau's group and intended to become a postwar branch of victorious Japan's own Comintern, the Greater East Asia Co-prosperity Sphere. From then until today, the major power struggle in Vietnam has lain between the Dai Viet, the VNQDD, and the Indochinese Communist Party, whatever other names might appear on the surface.

In 1941, the "members" of the Indochinese Communist Party were scattered all through Vietnam, with neither headquarters nor politburo. Groups in the far south and the far north attempted futile 1931-style uprisings; luckily for Ho-chi-Minh, Le-hong-Phong was killed. All the same, upon his arrival at the frontier from Yenan (probably the last instruction he received under the Comintern),[26] Ho, an exile for thirty years, faced the necessity of carrying out two *coups d'état* before he could bring a "Red October" to fruition: one within the Indochinese Communist Party to secure his own leadership, and the other against rivals to the Communist Party for the succession to French authority. In preparation he expanded the little band of sixty men who guarded his frontier limestone cave (barely a dozen of them ethnic Vietnamese)[27] into a politburo which would command the adherence of the scattered comrades, he proclaimed a "general uprising," and then he established a line of supply to Yenan through Maoist agents inside the Kuomintang.[28] His comings and goings in Kwangsi province led to his arrest by the Chinese authorities; after a year in prison—with no capitalist press to take up his case this time—he made a bargain with his captors for his freedom, a bargain whose conditions are still not known.[29] The Comintern was dissolved during his detention, and from this moment he co-operated overtly with the Kuomintang in China; he also collaborated with the VNQDD, supporting the Kuomintang's revival (in 1944) of the Liang-Phan idea for a "provisional government in exile" to legitimate the eventual invasion of Tonkin by a Chinese expeditionary force.[30]

---

[26] Vo-nguyen-Giap writes of his admiration for Maoist ways in *Nhan Dan*, May 15, 1960.

[27] *Lao Dong*, Hanoi, May 16, 1960. Read with Vo-nguyen-Giap, *The Military Art of People's War*, ed. by Russell Stetler, New York, 1970, pp. 50 ff.

[28] The Indochinese Communist Party's debt to the 8th Route Army is acknowledged in *Nhan Dan*, February 4, 1963; Chinese Communist training for guerrillas was not confined to the Vietnamese, but was extended also to the Philippines (see Justus M. van der Kroef, "Philippine Communists and the Chinese," *China Quarterly*, London, No. 30, April–June, 1967, p. 119.)

[29] King C. Chen, *Vietnam and China, 1938–1954*, Princeton, 1969, p. 78.

[30] *Ibid.*, pp. 71 ff.

Back among the Tonkinese hill people, and camped strategically between the Kuomintang-VNQDD and the center of government at Hanoi, Ho made his politburo the nucleus for a Maoist guerrilla army in the one-time base area of De Tham.[31] It was a belated counterpart to the "resistance" groups in Burma, Malaya, Indonesia, etc., to which "Force 136" was channeling arms. Destined to fire hardly a shot against the Japanese, this little band could be held in reserve, qualifying for the Allies' money and weapons while Ho vetoed "adventurism" in its deployment.[32]

The evidence that cadres of the Indochinese Communist Party elsewhere in Vietnam still had not heard of "Ho-chi-Minh" in 1945 indicates that he was not yet in control of the Party.[33] Ho made contact with the Office of Strategic Services (OSS) in the "China Theater" and seems to have given the impression that he commanded a wide-ranging intelligence network and could therefore make himself useful in practical ways. Moreover, by 1941, the Indochinese Communist Party had abandoned class-struggle propaganda for "bourgeois democratic nationalism," in line with Stalin's change of policy, which was intended to justify the wartime sacrifices demanded of the Soviet people. With this change in Vietnam, there went overt abandonment of the aim of seizing power throughout Indochina, and limitation of the objective to founding an independent state in Vietnam alone.[34] Ho found the OSS eager to see in him, thus purified, the embodiment—in the context of postwar settlements—of supposed Indochinese aspirations for emancipation from French imperialism,which was temporarily identified with the Axis fascists. Through the OSS, Ho was probably well informed about the Atlantic Charter and other developments in the outside world; the VNQDD was less informed, and the Dai Viet (and indeed the comrades of Le-hong-Phong) not at all. It was certainly the OSS that recited, for him to copy out and play back to them later, the Declaration of Independence of 1776.

The August Revolution of 1945

The moment for action came with the Japanese *coup de main* of March 9, 1945. The French colonials, by now subverted to the Gaullist side, were poised to turn on the Japanese in support of anticipated Allied landings from Manila, when the Japanese pounced first and interned them. At the same time the Japanese ordered the Emperor, Bao Dai, to denounce the French treaties of suzerainty, and appointed a Japanese "supreme counse-

---

[31] Vo-nguyen-Giap, *Military Art, op. cit.*, pp. 50ff.
[32] Vo-nguyen-Giap, *People's War, People's Army*, Hanoi, 1961, pp. 82–87.
[33] *A Heroic People—Memoirs from the Revolution*, Hanoi, 1965, p. 253.
[34] *Our President—Ho-chi-Minh, op. cit.*, p. 113.

lor" over him.[35] French rule was at an end in Indochina. But the Japanese substituted no direct administration of their own, counting instead on working through the Dai Viet in the center and the north, and through a committee of the Cao Dai and other factions in the south. The prize of future power was up for the fastest runner to snatch. With Leninist decisiveness, Ho dispatched "armed propagandists" into the Red River plain to lay down a "line" of conduct for leaders in strategically chosen villages suddenly cut off from higher authority, and with instructions to eliminate any recalcitrant leaders and install substitutes for them. The Japanese had been requisitioning the harvests for export, the spring sowing was neglected, and the food shortage was aggravated by alternate drought and flood and by U.S. bombing of the railroad which usually brought supplies from the richer south; the cadres directed the rationing of whatever had been hoarded—directed it, gun in hand, to political effect, and had soon become the men-on-the-spot-who-knew-what-to-do.[36] Squads were detailed for action at Hué, Saigon, and possibly elsewhere, to take over the existing organization of the Indochinese Communist Party,[37] and to seize offices and murder persons as soon as Allied landings began, in order that the Party (now calling itself the Viet Minh)[38] should be there to welcome the invaders as an established authority. In the event, there were no landings, for Japan surrendered abruptly beneath the two atom bombs.

The main events of the "August Revolution" are well known. Throughout, Ho-chi-Minh founded his prestige in Vietnam *vis-à-vis* his rivals on the impression he gave of being one of the Allies in the World War—a pose adopted by the Communists in Indonesia, Malaya, and the Philippines at the same moment—and of having the droppers of the atom bombs behind him politically.[39] Foreseeing the chaos that would ensue, with so many arms now in circulation, Ho proclaimed a second "general uprising"—for the record and for foreigners, since he lacked publication media of his own—in order to take over the chaos, as it were, as well as to take advantage of the exhila-

---

[35] Françoise Martin, *Heures tragiques au Tonkin, 9 Mars 1945—18 Mars 1946*, Paris, 1948, p. 24.

[36] Truong Chinh, *The August Revolution*, pp. 11–14; *Thirty Years, op. cit.*, p. 91.

[37] Inference from dissensions between "new" and "old" cadres referred to in *A Heroic People*, p. 255.

[38] Short for *Viet-nam doc-lap dong-minh hoi* ("League for the Independence of Viet Nam"), supposedly founded at a plenum of the Indochinese Communist Party in 1941.

[39] The observations of Jean-Michel Hertrich in *Doc-Lap!—choses vues en Indochine*, Paris, 1946, p. 122, in Saigon are confirmed by many Vietnamese of that generation.

ration young people felt in the atmosphere of free-for-all graced by the slogan "*Doc-lap*" (Independence). He and his followers swooped on Hanoi to
forestall any similar move by the VNQDD, and cowed the Dai Viet imperial viceroy, Phan-ke-Toai;[40] Nguyen-chi-Thanh demanded of the collaborationist emperor (whom the Japanese could not or would not protect) that
he should "surrender" and abdicate,[41] permitting the proclamation by Ho at
Hanoi (in the language of 1776) of an independent state on September 2,
1945, with members of the OSS as prominent guests of honor.[42] The abdication not merely reassured Americans that Ho was, after all, a republican
émigré of Syngman Rhee or Count Sforza stamp; it also paralyzed the man-
darins and gendarmes loyal to the throne, who had been keeping order in
parts of the country where there had been no French officials for the Japanese to remove from the Indochinese Communist Party's path.[43] Besides
Phan-ke-Toai, other members of the government sponsored by Japan
were taken into the Vietminh; there was, in fact, a rush among the Dai Viet
to change sides, and key figures who stood out (Pham Quynh, Ngo-dinh-
Khoi, and others) were slain where they stood. It was a general time for
slaughter, and, apart from the murder of 100 or so Europeans by looters,[44]
the Indochinese Communist Party and the VNQDD paid off old scores
against Vietnamese witnesses at trials in 1930–1931 and against one another.[45] In the Tonkinese countryside, the Indochinese Communist Party
started two campaigns to mobilize the masses—one by day calling all hands
to the plow (justified by reports that two million people were dying of

---

[40] Duong-Chau, *The 17th Parallel*, Saigon, 1958, pp. 11 and 13.

[41] *A Heroic People*, p. 253. Thanh became senior Hanoi general in South
Vietnam from 1965 to 1967.

[42] The text of the abdication is known only from Indochinese Communist
Party sources; purporting to be signed by Bao Dai on his own, it is doubtful
whether it was in good constitutional form.

[43] Foreigners were given to understand at the time, and many writers still
repeat, that the abdication was a spontaneous patriotic gesture by Bao Dai. In
1972, however, it is admitted freely in Hanoi that the abdication was "demanded"
(*exigée*) of the emperor, in order, first, to prevent his alignment with the Allies,
and, second, to sow discord in the Vietnamese civil service (see *Histoire de la
Révolution d'Août*, Hanoi, 1972, pp. 109–110 and 131–132).

[44] Pierre Célerier, *Menaces sur le Viet-Nam*, Saigon, 1950, pp. 77–78; Jean
Sainteny, *Histoire d'une Paix manquée*, Paris, 1953/1967, p. 155; and *Thirty Years*,
op. cit., p. 91. Cadres had been given a general license to kill in a manifesto for a
"general uprising" in June, 1941; see Tran-huy-Lieu and Van Tao, *Phong trao
cong Phat xet cong Chien tranh*, Hanoi, 1957, p. 58; it was repeated in Cochinchina
in September, 1945; see Nguyen-duc-Tho, *Le Nam-ho libre*, Paris, 1949, p. 5.

[45] Duong-Chau, *op. cit.*, p. 15.

starvation),[46] the other by night to wipe out illiteracy (whose dimensions were conveniently exaggerated). The true purpose of both campaigns was undoubtedly to install the rule of the cadres in the villages. Guerrilla training for "self-defense" was inaugurated, with secret Japanese trainers, and within a few weeks was acknowledged to be "in preparation for resistance war."[47] In a "gold week," owners of nest-eggs were made to surrender their savings as voluntary contributions for the purchase of arms.[48] These moves quickly brought thousands of people under the domination of the Communist Party against whatever the future might hold.

Meanwhile, in a journey reminiscent of Paul Revere's ride, Ho's intimate, Hoang-quoc-Viet, drove down the coast in two days, carrying advance word of the politburo's proclamation of a government and of the credentials of its unknown president, in order to secure the obedience of Communist cadres in smaller centers of administration.[49] In Cochinchina, there were neither adherents of the Dai Viet nor the VNQDD to forestall, but the Party had few cadres outside Saigon and had to contend with the new syncretic sects, to whom the Japanese had given a free hand. Hoang-quoc-Viet arrived in time to effect the *coup d'état* within the Indochinese Communist Party in the southern capital, notably winning the leader Tran-van-Giau to the following of Ho-chi-Minh. Some of the government offices—thinly staffed since the French had been interned—were taken over. But Giau and the cadres dispatched ahead of Viet had been unable to get the better of the Trotskyites or of the sects, either by opposing them or by joining with them in a National Committee for government which the Japanese set up; nor had they at first any wireless links with Hanoi.[50] Nevertheless, when British Major General Gracey flew to Saigon to superintend the disarmament of the Japanese headquarters, Giau's representatives posed "as masters of the country to receive the Allies who came to disarm the Japanese,"[51] and Gracey was at first taken in.[52] Giau's men were able, on tactical occasions, to throttle

---

[46] Ho-chi-Minh in his Declaration of Independence.

[47] For Japanese trainers, see Ngo-van-Chieu, *Journal d'un Combattant Viet-Minh*, Paris, 1955, pp. 94–99; for the objective, see *Forty Years of Party Activity*, Hanoi, 1970, p. 27.

[48] Célerier, *op. cit.*, p. 77.

[49] *A Heroic People*, pp. 250 ff.

[50] Allan Cameron, *Vietnam Crisis*, Ithaca, N.Y., 1971, p. 57.

[51] *Thirty Years*, p. 94.

[52] Earl Mountbatten, *Post Surrender Tasks—Section E of the Report to the Combined Chiefs of Staff by the Supreme Allied Commander, South East Asia, 1943 to 1945*, London, 1969, p. 288. Although the Commander in Chief says that "outside the key areas" the Vietminh were in complete control, he specifies further on that this was their *claim* (p. 287).

the food markets of Saigon, but could not increase supplies at will, or control the shooting and looting, and they antagonized the mass of townsfolk.[53] To the relief of the latter, Gracey authorized the French, who had been released from internment, to repossess the administration; his action—which was correct, despite subsequent strictures[54]—tipped the balance against the Indochinese Communist Party. Although a large minority of Cochinchinese continued to believe that the Communist Party was the winning side, the majority, including the sects, sided with the French reinforcements soon sent in and acquiesced in the moves for Cochinchinese autonomy from rule by the Democratic Republic of Vietnam from Tonkin. The eventual attempt by the Communist Party to take over the Hoa Hao in 1947 by murdering its founder proved counter-productive.

The First Democratic Republic

Ho-chi-Minh's dealings with the provisional government in France during 1946 have been misunderstood by many Western authors, thanks mainly to his astute misrepresentations in his communications with pressmen at the time. The issue was not whether Indochina should be independent or remain perpetually under colonial (or protectorate) rule. True, there were large numbers of the French public, and some officials, who believed right down to 1954 that this was possible, but De Gaulle—at least since March, 1945—had committed France to handing over power after the war; the question was how soon and to whom. This was crystal clear to Ho, and, although for a while in 1945 he may have been misled by his OSS contacts into believing that France would not come back and thwart his Bolshevik coup, his actions all through 1946, until he and his "ministers" fled from Hanoi on December 19, were patently aimed at ensuring that the heir to France should be the Indochinese Communist Party, and the Indochinese Communist Party alone. His proposals that France should continue to exercise paramountcy over the Democratic Republic of Vietnam for five years or so are often portrayed as a generous concession to the interests of the colonists; this is ingenuous thinking. The five years, after all, might be needed to seat the Indochinese Communist Party firmly in power, and France, once her sovereignty had been upheld even by the United States—as it had to be, the OSS notwithstanding—could usefully be committed to seeing the process through financially, economically, politically, and inter-

---

[53] F. S. V. Donnison, *British Military Administration in the Far East 1943–46*, London, 1956, p. 409.

[54] For an analysis of Gracey's position, see Dennis J. Duncanson, "General Gracey and the Vietminh," *Journal of the Royal Central Asian Society*, London, October, 1968, pp. 288–297.

nationally. There were, after all, no precedents for the Communist take-overs of colonies, and if, as was confidently expected in Communist circles, the French Communist Party had won the elections in November, 1946, the association Ho proposed might in the event have been prolonged indefinitely.

Relations with China were similarly dictated by the aim of confirming the predominance of the Indochinese Communist Party, and not by the desire for independence for its own sake. When the Yunnanese Kuomintang army entered Tonkin, nominally as a counterpart to Gracey's little force in the south, it brought with it the VNQDD and other Vietnamese participants in the 1944 project for a Chinese-sponsored provisional government—less of course the Indochinese Communist Party, which had stolen a march on all the others. The VNQDD is alleged to have replaced cadres of the Indo-chinese Communist Party controlling villages along the route with nomi-nees of its own, but they apparently still expected to work with Ho and his politburo once they reached Hanoi. The Democratic Republic of Viet-nam proclaimed by Ho was legitimate only if recognized by the occupying power, China. But China, as represented by the Kuomintang army under its future (perhaps already) Communist political director, Hsiao Wen, had agreed in advance only to a coalition in which all the three chief émigré groups—known by this time as Vietcong, Vietquoc, and Vietcach[55]—would work together. It was expedient for the Indochinese Communist Party to conform to the Chinese specification. While still in China, Ho-chi-Minh had not only dropped the name "Indochinese Communist Party" in favor of "Vietminh,"[56] but had established his personal non-Communist credit by preparing a Vietnamese translation of Sun Yat-sen's *Three People's Prin-ciples*, the Kuomintang classic fashionable at the time.[57] On November 11, 1945, Ho issued a statement that the Indochinese Communist Party had ceased to exist—a step later admitted to have been a deception,[58] but one which proved useful in relations with Chinese, American, and French offi-cials, and easy to take since in any case the Party was not more than a con-cept and had neither membership lists, subscriptions, nor statutes.

---

[55] *Vietcong* was the Indochinese Communist Party; *Vietquoc* the VNQDD (of Yunnan); while *Vietcach* referred to the VN Cach-menh (i.e., "revolutionary") Dong-minh Hoi—rival clients of the Kuomintang in Kwangsi province. See Mei Kung-i, *Yüeh-nan hsin chih*, Chungking, 1945, p. 82.

[56] There was already a Kuomintang organization with exactly the same name among émigrés at Nanking, and the Indochinese Communist Party's adoption of it was undoubtedly meant to confuse.

[57] Chen, *op. cit.*, p. 60.

[58] E.g., Truong Chinh, *March Ahead Under the Party's Banner*, p. 23.

A fortnight later, the Party claims to have issued its directive to cadres "giving orders for a resistance war and strict adherence to the Party line."[59]

The maneuvers by which the Indochinese Communist Party absorbed candidates for power from rival groups sponsored by the Chinese are described in many books.[60] The provisional "cabinets" and "ministries" had more meaning as shadow offices to accommodate and neutralize rivals than as centers of authority for public administration, of which there were practically none.[61] The colonial regime had bequeathed no ministries to be taken over, and the so-styled "ministers," chosen from the Communist Party or one of the other parties, had more to do with foreigners than with the Hanoi—let alone the Vietnamese—public. With the same audience in mind, a supposedly nation-wide election was staged in Hanoi—staged, because it was made an occasion for bunting in the streets of the capital and demonstrations of solidarity with the Vietminh (in order to impress world opinion),[62] and was helped by a few selective murders,[63] whereas every one of the means for holding a genuine election (prior electoral registers, demarcated constituencies, competing candidates, returning officers, ballot boxes, and communications—trains, ships, or airplanes) was lacking. The published results were generally accepted by Western pressmen without inquiry as evidence that the Vietminh ruled by popular consent.[64]

Within a few weeks, however, it was apparent that the Vietminh neither ruled in fact nor enjoyed majority consent. There were still big areas from which no news arrived or where the Democratic Republic of Vietnam was unrepresented. Even in the cities, which lacked administrative machinery, Ho had made a virtue out of necessity by announcing abolition of taxes,[65] and a government which does not collect revenue is rarely a government in the eyes of the people it purports to govern. The proceeds of the "gold week," if brought to account at all, were handled by the Party cadres much as they had been in the habit of handling "protection" money from the "bourgeoi-

---

[59] *Forty Years*, p. 27.

[60] E.g., Bernard B. Fall, *Le Viet-Minh*, Paris, 1960, pp. 48–51.

[61] "Neutralize" is the word used for this purpose in *Etudes*, No. 7, p. 43. In ideological terms, the Indochinese Communist Party was running the February and October revolutions of Soviet history together.

[62] The sole purpose mentioned by *Our President—Ho-chi-Minh*, *op. cit.*, p. 130.

[63] *Christian Science Monitor*, January 15, 1946.

[64] Descriptions of the elections (on January 6, 1946) and of prevarications over the "results" are in Martin, *op. cit.*, pp. 245–246; Sainteny, *op. cit.* p. 186; and Célerier, *op. cit.*, pp. 51–52. Salmon, a sympathizer, explains the lack of evidence of polling in Saigon by saying that, though universal, it was conducted "in secret." See Malcolm Salmon, *Focus on Indo-China*, Hanoi, 1961, p. 108.

[65] Célerier, *op. cit.*, p. 40, and others.

sie."[66] The Vietminh made progress in rural areas in recruiting armed men among the unemployed, and had no difficulty drafting them into the militia in the towns as a protection against any counter-coup, but it made no progress with public administration, nor could it control the 120 newspapers pullulating in Hanoi.[67]

News of the Leclerc landings in the south to take over from the British put new heart into opponents of the various émigrés; on February 28 there was a demonstration in Hanoi in support of the emperor,[68] who by this time had taken refuge at the court of Chiang Kai-shek in Nanking and already had the nucleus of a fresh anti-Communist group forming round him there.[69] French officials were not at one in sorting the lies from the truth of the situation,[70] still less in burying their own hatchets,[71] but three elements of French policy emerged during 1946: that the unavoidable postwar devolution of power to the Indochinese peoples should conserve as much as possible of the French investment; that power should not be devolved decisively to a single group—however blandly Ho-chi-Minh might transfer his complaisance from Chiang Kai-shek and the OSS to the representative of France, Jean Sainteny—without the free vote of the mass of the people;[72] and that decidedly separatist Cochinchina (constitutionally annexed outright to France) should not pass under the control of Tonkin unless by voluntary accession. The selfish element in French policy cannot be disentangled from the paternalistic, but it is wrong to ignore the weight of the latter on that account. The issue between France and the Democratic Republic of Vietnam was not colonialism versus independence, but self-determination (Yalta-style) versus totalitarianism;[73] prejudices of press and

---

[66] See, for instance, Louis Roubaud, *Viet Nam*, Paris, 1931, p. 194.

[67] Jean Chesneaux, *Histoire de la Nation Vietnamienne*, Paris, 1956, p. 239; Ku Yen-shih, *Chung-kuo chih pi-mi chieh-she*, Hong Kong, 1969, p. 28.

[68] Célerier, *op. cit.*, pp. 53–54.

[69] Department of State, *Foreign Relations of the U.S.*, O.I.R. Report No. 3708, *op. cit.*, pp. 106–107.

[70] Sainteny, *op. cit.*, p. 124.

[71] The mutual enmities are described vividly by Jacques Le Bourgeois in *Saigon sans la France*, Paris, 1949, pp. 226–241.

[72] The postwar formula for new governments after "liberation" drawn up at the Yalta Conference, it may be recalled, was "the holding of free and unfettered elections as soon as possible on the basis of universal suffrage and secret ballot." Department of State, Publication No. 6199, *The Conferences at Yalta and Malta*, Washington, D.C., 1955, p. 980.

[73] Admiral D'Argenlieu is usually credited with trying to revive colonial rule in Cochinchina; as High Commissioner, he publicly repudiated such a policy in September, 1945 (Célerier, *op. cit.*, p. 86), and again early in 1946 (Pierre Gentil, *Sursauts de l'Asie—remous du Mekong*, Paris, 1950, p. 20).

intellectual tradition in a West nurtured on Byron and Mazzini conspired to spread the misinterpretation, which has been cultivated by the Indochinese Communist Party ever since with the seconding of the Soviet Union and China.

It is against this background that the events of 1946 should be viewed: the withdrawal of the Chinese occupation force by agreement with *France*, not the Democratic Republic of Vietnam; the conferences at Dalat and Fontainebleau, which faltered over the politburo's demand for a monopoly of power; the proclamations of autonomy in Cochinchina and the hill country; French efforts to get Bao Dai to preside, above politics, over the contending Vietnamese factions, of which the Indochinese Communist Party and its Democratic Republic of Vietnam were but one—whereas Ho-chi-Minh demanded that role for himself, as head of the Vietminh "coalition" to which Bao Dai had "abdicated" and for which the people had "voted"; the mounting fiscal problems and eventual bankruptcy of the Democratic Republic of Vietnam,[74] which Ho's inexperienced helpers sought to rectify unilaterally;[75] finally, the French resistance with force at Haiphong to Ho's cruder remedies, once the bulk of the national leaders had recoverd their nerve from "Red August." On December 19, after the last-straw disappointment of the poor Communist showing in the election in France in November, the Rubicon was crossed: Hanoi was abandoned by the politburo, and the Indochinese Communist Party fell back on Maoist protracted war while maintaining the fiction of a Democratic Republic of Vietnam "somewhere in the highlands."

The First People's War

Ho-chi-Minh's temporizing radio dialogues during 1947, with the French authorities busy persuading Bao Dai to negotiate the independence settlement and setting up provisional regimes in Hanoi and Saigon (under Vietnamese political leaders but with French administrators to do the work) testify in part to Vietminh unpreparedness for an armed struggle, but perhaps also in part to the persistence of Soviet influence. Moscow did not give the signal in Southeast Asia for abandonment of the wartime alliance until American demobilization was complete. The shooting began in earnest in Vietnam with the declaration of the Cold War implicit in the "Zhdanov line" and the launching of the Cominform, quickly followed by the controversial

[74] Attested by several sources, notably Célerier, *op. cit.*, p. 168. Money had been raised by looting installations and selling the fittings in some places (Gentil, *op. cit.*, p. 39) and by illicit deals with the Chinese occupation forces, which necessarily came to an end when the latter went home.

[75] Sainteny, *op. cit.*, p. 214.

youth conferences at Delhi and Calcutta, at the latter of which Vietminh delegates were lionized as exemplars of the new "nationally liberating" style of socialism.[76] The shooting assumed recognizably military proportions after the Red Army of China reached the Tonkin frontier and squeezed out the garrisons under French command.

The chief battles of the war are well known, but their strategic significance is commonly misinterpreted. The biggest error has been to view the campaigns in *vox-populi, vox-dei* terms—that is to say, as if the Indochinese Communist Party was victorious in 1954 (if it was) because its patriotic aims, real or stated, "appealed" to the sense of what was right among the majority of the Vietnamese people. The decisive factor was not the aims but the chances of winning; the Vietquoc and Vietcach had lined up with the Vietcong in the Vietminh because that seemed the best road to office and power, but they disengaged themselves when the Vietminh itself abandoned office and power. Further defections of intellectuals occurred as soon as it became safe to go, and notably when the Republic of Cochinchina and the State of Vietnam began to offer more credible political opportunities. As the Vietminh had taken over platoons of the *Garde Indochinoise*, so now it lost some of them again to the new royal forces, which offered better pay and conditions. Foreigners are often told in Saigon today that their interlocutors broke with the Vietminh after it revealed its solidarity with Maoist China, either because they disliked communism or because they disliked China; but that moment coincided with the hardening attitude of the United States, which had intervened in Korea, and which had given material support to the anti-Communist cause in Indochina. How then explain that, throughout these years, the Vietminh could make increasing numbers of recruits and "mobilize the masses" even in the Tonkinese delta? The answer is that the recruits never amounted to a majority of the "masses" and were peasants tied to their land, with nowhere else to escape to.[77] The French commanders missed the point that guerrilla operations were invariably planned with a psychological objective, namely to dissuade the garrisons from interfering with the "armed propaganda" of cadres mobilizing the peasants, and to persuade the peasants that there was consequently no safe alternative to compliance with orders from the Communist Party. Fear, not bravery, mobilized the famous trains of porters on bicycles: in guerrilla warfare, in which no strongholds are guarded, attack is safer for the fighting man than

---

[76] J. H. Brimmell, *Communism in Southeast Asia*, London, 1959, pp. 252ff. For passages in Zhdanov's speech of September 22, 1947, specially referring to Southeast Asia, see Cameron, *op. cit.*, pp. 114–115.

[77] The overwhelmingly peasant character of both fighters and coolies is acknowledged in *Etudes vietnamiennes*, No. 7, p. 177.

defense, and the peasant who does his stint of transporting in the jungle-covered hills has less to fear than the one who stays at home and may have his throat cut as a "traitor."[78] In their hearts, all Vietnamese concerned understood that nationalist ideology was a justification for strategy and tactics, not the motive; their actions from day to day were prompted by deceptions and intimidations over matters much more down-to-earth and immediate.[79]

The extent of Communist Chinese aid to Ho-chi-Minh has been much debated. The basic detective work has been done;[80] whether the Chinese expeditionary force supporting General Vo-nguyen-Giap in the final campaign (Dien Bien Phu) numbered 20,000 or more or less, and whether all the Chinese were "pioneers" and sappers or included artillerymen, is unimportant; the certain thing is that Chinese help comprised whatever Ho and Mao (neither of them exposed to scrutiny by the press) judged to be necessary to bring victory to the revolution in Vietnam. Ex-prisoners of, and defectors from, Giap's forces bear witness to widespread Chinese technical assistance, which was sometimes resented because it was incompetent;[81] yet there is no evidence of greater friction than would be normal between allies anywhere. Common sense and his knowledge of Vietnamese history, ancient and modern, were enough without doctrinal conviction to tell Ho-chi-Minh that he must always trim the sails of the Democratic Republic of Vietnam to the prevailing Chinese wind. The Maoist model was the only practical one for the Democratic Republic of Vietnam, impelled as it was, not by calls on it for public administration, but by the necessity to mobilize resources, especially from zones administered by its adversaries. It was essential to forge suitable links between the politburo and its further-flung

---

[78] The continuous necessity of "armed propaganda" to maintain the psychological advantage among the masses is stressed over and over by Vo-nguyen-Giap in all the books attributed to him by publishers in the Democratic Republic of Vietnam; but the whole process was put on a *corvée* basis as early as 1950; see *Vietnam Information*, Bangkok and Rangoon, March 31, 1950.

[79] The French government afterwards sanctioned the publication of two psywar studies: A. Fossey-François, *La Guerre psychologique en Indochine de 1945 au "Cessez-le-feu,"* Paris, 1955, and Yvonne Pagniez, *Le Viet Minh et la guerre psychologique*, Paris, 1955.

[80] George K. Tanham, *Communist Revolutionary Warfare: The Vietminh in Indo-China*, New York, 1961/1967.

[81] An eminent Saigon doctor, in those days a divisional medical officer for the Democratic Republic of Vietnam, tells how he was allotted a Chinese adviser to teach him improvised surgical procedures; the Vietnamese was Paris-trained, the Chinese untrained.

"base areas" in the south[82]—links able to withstand "the perfidious schemes and maneuvers" of the defense (presumably intelligence penetration, as there had already been many defections); the reshaping of the Party on Maoist lines would make possible the sterner discipline of "criticism and self-criticism," "rectification," and so on.[83] From March, 1951, the name Vietminh was dropped, and "Vietnam Workers' (Marxist-Leninist) Party" substituted for it.[84] In relations with China, the major point was not that Ho-chi-Minh had not been obsequious to Chiang in 1945 and conformist over "style of work" with Mao in 1950, and had to reckon with invasion or other chastisement, but that, without practical demonstrations of mutual solidarity in the traditional relationship of "southern court" to "northern court," in a single ideological "East," Ho would have lacked credibility as the head of the winning side in the eyes of his own supporters.

Few people would today deny that Vo-nguyen-Giap outgeneraled Navarre in the siege of Dien Bien Phu; Chinese artillery—not reckoned with in the "Plan Navarre"—if not Chinese artillerymen, was decisive. This was the culminating battle of a war in which European professional soldiers had failed to come to terms with the distasteful truth that for their enemies fighting was incidental to politics, that defense doctrine which derived from European conflicts over territory like Alsace-Lorraine was irrelevant in Vietnam. All the objectives of people's war had something to do with somebody's morale: to demoralize the people, to demoralize the central government, to demoralize the colonial power; territory would not change hands until the peace settlement. To Navarre, the final battle was for "the gateway to Laos"; for Giap, it was for the slaughter or capture of 14,000 hostages for whom Paris would be answerable, not Saigon. When Mendès-France took office in Paris with the brief to reach a settlement at the 1954 Geneva Conference, he had to speed the release of Europeans subjected to deliberately inhuman conditions,[85] of North Africans available for subversion so long as they stayed in Communist camps,[86] and of Vietnamese, some of whom had gallantly parachuted in to the side of their besieged overseas allies in the last desperate days and all of whom were liable, from the example of 1945, to be dealt with by the politburo as "traitors." What the polit-

---

[82] A similar problem and solution in China are described by Michael Lindsay in *Notes on Educational Problems in Communist China, 1941–47*, New York, 1950, pp. 11–17.

[83] *Our President—Ho-chi-Minh, op. cit.*, pp. 144–145.

[84] The name "Workers' Party" was taken from Korea, which had taken it from Poland, etc.

[85] Pierre Richard, *Cinq ans prisonnier des Viets*, Paris, 1964, p. 163.

[86] Bernard B. Fall, *Street Without Joy*, Harrisburg, Pa., 1961, pp. 264–279.

buro had to negotiate at Geneva was the best price for these prisoners in terms of a takeover of Vietnamese (or all-Indochinese, but that was quickly dropped) territory, no longer by unilateral action, but with the recognition, and the guarantee against being disturbed in its rule thereafter, of the five great powers.

Were the Vietnamese Communists cajoled by their Russian and Chinese allies into accepting a lower price (the 17th parallel for the time being) than their strategic position warranted? The death of Stalin the previous year and the movement of the Socialist bloc towards a phase of "peaceful coexistence" was certainly important, for it lessened the demands which could be made on France without provoking an American reaction with greater force than Russia and China were then prepared to meet. But it is untrue that the Democratic Republic of Vietnam was induced to *forgo* territory it had already won through its victory in the siege: that victory had not enlarged its territory by an acre. There were historical reasons for the partition of Vietnam somewhere north or south of Hué, and possibly—although the evidence for this has yet to be explored and evaluated—a diminishing Chinese interest in furthering Marxist-Leninist rule in Indochina the greater the distance from the territory of the People's Republic of China. But the crucial consideration was almost certainly how much of the densely populated areas of Vietnam the politburo judged it could take over in one chunk—in exchange for the further-flung base areas—without so extending the Party machine that the old schisms of the 1930's and 1940's would reappear and expose it to fatal "perfidious schemes" by the large number of Vietnamese who opposed it.

If the commander in chief of Bao Dai's forces had been Vietnamese instead of French, the cease-fire might well have been less, not more, favorable to the Indochinese Communist Party; to that extent the politburo was able to turn French opposition to itself to ultimate advantage as a means of exacting from its real enemies in Vietnam more than it had won on the battlefield. On a second point as well, the election issue, France's good intentions on behalf of her protégés seemed similarly to turn to the Indochinese Communist Party's advantage. The third of the elements in French postwar policy—respect for the regionalism of Cochinchina—could be negatived by demanding compliance with the second element, the principle of self-determination. So long as the "self" which was to determine the future of Vietnam included both zones, the Democratic Republic of Vietnam would control more than half the population, and control them through a social mechanism not open to scrutiny from outside, while Bao Dai's government would administer less than half the population and be open to constant scrutiny; thus, the elections could hardly fail to bring the entire country under the rule of the Indochinese Communist Party, by "peaceful means," as soon as the politburo was ready to take over—a situation very different from the ideal of Yalta envisaged by France and the United States. As it turned out, with political troubles even in the area the Democratic Republic of Vietnam did take over, Ho and the politburo had some cause to be thankful, despite their crocodile tears over the matter, when Bao Dai's successor, Ngo-dinh-Diem, lacking their own subtlety of deception, denounced out of hand this part of the Geneva "Agreement."[87]

The Second Democratic Republic and the Second People's War

Fortified with the blessing, example, money, and technical assistance of a Socialist bloc which still included the People's Republic of China, the Democratic Republic of Vietnam reinstated in Hanoi in the fall of 1954 was a more sophisticated apparatus for rule than the Democratic Republic of Vietnam overwhelmed by its burdens in 1946. From the start, two elements of policy were announced and have been adhered to ever since: the Marxist reorganization of the territory taken over under the cease-fire, and reunification with—that is, takeover of—the remainder of Vietnam. When Lenin began his political career, he envisaged the party as the organ which would establish the ideal Marxist state; before he died, the Marxist state had become, contrariwise, the organization by which to keep his party in power. So it was with the Democratic Republic of Vietnam: the Vietnamese are second to no nation, when left to themselves, for dissension and factionalism, so that social discipline of the people was indispensable if monopoly of power was to be achieved. The flight to Saigon of nearly a million citizens, although it threatened the electoral advantage of the North, reduced the problem of potential "resisters" but did not solve it; collectivization of the entire economy, after ruthless liquidation of landowners (by Maoist, not Stalinist, procedures) cowed the masses for an indefinite period, as it did in China. The subsequent disowning by the politburo of the Communist Party's secretary-general, Truong Chinh, as responsible for excesses which made the more foolhardy peasants turn on the cadres, did not invalidate the intimidating effect of the "land reform." The people had gotten the message: terror might have to be subtler in the future, but discipline not less thorough.

Pursuit of other Chinese policies similarly had parallel consequences in Vietnam: integration of army and Party, "autonomy" for hill regions border-

---

[87] The fullest study of the Geneva Conference is Robert F. Randle, *Geneva 1954*, Princeton, 1969; on the election question see Dennis J. Duncanson, "Two Vietnams or One?" *The World Today*, London, September, 1969, pp. 405–414.

ing on Chinese "autonomous" regions, reinterpretation of the national saga in Marxist terms as the sole non-materialist outlet for speculation allowed to the intelligentsia, and even the Hundred Flowers.[88] Like China, the Democratic Republic of Vietnam reached some kind of watershed in 1960 which has not been adequately explained yet; its chief feature, however, was certainly that the political advantages of collectivization had been bought at the cost of the economy. But that is about as far as the parallel goes: Vietnamese circumstances—especially strategic circumstances—precluded a dispute with the Soviet Union, for example, while the very fact that China had to achieve autarky in economic fields where both countries had been looking to Russia for supplies meant that it could not make good the Democratic Republic of Vietnam's deficiencies in addition to its own. Furthermore, whatever the problems actually were which Mao set about resolving with the Great Proletarian Cultural Revolution, the place of that event in the Indochinese Communist Party's historical development has been taken by the renewal of the people's war.

The origins of the second Vietnam war are much disputed but little researched.[89] The argument that the Democratic Republic of Vietnam became involved reluctantly in the practical fulfilment of the "general Party line" on reunification, and that the cause of the war was the defensive measures taken unreasonably against that "line" by Ngo-dinh-Diem, though recognizable to students of Marxism-Leninism as a stock deception, has become the conventional wisdom of academe throughout the West in the *credo-quia-incredibile* mood of contemporary political science. In the later stages of the war, the prevalence of this belief has become the chief weapon in the Democratic Republic of Vietnam's psychological-warfare armory. The nation-wide elections were the most direct, but not the only, path to reunification written into the Geneva Agreement. Freedom of movement between the two zones, freedom of communication between them by post, and exemption from reprisal in each zone for former supporters of the other zone were all humane provisions which could have been used either to reinforce, or to substitute for, takeover by election: a whole army could have been moved from North to South in mufti (with absolute right of entry), along with a postal deluge of intimidatory propaganda covering a concealed network of intelligence links in the days before transistor radio receivers. Under the

---

[88] Known in Vietnam as the *Nhan Van* affair; see Hoang-van-Chi, *The New Class in North Vietnam*, Saigon, 1958. The incautious Vietnamese authors, though similarily pounced on in 1958, were not tried until the watershed year of 1960—with great severity (*Hoc Tap*, Hanoi, September, 1960).

[89] Only one field inquiry has been conducted under university auspices—by Jeff Race, "Origins of the Second Indochina War," *Asian Survey*, Berkeley, Calif., May, 1970, pp. 359–382.

third provision of the agreement, the whole force would have been protected from government interference as it mobilized the villagers of the South under the direction of the North. Ngo-dinh-Diem's comprehension of what the provisions implied, and his refusal to let them stand, was, therefore—in a different sense from the one usually meant—a reason for the politburo to switch to reunification by front tactics. But the National Liberation Front for the Liberation of South Vietnam and the People's Revolutionary (Marxist-Leninist) Party might have carried little weight with peasants in doubt whether they really had the backing of the Democratic Republic of Vietnam; so the call to "peaceful" (that is, subversive) reunification was eloquently renewed by Ho-chi-Minh at the Third Party Congress in 1960, as the opening of a new phase of national history analogous to the escalation of the first people's war, with China's help, which had followed the Second Congress in 1951. This message has remained enigmatic to foreigners; it has always been abundantly clear for natives. It was not the National Liberation Front's independence from the Democratic Republic of Vietnam which secured it recruits in the South, but its known dependence—with China ranged as "a great rear base area" beyond—just as had been true with the Kuomintang and the OSS, who gave Ho—the émigré coming home—his credibility in 1945.

If, at grips with the politburo, the French generals proved innocents abroad, so did the Americans, freed by consciousness of a nobler enlightenment from learning from "colonialist" example; the truth that any fighting that had to be done would be, in the aggressors' eyes, incidental to its political effect again proved especially distasteful. The second war has been in all respects a refinement of the first. The State (later Republic) of Vietnam was not ready for self-government as an open, parliamentary, society; the same difficulties of dissension which threatened the North dogged the South; dissenters neglected few chances to tittle-tattle with foreign advisers and pressmen for favors. Administrative shortcomings were made good with foreign aid, which drew in more advisers and journalists. Appreciation by the politburo, which possibly had been tipped off by European friends, that the mounting concern of the foreign press, compounded by the voracity of television, opened up novel scope for psywar, far beyond the days of Dien Bien Phu and Korea, was the greatest of the people's war refinements. We may never have a true Indochinese Communist Party version of the Buddhist crisis which overthrew Ngo-dinh-Diem, but its high point was the world-wide distribution of pictures of the burning bonze; after that, Diem had to be repudiated by Kennedy, which was the signal for his murder, and, with him dead, the rural security apparatus blocking the advance of the Indochinese Communist Party crumbled. The United States tried to redress the balance by infusions of aid, but this only nourished the Communist Party further; finally, a foreign expeditionary force had to be introduced to hold the line against the regular army of the Democratic Republic of Vietnam moving in for the kill.[90] By the end of 1970, the American force had turned the tide; it had repulsed the "high-point" of Vo-nguyen-Giap's calculated escalation, the Tet offensive of 1968—with Khe Sanh a would-be Dien Bien Phu[91]—and had seen the army of the South through the crises in Cambodia and Laos. However, Hanoi's 1972 offensive introduced Russian tanks and artillery which outgunned the South Vietnamese, by now alone on the ground; the latter held on but were unable to roll the invaders back, despite renewed American strategic and tactical bombing.

Strategic bombing of North Vietnam did such damage to installations and communications, especially Haiphong docks, that not only the flow of essential food and war supplies from China and Russia but the very production collectives on which the Indochina Communist Party's political control of the masses depended were threatened with disruption; getting it stopped became Hanoi's highest priority.[92] But skillful play on the humanitarian feelings of the Western press, including the grant of "scoops" to selected newsmen by the device of keeping all others out of Hanoi, created the impression in the U.S. that the bombing had had the opposite effect of rallying the masses spontaneously round the leadership.[93] First, President Johnson was obliged to stop the bombing and acknowledge the Tet victory as a defeat, and later, after resumption of the bombing, President Nixon had to stop it prematurely, at the cost of the peace terms negotiable with Hanoi over both South Vietnam and Laos. Yet the underlying reason why bombing had failed to deter Hanoi from keeping up its offensives was the tacit limitation set on it by China's strategic interests and by the known determination of the Soviet Union not to tolerate the overthrow of Com-

---

[90] For an analysis of the symbiosis between people's war and foreign aid, see Dennis J. Duncanson, *Government and Revolution in Vietnam*, London, 1968, pp. 272–342.

[91] According to surrendered personnel. This was the second such disappointment, if we may credit Truong Chinh in *Quan Doi Nhan Dan*, Hanoi, February 4, 1965.

[92] Acknowledged by Truong Chinh in *Hoc Tap*, Hanoi, February, 1969.

[93] Dennis J. Duncanson, "The Mass Media War," in A. J. P. Taylor and J. M. Roberts (eds.), *History of the 20th Century*, Vol. VII, No. 99, London, January, 1970, pp. 72–75. *Outline History, op. cit.*, p. 129, speaks of the tightening up of compulsory mobilization as a result of damage to communications. Loss of civilian life has not been featured in accounts of the bombing published in the Democratic Republic of Vietnam.

munist regimes, once established. In 1945, Hitler's and Tojo's citadels could be deliberately blasted so as to destroy their regimes, whereas destruction of Indochinese Communist Party rule in North Vietnam would have threatened world peace; but, short of physical destruction, bombing could not deter a totalitarian regime, untroubled by that phenomenon of open societies, public opinion.

Have the 1973 cease-fires, in Laos as well as Vietnam, made the second people's war worthwhile for the Party? The politbureau has suffered only one casualty, General Nguyen-chi-Thanh, and, except for bomb damage and for Russian and Chinese aid, the whole cost of war has been paid by the side of the defense. On the other hand, the Party's first gain is security in power. The Geneva Agreement envisaged that the Democratic Republic no less than South Vietnam was to submit, Yalta-wise, to expression of the popular will of the *whole* nation; that has been left out of the new cease-fire, and the Paris Twelve-Power Conference, in effect, reduced the territory up for settlement to the South, while bringing the North diplomatic re-cognitions withheld for a decade and a half because of the uncertainty left by Geneva. Within the area of the South, the Party has claimed for the National Liberation Front recognition as a full fledged Provisional Revolu-tionary Government over the narrow strips of territory they occupied before and just after the cease-fire. Disappointingly, lack of the usual attributes of a government has drawn a negative response from all but distant countries concerned primarily to please the Soviet Union or China. As between Government and pseudo-Government, the people are to decide by internationally observed (not *managed*) elections; confident of its constituents now, but anxious about subversion in the future, the Government presses for them to occur quickly, but the Party declines.

How the struggle will end is still unpredictable; but if, stalemated, the Party should plan yet another grand offensive, possibly with air support, as Saigon purports to fear, would anything at all remain of Yalta and the Truman Doctrine? Or has the shock of Vietnam-on-television, not merely to American self-esteem, but to the political philosophy of all Christendom (the shock less of the realities than of the misperceptions of Indochina) cleared the last obstacles from the path of "national liberation," which both Russian and Chinese party leaders have lately assured their followers détente is, on their side, meant to promote?

The Model for Revolutionary People's War: The Communist Takeover of China

Jürgen Domes

In the history of Communist revolutions, the case of China is unique in that the struggle for power took so long. After two periods of civil war, lasting ten years and four years respectively, and after eight years of international war with Japan, the Communist takeover of China climaxed armed efforts of twenty-two years. In comparison, the total takeover of power by the Communist Party in Russia took only seven years. The extreme length of time that it took the Chinese Communists to come to power suggests the enormous stresses and strains that went into the making of their revolution. These hardships were to have important repercussions on the structure and political style of the victorious Chinese Communist Party.

The situation of the Chinese Communist Party at the outset of this twenty-two years was rather desperate, for the united front with the Kuomintang (Chinese Nationalist Party) had collapsed in April, 1927, when Chiang Kai-shek threw off the Communist alliance and set up a government in Nanking.[1] In the first three months of 1927, the Chinese Communists had come very close to power. They had infiltrated many parts of the Kuomintang organization and its propaganda network. Membership of the Chinese Communist Party had increased from a little over 1,000 in 1924 to more than 58,000 in 1927.[2] There were Communists in almost all the central organs of the nationalist revolutionary leadership, and Communist influence had even extended into the ranks of the Kuomintang armed forces. But what had been gained from more than three years of coexisting in a united front with the Kuomintang was lost in only three months of conflict. The organization of the Communist Party in the big cities along the coast and in the Yangtze Valley broke down, the Communist-led mass

---

[1] Cf., among others: Conrad Brandt, *Stalin's Failure in China*, Cambridge, Mass., 1958; Martin C. Wilbur and Julie How (eds.), *Documents on Communism, Nationalism, and Soviet Advisers in China: 1918–1927*, New York, 1956; Harold R. Isaacs, *The Tragedy of the Chinese Revolution*, 2nd ed., Stanford, Calif., 1951; Xenia J. Eudin and Robert C. North (eds.), *M. N. Roy's Mission to China*, Berkeley, Calif., 1963; Tang Leang-li, *The Inner History of the Chinese Revolution*, London, 1930; Hsiao Tso-liang, *Chinese Communism in 1927—City vs. Countryside*, Hong Kong, 1970.

[2] Isaacs, *op. cit.*, pp. 113 ff.; Brandt, *op. cit.*, pp. 100 f.

organizations were nearly all liquidated, and the future of the Communist movement in China—at least for the time being—seemed very dim.

The Chinese Communists nevertheless made a number of impulsive attempts to rekindle the flames of revolution. They staged a spectacular if abortive uprising of units of the Kuomintang army in Nanchang in August and led an unsuccessful revolt of worker's militia in Canton in December.[3] A third uprising also failed, but it generated a small and fiercely dedicated group of partisans who formed the core of subsequent revolutionary activities in China. This third revolt, the Autumn Harvest Uprising, took place in the southern province of Hunan in September and October, 1927. Armed units of Kuomintang soldiers, worker's militia from the local mines, and peasants led by Mao Tse-tung took part.[4] Remnants of these defeated forces sought refuge in the mountainous area of Ching-kangshan, and after unification with other, scattered groups of guerrillas, they launched—under the political leadership of Mao Tse-tung and the military leadership of General Chu Teh—the stubborn campaign that was to culminate twenty-two years later in the accession of the Communist Party to supreme power.

In analyzing the long process that brought the Chinese Communists to power, this study will briefly review the historical events and then examine the ways and means by which the Communists were able to recruit their revolutionary forces. Finally, some systematic conclusions about the strategy and tactics of the Chinese Communists will be drawn.

The twenty-two years that it took the Communists to come to power in China can be roughly divided into six stages. During the *first stage*, from late 1927 to late 1931, the development of the Communist Party took place along two sharply differentiated lines. On the one hand, in some eastern Chinese cities, the official Party leadership, under the influence of the Comintern (the Communist International) in Moscow, worked to re-establish an underground organization. Though initially successful, this underground system was eventually crushed by the secret police of the Kuomintang, and the Central Committee of the Chinese Communist Party had to flee to guerrilla bases in southern China.[5] Here, in comparatively

---

[3] Cf. Hsiao, *op. cit.*, pp. 135–156; Brandt, *op. cit.*, pp. 162 ff.

[4] Benjamin I. Schwartz, *Chinese Communism and the Rise of Mao*, Cambridge, Mass., 1958, pp. 99 ff.; Jacques Guillermaz, *Histoire du parti communiste chinois (1921–1949)*, Paris, 1968, pp. 157 ff.; Warren Kuo, *Analytical History of the Chinese Communist Party*, Vol. I, Taipei, 1966, pp. 292–300.

[5] Li Ang, *Hung-se wu-t'ai*, Chungking, 1942, p. 143; Schwartz, *op. cit.*, pp. 184 f.; and Charles B. McLane, *Soviet Policy and the Chinese Communists : 1931–1946*, New York, 1958, p. 40.

remote areas, nuclei of the Communist movement had not only persisted, but also had been able to consolidate and slowly extend their power in the shadow of major civil wars between the Kuomintang and competing groups of warlords. Capitalizing upon the dire needs of the poor peasants, Mao Tse-tung and his military supporters were able to re-create the Communist movement, transforming it into a formidable political force. Having spread their influence into the southern part of Kiangsi province, they successfully repulsed three so-called extermination campaigns waged by the Kuomintang army.[6] When the central government was forced to divert its attention to the north following the Japanese invasion of Manchuria in September, 1931, the Chinese Communist Party gained a period of relief, which it used to prepare for the establishment of a Chinese Soviet Republic in November, 1931.

The new Chinese Soviet Republic was formed by guerrilla forces in such areas as the southeastern province of Kiangsi, the southeastern maritime province of Funkien, the eastern province of Anhwei, the southern province of Hunan, and the central provinces of Hupeh and Szechwan. These guerrilla forces controlled areas with a total population of close to 60 million inhabitants. The principal base of their support lay in the southern part of the Kiangsi province and its neighboring border regions. Called the Central Soviet area, it encompassed 47 counties with a combined population of some 15 million persons. Representatives of these guerrilla forces chose Mao Tse-tung as the head of the newly created Communist state. Thus, by late 1931, a relatively small group of desperadoes had proliferated into a sizeable movement. As before 1927, the Chinese Communist Party had again become an important political force in China, with 250,000 active guerrillas posing a considerable threat to Kuomintang rule.

The *second stage* in the Communist struggle for power, from late 1931 to autumn 1934, marked the further strengthening of the base area in the Kiangsi province. A drastic land reform increased the support from the peasants, and the size and capability of the Communist military forces grew steadily. But when the official Party leaders fled from the cities to the Chinese Soviet Republic, Mao Tse-tung's authority met with a strong challenge. At this time the official Party leadership was largely made up of young people who had been trained in Moscow and viewed Mao Tse-tung as a farmer-revolutionary with little knowledge of Marxism and even less of politics. By early 1934, the Moscow-trained civilian leaders in the Party machine had succeeded in substantially diminishing the power of the

---

[6] Cf. Guillermaz, *op. cit.*, pp. 223–231.

military-oriented guerrilla leaders and of Mao in particular. Their decision to switch from mobile guerrilla warfare to conventional, front-line encounters in effect meant relinquishing the basic tactical advantage that had been successfully exploited by the partisans. During the fourth extermination campaign, the Kuomintang army, under the personal leadership of Chiang Kai-shek, was able to destroy minor Communist installations in Hupeh, Hunan, and Anhwei, but was still unsuccessful in its thrust against the major guerrilla base in the southern part of the Kiangsi province. With the decline of Mao's influence, the fifth extermination campaign, begun in March, 1934, scored decisive successes, with Communist forces being consistently defeated in conventional battles.[7] By the end of September, the central Soviet area had been reduced to only six counties, and in early November government troops entered Juichin, the capital of the Chinese Soviet Republic. Even so, two weeks before, crack units of the Red Chinese Army had been able to break through the encirclement by the Nationalist army and invade southern Hunan with a force 290,000-strong.

Thus began the *third stage* in the Communist struggle for power, extending from 1934 to 1936. This was the heroic phase in the history of the Communist movement in China, dominated as it was by the legendary Long March. With the Long March came a return to mobile guerrilla warfare and the rise of Mao Tse-tung to the topmost Party leadership. The guerrilla army walked more than 6,800 miles—through Hunan, Kweichow, Yünnan, Szechwan, Eastern Tibet, and the fringe areas of the Gobi Desert and Kansu—finally to find refuge in the vicinity of Yenan in the northern part of the Shensi province. Less than 20,000 guerrillas survived this fantastic trek; relatively few in number, they nevertheless constituted a highly seasoned, hard-core revolutionary élite. In exchanging a comparatively fertile base in the south for a remote and—even by Chinese standards—very poor strip of land in the north, the Chinese Communist Party nonetheless managed to preserve a key group of men necessary to establish and train new forces.[8] But anticipating a possible assault on its new sanctuary, the Party sought to conclude an armistice with the Nationalist government. Constant Japanese intrusions into northern China had roused

---

[7] *Ibid.*, pp. 233 ff.; Franklin M. Osanka (ed.), *Modern Guerrilla Warfare*, 2nd ed., New York, 1962, p. 149; Gustav Amann, *Bauernkrieg in China—Chiang Kai-sheks Kampf gegen den Aufstand 1932–1935*, Heidelberg, Berlin, and Magdeburg, 1939, p. 84; and Hollington K. Tong, *Chiang Kai-shek*, 2nd ed., Taipei, 1953, p. 179.

[8] *Ibid.*, pp. 183–185; Amann, *op. cit.*, pp. 90–107; Osanka, *op. cit.*, pp. 150–158; Guillermaz, *op. cit.*, pp. 247–258; and F. T. Ishimaru, *Chiang Kai-shek ist gross!*, Berlin, 1938, pp. 130 ff. (The latter is a much more detached account than the title would imply).

nationalistic feelings among the Chinese, and in this climate the new proclamations of a united front by the Communists found support. In December, 1936, Chiang Kai-shek was temporarily arrested in the northwestern
city of Sian by a group of generals who hoped to force the conclusion of an
agreement between the Communist Party and provincial military authorities. No such agreement was reached, but Kuomintang military activities
against the Communists slackened in the early months of 1937, and initial
negotiations for a possible future arrangement took place.[9] There are
indications that notwithstanding these developments Chiang Kai-shek
intended to launch a sixth extermination campaign against the Communists
in June, 1937.[10] At this point, however, the Sino-Japanese war broke out,
and the Communists were welcomed to join forces with the Kuomintang
in a new, anti-Japanese united front.

The *fourth stage*, from September, 1937, to January, 1941, saw the
operation of the new united front. While the Kuomintang struggled to
defend itself against the major thrust of the Japanese offensive along the
Yangtze and in southern China, the Communist Party developed highly
effective methods of guerrilla warfare, gradually enlarging its sphere of
influence in the northern and northwestern provinces. During the first
three years of the war, the Communist troops contributed substantially to
tying up Japanese forces by constantly provoking the Japanese with
attacks on their garrisons.[11] From 1940 to 1941, however, rivalry between
the Kuomintang and the Communist Party flared up again, and led to
open clashes between their forces in January, 1941. From then on, the war
effort of the Communists against the Japanese diminished, with the Chinese
Communist Party committing most of its forces to a build-up aimed not
so much at defeating the Japanese as at preparing for a major conflict with
the Kuomintang after the war.

The *fifth stage*, from 1941 to 1945, was, consequently, a time of intensified efforts to strengthen the military and political organization of the
Communist movement, especially in northern China. These efforts proved
to be highly successful. Thousands of young intellectuals from the universities in Peking and Tientsin were indoctrinated, a strong conventional

---

[9] Balanced accounts of the "Sian Incident" can be found in: McLane, *op.*
cit., pp. 79–91; and Lyman P. Van Slyke, *Enemies and Friends—The United Front
in Chinese Communist History*, Stanford, Calif., 1967, pp. 75–91.

[10] For documentation, cf.: Jürgen Domes, *Vertagte Revolution—Die Politik
der Kuomintang in China, 1923–1937*, Berlin, 1969, pp. 679 f.

[11] Cf. Chalmers A. Johnson, *Peasant Nationalism and Communist Power—The
Emergence of Revolutionary China : 1937–1945*, Stanford, Calif., 1962, and Guillermaz, *op. cit.*, pp. 302 ff.

military force was built up, and procedures for administrative change of command were established, in anticipation of a rush for control of northern China immediately after the Japanese defeat. In 1937, the Communist Party controlled areas with only about four million inhabitants, and its army comprised little more than 100,000 men. By the summer of 1945, the Communist Party controlled areas with a population of 95.5 million, and there were 900,000 soldiers in the Red Chinese Army. In addition, a militia consisting of some 2.2 million citizen soldiers had been organized and trained.[12] The stage had thus been set for a final showdown between the Nationalists and the Communists.

The showdown took place during the *sixth stage*, from August, 1945, to late 1949, ending with the Communist takeover of the whole Chinese mainland. When Japan surrendered, the two rival forces in China were no longer challenged from outside, and they prepared for a final thrust against one another for overall control. The Kuomintang, operating from its wartime base in the southern and southwestern provinces brought most of the area south of the Yangtze under its control and managed to occupy the cities in the northern provinces. At the same time the Communists succeeded in expanding their rule over most of the countryside in the north. In the rush to gain control of territory, few clashes occurred between the two contending armies. The occupation of Manchuria by the Soviet Union halted the efforts of the Nationalists to extend their control into that region. Forced to comply with Soviet demands for joint operation of the Manchurian railways and the naval base at Port Arthur, the Nationalist government had also to agree to recognize the independence from China of Outer Mongolia, which meant in fact the recognition of continued Soviet dominance of Outer Mongolia.[13] For its part, the Soviet Union promised to withdraw its troops from Manchuria within three months after the end of the war—that is, by early December, 1945—and to render economic and military support only to the Nationalist government.

These were the main provisions of the Sino-Soviet treaty concluded in Moscow in August, 1945. The conclusion of the treaty could not help but widen the differences between the Kuomintang and the Nationalist Chinese intelligentsia, for it was clear that the Nationalist government was obligated to sacrifice too much.

The Soviet Union did not fail to exploit its position in Manchuria in order to provide support to the Chinese Communist Party. Under Soviet cover, units of the Red Chinese Army commanded by Lin Piao spread

---

[12] Mao Tse-tung, *Selected Works*, Vol. IV, New York, 1955, pp. 253 f.
[13] Cf. Tang Tsou, *America's Failure in China*, Chicago, 1963, pp. 273 f.

into Manchuria, where they mobilized bands of guerrillas and remnants of "Manchukuo" military forces, creating a powerful army of more than 250,000 soldiers. Soviet advisers assisted in the formation of this army, and Soviet troops equipped it with matériel captured from the 700,000 Japanese soldiers who had surrendered in Manchuria.[14] In early November, Soviet authorities prevented the landing of Kuomintang troops in the harbors of southern Manchuria. By January, 1946, when the first units of the Nationalist army were finally able to reach the strategically located city of Mukden (Shênyang), the Communist hold over the northeastern part of China had already been firmly established.

After eight years of devastating war, China's economy was a shambles. Mounting inflation had destroyed the value of the country's currency. Prices in the cities had increased in such a way as to encourage corruption among the underpaid members of the Kuomintang administration. Facing seemingly insurmountable difficulties and under considerable pressure from the United States, the Kuomintang was driven to seek a reconciliation with the Communists and a number of small, middle-of-the-road parties.

With the aim of forming a coalition government, the U.S. Ambassador to China, Patrick Hurley, arranged for direct talks between Chiang Kai-shek and Mao Tse-tung. Begun in Chungking in late August, the talks resulted in a general agreement to form a coalition government. The military forces of the Kuomintang and the Communists were to be integrated in a single, non-political, national army. The agreement was signed on October 11, but the details had yet to be worked out.[15] Towards this end, a joint committee headed by President Truman's special representative, General George C. Marshall, was appointed. Marshall was able to achieve a preliminary commitment from both parties to suspend hostilities temporarily and to convene a national assembly for the purpose of drafting a new constitution. But when the Soviet Union—after a delay of five months—finally evacuated Manchuria, new fighting broke out in that region. By this time roughly ninety percent of Manchuria was under the control of the Communists.[16] In April the Kuomintang forces launched a general offensive, and in May they won a major battle at Ssupingchieh. In a state of dissolution, Lin Piao's army was forced into a disorganized retreat, while the Kuomintang army occupied the major Manchurian center of Changchun.[17]

---

[14] Carsun Chang, *The Third Force in China*, New York, 1952, pp. 168 f.
[15] *Ibid.*, pp. 137 ff.
[16] McLane, *op. cit.*, pp. 229 f.
[17] Tsou, *op. cit.*, p. 419.

It seemed as if the Nationalists would be able to drive the Communists out of Manchuria. But at this very moment, the Communist Party was indirectly aided by the United States. Bringing enormous pressure to bear, Marshall persuaded the Nationalist government to agree to a cessation of hostilities in Manchuria in June, precisely at the time when Kuomintang troops were on the verge of occupying Harbin. This development has come to be looked upon by some authorities as the major turning point in the whole civil war in China.[18] Because the victorious Nationalist army halted its offensive, Lin Piao's forces gained a period of respite, enabling them— not without Soviet support—to reorganize and strengthen their ranks. When fighting flared up again early in July, the United States decided to press for an unlimited armistice, and in order to back up this move, imposed an arms embargo on China.[19] As the Kuomintang forces were almost entirely dependent on the United States for weapons and spare parts, the embargo primarily served to hurt the Nationalist side. Yet in spite of heavy pressure from the United States, neither side proved ready to reconcile the differences, and no agreement could be reached on the formation of a coalition government. As a result, in January, 1947, full-scale civil war broke out. Admitting the failure of his mission, Marshall left China, resigning the fate of the country to a decision on the battlefield.

From 1945 on, the Chinese civil war was thus influenced by the emerging conflict between the two major world powers. The policy of the Soviet Union was one of formal co-operation with the Kuomintang, but in fact Moscow never lived up to its promises of economic and military support. It may be that Stalin was not interested in an overall Communist victory in China but rather in Communist domination of the northern part of the country. Such an outcome would have left the country divided and given the Soviet Union a largely dependent satellite in northern China and Manchuria. For this reason, the Soviets gave strong support to the Communists in Manchuria, and for the same reason did not help the Kuomintang. There is no indication that the Soviet Union was willing to help the Communists take over all of China, but Soviet assistance in the north must be viewed as an important contribution to the subsequent Communist victory. The United States, on the other hand, continued to entertain illusions about the possibility of a coalition government in China—even after the major conflict for control of Manchuria had begun—and was, therefore, unwilling to give the Kuomintang the support it needed. The Nationalists themselves proved unable to cope with the major economic and social problems resulting from World War II and the civil war.

---

[18] *Ibid.*, p. 421.
[19] *Ibid.*, p. 428.

In this situation, the Communist forces, highly indoctrinated and led by cadres deeply committed to an ideological cause, soon gained the advantage in the conflict, notwithstanding initial military successes by the other side. (In March, 1947, Kuomintang troops conquered the Communist capital, Yenan, a victory that was greatly overestimated by Chiang Kai-shek.) The Communist Party was able to conduct major offensives in Manchuria and northern China late in 1947. At the beginning of 1948, a large part of the Kuomintang army was encircled in Changchun and Mukden, where Chiang insisted that it defend itself instead of evacuating to "China proper" for reorganization and reinforcement. All attempts to lift the siege failed,[20] and on October 19, 1948, Changchun fell. This defeat was followed by the surrender of 400,000 Nationalist soldiers in Mukden on November 1, and thus the Kuomintang not only had lost Manchuria, but also had sacrificed so many soldiers that the military forces of both sides were now almost equal in numbers, with the Communists having much higher morale.

In December, 1948, Lin Piao's army began its attack across the Great Wall towards Peking. About the same time, Communist divisions under P'eng Tê-huai, Liu Po-ch'eng, Ch'en Yi, and Nieh Jung-chen started an all-out offensive towards the Central Chinese Plains. It was in this area, near Hsüchou and Huaihai in northern Kiangsu, that the decisive battle was fought. Chiang sent most of his remaining units into the battle one by one, and the Communists skillfully exploited local numerical superiority to defeat them one by one. To make matters worse, the chief adviser on military strategy to the Kuomintang defected to the Communists and disclosed all information on the Nationalist army's operational plans. As a result, the battle of Hsüchou-Huaihai was a catastrophe for the Kuomintang, which sustained losses of more than 600,000 persons, as compared with 250,000 casualties on the Communist side.[21] After this defeat, the resistance of the Nationalists broke down rapidly, in spite of a number of successful local encounters indicating that some units of the Kuomintang army were still inspired to fight.

On January 31, 1949, Peking surrendered, after Chiang himself had "temporarily" resigned from the presidency of China ten days earlier. By late March, the Chinese Communists had reached the Yangtze, and Stalin again suggested that they discontinue their southward offensive in order to avoid a protracted continuation of the war. But Mao Tse-tung did not follow Moscow's advice, which he had already ignored more than a year

---

[20] *Ibid.*, p. 483; and Cheng Tien-fang, *A History of Sino-Russian Relations*, Washington, D.C., 1957, pp. 306 f.

[21] Tsou, *op. cit.*, p. 419.

before.[22] Attempts on the part of the Nationalists to lure the United States into a last-minute intervention and thereby stabilize the line of defense along the Yangtze also failed. Thus, both world powers were practically disengaged from the final phase of the civil war in China. On April 21, 1949, the Communists crossed the Yangtze. On April 23, they conquered Nanking, and in May they marched into Shanghai and Wuhan. From then on the Kuomintang had no chance of stopping the Communist onslaught. Within four months, the Red Army, now called the "People's Liberation Army," had gained control of all southern China, and by the end of 1949 almost the whole Chinese mainland was in its hands. Chiang Kai-shek retreated to Taiwan with more than half a million soldiers and over a million and a half civilian refugees. Mao Tse-tung's proclamation of the People's Republic of China on October 1, 1949, symbolized the final overthrow of Nationalist rule in China. The Kuomintang had failed, and the Communists were now in a position to try their way of modernizing the most populous underdeveloped country in the world.

Many explanations have been offered for the failure of the Kuomintang. The Nationalist leaders themselves, together with many of their foreign supporters, have tried to place the major share of the blame on the policies of the United States in China. The critics and enemies of the Kuomintang have in turn pointed out the corruption of the Nationalist government and the inability of its leaders to secure the support of the intellectuals. These and other such explanations all seem to have some degree of validity. Yet what they suggest is that a monocausal approach to explaining the Communist takeover of China is inadequate. In fact, there seem to have been at least eight different elements which contributed to the Communist victory:

(1) Eight years of devastating war with Japan had disrupted the tenuous economic infrastructure of the country and debilitated the economically important areas along the coast and in the Yangtze valley. These dislocations had caused serious inflation, with which the Nationalist government was unable to deal effectively. In 1937, 3.42 yuan were equivalent in value to a single U.S. dollar. By 1945, the rate was 1,705 yuan to the dollar; in March, 1948, 450,000 yuan to the dollar; and in August, 1948, as much as 8.6 million yuan to the dollar. At this point, the National government enacted a drastic currency reform. On August 19, 1948, a new yuan, based on gold and valued at four dollars, was introduced. But the government's attempt to sustain a gold reserve was unsuccessful. With the support of some leading Nationalist politicians, smugglers and speculators destroyed the basis of the new currency, and by March, 1949, the ratio between the

---

[22] Vladimir Dedijer, *Tito*, New York, 1953, p. 322.

new yuan and the dollar was 17,700 to one. By mid-May, the ratio had reached 22.3 million new yuan to the dollar.[23]

(2) Inflation caused widespread corruption within the administrative machinery of the government. Underpaid and underfed, many government officials accepted bribes in order to survive; others spent most of their working hours pursuing more lucrative occupations. In consequence, the government became increasingly inefficient, and no longer enjoyed the confidence of the people. Nonetheless, the importance of corruption as a factor in the downfall of the Kuomintang should not be exaggerated, as is sometimes done by Western observers, for there were many scrupulous persons in the higher echelons of the Nationalist government. The corruption in the Nationalist government would not by itself have brought about the defeat of the Kuomintang.

(3) Since 1927, the Kuomintang had been short of cadres to establish and train new military units, and their number was further diminished during the war against Japan. More than 100,000 officers were among the casualties of the Sino-Japanese war, and it took the Kuomintang army until 1949 to make up this loss.[24] Of the officers lost, more than two-thirds were graduates of the Central Military Academy. The casualties also included 19,000 out of 24,000 members of "special units" (*Pieh-tung-tui*) trained for mass mobilization. The result was that the Nationalists sorely lacked the professional military framework which the Communists had so effectively built up during the war.

(4) Even before the Sino-Japanese war, the Kuomintang had proven unable to implement long overdue social reforms, especially the redistribution of land. To stabilize his rule and consolidate resistance to Japanese aggression, Chiang Kai-shek was obliged to co-operate with ultra-conservative regional powerholders and various lobbies of landholders. Such co-operation precluded the enactment of thoroughgoing social legislation, and after the war Chiang found it difficult to disengage himself from his conservative allies. When full-fledged civil war broke out, attempts to take the initial steps towards land reform were again made, but with a critical shortage of cadres to mobilize the people, and while fighting a war, the reform efforts of the Kuomintang once more came to nothing.

(5) As an agglomeration of diverse social forces, the Kuomintang was weakened by internal conflict and intrigue. Even in the last year of the

---

[23] Cf. Chang Kia-ngau, *The Inflationary Spiral—The Experience in China, 1939–1950*, Cambridge, Mass., New York, and London, 1958, p. 383.

[24] Ho Ying-ch'in, (Nationalist Chinese Minister for Army Affairs from 1929 to 1946), in *Chung-yang jih-pao*, Taipei, September 3, 1965.

civil war, its several factions were not willing to co-operate with one another unconditionally. Unity of purpose and action, a prime requisite for a successful military campaign, was not a distinguishing feature of the Kuomintang. Some of its competing factions invested more energy in internecine rivalries than in mapping a comprehensive strategy to win the war.

(6) Soviet aid to the Chinese Communist Party in Manchuria in 1945-1946 created a strong territorial base for the Communists and provided them with the weapons needed to arm a sizeable conventional military force. Though the final victory of the Chinese Communists was unquestionably won by their own efforts, the groundwork for their success was at least partly laid by the support they received from the Soviet Union immediately after the Pacific War.

(7) The attitude of the United States towards China in the summer of 1946 proved detrimental to the cause of the Nationalists. Just after the Kuomintang forces had scored an important victory in Manchuria, Washington brought pressure to bear on the Nanking government to conclude an armistice, and even imposed an embargo on shipments of arms to the Nationalists. Psychologically and to some degree materially, these measures broke the back of the Kuomintang's military effort.

(8) From early 1947, Chiang committed a number of regrettable strategical mistakes. Instead of fighting the Communists in their base areas, closer to the Central Chinese Plains, he diverted a sizeable part of his army for the spectacular but strategically irrelevant conquest of Yenan. Instead of evacuating his first-rate troops from Manchuria, he forced them to try to hold an encircled position until they had no choice but surrender. Finally, instead of then withdrawing south of the Yangtze to establish a strong line of defense without a major Communist guerrilla base in the rear, he threw the remainder of his best troops piecemeal into the mill of the Hsüchou-Huaihai battle. These three moves were precisely what the Communists hoped for, and they had prepared effective strategies to counter them. Chiang's unchallenged prestige, which nurtured conventional, unexamined, and unjudged thinking, thus contributed strongly to his defeat.

Of these eight major factors, the disruption of the Chinese economy, the decimation of the Nationalist cadres, the inefficiency and corruption of the Kuomintang, and the aid given to the Chinese Communists by the Soviet Union appear to be the most important in explaining the failure of the Kuomintang. It has been argued, however, that if the United States had taken a different approach to the Chinese civil war, the Communist takeover of China might have been averted. Given the ramifications of all the factors just discussed, it seems highly unlikely that this would have proved to be the case. Nonetheless, the question might be raised whether an American decision to intervene in China could have resulted in the stabilization of Kuomintang rule south of the Yangtze. A careful consideration of the overall military and political situation in China in the winter of 1948–1949, before the Communist conquest of Peking, suggests that at the time decisive intervention by the United States could still have led to a stalemate in the conflict along the Yangtze. A stalemate would have meant the division of China, at least temporarily, but it is hardly thinkable that with a divided China the Korean and Vietnam wars would have followed. Indeed it might be argued that the investment in man power and resources needed for such an intervention in China would scarcely have reached one-fifth of that which subsequent United States administrations have been willing to invest in the two smaller countries.

A revolutionary takeover of power is highly dependent on the ways and means at the disposal of the insurgent party for recruiting revolutionary personnel. A review of the practices followed by the Chinese Communist Party during the civil war shows that industrial workers played an extremely minor role in the Communist movement in China. But it also indicates that it would be an oversimplification to state that the Communist takeover of China was a peasant revolution, even though numerically the peasantry was the major group contributing to the movement. The truth is that the Communist Party relied on shifting social groups in a predominantly upper-class and peasant-oriented context.

Before 1927, university and secondary school students and children of Kuomintang members in urban areas were the principal targets of Communist recruitment. Following the collapse of the first "United Front" in 1927, the emphasis shifted to recruiting soldiers of the Nationalist army and rural bandits. Coming largely from the poor peasantry in the villages, these elements were the cadres of the original Chinese Communist guerrilla army. It was only after the Communist base in the south had been consolidated that peasants from other social strata rallied round the Communist Party.

The Chinese urban intelligentsia, from which much support had been drawn by the Communists before 1927, did not play an important part in the initial phase of the civil war. It was only after the Long March that Communist agitation again turned towards the basically nationalistic intellectual circles. Posing as the most anti-Japanese political force in the country, the Chinese Communist Party then began to win new support from the intelligentsia. After the major cities in northern China fell to the Japanese in 1937, Communist recruitment among students at the universities in Peking and Tientsin became increasingly successful. This was mainly because the territorial base of the Communist guerrillas was close to these cities. The intellectuals who joined the movement after 1937 were much more nationalistically than ideologically motivated.

To indoctrinate newcomers to the movement, the Chinese Communists developed a highly effective method for transforming general political and social discontent into active revolutionary conduct.[25] This process of "thought reform" (*Ssu-hsiang kai-tsao*) usually unfolded in five steps. First, the newcomer was exposed to intensive propaganda specifically focused on his particular political demands and expectations. The aim of this propaganda was to induce in him a state of mind in which acceptance by the Communist Party would become an urgent personal objective. Second, making minimum demands in its own behalf, the Party granted the target special recognition as a supporter of the Communist movement and asked him to prepare himself for active, armed participation in it. Again, the aim was to transform the expectation of becoming an active participant in the Communist movement into a fervent personal objective of the newcomer. Third, the newcomer was accepted as an *armed* supporter of the Communist Party. While he was fighting side by side with Communist forces, differences in the decision-making influence of mere supporters of the Party and full members of the Party were made apparent to him. Devised with the idea of encouraging the initiate's ambitions, these differences usually succeeded in bringing him to the point of placing membership in the Communist Party above all else. Fourth, the target was made a member of the Party. Fifth, and only then, the most important step was enacted: the social and political consciousness of the target was remolded. Under the rubric of a "rectification campaign" (*Cheng-feng*), this five-step process was used on an extensive scale to create active cadres for the Chinese revolutionary movement.

Based on this pattern of recruitment and training, the Chinese Communist Party forged its cadres from a largely intellectual, upper-class élite. Under the leadership of these cadres, as Chalmers Johnson has pointed out,[26] a rudimentary peasant nationalism, given new impetus by Japanese atrocities committed in the villages of northern China, could be mobilized into an effective movement for social and political change. Johnson draws a comparison with the Communist movement in Yugoslavia during World War II, and indeed there are striking similarities. But the differences have to be borne in mind also. Although suffering setbacks as a result of Japanese aggression, the Kuomintang government did not completely fall apart, as

---

[25] Cf. Boyd Compton, *Mao's China—Party Reform Documents*, Seattle, 1952.
[26] Cf. Johnson, *op. cit.*, pp. 176–185.

the Yugoslav government did. Moreover, the competition offered the Chinese Communists by the Kuomintang army in the fight against the Japanese was much stronger than the competition offered Tito's guerrillas by the Chetniks in the struggle against the Axis occupation. Tito's partisans in Yugoslavia were the most active and formidable enemy of the German and Italian occupation forces in the final phase of World War II. But in China the brunt of the war effort from 1941 on was borne by the Kuomintang, while the Communists saved their strength for the domestic showdown after the Japanese surrender. In the event, the force that prevailed in China was a guerrilla-trained army recruited from the peasantry, operating for the most part conventionally, and led by a highly indoctrinated élite whose members had divorced themselves from their social origins.

To turn finally to the strategies used by the Communists in their long drive to power in China, it is useful to recall the basic Maoist assumption that all political power proceeds from the barrel of a gun and that power must therefore be seized by an armed revolution. Within the bounds of this central thesis, a scheme of diversified political and military strategies can be applied to achieve the objective of the revolutionary effort.

The *political strategy* of the Chinese Communists was grounded in the theory that in every situation there is only one main enemy. From 1927 to 1933 the main enemy was the Kuomintang and its following, symbolized by the Nanking government. From 1933 to 1936 Chiang Kai-shek was viewed exclusively as the main enemy, with the term no longer applied to other generals and politicians in the Kuomintang, since the Communists wished to lure them into an alliance against Chiang. In 1936 Japan was cast in the role of the main enemy, and despite a number of clashes between Nationalist and Communist forces during the war, it was only when the Japanese surrendered in 1945 that the Kuomintang again became the main enemy. To isolate the main enemy from potential allies, the theory provides for the conclusion of temporary alliances with every group which may be considered a minor enemy. The principle of concluding temporary alliances to isolate the main enemy was developed into a highly effective united front tactic by the Communists, enabling them to diminish the ranks of their adversaries, who did not realize that they in turn might be regarded as main enemies at any time. In exploiting this principle, the Communists dwelt on the enormous social and economic problems of China to gain support from different strata of the population, but mainly from the peasantry. They had some answers to the problems, but never made them too explicit, since in striving for broad backing among the population, they could hardly promise to alleviate the burdens of one group if it implied increasing the burdens of another.

The *military strategy* of the Chinese Communists was grounded in the principle of progressive warfare in three stages. The first stage comprehended mostly roving guerrilla warfare, which made it possible for the revolutionaries to survive and safeguard their cadres. At an appropriate moment, and after concerted propaganda efforts, the second stage, that of guerrilla warfare from consolidated base areas, was entered. This stage called for harassing the enemy in his own area of control by surprise raids, attacks on communication and supply lines, etc., while building up strong conventional forces in the Communist base areas. Only then could the third stage, a large-scale conventional offensive, begin. And it was only in this third stage that the final victory could be won. In other words, Mao's strategy did not have in view a takeover *by guerrilla warfare*, but sought—through different stages of guerrilla warfare—to *prepare* for a takeover in a conventional civil war employing large armies in open battles.

These basic political and military strategies were reinforced by a particular set of *tactics*, some of which were devised for use under the peculiar socio-political conditions of China, but many of which have been in common use wherever the Communist movements have sought to seize power. The Chinese Communists relied on three important tactics. First, they followed the principle of combining negotiations with preparations for a new onslaught. This tactic provided for proposing an armistice or a united front whenever the movement was really in trouble. The Chinese Communists were particularly successful on this score in 1935–1936. Threatened by impending annihilation, they proclaimed the slogan "Chinese do not fight Chinese!" (*Chung-kuo-jen pu ta Chung-kuo-jen!*) to secure support from Nationalist intellectuals in an anti-Japanese united front.[27] Again, when the Nationalist offensive in Manchuria dealt heavy blows to crack units of the Red Chinese Army in 1946, the Communists called for an armistice to give themselves time to reorganize their battered ranks, and with the support of the Marshall mission they were successful in their effort.[28]

Second, the Chinese Communists adhered to the principle of broadening the social and political base of their movement while it was on the upsurge but not yet fully victorious, and of reducing this base when the victory had been won. For example, in 1949 they concluded temporary alliances with democratic parties and groups, as well as with a number of Kuomintang generals and officials. But after control of the Chinese mainland had been achieved, these groups and individuals were dropped one by one. By late 1957, most of those who had joined the anti-Kuomintang alliance

---

[27] Cf. McLane, *op. cit.*, pp. 66 ff.

[28] Tsou, *op. cit.*, pp. 421 ff.

in 1949 had been purged or at least criticized, and their influence on the political process in China had become negligible.[29]

Third, the Chinese Communists relied on the principle of formulating attractive promises by means of sociological analysis to gain at least tacit support from large segments of the population. The most sucessful of these promises proved to be the old slogan of Sun Yat-sen: "Land to the tiller!" (*Kêng-che yu ch'i t'ien!*), implying that agricultural property should be given to the peasants who actually cultivated the land. As early as 1947–1948, the redistribution of land to the peasants had been started in Manchuria, and a similar land reform was implemented throughout China from 1950 to 1953. But as soon as the land reform was finished, agricultural collectivization was begun, again depriving the Chinese peasants of their property. By 1957–1958, the peasants were organized on collective farms employing cheap agricultural labor, and after eight years of Communist rule, found themselves in a situation not so different from that before the Communist takeover. But by then they had served their purpose as instruments of the takeover, and were fulfilling their new role as instruments of developmental policies based on mass mobilization.

It can thus be said that the Communist takeover of China differs in some important ways from Communist takeovers in other countries. The Bolshevik revolution in 1917 scored quick successes in the cities, where it began with the support of the workers and the soldiers, and only later spread to the rest of the country, where it was resolved by a comparatively short, largely conventional civil war. In contrast, the Communist revolution in China first gained a foothold in remote areas, where it relied exclusively on guerrilla tactics. Only after a protracted period of civil and international war were the Communists successful in conquering the cities, where they had very limited support among the workers. Unlike Yugoslavia, where guerrilla warfare was directed mainly against foreign invaders and their collaborators, in China the major enemy of the Communists was an indigenous nationalist party with comparatively strong support from the upper and middle strata of the population.

Since the autumn of 1949,[30] and particularly since 1965,[31] the leaders of the Chinese Communist Party have recommended their strategy and

---

[29] Roderick MacFarquaar, *The Hundred Flowers Campaign and the Chinese Intellectuals*, London, 1960.

[30] Lui Shao-ch'i, "The Opening Speech at the Asian and Australian Trade Union Delegates' Meeting" (November 16, 1949), in Union Research Institute, *Collected Works of Liu Shao-ch'i, 1945–1957*, Hong Kong, 1969, pp. 175–182.

[31] Lin Piao, "Long Live the Victory of People's War," first English translation in: *Current Background*, Hong Kong, September 13, 1965.

tactics for "revolutionary people's war" to the underdeveloped areas of the world. It might be argued that the so-called Chinese model has been successfully applied in North Vietnam, Cuba, and—under entirely different circumstances—in Algeria. But in Laos, Cambodia, and South Vietnam, the final success of the model is still uncertain, and its application has failed so far in Malaya, the Philippines, Burma, Thailand, and Congo-Kinshasa. The Chinese model for an armed revolutionary takeover therefore does not seem to be a safe and sure prescription for a seizure of power. Its success in China itself certainly depended as much on the outbreak and outcome of the Sino-Japanese war as on domestic political factors, and just as certainly was influenced to a significant degree by the attitude of the two great powers. Soviet support was not decisive but nevertheless very important, and the reluctance of the United States to intervene seems to have accelerated the breakdown of the Kuomintang.

All the same, the Chinese Communists still believe in the invincibility of their revolutionary model, and the effects of their victory on their strategic thinking in world politics can hardly be overestimated. Having prevailed against a materially superior enemy in a protracted war, the Chinese Communists believe that this achievement can be repeated on a world-wide scale. It might be asked, however, what event in today's world could assume the role played by the Sino-Japanese war in the Communist victory in China. It would seem that only a nuclear confrontation between the two superpowers could play such a role, and all indications are that neither the United States nor the Soviet Union is willing to risk that. Could it be, then, that Mao Tse-tung was right in the judgment he pronounced on the contemporary international situation in a few words exclaimed in 1934 in an entirely different context? At that time, he said, complaining to a friend about his temporary defeat in southern Kiangsi: "Alas, this is no longer the world of the comrades of Chingkangshan!"[32]

---

[32] Quoted in John E. Rue, *Mao Tse-tung in Opposition, 1927–1935*, Stanford, Conn., 1966.

The Wages of Ambiguity: The 1965 Coup in Indonesia, Its Origins and Meaning

Justus M. van der Kroef

On the night of September 30—October 1, 1965, a *coup d'état* was attempted in Indonesia's capital city of Djakarta, as well as in a number of localities throughout the country, but mainly in Central and East Java. The attempt was made by several hundred army dissidents together with members and supporters of the Indonesian Communist Party (*Partai Komunis Indonesia* or PKI) and its women's, youth, and other front organizations.[1] Usually referred to by acronym-minded Indonesians as the *Gestapu* affair (from *Gerakan Tigah Puluh September* or "Thirty September Movement"), the uprising was virtually suppressed within three days, leading eventually to drastic alterations in Indonesia's domestic balance of power, including not only the slide into ignominy of President Sukarno—widely suspected of having condoned the coup—but also the shattering of the Indonesian Communist Party in a bloody nation-wide pogrom. Thus, for the third time in its fifty-two year history, Indonesian communism was plunged into disrepute and disaster after an abortive coup. This is perhaps the more remarkable because the policies which led to the debacle in 1965 had in many respects been a conscious reaction to and implicit repudiation of the tactics which on two occasions in the past had similarly precipitated elements of the Indonesian Communist Party into unsuccessful ventures to seize power. Though many details of *Gestapu* are still not clear, it would seem that the Indonesian Communist Party had apparently become a prisoner of the very ambiguities of policy which, ironically, had appeared so ideally suited to its rise to unprecedented power during the previous decade.

The Indonesian Communist Party was founded on May 23, 1920, and is the oldest Communist Party in Asia. It at first participated in agitation among the trade unions, with the aim of encouraging Indonesian nationalism during the Dutch colonial period, but the Party virtually destroyed itself by ill-planned and easily suppressed coups in West Java and West

---

[1] The literature on the coup of September 30, 1965, is growing rapidly. For summaries and evaluations, see Donald E. Weatherbee, "Interpretations of Gestapu, the 1965 Indonesian Coup," *World Affairs*, Washington, D.C., Vol. 132, March, 1970, pp. 305–317; Jerome R. Bass, "The PKI and the Attempted Coup," *Journal of Southeast Asian Studies*, Singapore, Vol. 1, March, 1970, pp. 96–105; and Justus M. van der Kroef, "Interpretations of the 1965 Indonesian Coup: A Review of the Literature," *Pacific Affairs*, Vancouver, Winter, 1970–1971, pp. 557–577.

Sumatra in 1926–1927.[2] Not recovering until the Indonesian revolution against the Dutch (from 1945 to 1949), the Party again saw its growth interrupted when some of its leaders staged yet another abortive coup in September, 1948, in East Java, discrediting it at the very time that Indonesian nationalist ambitions were about to be realized by Dutch recognition of the country's independence. Erasing the image of having "stabbed the revolution in the back" was slow and difficult, even though the Indonesian Communist Party was not formally banned. But by January, 1951, a group of younger Party leaders, dominated by the twenty-seven-year-old Sumatran, D. N. Aidit, acquired preponderant influence in a newly formed politburo, and the Communist resurgence began to quicken. In the national parliamentary elections in 1955—Indonesia's first—the Indonesian Communist Party emerged as the fourth strongest among the dozen or so parties in the country, polling more than six million votes (16.4 per cent of the ballots cast).

Under Aidit as Party chairman, three fundamental considerations motivated the strategy of the Indonesian Communist Party and contributed greatly to its rapid attainment of a position of power unparalleled in its history.[3] But in retrospect they also provided much of the matrix for the eventual disaster of 1965. The first tactical consideration was the Party's concern to legitimize itself again, and thus stabilize and extend its sphere of operations in the new national Indonesian political system. This meant participating actively in parliamentary affairs, seeking representation in local government and other bureaucratic positions, developing a Party press and new organizational appeals to the public, and striving for maximum "openness" and extensive dissemination of Party aims and programs. In short, the Indonesian Communist Party wanted to construct an image of constitutionalism suited to the origins and aspirations of the newly independent Indonesian Republic. These steps were intended to create the impression that the Indonesian Communist Party, despite its previous coup ventures, was a *national* party, concerned with Indonesian affairs like any other party, and not a foreign conspiratorial agency, as its enemies were wont to stress.

---

[2] For the history of the Indonesian Communist Party, see Arnold C. Brackman, *Indonesian Communism: A History*, New York, 1963; Donald Hindley, *The Communist Party of Indonesia 1951–1963*, Berkeley and Los Angeles, 1964; Ruth T. McVey, *The Rise of Indonesian Communism*, Ithaca, N. Y., 1965; and Justus M. van der Kroef, *The Communist Party of Indonesia: Its History, Program and Tactics*, Vancouver, 1965.

[3] The following description is largely drawn from my chapter, "D. N. Aidit—Indonesian Architect of Success and Failure," in Rodger Swearingen (ed.), *Leaders of the Communist World*, Glencoe, Ill., 1971, and from the literature cited therein.

Aidit also emphasized that the Indonesian Communist Party now eschewed the *coup d'état*; for example, he argued that the Party's involvement in the coup of September, 1948, had been due to "provocations" by its enemies.[4] In an address to the Sixth Congress of the Indonesian Communist Party in September, 1959, Aidit expressed amazement over recent rumors that his Party was again planning a coup. He declared that nothing could be further from the policy of the Indonesian Communist Party, asserting that the *coup d'état* is a way out for persons "who have lost all hope," and "who have no confidence in the people and in democracy," whereas the Indonesian Communist Party "has boundless confidence in the people as the source of all strength." Aidit went on to say that there were no "coup-ists" within the Indonesian Communist Party.[5] Moreover, Aidit now seemed to be equating the Communist rebellion in 1926 with Communist resistance to the Japanese occupation during World War II and with Indonesia's national struggle for independence following the Japanese interregnum— both of which were necessitated because "at that time there was no democratic path" for the Indonesian Communist Party to follow.

Though professing not be a leader of "coup-ists," Aidit could subsequently also remark that the Indonesian revolution had taught the Communist Party that in a revolution "armed struggle is the most important form of struggle."[6] Still, such talk of the importance of "armed struggle" was relatively rare, at least in the 1950's, and in any case tended to be placed in the context of specifically national, Sukarno-approved and army-backed objectives, such as the "liberation" of Dutch-held West New Guinea (Irian Barat) or the subsequent campaign of "confrontation" against the new Federation of Malaysia. Yet later, in the period from 1963 to 1965, Communist emphasis on militant revolutionary activity went hand in hand with Djakarta's rapidly developing ties with Peking and with the new revolutionary mission which Indonesia seemed to be assigning itself in Southeast Asia.

Meanwhile, in order to gain political legitimacy, the ideology of the Indonesian Communist Party had to be adapted as harmoniously as possible to the Indonesian environment. In many of his writings and speeches, Aidit tried to bring the Indonesian Communist Party's own program of "Indo-

---

[4] Cf. *Aidit Menggugat Peristiwa Madiun*, 4th edition, Djakarta, 1964.

[5] D. N. Aidit, "The Success of the Sixth National Congress of the C.P.I. is a Mighty Victory of Democracy," pp. 10–11, in *C.P.I. Sixth National Congress. Congress Issue.* Supplement to *Review of Indonesia*, Djakarta, September–October, 1959. *Review of Indonesia* was the principal English-language news periodical of the Indonesian Communist Party.

[6] D. N. Aidit, *Peladjaran dari Sedjarah PKI*, Djakarta, 1960, p. 12.

nesian socialism" into accord with Indonesia's official national ideology—as expressed, for example, in Sukarno's "Political Manifesto" (or *Manipol*) of 1959, or in Sukarno's concept of the world struggle between OLDEFOS ("Old Established Forces," particularly in the Western countries) and NEFOS ("New Emerging Forces," or Communist nations and those Third World countries whose brand of left nationalism Sukarno agreed with). At the same time, Aidit also tried to "Indonesianize" Marxism-Leninism—that is, to apply Marxist-Leninist doctrine to "concrete" Indonesian economic and social conditions and to problems of Indonesian foreign policy, demonstrating its national relevance.[7] One consequence of this tactic was the Indonesian Communist Party's consistent attempt to identify itself with and—particularly in times of difficulty—to lean on President Sukarno. The acceptance by Indonesian Communists of Sukarno's most widespread ideological concepts, such as *Pantjasila* (the so-called "five pillars" of the Indonesian state, including belief in God, nationalism, democracy, social justice, and humanism or internationalism), and *demokrasi terpimpin* ("guided democracy"), permitted the incorporation of communism along with nationalism and religion (*agama*), into such Sukarnoist doctrines of national unity as *nasakom*. Perhaps more important, because of its support of his policies, Sukarno on occasion felt a tactical obligation to protect the Indonesian Communist Party from its army enemies.

An example of Sukarno's intervention is the furor that followed the publication by the politburo on July 8, 1960, of an "evaluation" sharply criticizing the policies pursued by the cabinet of Premier Djuanda (Sukarno, significantly, was not mentioned in this "evaluation"). Prominent leaders of the Indonesian Communist Party were briefly arrested, the Party daily newspaper was suspended amidst a barrage of attacks on the Party in the Djakarta press, and a number of regional military commanders in Sumatra, Kalimantan (Borneo), and Sulawesi (Celebes) suspended the Party's operations. It was, however, largely President Sukarno's influence and public support of the Indonesian Communist Party that restrained the Party's enemies. In the course of the furor over the "evaluation," Sukarno publicly upbraided those who, in his opinion, were suffering from "Communist phobia." In his speeches he also stressed the identity of his views with those of the Indonesian Communist Party, though admitting some "differing" emphasis, and declared that his own philosophy was "Marxism adapted to the Indo-

---

[7] Cf. D. N. Aidit, *Sosialisme Indonesia den Sjarat-Sjarat Pelaksanaannja*, Djakarta, 1962, pp. 6–8, 11–37; *Untuk Demokrasi, Persatuan dan Mobilisasi*, Djakarta, 1962, p. 75; *Marxisme-Leninisme dan Peng-Indonesiaannja*, Djakarta, 1964, pp. 39-62; and *Politik Luar Negeri dan Revolusi Indonesia*, Djakarta, 1965, pp. 51–55.

nesian situation."[8] Behind the scenes Sukarno also pressured cabinet members and army commanders to mitigate the anti-Communist campaign. And, though much of the regional ban on the activities of the Indonesian Communist Party lasted well into 1961, by the end of August, 1960, with the appointment of Aidit and other prominent Party figures to the executive of the new National Front organization, which was designed to unify the country and "complete" its revolution, the Party, thanks to Sukarno, could already be said to have successfully weathered the storm. Sukarno's efforts on behalf of the Indonesian Communist Party at this time seemed but a prelude to similar but unsuccessful attempts made by him to save the Party in the months after the coup of September 30, 1965.

Before proceeding with an analysis of the remaining two tactical considerations of the Indonesian Communist Party it seems desirable to take a closer look at President Sukarno's policies. Why did Sukarno protect the Indonesian Communist Party? Why did he neutralize or eliminate many, though not all, of its opponents? Why, indeed, did he—only weeks before the 1965 coup—publicly encourage the Party to "Go ahead! Go on!" and to "Grow! Grow further!"?[9] Does his role compare, perhaps, with that of Cuba's Castro—i.e., that of a leftist nationalist leader, not initially a Communist, who for tactical reasons increasingly relies on Communist support at home and abroad? Complete answers to these questions would far exceed the scope of this study, but two reasons for Sukarno's conduct might be very briefly noted here. The first involves the changing Indonesian constitutional structure after the country formally attained its independence from the Dutch in December, 1949. The second concerns Sukarno's own preferred political style, which was also an expression of his personality.

Principles of parliamentary government, a structure of ministerial responsibility, and constitutional limitation of executive powers were—however inadequately implemented by Western democratic standards—already in existence in the government of the revolutionary Indonesian Republic during its struggle with the Dutch. But after independence, factional political struggles in an ineffective multiparty system and regional discontent, which had already flared into open army-led rebellions against the central government by 1956, soon caused the new Indonesian polity to be dominated by extra-parliamentary and extra-constitutional forces. The job of balancing these forces increasingly fell to Sukarno as the country's first

---

[8] *Indonesian Observer*, Djakarta, July 26, 1960, and Justus M. van der Kroef, *The Communist Party of Indonesia*, p. 237.

[9] *Bintang Timur*, Djakarta, May 24, 1965, and Sukarno, *Subur, Subur, Suburlah PKI*, Djakarta, 1965.

president and prestigious *bapa Indonesia* ("father of Indonesia").[10] The economy declined under nationalist attempts to restrict the scope of foreign enterprise and the burdens of inefficient, over-bureaucratized management. Risky but headline-catching foreign ventures such as the "confrontation" campaign to acquire Dutch-held West New Guinea and, later, a similar campaign to crush the new Malaysian Federation (described as a "neo-colonialist plot"), increasingly diverted domestic resources and attention from the arduous, humdrum problems of national development to the warding off of real or imagined dangers to the country.

In the meantime, Sukarno's own executive power steadily increased. Sukarno emerged as a much decorated, streamlined version of the traditional Indonesian potentate, a living embodiment of such precarious unity as the Indonesian nation retained. Not parliamentary democracy—"free-fight democracy," as Sukarno termed it—but rather "guided democracy," in keeping with the paternalism of traditional Indonesian society, was what the country was believed to need and, under Sukarno's leadership, soon got. Apart from the army, the principal beneficiary of this development was the Indonesian Communist Party. No other political party seemed to be so eager to try to develop a mass base by promoting anti-Western and, especially, anti-American agitation, and by providing a radical nationalist rationale for an as yet "unfinished" Indonesian revolution—steps that blended easily with Sukarno's own ideologizing and nigh ceaseless production of new slogans for his nation. As will be argued presently, there were serious organizational weaknesses in the Communist power structure. But by 1962, the Indonesian Communist Party, rightly or wrongly, was popularly considered to be the most influential and strongest of the political parties. Maintaining himself in power by balancing the army against the Indonesian Communist Party, while reacting with ever sharper hostility to Western political and economic interests (the nationalization of Dutch, British, and Belgian estates and enterprises in Indonesia was soon to take place), Sukarno also seemed to evolve naturally into Peking's principal partner in Asia.[11]

This new role, it should be added, seemed to fit well with Sukarno's own personal political preferences and character. His, after all, was a highly personal, romantic-authoritarian concept of leadership, predicated on a Rousseauist mystique of revolutionary nationalism and massive deployment of the popular will, of which he felt himself (often with a fine sense of the dra-

---

[10] For this development, see Herbert Feith, *The Decline of Constitutional Democracy in Indonesia*, Ithaca, N.Y., 1962.

[11] Justus M. van der Kroef, "The Sino-Indonesian Partnership," *Orbis*, Philadelphia, Pa., Vol. 8, Summer, 1964, pp. 332–356.

matic) to be the principal symbol and articulator.[12] A more formal, legalistic, and carefully circumscribed concept of executive authority, necessitating close and patient attention to the unspectacular "nuts-and-bolts" problems of national development, was never to his liking—it simply did not accord with his personal *élan* and sense of grandeur. Whether or not he actually believed that the Indonesian Communist Party, held in check by the army, would continue to remain manageable and stay within permissible tactical boundaries, as he defined them, is likely to be debated for many years to come. But there is, in retrospect, little doubt that the net effect of his role—not only as the "balancer" of Indonesia's domestic power alignments, but also as the self-conscious purveyor of its official national ideology—was to accentuate a climate of political authoritarianism in which the Indonesian Communist Party could flourish. In turn, Sukarno was well aware of the powerful critics in the army who had little patience with his flamboyance and extravagance; in confronting the army, the support of the Indonesian Communist Party was quite useful to Sukarno. Thus a curious, symbiotic relationship came to exist between Sukarno and the Communists, and the destruction of the Communist Party in the aftermath of the coup in 1965 would inevitably affect his fate. Like the Indonesian Communist Party, Sukarno was to be the prisoner of his own ambiguous position: simultaneously depending on the forces he sought to balance and attempting to rise above them as the nation's father figure. The ambiguity was to express itself fully in Sukarno's role during the *Gestapu* affair: he unquestionably knew of the coup, yet was not really a part of it,[13] just as important segments of the

---

[12] Sukarno's role and political style are controversial. For various views, see Berhard Dahm, *Sukarno and the Struggle for Indonesian Independence*, Ithaca, N. Y., 1969; *Sukarno. An Autobiography, as told to Cindy Adams*, New York, 1965; T. K. Tan (ed.), *Sukarno's Guided Indonesia*, Sydney, 1967; Donald E. Weatherbee, *Ideology in Indonesia: Sukarno's Indonesian Revolution*, Monograph Series, No. 8, New Haven, 1966; and Justus M. van der Kroef, "Sukarno—the Interpreters," *Quadrant*, Sydney, May-June, 1967, pp. 34–48, and "Sukarno—the Ideologue," *Pacific Affairs*, Summer, 1968, pp. 245–261.

[13] John Hughes, in his perceptive account of the *Gestapu* affair, notes: "There is not much doubt that Sukarno did have advance warning of pending trouble." But, Hughes adds, this does not mean that Sukarno wrote out the order for the killing of the army generals who were murdered by the *Gestapu* plotters. "It does not mean the plotters came to Sukarno, asked for his assent and got it. In Indonesia, things are not done that way." (John Hughes, *Indonesian Upheaval*, New York, 1967, pp. 113–114.) According to one specialist, an understanding existed between Sukarno and the Indonesian Communist Party since 1964, by which the Party pledged support to Sukarno during his lifetime, "in exchange for his special help to the Communists in the struggle for his succession." Guy J. Pauker, "Indonesia: The Year of Transition," *Asian Survey*, Berkeley, Calif., February, 1967, p. 140.

Indonesian Communist Party were deeply involved in it, and yet the Party as a whole was not committed to it.

Returning now to our dicussion of the strategy of the Indonesian Communist Party under Aidit, it may be noted that the second basic consideration of that strategy was constantly to maximize Communist power and organizational strength through judicious exploitation of each opportunity presented by the post-independence political kaleidoscope, and to adjust Party theory accordingly.

Examples abound. In the early 1950's, for instance, well before the national elections in 1955, the Indonesian Communist Party identified itself with the problems of the Indonesian entrepreneurial element, which was chafing under the restrictions imposed on it by the heavy dominance of Western (especially Dutch) import-export, estate, and industrial concerns. This tactic brought an informal alliance with such influential parties as the *Partai Nasional Indonesia* (PNI), with which Sukarno himself was more or less identified and which was an important fulcrum of the national Indonesian bourgeoisie. But, more important, it also fused the Indonesian Communist Party with the rising public temper of anti-Western nationalistic feeling grounded not only in resentment of Western economic and political influences, but also in disappointment over the absence of prosperity and national progress, which, it was generally believed, would follow *merdeka* (liberty). There is little doubt that the successes of the Indonesian Communist Party in the elections in 1955, achieved only a few years after the abortive East Java coup, were in part due to this nationalistic feeling and to the new respectability which the Party had won in some middle-class business and professional circles.

Shortly after the elections regional rebellions broke out against the central government in Djakarta. The Indonesian Communist Party correctly assessed that its principal opponents, the anti-Communist Socialist and Masjumi (Muslin Federation) parties (which were increasingly restive under Sukarno's authoritarian scheme of "guided democracy"), would covertly sympathize with, if not overtly support, the rebels. By siding at this critical time with Sukarno and much of the army against the provincial insurgents (who in February, 1958, proclaimed a rival "Revolutionary Government" in Sumatra) the Indonesian Communist Party purchased a greater degree of legitimacy. Also, these rebellions led to increased ideological polarization of avowed anti-Communists and anti-Sukarnoists on the one hand and Sukarno, the Indonesian Communist Party, and the main elements of the army on the other. The result of this alignment of loyalties was a further accommodation of communism by the government when the provincial rebellion collapsed.

In much the same way, the Indonesian Communist Party identified itself with the campaign, accelerating since the middle of 1959, to acquire Dutch-held West New Guinea (Irian Barat), and attempted, with some success, to turn it into a general anti-imperialist movement designed to radicalize mass opinion into opposition to all remaining Western interests in Indonesia. The momentum generated by the Irian campaign steadied the domestic balance of power between the president, the army, and the Indonesian Communist Party and their respective ancillary organizations, and so further strengthened the authoritarian scope of Sukarno's "guided democracy." However, by May, 1962, the relatively abrupt Dutch willingness to surrender West New Guinea to the Indonesians (as a result of strong pressure from the United States) created the need for a continuing "external" crisis to maintain prevailing leadership patterns. Even before the end of the Irian campaign, the Indonesian Communist Party had already pointed to the new target of such a continuing external campaign of "confrontation": the impending formation of the Federation of Malaysia. By the beginning of 1963 the Indonesian Communist Party could feel pleased that its anti-Malaysian campaign had indeed become official Indonesian policy. With Sukarno in the lead, and with the grudging support of the army, Indonesians were now called upon to *ganjang* ("crush") Malaysia.

The anti-Malaysian campaign of Indonesia dismayed the United States, Britain, and the other Western powers which had hoped that the acquisition of the Irian *irredenta* would mitigate the radicalization of the domestic Indonesian political climate in which the Indonesian Communist Party could prosper. But the Djakarta government had seemingly become addicted to the politics of "confrontation," and soon official pronouncements of Indonesian foreign policy, including Sukarno's and Foreign Minister Subandrio's, began to refer to the country's new revolutionary and anti-imperialist mission among its Asian and world neighbors.[14] This, it need hardly be emphasized, was grist for the Indonesian Communist Party's mill, and Party theory as well as tactics reflected a new emphasis on the need to broaden the revolutionary, anti-imperialist movement in Southeast Asia. The whole of Southeast Asia, declared Aidit in September, 1963, had now become the focus of the most acute anti-imperialist struggle going on in the world, and

---

[14] See, especially, Sukarno's independence day address of August 17, 1964, *Tahun "Vivere Pericoloso" Pidato 17 Agustus 1964, Presidèn Sukarno*, Djakarta, 1964; Sheldon W. Simon, *The Broken Triangle : Peking, Djakarta and the PKI*, Baltimore, 1969, pp. 24–25, 30–32; and Justus M. van der Kroef, "Indonesian Communism's Expansionist Role in Southeast Asia," *International Journal*, Toronto, Spring, 1965, pp. 189–205.

as conditions "both objective and subjective" were very favorable in Southeast Asia, the Communists and other Indonesian revolutionaries should feel fortunate to be living in the front-line area of the anti-imperialist struggle.[15]

Not just in Malaysia, but also in India and the Philippines, agents and supporters of the Indonesian Communist Party began assisting local Communist or anti-government insurgent movements.[16] Meanwhile, the anti-Malaysian campaign afforded the Indonesian Communist Party an opportunity to demand creation of an armed civilian organization at home, a kind of embryo "people's army" which would function as a so-called "Fifth Force," side by side with the other four services (army, navy, air force, and police) in the defense of the nation against the new "imperialist" danger of a British-backed Malaysian Federation. The armed forces opposed the "Fifth Force," but Sukarno seemed to be coming around to approving it, though the *Gestapu* affair itself cut short the gradual move towards its total acceptance.[17] Even so, the "Fifth Force" argument of the Indonesian Communist Party, bolstered by recommendations from a number of Chinese Communist leaders, provided significant impetus to the Party's efforts to neutralize the armed forces by creating a legitimate fighting arm of its own, while at the same time in a number of areas "civil defense" and "village guard" units had already fallen under the effective influence of the Party.

---

[15] D. N. Aidit, *Langit Takkan Runtuh*, Djakarta, 1963, pp. 24–40, and *Peking Review*, October 11, 1963, pp. 17–18.

[16] On Indonesian Communist infiltration of India, see *Straits Times*, January 9, 1965, Seymour Freidin, "Peking Sets Up Rival Comintern to Soviets," *The New York Herald Tribune*, January 4, 1965, and K. Krishna Moorthy, "Aidit Assailed," *Far Eastern Economic Review*, Hong Kong, January 30, 1964, p. 193. On Indonesian Communist activity in the Philippines, see *Manila Bulletin*, May 26, 1964, and May 31, 1965, *The Manila Times*, May 26, 1964, *The Sunday Times*, Manila, October 4, 1964, and Senator Rodolfo Ganzon, "Indonesia and the Philippines," *Philippines Free Press*, April 3, 1965. On Indonesian Communist subversion in the Malaysian area, see the Malaysian government's "White Paper," *Indonesian Intentions Towards Malaysia* (Di-chetak Di-Jabatan Chetak Kerajaan oleh Thor Beng Chong, A.M.N., Penchetak Kerajaan, Kuala Lumpur, 1964).

[17] After originally rejecting the "Fifth Force" proposal of the Indonesian Communist Party on January 14, 1965, Sukarno, a month later, declared that, if necessary, workers and peasants would be armed to defend the country "shoulder to shoulder" with the regular armed forces (*Antara Daily News Bulletin*, February 15, 1965; cf. also *The New York Herald Tribune*, January 22, 1965). Meanwhile, Aidit declared that if Britain was massing its troops in Malaysia in order to attack Indonesia no patriot in Indonesia would object to arming the workers and peasants (*Harian Rakjat*, Djakarta, February 8, 1965).

With the anti-Malaysian campaign, as has already been indicated, the Djakarta-Peking axis began to emerge, allied in the purpose of launching an anti-Western offensive in the Third World. It was undoubtedly the enlarged prestige and influence which the whole anti-Malaysian campaign of "confrontation" was bringing to the Indonesian Communist Party and the attendant momentum generated by Indonesia's new self-conceived revolutionary mission in the world that provided a significant reason for the Party leaders to consider turning the wheel of national Indonesian leadership still further towards establishment of an outright "People's Democracy." In a sense, and certainly insofar as the Indonesian Communist Party was concerned, *Gestapu* was born out of the rising prestige of the Party in the context of the anti-Malaysian "confrontation," and the domestic as well as the international revolutionary role which the Party felt emboldened to assume as a result of that campaign.

This bold new role was circumscribed, however, not only by the two other strategic aims of the PKI noted earlier (i.e., the Party's need to legitimize itself, plus its need to maximize its strength by exploiting political opportunities), but also by a third motivating factor. This was the necessity of forging—theoretically, and from the point of view of ideological appeal, as well as structurally—an effective organizational weapon, composed of the Party and its front group complex. Cadre training and recruitment of neophytes, financial control and administration of internal committees, co-ordination with Party branches on outlying islands, and skillful formation of new *ad hoc* front groups—all these became objects of concern for the Party leadership as they had never before been in Party history. Insistence on regular meetings and conferences at all levels reflected the growing bureaucratization of the Party. Aiditism, synonomous with Indonesian communism at this time, also meant a Party outreach to such groups as the peasantry, which prior to Aidit had only figured haphazardly and ineffectively in the Indonesian Communist Party's tactics. For Aidit, however, the Indonesian peasants were not simply the "basic force of the revolution." He subscribed to the view: "Without the active participation of the peasant the revolution cannot possibly succeed."[18] This tactic involved construction of an effective peasants' front organization, systematic analysis of inequitable land tenure patterns and of the exploitation of tenants and landless workers by landlords, and continuous agitation by Party cadres for the implementation of dormant land-reform legislation. The land-reform campaign included the so-called *aksi sepihak* or "arbitrary action," by

---

[18] D. N. Aidit, "Kibarkan Tinggi Pandji-Pandji 'Tanah Untuk Petani' dan Rebut Kemenangan Satu demi Satu," *Bintang Merah*, Djakarta, Vol. 15, April-May 1959, pp. 217, 219.

which peasants, led by Party cadres, seized landlords' land, and which occasionally led to bloodshed in 1963–1964.[19]

With each passing year, and in particular in the period from 1963 to 1965, when Maoist themes appeared to become more and more prominent in Aidit's speeches generally, the revolutionary potential of the peasantry, also in an international sense, came to be more frequently stressed. For example, in an address to the Central Committee of the Indonesian Communist Party in December, 1963, Aidit, after again emphasizing the crucial importance of mobilizing the peasantry, said:

> On a global scale, Asia, Africa, and Latin America are the village of the world, while Europe and North America are the city of the world. If the world revolution is to be victorious, there is no other way than for the world proletariat to give priority to the revolutions in Asia, Africa, and Latin America, that is, the revolutions in the village of the world. In order to win the world revolution the world proletariat must "go to these three continents."[20]

While other interest groups—from trade unions and women to youth and veterans—were also organized by the Party, and the theoretical principle that the proletariat remained the spearhead of the revolution was never abandoned, it remains true to say that under Aidit political dialectics came increasingly to be appreciated in terms of an urban-rural antithesis. In this scheme the village world, where the great majority of Indonesians live, becomes the staging area for revolutionary (including, eventually, guerrilla) action. This too was the larger meaning of the earlier mentioned "Fifth Force." In the months before the *Gestapu* affair, as Party-directed agitation against landlords, alleged Western espionage, films from the United States, the anti-Party press, and other manifestations of "cultural imperialism" all intensified, it was quite evident that the Party had succeeded to a considerable degree in radicalizing various segments of Indonesian society and had begun to prepare its followers for a radical new revolutionary move.[21] Meanwhile, Aidit, at the plenary session of the Central Committee in May, 1965, urged ever greater militancy in the "revolutionary offensive" undertaken by the Party in the country, adding also that "Indonesia is duty-

---

[19] *Harian Rakjat*, November 10–12, 1960, Asmu, "Masalah Landreform," *Bintang Merak*, January 1960, pp. 14–28, and "Aidit Completes Research into Conditions of Peasants and Peasants' Movement," *Review of Indonesia*, May-July, 1964, pp. 27–30.

[20] D. N. Aidit, *Kobarkan Semangat Banteng! Madju Terus, Pantang Mundur!*, Djakarta, 1964, p. 59. (Original in italics.)

[21] Justus M. van der Kroef, "Indonesian Communism's 'Revolutionary Gymnastics,'" *Asian Survey*, May, 1965, pp. 217–232.

bound to maintain and further develop the revolutionary situation in Asia and Africa."[22]

Still, for all this aura of militancy, stress on organizational development, and the popular acceptance of its great and still growing power in the country, the Party also continued to represent itself in constitutional terms. And while no doubt straining the patience of army commanders and their anti-Communist political allies (though cowed and quiescent, these were numerous!), the Party never presented them with a vantage point—such as the "evaluation" of the government in 1960—from which an attempt could be made again to restrict Communist freedom of operations or to attack the Party's new legitimacy. At the same time that Aidit was urging an accelerating "revolutionary offensive," he was also calling for the holding of the overdue general parliamentary and regional elections, saying that if the government felt these to be unfeasible, then elections could and should be held for village chiefs, a process which he claimed would entail little or no expenditure.[23] When it became apparent in the middle of 1964, that the militant campaign of the Party's peasant front against landlords who resisted redistribution of their excess holdings was beginning to bring police and military counteractions, the campaign was moderated. Caution remained one side of the coin of revolutionary success for the Party.

Despite the Party's newly won prestige, its leaders themselves were quite careful, not just because of opposition in the army, in Muslim political and business circles, and in some of the lesser political parties, but also because of its own internal organizational weaknesses, stemming in part from a too rapid overextension of its operations. The post-*Gestapu* assessment of one observer of Communist activities in East Java was that the strength of the Indonesian Communist Party had been vastly overrated, and that though the Party "gave an impression of invincibility" a "more accurate appraisal was that it consisted of a small, well-organized and well-financed group of activists without consistent mass following."[24] But this would have applied, *pari passu*, to all Indonesian political parties. The point is that by 1965 the Indonesian Communist Party was no longer regarded in the same way as other political parties; it had indeed acquired something of an aura of "invincibility" and was politically trading on it like no other party could.

---

[22] Cf. Aidit's report in *Harian Rakjat*, May 12–15, 1965, and *Antara Daily News Bulletin*, May 17, 1965.

[23] *The Straits Times* (Singapore and Kuala Lumpur), May 13, 1965, and *Antara Daily News Bulletin*, May 18, 1965.

[24] Jacob Walkin, "The Moslem-Communist Confrontation in East Java, 1964–1965," *Orbis*, Vol. 13, Fall, 1969, p. 822.

And yet leaders of the Communist Party, judging by their exhortations to their cadres to work harder among the masses and to develop better organizational discipline, appeared to be well aware of the tenuous nature of their control over the Party's broad following.[25]

This problem of whether, in an actual test, Party strength and action could live up to Party rhetoric, also influenced (it may be surmised) the Indonesian Communist Party's attitudes towards other Communist Parties and more especially towards the Sino-Soviet dispute. An analysis of the theses contained in the speeches of Aidit and other Party leaders and an examination of the Party's enthusiastic response to the developing Djakarta-Peking axis after 1963 can leave little doubt that for all practical purposes Indonesian communism had embraced Maoism, both ideologically and tactically.

For example, there was a call for a new revolutionary offensive, especially in the focal area of the anti-imperialist struggle—that is, in what Indonesian Communists were increasingly beginning to call the "Triple A" (i.e., Asia, Africa, and Latin America), and in particular in Southeast Asia. This significantly linked Indonesian and Chinese Communist thought, but the Soviet theorists specifically rejected such an offensive. Thus, in the middle of 1964, a national conference of the Indonesian Communist Party again emphasized the importance of struggle against American imperialism in the "Triple A" region, and singled out Southeast Asia as among the "most vulnerable areas," and as being a center of "revolutionary storm." According to a resolution passed at this conference, contemporary events demonstrated

> how dangerous it is to emphasize one-sidedly and give prominence to the "peaceful road," as the experience of the struggle of the Indonesian people themselves has also proved that only when they do not give up the weapons in their hands can they carry the struggle against imperialism and old and new colonialism through and win success.[26]

---

[25] See D. N. Aidit, *Berani, Berani, Sekali Lagi Berani (Laporan Politik Ketua CC PKI Kepada Sidang Pleno 1 CC PKI PKI, Disampaikan Pada Tanggal 10 Februari 1963)*, Djakarta, 1965, pp. 63–67; also D. Amrin, "Organisasi: Beberapa Peladjaran Tentang Pembangunan Partai Sedjak Revolusi Agustus," *Kehidupan Partai*, August, 1960, pp. 166–168. Amrin notes: "The larger our Party becomes, the greater our responsibilities and the more difficult our duties in consolidating and preserving the unity of our Party." On the question of the Indonesian Communist Party's organizational problems in relation to the coup, see also Arthur J. Dommen, "The Attempted Coup in Indonesia," *The China Quarterly*, London, January-March, 1966, pp. 165–166.

[26] *Harian Rakjat*, July 15, 1964. Significantly, this resolution was also reprinted in full in, and is here cited from, *Peking Review*, July 24, 1964, pp. 14–15.

These thoughts seem but an echo of the well-known letter of the Central Committee of the Chinese Communist Party to its Soviet counterpart, dated June 14, 1963, in which the "vast areas of Asia, Africa, and Latin America" are also considered to be "the storm centers of world revolution," and in which those who are said to deny this (the Chinese here refer to the Soviets) are excoriated.[27] Considering that no less a Soviet theoretician than M. A. Suslov, in an address to the Soviet Party's Central Committee on February 14, 1964, saw focusing revolutionary attention on the "Triple A" region as clearly revisionist and as doing "only harm" to the entire socialist struggle and the international proletarian struggle,[28] the persistent obeisance of the Indonesian Communist Party to this line can only be considered as a conscious choosing of the Chinese ideological position in the Sino-Soviet dispute. "The mounting struggles in Asia, Africa, and Latin America are shaking and weakening imperialism and will finally crush it," Aidit declared again at an international labor rally in Djakarta on May 2, 1964, adding meaningfully that "in the areas where the revolutionary movement is rising there is no market for revisionism."[29]

And yet, despite such avowed preference for the Chinese line, the Indonesian Communist Party also tried to maintain formally correct relations, if not friendship, with the Soviet Union, meanwhile placing the "independence" of the Indonesian Communist Party in the foreground and declaring that the Sino-Soviet rift ought to be considered a "dispute within a family" to be resolved "in a family spirit."[30] Holding simultaneously to all of these positions did not always make for consistency. In his brief history of the Indonesian Communist Party, Aidit had already remarked that "one of the basic mistakes" of the Party during the revolutionary period against the Dutch was its preoccupation with finding similarities between the Chinese and Indonesian revolutions, and its lack of concern for the unique conditions prevailing in Indonesia.[31] Though never altering his open attack on Yugoslav revisionism, Aidit at no time directly or openly criticized the

---

[27] *A Proposal Concerning the General Line of the International Communist Movement, the Letter of the Central Committee of the Communist Party of China in Reply to the Letter of the Central Committee of the Communist Party of the Soviet Union of March 30, 1963*, Peking, 1963, pp. 12–13, 26.

[28] M. A. Suslov, "Struggle of the CPSU for the Unity of the World Communist Movement," *Soviet Documents*, Vol. II, No. 16, April 20, 1964, p. 9.

[29] D. N. Aidit, "Indonesian Communist Party Will Never Forgive Revisionists," *Peking Review*, June 26, 1964, p. 14.

[30] D. N. Aidit, "Indonesian Communists March Forward for Full National Independence," *World Marxist Review*, Toronto (English Edition), Vol. 6, June, 1963, p. 16.

[31] See Aidit's essay, "Lahirnja PKI dan Perkembangannja," in the collection *Pilihan Tulisan*, 1959, Vol. I, p. 421.

Soviet Union by name, despite the Indonesian Communist Party's increasingly pro-Maoist leanings. After attending the Twenty-first Congress of the Soviet Communist Party in 1959, Aidit reported on Nikita Khrushchev saying at the Congress that in the world Communist movement there are no superior or inferior parties. This was entirely correct, Aidit noted, adding that it was the "imperialists" who were spreading the slander about the Soviet Communist Party leading the other Communist Parties. Aidit went on to say that Indonesian Communists had to stand on their own feet as they had always done, ever since the founding of the Indonesian Communist Party.[32] By the end of 1961, however, one could hear Aidit also saying: "There is only one vanguard of the world Communist movement and let there be no doubt about it that that vanguard is the Communist Party of the Soviet Union." Almost simultaneously he would reiterate that the Indonesian Communist Party "is an independent Marxist-Leninist party which has equal rights with other communist parties," and which was neither leading nor being led by any other party.[33]

At the Twenty-second Congress of the Soviet Communist Party in 1961 Aidit was fulsome in his praise of the USSR, declaring that Soviet-Indonesian relations were "blossoming rapidly like flowers in spring," and concluding that neither anti-Soviet slander nor imperialist intrigue could destroy Soviet-Indonesian friendship. However, after his return to Djakarta at the end of the Twenty-second Congress, Aidit declared that it was "imperialists," "revisionists," "Trotskyites," and "reactionaries" who had been gleeful over Khrushchev's attacks on Albania and on Stalin; the Indonesian delegation had deplored such attacks, Aidit said, believing that as long as a country genuinely possessed a socialist system—and Albania was to be looked upon as such a country—it belonged inside the Socialist camp, even though there might be conflict between one Socialist country and another.[34] Loyalty to the Moscow Declaration of 1957 and the Moscow Statement of 1960, Aidit affirmed, was "the main measurerod" of the purity of a Communist party.[35] (In view of the similar stress placed by the Chinese and Albanians, in their dispute with the Soviets, on the Declaration of 1957 and the Statement of 1960, Aidit's "measurerod" again seemed to underscore his Maoist preferences.) Yet, in an address to a training school for cadres of the Chinese

[32] "C.P.I. Fraternal Delegation to Twenty-first CPSU Congress Returns Home," *Review of Indonesia*, April-May, 1959, p. 10.

[33] *Strengthen National Unity and Communist Unity. Documents of the Third Plenum of the Central Committee of the Communist Party of Indonesia*, Djakarta, 1962, p. 24, and *Serba-Serbi Dokumen Partai 1961*, Djakarta, 1962, p. 114.

[34] *Strengthen National Unity and Communist Unity*, pp. 75–76.

[35] D. N. Aidit, *Berani, Berani, Sekali Lagi Berani!*, p. 46.

Communist Party in September, 1963, Aidit also professed to believe that with "a proper attitude" the internal polemics within the international Communist camp "would strengthen the ranks of the Communists," and also that Indonesian Communists had been given "all available material" on the international Communist movement, in keeping with "the independent attitude" which the Indonesian Communist Party had adopted towards the "problems" in that movement.[36] Aidit was also strong in his praise for the Soviet Union after his trip there in August, 1963 (the journey also included stopovers in Cuba, East Germany, China, and North Korea), and the following year, in an address to the Indonesian-Soviet Friendship League in Djakarta, he expressed his hope for a long life of friendship between the Indonesian and Soviet people.[37]

Khrushchev's downfall could safely be hailed by Aidit as opening "new possibilities" in the Communist movement; but the Indonesian Communist Party refused to attend the avowedly anti-Peking International Communist and Workers' Parties Conference in Moscow in March, 1965, ostensibly because not all such parties and Socialist countries in the world had been invited.[38] Aidit's commitment to a line of revolutionary militance in the "Triple A" region (by the middle of December, 1963, the Indonesian Communist Party daily newspaper *Harian Rakjat* had even referred to the Moscow statement of 1960 as providing the sanction for the stepped-up revolutionary struggle in Asia, Africa, and Latin America) undoubtedly, in Moscow's opinion, began to mark the Indonesian Communist Party as suffering from the risky "left-wing communism" which Lenin had described as an "infantile disorder." Soviet observers probably felt that remarks by Aidit such as the following, made early in April, 1965, a few weeks before the Indonesian Communist Party began planning for the *Gestapu* affair in earnest, were—however veiled—actually directed at them:

> Not long ago a modern revisionist debated with me that it was more important to have factories than spirit. What function could spirit have? What role would street demonstrations have? It would be better to carry on with production in the factories. I rebutted: factories would become like those of capitalism. But even if there were no factories at first, they would appear later if there is a revolutionary spirit . . We are now in a very favorable revolutionary situation. In this kind of situation the best way for us is to launch a revolutionary offensive and only by so doing can we win victory every day.[39]

---

[36] D. N. Aidit, *Kibarkan Tinggi Pandji Revolusi!*, Djakarta, 1964, p. 39.
[37] *Review of Indonesia*, October-December, 1963, p. 3, and May-July, 1964, p. 30.
[38] *Peking Review*, November 27, 1964, p. 18, and December 25, 1964, pp. 17–18.
[39] *Harian Rakjat*, April 6, 1965.

Just the same, all such sanguine rhetoric could not hide a realization of the compelling need for caution among the leaders of the Indonesian Communist Party. Moscow not only had avowed friends in the Indonesian Communist Party (e.g., Party vice-chairman Muhammad Lukman was said to be leaning towards the Soviets in the Sino-Soviet dispute), but more important, an open attack on Moscow at this time would have been quite dangerous considering the large Soviet military and economic assistance program for Indonesia and the place of the Soviet Union among Sukarno's "New Emerging Forces," with which Indonesia was seeking to ally itself in the world. Enemies of the Party were already making much of its attacks on Yugoslavia, claiming that such attacks on a government friendly to Indonesia, and a Socialist "non-aligned" state at that, were clearly in violation of official national policy. Initial Soviet credits of $100 million to Indonesia in 1956 were followed, in February, 1960, by an additional $700 million to $800 million in aid, of which around $500 million was in military credits alone; subsequent assistance agreed to in 1963 and 1964 brought the total Soviet aid package to well over a billion dollars making Indonesia one of the principal beneficiaries of Russian largesse.[40] (According to a Soviet-Indonesian protocol signed in Moscow on November 22, 1966, more than a year after the *Gestapu* affair, total Indonesian indebtedness to the Soviet Union was set at $804 million in long-, medium-, and short-term obligations.)[41]

Missile-firing MIG-19 and MIG-21 jets, TU-16 bombers, transport planes, PT-76 light tanks, frigates, destroyers, minesweepers, and even a complete, if overaged, 19,000-ton Sverdlov-class cruiser were some of the basic elements in the Soviet Union's military aid to Indonesia. Support for Indonesia's claim on West New Guinea was stated as an important consideration in granting this aid and in enhancing Soviet prestige in Indonesia. Fearful of losing such influence as it had gained in Indonesia, Moscow continued to be willing to negotiate new assistance programs with Djakarta beyond 1963, even though by that time Sino-Indonesian friendship was becoming noticeably warmer, and even though the Soviet Union, which had given Djakarta complete backing in its "confrontation" campaign for West New Guinea, was far less enthusiastic about continuing that campaign against Malaysia.[42] The seeming Indonesian recklessness (particularly the disregard of runaway inflation and food shortages), coupled with "confrontation" militancy readily backed and exploited by Peking and nourished by

[40] Cf. Guy J. Pauker, "The Soviet Challenge in Indonesia," *Foreign Affairs*, New York, July, 1962, pp. 612–626.

[41] Antara dispatch, Djakarta, May 20, 1968.

[42] Stephen P. Gibert and Wynfred Joshua, *Guns and Rubles, Soviet Aid Diplomacy in Neutral Asia*, New York, 1970, p. 35.

Djakarta's own self-proclaimed revolutionary mission in Southeast Asia, could not do anything but alarm the Kremlin. Yet, officially, Soviet relations remained cordial, and under the circumstances the Indonesian Communist Party could go no further than cautious ideological identification with Maoism, as well as full support for combined Chinese and Indonesian efforts to control various Afro-Asian "solidarity" conferences and special interest groups (e.g., workers and journalists).

Could the Indonesian Communist Party have opted for the Soviet side in the dispute with China? Any complete answer to this question would have to note first that up to 1963 and the beginning of the anti-Malaysian "confrontation" campaign, the Indonesian Communist Party on the whole did preserve genuine impartiality in the Sino-Soviet quarrel, and even after 1963 did not become another Albania. The anti-Malaysian "confrontation," as a continuation of the "confrontation" to acquire West New Guinea, was dictated largely by pressing Indonesian domestic considerations, such as the need to maintain the relatively stable relationship between Sukarno, the army, and the Party, and the sense of national purpose developed in the "crisis" of the West New Guinea question. But commitment to a new crisis policy, this time over the Malaysian problem (an issue which, *nota bene*, the Indonesian Communist Party had been the first to raise publicly), only radicalized government policy and the public temper still more—a development from which the Indonesian Communist Party again benefited considerably. Both Sukarno (in his role as his nation's chief ideologue) and the Indonesian Communist Party inevitably began rationalizing this latest turn in "crisis" policy, and the resulting barrage of verbal pyrotechnics pointed, with Maoist vocabulary, to Indonesia's "unfinished revolution"—not only at home but also in the world—against the *nekolim* (a Sukarno acrostic standing for *neo-kolonialisme, kolonialisme, imperialisme*), of which the Malaysian Federation was held to be representative. At the same time, the seemingly growing recklessness and destabilizing effects of Indonesian policy, manifested, for example, in Indonesia's departure from the United Nations in early January, 1965, greatly pleased Peking and alarmed both the United States and the Soviet Union. With the anti-Malaysian campaign of "confrontation," it was the Chinese People's Republic, not the USSR or any of the Western powers, that became Indonesia' natural ally.

It is against this background that the nodal developments of the *Gestapu* affair may now be briefly examined. With the anti-Malaysian campaign, an emboldened Indonesian Communist Party launched an intensified revolutionary offensive. The Party initiated peasant front-action against landlords, demanded the banning of Western "cultural imperialism" (e.g., American films and USIS libraries), suppressed covert anti-Communist organizations which were encouraged by the army, and urged instead the creation of an armed "Fifth Force," stepping up its assistance to Communist insurgents who were infiltrating from the Philippines to India.[43] At the same time, however, the Party still tried to remain cautious, slowing and then stopping the peasant action in the face of violent opposition and continuing to identify itself with Sukarno.

By the end of 1964, the need for caution was demonstrated again when an allegedly secret document of the Indonesian Communist Party became known. This document detailed the Party's plan of operations for 1965, including infiltration of the government for an eventual coup.[44] All the details of the document are not yet clear, but as subsequent trial testimony of captured Indonesian Communist Party leaders has revealed, the Communists had established a secret *Biro Chusus* (Special Bureau), with a central directing group and branches in Java functioning immediately under Aidit, as early as November, 1964. The *Biro's* purpose was to infiltrate and win over to the Communist cause various "progressive" officers of the armed forces, and possibly members of other government services.[45]

Then, by the middle of 1965, the tactic of "gradualism" was confronted by a serious crisis—presumably reliable reports of Sukarno's rapidly deteriorating health. In early August, 1965, Aidit prematurely ended a journey to a number of Communist countries upon receiving word from the Indonesian Foreign Ministry of Sukarno's illness, and it is generally assumed that Sukarno's Chinese doctors later confirmed the President's deteriorating condition in conversations with Aidit.[46] Subsequently, in a number of special conferences of politburo members and other Party leaders during August, 1965, Aidit called attention to the fact that leaders of the armed forces had also become alarmed over Sukarno's declining health and that they were allegedly getting ready for a seizure of power through a so-called "Council of Generals." The question of whether Aidit actually believed

---

[43] Cf. again notes 16, 21, and 22, *supra*.

[44] *The Straits Times*, December 24, 1964.

[45] Nugroho Notosusanto and Ismail Saleh, *The Coup Attempt of the "September 30 Movement" in Indonesia*, Djakarta, 1968, pp. 10–12, and Donald Hindley, "Indonesian Politics 1965–67: The September Movement and the Fall of Sukarno," *The World Today*, London, August, 1968, p. 348.

[46] See the trial record of former Foreign Minister Subandrio: *Mahkamah Militèr Luar Biasa. Berkas No; PTS–013/MLB — XI/BDR/1966. Tanggal 23 Oktober 1966 Perkara : Hadji Dr. Subandrio Ex. Wakil Perdana Menteri I/Menlu Dalam Peristiwa : Gerakan 30 September*, Djakarta, 1966, Stencil, Vol. I, pp. 3 and 159. See also Basuki Gunawan, *Kudeta. Staatsgreep in Djakarta*, Meppel, 1968, pp. 134–135, and John Hughes, *Indonesian Upheaval*, pp. 14–15.

that Sukarno's physical incapacitation or death was imminent is likely to remain controversial for some time to come; rumors about Sukarno's failing health had been rife for years, yet Indonesia's President seemed to continue to be able to function, and it is possible that the story of Sukarno's illness, like the alleged "Council of Generals," was but a ruse on Aidit's part to justify accelerating the Indonesian Communist Party's revolutionary offensive. Army spokesmen have generally denied that a "Council of Generals" existed, at least for the purpose of staging a coup. (Army commander, Lieutenant General Ahmad Yani, according to one report, did admit to Sukarno possibly as early as May, 1965, that there was a "committee" of generals, but said it was only concerned with regulating promotions of army officers.)

Evidently to forestall the "Council of Generals," Aidit's emissaries began a series of meetings during the second half of August and most of September, 1965, with sympathetic army officers, and notably with Lieutenant Colonel Untung, a Sukarno protegé who had served briefly on the side of the Communists during the Indonesian Party's coup in Madiun, East Java, in 1948, and who now commanded the First Batallion of the Tjakrabirawa Regiment of Presidential Guards. Meanwhile, some 4,000 members of *Pemuda Rakjat*, the youth front of the Indonesian Communist Party, and *Gerwani*, the Party's women's front, had covertly been getting military training at Lubang Buaja, on the remote outskirts of Halim air force base in Djakarta, under the supervision of the pro-Communist commander of Halim's security forces. In addition to these Communists the plotters could count on the support of elements of the First Infantry Brigade in Djakarta, two Communist-controlled paratroop batallions coming from East and Central Java to the capital, and miscellaneous air force units, the last amounting to about a batallion in strength. Co-ordination with coup supporters in Djokjakarta and Surakarta was largely left to *Biro Chusus* branches.

A reading of the trial records and testimony of some of the principal military and Communist Party figures charged with extensive knowledge of the coup or collaboration with *Gestapu* leaders conveys a strong impression of poor planning, haphazard organization, and a kind of "*ad-hocery*," if not half-heartedness, even on the part of the small inner circle of plotters.[47]

---

[47] In forming this impression I have benefited not only by the trial record of Subandrio cited in note 46 above, but also by the testimony in the trials of politburo members Njono and Sudisman, *Biro Chusus* head Sjam (Kamarusaman), Central Java Party leaders Wirjomartono and Utomo Ramelan, and such military *Gestapu* plotters as Major Moeljono and Brigadier General Supardjo. I am grateful to Mr. Oejeng Suwargana of Bandung, Indonesia, for making these verbatim trial records available to me.

A number of top politburo members knew, in general terms, of the plot, yet were left not only unaware of essential details (even of the date of the coup) but also had no assigned responsibilities to assure its success. Nor apparently did they insist on knowing more. No plans were laid for a popular uprising or even a demonstration in Djakarta after the leaders had announced the coup. Indeed, the need for mobilization of a critically important "back-up" force drawn from the trade unions or the peasantry, or from the youth, women's, and other front groups apparently was never really considered. This vital step may have been avoided in order to prevent leakage of the insurgents' plans, but it is just as possible that none of the plotters had the necessary organizational expertise or control over potential followers. Any co-ordination that may have existed between the *Biro Chusus* branches in Central and East Java and the chief plotters in the capital (including Aidit) seems to have existed mainly on paper.

Even the day for the coup appears to have been selected on the spur of the moment. September 19 or 20 was originally the choice, according to the testimony of some of the plotters, but for some unknown reason it was rescheduled, possibly because Indonesia's Central Intelligence Office, headed by a friend of the Communist Party, Foreign Minister Subandrio, had gotten wind of the date,[48] possibly because Untung expected further additions to the rebel striking force which was expected to occupy Djakarta. There is still controversy over why September 30 was ultimately chosen as the day for the coup. According to the testimony of some of the plotters, the decision to start the coup on that date was made by Untung the day before, with the concurrence of Aidit's emissaries. Another version has it that the decision to launch the coup was made by Aidit himself when, on September 30, Sukarno briefly became unwell during a public speech, and Aidit, thinking the President would not recover, decided to act that very night.[49] Whatever the actual motivation was, Untung and his forces occupied the government radio station in the early morning hours of October 1, 1965, and a little

---

[48] See the Subandrio trial record (cited note 46) *Mahkamah Militèr Luar Biasa*, *op. cit.*, Vol. I, pp. 65, 123, 175; Vol. II, pp. 119, 123–128. Subandrio passed this information on to others, including military intelligence personnel, but not to Sukarno, because he felt that the President had already been made aware of it. Neither Subandrio, nor indeed Sukarno, seemed particularly concerned about the impending plot. What Hughes has written about Subandrio really could be said to apply to both Sukarno and Subandrio, namely that they acted like men "with inside knowledge of what was happening and no fear for either the President or the government." John Hughes, *Indonesian Upheaval*, p. 113.

[49] Basuki Gunawan, *Kudeta*, p. 153, and Brian Crozier, *Since Stalin: An Assessment of Communist Power*, New York, 1970, p. 149.

after 7:00 a.m. announced to the startled Djakartanese that a "Thirty September Movement" had seized control of the government in order to forestall a planned coup by army generals, and that the movement would shortly establish a "Revolutionary Council" to handle affairs. Indecisive action and inadequate organization doomed the coup attempt to failure, although army reaction to the coup may have been delayed if the rebels' plan to assassinate Defense Minister A. Nasution and six generals had succeeded. The generals were, in fact, killed; however, Nasution escaped, and he assisted the commander of the Army's Strategic Reserve Forces, Major General Suharto (who had not been on the list of those to be killed—largely, it seems, because he was not deemed important enough), in quickly mobilizing loyal army units and breaking up the rebel forces in and around Djakarta within forty-eight hours. Sukarno had gone to Halim airbase during the early hours of the coup and reports of his presence and conversations there with principal *Gestapu* figures gravely compromised him, confirming well-founded suspicions that he had known of the coup much in advance and had actively or tacitly approved of what the plotters were doing.

Aidit too had gone to Halim and had flown to Central Java, where according to some reports he attempted to persuade rebels to lay down their arms, but according to others sought to give assistance and direction to the brief and wholly ineffectual *Gestapu* episode in the Djokjakarta and Surakarta area.[50] Within days, however, the chairman of the Indonesian Communist Party became a hunted criminal and was ultimately captured and shot by the army on or about November 24, 1965. By this time a massive anti-Communist pogrom had gotten under way, especially in Java, and at least 150,000 (and probably far more) members of the Indonesian Communist Party, known sympathizers, suspects, and even innocents were slaughtered by Muslim youths and village defense units, frequently with the open support of the army.

In retrospect, the purpose of the coup as well as the manner of its execution reflected the ambiguities of the Indonesian Communists' position and politics. The Indonesian Communist Party was very much in the coup, yet somehow not wholly of it. Elements of the Party were committed to it; yet despite the present Indonesian government's claims that there existed overt or covert *Gestapu* supporters in all walks of life, it is difficult, on the evi-

---

[50] Though Djakarta and sections of Central and East Java were the centers of the most important *Gestapu* activity, army sources have claimed that in Kalimantan (Borneo) local Communist Party cadres had also been making preparations for the coup. See *Djakarta Daily Mail*, November 22, 1965.

dence, to say that the Party or even most of its cadres were involved in the coup.[51] One rather gets a picture of Aidit wanting an acceleration of the government's gradual slide towards an outright "People's Democracy,"[52] but not at the cost of jeopardizing the Indonesian Communist Party or its hard-won legitimacy, nor so abruptly or incisively as to run ahead of a still-radicalizing public temper. In other words, if the coup failed, the Party hoped to remain relatively unscathed, counting as in the past on Sukarno's protection; if the coup succeeded the Party would of course greatly benefit from having assisted in turning the Indonesian state in the direction of the Communist bloc.

In keeping with this "acceleration" tactic, the purpose of the coup was *not* to establish a full-fledged "People's Democracy" overnight (this would have run ahead of expected support in the prevailing political climate), but rather to take a long stride towards it. After the coup, at least one segment of the now underground and badly divided Party admitted as much. The purpose of *Gestapu*, one spokesman of this Party group declared, was not only to frustrate the "Council of Generals" but also to establish a "Revolutionary Council" as the new government for Indonesia. The "Revolutionary Council" was to be composed of nationalists, Muslims, and Communists who "would work together *as a preliminary to People's Democracy*."[53] This reference to the "Revolutionary Council" serves to underscore another aspect of the plotters' and the Communist Party's ambiguity of policy in the coup.

---

[51] Cf. "Communists Behind Every Bush," *The Economist*, London, July 20, 1968, pp. 29–30. In January, 1970, the government announced that no less than 800 members of the Indonesian air force, including four senior officers, had been detained "on charges of involvement in the Communist coup attempt in 1965." The following March it was announced that a "just concluded rescreening" of Public Works and Electricity Department personnel had shown that "8,549 of the total 20,000 officials of the department are Communist elements." An initial screening under an army colonel had "only counted 3,265 Communists," but the colonel in question had himself been arrested subsequently "for alleged involvement in the 1965 Communist coup attempt." *Antata Daily News Bulletin*, January 27 and March 4, 1970.

[52] As one specialist put it, at the beginning of 1965, though the military might succeed Sukarno "the probability that Indonesia will become a Communist state has been increased by the political events of 1964." Guy J. Pauker, "Indonesia in 1964: Toward a People's Democracy?" *Asian Survey*, February 1965, p. 95.

[53] Suchahyo, "The 'New Order' in Indonesia," *World Marxist Review*, Vol. 10, October, 1967, p. 47 (Italics supplied). This view may be said to represent the thinking of the pro-Moscow faction of the underground émigré Indonesian Communist Party.

In the four announcements read over Djakarta radio by *Gestapu* spokesmen in the morning and early afternoon of October 1, 1965, there is mention of a "Revolutionary Council" and of subsidiary councils in the provinces and at the local level as constituting the new Indonesian government.[54] The third *Gestapu* rebel broadcast listed forty-five persons who had been appointed to the "Revolutionary Council." As a whole the Council lacked distinction; only a few prominent persons, such as Foreign Minister Subandrio, had been named, along with relatively minor figures like Sirad-juddin Abbas, the leader of a small Muslim party, and a bevy of relatively unimportant military men. Only four of the Council members—and these, with one exception, did not loom particularly large in the public eye—could be considered as members of the Indonesian Communist Party or as strong fellow travelers. Moreover, some of the Council members later claimed that they had been appointed without their knowledge and consent. Nonetheless, taking the "Revolutionary Council" as a symbol, it served the *Gestapu* plotters very well, in that it conveyed a vague, general impression of political "progressiveness," since most Council members were more or less known as supporters of the current and more militant phase of Sukarnoism, but did not project definite policy positions associated with more outstanding personages in public life and therefore avoided giving the Council too specific a political coloration. In the same vein it is noteworthy that in their first Djakarta radio announcement on the morning of October 1, 1965, the *Gestapu* rebels took care to identify themselves by using Sukarno's slogans and by referring to the continuing confrontation against Malaysia and the *nekolim*. Thus, as much as their coup proclamation allowed, the *Gestapu* leaders sought to remain within the official ideological climate. The statement of the immediate aims of the *Gestapu* plotters, as revealed in these radio broadcasts, reaffirms the accuracy of Luttwak's shrewd advice to practitioners of *coup d'état*:

> We will not, of course, identify our coup with any particular party (whose policies would be known) nor with any political faction (whose leading personalities will be known). We will, instead, state the aim of the coup in terms of a political attitude rather than in terms of policies or personalities, because the latter are necessarily more specific and therefore liable to specific opposition. The attitude which we will project will have to be calculated carefully: it should reflect the preoccupations of the target country, implying a solution to the problems which are felt to exist, and in *form* it must reflect the general political beliefs of the majority of the people.[55]

[54] For the text of these four *Gestapu* announcements over Djakarta radio on October 1, 1965, see *Indonesia*, Ithaca, N. Y., April, 1966, pp. 134–139.

[55] Edward Luttwak, *Coup d'Etat. A Practical Handbook*, Greenwich, Connecticut, 1969, p. 80. (Italics in original.)

For the Indonesian Communist Party, the "Revolutionary Council," no less than the *Gestapu* attempt itself, represented what was hoped to be a cautious quickening of its revolutionary drive. It was a move calculated to be just within the limits of the radicalization of the public temper, to which the appalling economic retrogression was also steadily contributing.[56] As such, it was not a truly revolutionary action, despite the rebels' and even the Indonesian Communist Party's rhetoric. For example, also in their first radio announcement on the morning of October 1, 1965, the *Gestapu* leaders declared Sukarno to be safe and under their protection. Deposing the President was certainly never part of their plan.

Precisely because of its ambiguities of policy in relation to the coup, the Indonesian Communist Party was not only unwilling or unable to mobilize mass support, but it also permitted itself to become dependent on ineffective allies, such as the easily dispersed and poorly co-ordinated *Gestapu* military, not to mention Sukarno. It should be said that after debacle had overtaken the plotters, Sukarno tried to protect the Indonesian Communist Party as best he could, even as the bloody anti-*Gestapu* pogrom began. In speeches and exhortations, the President, though declaring himself to be "anti-*Gestapu*," repeatedly insisted that Indonesia's was a "left revolution," warned the nation not to "deviate to the right," urged that communism be retained as an element in the earlier mentioned concept of *nasakom*, and as late as February 14, 1966, declared publicly that in his view the "Indonesian Communist Party was the only political party in Indonesia which rendered considerable contribution and sacrifice for the independence of the country."[57] It has also been authoritatively reported that after the coup Sukarno

[56] One day before the *Gestapu* coup, the youth front of the Indonesian Communist Party organized mass demonstrations in Djakarta against soaring prices caused by "corruptors and swindlers," with Aidit declaring that such elements would be crushed. Sukarno almost simultaneously asserted that only increased production could bring the rising prices down, but that in the meantime he had ordered that "swindlers be shot dead in public." See the *Sabah Times*, Kota Kinabalu, October 1, 1965, and *The Straits Times*, September 29, 1965. Between March, 1961, and September, 1965, the cost of living, including food and clothing, rose in Djakarta from 239 (1957–1958 is 100) to 14,371! (J. Panglaykim and H. W. Arndt, *The Indonesian Economy : Facing a New Era ?*, Rotterdam, 1966, p. 30). Approximately half a year after *Gestapu*, and on the basis of authoritative assessments of the state of the Indonesian economy made by the new government, Panglaykim and Arndt wrote (p. 7) that "a picture of economic breakdown has been revealed to the Indonesian people and to the world which can have few parallels in a great nation in modern times except in the immediate aftermath of war or revolution."

[57] *The Sarawak Tribune*, February 15, 1966 (Reuter's dispatch, Djakarta, February 14, 1966), and *Antara Daily News Bulletin*, November 2 and 10, December 9, 15, 21, and 28, 1965.

either maintained contact with or personally protected some fugitive Communist Party leaders for a while, among them Party chairman Aidit. But since the army command had not collapsed with *Gestapu*'s assassination of leading generals (in fact, Nasution and Suharto were immediately able to capitalize on the plotters' failure and tacitly endorse if not actively encourage the developing anti-Communist pogrom), Sukarno's pro-Communist pronouncements only goaded his and the Party's enemies to greater fury, and in the end contributed significantly to the President's own fall from power.

Many observers of the Indonesian scene, accustomed to the seeming mass adulation of the President during his public appearances, and convinced also of the invincibility of the resurgent Indonesian Communist Party, were surprised after the coup by the intensity with which anti-Sukarno and anti-Communist feelings burst forth among the people, particularly within the student movement. (This surprise was probably shared by Sukarno and many in the Indonesian Communist Party as well.) Partially organized and clearly encouraged by the army, the anti-Sukarno and anti-Communist student movement became a principal weapon against any effort by the President or anyone else to protect the plotters and the Party following the coup's failure.[58] Yet the sudden eruption of anti-Communist and anti-Sukarno popular sentiment should not have been wholly unexpected. As indicated earlier, the growing "revolutionary offensive" of the Indonesian Communist Party, especially during 1964–1965, and the moves against the landlords had aroused deepening hostility against the Party, while Sukarno's charismatic posturing and his oratorical rodomontades could no longer hide the deepening economic misery of his people.

Perhaps what helped to accentuate the anti-Communist fury was the discovery that the Chinese Communists had assisted the *Gestapu* plotters. Two weeks before the coup, Thai and Malaysian newspapers had carried reports from sources in Hong Kong that Communist China was sending secret supplies of arms and explosives to the Indonesian Communists via small West and East Java ports.[59] During the trial of former Foreign Minister Subandrio evidence was introduced showing that early in 1965 he had agreed to the secret import of 100,000 small arms from China, without the knowledge of the Indonesian armed forces, and during the round-up of Communist guerrillas after the *Gestapu* affair Indonesian troops reported

[58] Cf. Gunawan Mohammad and Ivan Kats, "The Indonesian Student Movement: How it Helped Topple the Sukarno Regime," *Solidarity*, Manila, Vol. 4, July, 1969, pp. 28–51, and H. W. Bachtiar, "Indonesia," in Donald K. Emmerson (ed.), *Students and Politics in Developing Countries*, New York, 1968, pp. 180–214.

[59] *Sabah Times*, Kota Kinabalu, September 14, 1965.

having found Chinese weapons on them.[60] The Party's enemies had no difficulty in using such reports not only to discredit the Communist Party's claims that it was an Indonesian party concerned with "Indonesianizing" Marxist-Leninist doctrine, but also to launch an effective campaign of demonstrations against China which eventually ended with the progressive suspension of diplomatic relations between Djakarta and Peking in October, 1967.[61]

With Sukarno's failure to save the Indonesian Communist Party, it was formally banned on March 12, 1966, by General Suharto, leader of the anti-*Gestapu* forces and Indonesia's emerging strong man, who would shortly succeed the discredited Sukarno as President. But, though outlawed, the Party continued to exist underground, led by second- and third-echelon leaders, and it remained active, briefly establishing a Maoist-style guerrilla "counter-government" in parts of Central and East Java in 1968.[62] Meanwhile, separate Moscow- and Peking-oriented factions of the scattered Party cadre structure sprang up, both issuing publications from abroad, and each delivering its particular judgment on the failure of *Gestapu*. The Moscow faction contended that failure of the coup was due to a "revisionist leftist point of view" that had come to prevail in the Party; as a result, "a rash decision" to play "savior" was made by the Party, although no true revolutionary situation existed in Indonesia; and then, everything came simply to hinge "on Sukarno's lesioned kidneys." For the pro-Peking faction, the failure of the coup lay in the debilitating tendency of the Party to become "bourgeois," in the undue stress it had placed on peaceful tactics as opposed to armed struggle, and in its serious lack of organizational strength and cadres. Only Mao-style tactics, relying on rural base areas and employing the peasant masses, are now said to be able to save the Indonesian revolution and the Party's place in it.[63] Which tactical course the Party underground

---

[60] *The New York Times*, October 11, 1966; *Sarawak Tribune*, January 26, 1972.

[61] Justus M. van der Kroef, "The Sino-Indonesian Rupture," *The China Quarterly*, London, January-March, 1968, No. 33, pp. 17–46.

[62] See the press surveys of resurgent underground activity by the Indonesian Communist Party in *Review of Indonesian and Malayan Affairs*, Sydney, January-March, 1968, pp. 33–37; April-June, 1968, pp. 69–71; and July-September, 1968, pp. 21–32.

[63] Justus M. van der Kroef, "Indonesia's Gestapu: The View from Moscow and Peking," *The Australian Journal of Politics and History*, St. Lucia, Brisbane, Vol. 14, August, 1968, pp. 163–176. For the Moscow faction's point of view, see *Information Bulletin*, Prague, 1967, No. 18, pp. 40–65, and 1969, No. 7, pp. 23–42. For the Peking group's position, see *Peking Review*, July 14, 1967, pp. 18–22, and July 21, 1967, pp. 13–22; *Pacific Community*, Melbourne, Vol. I, June, 1969, pp. 83–91 and Spring, 1969, pp. 163–184; *Indonesian Tribune*, Tirana, Albania, Vol. 3, No. 1, 1969, pp. 9–14, 25.

will finally settle on and whether the Party can emerge any time soon as a legal organization (a possibility some Indonesians do not see as likely for at least a generation) are questions whose answers lie in what will probably be the mercurial future of Indonesian politics.

Gestapu marked the end of an era for the Indonesian Communist Party in which it was supposedly repudiating its "coup-ist" past and embracing constitutional and national Indonesian ideological principles. Ironically, the very success which this tactic brought also created the temptation to hasten the slide towards "People's Democracy," particularly in view of Sukarno's presumably declining health. But having made the decision to "accelerate," i.e., to organize and join an attempt at a coup, Party leaders did not wish to gamble with all their hard-won gains. After all, legitimacy had brought them so much in the past few years, and, organizationally, the Party was probably a lot less invincible than its popular image made it out to be. Out of these considerations arose the ambiguity of the Indonesian Communist Party's political position in the Sukarno years. It was a party ideologically committed to a revolutionary doctrine, but trying also to act as a constitutional, parliamentary, and—above all—national political force. This ambiguity became intertwined with an equally ambivalent and incomplete commitment to its own (much-touted) "revolutionary offensive" and to the attempt at a coup as part of that offensive. It is not just facile hindsight which permits one to conclude that such a course would lead to the disaster which in fact overtook the Communists in Indonesia.

Guatemala: An Aborted Communist Takeover

Ronald M. Schneider

From 1951 to mid-1954 a relatively small group of native Communists strove to mount the base for a takeover of Guatemala. Although this bid for power was frustrated by a combination of belated opposition from the Guatemalan military establishment and an invasion by exiles who had the backing of the United States, the experience opened the eyes of other Communists in the Western Hemisphere to the revolutionary possibilities inherent in the very backyard of the capitalist camp's leading exponent. More important, it may also have awakened the Soviet Union to the same possibilities, ensuring a more positive attitude on its part towards the revolution led by Fidel Castro a scant four-and-a-half years later in Cuba. On the other hand, the ease with which the government of Colonel Jacobo Arbenz was overturned in Guatemala in June, 1954, helped lull the policy-makers of the Eisenhower administration into a false sense of security which partially accounted for the gross inadequacies, not to mention the fundamentally unrealistic nature, of the "Bay of Pigs" invasion in April, 1961. Compounded, the Guatemalan and Cuban experiencies go far towards explaining the direct and drastic nature of the intervention in the Dominican Republic by the United States in April, 1965. On the domestic Guatemalan scene, the incomplete national social revolution of the decade from 1944 to 1954 and the subsequent inability of the country to return to the *status quo ante* contributed mightily to the escalation of political violence and brutal repression which characterized the 1960's and became even more accentuated at the beginning of the 1970's.

As seems appropriate for the study of a Communist takeover which did not succeed, this reassessment of the Guatemalan case,[1] while centering on Communist strategy and tactics, will also treat the conditions differentiating Guatemala from countries in which the Communists *did* come to power, particularly Cuba and Chile. It will also briefly trace the course of events in Guatemala since the indirect "therapeutic" intervention by the United States in 1954, in order to assess the long-range efficacy of such anti-

---

[1] Ronald M. Schneider, *Communism in Guatemala, 1944–1954*, New York, 1959, contains a very detailed assessment of this subject and serves as the foundation for the re-examination contained in this paper.

Communist interventions. Finally, an attempt will be made to analyze the interrelationships between the Guatemalan case and subsequent developments, not only in Cuba and Chile, but also in the Dominican Republic, and tangentially in Bolivia.

The Guatemalan Revolution: 1944–1950

What happened in Guatemala demonstrated the opportunities afforded to communism in a small agricultural country where Communists have no previous experience or apparatus upon which to build. The chief lesson of the period from 1944 to 1954 may be that in the aftermath of an entrenched dictatorship the important equation for power involves the *relative* capabilities of the contenders, and that in the Guatemalan case at least, the initial weakness of the Communists was perhaps more of an advantage than a drawback.

Over ten years ago, I wrote:

> Within the short space of a single turbulent decade, Communism in Guatemala was born and grew until it exerted greater influence than in any country outside the Iron Curtain. Whereas in 1944 there were no Communists in Guatemala except for a small group who had been rotting in prison for a dozen years, less than ten years later there were perhaps 4,000 card-carrying party members and several times that number of sympathizers. By the end of 1953, the Communists held commanding positions in the labor movement, the coalition of political forces upon which the government rested, and even in the government itself.[2]

I also pointed out:

> The Guatemalan experience is particularly significant since it casts doubt upon the validity of certain widely-held generalizations concerning the relatively low vulnerability of Latin American society to Communist penetration. It has been frequently argued that the low level of industrialization, the strength of Catholicism, the decisive political importance of the army, the stubborn individualism of the Latin Americans, and the existence of a large Indian population clinging to their traditional way of life, particularly when backed up by the proximity of the United States, would serve as an effective bar to the growth of Communist influence in this vital area.[3]

It is true that in spite of these factors, a handful of young and relatively inexperienced Communists with quite limited material resources and only sporadic outside guidance was able to seize the leadership of a national social revolution and in a remarkably short period of time gain a position of influence and even control over the political processes of the country. A large

---

[2] *Ibid.*, p. 1.
[3] *Ibid.*, p. xi.

part of the answer to this seeming paradox lies in the ability the Communists had to exploit the social disunity and political backwardness which were the legacy of the dictatorship of Jorge Ubico and its forerunners. The key to the Communists' rapid progress in Guatemala under the governments of Juan José Arévalo and Colonel Jacobo Arbenz was the manner in which they captured the leadership of the urban workers and the lower middle-class groups which were entering the political arena for the first time.

Although the Communists did not become an influential political force until the government of Colonel Arbenz ruled the country, their success depended heavily upon the peculiar character of the national social revolution at that critical juncture. Prior to World War I, Guatemala had alternated between long periods of dictatorial rule and briefer interludes of instability. The 1920's were a time of relative prosperity and incipient democracy, but when the full impact of the world depression was felt, Ubico entrenched himself in power. An efficient administrator deeply concerned with sanitation and public security, Ubico brooked no resistance to his wishes. While liberal dictator Justo Rufino Barrios (1871–1885) was his professed hero, there was a good deal more of the despotic Manuel Estrada Cabrera (1898–1920) in his makeup.

Opposition to Ubico rose throughout World War II, and following the fall of the military strongman in neighboring El Salvador in April, 1944, a civil protest movement sparked by university students and young professional men threatened to topple the Guatemalan dictator. After a month-long crisis, Ubico resigned on July 1, 1944. In mid-October these same groups, in alliance with young, progressive army officers, ousted General Federico Ponce Vaides from the provisional presidency, thus opening the way for the election of a democratic, civilian regime. Juan José Arévalo, an educator living in exile in Argentina, was the overwhelming popular choice for the presidency in the elections in December, 1944. During the next few years long overdue reforms and welfare programs were enacted by this self-professed "spiritual socialist," who fostered the widest degree of political liberty Guatemala had yet experienced. Arévalo became the second president in the history of the country to turn power over to a constitutionally elected successor, but the seeds of political radicalization were sown during his incumbency.

Arévalo was a strong anti-imperialist who viewed democracy as the unrestrained competition of rival ideas. Though he did not permit the Communists to become a legal party during his administration, he utilized a number of foreign Communists—chiefly Salvadorean, Honduran, and

Chilean—in his government, along with many other Latin-American political exiles. Unwilling to retain those individuals who had collaborated with the Ubico regime, he had little choice but to rely on the organizational skills and administrative experience of these foreign elements until the bright young Guatemalans he had recruited for service in the government developed a modicum of expertise and political maturity. In the end a significant proportion of this new political generation evolved towards communism by one road or another.

> In short, after the destruction of the old regime there was no organized group to inherit power, furnish leadership, and put forth a practical program suited to the needs and capabilities of the Guatemalan nation. Owing largely to the political, social and economic backwardness of Guatemala, no homogeneous force evolved to back the revolution. Lacking experience and having to fight against an intransigent and often conspiratorial opposition, the revolution under Arévalo never fulfilled its early promise.[4]

In the early years of the Arévalo administration, the Communist movement recruited cadres for the day when they would be able to strike a more advantageous bargain with Arévalo's successor. These years were still part of the era of good feelings which followed the victory of the Allies in World War II and preceded the outbreak of the Cold War. In Chile, Costa Rica, and even Brazil, presidents went at least as far as Arévalo in tolerating the Communists and even in bargaining with them for support. But while both the Communist Parties and rival political forces in these countries were reasonably well organized, in Guatemala the Communists were still only "a small, select group of able young politicians and labor leaders whose only organization was in the form of study groups and clandestine cells within the revolutionary organizations."[5] José Manuel Fortuny, future General Secretary of the Communists' Guatemalan Labor Party (PGT), served as head of the chief party in the administration until ousted in March, 1949, by a socialist slate; Alfredo Guerra Borges, later the Communist Party's top propagandist, was Guatemala's first Inspector General of Labor and managed the President's news and public relations staff; Victor Manuel Gutiérrez, the outstanding Communist labor leader, was a director of the Social Security Institute; and after holding a diplomatic position in Paris, the future agrarian reform expert of the Party, Carlos Manuel Pellecer, was appointed to supervise the extension programs of the Ministry of Education.

Widespread resentment of "Yankee imperialism" as represented by the United Fruit Company was of substantial importance in paving the way for

---

[4] *Ibid.*, p. 21.
[5] *Ibid.*, p. 25.

the growth of Communist influence in Guatemala. To many Guatemalans the United Fruit Company was synonymous with the United States, and the initials UFCO and USA symbolized the same kind of domination and exploitation. *La Frutera* was frequently referred to as an octopus, since it seemed to have a stranglehold on the economy, being the chief stockholder in the railroad company, possessing a virtual monopoly over the country's shipping through its "great white fleet," and even controlling internal telegraphic communications through a subsidiary. Many Guatemalans believed that the electric utilities were also controlled by United Fruit, and a good part of the urban population even felt that UFCO somehow determined United States policy towards their country. Prodded by the agitation of Communists and other extreme nationalists, Guatemalan workers and many intellectuals were aware how UFCO had pressured governments, bribed politicians, and intimidated opponents in the past to gain valuable concessions and extremely advantageous terms. As so vividly portrayed in the novels of Miguel Angel Asturias, winner of the Nobel Prize for literature in 1967, United Fruit had extracted huge profits from Guatemala while working with dictatorial regimes to block reform and modernization. Ultimately, perceived reality and past sins were much more important in shaping the course of events than any "objective" balance sheet of United Fruit's actions and performance in the early 1950's:

> Under the "cold war" situation which prevailed on the international scene, hostility towards the United States was perhaps more important to the Communist cause than the development of pro-Soviet sentiment. By fanning the latent hostility into flames, the Communists created a mental and emotional climate in which their Leninist explanation of imperialism would be accepted by many nationalists.[6]

During the last years of the Arévalo administration, the Communists sought with success to establish a solid base within the labor movement and among students in secondary schools and universities. Having themselves found in Marxism a ready rationalization for the country's economic and social backwardness, plus a blueprint for revolutionary change, the Communists quickly developed a facility for drawing reform-minded and anti-imperialist youth along the same path. For those in their early and midtwenties, communism projected an image of idealism and self-sacrifice, and appealed to them as "children of the revolution in 1944."

---

[6] *Ibid.*, p. 47. Guatemalans were aware of John Foster Dulles' earlier ties to the United Fruit Company and generally accepted the claim that he and his family continued to have a major financial interest in that concern. Then, too, UFCO did come under anti-trust litigation in the United States, subsequently being ordered to divest itself of its controlling interest in International Railways of Central America.

The Communists met little organized opposition among the workers, because the working class in Guatemala was relatively unsophisticated and lacked previous political commitment. Carefully singling out the informal leaders among the working class, the Communists assiduously cultivated them, counting on them to use their influence within the unions and government apparatus to bolster the formal positions of converts. Thus, while playing upon the normal aspirations and ambitions of the more politically aware workers, the Communists introduced an element of organization into what was previously an amorphous mass. By winning the backing of important elements in the labor movement, the Communists were able to prevent Guatemalan workers from lending substantial support to any other political party.

Organizationally, the key to control of the labor movement was the teachers' union (STEG), through which the Communists exercised direction over the General Confederation of Guatemalan Workers (CTG). When the legality of the Party and the unification of the labor movement were achieved under the Arbenz government, most of the top positions in both were held by former activist members of the teachers' union. Four of the five members of the Party secretariat, as well as two members of the eleven-man political commission, had held office in STEG. The General Secretary of the National Campesino Confederation had been one the founders of the teachers' union. This organization, with nearly 5,000 members, formed a nation-wide network of propagandists.

Notwithstanding their strength within the labor movement, the influence of the Communists under the Arbenz regime functioned chiefly from the top down, with the favor and co-operation of the President. Clearly, it had been essential to their designs that Arbenz, and not someone else, succeed Arévalo. As Minister of Defense, Arbenz was a strong contender for the presidency from the early days of the revolutionary regime, but until mid-1949 he faced formidable competition from Colonel Francisco Javier Arana, the Chief of the Armed Forces. Like Arbenz, Arana had been a member of the junta government in 1944. The assassination of Arana in June, 1949, by elements linked closely to Arbenz not only removed the chief rival of Arbenz for the presidential office, but also triggered an army revolt that justified a purge of anti-Arbenz forces from the military. Given the failure of other attempted coups in June and November, 1950, the accession of Arbenz to the presidency in March, 1951, was all but a foregone conclusion. (By the same token, these developments, which facilitated the rise to power of radical elements, postponed the day of reckoning until, as was to be the case, the normal balance of forces had been more or less reestablished by 1954.

The Communist Bid for Power: 1951–1954

During Arbenz's first year in power, the Communists concentrated on healing the split within their own ranks, which had resulted in the existence of two parties, and in consolidating their hold over the labor movement.[7]

Then, in mid-1952 they used the strategic position they had gained to aid the President in the implementation of an agrarian reform and in the mobilization of peasant support to compensate for the backing of the moderates, who had abandoned the administration on this controversial issue. In return, at the end of 1952 Arbenz granted the Communists full legality as the Guatemalan Labor Party, and included several of the Party's leaders in the government's coalition ticket for the congressional elections to be held in January, 1953. Exploiting nearly exclusive control over the machinery of the agrarian reform, the Communists sought to build a nation-wide base for electoral support and to establish hegemony over the other revolutionary parties. In this respect, the increasing dissension within the official parties and the bitter rivalry between the two largest of them played into the hands of the Communists. The Communists were counting on three more years under the patronage of President Arbenz. In this time they hoped to increase their strength throughout the country and to find a successor to the President who would be at least as dependent as Arbenz on their support, even if he should not be as fundamentally favorable in his attitude towards communism.

In the pattern of politics which emerged by 1954, the unions and peasant organizations, rather than the parties, functioned as effective instruments, centralized under Communist leadership, for turning the rural masses into a national political force. These two bodies together with the Guatemalan Labor Party made up three of the five organizations represented in the National Democratic Front (FDN), which by 1954 had supplanted the cabinet as the chief policy-making body in Guatemala. The other two organizations were the Revolutionary Action Party (PAR), a large amorphous political conglomerate, weakened by dissension and opportunism, and the Party of the Guatemalan Revolution (PRG), a considerably smaller group, but one much less subject to the ravages of internal strife. Compared with the Communists, both these parties lacked a well-defined program or coherent ideological foundation, and suffered from a shortage of effective leaders, weak discipline, and a tendency to dissipate their energies in short-sighted struggles over spoils and patronage. Each contained an influential group of

---

[7] This section is essentially a summary of Chapter 3 of my earlier work, *Communism in Guatemala*, entitled "The Revolution under Arbenz: Toward a New Pattern of Politics."

Communists or Communist-sympathizers within its ranks, working to thwart its development into a dynamic rival of the Guatemalan Labor Party.

Perhaps the most distinctive characteristic of the Arbenz regime was the close relationship between the President and the Communists. Benefiting from the sympathy of the President's wife, the Communists had drawn around Arbenz while he was still Arévalo's Minister of Defense. They had subsequently demonstrated their usefulness to him during the election campaign, and their stock rose further in his eyes as they provided him with the background studies, technical advice, and talent for mobilization that were required for the project he regarded as his top priority—agrarian reform. More concerned with immediate problems than the shape of things to come, Arbenz valued the Communists for their loyal support and technical skills more than for their ideology. In contrast to the other political groups, the Communists brought him plans and answers rather than problems and constant demands for patronage. In picturing Arbenz as the "soldier of the people," in hinting that the working class considered him indispensable and might even demand that he be given a second term, and in effectively organizing mass demonstrations in support of his policies, the Communists strengthened their links to the chief arbiter of power in Guatemala at the time—the one individual who could neutralize military opposition to their growing influence. With the agencies in charge of the agrarian reform, much of the educational bureaucracy (including some 1,600 teachers who were Party members), and the labor unions—both urban and rural—largely in their hands, at least at the top, the Communists were able to establish an interlocking network of front groups and mass organizations. By 1954 the General Confederation of Guatemalan Workers claimed 100,000 members and the National Campesino Confederation nearly twice that number, with youth, women's, and peace organizations adding several thousand others.

In general, communism in Guatemala seems to have thrived upon new groups that were misfits in the traditional socio-political order. At first, Communist cadres came from young intellectuals of lower middle-class origins, then incorporated increasing numbers of militant urban workers, and in the final months of the regime reflected recruitment of "mobile" rural workers. The young intellectuals were the sector of Guatemalan society perhaps most acutely frustrated by the system of government up to 1944, for in their eyes it sought to doom them to a life as poorly paid teachers or office employees. Conscious of the marked gap between their level of education and their socio-economic status in a stratified society, they believed the Communist Party offered them an opportunity to gain recognition and advancement commensurate with their own estimates of their ability. Many of them also came to see in communism a blueprint for social and political change, though by European standards (or even by those of the Chilean or Cuban Communist Parties of the day) their ideological orientation was still quite primitive.

Among the working class the greatest susceptibility to communism was shown by so-called uprooted persons. In leaving their native villages to work on coffee *fincas* or in textile factories, these persons had usually given up their accustomed way of life for the elusive promise of material betterment. Very often the new life was not as satisfying as the one they had left behind in their Indian communities. Confused by the new environment with its host of strange demands, and prey to the uncertainties of existence as poorly paid wage laborers, they needed the Communist labor leaders to act as a buffer between them and the authorities and to extend to them a sense of belonging to a new community. Together with westernized rural workers who were attracted to the Guatemalan Labor Party by the chance it offered for political activity and advancement, these mobile laborers provided local leadership for the Communists in areas outside the easy reach of the capital. The stage of rapid expansion of Communist influence was just getting well under way at the time of the counter-revolution in 1954, and with the promise of land the Communists were beginning to attract many of the Indians, who had finally been affected by the decade-long process of social mobilization. Thus, to a large extent, the shrewd application of the standard techniques of machine politics to hitherto non-participant groups enabled the Guatemalan Communists to progress towards a position of electoral strength. The workers and *campesinos* were not concerned about international affairs or life in Communist countries, but they were very much motivated to improve their own day-to-day existence. Essentially, the Guatemalan Communists adopted an instrumental rather than Messianic approach to the workers' problems, in keeping with the realities of the situation.

Organized anti-Communist opposition in Guatemala was largely a negative phenomenon, as it was too closely linked to retrograde forces to be effective among the population. By denouncing social security, the labor code, and agrarian reform as Communist-inspired, the anti-Communists actually facilitated the Guatemalan Labor Party's effort to identify itself as the champion of popular demands. Moreover, since the anti-Communist movement was dominated by opponents of social reform, it could not make common cause with the moderate and centrist elements who supported the revolution but were opposed to the growth of Communist influence. As a result, Guatemala never developed an opposition party willing or able to face up to the changing facts of political and economic life, to accept reform as legitimate, and to provide better solutions to the nation's pressing problems than those offered by the Communists and their *Arbencista* allies. Nor, as we have seen, was there any really effective competition for the Communists from an advanced left-wing party of an essentially nationalist orientation. The result of this situation was that those groups that wished to curb Communist influence within the regime but had no desire to overthrow the elected government were caught on the horns of a dilemma. Loyal to the principles and aims, however vague and nebulous, of the revolution of 1944, these moderates could not join hands with the self-styled anti-Communists who insisted upon denouncing everyone and everything concerning the government or organized labor as Communist. Nor could they find sufficient support within the government, organized labor, and the revolutionary parties to effectively contain Communist growth. Many resolved their ambivalent feelings by rationalizing that the regime needed Communist support to avoid overthrow by the intransigent opposition and the subsequent destruction of all the gains made since 1944. Others followed the negative policy of dissociating themselves from the regime and withdrawing to the margin of the political arena.[8]

By and large the Guatemalan nationalists accepted the Communists as fellow revolutionaries to be tolerated in the name of democracy and common anti-imperialist objectives. While avoiding a rupture with the bourgeois parties, the Communists strove to intensify the pace of revolutionary change and to emphasize the elements of class struggle present in the Guatemalan situation. Enjoying the President's favor in a system which concentrated much political power in the hands of the chief executive, they made it appear to other progressive forces that is was more profitable to collaborate with them than to oppose them.

Even as late as 1954, Arbenz was almost certainly not a Communist, and there was a strong rational element in his decision to work closely with the Communists. His wife was clearly much closer to communism than he, though it ought to be said that her involvement was more emotional than ideological. While the President relied heavily upon Communist advisers, his regime was subject to Communist influence rather than Communist control. That this influence was increasing rapidly during the latter part of 1953 and the first part of 1954 is clear, and Arbenz emphatically rejected suggestions from various quarters that he dissociate his government from the Communist leaders and organizations. Arbenz had progressed from finding the Communists useful in 1950 and 1951 to considering them, and particularly his confidant José Manuel Fortuny, indispensable in 1954. Not

---

[8] *Ibid.*, p. 50.

heading a party of his own, Arbenz felt a need for the reliable organizational support of the Guatemalan Labor Party and the labor movement which it controlled. The leaders of the other "revolutionary" parties were already concerned with their bids to succeed him in power. In the short run at least, the interests of the Communists most closely coincided with Arbenz' own. In sharp contrast with Fidel Castro or even Salvador Allende, Arbenz lacked not only charisma, but also ability as a public speaker, being essentially a quite introverted, if not insecure, individual.[9]

Intervention and Collapse of the Regime: June, 1954

The Guatemalan Communists were looking ahead with optimism to the elections in 1956. Whether they would have increased their already substantial influence at that time or would have found Arbenz' successor less favorably disposed towards them remains an unanswerable if a nonetheless tantalizing question. As it was, the United States was prepared to invest an estimated $7 million to finance an exile invasion and internal uprising to overthrow this transitional regime.[10]

Substantial opposition to the regime of Arbenz had persisted after his election; as late as the congressional balloting in January, 1953, the parties opposed to Arbenz polled 105,000 votes compared with 130,000 votes for his coalition. In November, 1950, Lieutenant Colonel Carlos Castillo Armas had led an unsuccessful attempt to oust Arévalo and prevent Arbenz from taking office. In mid-1951 Castillo Armas escaped from prison and by late the next year was organizing one of several exile movements directed at overthrowing Arbenz. Viewed as an heir to the murdered Colonel Arana, Castillo Armas was preferred by the U.S. government over several conservative civilian aspirants. By early 1953, CIA support was being received in Honduras by Castillo Armas, and within a year a force of roughly 160 men was in training to invade Guatemala in a move to be co-ordinated with internal uprisings. While the unsatisfactory negotiations over compensation to be paid to the United Fruit Company for expropriated lands were certainly a factor in the Eisenhower administration's decision to intervene

---

[9] *Ibid.*, pp. 186–202, contains a detailed discussion of these considerations. Subsequent indications that Arbenz, who died in Mexico in January, 1971, may have become a drug user while still in office further cloud the matter. His various statements while residing in Cuba during much of the 1960's are not very useful in the quest for a more precise definition of his relationship with the Communists.

[10] In addition to my own book, this episode is discussed by Marta Cehelsky in her Master's Essay on "Guatemala's Frustrated Revolution: The 'Liberation' of 1954" (Columbia University, Department of Political Science, 1967, pp. 47–53).

indirectly, security considerations weighed more heavily.[11] And of the several types of support given to the "Liberation Movement," the most crucial was several World War II fighters, which had a profound psychological impact upon the population of Guatemala City and severely undercut the morale of the regime. (Seven years later the CIA was content to employ a somewhat larger-scale version of the Guatemalan operation against the Castro regime at the Bay of Pigs. The Cubans, however, seem to have learned a good deal from the fall of the Arbenz regime, and what worked in 1954 failed abjectly in 1961.)

Relations between the Arbenz government and the United States had begun badly and worsened sharply after mid-1952 on the interrelated issues of communism and agrarian reform. In contrast with other Latin-American countries, no military assistance from the United States was available to Guatemala, and efforts to procure arms in Western Europe proved frustrating enough to convince Guatemalans that John Foster Dulles had a hand in the matter behind the scenes. With conspiracies against the regime in the making, the situation was clearly becoming grave from Arbenz' point of view.

The Soviet Union, still under the firm control of Stalin, and not yet faced with competition from China for the leadership of the world Communist movement,[12] was quite cautious towards Guatemala, making no significant material or even psychological investment in the Arbenz regime. The emergence of the Communists as the orienting force in the Arbenz government during its last year in power coincided with the power struggle ensuing from the death of Stalin. While Beria was being eliminated by Stalin's other heirs and Khrushchev was beginning to consolidate his control over the apparatus of the Soviet Communist Party, the Soviet leadership was not inclined towards a major adventure so close to its principal Cold War adver-

---

[11] The most nearly adequate published discussion of U.S. involvement in the Guatemalan affair is David Wise and Thomas B. Ross, *The Invisible Government*, New York, 1964, which devotes a chapter to "Guatemala: CIA's Banana Revolt." In the Guatemalan case the critical factor was the failure of the army to make any serious attempt to defend the regime and its refusal to accept the co-operation of the Communist-oriented mass organizations. In Cuba, by the time of the Bay of Pigs invasion the old professional military had been replaced by the "Revolutionary Armed Forces" under the control of individuals whose personal loyalty to Castro had been tested and proven. Moreover, the Cuban security apparatus was much more effective than Arbenz's had been, and Castro had been decisive where Arbenz had vacillated in the face of such a challenge.

[12] Cecil Johnson, *Communist China and Latin America, 1959–1967*, New York, 1971, is the most reliable treatment of Chinese interests and activities in the region.

sary.[13] Kremlin policy-makers apparently assumed—and correctly assumed, as events soon proved—that the Eisenhower administration would take effective action to eliminate the Arbenz regime before it could become a model for other Latin-American countries. Thus, the Soviets decided to exploit the opportunity for the not inconsiderable nuisance value it possessed rather than to attempt to bolster materially—or even diplomatically—a non-viable outpost of Communist influence in Central America.

Diplomatic ties between Guatemala and Communist countries were not yet of a close nature when the Arbenz regime was overthrown, but it should be borne in mind that this was a period when most Latin-American countries had severed diplomatic relations with the Soviet Union in response to prompting from the United States, and when the shadow of the Korean War was only beginning to dissipate. In March, 1953, the Commercial Attaché of the Czechoslovak Legation in Mexico paid an extended visit to Guatemala, and ten months later a Minister from the Prague government presented his credentials to President Arbenz. As the Soviet Commercial Attaché in Mexico had enjoyed a lengthy private interview with Arbenz in October, 1953, there was some speculation over the possibility that diplomatic relations would be established with Moscow should the regime prove able to survive the crisis which was clearly brewing.

Needing arms both for his restive army and for the Communist-oriented worker and peasant militia which the Guatemalan Labor Party was urging him to form, Arbenz was finally able to conclude an agreement for just over 2,000 tons of weapons of Czechoslovak origin. Unloaded at Puerto Barrios in mid-May, 1954, these munitions arrived too late to help the government, but in time to create a major headache for it. The Guatemalan army, which had previously balked at sharing its limited supply of weapons with the militia units the Communists were seeking to organize, appears to have been aware of the threat posed to the interests of the military in Bolivia by both armed miners and a peasant militia after the revolution in that country in 1952. The army also seems to have recalled how railroad workers and members of other labor unions in Guatemala had held the balance of power in the capital in the civil strife in June, 1949, after having been armed by Arbenz in his role as Arévalo's Defense Minister. In any event,

---

[13] Nikita Khrushchev (?), *Khrushchev Remembers*, Boston, 1970, the authorship of which is unknown, contains no mention of Guatemala at all in dealing with this period. Interestingly, in a recent international symposium entitled *The Soviet Union and Latin America*, edited by J. Gregory Oswald and Anthony J. Strover, New York, 1970, not one of seventeen contributors makes any mention of the Guatemalan experience prior to the guerrilla movements of the 1960's (and only one touches upon that).

the army decided to keep control of the war matériel purchased from Czechoslovakia, creating a showdown with the President's Communist advisers, some of whom suspected that Arbenz had too much confidence in the loyalty of young officers who had been his students in the military academy. On June 5 the army commanders suggested to the President that he should curb the influence of the Communists, a suggestion which he energetically rejected, thus increasing the army's uneasiness. Even after the invasion of Guatemala by exiles began, the army commanders rejected offers of assistance from the Guatemalan Labor Party and the Labor unions if they called for furnishing arms or providing military training. When his loyal Chief of the Armed Forces reported that his fellow officers would not permit him to arm civilian elements even for the defense of the capital, Arbenz resigned on June 27, and most of the Communist leaders were far from the last to seek safety in friendly embassies. Thus one can only reach the judgment that the events of the last week of the Arbenz regime showed that communism in Guatemala had not developed into a successful popular movement. Although the Communists exercised great influence through the key positions which they had attained in the country's rather simple political structure, they had not found sufficient time to build a broad base or to sink their roots deeply. To a considerable degree, the same conditions which facilitated the Communists' rapid rise to power contributed to their ineffectiveness in the final crisis.[14]

The Post-1954 Record: Political Regression and Violence

While the short-run outcome of the intervention in 1954 was viewed at the time as a success for the United States in the Cold War, even if perhaps a relatively minor one, in longer perspective it is increasingly difficult to see it as such. Indeed, in light of subsequent events it might reasonably be considered little short of a disaster.[15] Unlike Vietnam, there has not been a fundamental problem in the viability of the government, but the political record of the past seventeen years in Guatemala is grim and even dismal, for the ouster of the Arbenz regime and the dismantling of the Guatemalan Labor Party and its mass organizations did not spell the end of the revolution's impact on Guatemala's political life. Not only was it impossible to turn the clock back fully, but also the heritage of bitterness between revo-

---

[14] Schneider, *op. cit.*, p. 318.

[15] Richard N. Adams, *Crucifixion by Power: Essays on Guatemalan National Social Structure, 1944–1966*, Austin, Texas, 1970, is the richest convenient source on post-1954 developments. His interpretations essentially support the factors covered in the present paper. See particularly pp. 141–143, 184–197, and 203–205.

lutionaries and liberationists contributed to the bloody turn taken by Guatemalan politics since then, as left-wing terror and right-wing counter-terror have come to characterize Guatemala.

Castillo Armas, who succeeded Arbenz, personally accepted the basic tenets of the revolution in 1944 and many of the specific reforms of the Arévalo period, but he was caught in the cross-fire of those who wanted to restore the old order and those who felt that his movement represented forces of reaction.[16] Under his tutelage political democracy regressed. A single pro-government party dominated politics, elections were carefully controlled, and power was concentrated in the hands of the President, supported by the army.

The "liberation" had been accepted rather than supported by the largest segment of the population, and the punitive actions taken by the government of Castillo Armas perhaps alienated as many people as were won over by its subsequent positive actions in the spheres of housing, education, and rural development. Once past the end of Arbenz' constitutional term, Castillo Armas adopted a more positive, centrist orientation, which earned him the enmity of right-wing elements, who, with support from the Dominican Republic, plotted his elimination. When Castillo Armas' career was cut short by his assassination on July 26, 1957, the next eight months were marked by political instability under two interim regimes. In the elections of January, 1958, Miguel Ydígoras Fuentes, a long-time aspirant to the presidency who had run against Arbenz in 1950, won a plurality with his personalist "Redemption" party.

Under Ydígoras, political maturity in Guatemala remained a distant goal, as the President's "divide-and-conquer" tactics brought increasing chaos and accentuated arbitrary authority. In 1962 it became increasingly evident that the administration was failing to resolve the country's pressing problems with constructive solutions. Moreover, the corruption of the Ydígoras regime became blatantly apparent. In April, 1962, the President was forced to fall back upon the device of an all-military cabinet; in November, 1962, there was an abortive air force revolt; on March 31, 1963, the army, with the backing of most political parties and other civilian groups, ousted Ydígoras from office, arguing that his malfeasance might have led to a return to power by Arévalo in the scheduled elections.

The caretaker regime headed by Colonel Enrique Peralta Azurdia, Ydígoras' Defense Minister, only partially fulfilled its promises to set the financial and administrative house in order and to combat vigorously the

---

16 Cehelsky, *op. cit.*, pp. 51–153, provides the most comprehensive treatment of the Castillo Armas regime.

Communist-supported insurgency which had been on the rise since Castro's victory in Cuba. Managed elections for a Constituent Assembly were held in May, 1964, and a new constitution was adopted in September, 1965. In the general elections on March 6, 1966, the candidate of the moderately leftist Revolutionary Party (PR), Julio César Mendez Montenegro, polled some forty percent of the popular vote and became the new President.

During the second half of 1966 the armed forces, assisted by large numbers of U.S. Special Forces "Green Berets," energetically repressed the pro-Castro guerrillas. In the Zacapa area, where the Sierra de las Minas had all but become a rebel enclave, the army countenanced and even encouraged right-wing counter-terrorist organizations, which subsequently spread into other parts of the country. In 1967 at least a thousand deaths could be attributed to these groups, collectively known as "The White Hand." In reprisal, the guerrillas assassinated the two top-ranking officers of the United States Military Assistance Group in January, 1968, and seven months later killed U.S. Ambassador John Gordon Mein. Mendez Montenegro continued to sacrifice his reformist policies for the goal of surviving in office until the end of his term and turning the presidency over to a freely elected successor. While the Communist guerrillas were nearly wiped out, they continued to carry out acts of terrorism in the capital throughout the election campaign of 1969–1970.

In March, 1970, Colonel Carlos Arana Osorio, a rightist sponsor of the "White Hand," was elected to the presidency, succeeding Mendez Montenegro, the relatively mild-mannered former Law School Dean. After a brief political honeymoon under Arana, violence rose to the point where extremists of the left and right were responsible for several thousand deaths by the end of his first year in office.[17]

Guatemala's Impact on Cuba, the Dominican Republic, Chile, and Bolivia

The late Ernesto "Che" Guevara served as the major link between Guatemalan and Cuban revolutionary activities, or, better said, as the chief interpreter of the lessons of Guatemala for the subsequent Cuban case. Arriving in the Guatemalan capital late in January, 1954, after a relatively long visit to Bolivia, he experienced the frantic last months of the Arbenz

[17] Of several recent assessments of the Guatemalan situation, the most balanced and useful is Victor Perera, "Guatemala: Always *La Violencia*," *The New York Times Magazine*, June 13, 1971, pp. 13, 50, 57, 59, 61, 64, and 71–72. A Guatemalan living in the United States, the author estimates deaths from political violence at 4,000 in 1966–1968 and 700 to 1,000 from mid-November, 1970, to mid-February, 1971.

regime, including the government's denunciation of an international conspiracy against it and the intense internal reaction to the Tenth Inter-American Conference held in Caracas during March. Denied employment with the Health Ministry since he was not a Party member, he subsequently may have been appointed to a low-level position in the rapidly expanding agrarian reform agency, although even this direct link to the Arbenz regime is doubtful.[18] Seeking without success to organize armed resistance in Guatemala City, he subsequently found asylum in the Argentine Embassy.

Guevara met some Cuban veterans of the uprising of July 26, 1953, while still in Guatemala, but the most important contact he made during his few months there was with Hilda Gadea Acosta, a Peruvian leftist whom he subsequently married while they were both living as political exiles in Mexico. Paradoxically, he did not meet the Guatemalan who was to have the greatest influence on him until they were both on a train heading for the Mexican border. Julio Roberto Cáceres Valle, whom Che affectionately dubbed "el Patojo" (the Kid) became his intimate friend, working with him during the day as a street photographer and living with him and his wife Hilda in a shabby apartment. The young Guatemalan Communist student did not keep Guevara in close contact with the leadership faction of the Guatemalan Labor Party in Mexico City, for Che soon became more interested in the forward-looking Cuban political refugees than in the Guatemalans, who had shown an unwillingness to fight when the chips were down in June, 1954. By early 1955, Che had met Raul Castro, and he came into contact with Fidel himself in November of that year.

When Castro and his followers came to power in Cuba, they did not ignore the Guatemalan Labor Party's self-criticism of its work in Guatemala. Meeting in Mexico in early 1955, the Guatemalan Communist leaders agreed that they

> had relied too heavily upon the middle class, which had proved unable to withstand "imperialist pressures." Other mistakes which, in their eyes,

---

[18] Ricardo Rojo, *My Friend Che*, New York, pp. 42–63, is the closest we have to a first-hand report on Guevara's months in Guatemala. Che's personal tribute to a Guatemalan friend upon the occasion of the latter's death at the hand of government forces can be found in "El Patojo," pp. 99–103, of Ernesto Che Guevara, *Episodes of the Revolutionary War*, New York, 1968. See also Daniel James, *Che Guevara : A Biography*, New York, 1969, pp. 76–83, and Martin Ebon, *Che : The Making of a Legend*, New York, 1969. Leading Guatemalan Communists such as José Manuel Fortuny and the late Jacobo Arbenz lived in Cuba after Castro came to power and in the early 1960's were paraded out on ceremonial occasions or interviewed on appropriate topics. An interesting Guatemalan ex-Communist leader's perspective on Castro's regime is Carlos Manuel Pellecer, *Utiles Despues de Muertos*, Mexico City, 1966.

contributed to the downfall of the regime included: failure to pay sufficient attention to the army or to effectively neutralize it; allowing the opponents of the regime too great freedom; and expectance that the Organization of American States or UN would act to prevent the "aggression" against Guatemala. In addition the party leaders felt that they had placed too much faith in Arbenz's revolutionary determination. [They] criticized his "typically bourgeois attitude" in underestimating the role which the masses could play and relying too greatly on the army.[19]

If Che or the Castros did not pay attention to these views at the time, they apparently did at a subsequent date, for immediate replacement of the army by a revolutionary militia, rapid implementation of a drastic agrarian reform, and disregard for the sensibilities of the economically comfortable middle class were hallmarks of the 1959–1960 policies of the Castro regime. It seems clear that the orthodox Communists in Cuba, who had contributed significantly to the earlier Communist successes in Guatemala by mediating intra-party rivalries and tactical disputes, drew important lessons from the ultimate debacle.

Perhaps the most disastrous effects of U.S. policy-makers' perceptions of the Guatemalan experience were to be felt in 1965 in the Dominican Republic rather than earlier in Cuba. When faced with the question whether Juan Bosch's restoration to power through the Constitutionalist movement would open the way for Communist penetration of the Dominican political system, the ranking U.S. diplomat on the scene decided that this would indeed be a strong possibility if not a distinct probability. Quite recently arrived in the Dominican Republic, after having headed the State Department's Operations Center, a twenty-four-hour-a-day command post dealing with international crisis situations, William B. Connett, Jr. apparently drew heavily on analysis by analogy with his previous Latin-American experience as chief of the Political Section of the U.S. Embassy in Guatemala in 1956 and 1957. While in that post Connett had engaged in a re-examination of the political dynamics in Guatemala in the period from 1944 to 1954. The lesson which he drew from this was that the non-Communist left in a small, agrarian Central American country was at a decided disadvantage in competing with the more disciplined, better organized, internationally supported Communists. In the case of the Dominican Republic assistance from Communist countries was much closer at hand than had been the case in Guatemala.[20] When President Johnson and Under Secretary of State

---

[19] Schneider, *op. cit.*, p. 319.

[20] The author had an opportunity to talk with Mr. Connett in Guatemala City in June, 1957, at which time he expanded upon this interpretation of the Guatemalan experience. The tone of his cable of April 25, 1965, as Chargé d'Affaires in Santo Domingo (during Ambassador W. Tapley Bennett, Jr.'s

Thomas Mann determined that the Dominican Republic should not become a second Cuba, the stage was set for a direct, preventive intervention using U.S. troops, a reversion to the practices of the pre-1930 period.

In contrast to the Cuban experience, or even to that of the Dominican Republic, the Guatemalan episode has had little direct impact upon the situation in Chile. Although a significant number of Chilean leftists worked in the Arévalo administration and a few stayed on in the Arbenz regime, they were not destined to play any major role in the Chilean Socialist or Communist Parties upon their return home. The U.S. indirect intervention in Guatemala may have marginally reinforced the already dominant view among Chilean Communists that a *via pacífica* offered the most promising path towards eventual power, especially with participation in the elections of 1958 open to them, unlike in 1952. But their participation in a coalition cabinet, after providing the margin for Gabriel González Videla's electoral victory in 1946, was a much stronger factor in this regard. Moreover, throughout the 1960's, the Cuban revolution was an important factor in Chilean politics, with Guatemala all but forgotten. Possessing a relatively strong and deeply rooted Communist Party, one drawing on a substantial urban working class, as well as on an intellectual community many times larger than that of its Guatemalan counterpart, Chile's path towards communism was bound to differ greatly from that of much more underdeveloped Guatemala.

As sharply as Guatemala differs from either Cuba or Chile, it is not so atypical when compared with the other Indo-American countries both in Central America and in the Andean region—particularly Bolivia, Ecuador, Honduras, El Salvador, Nicaragua, and possibly even Peru. While Bolivia's geographic position (bordering on Brazil, Argentina, Chile, Peru, and Paraguay) and Che Guevara's relative familiarity with the country, dating back to 1953, probably go far towards explaining why he selected it as the base for his guerrilla operations in South America, its gross similarity to Guatemala may also have been a factor.

Ironically, Guevara met his death during the collapse of an attempted guerrilla movement in a country in which—perhaps because of the relative absence of investment at the time—the United States had accepted a national

---

absence in the United States) strongly indicates a carry-over of this attitude to the contemporary Dominican situation. Connett's cable is analyzed by Theodore Draper in "The Dominican Intervention Reconsidered," *Political Science Quarterly*, New York, Vol. LXXXVI, No. 1, March, 1971, pp. 1–36, and particularly pp. 5–9. Draper's article serves as a useful introduction to the literature and controversy concerning this U.S. military intervention to gain political aims.

social revolution in 1952 and worked closely with the governments which emerged out of it.[21] In contrast, despite extensive U.S. aid to security forces, Communist-Castroite insurgency in Guatemala has remained alive long after the organization and financing of an armed intervention to "end" a perceived Communist threat there. And Guatemala today has by far the more repressive of the two governments. Add to this the Bay of Pigs debacle and the unfortunate Dominican intervention, and one is forced to ask whether the United States did not read the wrong lessons out of the Guatemalan experience.

---

[21] James M. Malloy, *Bolivia: The Uncompleted Revolution*, Pittsburgh, 1970, is the most comprehensive study of political developments between 1952 and 1964 in that country. For the impact of Che's death on Cuban revolutionary strategy, see James F. Petras, "Socialism in One Island: A Decade of Cuban Revolutionary Government," *Politics & Society*, Los Altos, Calif., Vol. 1, No. 2, February, 1971, pp. 203-224.

Radicalization of a Latin-American State: The Establishment of Communism in Cuba

Boris Goldenberg

In discussing the Cuban revolution it may be best to begin by refuting certain current misconceptions about it. In the main these stem from the attempt to apply the wrong sociological categories to the particular series of historical events that has come to be called the Cuban revolution. Though one could very well maintain that the revolution in Cuba is still going on, this study is limited to the period from 1957 to the spring of 1962—i. e., from Castro's flight to the Sierra Maestra until the purge of the leading old Communists. This period saw what one may call the successful establishment of communism in Cuba, including the emergence of a number of peculiarities distinguishing Cuban communism from official Moscow-oriented communism. No one would deny that Cuba has experienced a genuine revolution—a political, social, and economic transformation more radical than any other in Latin America—but a proper understanding of what has happened requires correctly grasping the uniqueness of the Cuban situation.

Three common views are held about revolution: (1) A revolution is distinguished from a *coup d'état* in that it is looked upon as the work of the masses and not of a minority. (2) Many persons still suppose that revolutions result from the misery of popular majorities who rebel against their fate. (3) There is an inclination to differentiate between revolution and reform by the presence or absence of violence. None of these descriptions fits the case of Cuba. We may, and should, perceive two phases in Fidel Castro's revolution—a democratic phase and a socialist one. But it must be stressed that both phases were the work of small minorities. The masses never played a bigger role than that of a Greek chorus, acclaiming and approving, but not making history. This characteristic sets Castro's revolution apart from other revolutions in the recent history of Latin America, including the Mexican revolution in 1910, the Cuban revolution against the dictatorship of Gerardo Machado in 1933, and the Bolivian revolution in 1952.

An important reason why the masses did not become active in Cuba was that the majority of the Cuban people lived considerably better than most other Latin-Americans. Cuba was one of the most advanced countries of Ibero-America, and the lower strata of its population largely enjoyed a living standard, which, although very poor by comparison with the developed industrial countries, was higher than that of Spain, Portugal, or southern Italy. The dictatorship of Fulgencio Batista had done much to improve the lot of the workers and even in part of the peasants, so that most of them were rather satisfied with their way of life. Besides, the economic situation on the whole was favorable in 1957 and 1958. Thus, Cuba is one illustration of the fact that revolutions are hardly ever born out of mass misery.

Furthermore, though there was some violence in Cuba, it did not reach anything like the proportions of a civil war during the first or democratic phase, and there was practically no resistance to the revolutionary transformation that took place in the second or socialist phase, which was accomplished for the most part peacefully. It might fairly be said that the revolution was *violent* only in its democratic phase and *non-violent* in its socialist phase. But even the violence of the period from 1956 to 1959 should not be exaggerated. After the victory of Castro, the revolutionaries claimed that 20,000 people had died in the struggle against Batista, but this is a ridiculous overstatement of casualties without any basis in fact. The total number of victims from 1952, when Batista took power, until he fled to the Dominican Republic on January 1, 1959, almost certainly did not exceed 3,000, and many of these died committing acts of urban terrorism or wasting in the prisons of Batista. Castro's guerrillas did not number more than 300 in the spring of 1958, and the size of the force grew to some 800 or 1,000 only during the last weeks of the year. Therefore to speak of a civil war is to perpetuate a myth. As a matter of fact nothing like a civil war took place, and Castro was able to take over a country which was in no way destroyed and had a flourishing economy. This circumstance defines an essential difference between the Cuban revolution on the one hand, and the Russian, Yugoslav, and Chinese revolutions on the other, and explains much of what followed in Cuba.

Other misconceptions about the Cuban revolution arise from the attempt to bend what happened to make it fit into ready-made Marxist categories. According to Marx, a democratic revolution is a *bourgeois* revolution, and a socialist revolution is a *proletarian* revolution. Now the term "bourgeois" acquires meaning only if a revolution is directed against feudalism or absolutism. But there was no feudalism in Cuba, as the big plantations were capitalist in character. Neither was there anything like "absolutism." What may be called the "bourgeoisie," i. e., the capitalists and the upper middle class, never lacked influence in the government. It would also be wrong to think that the Cuban bourgeoisie was "anti-imperialist." It had been strongly anti-North American in 1933, but its vast majority was pro-American in the period from 1957 to 1959 because many of the grievances existing in 1933 had disappeared. In fact, the change of government imposed by Castro in the course of 1959, after the deposition of President Urrutia (who had practically been nominated to his post by Castro), was explained by saying that most of the displaced ministers were "pro-Yanqui."

If it does not make sense to speak of the first phase of the Cuban revolution as a "bourgeois" revolution even though the middle class, and especially its younger generation, was among the most ardent partisans of Castro and his guerrillas, it hardly makes any more sense to speak of it as a "peasant" revolution. The majority of Cubans engaged in agricultural production were not peasants but workers, and most of those who could really be considered independent farmers played only a minor role in the overall agricultural effort. Moreover, as was the case in Mexico and Bolivia, neither the agricultural workers nor the peasants became active in the revolution in Cuba, though some young peasants, naturally enough, found their way into Castro's guerrilla forces. Finally, it might be added that nobody has ever presumed to describe what happened in Cuba as a "proletarian" revolution. For all these reasons, it would be a mistake to see the first phase of the Cuban revolution as the uprising of a *social class* or even a combination of classes. It would be equally misleading for the *socialist* phase of the revolution, which very rapidly grew out of the democratic phase, to be characterized in this way. According to Marx, it should have been a "proletarian" revolution, but as a matter of fact it was nothing of the kind. It was imposed from above, by Castro, on a rather unwilling working class which lost its free trade unions, its right to strike, and many of its other advantages and privileges in the process.

The Cuban revolution was not directed by any *party*, either in its initial democratic phase or in its phase of socialist transformation. Castro's "Twenty-sixth of July Movement" certainly cannot be considered a party. It never had a constituting congress, was far from being Marxist, did not have a clear-cut program, and lacked both a defined organizational structure and a dues-paying membership. The Cuban Communist Party, which was founded in 1925, but forced underground by Batista in 1953, originally disdained the young intellectuals who formed the kernel of the "Twenty-sixth of July Movement," viewing them as irresponsible adventurers. The reciprocal attitude of the "Twenty-sixth of July Movement" was antipathy towards the Communists. The first contacts between the two groups date from the middle of 1958, but until the end of that year the Communist group, officially known as the Popular Socialist Party, still looked upon a victory of the Castroists as highly improbable. Instead, the Communists placed their hope in the formation of a democratic "Popular Front" in which all parties and groups inimical to Batista would be united under the banner of democracy. But the majority of these groups, even the ones with a left-wing orientation, had as little sympathy for the Communists as Castro had. This can be explained by a quick glance at the history of the Cuban Communist Party.

The Cuban Communists made their first fundamental mistake in 1933, during the events that led up to the overthrow of the Machado regime. A general strike took place in August, 1933, in which not only the workers but also the middle classes participated actively. Teachers, as well as most bank employees, stopped working, shops were closed, and there was a good deal of unrest among students. Machado seemed lost. He met with leaders of the Communist Party, which had some influence in the trade unions, and offered to make a bargain with them if they would call off the strike. The Communists tried to end the strike, but it went on, and Machado had to flee Cuba. The prestige of the Communists suffered as a result, and Cuban democrats continued to resent what the Communists had tried to do.

Under the provisional government which came to power in 1933 and which was headed by Professor Grau San Martin, the Communists made other basic mistakes. The Grau government was radically nationalist and anti-imperialist, but it was not socialist. The Communists attacked it from the beginning despite its popularity among the middle and lower classes. The government proclaimed a law on the "nationalization of work," decreeing that all people employed in industry, commerce, and banking should be Cubans, fifty percent of them Cubans by birth. The significance of this law was that many workers and employees were foreigners—mainly Spaniards—and unemployment in Cuba was high. But the Communists, acting within the framework of internationalist considerations, objected to the law, condemning the nationalism of the Grau government. This obviously did not make them popular among Cuban workers.

The Communists also attacked the Grau government on additional grounds, usually from a radical Communist point of view, while other elements opposed to the government, including wealthy Cubans and North Americans, criticized it from a more conservative point of view, seeing it as too revolutionary. As it turned out, the Communists found themselves for all practical purposes joined in a "United Front" with forces considered to be reactionary, and were instrumental in contributing to the downfall of Grau in January, 1934. The policy of the Communists in these years explains the split which eventually occurred between them and the anti-imperialist and democratic radicals, who soon were to form an organization called the Cuban Revolutionary Party, otherwise known as the Autentico Party. The split went deep, with the Communists denouncing the most radical among the democrats—people who were indeed very near to socialist positions—as dangerous "social-fascists."

From 1935 on the world Communist movement, including its Cuban branch, pursued the new political line of the "Popular Front." Cuba's government at this time was dominated behind the scenes by the strong man who had emerged from the revolution, Fulgencio Batista. A former sergeant, later promoted to general, Batista had persecuted the revolutionaries in 1934–1935, and they regarded him as an arch enemy. The Communists tried in vain to form a popular anti-Batista front with the same nationalists and democrats they had so violently opposed during the revolutionary upheaval. But when it was evident that the formation of such a front would be impossible, the Communists came to terms with Batista himself, who was eager to rule on the basis of broad support, and wanted to use the Communists to acquire a leftist image for himself. Batista also aspired to be elected President of Cuba in democratic elections. He legalized the Communist Party, which took the name Popular Socialist Party, and gave its leaders control of the trade-union movement. Subsequently, the Popular Socialist Party was included in the so-called Social-Democratic coalition which put forward Batista as its candidate for the elections. Batista was elected President for the term 1940–1944, and later even named two Communists as ministers in his cabinet.

At this time Batista was far from being a reactionary. He not only proclaimed himself a champion of democracy, but laid the ground work for a democratic order in Cuba. Elections were held on schedule, most political parties functioned openly, and the press was more or less free from interference. In addition, Batista fathered a number of social reforms favoring the workers. Nonetheless, the collaboration of the Popular Socialist Party with Batista only deepened the rift between the Communists and the Autenticos of the Cuban Revolutionary Party, to which most of the radical democrats and nationalists belonged, or with which they sympathized. In 1944 the leader of the Autenticos, Grau San Martin, was elected President. He was succeeded in 1948 by another prominent member of the Cuban Revolutionary Party, Carlos Prîo Socarrás. Though the Communists at first tried—not wholly without success—to reach an understanding with the Autentico government, relations between the Popular Socialist Party and the Cuban Revolutionary Party continued to be strained and reached a critical low point in 1947–1948, when the Communists again switched to the revolutionary policies dictated by Moscow.

The Autentico Party had meanwhile undergone a split resulting in the formation of a new, essentially middle-class party. Known as the Party of the Cuban People or more commonly as the Ortodoxo Party, it was led by Eduardo Chibás. The Ortodoxos accused the Autenticos of having betrayed the ideals of democracy. In particular, the Ortodoxos attacked the corruption of the government. Chibás had always been strongly anti-Communist. He was a radical democrat and disliked any kind of totalitarianism. Fidel Castro became a prominent member of the Ortodoxo Party under Chibás and was supposed to run for parliament in the elections of 1952, but the elections never took place because Batista suddenly seized power in a *coup d'état*.

All this suggests why Castro could not have had much sympathy for the Communists in 1952. His antipathy was further aggravated by what happened under the new Batista government. On July 26, 1953, Castro organized an armed attack on the Moncada Barracks in Santiago in eastern Cuba. The attack misfired and dozens of people were killed. Castro was arrested, and at his trial he made a long speech which was to serve as a program for the movement he was later to form. This movement took its name from the date of the attack on the Moncada Barracks. The Communists, whose party was outlawed soon after the Moncada affair, were not slow in criticizing the attack as foolish and characterizing its authors as petty bourgeois adventurers, in accordance with Communist theory. As already mentioned, the Communists maintained a highly critical attitude towards the "Twenty-sixth of July Movement" right up to the victory of Castro at the beginning of 1959. This was true even though a minority of the Communist leadership, headed by Carlos Rafael Rodriguez, seems to have had sympathy for the guerrillas from 1957 on.

This brief historical background explains why Castro cannot be considered a "Communist" if by this term is meant an official, pro-Soviet Communist. Castro was never a member of the Cuban Communist Party. His brother Raul belonged at one time to the Communist youth organization, but was certainly not a disciplined Communist. Neither can Castro be considered an adherent of "theoretical" communism. He had read very little Marxist literature, given little thought to the theoretical and strategical concepts of Marxism-Leninism, and did not collaborate with the Communist Party, for which he had little regard. The Communist Party played a very minor role in the two phases of the Cuban revolution, but Castro soon saw the advantage of being able to use the Communists for his own purposes. Cuba became Communist not because of the work of the Popular Socialist Party, but primarily as a result of certain processes in Castro's mind and in Cuban reality.

Castro rose to power in 1958–1959 because he presented himself as a democrat and proclaimed as his main aim the re-establishment of the constitution of 1940, a document enshrining pluralistic democracy. Batista's government had become more dictatorial and unpopular, and though Castro's partisans were but a small group, they could count on growing sympathy among all strata of the Cuban population. Moreover, though the masses never became active in the fighting, they gave their moral support to Castro. Castro won so easily because the entire military and administrative machinery of the state was infused with the popular feelings and thus could no longer hold Batista in power. The historical background sketched above shows that the Cuban revolution cannot easily be compared with other Communist takeovers. In Indonesia, for example, the Communist effort had its beginnings in the struggle against the colonial government of the Dutch and developed under totally different social and historical conditions. Similarities may exist between the Cuban revolution and other Communist seizures of power, but they are rather misleading.

To state that Castro was a democrat and that he was not a Marxist-Leninist does not, however, mean that he was not a radical, or that he did not desire a profound social transformation of Cuba, even if he was not very clear about how profound such a transformation should be and how he should act in order to realize it. Castro never had a well-defined ideology or carefully elaborated plans. He was a pragmatist, inspired with the vague idea of a "genuine" revolution, and he certainly was not interested in maintaining a facsimile of a capitalist market economy for theoretical reasons. His lack of clear concepts, the vagueness and emotionalism of his ideology, his quest for "social justice," and his nationalism and anti-imperialism explain why he could turn increasingly radical, socialist, and "anti-Yanqui." The flourishing state of the Cuban economy explains why he could satisfy many popular desires and win the confidence of the lower classes for the next, socialist phase of the revolution. As he turned towards socialism, he not only came to terms with the Communists, but also needed them as the only well-organized political force in the country.

To understand why Castro did become a Communist and did impose a radical transformation on Cuban society it is necessary to understand the sort of dialectical relationship that existed between Cuban reality as it was developing at the time and Castro's ideas as they were evolving. Driven by his wish to realize social justice and national independence as quickly as possible, Castro carried out fundamental economic and social changes in Cuba which placed before him the alternative of either halting and entering into compromises with non-revolutionary forces or else going forward towards a state of things that would be incompatible with the maintenance of a capitalist market economy and with friendly relations with the United States. The second alternative, which he chose, led him to undertake further revolutionary changes, and in turn his thinking grew more radical, until finally he arrived at communism, but a very peculiar kind of communism.

The peculiarity of the Castro brand of communism can be illustrated by a series of examples. Castro had promised to punish all the followers of Batista by expropriating their property. But it was nearly impossible to define with any precision who was and who was not a follower of Batista, and the revolutionaries simply began to expropriate factories, hotels, shops, and other commercial undertakings at will. The result was that some six months after Castro's victory there already existed a vast and incoherent "socialized" sector of the economy which did not lend itself to the functioning of a capitalist market economy. Then Castro decreed a reduction in rents ranging from thirty percent to fifty percent, a move that immediately led to the cessation of private building and the threat of extensive unemployment among construction workers. This situation led in turn to what was for all practical purposes the socialization of the building industry. Castro arbitrarily lowered property values, so that a piece of land which had previously been worth, say, $300, was suddenly priced at $30. The result was a total undermining of mortgages. Castro raised wages and salaries considerably, while at the same time he increased taxes on the rich and enforced the payment of tariffs, something which had never been done before in Cuba. The export of capital was prohibited, making the functioning of private enterprise very difficult, if not impossible, since a private enterprise economy, which needs a framework of law, order, and security, was suddenly replaced by revolutionary arbitrariness.

Last but not least, attention must be called to the famous agrarian reform. The original law proclaimed in the spring of 1959 was very radical indeed, and even included some provisions which pointed towards the socialization of agriculture, including the establishment of a powerful state institute of agrarian reform and the creation of co-operative farms. The law also stated that compensation was to be provided for confiscated land, with tribunals set up for this purpose deciding just how much was to be paid in each case. But the law never was put into effect, and out of the agrarian reform rapidly grew an agrarian revolution directed by inexperienced and radical young people who confiscated whatever they wanted without any tribunals being established or any compensation paid. It must be noted that the agrarian revolution was far more radical than even the Communists had proposed in 1960, thus offering additional proof that while collaborating with Castro, the Communists did not really insist their point of view on him or even know exactly what he was planning to do.

At each point along the road towards radicalization, Castro might have chosen to stop but this would have meant going back, a prospect that was alien to his mentality. Lenin had been obliged to abandon War Communism and introduce NEP (the New Economic Policy) because the Russian economy was ruined, but Cuba's economy was intact, with an enormous quantity of goods and resources available. Besides, Lenin was a realist, whereas Castro was a radical voluntarist. For Castro, to go forward at each definite point along the road towards socialism meant multiplying his conflicts with the less radical democrats of Cuba, including those who constituted a majority in the government during the first months of 1959. These functionaries were actually rather powerless, however, for they had been put into their ministerial jobs by Castro himself, and had to govern without an effective administration or the political backing of organized parties. Indeed, Castro was somewhat like a locomotive at the head of a train without any brakes. His radicalization provoked the growing resistance of the United States, which nonetheless did not enter into an open conflict with Cuba until 1960, when most of the revolutionary changes in the country were already under way, if not completed. When Castro nationalized the oil companies at the end of June, 1960, the United States reacted by cutting its imports of Cuban sugar. Castro responded by dispossessing all American companies, and immediately thereafter took over most of the big Cuban enterprises too. As a matter of fact, Cuba was already socialist by October, 1960, or half a year before the socialist character of the revolution was officially proclaimed.

It is impossible to determine exactly when Castro turned finally towards socialism and whether or not the shift was from the first a conscious breach with democracy as democracy is understood in Western societies. What is clear, however, is that he made the move in the course of 1959, or long before the United States turned against him. It would be entirely wrong, therefore, to view Castro's radicalization as a reaction to North American pressure. After a rather brief flirtation with the United States, which took place immediately before and during his visit to America in the spring of 1959, Castro condemned those who seemed to him too "pro-Yanqui," too anti-Communist, or insufficiently radical. He proclaimed anti-communism to be a counter-revolutionary ideology and removed former allies and friends who were anti-Communist from responsible posts, replacing them with Communists or pro-Communists. In July, 1959, this even happened to President Urrutia, whom Castro himself had put in the post of Cuba's chief executive.

The most famous case of a prominent Cuban figure who was purged by Castro is that of Major Hubert Matos. A member of the "Twenty-sixth of July Movement," Major Matos had distinguished himself in the guerrilla struggle and had later been appointed Governor of the province of Cama- guey. In October, 1959, he protested against the growing Communist influence in Cuba, and resigned, together with some of his officers. For this reason only, he was arrested as a counter-revolutionary and subse- quently sentenced by a revolutionary tribunal to a prison term of twenty years. Soon after, leading members of the trade-union movement who were also veterans of the "Twenty-sixth of July Movement" were removed from their posts, even though they had obtained a huge majority in the elections to the trade-union congress which took place in November, 1959. They too were replaced by Communists or Communist sympathizers.

It should be evident, then, that the Cuban revolution had become potentially "Communist" as early as 1959, long before any conflict between Cuba and the United States. It would, in fact, be a mistake to regard the United States as responsible for the split between the two countries, for Castro had long before indulged in many provocative actions and state- ments against "American imperialism." In other words, the reasons for the radicalization did not lie in anything the United States had done. It would be equally mistaken to explain the radicalization as motivated by Castro's desire to receive economic aid from the Soviet Union, which probably would have assisted Cuba if Castro had merely shown his inde- pendence from the United States in the same way that Nasser and others had done. Close contacts between Cuba and the Soviet Union began only in 1960, after the Soviet exposition in Havana and the visit by Anastas Mikoyan, First Deputy Chairman of the USSR Council of Ministers. At first, the amount of Soviet aid was quite modest.

To carry out the radicalization he wanted, Castro had to rely on the cadres of the Popular Socialist Party (i.e., the Communist Party), but this did not mean that the revolution, as it was becoming Communist, was in any way dominated by the Popular Socialist Party or its policies. It has already been mentioned that the Popular Socialist Party was poorly informed about what Castro did and what he intended to do, and that it was, on the whole, rather less radical and more moderate—or, to put it another way, more timid—than Castro. It was Castro who used the Communists, and not the other way round, as the year 1962 was to make clear. In March, 1962, Castro attacked the leaders of the Popular Socialist Party and de- posed the most important figure among them, Anibal Escalante, from the secretariat of the new revolutionary party being formed. Called the Inte- grated Revolutionary Organizations (ORI), this new revolutionary party merged the "Twenty-sixth of July Movement," the Revolutionary Directorate (a radical student organization), and the Popular Socialist Party. Out of the ORI, in which the influence of the Popular Socialist Party was weakened by absorption, there emerged the United Socialist Party of the Cuban Revolution (PURS), which was eventually replaced by the *new* Cuban Communist Party. The new Cuban Communist Party was dominated entirely by Castro, and former members of the Popular Socialist Party made up only an insignificant minority in it. More than a decade after the victory of Castro, the Party has not even had its founding congress and therefore has no existence independent from that of its charismatic leader, Fidel Castro, who continues to dominate the Cuban scene.

Whether the Castro regime can be considered Communist is a question that depends on the definition given to this term. There is no doubt that the regime is a totalitarian system in which all power is concentrated at the top, in Castro's hands; in which all social organizations are directed by him; in which the economy, as well as the whole cultural establishment, including the press and all means of communications, is in the hands of the state; and in which practically no sphere of life remains private for the individual. It is true that certain aspects of the system might be called democratic, and that, indeed, a model of "totalitarian democracy" might be constructed after the example of Cuba. The masses, organized in a multiplicity of groups such as the Committees for the Defense of the Revolution, are forced to be in almost constant activity. If such activity is to be viewed as democratic, then the system is to be viewed as democratic. Furthermore, if equality is to be regarded as a characteristic of democracy, then it must be said that Communist Cuba is more democratic than Cuba has ever been before, for there is no new "ruling class" with special privileges. Educational opportunities exist for all, everyone gets medical care, and so on. But the whole society is directed from above, all citizens are submitted to an unending process of "revolutionary re-education" ("brain-washing," if you want), and they are under constant surveillance. Though in a sense there is more freedom to criticize the regime in private, though there seems to be no postal censorship, and though small numbers are permitted to leave the country (after renouncing all their possessions and working a long time in the cane fields), it is still necessary to speak of a dictatorship which is totalitarian.

In some ways Cuba tries to be more Communist than the socialist countries of Eastern Europe, and is rather more like China in this respect. Moral incentives are prevalent and material incentives looked down upon, there is no room for private economic activity such as that permitted on the peasant plots in most East European countries, and the Cuban government even tries to do away with money. In all this, Castro reveals himself as a voluntarist who is more radical than the orthodox Marxist-Leninists and the revisionist Communists of the Moscow type. Voluntarist radicalism also characterizes Castro's strategic thinking, his *guerrillerismo* as formulated first by Che Guevara and then by Regis Debray in his famous booklet *Revolution in the Revolution*. This concept took the Cuban revolution as a model, but it could not be applied in other countries precisely because the Cuban revolution was unique.

Castro, a gifted leader who was already known in Cuba because of the important role he played in pre-Batista politics, rose against an unpopular and inefficient dictatorship, brandishing the promise of re-establishing a representative democracy. As a result, he was able to count on the sympathy of a growing majority of the Cuban population and on the material and moral support of the upper classes in Cuba and democrats in other Latin-American countries. He even found backing inside the United States administration, which, it might be mentioned, declared an embargo on arms shipments to the Batista regime in March, 1958. Castro's forces were matched against a corrupt and inefficient army which was unwilling to fight seriously, and they did battle in a rather small and homogeneous country, operating from the mountainous region of the Sierra Maestra, which was climatically and topographically suited to guerrilla war. Not a single one of these conditions maintains in other Latin-American countries. Apart from this, counter-revolutionary forces elsewhere in Latin America have learned something from the Cuban experience, making a repetition of it impossible even supposing that other Latin-American armies were as inefficient as Batista's and that the Andes were more like the Sierra Maestra than they are. But even given the likelihood of a revolutionary victory like that of Castro in any other "underdeveloped" country, the subsequent course of the revolution would inevitably be quite different from that in Cuba. It is, therefore, wrong to speak about a Cuban *type* of revolution, because the uniqueness of the circumstances and events in Cuba then get lost in a rather meaningless generalization.

It might, finally, be said that in general the Soviet Union seems not to favor revolutionary tactics such as those propagated by Castro. There would appear to be three reasons for this attitutde. First, Soviet leaders consider these tactics as adventurous and doomed to failure; second, the Soviet Union is interested in maintaining a condition of peaceful coexistence with the United States, and this would hardly be possible if the Russians should overtly meddle with revolution in Latin America; and third, Moscow evidently does not want to dispense the tremendous amount of economic aid that a new Communist state in the Western hemisphere would require, especially since Cuba already costs the Soviet Union so much. In any event, it is not the Russians who make history in Latin America; they have to adapt their policy to the circumstances and events arising there.

It is therefore pointless to ask if the Soviet leadership would have preferred a Nasser-type revolution to Castro's revolution, because it had no choice in the matter. Once Castro had won and Cuba had turned towards the Soviet Union for political and economic help, Soviet leaders could hardly have refused to give it, though only practical experience over a number of years would show precisely what could be done to help Cuba without getting into an open conflict with the United States. The balance was found only after the missile crisis of 1962 and was difficult to keep, for Castro's policy conflicted with that of the Soviets and their Communist friends in the hemisphere, and the conflict became acute in the years 1966 and 1967. To speculate a bit, it would seem that the conflict will become less acute and that the Soviet Union and Cuba will achieve a sort of "revolutionary" coexistence without endangering Cuba, a country which is obviously dependent economically on Soviet assistance. Thus, Castro will be prepared to avoid antagonizing the Soviet leadership seriously in the future and will concentrate more and more on the domestic problems of Cuban development.

The Hungarian Revolution of 1956

Andrew Gyorgy

Major General Béla K. Király, Commander in Chief of Hungary's land forces during the revolution of 1956, rightly characterized the bitter clash between the Soviet Union and Hungary as "the first clash between Socialist states."[1] The Moscow regime has steadfastly denied that the provisional revolutionary government of Imre Nagy was "Socialist," but the fact remains that the Nagy government was composed of lifelong, ardent Communists, who believed in the cause of Marxism-Leninism while attempting to oppose the Soviet Union. Thus the tragic events of October and November, 1956, can well be described as an internecine civil war among Communists, a "counter-revolution" staged by the Hungarians against the Soviet Union.[2]

In historic perspective, there is no question that the takeover of 1956 was entirely different from the Communist conquest of Hungary in 1944–1945. As in the other East European states which became Communist after World War II, in Hungary the earlier revolution was imposed from the outside by the might of the Red Army and spearheaded by Stalin's well-trained advance agents and specialists. In Hungary, moreover, there was nothing indigenous about the takeover, unlike in Yugoslavia, China, Czechoslovakia, Vietnam, and Cuba. A totally devastated and war-torn country, Hungary surrendered without any fighting, yielding as it were to the surgeon's knife like a semi-paralyzed patient. The takeover of 1944–1945 was carried out despite the specific conditions in the country, in a situation in which local factors were largely irrelevant. In truth, it lived up to all the expectations of Stalin's theory of "prefabricated" revolutions "from above," which, for the purpose of this study, is to be interpreted as the imposition by external force of an alien ideology and political system upon a largely non-resisting and apathetic population.

The takeover of 1956 was not only totally different from that of 1944–1945, but also at variance with the two major prototypes for Com-

---

[1] See Béla K. Király, "Stalin's Plan to Invade Yugoslavia," *The New York Times*, December 11, 1970, p. 46.

[2] The author of this article has used the terms "counter-revolution" and "revolution" synonymously. The events in Hungary in 1956 should be assessed as elements of a nationalist, anti-Communist revolt and not as a Communist-led counter-revolution. The concept of a counter-revolution is itself a Communist notion, and must be handled carefully by Western observers.

munist takeovers in the period immediately following World War II—namely, the other military takeovers by the Red Army in such countries as Poland, Rumania, and Bulgaria and the indigenous Communist revolutions in such countries as Yugoslavia, China, and Cuba. Assuming that the details and facts surrounding the events of October and November, 1956, in Hungary are generally known,[3] the two most important questions to be asked are: (1) What external factors helped to set in motion the Hungarian counter-revolution? and (2) What internal factors caused the social, political, and military upheaval that brought heroic "freedom fighters" into direct conflict with Soviet tanks and artillery? In answering these questions it will become clear in what ways this popular uprising was unique, to what extent it was modeled after other revolutions, and—last but not least—how far it has served as a model for subsequent mass revolts against Soviet communism.

The International Scene

Several external factors contributed directly to the revolutionary events in Hungary in 1956. Probably most notable among these was the Soviet Union's general ideological and economic relaxation—popularly referred to as the "New Course"—following Stalin's death in 1953. Revolutions do not erupt in the face of political situations characteristic of totalitarian dictatorships. They come suddenly and unexpectedly, when temporary periods of "thaw" or relaxation occur and the chances of accomplishing popular goals, even if by preponderantly violent means, seem promising and realistic.

In addition to the post-Stalinist "New Course," which sent strong shock waves throughout the satellite countries of Eastern Europe, Nikita Khrushchev's calculated gamble in his "secret speech" of February, 1956, turned out to be poorly timed. The violence with which the incumbent leadership de-Stalinized even Stalin, denigrating both his character and the political system which he so tyrannically represented, astounded the non-Soviet public of continental Europe. Moreover, it helped to launch a process of skeptical re-evaluation of the system—even among the most fanatical Communists—from France to Hungary, Albania, and Bulgaria. Suddenly the mask was torn off the Soviet political élite. Not only was the image of Stalin destroyed; the image of the entire Soviet leadership, including the author of the secret speech himself, stood deflated in the

---

[3] For the best interpretive analyses, see Ferenc A. Váli, *Rift and Revolt in Hungary, Nationalism Versus Communism*, Cambridge, Mass., 1961, and his "Hungary Since 1956: The Hungarian Road to Communism," in *Issues of World Communism*, edited by Andrew Gyorgy, Princeton, N.J., 1966, especially pp. 86–107.

eyes of the public, particularly the non-Communist public, as a result of guilt by association. Instead of enhancing his own image with his pious protestations, Khrushchev succeeded in destroying the myths of Stalinist infallibility and Marxist-Leninist integrity. In Hungary, the de-Stalinization was clearly responsible for a large degree of the political antagonism, literary dissent, and popular unrest that are essential preconditions for revolutions and counter-revolutions. Khrushchev's gamble not only did not pay off, it actually helped to exacerbate the latent dissatisfaction found in both Hungary and Poland, in turn producing a popular backlash in each country.

Poland and Hungary, in this context, offer examples of the external linkage of domestic events. The uprising of the "Poznan workers" in Poland in June, 1956, was carefully studied in Budapest, and it taught the Hungarians a number of lessons soon to be drawn on for revolutionary ends. Even the initial date of the Hungarian uprising (Tuesday, October 23, 1956) is linked to the gathering of Budapest students and workers in front of the statue of a famous Polish military hero, General Louis Bem, to commemorate the four-month anniversary of the Poznan uprising. The crowd moved on from the statue to march in a silent demonstration through the streets of Budapest, and events rapidly escalated from then on until they became uncontrollable. It is important to remember that what happened in Hungary in October, 1956, was closely tied to what happened in Poland in June, 1956.

The irrationality of Khrushchev's de-Stalinization speech, both in substance and timing, was only one indication of the hesitant and confused leadership in the USSR. Again, it is worth stressing the generally deplorable public image of the Soviet political élite at this juncture. Khrushchev's "airport speech" in Belgrade in 1955, in which he humbly apologized to Tito for past Stalinist sins and begged his forgiveness in front of television and movie cameras, was a most undignified performance for a Soviet leader. Later that year, in the course of the Geneva summit meetings, the Khrushchev-Bulganin duo acted in a vacuous and feeble manner. Their subsequent tandem visit to Great Britain turned out to be a disaster, ranging from Khrushchev's drunken performance at a Labor Party reception to the mysterious "frogman" incident. Last but not least, the ideological stirrings within the French and the Italian Communist parties also contributed to the events of October in Budapest. The critical attitude of the French Communists (including Party Secretary General Maurice Thorez), compounded by the public soul-searching of Palmiro Togliatti and his colleagues in Rome, added further to the unrest in Eastern Europe. The deviationist ideological slogans "Polycentrism!" and "Unity in Diversity!" grew out of this international "second-thinking." First articulated by Togliatti and enthusiastically taken up by Hungarian and Polish writers, artists, and moderate ex-Social Democrats, these catch phrases, when forcefully articulated on the eve of revolutionary unrest, were turned into important manipulative weapons aimed against an autocratic system and its vacillating leaders.

The Internal Scene

While these external factors were helping to create unrest in Hungary, domestic events were already propelling the country towards a counter-revolution. It is more difficult to analyze and categorize revolutions "from below" than it is artificially and militarily imposed revolutions "from above," but such a nationalistic counter-revolution as the one that took place in Hungary can usually be seen as the result of two types of preconditions: long-term and short-term pressures.[4]

The following long-term conditions appear to be important in setting off anti-Communist popular uprisings:

1. An essentially unpopular regime antagonizes broad segments of the population under its control by arbitrary rule. Frequently irrational and unfair enforcement of laws and systematic discrimination between first- and second-class citizens (the "class friend" versus the "class enemy") tend to alienate the marginal Communist or non-Communist elements in such a captive society. In this context unpopularity becomes a highly personalized concept: the dissatisfaction and wrath of the population focuses on one or two key members of the leadership who come to stand for all the evils and abuses of the system, which is often too abstract a notion to arouse open violence by itself. In East Berlin, Walter Ulbricht epitomized such unpopularity and in Poland, Boleslaw Bierut and Marshal Rokossovsky. In Hungary, Mátyás Rákosi and Ernö Gerö emerged as the visible targets of the counter-revolutionaries.[5]

2. A constant and all-pervasive threat of police terror helps to incite a dissatisfied population. In one way or another, this has been true of every revolution and counter-revolution of modern times. This terror often diminishes just prior to a mass movement, as it did during the "New

---

[4] The term "usually" is consciously applied here in a restricted sense. What follows is an attempt to compare the uprising in Germany in 1953 and that in Poland in 1956 with the events in Hungary in 1956.

[5] For a discussion of Rákosi's role in Hungarian politics, see Váli, *op. cit.*, and Andrew Gyorgy, *Governments of Danubian Europe*, New York, 1949, *passim*. Rákosi died on February 5, 1971, in Gorky, USSR, but was apparently interred in Budapest. See the obituary in *The Washington Post*, February 6, 1971, "Mátyás Rákosi, Ex-Premier of Hungary, Top Communist."

Course" following Stalin's death, but the threat of its potential reappearance at any time feeds the widespread exasperation and fear which can send the citizenry to the barricades. Just the possibility of a return to Stalinist terrorism was enough to give effective momentum to the tension and anger among the peoples of East Germany, Poland, and Hungary.

3. A protracted failure to relieve the economic difficulties of the population consolidates the rejection of the regime from below. Even if economic conditions improve on the eve of revolutionary upheavals, people are convinced by that time that the government's efforts are too sporadic, too slow-paced, and too limited in scope. Thus the uprisings in East Germany, Poland, and Hungary may also be viewed as "revolutions of rising expectations." The far-reaching impact of economic conditions is obvious in open and democratic societies. In "Iron Curtain" countries its importance is harder to evaluate, but certainly material want is a force that heightens popular impatience and dissatisfaction everywhere. Moreover, people do not easily forget hardship and impoverishment, and are often easily incensed even by the recollection of economic injustices.

4. A growing literary ferment, which takes place against a background of infectious and attractive slogans, builds the case against the regime. With calls for "Polycentrism!" and "Diversity!" such ferment found expression in Hungary in 1956 and in Czechoslovakia in 1968 in a barrage of angry poems, fiery editorials, and protest plays that accompanied the revival of dissenting literary circles. As the intellectual climate of a Communist country improves, these latent forces emerge, frequently displaying a surprising degree of nationalist and anti-Communist aggressiveness, as did the Petőfi Circles in Budapest and the various writers' and students' clubs in Warsaw in 1956 and in Prague in 1968. A demand for cultural and intellectual diversity lies at the heart of this frenzied literary activity, and the ultimatum is addressed to the leaders of the Communist regime.

Without these four long-term conditions the stage would not have been set for the popular counter-revolution in Hungary. But in addition, at least two short-term conditions appear to be important in triggering anti-Communist popular uprisings:

1. As suggested above, it seems necessary for a sudden (and illusory) improvement to take place in the whole national outlook. At least three of the recent revolutionary stands taken in Eastern Europe were closely linked to the period of the "New Course" following Stalin's death, that brief era of socio-economic relaxation which turned popular attention to the silver lining of the clouds, and away from the gathering storm of renewed totalitarian repressive acts. Such unfounded optimism about the possibility

of rapid social and political change led eventually to the unsuccessful attempts at effecting that change by revolutionary means.

2. An irrational and often meaningless small incident seems needed to touch off the revolt itself. This catalytic factor varies from situation to situation. The Polish uprising in June, 1956, began when transport and steel workers protested high prices. In East Berlin in 1953, the spark occurred when the production norms of construction workers were suddenly doubled. In Hungary in 1956, an unusually insulting and ill-judged speech by Ernö Gerö, the Party's second leading spokesman, precipitated the uprising. While it is dangerous to generalize, it would seem that in order for the masses to reach the boiling point such a catalytic incident must occur in each pre-revolutionary situation.

These then were the preconditions for the outbreak of counter-revolution in Hungary and elsewhere in Eastern Europe. As a model for counter-revolutionary failure, the uprisings they germinated suggest three lessons. First, to have a chance of attaining success, the counter-revolution must yield a dynamic revolutionary leader of its own. He should have considerable courage, a good sense of political timing, enormous public appeal, and exceptional speaking and administrative abilities. Unhappily, these superhuman requirements make the sudden emergence of such a figure unlikely. "Events have to make the man," as Sidney Hook has suggested about Lenin.[6] As it turned out, neither the East Germans, the Poles, nor the Hungarians were able to produce a counter-revolutionary hero of these dimensions. Imre Nagy and Wladyslaw Gomulka hardly fulfilled any of the requirements for such revolutionary leadership. Furthermore, the scarcity of charismatic leaders was matched in an inverse ratio by the availability of quisling-type collaborators, who, with the aid of the Soviet military and civilian authorities, managed to displace the popular leaders and reinstitute the *ancien regime*. This is precisely the way in which Imre Nagy was forced to defer to János Kádár and Alexander Dubček to Gustáv Husák.

Second, the chances of these counter-revolutionary regimes for stability and survival on their own are distinctly limited. The difficulty of safe-guarding gains quickly enough in the face of a powerful and oppressive opponent is clear. Freedom, even in a restricted sense, survived for less than seventy-two hours in East Germany in 1953; it lasted no more than twelve to thirteen days in Budapest in 1956. Six to seven months was the limit for Gomulka's Poland of the 1956–1957 period. In a different set of circumstances, Dubček's "Spring in Prague" signaled a brief, eight-month

---

[6] See Sidney Hook, *The Hero in History. A Study in Limitation and Possibility*, Boston, 1955, especially chap. i, "The Hero as Event and Problem," pp. 3–26 and chap. x, "The Russian Revolution: A Test Case," pp. 184–228.

(January to August) respite between two rounds of Soviet-dictated communism. Even in the case of a successful counter-revolutionary coup the
chances of both chronological and ideological survival seem to be slim
at best.

Third, a brief, transitional period of hesitancy and vacillation on the
part of the Soviet Union clearly indicates a debate on whether to intervene
openly and forcibly in order to quell the counter-revolution. This indecision
should not be mistaken for benevolence or regard for world opinion;
rather, it reflects some kind of tugging contest between the Soviet Union's
versions of "doves" and "hawks": military leaders versus civilian politicans,
hardliners agains potential compromisers. Whatever the hidden and
unpublicized reasons, there has been a tactical delay of varying length in
each case of forcible Soviet intervention in East European revolutionary
situations. The delays, marking debate, indecision and the weighing of
relative consequences, have ranged from twelve hours in East Berlin (1953)
to about ten to twelve days in Budapest (1956) and Prague (1968). In
Hungary, the drama was compounded by the open and formal withdrawal
of Russian troops from Budapest on October 25 and 26, only to witness
their surreptitious return in the morning hours of November 4. The Soviet
response in Hungary, which included initial troop concentrations, a subsequent *visible* withdrawal of Warsaw Pact forces, and finally a swift surprise
attack on a fellow Socialist country, was followed in Czechoslovakia in
August, 1968, with improvements and refinements on the part of the Soviet
military. But no resistance was made by Czech "freedom fighters," nor was
there any national mobilization against the invaders. Thus the Hungarian
model, unique in October and November, 1956, remained so despite the
fact that it was copied during the next intra-Socialist bloc intervention in
1968. It would have served as even more of a true model for the Prague
invasion had the Czech civilians and military chosen to resist the Warsaw
Pact forces, or at least complicated the invasion by spirited (even if hopeless)
urban guerrilla fighting.[7]

Reasons for the Soviet Victory in Hungary —
Soviet Attitudes Towards the Second Takeover

The determination of the Soviet Union to keep Hungary within its
sphere of influence was thus the overriding factor in the failure of the
counter-revolution of 1956. Once the Soviet Union had resolved to use

---

[7] For an excellent account of the Czechoslovak events of 1968 and their
historic background, see Tad Szulc, *Czechoslovakia Since World War II*, New York,
1971, especially "Book Four: The Day," pp. 217–374, and "Book Five: The
Night Again," pp. 377–480.

military force, Soviet troops and armor moved swiftly, and in a few days of brutal fighting the attempted revolution was drowned in blood. The reasons for the thoroughness and ease with which this second takeover was accomplished are numerous, but the major external and internal factors that played a role will now be briefly listed.

International events, such as the Suez crisis and the American presidential elections helped to obscure the Hungarian tragedy by calling attention to themselves. Occurring during the first week of November, 1956, they indeed diverted world attention from events in Hungary. The inability of the United Nations to do anything but engage in lengthy moralistic debates and literally talk the issue to death did not further the Hungarian cause. Although far from indifferent, the Western powers were unable to help the revolutionaries, thus making long-term resistance to the Soviet Union impossible. In the face of ruthless military and political intervention by the Soviet Union, other nations had to lapse into the insignificant stance of offering mere moral—or, more accurately, oral—support to the beleaguered freedom fighters of Hungary. The second takeover was accomplished in a manner similar to the first: a single-handed and single-minded occupation was carried out by the dominant power in Eastern Europe, the Soviet Union.

It is also important to note the similar tactics employed in Hungary in 1956 and Czechoslovakia in 1968. In both countries there was a parallel use and exploitation of the Warsaw Pact, as the Soviets retroactively justified military intervention, by invoking their rights under the East European alliance system. Both the intervention in Hungary in 1956 and that in Czechoslovakia in 1968 were supposedly Warsaw Pact operations, although in Hungary only Russian troops were involved in the fighting. In both cases Soviet leaders repeatedly stressed that their troops were invited by local authorities opposed to the counter-revolution. In these ways the interventions were politically alike, except that the intervention in Czechoslovakia in 1968 was dignified by the enunciation of the Brezhnev doctrine. In major operational features, the substantive framework was the same. The fact that the Hungarians fought violently while the Czechs and Slovaks surrendered with relative placidity does not place the Soviet role in a different perspective.

It is also noteworthy that "friendly agreements" were forced upon both the post-revolutionary Hungarian leaders and the post-Dubček collaborators, calling for the long-term stationing of Russian troops on Hungarian and Czechoslovak soil and for a series of political restrictions with the general aim of "normalizing" the situation. In exchange, the Soviet leaders promised in both cases that there would be no direct Warsaw Pact

(Soviet) interference in the domestic affairs of these countries—a promise that was immediately violated and became, in the Czechoslovak case, the basis of lengthy wrangling between occupier and occupied. János Kádár avoided such arguments with his Soviet masters, and proved to be a pliant and enthusiastic collaborator on all points.[8]

Internal factors were equally decisive in undermining the counter-revolution in Hungary. It is a fact that Hungary's already shaky Communist Party—about 900,000 members strong on the eve of the revolution—collapsed and disintegrated almost immediately after it. Yet the obviously weak and hastily formed revolutionary government of Imre Nagy was no substitute. This coalition cabinet suffered from the twin handicaps of the inadequacy of Nagy himself (who lacked most of the leadership essentials discussed above) and from the presence of such potential pro-Soviet quislings as János Kádár and Ferenc Münnich.[9] The word "potential" may have to be amended to read "actual"; even sixteen years later it is not known exactly when these two men were approached by Soviet leaders to subvert the Nagy government and to form a new "Revolutionary Workers' Government," which would be supported by the Soviet occupation forces. What is clearly known is that by Sunday, November 4, when Russian tanks ringed Budapest, Kádár was already firmly established as First Secretary of a new Workers' (Communist) Party and as head of a new and carefully purged "coalition" government.

Other problems among the counter-revolutionaries helped to expedite their downfall. The inexperience of the Hungarian "freedom fighters" was an important one. These men were mostly young workers, high school and college students, and dissident intellectuals. In spite of their lack of training and organization, they fought courageously, many of them literally to the end. When they ran out of ammunition they were forced to surrender. "Molotov cocktails" have little effect against armored divisions using thousands of tanks in inner-city, urban guerilla fighting. Adding to the feeling of frustration and hopelessness was a growing sense of isolation. The total absence of any Western help, except for a few inflammatory

---

[8] For a more detailed discussion of these points, see A. Gyorgy, "Cohesive and Disruptive Forces in Soviet-East European Relations," in *Problems in International Relations*, 3rd ed., Englewood Cliffs, N.J., 1970, edited by Andrew Gyorgy, Hubert S. Gibbs, and Robert S. Jordan. See especially pp. 86–96.

[9] There were no such readily available quislings in Czechoslovakia. The absence of collaborators in Czechoslovakia was amazing and novel to the Russian leaders. Husák did not become Party leader until late April, 1969, which is a time lag of eight months. These months were spent in an unceasing search for collaborators by the Soviets. Furthermore, Gustav Husák is no János Kádár. He is a tough-minded realist and an ardent Slovak nationalist.

broadcasts from West Germany, paralyzed several of the counter-revolutionary nuclei and made further resistance or fighting seem absurd. A final drawback was the weakness of the Budapest revolutionary leadership on the one hand, and the politically disorganized and unco-ordinated nature of the rural and small-city revolutionary centers on the other. Hungarians are excellent fighters and are willing to engage in acts of violent heroics, but they are not noted for cool, long-term resistance movements or for administrative and organizational talents. The revolution was born as a leaderless, spontaneous mass movement expressing a nation-wide grass-roots sentiment, and unfortunately it expired in the same condition: still leaderless and spontaneous, courageous, but utterly lacking in central control and tight organization.

Two final questions remain to be answered. First, was the victory due mainly to domestic or to international factors? From the brief analysis of the various factors listed above we must conclude that it was a peculiar combination of both that helped to defeat the Hungarian uprising. Such far-ranging circumstances as the Suez Crisis, the indecisiveness of the United Nations, and unbeatable Soviet military strength combined to undermine any hopes for a successful counter-revolution. The ready availability of pro-Soviet opportunists and pliable collaborators cannot be overstressed, particularly since several of these masqueraded as ardent Hungarian nationalists.

What was Moscow's attitude towards the second takeover of Hungary? Repressively punitive at first, it allowed for subsequent moments of moderate permissiveness. The repression, in terms of purges, executions, and deportations, is a sad and sordid story known in great detail. The so-called Hungarian question in the United Nations focused world attention on these Soviet abuses and acts of mass terrorism. Yet it must be pointed out that over 200,000 Hungarian citizens were allowed to escape to the West (about two percent of the total population!) via a more-or-less open border. It is also clear that in the sixteen years which have elapsed since these tragic and heroic events, conditions in contemporary Hungary have improved considerably. Although initially considered a traitor of the revolution and of his immediate colleagues, even János Kádár has progressed to the point of exercising a moderate and not unpopular control over his people. Under prevailing conditions (that is, continued Soviet-oriented communism), Hungarians repeatedly assert that Kádár may be their least objectionable alternative. There are some who would go so far as to remark that Hungary lost the uprising of 1956 but in the course of the next sixteen years managed to win the revolution.

The Prague Spring and the Soviet Intervention in Czechoslovakia

William E. Griffith

Ubi solitudinem faciunt pacem appellant. Thus Tacitus on the Roman conquest of Britain.[1] Will this also be the final verdict of history on the Soviet invasion of Czechoslovakia in August, 1968? It is unlikely, I think, but uncertain: we are still too close to the event. Many observers thought, in late 1956, that this would be the verdict on the Soviet crushing of the Hungarian revolution in October, 1956; and yet today Hungary is the most liberalized country in the Warsaw Pact, and János Kádár has performed that rarest feat, the self-rehabilitation of a quisling. On the other hand, the Tsarist suppression of the Polish rebellions in 1830 and 1863 not only kept Congress Poland under the Russian heel until 1914, but it was the kind of Russian domination which only defeat in a world war could bring to an end.

Historical analogies are usually illuminating but never conclusive. This is the more so in the case of contemporary Eastern Europe, since the existence of atomic weapons has not only helped preserve the peace in postwar Europe but has frozen postwar European boundaries and thus made more permanent the Soviet sphere of influence in that part of the world. No power in the West, understandably, is willing to risk nuclear war to displace Soviet control over Eastern Europe. Therefore, as all postwar history has demonstrated, only a drastic weakening of the imperial Russian center, comparable to the defeat in 1917 of Imperial Russia by the Germans, can remove Russian hegemony over those areas of Eastern Europe which the Soviet leadership considers vital to Russian security—an unlikely occurrence.

The developments in Czechoslovakia in the 1960's have often been analyzed, and at greater length than this paper affords, even if that were its purpose.[2] My aim here is different: it is to analyze why the Soviet Union intervened in Czechoslovakia, how it intervened, and what the results have been to date.

---

[1] *Agricola*, 30.

[2] See the annotated bibliography in Robin Alison Remington (ed.), *Winter in Prague*, Cambridge, Mass. and London, 1969, pp. 461–464. Since that bibliography was prepared, the following seem to me to be the most illuminating recent studies: Hanus Hajek, "August 1970: Two Years After," *Radio Free Europe Research*, Munich, August 18, 1970; Heinz Brahm, *Der Kreml und die CSSR*

One cannot understand the Soviet intervention in Prague in 1968, or that in Budapest in 1956 or in East Germany in 1953, unless one views such actions within the context of Russian history. Russia has always been an autocracy, deriving from Byzantine caesaropapism. Its Westernizers have always been defeated by its Slavophiles, and authoritarianism in Russia has always won out over liberalization. Moreover, modern Russia has been a multinational state, and the difference between Great Russians ruling Ukrainians, or Balts, or Georgians and ruling Poles, or Hungarians, or Czechs is seen as only a relative one by the overwhelming majority of the Soviet élite.[3]

Soviet counter-revolutionary interventions have not been the first ones in Russian history in which imperialism and ideological commitment have been combined. Tsar Nicholas I not only intervened in Hungary in 1848 in order to preserve autocracy but also seriously proposed a multilateral intervention in Belgium in 1830 in order to preserve the rule of the House of Orange. One of the principal arguments for the Russian repression of the Polish risings in 1830 and 1863 was that St. Petersburg could not permit the Poles to have more extensive liberties than those few enjoyed by its own Russian subjects. Finally, the whole history of Soviet military interventions before 1968—within or without the Soviet Union—to put an end to developments which Moscow has felt inimical to its policies, from Lenin's ruthless liquidation of the Kronstadt Rebellion in 1921 to the Soviet intervention in Budapest in 1956, has shown that the Soviet leadership is inclined not to abstain from intervention but rather to embrace it, as principle and practice, when convinced that intervention is necessary in order to maintain its rule.

1968–69, Stuttgart, 1970; Antonin Kratochvil, "The Cultural Scene in Czechoslovakia, January-June, 1970," *Radio Free Europe Research*, August 27, 1970; Edward Taborsky, "Czechoslovakia: The Return to 'Normalcy,'" *Problems of Communism*, Washington, D.C., Vol. XIX, No. 6, 1970, pp. 31–41; Adam Roberts, "Socialist Conservatism in Czechoslovakia," *The World Today*, London, Vol. 26, No. 11, 1970, pp. 468–487; Michael Mudry-Sebik, "Czechoslovakia: Husák Takes the Helm," *East Europe*, Vol. 18, No. 5, May , 1969, pp. 2–8; Jan Provaznik, "The Politics of Retrenchment," *Problems of Communism*, Vol. XVIII, Nos. 4–5, 1969, pp. 2–16; Peter Ludzm, "Philosophy in Search of Reality," *Problems of Communism*, Vol. XVII, Nos. 4–5, 1969, pp. 33–42. The most penetrating analysis of the post-invasion period remains, in my view, Pavel Tigrid's *La chute irrésistible d'Alexander Dubček*, Paris, 1970, of which part has appeared in English in *Survey*, London, No. 73, 1969, and Nos. 74–75, 1970. Professors Gordon Skilling and Paul Zinner are now working on major studies of recent Czechoslovak developments.

[3] See the discerning analysis by Richard Pipes, "Russia's Mission, America's Destiny," *Encounter*, London, Vol. XXXV, No. 4, 1970, pp. 3–11.

One may point out, of course, as many Czechs and Slovaks did to me in Prague and Bratislava in June, 1968, that the Soviet Union did not intervene militarily in Yugoslavia after 1948 or in Rumania in the 1960's, and hold that the Soviet Union intervened in Hungary in 1956 only because Nagy had dissolved the Communist Party, reinstated a multiparty system, withdrawn from the Warsaw Pact, and declared neutrality[4]—none of which Czechoslovakia had done, would want to do, or would undertake to do. Therefore, these Czechs and Slovaks argued, they had no reason to fear Soviet intervention. Why were they so wrong?

To answer this question, one must begin by distinguishing between: first, what actually happened in Czechoslovakia from January to August, 1968; second, how the Soviet leadership perceived these developments; third, what probably would have been the consequences of these developments had the invasion not occurred; and, fourth, what the Soviet Union saw as the likely consequences and potential impact of the invasion upon its foreign and domestic policies. For our purposes, Soviet perceptions are more important than realities, but one cannot understand the former without first understanding the latter.

I have analyzed elsewhere[5] what in my view were the main causes of the developments in Czechoslovakia in the spring and summer of 1968, and need only summarize them here. What happened was the collapse of the police terror; the end of the censorship, bringing a wave of criticism of past Stalinist measures accompanied by demands for institutional, systemic changes to prevent their recurrence; the democratization of the Communist Party, including, in the new draft statutes of the Party, official tolerance of factions within it; the growth of interest groups, political and otherwise, besides the Communist Party; the decentralization of the economy; the assertion of autonomy for Slovakia; the improvement of relations with the West, specifically with West Germany; and, finally, the readjustment of relations with the Soviet Union so as to maintain the alliance but end the universal validity of the Soviet model for socialism.

These developments were caused by the economic crisis of the early and mid-1960's; by the destruction of the authority of Novotný and his group because of the economic crisis and as a result of the continuation of de-Stalinization (the group's complicity in the trials of the 1950's was publicly revealed); by the impact of West European prosperity and unity (the technological gap) on Czech aspirations; by the changing attitude of the Czech

---

[4] In my view the best study on the Hungarian thaw and revolution, 1953–1956, is Paul Zinner, *Revolution in Hungary*, New York, 1962.

[5] In my introduction to Remington, *op. cit.*, pp. xi-xx.

and Slovak intellectuals towards the Russians and the Germans; and by the reviving Slovak demand for autonomy. Sociologically, these factors resulted in a recoalescence of the Czech and Slovak intelligentsias and a revival of the traditional Czech and Slovak political cultures. In the case of the Czechs, this implied a primarily nationalistic and democratic posture in the tradition of T. G. Masaryk or, for the Czechoslovak Communist Party, of its first head, Šmeral; in the case of the Slovaks, a primarily nationalistic and authoritarian posture in the tradition of Gustáv Husák. Ideologically, the Prague Spring was characterized by a rigorous, almost existentialist morality; a radical rejection of bureaucratism (indeed, unrealistically, of bureaucracy itself); and a democratic, humanistic socialism, which offered a model for developed European countries.

In Czechoslovakia in 1968, as in Hungary in 1956, a social revolution from below confronted a weak and divided leadership. Its new head, Alexander Dubček, was, like Imre Nagy, a man of honesty and integrity but also of weakness and indecision, a "true believer" in communism who was convinced that he could and would purify and revitalize communism while maintaining, and indeed strengthening, the alliance with the Soviet Union. Neither man was anti-Leninist or anti-Soviet, but both were primarily objects, not subjects, of events. Like Nagy, Dubček was confronted by a social revolution which he could neither understand nor control, and towards which he inevitably was ambivalent: on the one hand, he needed the revolutionary forces as allies against his dogmatic, neo-Stalinist opponents; on the other hand, he had to oppose these forces lest they go further than he wanted or than Moscow, in his view, would permit.

Moscow's perception of these developments was different from Dubček's and *a fortiori* from that of the Czech and Slovak peoples; it was also increasingly negative. At first the Soviet leaders probably realized even less than Dubček and his "progressive" colleagues what was going on. As a result, when they did become aware of it, their disillusionment and hostility was all the greater, and was reinforced by the severe disenchantment and enmity of Ulbricht and Gomulka, who were convinced, and in my view rightly, that if these trends in Czechoslovakia continued, they were bound to infest East Germany and Poland, just as developments in Hungary in 1956 had done. Moscow's disillusionment and hostility must have been intensified still more because the Czechs, unlike the Poles, Hungarians, and Germans, had never been anti-Russian, had no tradition of risings against Russian rule or hegemony, and had—until 1968, and even in 1956—been a near-model of conformity and stability. Dubček's neo-Stalinist opponents at home were working feverishly to turn Moscow against him. The Soviet Union was confronted with a situation in which Dubček and the Czechoslovak Communist Party were gaining more and more popular support by following, *nolens volens*, policies which Moscow considered antagonistic. Anti-Soviet sentiment in Czechoslovakia only increased when the Soviet Union began to exert pressure on the leadership of the Czechoslovak Communist Party in the spring and summer of 1968 to restrain and reverse the Prague Spring. In addition, Dubček had made one move which the Soviet Union regarded as directly menacing: he had obtained the removal of most of the Soviet "advisers" in the Czechoslovak security, intelligence, and military bureaucracies.

On the international scene, Dubček in fact undertook only the most minor, almost timid steps towards *rapprochement* with the West, but the Soviet Union became convinced that this was only the beginning, that Soviet influence in Czechoslovakia was declining, and that Dubček either could or would do little or nothing about it. Moscow was the more concerned because, urged on by Ulbricht and also at that time by Gomulka, it had become increasingly alert to the disruptive effects of the new West German *Ostpolitik*, which, it feared, was being carried on, without its agreement and over its head, *vis-à-vis* the less pro-Soviet East European countries. (That this was not Brandt's intention was not the point.)

Finally, and in the last analysis most important, the Soviet leaders lost all confidence in Dubček and his closest associates, as they had done in Nagy and his followers in 1956. Whether or not they had become convinced that Dubček was deliberately working against them, or only that he was so weak and indecisive that he was "objectively" sacrificing their interests, is not known, nor is it really important. What is evident is that by midsummer they had come to believe that Dubček would always promise to execute their wishes but then would renege on his promises. No effective imperial power can tolerate such a proconsul, and Moscow did not.

Ultimately, then, the Soviet Union became persuaded that the internal developments in Czechoslovakia were moving in a direction that not only imperiled Communist rule there, but also called into question the whole Soviet model for socialism and did so in such a way as to jeopardize the stability of Soviet control over Poland and East Germany, and even over the Ukraine inside Soviet borders. The Soviet leaders were persuaded, moreover, that the internal developments in Czechoslovakia were bound to have certain implications for Czechoslovak foreign policy, with the probable result that not only would Soviet influence in Czechoslovakia decline but also would gradually be replaced by Western—and specifically by West German—influence within a context in which the Soviet Union had not come to an agreement with West Germany. The balance of power in a key area of their European imperium would, they believed, shift decisively against them and in favor of Washington and Bonn—a development they were not prepared to tolerate.

Clearly, Dubček did not anticipate the Soviet invasion. Until almost the last moment, conversely, the Soviets hoped that it would not be necessary. It is likely that there was some opposition to the invasion in the Soviet leadership, quite possibly centering around Suslov and Shelepin, but the final decision in Moscow was probably unanimous. The efforts of the Communist Parties in Western Europe, and of Kádár, to prevent the invasion succeeded, at best, only in postponing it. Moscow was, one may assume, aware of the losses it would suffer in the promotion of international communism—in Western Europe, Australia, and Japan, and to a lesser extent in the underdeveloped world—as a result of the invasion. It must also have known that the invasion would interrupt, at the least, the negotiations and the partial *détente* with Washington, but it correctly calculated that these losses would only be temporary. Bolsheviks have always preferred being respected and feared to being loved, and the present Soviet leadership is particularly suspicious of the West and of liberalization at home.

The Soviet invasion was a brilliant military success, and over the next two years its initial political failure was converted by Moscow into the realization of its political objectives. Militarily, the Czechs had neither expected the invasion, nor had they any intention of fighting if it were to come; the deployment of Soviet forces was rapid and complete.

From the viewpoint of the Soviet leaders, the invasion was initially a political failure for three reasons. First, contrary to their expectations, their supporters did not obtain a majority in the presidium of the Czechoslovak Communist Party on the eve of the invasion, and thus were not able to make an official plea for Soviet intervention. Second, after the Soviets had dragged away Dubček and his closest associates, the pro-Soviet leaders went to see the new President, General Svoboda, to demand that he appoint them heads of a new government, but Svoboda refused and demanded to be allowed to go to Moscow to negotiate directly with the Soviet leadership. Third, these first two developments, and the passive resistance of the population, led by students and intellectuals and co-ordinated in an amazingly effective fashion by the mass communication media, strengthened the hand of the Czechoslovak Communist Party leadership and for a time prevented the Soviets from winning the support of any significant collaborators. Indeed, the initial drama and effectiveness of this passive resistance, particularly as communicated to the West by television, caused many Western observers, not all of them pacifists, to think that it could effectively prevent the Soviet

Union from restoring complete control over the country. Subsequent events, however, have shown that this view was a mixture of hope and sentimentality.

The Soviet Union had already shown in the negotiations in Moscow late in August, 1968, what its tactics would be: to divide and then eliminate the Dubček group. Svoboda and Husák had already taken a more compromising position in Moscow than had Dubček and his other associates. The subsequent Central Committee plenum in Prague reluctantly endorsed the Moscow agreement and limited somewhat the freedom of expression of the communication media; otherwise, the "progressives" remained in control.

But this was not to last. The Soviet Union pursued its tactics of first splitting and then disposing of the progressives, and of constantly encouraging the dogmatists in their struggle towards the same end. Soviet "salami" tactics were reminiscent of Rákosi's prescription in 1949. In September, 1968, and thereafter, the Dubček leadership was persuaded or forced to co-operate in preventing the Czechoslovak issue from being raised at the meetings preparatory to the international Communist conference to be held in Moscow in June, 1969. More importantly, at the plenum in November, 1968, Dubček joined Husák and Svoboda in distancing himself from Smrkovský and the other progressives, thus furthering Soviet objectives. This process continued thereafter. At the plenum in January, 1969, Husák succeeded in displacing Smrkovský as president of parliament by insisting that a Slovak occupy the position, and censorship was re-established. The key crisis occurred in April, 1969, when the Soviets used a riot in Prague after a Czechoslovak victory over the Soviets in a hockey game as a pretext to get rid of all the liberals in the presidium and to have Dubček replaced by Husák as First Secretary. Thus, the centrist group itself was split, and Husák and the moderate conservatives took over. Since then, the purge has continued: the progressives were removed from the Central Committee and replaced by Novotnýites and proponents of the Soviet invasion. The process culminated in June, 1970, with the expulsion of Dubček from the Czechoslovak Communist Party.

Has, then, the victory of the dogmatists been complete? No, no more than was the case with the Rákosites in Hungary in 1957. Husák was able to preserve some remnants of the gains made in 1968. There were no mass arrests or political trials, even of the most extreme liberals (one which had been scheduled was postponed in late 1970); the great mass of the intelligentsia and the Party liberals refused to confess and make self-criticism; and police measures were not used to force them to do so. Cold comfort, but something.

Otherwise, however, winter in Prague is cold and dark indeed. The overwhelming majority of the gains made in 1968 were reversed. Husák and the Czechoslovak Communist Party welcomed and endorsed the invasion and the "Brezhnev doctrine" of limited sovereignty. Most of the Novotný dogmatist clique returned to power, although not entirely to predominance. Strict censorship was reintroduced; the heads of the élite and mass communication media were ruthlessly purged and replaced by dogmatists; and conformity reigned supreme. The legal system was re-politicized, demonstrations were suppressed, and their leaders persecuted. Cultural life in general—literature, the creative arts, and education—was purged and returned to a rigid neo-Stalinist mold. (Here, too, however, the overwhelming majority of spokesmen fell silent and refused to conform.) The purge of the intelligentsia within and without the Party was massive indeed: all those who had exposed themselves in 1968 and who refused to confess and conform were condemned to manual labor, if indeed they could get that. The economy was largely recentralized; the economic reformers were denounced and purged; foreign trade was reoriented towards the Council for Economic Mutual Assistance (Comecon), and particularly towards the Soviet Union; and the moves made in 1968 towards workers' self-management were reversed.

Of all the gains of 1968, aside from the absence of police terror and trials, the only one which partially remained was Slovak autonomy, presumably in large part because of Husák's Slovak nationalism, but also because in 1968 liberalization had been overshadowed by nationalism in the Slovak part of the Republic. Even this autonomy, however, though preserved to a considerable extent in theory, was greatly limited in practice by the recentralization of the Party and economy in Prague.

Czechoslovak foreign policy again became completely conformable with Moscow's. All attempts to resume political and economic ties with the West on any other basis than that approved by Moscow were abandoned. This was particularly true of any resumption of ties with West Germany. In fact, the invasion of Czechoslovakia was largely responsible for the decision of the Brandt government to give priority to an agreement with Moscow before agreements with the East European allies of the Soviet Union. Thus, at the end of 1970 the signs that Bonn would shortly begin negotiations with Prague on the re-establishment of diplomatic relations were the result of, rather than being undertaken independently of, the agreement between Bonn and Moscow. The foreign policy aims of Moscow in invading Czechoslovakia had in the course of time been as successful as its aims within the re-subjected country itself.

And what of the future? In my view the Prague Spring (not of Dubček and his associates but of the intelligentsia which was leading it) was moving rapidly in the direction of social democracy at home and of a semi-Finnish policy abroad: that, is, of maintaining a primary alliance with the Soviet Union, but of also improving political and economic relations with the West. Brezhnev, Gomulka, and Ulbricht were correct in believing that these developments would indeed have endangered the political systems in East Germany and Poland, and, eventually, in the Soviet Union itself. As Thucydides had Cleon say of the Mitylenians:

> If they were right in rebelling, you must be wrong in ruling. However, if, right or wrong, you determine to rule, you must carry out your principle and punish the Mitylenians as your interest requires, or else you must give up your empire and cultivate honesty without danger.... Punish them as they deserve, and teach your other allies by a striking example that the penalty of rebellion is death. Let them once understand this and you will not have so often to neglect your enemies while you are fighting with your own confederates.[6]

To say that Dubček wanted a purified Leninism is true but irrelevant: for he was swept along by, but did not control, events, and in any case it is very doubtful, particularly in a developed country like Czechoslovakia, with a democratic tradition, whether "purified Leninism" or revisionism can become stable. It is much more likely to evolve rapidly into social democracy. What Dubček and his associates seem to have envisaged was a Communist Party which would lead but not command, inspire but not dominate, and set policy by persuasion and education rather than by compulsion and "administrative measures"—in short, an élite of philosopher-kings whose authority and legitimacy would be recognized by the intelligentsia and the masses. Moreover, Dubček and his associates seem to have relied upon a universal consensus to prevent attacks on the Soviet Union and the other East European socialist states. There is no doubt that the Czechoslovak Communist Party greatly increased its prestige during 1968, but it did so at the price (for Moscow an unacceptable one) of following, rather than commanding, the intelligentsia. Indeed, such liberal figures as Smrkovský, Slavík, and Mlynár were probably, from a sociological viewpoint, at least as much a part of the reformist intelligentsia as of the Communist Party leadership. Though the overwhelming majority of the intelligentsia probably recognized the necessity of not unduly offending the Soviet Union, what they thought would, or should, offend Moscow and what Moscow found unacceptable were very different indeed. Finally, there was a minority, within and—to a greater extent—without the Czechoslovak

---

[6] *History of the Peloponnesian Wars*, III, 40 (tr. Crawley).

Communist Party (such a figure as Sviták, for example), who were for liberty *à outrance*. They were not prepared to remain silent for the sake of *raison d'état*; the revisionist heads of the communication media were not prepared to silence them; and there was no censorship or mechanism by which the Communist Party could or would silence them.

In my view, then, if Brezhnev, Ulbricht, and Gomulka wanted to keep their political systems intact and were unprepared to make major, systemic changes in them, they were, given these policies, quite right in invading Czechoslovakia. *Tertium non datur*. Furthermore, although Soviet political bungling in August, 1968, prevented them from initially attaining their political objectives, they could afford to bungle, and Dubček and his associates could not, any more than Beneš and his associates could in 1938 or 1948, or for that matter the Melians *vis-à-vis* the Athenians. For once the Red Army had overrun Czechoslovakia, the Soviets had only to pursue vigorously their policy of *divide et impera* in order to gain their objectives.

One must, therefore, turn next to two questions with respect to Dubček and his associates. First, what if anything could they have done before or during the invasion to prevent it or change its outcome? And, second, what if anything could they have done after the invasion to avert the re-establishment of total Soviet control? Was, in short, the Soviet counter-revolution both inevitable, and inevitably successful?

Before the invasion, the only thing that Dubček and his associates could have done (and the only thing that Nagy could have done in Hungary in 1956) was to restrain—by a combination of persuasion, authority, and, if necessary, force—those elements that most directly challenged the Soviets. On balance, it seems highly unlikely that Dubček and his associates could have done so. They were followers, not leaders; they needed the revisionists against the dogmatists; and they, like all other Czechs and Slovaks, greatly overestimated Soviet tolerance, and could not imagine that the Red Army would march in. Finally, it is even doubtful whether Dubček could have restrained the Prague Spring even if he had wanted to, for he would probably have been swept away, at least after April, by the social revolution taking place.

The most difficult question to answer, and one which an outside observer like this writer touches on only with great diffidence, is whether the Czechs and Slovaks should have fought when the Red Army invaded. That they did not, considering their history, is not at all surprising, just as it would be surprising if the Yugoslavs, given their history, would not fight if they were invaded. The Czechs last fought to defend their independence in 1620, when they were defeated by the Austrians in the Battle of the White Mountain. They did not fight in 1938, they did not fight in 1948, and it is therefore not surprising that they did not fight in 1968.

Yet, by not fighting, and therefore, in my view, inevitably falling prey again to neo-Stalinism and Soviet domination, the Czechs suffered a shock to their national pride and indeed to their national identity that was perhaps even greater than in 1938 or 1948. After all, they had always hated and feared the Germans, and the long-range result in foreign policy of the Munich crisis in 1938 was the disillusionment of the Czechs with Britain and France. In the inter-war period, the Communist Party had always been viewed as a national party in Czechoslovakia, not as a group of Soviet agents; it had received the highest number of votes in the free elections of 1946; and its takeover in 1948 was supported by large elements of the leftist intelligentsia within and without its ranks. What is more, the Czechs had always been pro-Russian. Russia, they felt—whether rightly or wrongly is another matter—had not deserted them in 1938; it had liberated them from the Nazis in 1945, and thus prevented their intelligentsia from being killed and their masses from being Germanized or enslaved; it had always preached proletarian internationalism; and, they were convinced, they had no intention of breaking their alliance with the Soviet Union. Thus in Czech and Slovak eyes, in 1968 Moscow joined hypocrisy to imperialism in invading their country.

Had they fought they clearly would have been overwhelmed. Prague, that almost uniquely preserved jewel of Central European cities, might well have been largely destroyed. Their leaders would, like Nagy and his associates, probably have been executed, if they had not fled. The resultant terror would probably have been much worse than it has been since the invasion. For one should have no illusions that Moscow would have been deterred by Czech resistance from destroying them; on the contrary, fighting would have made their destruction certain. The Czechoslovak Communist Party would have been largely wrecked and then re-established, as in Hungary in 1957, becoming an even smaller and more dogmatic clique than it now is. Yet from the point of view of communism in Czechoslovakia, it would not be nearly as discredited; on the contrary, it would have at least the beginnings of a heroic tradition. So, more generally, would the Czech and Slovak people. Moreover, had Dubček convinced Moscow before the invasion that he would fight, instead of making it quite clear to them that he would not, perhaps Moscow would not have invaded. All in all, then, one can make a good, although not necessarily a convincing, case that the Czechs and Slovaks would have been better advised to fight.

Finally, what if anything could Dubček and his associates and the Czechoslovak people have done, once the invasion had been militarily successful, to have prevented the re-establishment of Soviet domination of the country? Very little, it would seem. The popular passive resistance was doomed from the start. The Soviets had only to wait it out and use their Czech and Slovak collaborators to suppress it. Passive resistance worked against the British in India because the British people, and therefore the British government, were unwilling to use the degree of force necessary to repress it. The Soviet leadership has not, and never has had, any such compunctions. When Lenin had crushed his own people in the Kronstadt Rebellion, why should Khrushchev not have done the same against East Germans and Hungarians, and Brezhnev against Czechs and Slovaks? From what we know of sentiment in the Soviet Union about the invasion of Czechoslovakia, opposition to it seems to have been confined to a small group of intellectuals; the majority of the Great Russian intelligentsia, and certainly of the masses, probably supported it. But this is not surprising either: the same was the case with the Tsarist suppression of the Polish rebellion in 1863, when Alexander Herzen found himself isolated and vilified for his support of the Poles; and Pushkin, otherwise anything but a reactionary, wrote a poem denouncing the 1830 Polish rebellion:

> What are you clamoring about, bards of the people?
> Why do you threaten Russia with your curses?
> What has aroused you? The disturbances in Lithuania?
> Leave that all alone: it is a quarrel of Slavs among themselves,
> An old domestic quarrel already weighed by Fate,
> A question which you will not solve.
> ....
>
> Who will survive in the unequal conflict—
> The arrogant Pole or the true Russian?
> Shall the Slav streams merge in the Russian sea?
> Shall it dry up? That is the question
> ....
>
> Leave us alone: you have not read
> These bloody tables; this family
> Animosity is incomprehensible and strange to you; ...
> You are senselessly attracted by all that is valiant
> In the desperate struggle
> And you hate us ...
> ....
>
> You menace us with words—just try to act![7]

---

[7] "To the Slanderers of Russia" (tr. John Fennell in *The Penguin Pushkin*, New York, 1964).

Dubček could not have counted on the Russians relenting. On the contrary, their pressure on him was bound to increase. Nor was it likely that he could have kept his associates united and loyal to him. He had been a compromise choice as First Secretary, voted for by many exactly because he was felt to be weak and indecisive, and therefore unlikely to make any major changes. Already in the Moscow negotiations in August, 1968, Svoboda and Husák had begun to distance themselves from him. He was prepared to sacrifice his more liberal associates in the hope of saving what he could. The eternal argument of collaborators—*pour éviter le pire*.

But this is not the whole story. Two final factors must be taken into consideration: the possibilities of eventual liberalization in Czechoslovakia parallel to what has occurred in Hungary since the mid-1960's, and the eventual legacy of the events in Czechoslovakia in 1968 in the decades to come. As to the former, Gustáv Husák certainly does have some parallels to János Kádár. He is a prewar, "native" Communist, who was imprisoned under the Stalinist regime and is desirous of avoiding a return to Stalinist terror. (Unlike Kádár, however, he is an intellectual, but he is also more dogmatic and inflexible). He has been waging a struggle on two fronts, as Kádár did: against the revisionists and the neo-Stalinists. He is probably a Czechoslovak, and certainly a Slovak, patriot. He is ambitious; he can be ruthless; and he is certainly limited to the Leninist framework. Yet he, too, probably feels that he is following the only policy, given the invasion, which offers any possibility of eventual improvement for Czechoslovakia. He is, unlike Dubček, not weak; on the contrary, he is strong and scheming. He never shared the views of the progressives in the Czechoslovak Communist Party in 1968: he is authoritarian by temperament, training, and experience. He has clearly given priority to re-establishing the Soviet leadership's confidence in his person and in his leadership. It may be, but it is too early to tell, that perhaps five to ten years from now he will be willing and able and get Soviet approval to launch the kind of limited, primarily economic liberalization that has occurred recently in Hungary. Moreover, the Czechs and Slovaks, like the Hungarians, have had their lesson as far as Soviet tolerance is concerned; they are unlikely to defy Moscow again in this generation. Indeed, in Eastern Europe, Czech tradition is probably, except for the Germans, uniquely adaptable to the kind of long-range passive survival which kept them a nation from 1620 to the end of the eighteenth century—a tradition, like that of the *Ausgleich* in Hungary, which gives them some justification, *faute de mieux*, for co-operation, if not collaboration, with the inevitable. Yet in the long run there is, as 1968 showed, much more potential for uncontrolled liberalization leading to social democracy in Czechoslovakia, a developed Central

European country with a strong democratic tradition, than in more agrarian Hungary, which has never enjoyed a functioning democracy. One should thus be cautious in assuming that Prague will necessarily go the way of Budapest.

Finally, the Prague Spring, its "socialism with a human face," will not soon be forgotten, within or outside of Czechoslovakia. It was a dream probably doomed to destruction from the beginning. It was in many respects romantic, and in many aspects of its ideology almost irrelevant to the bureaucratic society of our industrial era. Yet for a few months it revived the belief of many leftists, in and out of the country, that a new, humanist model of socialism was possible. That the Soviet Union so ruthlessly crushed it has been an immense and lasting blow to Moscow's already tarnished claim to be the center of a genuinely socialist and internationalist world movement. That, up to now, its main exponents have consistently and heroically refused to recant has kept its luster alive in the midst of its destruction. Idealism has been frequent in Czech history. It has normally, except in the First Republic, been cruelly deceived and frustrated. It is probably now not too fashionable in Prague. But in the perspective of generations to come it is not something to be dismissed too lightly. Certainly the memory of the centuries-long struggle of the Poles played a role in their partial regaining of independence in 1956. Certainly the memory of the wartime partisan struggle played a role in the clear determination of the Yugoslavs in 1948 to fight if the Soviets invaded them, and thereby contributed greatly towards the Soviet decision not to invade.

If nothing else, the invasion of Czechoslovakia in 1968 ended the centuries-long tradition of pro-Russian feeling in that country, and provided an idea, with a group of exponents, to which for generations to come Czechs and Slovaks will look back with pride and honor. Such achievements cannot be quantified or their future impact predicted. But that they will play a significant role, some day, in the future history of the Czechs and Slovaks can already, it seems to me, be taken for granted.

The Sources of Communist Political Power in Kerala

Gerald Heeger

A democratically elected Communist government assumed power in Kerala on April 5, 1957. The swearing-in of a Communist ministry was watched with gloom by a number of observers, for in the example of Kerala, many saw portents of the Indian future. Kerala had turned to communism first, so it was argued, only because the problems endemic to all of India were particularly great in that state. Kerala had the highest unemployment rate in India and the lowest per capita income. Kerala's birth rate was (and continues to be) the highest in India, while its population density averages over 1,100 per square mile. The average landholding in Kerala, which is one of the smallest states in India, is 1.9 acres, as compared with 7.5 acres for the country as a whole. The explosiveness of Kerala's economic situation seemed to be heightened by the fact that it also possessed the most educated and, by implication, the most politically aware population in India.

The gloomy predictions have not been fulfilled. The variables of poverty, of pressure on land, and of growing literacy have—to different degrees —been replicated elsewhere in India and have produced little long-term support for the Communists. More important, the Communists in Kerala have been just as susceptible as the other political parties to shifts within the political system of the state.

Many students of Indian politics have, as a result, come to view the growth of communism in Kerala as simply the result of the particular communal rivalries which have characterized the state. The Communists, in this view, are less a Communist Party than an Indian party, and it is the Communist Party's operation as an Indian party—in particular, its existence within a framework of caste and communal conflict—that yields the clue to explaining its success.

Such explanations may be as erroneous as earlier explanations. While communalism is a primary characteristic of politics in Kerala and is critical to an understanding of the basis for Communist support in the state, the electoral success of the Kerala Communist Party in 1957 was not simply the result of inter- and intra-community coalitions. The Communist Party in Kerala may be said to be unique in that it was Communist and, as such, was concerned to formulate particular political programs and particular political tactics consistent with an overriding ideological formula.

Party-Building in Kerala

Despite efforts to make typological distinctions between various political parties in India, the processes of building a party and mobilizing electoral support continue to be analyzed in terms of the pattern established by the dominant actor in the Indian political system, the Congress Party. The successes of the Congress Party are attributed to the willingness of its leadership to accommodate a diversity of groups, with little or no concern for ideology. That is to say, the Party aggregates support by means of accommodation and co-optation instead of mobilizing support through ideological fervor. Accordingly, the electoral victories of opposition parties and the emergence of non-Congress party governments are generally explained as beating the Congress Party at its own game, i.e., as having simply aggregated communal group support more effectively.

Such an analysis is inadequate for an understanding of the Communist successes in Kerala. Communal alignments were an important ingredient of the Communist victory in Kerala in 1957 and continue to be a critical element in determining the fortunes of the Kerala Communist Party, but the Communists in Kerala operate within an ideological as well as a social environment. It is with reference to this environment that the Kerala Communist Party derived the tactics making it the preponderant political organization of the left in Kerala.

Origins of the Kerala Communist Party:
The First United Front

Kerala was created as a Malayalam-speaking linguistic state in 1956, combining most of the territories of the former princely states of Travancore and Cochin with the Malayalam-speaking portion of the state of Madras (now Tamil Nadu). Communism in the area, as a result, has diverse origins. In the states of Travancore and Cochin, trade-union activity and agrarian unrest provided the major vehicles for Communist growth. While such activities played a role in Malabar as well, the Communist Party there emerged primarily as a linear descendent of the Indian National Congress movement.

Communists in the Malayalam-speaking area and in India in general were relatively disorganized throughout the 1920's and 1930's. There was no Communist Party center, and the Party, as such, was merely an amalgam of local groups. Even after a "Platform of Action" was adopted by the Indian Communist Party when it became affiliated with the Comintern (the Communist International) in 1930, the overall pattern of organization remained minimal.[1] More damaging than this weakness, however, was the growing isolation of Indian Communists from the Congress-led nationalist movement. Following the Comintern recommendation in 1930 that the Indian Communist Party "sever contact with the National Congress . . . and show [Congressmen] up . . . as assistants of British imperialism," Indian Communists formally broke with the Congress.[2]

In 1935 this isolationist trend, which had been established during the "leftist" Sixth World Congress of the Comintern, was reversed. At the Seventh Comintern Congress, the Indian Communist Party was accused of left-sectarianism and criticized for isolating itself from the general population.[3] The Comintern instructed Indian Communists to join mass, "anti-imperialist" movements headed by nationalists and to seek to initiate a "united front" of Congress and Communist groups.[4] The united front which ultimately resulted was a coalition of Communists and the Congress Socialist Party, a leftist "pressure group" organized in 1934 within the Indian National Congress. Although the Congress Socialist Party had adopted leftist unity as a primary purpose of its organization, the hostility of the Communists towards the Socialist group had previously kept the two parties apart.[5] The Comintern shift away from isolationist tendencies and the hesitant endorsement of the new line by the Indian Communist Party brought the two groups together. After extensive contact between Communist and Socialist leaders, the Congress Socialist Party formally committed itself to a united front.[6] The front was simultaneously one "from above" and "from below," i.e., at Socialist initiative the front linked the two parties as separate entities and admitted individual Communists to membership in the Congress Socialist Party.[7]

The Congress Socialist Party was particularly important in Malabar. Malabar district provided the nucleus of the Congress movement in the Malayalam-speaking area (the Congress movement was not officially organized in the princely states of Travancore and Cochin), and it was under the auspices of the Malabar Congress organization (called the Kerala Provincial Congress Committee) that most of the activities and conferences of the Con-

---

[1] T. P. Sinha, *The Left Wing in India, 1919–1947*, Musaffarpur, 1965, p. 245.

[2] *Ibid.*, p. 249.

[3] *Ibid.*, p. 419.

[4] *Ibid.*, p. 420.

[5] Jayaprakash Narayan, *Socialist Unity and the Congress Socialist Party*, Bombay, 1941, p. 2.

[6] Jayaprakash Narayan, *Towards Struggle*, edited by Yusuf Meherally, Bombay, 1946, pp. 169–170.

[7] Minoo Masani, *The Communist Party of India*, New York, 1954, pp. 67–68.

gress movement were held. Trade-union and peasant activists and young Socialists were particularly influential in the Malabar Congress, and by 1934, had emerged as the leading elements in the Kerala Provincial Congress Committee. When the Congress Socialist Party was formed as an all-India body, the Kerala Provincial Congress Committee was the only subsidiary Congress group dominated by members of the Congress Socialist Party.[8]

The united front strategy stimulated both Communist penetration into the Kerala Provincial Congress Committee and co-optation of major Kerala Socialists by Communists. As a result, the Socialist-dominated Kerala Provincial Congress Committee provided the basis for Communist organization in Kerala. It is not wholly clear whether the major Kerala Communist leaders were Communists prior to the united front period, although some undoubtedly were. Biographical sketches of many Kerala Communist leaders link them to the Communist Party during the early 1930's.[9] Other leaders such as E. M. S. Namboodiripad, who became the first Communist Chief Minister in Kerala in 1957, were not officially tied to the Communist Party until 1939–1940.[10] Most of these leaders were, however, active in the Congress movement. A. K. Gopalan joined the Congress Socialist Party in 1935 and was president of the Kerala Provincial Congress Committee.[11] Namboodiripad was one of the national joint secretaries of the Congress Socialist Party when it was formed in 1934 and later served as secretary of the Kerala Provincial Congress Committee.

Control of the Kerala Provincial Congress Committee gave the Congress Socialists and in particular the Communists room for a wide range of political activities. According to Namboodiripad, Communist and Socialist activists succeeded in organizing a considerable number of trade unions in Malabar through the various Congress committees.[12] Communist peasant activists, acting as Congress "volunteers," sponsored peasant conferences throughout the area.[13] Perhaps more important, the leftist-led Kerala Provincial Congress Committee succeeded in gaining control of the important local Congress Committees in the area.[14]

---

[8] K. P. Karunakaran, "Social Background of Political Radicalism in Kerala," in Igbal Narain (ed.), *State Politics in India*, Meerut, 1965, p. 163.

[9] See Gene D. Overstreet and Marshall Windmiller, *Communism in India*, Los Angeles and Berkeley, Calif., 1959, pp. 555–575.

[10] *Ibid.*

[11] *Ibid.*, p. 563.

[12] E. M. S. Namboodiripad, *Kerala : Yesterday, Today, and Tomorrow*, Calcutta, 1967, p. 163.

[13] *Ibid.*, p. 164.

[14] *Ibid.*, p. 167.

Communist activities in the native states of Travancore and Cochin focused on trade unions, agrarian associations, and general demonstrations against the state governments. A Communist League was formed in Travancore in 1931–1932, with the objective of co-ordinating union activities.[15] Communists helped organize peasant protest movements in the two states in 1933.[16] Following the refusal of the government to implement democratic reforms in Travancore, Socialist and Communist elements mobilized a number of strikes and gained considerable influence in the Travancore State Congress.[17]

By the late 1930's, then, the Communists had established a sizeable basis of support in Malabar, Travancore, and Cochin. When the united front of the Congress Socialist Party and the Indian Communist Party collapsed in 1939, it left behind a powerful Communist organization. As early as 1936, the National Executive of the Congress Socialist Party had begun to express concern over Communist activities within its organization, particularly in South India.[18] In 1939, citing an allegedly secret document of the Indian Communist Party, the Socialists accused the Communists of attempting to take over the Congress Socialist Party and barred any more Communists from joining. Communists already in the Congress Socialist Party were allowed to remain.[19] But relations between the Communists and the Socialists continued to deteriorate, and following Communist efforts to mobilize mass action against the British in the early part of World War II, the National Executive of the Congress Socialist Party expelled all Communist members. The Kerala branch of the Congress Socialist Party, almost completely dominated by Communists, responded to this move by converting its organization into the Kerala Communist Party. Since the Communist Party was illegal at the time, the Kerala group remained part of the Congress movement, and, led by Namboodiripad, continued to be the dominant group in the Kerala Provincial Congress Committee. Subsequently, the Communists, as Congress leaders, launched a major anti-war protest without authorization from the National Congress leaders, who in turn responded by dismissing the Communist-led Kerala Provincial Congress Committee. The Kerala Communist Party crystallized as an independent political party. As it embraced the major political figures and a sub-

---

[15] *Ibid.*, p. 169.

[16] *Ibid.*

[17] *Ibid.*, pp. 171–173.

[18] Overstreet and Windmiller, *op. cit.*, p. 165.

[19] The document, "Communist Plot Against the C.S.P." can be found in Democratic Research Service, *Indian Communist Party Documents, 1930–1956*, Bombay and New York, 1957, pp. 36–45.

stantial portion of the Congress political organization in Kerala, it established a claim to being the inheritor of the National Congress movement in that area.

The Second United Front

The united front strategy was not revived for more than fifteen years, during which time the Communist Party—both nationally and in Kerala—was increasingly isolated. A return to this strategy in the early 1950's, in the context of "constitutional communism," resurrected the fortunes of the Party, establishing it as the ascendent party of the left in Kerala and, by 1957, as the only opposition party organizationally strong enough to assume power.

After 1942, when the Communists shifted to support the "peoples' war," all connections between the Congress movement and the Communists were broken. Communists were formally barred from holding Congress offices.[20] The Communists, then a legal party, made considerable inroads into the trade unions and student and peasant groups at the Congress' expense (the British authorities declared the Congress illegal, and most of its leaders were arrested in 1942 for resisting the war effort.) These gains were a Pyrrhic victory, however, for the Communists lost considerable public support in India and fared poorly in the first elections held immediately after the war.

The isolation of the Communists from the nationalist movement was exacerbated in the immediate postwar years as the Party shifted leftward and became openly hostile to the Congress and to Nehru especially. Supported by a change in the Party line in Moscow, which now argued that imperialism was the principal enemy and saw the Congress in India as linked to imperialist forces, a "leftist" faction in the Indian Communist Party deposed the Party's moderate Secretary-General P. C. Joshi, who had favored collaboration with the Congress, and replaced him in February, 1948, with a militant trade unionist, B. T. Ranadive. Under Ranadive, the Party launched a series of labor strikes, notably in Calcutta and Bombay, and supported the agrarian violence occurring in some areas of southern India.

The Ranadive strategy resulted in a severe government repression that almost broke the Party. The strategy itself seemed divorced from Indian reality. Despite Ranadive's attack on the Chinese Communist agrarian-based revolution as "erroneous" and "counter-revolutionary,"[21] the momen-

---

[20] N. N. Mitra (ed.), *Indian Annual Register*, 1945, II, 112–122.

[21] B. T. Ranadive, "Struggle for People's Democracy and Socialism—Some Questions of Strategy and Tactics," *Communist*, II, June-July, 1949, p. 71.

tary success of the agrarian uprising in the area of Telengana (Hyderabad) in southern India gave the impression that the Chinese model of revolution was the more appropriate one for India. When the Soviet Union formally endorsed Mao's strategy in November, 1949, and recommended it as the path to be taken by the former colonial nations of Asia, "agrarian leftists" (termed "violent neo-Maoists" by John Kautsky) ousted Ranadive and took control of the Indian Communist Party.[22]

The switch of the Indian Communist Party from a leftist urban revolutionary strategy to a leftist agrarian strategy did not alter the position of the Communists in the Indian political system. Communists were no longer attacking a British ruler; they were in confrontation with an Indian-controlled government. This period, as a result, marked the nadir of Communist popular support.

The suppression of the Telengana revolt by the Indian government deprived the agrarian leftists in the Communist Party of the initiative. With the first general elections to be held in February, 1951, and with the atmosphere increasingly hostile to guerrilla activity, the various factions within the Indian Communist Party compromised. "Centrists" took over the Party Secretariat, and the General Committee adopted a "Statement of Policy" committing the Party to "throw all its resources into parliamentary elections and elections in every sphere where broad strata of people can be mobilized and their interests defended."[23]

The Indian Communist Party not only hesitantly adopted constitutional tactics, it also committed itself completely to the neo-Maoist strategy endorsed by the Soviet Union. That strategy, stressing the "union of four classes" (proletariat, peasantry, petty bourgeoisie, and anti-imperialist bourgeoisie) resulted in a renewed emphasis on united fronts created by alliances between Communist and other political parties.[24] In December, 1950, the Central Committee of the Indian Communist Party called upon "all Democratic and anti-imperialist parties to come together on the basis of an agreed programme . . . and to build up united mass organizations."[25]

Communists in Malabar, Travancore, and Cochin, participating in the general leftist swing of the Indian Communist Party after World War II,

---

[22] See John Kautsky, *Moscow and the Communist Party of India*, Cambridge, Mass., 1956, pp. 122–127, for a discussion of "violent neo-Maoism."

[23] Communist Party of India, *Statement of Policy of the Communist Party of India*, Bombay, 1951.

[24] An elaboration of the neo-Maoist strategy can be found in Kautsky, *op. cit.*, pp. 16–157.

[25] Quoted from Masani, *op. cit.*

had been active in numerous strikes and protests. Efforts were made to mobilize a general strike in Malabar in 1946. In Travancore and Cochin, Communists attempted to take over nationalist efforts to get the two princely states to accede sovereignty to the Indian Union. The result of such activities was, as generally admitted by Party activists, disastrous for the Party.[26] The various agitations were unco-ordinated and sporadic, and the government response was vigorous. All of the governments in the area banned the Communist Party and launched efforts to arrest the Party leaders. The Malabar Communists were released and allowed to contest the elections of 1951, but the Communist Party in the state of Travancore-Cochin (which was created in 1949 by the merger of the two former princely states into a single Indian state) remained illegal. As such, it was threatened with isolation from the primary arena of the state political system—the legislature.

By adopting the united front strategy in 1950, the Communists were able to purchase respectability and gain access into the system. Contesting as independents, the Communists formed a United Front of Leftists with the Kerala Socialist Party (formed in 1950) and the Revolutionary Socialist Party. The United Front of Leftists contested seventy-two state legislative seats and eight parliamentary seats. In Malabar, the Communists formed an electoral alliance with the newly formed Peasant, Workers', and People's Party, which had been created by several former national Congress leaders. Though the two parties were hostile to one another at the national level, they jointly sponsored twenty-four candidates for the State assembly (fourteen of whom were Communists) and six candidates for Parliament (including four Communists). The Malabar coalition was short-lived, but the United Front of Leftists in Travancore-Cochin persisted, even after the Communist Party regained legal status. The Party's purpose for participating in the Front underwent considerable change, however. At the Third Party Congress held in Madurai (Madras State), the Party executive ruled that while united fronts from above should be continued, the Communist Party was to retain its separate organization and program.[27] More important, state Communist parties in such fronts were instructed to seek to dominate their coalitions.

By 1954, the Kerala Communist Party had achieved more than dominance; it had also undermined its major competitors on the left. By the time the Congress-backed minority government in Travancore-Cochin had

---

[26] Namboodiripad, *op. cit.*, pp. 192–193, 206.

[27] Communist Party of India, *Review Report of the Politbureau* (presented to the Third Party Conference at Madurai, December, 1953). Discussion is drawn from the report as published by Democratic Research Service, *op. cit.*, pp. 142–160.

collapsed in 1954 and the mid-term elections had been held, the Communists had become an overwhelmingly preponderant element in the United Front of Leftists. Of the thirty candidates of the Front winning seats in the State Assembly, twenty were Communists, eight were Revolutionary Socialists, and three were Kerala Socialists. In May, 1954, the Revolutionary Socialist Party seceded from the Front, accusing the Communists of "seeking to strengthen themselves at the expense of the other coalition members."[28] The break came too late, for virtually all of the leftist parties in Kerala—with the exception of the Communists—had been weakened considerably.

By 1956, then, the Communist Party had emerged as the primary party of the left in Kerala and, as a result, as the primary party opposing the Congress. Initially, the development of the Kerala Communist Party was not, however, so much the result of creating an effective coalition of support as it was building an organization, a process occurring with particular reference to the "wider" environment of Communist ideology. That same environment provided the basis of linkage between Party and society in Kerala.

The Mobilization of Electoral Support

In Kerala, religious or caste communities, or coalitions of them, have tended to shape party behavior.[29] Caste and religious groups have mobilized themselves politically and have become concerned with the distribution of power and resources in the political system. The role of political parties in such a context can vary. At times, a party can act as a "broker" between disputing communities. More often than not, however, political parties have, against a background of great communal rivalry, become associated with one particular communal group. In Kerala, the latter situation has generally been the case. Political parties—in their appeals, electoral support, and selection of candidates—have tended to be dependent on the major ascriptive communities: the Communist Party on the Ezhavas and Scheduled Castes; the Congress on the Christians and Nairs; the Socialists on the Nairs; and the Muslim League on the Muslims.[30]

The association of the Communist Party with the lower end of the spectrum defined by the caste-class system in Kerala is not, however, so much a result of the Party's being "captured" by the increasingly politicized low-caste groups as it is a linkage of ideological appeal and economic

---

[28] *Hindustan Times*, New Delhi, May 27, 1954.

[29] Lloyd I. Rudolph and Susanne Hoeber Rudolph, *The Modernity of Tradition*, Chicago, 1967, p. 71.

[30] *Ibid.*

circumstance. Just as ideology influenced the tactics used to build the Party organization, it also "decreed" the Party's focus on the lower classes and castes. Of equal importance, however, has been the context within which the Communist demands for major economic reforms were made. Caste rank, despite increased social and economic mobility in India, is still closely related to socio-economic class. Communist rivalry in Kerala has increasingly been expressed in the vocabulary of class rivalry. The result has been an increased saliency of Communist appeals as they have become more comprehensible to the lower castes.

The social structure of Kerala is highly complex. In a country where "caste is . . . so completely accepted by all, including those most vocal in condemning it," and where caste "is everywhere the unit of social action," Kerala has often been cited as an extreme case, exacerbated by the presence of sizeable non-Hindu communities as well.[31] There are three major religious communities in Kerala. Sixteen percent of the population is Muslim; twenty-three percent, Christian; and sixty-one percent, Hindu. The principal groups in the Christian community are the Syrian Christians (Roman Catholic and Protestant groups using a Syrian liturgy) and Latin Catholics. Syrian Christians comprise seventy-five percent of the Christian population of Kerala and have been a dominant business community in Travancore since the sixth century. In Malabar, Muslims rather than Christians comprise the second largest religious community. Descendents of the traditional coastal traders of the area, Muslims continue to be engaged primarily in commerce in the region although they have more recently become involved in other occupations. A large percentage of the community belongs to the poor peasantry, which includes tenant farmers and agricultural workers.

The Hindus comprise the largest and most complex of the religious communities in Kerala. There are 420 castes in Kerala, ranked in a ritual hierarchy and separated from one another by endogamy, commensality, and dialectual variation.[32] Only several need mentioning as having particular ritual or political importance. In terms of the ritual hierarchy, Namboodiri Brahmins rank highest. This relatively wealthy community, however, has become politically unimportant because of its small size (eight percent of the Hindu population).[33]

---

[31] The quote is taken from M. N. Srinivas, "Caste and Modern India," *Journal of Asian Studies*, Durham, N. C., Vol. XVI, p. 548.

[32] Robert L. Hardgrave, Jr. "Caste in Kerala: A Preface to the Elections," *The Economic Weekly*, Bombay, November 21, 1964, p. 1841.

[33] For material on this community, see Joan P. Mencher, "Namboodiri Brahmins: An Analysis of Traditional Elite in Kerala," *Journal of Asian and African Studies*, Leiden, Vol. I, 1966, pp. 183–196.

Of the castes ranked below the Namboodiris, several are particularly important. The Nairs (also spelled Nayars) are a prosperous landowning community who are descendents of the traditional military caste of Kerala.[34] Their prosperity and their numbers (twenty-five percent of the Hindus in Kerala) have established the Nairs as pivotal in Kerala politics. The Nairs have increasingly come into conflict with the Ezhavas, a by-and-large economically depressed caste, who were considered untouchable and were barred from Hindu temples. Despite the economic weakness of the Ezhavas, their numbers (forty-four percent of the Hindu population) have, in an era of mass franchise, made them a major community in Kerala politics. Below the Ezhavas are the Scheduled Castes (so called because they are listed as being entitled to special benefits under the Indian Constitution) who comprise a little over twenty percent of the population.

While identification of these large communities and of their numbers implies a long history of caste and communal competition, in actuality such conflict is comparatively recent. Caste in traditional Kerala society was relatively localized. The local caste or subcaste, as it is usually called, established by birth an individual's place in a local hierarchical authority relationship between an upper-class, upper-caste landlord family and lower-caste families who worked as tenant farmers, coolies, and servants. The interdependence of groups in this structure worked against the emergence of any broader sense of identity between members of the same caste in different areas.

Modernization, with its expanded communication facilities, its cash economy, and its creation of jobs external to the local village system, altered this system of localized hierarchies. This transition, which brought caste groups of similar status increasingly into contact with one another, coupled with the discontent felt by caste élites who had achieved economic status without commensurate social status, and who actively sought to mobilize their castes in an effort to better their position in the ritual hierarchy, provide the basis for the emergence of regional caste communities. The emergence of such communities was accompanied by increasing communal conflict. In Kerala such conflict was expressed primarily through caste associations, which were organizations created to articulate caste demands and mobilize widespread support within a particular caste for these demands. In 1902, a Ezhava caste association, the SNDP, was formed with the purpose of ending restrictions placed upon the Ezhavas, who, as untouchables, were denied government jobs and access to government schools. The SNDP attempted to upgrade the ritual status of the Ezhavas by both espousing a creed repudiating

---

[34] See Kathleen Gough, "Changing Kinship Usages in the Setting of Political and Economic Change among the Nayars of Malabar," *Journal of the Royal Anthropological Institute*, London, Vol. LXXII, 1952, pp. 71–88.

caste inequality and by "sanskritizing" Ezhava ritual to imitate the rituals of higher castes. It also actively sought to secure economic reforms to improve the lot of the Ezhava peasant. In 1914, the Nair Service Society was organized. Among other purposes, it sought to establish schools so that Nairs could compete effectively for civil service positions with Syrian Christians, who had already organized an extensive church-managed high school and college system.[35] In 1928, the more advanced communities in Travancore began to agitate and compete for greater access to government jobs. The rivalry increased after the legislative elections in 1931, in which the Nairs secured fifteen seats compared with four for the Christians and none for the Ezhavas.[36] In 1932, Christians, Ezhavas, and Muslims formed a Joint Political Congress to press their demands. The Nairs, in turn, organized the Travancore State Congress. Unity was momentarily achieved during the independence period as both parties grew increasingly antagonistic towards the Travancore government and, as a result, merged.[37]

It should be noted that mobilization along the communal lines of caste and religion was not essentially a class phenomenon. While caste and religion in Kerala are linked to socio-economic class, the élites responsible for the emergence of all the communal associations were largely members of an urban bourgeoisie. The SNDP, for example, linked Ezhavas of differing economic circumstance. In the late 1940's and early 1950's, however, the social and political environment of Kerala underwent massive change. Limited economic growth and a massive increase in the population impoverished the rural lower castes.[38] The political manifestions of this were profound.

The Communists had long made appeals to Ezhava economic interests and had made considerable inroads into that community during the 1930's and 1940's, usually through peasant unions organized by leftist Congress activists such as Gopalan. When the Kerala Communist Party was formed in 1940–1941, these same groups became Communist auxiliaries.[39] Univer-

[35] V. K. S. Nayar, "Communal Associations in Kerala," in D. E. Smith (ed.), *Religion and Politics in South Asia*, Princeton, N. J., 1966, p. 178.

[36] Horst Hartmann, "Changing Political Behavior in Kerala," *Economic and Political Weekly*, Bombay, January, 1968, p. 165.

[37] V. K. S. Nayar, "Kerala Politics since 1947: Community Attitudes," in Igbal Narain, *State Politics in India*, p. 157.

[38] For one case study, see Katherine Gough, "Village Politics in Kerala—I," *The Economic Weekly*, February 20, 1965, p. 369.

[39] Kathleen Gough, "Palakkara: Social and Religious Change in Central Kerala" in K. Ishwaran (ed.), *Change and Continuity in India's Villages*, New York, 1966, p. 160.

sal franchise after independence, resurgence of legal Communist activity, competition among the political parties, and growing economic divisions in Kerala society increasingly yielded a tendency to define social conflicts in economic terms. To some degree, there was a widening of the cleavage between propertied and unpropertied groups within each caste.[40] More generally, however, the vocabulary of class analysis was conveniently applied to the caste conflict to explain it in terms of propertied versus property-less.[41] The result of this was a growing congruency between Communist Party appeals, which defined the communal conflict in class terms, and the Ezhava and Scheduled Castes' definition of their own interests.

The Ezhava-Communist linkage was solidified by the effect of the communal rivalry on the Congress, a rivalry which, by 1954, seemed to leave the Syrian Christians an increasingly predominant element in the Congress Party. The mid-term elections in 1954, held after the collapse of the Congress ministry in Travancore-Cochin, were fought largely along communal lines with a group of Nair Congress defectors allied with the United Front of Leftists against the Congress. That alliance stressed in particular the role of the Syrian Catholic Church in the Congress. The Congress won forty-five of the 118 seats being contested, leading primarily in heavily Christian constituencies. The United Front of Leftists won forty seats (twenty-three were won by Communists), leading in constituencies with large Ezhava and Scheduled Caste populations.

The Communists did not monopolize Ezhava support, however; many Ezhava élites, especially those active in the SNDP, tended to be Congress supporters. One former SNDP official was Congress Chief Minister in Travancore-Cochin in 1951–1952. The creation and maintenance of communal solidarity was the principal concern of the Ezhava caste association; and, for the most part, SNDP support was given to candidates on the basis of caste rather than on the basis of party.

Communal-based rivalries and defections continued to topple ministries. In March, 1956, the President of India, under Article 256 of the Constitution, vacated the Assembly of Travancore-Cochin and assumed administrative control of the state until a government could be formed after the second general elections to be held a year later.

In November, 1956, a major alternation occurred in the politics of the area when the Malayalam-speaking linguistic state of Kerala came into being.

---

[40] Kathleen Gough, "Village Politics in Kerala—II," *The Economic Weekly*, February 27, 1965, shows strong association between caste, class, and party in her examination of two Kerala villages.

[41] *Ibid.*

The demand for such a state had been widely backed, but the Kerala Communists and the Indian Communist Party had long been supporters of the creation of Kerala in particular and linguistic states in general. Such support no doubt served to enhance the Party's mass appeal. More than that, however, with the creation of Kerala the Communist position was strengthened through the radical alteration of the political and communal balance in the area. The formal linkage of Malabar with the Malayalam-speaking areas of Travancore-Cochin brought into the political system an area in which, as seen above, the Communists had long been established and in which Communist political leaders such as Gopalan and Namboodripad were preeminent political figures. Malabar was also a major Ezhava area as well.

The Elections in Kerala in 1957

The elections in 1957 produced a major victory for the Kerala Communist Party. The Party won sixty seats outright and succeeded in electing five Communist-supported independents as well. The Congress, which contested more seats, received a slightly larger percentage of the vote but carried only forty-three seats.

The Elections in Kerala in 1957

| Party | — SEATS — | | — VOTES — | | Deposits |
	Contested	Won	Number	Percent	Forfeited
Communist Party	100	60	2,060,665	35.3	4
Congress Party	124	43	2,206,604	37.8	5
Praja Socialist Party	62	9	630,458	10.8	28
Revolutionary Socialist Party	28	0	186,802	3.2	22
Muslim League	19	8	274,366	4.7	0
Communist-Supported Independents	19	5	321,067	5.5	0
Others	37	1	157,615	2.7	31
Total	389	126	5,837,577	100.0	90

The elections seemed to mark the merger of good fortune with pay-offs for tactics used by the Communists. The non-Communist left—particularly the Communist Party's former allies in the United Front of Leftists— was almost obliterated. The Kerala Socialist Party had become virtually non-existent even prior to the elections and did not contest; but the Revolutionary Socialist Party contested 28 seats, winning none. Twenty-two candidates of the Revolutionary Socialist Party failed to gain the required number of the votes cast and forfeited their deposits. The Praja Socialists fared poorly as well, dropping from nineteen seats in 1954 to nine seats in 1957. Made up of Nair Congress defectors, the Praja Socialist Party had been severely damaged by Congress maneuvers after the elections in 1954. The

Congress had first supported and then undermined a Praja Socialist minority government. Competing with the Communists for dominance of the Kerala left, the Praja Socialist government had attempted to pass a number of land reform bills, and incurred opposition from the Nair Service Society élites who had initially supported its formation. At the same time, the Praja Socialist Party's identification with the Nair community and the Communist influence among the Ezhavas and other low castes isolated the Praja Socialists from support in those communities.

The Communists' primary competitor for control of the government, the Congress, entered the elections in disarray. The Congress had been widely denounced for first supporting the Praja Socialist ministry and then subverting it, and the chronic instability which had characterized politics in the area was largely blamed on the Congress. While the Catholics strongly endorsed the Congress during the election campaign (the Congress won heavily in the Christian-dominated constituencies in the state, and nearly half of the winning Congress candidates were Christians), Nair support was more equivocal. The Nair Service Society leader was in open dispute with the Nair Congress Party leader; and it appears that the disagreements involved may have turned several marginal constituencies against the Congress.

To summarize, the Communist victory in 1957 grew out of a linkage between changing party strategies (primarily resulting from circumstances external to the Indian political system), the evolution of a particular kind of communal conflict, and an untimely decision by the Indian government to alter Kerala's political boundaries. The shift in strategies, marked in particular by the evolution of "constitutional communism" and the achievement of respectability through the united front of 1951–1954, allowed the Party to adapt to the Indian environment. More than that, however, the shift in strategies allowed the Party to achieve several primary ideological goals—the formation of an effective Party organization, the establishment of influence in peasant and worker groups, and the achievement of dominance in the Kerala left. The favorable impact of the boundary alterations on the Communist vote was a direct consequence of the achievement of these goals by bringing an area of high Communist organizational strength and support into the political system. Communist strategy and the Kerala environment dovetailed with the congruency of Communist economic appeal and a growing tendency of communal conflict to be expressed in terms of class conflict. Organizationally dominant in the Kerala left, the Communists secured a monopoly of voter sentiment mobilized by concern over low caste and class status.

Stability and Instability: 1957 and After

Kerala politics since 1957 has revealed both stability and instability in the Kerala Communist movement and in the political system in general. The instability is apparent in a recitation of major political events since 1957. In 1959, after two years in office, the Indian Communist Party government was removed from office by the government of India. The action was the culmination of a struggle begun after the Communist government succeeded in passing the Kerala Education Act in 1957. Aimed at increasing government control over some 7,000 state-aided private schools, the Act was viewed as an attack on the Christian and Nair communities, which ran most of the schools; and those communities, with the support of the Congress and Muslim League Parties, launched a "Liberation Struggle" against the Communist government. Reacting to the Governor of Kerala's report that the legal machinery of the state had broken down and to a recommendation of the national Congress leadership, the President of India dismissed the Communist government and placed the state under administrative rule. The subsequent mid-term elections of 1960 pitted the Indian Communist Party against a Congress-Socialist-Muslim League coalition which won ninety-four seats while Communist strength declined to twenty-six seats.

The Congress-Praja Socialist ministry that followed lasted only two years, being toppled by a Nair-Christian defection in protest over efforts on the part of the Congress leadership to break the Communist hold on the Ezhava community. The mid-term elections in 1965 pitted the Nair-Christian defector group (organized as the Kerala Congress), the Congress, and the Communists, who had split in 1964 into two parties—the Indian Communist Party and the Communist Party (Marxist)—all against one another. Because no party or coalition of parties was able to form a government, the elections were inconclusive except to demonstrate that the Communist Party (Marxist), led by Namboodiripad and Gopalan, was the united, pre-1964 Communist organization in Kerala. Members of the Communist Party (Marxist), in coalition with the Socialists and the Muslim League, won forty seats as opposed to three for the Indian Communist Party.

In the general elections in 1967 a conclusive result was achieved, however. Namboodiripad forged a seven-party coalition that, on the one hand, consolidated the left to prevent fragmentation of the Ezhava-Scheduled Caste vote and, on the other hand, secured the Communist vote in Malabar by accommodating its only real rival in the area, the Muslim League. The Congress and the Kerala Congress, in contrast, continued to compete for Nair and Christian support. The coalition led by the Communist Party (Marxist) won decisively, capturing 113 seats (out of an assembly of 133) with 51.4 percent of the vote. Of this, the Communist Party (Marxist) won 52 seats with 23.5 percent of the vote, while the Indian Communist Party won 19 seats with 8.5 percent of the vote. The Congress was reduced to 9 seats with 35.4 percent of the vote. After a decade out of office, Namboodiripad had again formed a government.

But the events of 1967 did not end political instability in Kerala. In October, 1969, the united front government collapsed after the resignation of seven of the twelve ministers; the withdrawal of four parties, including the Indian Communist Party, from the coalition; and the defeat of the Namboodiripad government on the "smoke-screen" issue of corruption. Subsequently, an Indian Communist Party member of Parliament, Achutha Menon, forged an anti-Communist Party (Marxist) front and assumed power, supported by the Congress (an alliance facilitated by the Congress split and the support of the Indian Communist Party for Indira Gandhi's progressive faction of the Congress). In 1970, Mrs. Gandhi's supporters in Kerala, the predominant Congress group, formally joined the coalition led by the Indian Communist Party.

The instability of party politics in Kerala and the changing fortunes of the Communists are not, however, wholly revealing. Support for the Communists has been highly stable. The Indian Communist Party achieved power in 1957 with Ezhava and Scheduled Caste support. That support was deepened through various administrative programs after the accession of the Party to power. Since 1957, the Communists have, with fluctuations, secured approximately one-third of the vote in each election. The Communists continue to benefit from a high congruency between their appeals and economic-caste divisions in Kerala society. Even though the Communist Party (Marxist) lost nineteen seats in the Assembly in the mid-term elections in 1970, a loss which kept the Congress-Indian Communist Party coalition in power, it emerged as the largest political party in Kerala, a position which had been enjoyed by the Congress Party since independence.

The Continuing Sources of Communist Political Power in Kerala

The present paradox of instable Communist Party fortunes and stable support for the Communists can be explained by reference to the reasons for the Communist success in the elections of 1957. The reasons were the Indian Communist Party's preponderance in the Kerala left, a preponderance secured in part by united front strategies; the growing tendency of social conflict to be expressed in terms of "propertied versus propertyless," a consequence in part of the particular nature of communal mobilization in Kerala and in part of Communist influence; and the nature of Communist appeals. These reasons all conspired to create maximum strength for the Communists and led—in the context of the decision to form the linguistic state of Kerala and against a background of disunity among the groups traditionally linked with the Congress—to an almost inevitable electoral victory. In 1967 much the same process occurred but, by necessity, in a more complex way. The decade between the two elections had produced considerable fragmentation among the Communists when the Sino-Soviet split provided legitimation for already existing factions in the national Indian Communist Party to split from one another. In Kerala, the Communist Party (Marxist) soon emerged as the dominant Communist group, and to secure its position negotiated a wide leftist coalition, co-opting virtually the entire left. To secure its position in Malabar, the Communist Party (Marxist) evolved an agreement with a resurgent Muslim League. Thus, again, Communist ability to avoid a fragmentation of lower class support and to translate such support into Communist victories in Malabar secured success.

The united front government persisted thirty-one months, the longest tenure of any government in Kerala. Its collapse was not the result of a loss of support but rather the consequence of alternating attitudes on the part of the coalition partners towards one another. Under attack by more radical Communist groups for entering the government and by its own Central Committee for being too accommodating towards its coalition partners, the Communist Party (Marxist) responded by attempting to undermine its two principal allies, the Muslim League and the Indian Communist Party. Both ultimately left the coalition. Their subsequent alliance with the Congress denied the Communist Party (Marxist) further access to power.

Nonetheless, Communist political power continues to be a primary political force in Kerala. Kerala communism is a linkage of pay-offs for political strategy and communal conflicts increasingly understood in class terms. In this sense it is unique. Members of the Communist Party (Marxist) in West Bengal, who gained power as part of a united front in 1967, possess neither organizational preponderance on the left nor a stable social base. Elsewhere non-class conflicts have defied Communist efforts to develop support. In Kerala, however, caste, class, and organization have telescoped to produce power.

A Summing Up

Thomas T. Hammond

The Typology of Communist Takeovers[1]

It is clear from the articles in this volume that Communists have taken power under a great variety of circumstances, with tactics differing from country to country and from time to time. There are, however, some remarkable similarities. It might be useful at this point, therefore, to group the various takeovers according to type and see which ones fall into each category.

One major dividing line can be noted at the start—between exported revolutions and indigenous ones. There have been three types of *exported revolutions*—i. e., revolutions imposed from without by foreign armies:

Type 1—*Outright Annexation of Territory by a Communist State*. The instances of this type are numerous. For example, during the first years of the Bolshevik regime the Red Army was continuously engaged in conquering and re-annexing the borderlands of the former Tsarist empire—areas such as the Ukraine, the Caucasus, and Central Asia, where non-Russian peoples had established independent states. Many years later, as a result of the Nazi-Soviet pact of 1939, several more areas were annexed—western Ukraine, western Belorussia, the Baltic States, Bessarabia, northern Bukovina, and parts of Finland. During and after World War II other territories were annexed—Tannu Tuva, Carpatho-Ukraine, the Königsberg area of East Prussia, the Kurile Islands, and Southern Sakhalin. In this same category might also be included the absorption of Tibet by Communist China and the annexation by Poland of German lands east of the Oder-Neisse line.

Type 2 — *Installation of a Communist Regime Outside of Russia by the Soviet Army*. The first cases of this type were in Outer Mongolia and Tannu Tuva in 1921, while the others came in the aftermath of World War II—in Poland, East Germany, Hungary, Bulgaria, Rumania, and North Korea. This was the most common way in which countries became Communist during the period from 1944 to 1947.

---

[1] For somewhat different typologies of Communist takeovers see Cyril E. Black, "The Anticipation of Communist Revolutions," and R. V. Burks, "Eastern Europe," in C. E. Black and Thomas P. Thornton, (eds.), *Communism and Revolution; The Strategic Uses of Political Violence*, Princeton, N. J., 1964; and Hugh Seton-Watson, *The East European Revolution*, London, 1950, chap. viii.

Type 3 — *Counter-Revolutions in Heretical Communist Countries by the Soviet Army.* There have been three of these so far—in East Germany in 1953, Hungary in 1956, and Czechoslovakia in 1968.

The remaining types of Communist takeovers have been entirely or mainly *indigenous*; that is, they have been carried out primarily by native forces, although they may have received some help from abroad.

Type 4 — *A Revolution in the Urban Centers, Based Largely on the Proletariat, Followed by Conquest of the Countryside.* This type of Communist takeover has occurred in only one country—Russia.

Type 5 — *A Revolution in the Countryside, based mainly on the Peasants, Followed by Conquest of the Urban Centers.* This pattern of tactics was outlined by Mao in 1938 when he said: "Basically the task of the Communist Party here is not to...seize the big cities first and then occupy the countryside, but to take the other way round."[2] Such revolutions have occurred not only in China but also in Yugoslavia, Albania, and North Vietnam.

Type 6 — *A Completely Legal Takeover Through Free Elections.* So far Communists have been freely voted into power in only three small areas—San Marino, Kerala, and West Bengal—and in all three they were subsequently voted out. None of them are truly independent states.

Type 7 — *A Semi-Legal Takeover Through Considerable Popular Support, Combined with Armed Threats.* In Czechoslovakia the Communists hoped to take power through free elections, but never quite made it. Instead they threatened the country with civil war by mobilizing the police forces, the "Workers Militia," and the trade unions, while at the same time intimating that Soviet troops would intervene if necessary. Fearing bloodshed, President Beneš gave legal sanction to a Communist-controlled government. Czechoslovakia thus followed in many respects the pattern set by Hitler's takeover.

Type 8 — *A Non-Communist Leader Seizes Power and then Decides to Adopt Communism.* Cuba so far offers the only example of this type of takeover, which has been described by Prof. Robert C. Tucker as "communism by conversion." Similarities, have been displayed elsewhere, however: Sukarno in Indonesia and Arbenz in Guatemala seemed to be moving in this direc-

---

[2] Mao Tse-tung, "Problems of War and Strategy," *Selected Works*, New York, 1954, Vol. II, p. 267. The distinction made in this essay between the Russian and Chinese revolutions is also made by the Chinese. For example, in 1965 Lin Piao wrote:

> The October revolution began with armed uprisings in the cities and then spread to the countryside, while the Chinese revolution won nation-wide victory through the encirclement of the cities from the rural areas and the final capture of the cities.

Long Live the Victory of People's War!, Peking, 1966, p. 43.

tion until they fell from power, and it once seemed possible that Allende would become the Castro of Chile.

Why Communist Takeovers Have Succeeded or Failed

(1) *Military Force.* The most striking conclusion that emerges from this survey of Communist takeovers is that military force has been the key to success in almost every case, and usually this has meant the Red Army. Out of a total of twenty-two Communist takeovers beginning in 1917, the Red Army played some role in fifteen and played the leading role in twelve. Where the Red Army was not decisive, native armed forces generally were used, as in Yugoslavia, Albania, China, Vietnam, and Cuba. Indeed, there were only three instances in which armed force was not the crucial element— in the tiny states of San Marino, Kerala, and West Bengal. Moreover, in each of these three states the Communists were subsequently removed from office. Thus it can be said that armed force was the determinant of victory in *all* cases in which Communists have not only seized power but have managed to retain it.

If Lenin and Stalin emphasized the importance of military power, Mao stressed it even more. Indeed, since Mao was forced to fight a civil war for more than twenty years in order to gain power, his attachment to military power became an obsession. In 1938 he made his famous statement:

> Political power grows out of the barrel of a gun ...Anything can grow out of the barrel of the gun.... Whoever wants to seize and hold on to political power must have a strong army. Some people have ridiculed us as advocates of the "theory of the omnipotence of war"; yes, we are, we are advocates of the theory of the omnipotence of revolutionary war. This is not a bad thing; it is good and it is Marxist. With the help of guns, the Russian Communists brought about socialism....The working class and the toiling masses cannot defeat the armed bourgeois and landlord except by the power of the gun; in this sense we can even say that the whole world can be remolded only with the gun.[3]

Pointing out the importance of organized armed force may seem to some a case of belaboring the obvious. However, many people still have highly romantic notions about revolutions—they have visions of the poor, downtrodden masses, unable any longer to bear the poverty and tyranny under which they suffer, rising up spontaneously to overthrow their reactionary oppressors. Such has not been the case in a single Communist revolution. A similar mistake made by some writers has been to ignore

---

[3] Mao Tse-tung, *Problems of War and Strategy*, Peking, 1954, pp. 14–15; quoted in Stuart R. Schram, *The Political Thought of Mao Tse-tung*, 1st edn., New York, 1963, p. 209 .

or underestimate the importance of the Red Army. For example, Gar Alperovitz writes: "...revolutions are caused by the inability of governments to deal with their problems (rarely, in any serious sense, as Che Guevara's failure [in Bolivia] illustrates, by 'outside agitators' and 'foreign powers')...."[4] Such a statement is obviously nonsense if applied to Communist revolutions, as the figures given above about the Red Army illustrate.

Military force imported from outside has also played a key role in Communist defeats. In the first few years after the Bolshevik revolution, armed intervention from other countries helped to prevent Communist revolutions from succeeding in Finland, Estonia, Latvia, Lithuania, Poland, and Hungary. In the aftermath of World War II, military intervention (or the threat of intervention) was important in defeating attempted Communist takeovers in Greece, northern Iran, Malaya, South Korea, South Vietnam, Laos, Cambodia, and Guatemala.

(2) *Geographical Contiguity.* Since Communist victory or defeat has been determined in most cases by armed intervention from outside, the physical location of a country and the political complexion of its neighbors have naturally been important. Countries that have become Communist since 1917 have bordered on an established Communist state in every case except one—Cuba. Geography has been of equal importance in Communist defeats. To cite just two of the most striking examples: the Hungarian Soviet Republic of 1919 was overthrown largely because it was surrounded by hostile neighbors, while the attempt to make Guatemala Communist was foiled in part because of the proximity of anti-Communist neighbors, including the United States.

(3) *War.* Almost all Communist takeovers have occurred either during international wars or in the aftermath of such wars—wars which undermined the old political, economic, and social order and which, in many cases, provided an opportunity for a foreign Communist army (usually the Red Army) to intervene. Examples are numerous. The Bolsheviks' opportunity to seize power in Russia came because of World War I. Eastern Europe became Communist mainly because of World War II. "The decisive factor in undermining the Nationalist government in China and enabling the Chinese Communist Party to build up sufficient strength to overthrow it was the Sino-Japanese war."[5]

---

[4] *The New York Times Book Review*, November 24, 1968, in a review of *Intervention and Revolution* by Richard J. Barnet.

[5] Tang Tsou and Morton Halperin, "Maoism at Home and Abroad," *Problems of Communism*, July–August, 1965, p. 11. The only important Communist takeover that did not occur in connection with an international war was the Cuban

(4) *Free Elections*. Communists have been freely elected to power in only three small states—San Marino, Kerala, and West Bengal—and in all three cases the Communists subsequently fell from power. That these Communists gave up power peacefully can be explained by the fact that each of these states is located inside a larger political entity, ruled by democratic governments, which can intervene if necessary. (Indeed, the President of India did intervene and dismiss the Communist government of Kerala in 1959.) Aside from these three states where Communists have been voted into office, there are two countries of some importance—France and Czechoslovakia—where Communists have won pluralities (but not majorities) in free elections, and two others—Italy and Finland—where they have gotten about one-fourth of the votes.

(5) *Agrarian Countries*. Marx was of course wrong in expecting that Communist revolutions would occur first in advanced, highly industrialized countries. So far they have taken place in only two such countries—Czechoslovakia and East Germany—while the rest have been predominantly agrarian.

(6) *Camouflage*. No Communist Party has ever come to power on the basis of a platform which frankly admitted that it intended to introduce communism, including such measures as the collectivization of agriculture, the nationalization of small enterprises, and the establishment of a one-party dictatorship.

(7) *Retaining Power*. It is a remarkable fact that only one Communist regime controlling a whole country has ever been overthrown—Hungary in 1919. The only other exceptions are *parts* of countries, such as San Marino, Kerala, and West Bengal, plus the puppet regimes of Azerbaijan and Kurdistan in northern Iran. Guatemala and Indonesia do not qualify because there the Communists were not yet in control. This remarkable stability of Communist governments points to the conclusion that communism is a science not only of how to seize power, but also of how to *retain* power. Once a Communist regime is fully ensconced, it is almost impossible to remove it, except perhaps by foreign intervention.

---

one. Stalin often emphasized the relationship between war and revolution. For example, in 1934 he said : "... things are heading towards a new imperialist war .. war... is sure to unleash revolution and jeopardize the very existence of capitalism in a number of countries, as happened in the course of the first imperialist war." "Report to the Seventeenth Party Congress," J. V. Stalin, *Works*, Moscow, 1955, Vol. XIII, p. 300. For further discussion of Stalin's views on the connection between war and revolution, see the essay by "Historicus" (George A. Morgan), "Stalin on Revolution," *Foreign Affairs*, New York, January, 1949.

(8) *Indigenous Revolutions*. Finally, it might be noted that the Soviet Union has had the greatest difficulty in controlling those Communist regimes which rose to power mainly through their own efforts, rather than through the Soviet army. The examples are obvious—Yugoslavia, Albania, China, Cuba, and North Vietnam. Moscow has undoubtedly drawn the appropriate lesson from this fact—namely, that Communist revolutions carried out by the Soviet army and subject to Soviet control are usually desirable from the point of view of Russia's national interests, while indigenous Communist revolutions generally are not. The implications of such a conclusion for present Soviet foreign policy are clear—another Communist takeover in Latin America, for example, would be acceptable in Moscow's eyes only if there were reason to believe that the new regime would benefit the USSR or weaken the capitalist powers. No more Yugoslavias and Chinas are wanted, and perhaps no more Cubas either.

Thus Peking's charge that Moscow has abandoned the cause of world revolution is largely true. Since 1917 the Soviet Union has followed a dual policy—promoting revolutions when favorable opportunities arise, while at the same time promoting peaceful relations with capitalist states when it is advantageous to do so. In recent years the former goal has been almost completely sacrificed to the latter. Whether in the Middle East, Africa, Asia, Latin America, or Europe, the Soviet Union today seems to feel that its interests are usually better served by dealing with existing non-Communist regimes than by trying to overthrow them.

Successful Communist Takeovers

Russia	Rumania
Outer Mongolia	Hungary
Tannu Tuva	Czechoslovakia
Estonia	North Korea
Latvia	North Vietnam
Lithuania	China
Yugoslavia	Tibet
Albania	Cuba
East Germany	San Marino
Poland	Kerala
Bulgaria	West Bengal

Contributors

WERNER T. ANGRESS is Professor of History at the State University of New York at Stony Brook and the author of *Stillborn Revolution : The Communist Bid for Power in Germany, 1921–1923* (Princeton, 1963); a revised and extended version in German translation, entitled *Die Kampfzeit der KPD 1921–1923* (Düsseldorf, 1973); contributor of "Juden im politischen Leben der Revolutionszeit," in *Deutsches Judentum in Krieg und Revolution 1916–1923* (Tübingen, 1971); and articles in American, German, and British scholarly publications.

ALEXANDRE BENNIGSEN is Directeur d'Études at the École Pratique de Hautes Études, The Sorbonne, and Professor of Russian Turkish History at the University of Chicago. He is co-author of *Islam in the Soviet Union* (1967).

DAE-SOOK SUH is Professor of Political Science and Director of the Center for Korean Studies at the University of Hawaii. He is the author of *The Korean Communist Movement, 1918–1948* (1967) and of *Documents of Korean Communism, 1918–1948* (1970). He is currently writing a book on the Workers' Party of Korea.

KEVIN DEVLIN is Assistant Director, Communist Area Analysis, Radio Free Europe. He has contributed to *The Sino-Soviet Conflict* (1965), *International Communism After Khrushchev* (1965), *The Future of Communism in Europe* (1968), and *Die kommunistischen Parteien der Welt* (1969).

JÜRGEN DOMES is Professor of Political Science and Director of the Research Unit on Chinese and East Asian Politics at the Free University of Berlin. He is the author of *Von der Volkskommune zur Krise in China* (1964), *Politik und Herrschaft in Rotchina* (1965), *Kulturrevolution und Armee—Die Rolle der Streitkräfte in der chinesischen "Kulturrevolution"* (1967), *Vertagte Revolution—Die Politik der Kuomintang in China, 1923–1937* (1966), *Die Ära Mao Tse-tung—Innenpolitik in der Volksrepublik China* (1971 and 1972), and co-author of *Die Aussenpolitik der VR China—Eine Einführung* (1972).

DENNIS J. DUNCANSON is Reader in Southeast Asian Studies at the University of Kent, England. He is the author of *Government and Revolution in Vietnam* (1968) and *The Rise to Power of the Indochina Communist Party* (forthcoming).

ROBERT FARRELL. Formerly Editor of *Studies on the Soviet Union* and Assistant Director, Munich Center, University of Oklahoma. Editor, with Robert Rupen, of *Vietnam and the Sino-Soviet Dispute* (1967); with Vladimir G. Treml, of *The Development of the Soviet Economy : Plan and Performance* (1968); and, with Martin Dewhirst, of *The Soviet Censorship* (1973).

STEPHEN FISCHER-GALATI. Professor of History and Director of the Center for Slavic and East European Studies at the University of Colorado, editor of the *East European Quarterly*, and author of numerous books on East European history and politics, including *The New Rumania : From People's Democracy to Socialist Republic* (1967) and *Twentieth Century Rumania* (1970).

BORIS GOLDENBERG. Since 1964, Director of the Latin-American editorial department of the Deutsche Welle, Cologne, Germany. Author of *Lateinamerika und die kubanische Revolution* (1963), *Gewerkschaften in Lateinamerika* (1964), and *Kommunismus in Lateinamerika* (1971).

WILLIAM E. GRIFFITH is Ford Professor of Political Science, Massachusetts Institute of Technology, and Adjunct Professor of Diplomatic History, The Fletcher School of Law and

Diplomacy. He is the author of *Albania and the Sino-Soviet Rift* (1963), *The Sino-Soviet Rift* (1964), and *Sino-Soviet Relations, 1964–1965* (1967); and editor of *Communism in Europe* (2 vols., 1964–1966) and *Peking, Moscow and Beyond* (1973).

ANDREW GYORGY. Professor of International Affairs and Political Science at the Institute for Sino-Soviet Studies, George Washington University, he is the author of *Ideologies in World Affairs* (1967), *Eastern European Government and Politics* (1967), *Problems in International Relations* (1970), *Nationalism in Eastern Europe* (1970), and co-author of *Basic Issues in International Relations* (2nd edition, 1973).

THOMAS T. HAMMOND is Professor of History at the University of Virginia. Among his publications are *Soviet Foreign Relations and World Communism* (1965 and 1966), *Lenin on Trade Unions and Revolution* (1957), and *Yugoslavia Between East and West* (1954). He contributed to *Continuity and Change in Russian and Soviet Thought*, ed. by E. J. Simmons; *Yugoslavia*, ed. by Robert F. Byrnes; and *Essays in Russian and Soviet History*, ed. by John S. Curtiss.

GERALD HEEGER is Assistant Professor of Government and Foreign Affairs and Chairman of the South Asia Committee at the University of Virginia. He conducted research in India on political parties in 1968–69 and spent the academic year 1973–74 in Pakistan continuing his studies of South Asian politics.

PAUL IGNOTUS. A well-known liberal political writer, critic, and literary editor in prewar Hungary, he spent the war years in London on the BBC staff and the years of Rákosi's Stalinist dictatorship, 1949–56, in Hungarian prisons. After the crushing of the Hungarian revolution he took refuge in London again. His literary work over the last fifteen years includes three full-length books written in English: *Political Prisoner* (1964), *The Paradox of Maupassant* (1968), and *Hungary* (1972).

JOHN KEEP is Professor of Russian History at the University of Toronto. He is the author of *The Rise of Social Democracy in Russia* (1963); editor of *Contemporary History in the Soviet Mirror* (1964); and contributor to *Revolutionary Russia*, ed. by Richard Pipes (1968), and *Lenin*, ed. by Leonard Schapiro and Peter Reddaway (1967).

GOTTFRIED-KARL KINDERMANN. Since 1967, Director of the Institute for International Politics at the University of Munich, Germany. His doctoral dissertation at the University of Chicago was on "Chiang Kai-shek and the Causes for the Disintegration of the First Sino-Soviet Entente" (1959).

D. GEORGE KOUSOULAS is Professor of Political Science at Howard University, and a Professorial Lecturer at the National War College, Washington, D.C. A specialist on Greek political affairs, he is the author of *The Price of Freedom: Greece in World Affairs, 1939–1953* (1953), *Revolution and Defeat: The Story of the Greek Communist Party* (1965), and *On Government and Politics* (1971).

WARREN LERNER is Professor of History at Duke University and author of various works on Soviet history, including *Kark Radek: The Last Internationalist* (1970) and a forthcoming study on *The Revolution from Without: Soviet Russia's Quest for a Red Poland*. He edited *The Development of Soviet Foreign Policy* (1973).

SUSANNE S. LOTARSKI received her Ph.D. in political science at Columbia University and wrote her dissertation on "The Political Culture of Local Politics in Poland: Participation of

Citizens and Councillors in the People's Councils." She has taught at Vassar College and is presently employed in the Bureau of East-West Trade of the U.S. Department of Commerce. Her chapter was written while she was a Junior Fellow at the Research Institute on Communist Affairs at Columbia University.

MALCOLM MACKINTOSH. From 1944 to 1946, British liaison officer to the Soviet High Command in Rumania and Bulgaria. From 1946 to 1948 studied at the University of Glasgow. From 1948 to 1960 head of Bulgarian and Albanian sections of the BBC. From 1960 to the present Consultant on Soviet Affairs to the International Institute for Strategic Studies, London. He is the author of *Strategy and Tactics of Soviet Foreign Policy* (1962), *Juggernaut : A History of the Soviet Army* (1967), and *The Evolution of the Warsaw Pact* (1969).

NISSAN OREN taught at The Johns Hopkins University from 1960 to 1964 and presently holds a joint appointment in the Departments of International Relations and Soviet Studies at the Hebrew University of Jerusalem. He is the author of *Bulgarian Communism : The Road to Power, 1934–1944* (1971) and *Revolution Administered: Agrarianism and Communism in Bulgaria* (1973). He spent the academic year 1973–74 at the Center of International Studies, Princeton University, completing a volume tentatively entitled *Politics in Bulgaria, 1944–1948*.

STEPHEN PETERS served in 1944–45 as a member of the OSS Mission to Albania. He was with the Department of State from 1945 until 1966 and during 1966–70 was a Research Scientist at the American University, Washington, D.C. He is co-author of *Area Handbook for the Soviet Union* (1971) and *Area Handbook for Albania* (1971), and author of *USSR—Czechoslovak Relations, 1948–1968* (1969) and *Albania : Ingredients of Internal Stability* (1973).

ROUHOLLAH K. RAMAZANI is Edward R. Stettinius, Jr., Professor of Government and Foreign Affairs at the University of Virginia. He is the author of *The Foreign Policy of Iran, 1500—1941* (1966), *The Northern Tier : Afghanistan, Iran and Turkey* (1966), *The Middle East and the European Common Market* (1964), and *The Persian Gulf : Iran's Role* (1972).

ROBERT A. RUPEN is Professor of Political Science at the University of North Carolina and served as Director of East Asian and Western Pacific Studies at the National War College in 1969–70 and 1972–74. He is the author of *Mongols of the Twentieth Century* (1964) and *The Mongolian People's Republic* (1966), and co-editor of *Vietnam and the Sino-Soviet Dispute* (1967).

RONALD M. SCHNEIDER is Professor of Political Science at Queens College of the City University of New York. He is the author of *Communism in Guatemala, 1944–1954* (1959), *An Atlas of Latin American Affairs* (1965), and *Latin American Panorama* (1966). In recent years he has concentrated on studies of Brazilian politics, the most significant of which are *The Political System of Brazil: The Emergence of a "Modernizing" Authoritarian Regime, 1964—1970* (1971) and *Modernization and the Military in Brazil : Political Instability, Institutional Crises, and Army Intervention, 1822—1964* (forthcoming). He also co-authored *Brazil's Future Role in International Politics* (1973).

HANS W. SCHOENBERG. Visiting Professor in Political Science at the University of Maryland, Overseas Branch; Wagner College, Bregenz Study Center; University of Oklahoma, Munich Center; United Methodist Board of Higher Education, Study Center at the University of Graz, Austria (since 1957, 1964, 1968, and 1969 respectively). Author of *Germans from the East : A Study of Their Migration, Resettlement, and Subsequent Group History since 1945* (1970).

PAUL SHOUP is Associate Professor, Department of Government and Foreign Affairs, University of Virginia, and author of *Communism and the Yugoslav National Question* (1968).

C. JAY SMITH is Professor of History at Florida State University and served as King Professor of Maritime History at the U.S. Naval War College during 1965—66. He is the author of *Finland and the Russian Revolution, 1917—1922* (1958), *The Russian Struggle for Power, 1914—1917* (1956, 1969), and "Miljukov and the Russian National Question" in *Russian Thought and Politics* (1957).

EDGAR TOMSON is a research fellow at the Institut für Ostrecht of the University of Cologne. He has written several books on problems of international law and is the author of "La reconnaissance de l'indépendance de la Lettonie" in *Internationales Recht und Diplomatie* (1968).

PAVEL TIGRID is the author of *Why Dubček Fell* (1971) and *Le Printemps de Prague* (1968), which has been a best seller in a number of countries. He now lives in Paris where he edits the Czech-language quarterly *Svedectvi*.

JUSTUS M. VAN DER KROEF is Charles Anderson Dana Professor and Chairman of the Department of Political Science at the University of Bridgeport, Connecticut. He is the author of books on communism in Indonesia and Malaysia, including *The Communist Party of Indonesia : Its History, Program and Tactics* (1965), *Indonesia in the Modern World* (1956), and *Indonesia After Sukarno* (1971).

A Brief Bibliography

NOTE: This list is highly selective, being limited to broad, general works in English. Books dealing with only one country have been omitted. For additional titles see the footnotes in the text or refer to Thomas T. Hammond (ed.), *Soviet Foreign Relations and World Communism*; *A Selected, Annotated Bibliography of 7,000 Books in 30 Languages*. Princeton: Princeton University Press, 1966.

Andrews, William G., and Ra'anan, Uri (eds.), *The Politics of the Coup d'Etat ; Five Case Studies*. New York: Van Nostrand Reinhold, 1969.

Arendt, Hannah, *On Revolution*. New York: Viking, 1965.

Barnett, A. Doak (ed.), *Communist Strategies in Asia*; *A Comparative Analysis of Governments and Parties*. New York: Praeger, 1963.

Beloff, Max, *The Foreign Policy of Soviet Russia, 1929–1941*. London: Oxford University Press, 1947–49. 2 vols.

—— *Soviet Policy in the Far East, 1944–1951*. London: Oxford University Press, 1953.

Betts, Reginald R. (ed.), *Central and South East Europe, 1945–1948*. London: Royal Institute of International Affairs, 1950.

Black, Cyril E., and Thornton, Thomas P. (eds.), *Communism and Revolution : The Strategic Uses of Political Violence*. Princeton: Princeton University Press, 1964.

Bochenski, Joseph M., and Niemeyer, Gerhart (eds.), *Handbook on Communism*. New York: Praeger, 1962.

Borkenau, Franz, *The Communist International*. London: Faber and Faber, 1938. (Also published by the University of Michigan Press under the title, *World Communism*).

—— *European Communism*. New York: Harper, 1953.

Braunthal, Julius, *History of the International, 1914–1943*. London: Nelson, 1967.

Brinton, Crane, *The Anatomy of Revolution*. Revised and expanded edn., New York: Random House, 1965.

Brzezinski, Zbigniew, *The Soviet Bloc : Unity and Conflict*. Revised and enlarged edn., Cambridge: Harvard University Press, 1967.

Burks, Richard V., *The Dynamics of Communism in Eastern Europe*. Princeton: Princeton University Press, 1961.

Burmeister, Alfred. *Dissolution and Aftermath of the Comintern : Experiences and Observations, 1937–1947*. New York: Research Program on the USSR, 1955.

Calvert, Peter, *Revolution*. New York: Praeger, 1970.

—— *A Study of Revolution*. Oxford: Clarendon Press, 1970.

Carman, Ernest Day, *Soviet Imperialism : Russia's Drive Toward World Domination*. Washington: Public Affairs Press, 1950.

Carr, Edward H., *A History of Soviet Russia*. London and New York: Macmillan, 1950—.

Carsten, Francis L., *Revolution in Central Europe, 1918–1919*. Berkeley: University of California Press, 1972.

Cole, George D. H., *A History of Socialist Thought*. Vol. IV, *Communism and Social Democracy, 1914–1931*. Vol. V, *Socialism and Fascism, 1931–1939*. London: Macmillan, 1960.

Dallin, David J., *The Rise of Russia in Asia*. New Haven: Yale University Press, 1949.

—— *Soviet Russia and the Far East*. New Haven: Yale University Press, 1948.

Degras, Jane (ed.), *The Communist International, 1919—1943: Documents*. London: Oxford University Press, 1956—65. 3 vols.

—— *Soviet Documents on Foreign Policy*. London and New York: Oxford University Press, 1951—53. 3 vols.

Dimitrov, George, *The United Front*. New York: International Publishers, 1938.

Drachkovitch, Milorad M. (ed.), *The Revolutionary Internationals, 1864—1943*. Stanford: Stanford University Press, 1966.

—— and Lazitch, Branko (eds.), *The Comintern: Historical Highlights Essays, Recollections, Documents*. New York: Praeger, 1966.

Dunn, John, *Modern Revolutions: An Introduction to the Analysis of a Political Phenomenon*. Cambridge: Cambridge University Press, 1972.

Ellul, Jacques, *Autopsy of Revolution*. New York: Knopf, 1971.

Eudin, Xenia J., and Fisher, Harold H., *Soviet Russia and the West, 1920—1927: a Documentary Survey*. Stanford: Stanford University Press, 1957.

—— and North, Robert C., *Soviet Russia and the East, 1920—1927: a Documentary Survey*. Stanford: Stanford University Press, 1957.

—— and Slusser, Robert M., *Soviet Foreign Policy, 1928—1934: Documents and Materials*. University Park, Pa.: Pennsylvania State University Press, 1966—67. 2 vols.

Fischer, Louis, *Russia's Road from Peace to War: Soviet Foreign Relations, 1917—1941*. New York: Harper & Row, 1969.

—— *The Soviets in World Affairs: a History of the Relations Between the Soviet Union and the Rest of the World, 1917—1929*. Princeton: Princeton University Press, 1951. 2 vols.

Footman, David (ed.), *International Communism*. London: Chatto & Windus, 1960.

Friedrich, Carl J. (ed.), *Revolution*. New York: Atherton, 1966.

Gerassi, John (ed.), *The Coming of the New International*. New York: World, 1971.

Griffith, William E. (ed.), *Communism in Europe: Continuity, Change, and the Sino-Soviet Dispute*. Cambridge: The M. I. T. Press, 1964—66. 2 vols.

Gross, Feliks. *The Seizure of Political Power in a Century of Revolutions*. New York: Philosophical Library, 1958.

Gruber, Helmut (ed.), *International Communism in the Era of Lenin: A Documentary History*. Garden City, N. Y.: Doubleday, 1972.

Hulse, James W., *The Forming of the Communist International*. Stanford: Stanford University Press, 1964.

James, Cyril L. R., *World Revolution, 1917—1936: The Rise and Fall of the Communist International*. London: Secker and Warburg, 1937.

Janos, Andrew C., *The Seizure of Power: A Study of Force and Popular Conquest*. Princeton: Center for International Studies, Princeton University, 1964.

Johnson, Chalmers, *Peasant Nationalism and Communist Power*. Stanford: Stanford University Press, 1962.

—— *Revolution and the Social System*. Stanford: The Hoover Institution Press, 1964.

—— *Revolutionary Change*. Boston: Little, Brown, 1966.

Kaplan, Lawrence (ed.) *Revolutions: A Comparative Study*. New York: Random House, 1973.

Kase, Francis J., *People's Democracy: A Contribution to the Study of the Communist Theory of State and Revolution*. Leyden: Sijthoff, 1968.

Kennedy, Malcolm D., *A Short History of Communism in Asia*. London: Weidenfeld and Nicolson, 1957.

Kertesz, Stephen D., (ed.), *The Fate of East Central Europe: Hopes and Failures of American Foreign Policy*. Notre Dame: University of Notre Dame Press, 1956.

Kirkpatrick, Jeane J., *The Strategy of Deception: A Study in World-Wide Communist Tactics*. New York: Farrar, Straus, 1963.

Landauer, Carl, and others, *European Socialism*. Berkeley and Los Angeles: University of California Press, 1959. 2 vols.

Lazitch, Branko, and Drachkovitch, Milorad M., *Lenin and the Comintern*. Vol. I, Stanford: Hoover Institution Press, 1972.

Lenin, Vladimir I., *The Communist International*. New York: International Publishers, 1938. (Vol. X of his *Selected Works*).

Leonhard, Wolfgang, *Child of the Revolution*. Chicago: Regnery, 1958.

Lukacs, John A., *The Great Powers and Eastern Europe*. New York: American Book Co., 1953.

McKenzie, Kermit E., *Comintern and World Revolution, 1928–1943: The Shaping of Doctrine*. New York: Columbia University Press, 1964.

McLane, Charles B., *Soviet Strategies in Southeast Asia: An Exploration of Eastern Policy under Lenin and Stalin*. Princeton: Princeton University Press, 1966.

Malaparte, Curzio, *Coup d'Etat: The Technique of Revolution*. New York: Dutton, 1932.

Momboisse, Raymond M., *Blueprint of Revolution: The Rebel, the Party, the Techniques of Revolt*. Springfield, Ill.: Charles C. Thomas, 1970.

Nollau, Gunther, *International Communism and World Revolution: History and Methods*. New York: Praeger, 1961.

Page, Stanley W., *Lenin and World Revolution*. New York: N. Y. U. Press, 1959.

Possony, Stefan T., *A Century of Conflict: Communist Techniques of World Revolution*. Chicago: Regnery, 1953.

Scalapino, Robert A. (ed.), *The Communist Revolution in Asia: Tactics, Goals, and Achievements*. 2nd edn., Englewood Cliffs, N. J.: Prentice-Hall, 1969.

Selznick, Philip, *The Organizational Weapon: A Study of Bolshevik Strategy and Tactics*. New York: McGraw-Hill, 1952.

Seton-Watson, Hugh, *The East European Revolution*. 3rd. edn., New York: Praeger, 1956.
—— *From Lenin to Khrushchev: The History of World Communism*. New York: Praeger, 1960.
—— *Neither War Nor Peace: The Struggle for Power in the Postwar World*. New York: Praeger, 1960.

Survey of International Affairs, 1939–46, *The Realignment of Europe*, edited by Arnold Toynbee and Veronica M. Toynbee. London: Oxford University Press, for the Royal Institute of International Affairs, 1955.

Sworakowski, Witold S., *The Communist International and Its Front Organizations*. Stanford: The Hoover Institution Press, 1965.

Trotsky, Leon, *The First Five Years of the Communist International*. New York: Pioneer Publishers, 1945–53. 2 vols.

—— *The Third International After Lenin*. New York: Pioneer Publishers, 1936.

Tucker, Robert C., *The Marxian Revolutionary Idea*. New York: Norton, 1969.
—— *Paths of Communist Revolution*. Princeton: Center of International Studies, Princeton University, 1968.

Ulam, Adam B., *Expansion and Coexistence : The History of Soviet Foreign Policy, 1917—67.* New York: Praeger, 1968.

U. S. Congress, House, Committee on Foreign Affairs, *The Strategy and Tactics of World Communism.* Washington: Government Printing Office, 1948.

U. S. Congress, Senate, Committee on the Judiciary, *Study of the Anatomy of Communist Takeovers.* Washington: Government Printing Office, 1966.

Warth, Robert D., *Soviet Russia in World Politics.* New York: Twayne, 1963.

Wolff, Robert Lee, *The Balkans in Our Time.* Cambridge: Harvard University Press, 1956.

Index

Aaltonen, Aimo, 438
Africa: Chinese Communists in, 40
Agrarian Party: in Bulgaria, 328, 334, 335
Agrarian Reform: in China, 518, 526, 532;
    in Cuba, 590; in Guatemala, 569, 570;
    in Indonesia, 544; in Korea, 487;
    in Poland, 364—65
Aidit, D. N., 535—50, 553, 555—57, 560
Albania, 273—92; National Liberation
    Movement in, 273—74, 281—87, 291;
    and Yugoslavia, 273, 275—76, 279, 284;
    use of terror in, 275—76; Balli
    Kombetar (BK) in, 277—78, 280,
    282—87; National Liberation Army
    (ANLA) in, 277, 282—87, 292;
    Nationalist Legality Movement
    (NLM) in, 281—82, 285; Italian Army
    in, 283—84; and Kosovo-Metohija,
    284; classes in, 285; and United
    States, 286—87, 289—90; and USSR,
    286—88; and Great Britain, 286—88,
    290—91; and OSS, 287, 289; and
    Churchill, 288; and Teheran, 288;
    and Yalta, 288; Provisional Demo-
    cratic Government of, 289
Albanian Communist Party, 273—92
    passim
Allied Control Council: in Germany, 379
Allied Powers: and Germany, 373,
    382—83
Amagaev, 126
Annexations by the USSR, 19—20, 638
Anti-Communist movement:
    in Guatemala, 571—72
Anti-Fascist Council of National
    Liberation of Yugoslavia (AVNOJ),
    253, 255—57, 259, 261—62, 264
Antonescu, Marshall Ion, 310—11, 317
Arana, Colonel Francisco Javier, 568
Arana Osorio, Carlos, 578
Arbenz, Jacobo, 563, 566, 568—70, 572—75
Arévalo, Juan José, 566, 568
Armed Force: use of by the Communists,
    2, 23—24, 639, 640; in China, 530;
    Mao on the use of, 640
"Armed Propaganda": in Vietnam, 507—08

Armed resistance to Communists:
    in Poland, 358—62
Ataturk, Kemal, 194
August Revolution: in Indochina, 499
Austria, 32; revolution of 1919 in, 7;
    Red Army in, 379—81; elections in,
    380; and USSR, 380—82; neutrality
    of, 381
Azerbaijan, 61, 64, 66, 69, 448—74;
    Democratic Party in, 458—60

Balkan Federation, 333
Baltic States, 214—28; and Germany, 214;
    invasion of by Red Army (1940), 223;
    elections of 1940 in, 226; annexation
    of, 228, 231
Bao Dai, 498, 500, 506, 510
Bashkiria, 66, 69
Bavarian Revolution, 171—74
Bavarian Soviet Republic, 171—74
Batista, Fulgencio, 584, 587, 594
Bay of Pigs invasion, 563
Beneš, Eduard, 125, 404, 419, 424
Berlin: Communist Party in, 375
Berlin Blockade, 379
Berling, General Zygmunt, 120, 358, 359,
    360
Berling army, 358, 359
Bialystok, 101—03
Billington, James: on Finland, 443
Biriuzov, Marshall S. S., 327
"Blueprint" for Eastern Europe, 20—22,
    143
Bogdo Gegen, 111, 115, 117—19, 121—24,
    133, 155, 159
Bolivia, 581
Bolsheviks, 63—64, 81; in 1917, 53, 54—55,
    57; and Poland, 95, 98
Boris, King of Bulgaria, 324
Borisov, S. S., 115, 126
Borodin, Mikhail: and Mongolia,
    143—144; in China, 206—07
Brandler, Heinrich, 176, 178—79, 181—82,
    184, 187—88
Brest-Litovsk, Treaty of: and Finland,
    85—88, 91